CORONATION STREET

The Epic Novel

To the cast and crew who have made *Coronation Street* such a special phenomenon for over forty years and all Corrie fans everywhere, especially Frank and Sheila Dixon.

Acknowledgements

With grateful thanks to Gillian Holmes and Hazel Orme for their generous help, professionalism and expertise, in making this book possible. I could have never written it without them.

CORONATION STREET

The Epic Novel

Katherine Hardy

GRANADA

Coronation Street is based on an idea by Tony Warren and
is a Granada Television production for itv1

First published in Great Britain in 2003
By Granada Media, an imprint of Andre Deutsch Limited
In association with Granada Media Group Limited
20 Mortimer Street
London
W1T 3JW

A catalogue record for this book is available from the British Library.

ISBN: 0 233 05097 3

Typeset by E-Type, Liverpool
Printed and bound in the UK by Mackays of Chatham plc

IMPORTANT NOTE TO THE READER

All the events in the following pages took place on screen, but the timing of some events has been changed in response to the differing needs of the two mediums of screen and page.

Chapter One

Darkness had fallen early, even for December, and icy rain fell in a steady downpour over Weatherfield, drenching the terrace houses, transforming their sooty brick façades to glistening pewter. It wasn't an evening that encouraged anyone to linger in the streets, and those residents who weren't already indoors hurried home to stoke their fires and make their tea. But all was not peaceful: the clamour emanating from behind the doors of number eleven could be heard the full length of Coronation Street from the Rovers Return to the corner shop. As for breadth, Elsie Tanner's screeches rang out piercingly over the back yards to the inhabitants of Mawdsley Street who had grown accustomed to Elsie Tanner laying into her teenage son and Dennis Tanner answering his mother back.

Despite the bone-numbing cold and damp, pensioner Ena Sharples grabbed her lifelong friend Martha Longhurst's arm and they paused, huddled together in their shapeless army grey wool overcoats outside the

Tanners' door. Ena listened intently for a few moments, then nodded meaningfully to Martha. Elsie Tanner had generated more gossip for Ena to spread than the rest of the inhabitants of Coronation Street put together. She was a striking, voluptuous redhead and as Ena frequently said, everyone knew what redheads were like. Wild wasn't the word for it and Elsie had been after men from the day she had painted on her first dab of lipstick. She was also in what some would call the prime of life, her late thirties, and her reputation was somewhat suspect as her husband had left her years ago. With good reason, given the number of men who had been in and out of her house and her bed since she had moved into the street as a sixteen-year-old pregnant war bride, or so Ena and rumour had it.

Ena saw to it that everyone in the area, never mind the street, knew about Elsie's men. The only wonder was that she had stayed with Arnold Tanner long enough to give birth to the two children who resembled him: Dennis, a tall, dark, handsome lad who had turned out crooked – no surprise there, given the way Elsie had dragged up her kids – and Linda, whom Ena and Martha had just seen in the corner shop when they'd bought slices of ham for their tea. Not that they'd got anything more out of her than a cheeky 'You're looking well, Mrs Sharples, Mrs Longhurst.'

Linda had left the street months ago after marrying a

foreigner and Ena had already decided that her sudden reappearance meant she was going the same way as her mother. It was little wonder that Elsie's roving eye had been passed on to the next generation, given the number of men Elsie had brought home over the years. Perhaps Linda's husband had thrown her out . . .

An escalation of shouts, followed by a thundering of footsteps down the stairs behind the door, prompted Ena and Martha to move on. As Ena muttered to Martha as they headed for the Glad Tidings Mission Hall, where Ena lived rent free in exchange for performing the duties of caretaker, 'We'll find out more later on in Rovers Return.'

Elsie charged into the living room after her son and stood, hands on hips, in front of him as he flung himself into an easy chair. 'Come on, Dennis Tanner, where is it?' she demanded, at the top of her voice.

'Where's what?' Dennis fixed his handsome features into an expression that he hoped denoted innocence and met his mother's glare.

'Don't give me that sheep-eyed look. You know as well as I do.'

'I don't know what you're talking about,' he protested uneasily.

'There's two bob's gone from my purse.' Elsie's face darkened in anger.

Dennis turned aside and stared at the floor. 'That's nothing to do with me.'

To Elsie, the fact that he could no longer meet her eye was as good as an admission of guilt. Her temper escalated to breaking point. If only Dennis would tell her the truth she could cope, but his lies were worse than his thieving. 'Do you expect me to believe a cat burglar came in and nicked two bob?' she enquired caustically. When he didn't answer, she gripped the mantelpiece for support. 'Not half an hour ago you asked me for two bob for cigarettes.'

'And you wouldn't give it me,' Dennis retorted heatedly.

'So you stooped to go in a lady's handbag. Fine son you are,' Elsie railed.

Dennis's temper was slower than Elsie's but once roused it was equally fierce. He left the chair. 'You lost two bob. So, what am I supposed to do about it?'

'Get work!'

'Change the record, will you?' He moved towards the door.

'You know what your trouble is, don't you?' Elsie lectured. 'You just don't want a job. Here I am, working myself to death and you can't even be bothered to open a newspaper. There are plenty of jobs for those who look—'

'Yeh,' Dennis broke in acidly, 'and they ask what experience you have.'

'You have plenty of experience—'

'Not the right kind,' he interrupted bitterly, daring her to push him further. 'You know as well as I do why I can't get a job.'

'You've been out of that place seven weeks now.'

'Let's not wrap it up,' he mocked. 'If you mean prison, say prison. Everyone else does.'

Elsie's face crumpled in despair. The two shillings he had taken from her purse paled into insignificance beside the mess he had made of his life, which she had been powerless to prevent. 'Dennis,' she murmured softly, 'you can't go on like this . . .'

'What am I supposed to do, then?' he enquired acidly.

He stared at her and this time Elsie was the first to turn away. She didn't know which was worse: their increasingly frequent screaming matches, or moments like this, when her love for him was almost too much to bear. 'Why did I have to get lumbered with a son like you?' There was tenderness as well as complaint in her voice.

'I suppose you'd rather you had one like Kenneth Barlow,' Dennis taunted.

'And what's wrong with him? Let me tell you something. He'll have no trouble finding a job because he's got it up here,' Elsie pointed to her forehead, 'on the upper storey, and that's where it counts.'

Unwilling to listen to any more, Dennis opened the door.

11

'I wish we were more like the Barlows,' Elsie shouted after him. 'At least they're not rowing all the time.'

Ken Barlow heard Elsie and Dennis's raised voices, then the slam of the door of number eleven as he rounded the corner from Viaduct Street into Coronation Street and passed the corner shop. He turned up the collar of the duffel coat, which had almost become a uniform for university students, against the rain, and he looked at his own front door at number three. He had lived all his life in the street, and until he had won a scholarship to university he had been content enough. But since then his lecturers and fellow students had broadened his horizons, and he had learnt to question everything, especially the mind-rottingly dull existence his parents meekly accepted as their lot.

He could time their daily routine to the last minute. His father would have come home from work half an hour ago. By now he and his mother would be sitting in the cramped, dingy back room that remained gloomy even on bright summer afternoons because the sun never quite reached the window that overlooked the back yard. And the combination of stark utility furniture bought just after the war when nothing better was available, and beige and brown floral wallpaper blackened by smoke from the open fire for the last ten years did nothing to lighten the ambience.

His father, blue collar abandoned the minute he took off his coat after walking through the door, would be sitting at the tea table in braces and shirtsleeves; his mother would be in the uniform of the working-class woman – a flowered overall. They would be eating the same food they had eaten for the last twenty odd years and exchanging the same bleak, empty conversation, a continuation of the one they had shared the evening – or possibly even the year – before. His mother would fuss over him just as she had done when he'd been a child, in the vain hope that by monopolising the conversation she would prevent one of the increasingly bitter confrontations between him and his father, who'd decided university had turned him into a snob, and point-blank refused to listen whenever he tried to talk about the world that lay beyond the boundaries of Coronation Street.

If only they would read the newspapers or think for themselves once in a while . . . Bracing himself, he opened the door, stepped inside and hung his rain-soaked coat and college scarf on a peg in the hall.

'Your tea's all ready, Kenny.' Ida picked up her oven gloves and scuttled into the back kitchen as he walked in. She returned with a plate she'd lifted from the oven and set it on the table in front of the chair that had been his ever since he'd relinquished his high-chair to his younger brother David.

'Thanks.' He sat next to his father and picked up his knife and fork.

'Sauce, Kenny?' Ida smiled nervously as she set the bottle in front of him. She found it difficult to equate the handsome, confident young man Ken had become with the child she had borne and nurtured.

'No, thanks.' He returned her diffident smile.

'Oh.' Her disappointment was evident. 'I got it specially. You used to love it when you were little.'

'Did I?' He debated which was worse: his father's carping or his mother's reminiscences of a childhood he was anxious to forget.

His father glared at him. 'What's up now?'

Sensing an argument coming Ken struggled to keep his tone neutral. 'Nothing.'

'Then why have you got a dirty expression on your face?'

'I haven't.' He fought to keep his voice even.

'That new pullover's turned out a treat,' Ida prattled uneasily. 'Mind you, I'll not knit another that colour for you, Ken. Navy blue plays the devil with my eyes.'

Ostentatiously and deliberately Frank smothered his sausages, mash and gravy with bottled sauce. 'I bet they don't do this at college,' he goaded, 'or eat in their shirt-sleeves, neither.'

Ken cut into a sausage.

'I've noticed you looking at me,' his father continued, as if he'd spoken.

Ken looked up from his plate. 'I really don't know what you're talking about.'

'You *really* don't know?' Frank mocked mimicking Ken's voice and adding what he considered to be a 'posh' veneer. 'Oh, yes, you do. We're not good enough for you now.'

Ken looked to his mother in the hope that she would put an end to the argument before it started. 'I haven't said a word and he starts on me night after night—'

'Look, Dad,' she broke in, 'can't we have one meal in peace for a change?'

'You know he doesn't like you to call me Dad. It's common,' Frank added emphatically.

'Give over the pair of you.' She leant against her chair. 'My back's aching something awful again.' As soon as she'd spoken she realised that her health wasn't the best topic to bring up.

'That comes of you doing that rotten job,' Frank told her, then turned his attention to Ken again. 'I bet you don't tell those high and mighty pals you hobnob down the university with what your mother does to bring in money to keep you in the lap of luxury.'

'I don't make a secret of the fact that she works in a hotel kitchen.' Ken's temper rose at the implication that he was ashamed of his mother's job.

'What's got into you today, Frank?' Ida ventured, anxious to nip the row in the bud.

'Go on, blame me,' Frank challenged. 'It's him, just listen to him. Look what he said last night: "Why do we have to have cups of tea with our meals?" Well, I'll tell you why.' Frank poked his fork in Ken's chest. 'Because I like my grub swilled down properly, that's why. You'd best watch out, Ida, he'll have you changing into an evening gown to eat your meal next.'

Ida stared at the wall. 'Look at that clock! Wherever could our David have got to? Did you go into town this afternoon, Ken?'

'Yes, I got a record.' Ken was as anxious as her to change the subject.

'One I'd like?'

'You might. I'm not sure,' Ken replied cautiously.

'Oh, you know me.' Ida's hands shook as she set her knife and fork on her plate. 'I've always been one for a bit of good music. You can put it on when I've washed up and your dad's had his tea.'

Frank grunted disapprovingly as he shovelled a forkful of sauce-soaked mash into his mouth.

'Our David's meal will be bone dry in the oven.' Ida peered at the clock again.

Silence fell. Ken attempted to fill it: 'I shall be going out later.'

'Who with?' Ida hoped that Frank would have the sense to remain quiet.

'Just a girl in my year.'

'The one you had the letter from this morning?' she pressed. When he nodded, she murmured, 'Does she come from round here?'

'Not far away, the other side of town.' He gave his father a sideways glance.

'You'll be going round to their place, then,' Ida suggested.

'No.'

'Whereabouts you meeting her?'

'The Imperial.'

'Where?' Frank growled.

'The Imperial Hotel.' Ken knew he'd made a mistake but he couldn't lie. Not to his father.

'Now, listen here, squire,' Frank spat out, 'you'd best make your mind up now. You're not throwing no money away in no Imperial Hotel.'

'I'm not asking you for any money.'

'Oh, no? Then where did the money in your pocket come from?' he demanded.

'Dad—' Ida tried to interject, but Frank turned on her. 'Now look here, Ida, I'm not having you working in the stinking kitchens of the Imperial Hotel for him to go chucking our money about front of house. It's downright wicked, that's what it is.'

'He won't be spending much, will you, love?' Ida said, in a conciliatory tone.

'He won't be spending owt,' Frank said flatly, 'because

he can make his mind up now that he won't be going there at all.' He pushed his plate aside and left the table.

The door opened and David breezed in, bringing a draught of damp, freezing air with him. His brown hair was soaked, plastered to his skull, but a smile lightened his even pleasant features and, relieved to see a happy, friendly face, Ken instinctively smiled back.

'Hello, Ma.' David kissed her cheek before sensing frost in the atmosphere.

'And what time do you call this?' Ida asked briskly, as she picked up Frank's plate.

'I had another puncture. I thought it was just the valve at first.'

'The sooner you get yourself a decent bike the better,' Frank pronounced sternly. 'That thing's only fit for scrap-yard.'

'And that's just where it's going as soon as I've saved a deposit.' David peeled off his dripping wet coat and returned to the hall to hang it up.

'A deposit. What for?' Ida ferried her own and Frank's plates to the scullery.

'A motorbike.' David grinned as he walked back into the kitchen.

'Over my dead body,' Ida declared vehemently.

Frank left the table, went to the window and moved the curtain aside. He squinted into the darkness. 'Is it raining?'

'It was a minute or two ago but it's stopped now.' David

crouched in front of the fire and held out his hands to warm them.

'I'll take a look at that bike of yours. Where's your puncture outfit?' Frank muttered.

'In my saddlebag.' David took off his shoes and set them on the hearth to dry. 'But I told you, I'll see to it.' He tore up an old newspaper, crumpled the pages into balls and stuffed them inside his shoes so they would keep their shape.

'I'll just take a look.' Frank walked through the scullery and opened the back door.

'And how's our whiz kid?' David flicked Ken's head as he sat opposite him at the table.

'All right,' Ken mumbled.

'Do you want gravy, David?' Ida shouted from the scullery.

'I wouldn't mind.'

'You'll have to wait while I warm it up, then.'

David inclined his head towards the back door as their father closed it. 'What's up?'

'Nothing.' Ken pushed aside his half-eaten meal. 'Just had a bit of a set-to.'

'What about this time?'

'I was supposed to be meeting a girl at the Imperial Hotel.' Ken made a wry face. 'You can imagine what *that* started.' He left his chair. 'If anyone asks, I'll be in the Rovers buying a packet of cigarettes.'

Wishing he had the courage to defy his father, and upset because there was no way of letting Susan Cunningham know that he wouldn't be at the Imperial, Ken went into the hall and reached for his hat and scarf. The front door banged behind him, and he headed down the street.

When Ken walked into the Rovers Return, the landlady, Annie Walker, was tutting at her husband Jack's untidy ways as she cleared his football coupon from the bar. Annie had a soft spot for Ken, seeing him as a fellow intellectual with refined tastes beyond those of most of her regulars.

'Hello, love.' She gave him a rare smile.

'Hello, Mrs Walker.' Ken felt too miserable to return the smile.

'You do look happy,' she commented.

'I'm OK,' he lied. 'Twenty cigarettes, please, Mrs Walker.'

Dennis Tanner leant on the bar next to Ken. His dark shirt was unbuttoned at the neck and his hair, which was normally styled in a Billy Fury type quiff, lank, flat and soaking wet, dripped on to his collar, which was as sodden as the rest of his clothes. Ken shivered: he was cold in his woollen duffel coat and thick cardigan, yet Dennis seemed unconcerned by the freezing temperature and his drenched state.

'Half a mild,' Dennis said to Annie. He turned to Ken. 'How's our local genius?'

'All right,' Ken replied. He remembered the shouting he had heard coming from the Tanners' house when he had turned into the street earlier.

'Haven't seen you in paper recently. Haven't you been winning any more scholarships?' There was a sharp edge to Dennis's teasing.

'Here are your cigarettes, Ken.' In Annie Walker's eyes there were two kind of people, respectable and not, and she was anxious to rescue Ken, whom she put firmly in the first category, from Dennis, whom she regarded as one step away from the devil.

'I'll have twenty cigarettes an' all,' Dennis said coolly.

'That will be four and sevenpence ha'penny.' Annie stood, waiting for the money.

Dennis rummaged in his pocket, pulled out a handful of coppers and set it on the counter. 'That's for the mild. I'll give you the money for the fags another time.'

'No, you won't.'

'Don't you trust me?' Dennis asked aggressively.

'Trust has nothing to do with it,' Annie said firmly. 'This house doesn't give credit.'

Weary of arguments, and beset by a sudden feeling of sympathy for Dennis, who hadn't been given the start in life that he had, Ken handed over his packet. 'Here.'

Stunned, Dennis stared at him. 'Ta.' He took the

packet and tossed it into the air. 'When it comes down to it, it's all government money, innit?' He drained his pint and stalked out.

As Dennis left Annie fingered the string of pearls at her throat. 'Whatever did you want to do that for?' she admonished Ken. 'You don't want to go wasting your sympathy on him. It's Elsie I feel sorry for. Look at the trouble's he's brought to her door.' She shook her head sadly as she cleared away Dennis's glass.

Drained by her argument with Dennis, Elsie sat at the table in her living room and studied her face in her compact. She didn't like what she saw. There were wrinkles around her eyes that she was certain hadn't been there the day before. Was it her imagination or was her face sagging? She peered closer.

Without her noticing, some time during the last few years she had passed from being a smart young woman into a middle-aged – a middle-aged what? She held her mirror up to the light and examined her face even more intently.

'Here's your ham.'

Elsie glanced up as her daughter Linda walked in and dropped a paper bag on to the table. She reached for her handbag. 'How much do I owe you?'

'It's all right.' Linda slipped off her coat and tossed it on to a chair. 'I took two bob from your purse before I went to the shop.'

'Oh, hell! Talk about give a dog a bad name.'

'What?' Linda pulled an easy-chair closer to the fire and sat down.

'I have just wrongly accused your little brother of taking two bob from my purse. And you're a bit of a madam, going into my handbag without so much as a by-your-leave,' Elsie reproved her.

'I didn't have any change.' Linda stretched out her shapely nylon-clad legs in front of her and studied them.

Elsie tucked a stray strand of hair back into her French pleat, sighed and snapped her compact shut. 'I don't know what to do about our kid – or you.' She gave her daughter a hard look. 'Three of us can't manage on what I earn.'

'What do you mean, three?' Linda queried testily. 'I'm only here for the week.'

'Are you?' Elsie decided that she'd had enough of lies and subterfuge for one day. 'Out with it. You've left him, haven't you?'

Linda lifted her legs and tucked them beneath her on the chair. 'Supposing I have?' She tried to sound more blasé than she felt.

'What happened?'

'We had a bust-up.'

'What about?'

'We've had that many lately, I'm not sure.' Linda sighed. 'He's that moody.'

'Foreigners are,' Elsie asserted. 'But you must have done something to put him in a mood?'

'Absolutely nothing.'

'Give over.' Then Elsie remembered the rows she'd had with her husband Arnold before he'd left her: every one had been about other men but, then, she'd given him good cause to be jealous. 'It's no secret round here why your dad left me.'

'Well, in this case it's me who's done the leaving.' Linda swung her legs down and rose to her feet.

'What you going to do?' Elsie asked.

'I can't go back, Mam,' she pleaded. 'You don't know what he's like when he has one of his moods on him.' Tears started into her eyes and she turned to the mirror over the fireplace so her mother wouldn't see her cry.

'You know you're welcome here, so you can stay . . . Just one thing, though,' Elsie said. 'Don't go on at our Dennis, he's not had it easy lately.'

Linda's attention drifted as her mother continued to hector her over her attitude to her brother. She lifted a lock of her dark hair, examined it in the mirror. 'Mam, should I go blonde?'

'Why ask me? If you want to go blonde, go blonde.' Elsie was infuriated by the sudden change of subject and she wondered if either of her kids had ever listened to anything she tried to tell them.

'Ivan went mad when he found a bottle of peroxide in

the house. He's that narrow-minded. When the new short skirts came in I had to take mine up inch by inch so he wouldn't notice. He said he didn't want fellows staring at my legs.'

'If you're staying you'll have to get a job – you know that, don't you?' Elsie steered the conversation back on course.

'Anything going in your shop?'

'Nothing permanent, but we're looking for staff for Christmas.'

'And what do I do after Christmas?' Linda realised the significance of what her mother had said. 'Here, you think I'll go back to him, don't you?'

'You've been back to him before,' Elsie reminded.

'Not this time.' Linda folded her arms across her well-developed chest.

'All I know is, three months after you got married you came flying back here with your bedding, a brass companion set and a set of plastic ducks.' Elsie failed miserably to inject humour into the situation.

'This time it's different.'

Feeling that she had heard it all before, and further talk would accomplish nothing, Elsie reached for a magazine, opened it and began to read.

'Mam?'

'What?'

Linda saw she wouldn't get any more sympathy from her mother. 'Nothing.'

'What nothing?' Elsie looked up from the magazine. 'I'm trying to read here.'

'Go back to it then,' Linda said dully. She knew her mother's moods. The secret she was carrying would have to wait.

Chapter Two

Frank set the bike on the rug in the living room and scrutinised the tyre. He glanced at David, who was eating his tea. 'Well, it's not the valve and that's for sure.'

'I could have told you that.' David scooped the last forkful of food from his plate.

'We'd best get this tyre off and take a closer look.' Frank began to prise it off the wheel. 'Has our Ken said owt to you about going out tonight?'

'Yes.'

'Imperial Hotel,' Frank sneered. 'Cheek of the devil.'

'It's his life.' David carried his plate through to the scullery.

'Go on,' Frank snapped, 'take his side, gang up on me.' He fell silent as Ida walked in. She sidestepped the bike, pulled out her knitting from the side of her chair and sat down. 'Go on, then, Ida, blame me.'

'No one's blaming anybody,' Ida replied, tight-lipped.

Frank set down the wheel. 'Where is Ken?'

'He bought cigarettes in Rovers and now he's next door visiting Mr Tatlock.'

'He spends more time in Mr Tatlock's than he does here.'

'You leave Mr Tatlock alone,' Ida rushed to the old man's defence. 'He's all right, is Mr Tatlock.'

He had pushed Ida too far and Frank adopted a softer tone. 'Look, love, Ken's always making me look a proper fool. I think it's time he learnt to live in his own class. I saw what he was wearing today – *a silk tie* – and you can't get one of those for less than sixteen shillings. And don't try and tell me that came out of his grant.'

'No, I'll tell you straight it didn't.' Ida's temper boiled over. 'I bought it for him. And before you say any more he didn't ask for it. I'm no martyr, Frank Barlow, much as you'd like to think it. And our Ken's going to have the best chance I can give him.' At a knock on the door she fell silent.

'I'll go.' Glad of an excuse to leave the room, David returned with a shy and extremely pretty girl with short brown curls and bright hazel eyes. She was wearing a unisex duffel coat like Ken's and had the same college scarf. 'This is Susan, she's looking for our Ken.'

Ida smiled at the girl. 'I'll go and fetch him for you, love. You, sit yourself down.' Ida stood up and bustled out, leaving Susan hovering awkwardly in the doorway.

'Give us a hand here then,' Frank demanded of David.

Susan watched the two men wrestle with the tyre. 'Is there anything I can do?' she ventured.

David handed her a spanner. 'I'll need this in a minute. Can you hold it for me?'

Susan took the spanner and looked at the door, hoping that wherever Ken was, he wouldn't take much 'fetching'.

'Mrs Walker.' Martha Longhurst leant across the bar from the snug. Annie walked towards her from the far end in the public area. 'Have the Barlows got a car?'

'No, love, why?' Annie set a bottle of milk stout on the counter and took the shilling Martha handed her.

'Well, there's one outside their door.'

'Really.' Too superior to immerse herself in gossip with Martha Longhurst, Annie handed Martha her change and returned to the public bar as bus inspector Harry Hewitt entered in his uniform. Annie liked Harry and, along with everyone else in the Street, felt sorry for him. His wife had died a few months before and he was taking her loss hard, so hard he had made a very wrong decision: believing he had no other option he had sent his eleven-year-old daughter, Lucille, to an orphanage. Annie couldn't bear to think of the pretty, lively young girl confined to an institution for unwanted children.

'How's your Lucille, Harry?' Annie enquired as she pulled him a pint.

'Fretting,' Harry confided.

'That orphanage is no place for her,' Annie said. 'It's

time you were getting married again. There's plenty would be glad to have you.'

'Find me one, and I'll marry her, Mrs Walker.' Despite Harry's jocular tone there was a hint of seriousness in his voice.

Annie frowned as a tall, dark, good-looking young man entered the bar. 'Do you know that lad, Harry?'

'His face has a familiar look about it.'

'Terrible weather we're having,' Annie said, as the stranger approached the bar.

'Yes. Can I have a pint of bitter, please?'

Unable to place his foreign accent, Annie smiled. 'Excuse me asking but you're not English, are you?'

'No.'

Intrigued by his reticence, she pressed him further: 'Ukrainian?'

'No.'

'Some of them came to work round here,' she explained.

'I'm not one.'

But I've seen you before . . .' Annie winced as Ena shouted, 'Service,' from the snug. 'I give up.' She gave the man her most appealing smile.

'Sorry, I don't understand "I give up".'

'That,' Ena announced to Annie when she eventually reached the snug, 'is the Pole Linda Tanner married. And she came back here without him. The fact that he saw fit to follow her here means trouble. You mark my words, before the night's out there'll be more than words flying round Coronation Street.'

'As long as it's in the street, not in the Rovers Return.' A chill rippled down Annie's back as she glanced back at the man. She wished Jack would hurry up and finish his tea so he could take over the bar. As her mother had so often told her, 'A pub landlady's life is no occupation for a real lady.'

'Look at this mess! Whatever will you think of us, love?' Ida darted into the living room and scurried round, clearing up the newspapers and bike pieces Frank and David had strewn all over the floor.

Ken stood in the doorway. 'Hello, Susan.'

Susan faced him. There was a peculiar expression on his face that she couldn't quite decipher. 'Hello, Ken.'

'I'm sorry, love,' Ida cleared her knitting from her chair. 'We weren't expecting company.'

'Please, don't worry about me, Mrs Barlow,' Susan reassured her, embarrassed by Ida's fussing. 'I'm fine.'

'David, get this bike into the yard.' Ida shooed David towards the scullery. 'I don't know, I leave you men alone for five minutes and you turn the house into a tip.'

'What are you doing here?' Ken asked Susan.

'Well . . . when you didn't turn up at the Imperial . . .'

'That's a nice way to greet a person, I must say.' In an

attempt to compensate for Ken's cavalier attitude, Ida smiled at the girl. 'Do you fancy a cup of tea, love?'

'I'd love one.'

'Where are you off, Frank?' Ida asked, as he barged past.

'To put kettle on.'

'Well, that's a first.' She stared at her husband in disbelief.

Ken waited until his mother had followed his father into the scullery. 'Obviously you've got to have the tea or she'll be offended, but as soon as we've drunk it let's make a quick dash.'

'To where?'

'Town, where I was supposed to meet you.'

'Oh, don't let's bother about town,' she said. 'What about that funny little Victorian pub on the corner?'

'The Rovers Return.' His eyes rounded in horror at the thought of taking her into a place filled with people who had known him since he had worn short trousers. 'You should see inside the place.'

'That is exactly what I want to do.'

'Hey, is that your car outside, Susan?' David dashed into the living room.

'It's my father's. Why?'

'Kids have been at it.'

Ken clenched his fists. As if it wasn't bad enough that the girl he had been chasing for weeks and hoping to impress had seen his family and his working-class at its worst, the local street urchins had had to wreck her father's car.

'I am sorry about your car, love,' Ida sympathised, moving a photograph album along a shelf in the alcove next to the fire, so she could set Susan's tea down next to her.

'All I'm worried about is what my father is going to say.'

Ida frowned. 'Oh dear, are you going to get in bother?'

Susan picked up the album. 'Are these photographs, Mrs Barlow?'

'You don't want to look at those, Susan,' Ken said.

'Yes, I do.' Susan gave him a smile he didn't return.

'And you can turn over that page for a start,' Ken ordered his mother, as she opened the album.

'Why?' Ida said. 'You're wearing a clean nappy.'

David ran into the living room, leaving the door open. 'The blighters have hammered a six inch nail into your tyre, Susan. Have you got a jack?'

'No.' She bit her lip. 'Should I have?'

'No worries,' David said brightly. 'There's a fellow up the road I can borrow one off, but he's doing overtime. He won't be home until nine o'clock.'

'Then you're here for the evening, Susan, whether you like it or not.' Ken couldn't have looked more miserable if he'd been facing a hangman.

★

'Where's Dennis?' Linda asked, as Elsie stood in front of the mirror that hung over the fireplace applying Crimson Passion lipstick.

'I don't know, but he can't be far. He's got no money.' Elsie pushed down her lipstick and replaced the top. She lifted her eyebrows and gazed critically at herself. 'Eee, Elsie, you're about ready for the knacker's yard.'

'There's no point in us hanging about here.' Linda dropped the magazine she had been scanning. 'Let's go to the pub.'

'The Rovers?' Elsie asked.

'Where else?'

'God, and to think of some of the places I got taken to during the war.' Elsie's eyes misted over as she recalled the happiest days of her life. 'I passed one the other day. You should have seen the look the commissionaire gave me. He wouldn't have given me a look like that during the war if I'd swept in with one of my Yank officers, I can tell you. If it hadn't been for you and our Dennis, I'd have been shot of your father years ago and out in the Arizona desert now . . .'

'You getting ready or what?' Linda had heard too many of her mother's stories about Yank officers to want to listen to another when her own marriage was in tatters.

'Five minutes, and I'll be with you.' Elsie smoothed the skirt of the tight navy blue dress she had worn to work over her hips, straightened its enormous collar and reached for her scent.

★

'That's the spare wheel on,' David informed his mother, as he wiped his hands on an oily rag in the living room doorway. He looked around. 'Where's Ken?'

'He's taken Susan next door to meet Esther Hayes.' Ida picked up her knitting.

'What about our Ken, then?' David grinned.

'What about our Ken?' Ida asked, although she knew full well what David meant.

' "The bridegroom's mother was beautifully attired . . ." '

'Get out of it,' Ida interrupted, 'they're just friends. And I've been meaning to have a word with you about your pay packet. You had that rise?'

'Not yet.'

'When you do I want a bit more out of you than thirty shillings a week. You couldn't get full board anywhere else for that, and there's your washing. When I was your age I handed over my pay packet unopened. And do you know how much I got back—'

'There's no chance of getting a word in edgewise once you start.' David took the knitting from her hands. 'You can have a quid.'

'No.'

David pulled her from the chair and wrapped his arms around her waist. 'I'm not offering any more. A quid – going, going . . .'

'I only want ten shillings. I don't want you to think I'm grasping,' Ida said. 'I just want you to learn the value of money.'

'That's a fine thing to happen the first time our Ken brings a young lady home.' Frank had walked in through the scullery door.

'Young lady!' Ida tossed her head, as she broke free from David's grasp. 'I don't know what's got into you two. You're gossiping worse than Ena Sharples.'

'She's a nice girl, though, isn't she?' Frank looked to Ida for confirmation.

'She's all right,' Ida concurred.

Frank caught David's eye. They both knew what Ida meant. Susan was fine but Ida thought her Ken could do better.

'If your car's fixed, would you like to go into town?' Ken closed Esther Hayes's door behind them. A confirmed spinster, Esther had nursed her mother until her death a couple of years ago and continued to live on in her house. A teetotaller, she never went near the Rovers Return but she was the first to help any of her neighbours in time of trouble. She also loved having visitors and always made them feel welcome.

'Why do you keep on about going into town?' Susan asked.

Ken opened her umbrella and held it over her as the

rain started pouring down again. 'Because there's nothing amusing around here.'

'There's the fascinating little pub round the corner.' She linked her arm with his.

'I've heard the Rovers called some things in my time, but fascinating isn't one of them.'

'I'd still like to see the place for myself.'

Ken knew defeat when it was staring him in the face. 'All right, as you're so determined, I'll take you there.'

Dreading the comments he would get from the regulars when they saw him with Susan, Ken opened the pub door and ushered Susan inside. The public bar was crowded with neighbours who had braved the dismal night. He left her in a secluded corner and fought his way to the counter. He returned with a pint for himself and a half of shandy for Susan.

'Thank you.' She sipped it delicately. 'I can never make up my mind whether I prefer beer with lemonade or ginger beer.'

'You'll only get it one way in here,' Ken said, 'and there's no ice.'

'Will you stop it?' she said.

'Stop what?'

'Apologising. Give me credit for a bit of sense. I wasn't expecting to find the Duchess of Devonshire in here.'

'But this isn't the sort of place you've been used to,' he protested.

'What you mean is I live in what's known as a nice residential suburb.' She took another sip of shandy.

'Yes—'

'And you know as well as I do that there's people who look down their noses at me for that up at college.'

'Susan—'

'My grandfather lives in a house exactly like yours,' she broke in angrily, 'so don't go thinking that you've the sole rights on the Coronation Streets of this world, Ken Barlow, because you haven't.'

The second Elsie and Linda Tanner walked into the bar of the Rovers, Ena Sharples, who'd been watching the door intently from the snug, drained her glass. 'Same again, girls?' She kept her eye on Linda's husband, not wanting to miss anything.

'Don't mind if I do.' Martha followed Ena's example and set down her empty glass.

By the time Ena had collected Minnie's glass, Linda was staring at Ivan. Ena put the glasses on the counter and leant forward on tiptoe so she could see into the bar.

Linda was the first to speak. 'And what are you doing here, Ivan Cheveski?' she demanded.

Ivan looked Linda squarely in the eye. 'I've come to take you home.'

'If you expect me to come home with you, you've another think coming,' Linda retorted.

'Why did you leave?' he pleaded.

Elsie was conscious not only of all the bar customers watching and listening but also of Martha Longhurst, Minnie Caldwell and Ena Sharples standing at the snug bar, fresh milk stouts in hand as they lapped up Linda and Ivan's conversation. 'Let's go home and talk about this, shall we?' she said to Linda.

'If he goes back to our house, I'm not coming,' Linda answered.

'Don't be daft,' Elsie countered irritably. 'You've got to talk some time.'

'I never noticed you and my dad talking.' Linda turned her back on Ivan and Elsie.

'You leave me and your dad out of this.' Elsie glanced at Ena. 'If you won't go home, Linda, we'll talk about it here. We'll be as good as a concert for everybody,' she added derisively.

Annie walked down the bar to the snug. 'Ladies are kindly requested not to remain at the bar after being served.'

Ena slapped four pennies on to the counter. 'Then I'll have a packet of crisps.'

'Linda, please, love . . .' Ivan moved in front of his wife, lifting her chin with his fingertips forcing her to look at him.

'I've only one thing to say to you, Ivan Cheveski. Get out of here. And if you don't, I will.' When Ivan didn't make a move, Linda ran out.

Ivan focused his mournful Slavic eyes on Elsie. 'What am I going to do?'

'That's for us to think about.' She called to Annie, 'Two more drinks down here, love, please.'

'You can't talk to her,' Ivan said. 'If I say anything, she flies off the handle.'

'Our Dennis is just the same,' Elsie observed. 'He's gone off in a huff somewhere. I only hope he decides to come back soon. Tomorrow's his day for wood carrying.'

'Really?' Ivan answered, confused.

'Heck as like, pencil down labour,' Elsie joked. 'What time's your train back?'

'I'm not going back.'

'Don't be daft, Ivan. Just because you and our Linda have had a bit of a set-to there's no need to turn yourself out of work. Come on, what's the real problem? Has our Linda been knocking round with other fellows?' Elsie dreaded his reply, but she still had to ask the question.

'No, I don't think so,' he answered hesitantly, lowering his voice.

Elsie pushed a ten shilling note across the counter and took the drinks Annie handed her. 'If she's not, then what do you want to go saying such things for?'

'Just wanted to hear her tell me that she doesn't,' he admitted sheepishly.

'You haven't touched her?' Elsie bristled at the thought.

'No, nothing like that. I wouldn't hurt Linda.'

'I'm glad to hear it. Lamming into someone never did any good.' Elsie spoke from painful experience.

He stared down into his beer. 'She's just not the same person she used to be.'

'There's nothing like a cup of cocoa at the end of an evening, that's what I always say.' Martha Longhurst settled herself comfortably into the visitor's chair in Ena Sharples's private sitting room off the Glad Tidings Mission Hall.

'It's a good end to the day.' Ena tucked a stray hair under the hair net she always wore before setting milk on to boil.

There was a knock. 'Is that your door?' Martha asked.

'There was a committee meeting tonight, but I don't encourage them to disturb me this late.' Ena opened the door that connected her quarters to the hall and glowered at the short, stout, balding man standing in front of her.

'Good evening, Mrs Sharples.' Leonard Swindley, Chairman of the Glad Tidings Mission Hall Committee, greeted her formally.

'Mr Swindley, I didn't think anyone would be left in the hall this late. If you've come about those broken cups . . .' Ena began, pre-empting any complaint.

'No, it's not that.' He stepped inside and saw Martha. 'As you've company, Mrs Sharples, I'll come back another time.'

'I've no secrets from my friend Mrs Longhurst,' Ena said abruptly. 'Martha, this is Mr Swindley.'

'Very well, as you insist.' Leonard Swindley cleared his throat and faced Ena. 'The committee of the Glad Tidings Mission Hall feel that it is unseemly for the care-taker to be seen entering licensed premises.'

'You what?' Ena stared at him incredulously.

As he repeated himself, Ena regained her composure.

'Do you or your committee pay me anything?' she challenged.

'We give you free accommodation and coal,' Leonard blustered.

'Do you or do you not pay me anything?' she reiterated loudly.

'No actual money changes hands,' he conceded.

'Right, and what I do with my own bit of pension is no concern of you or anyone else.' She stepped closer to him and he retreated. 'Besides, who's to say that I ever cross the threshold of the Rovers Return? I've only one message for your committee, Mr Swindley, and it's from the good book. "Love thy Neighbour", that's what it says . . .'

Taken aback by Ena's vehemence, Leonard withdrew into the public hall. 'Now, now, Mrs Sharples, there's no need to carry on like this.'

Hearing a hiss from the stove, Ena turned just as the milk boiled over. 'Now look what you've done. Interrupting two old ladies having a cup of cocoa and a discussion on Handel's *Messiah*.'

'All I'm saying, Mrs Sharples, is mend your ways or we'll have to put you out.' He picked up his hat from the table behind him.

'Put me out? And who'll take this rotten job if I go?'

'We'll cross that bridge when we come to it.' Leonard had gone further than he had intended, but he couldn't back down now.

'Know some generals, do you?' Ena asked, as Leonard retreated to the outside door. 'Because if you don't, I'd like to know just who is going to put me out.' She closed the door behind him.

Chapter Three

Preoccupied with concern for Linda and Dennis, Elsie slept badly. She was awake long before the alarm clock shattered the stillness of the house at a quarter to seven. She turned back the bedclothes and shivered as the unheated air of the bedroom closed around her. She wrapped herself in her bronze nylon satin dressing-gown, left her chilly bedroom and walked down the narrow staircase, retrieved the morning newspaper from her letterbox and pushed open the door of the living room. It was cold but nowhere near as icy as her bedroom and she raked through the smouldering ashes in the fireplace to rekindle the flames.

Grateful for the residual warmth, she rummaged through the clutter on the mantelpiece in search of cigarettes, then discovered to her dismay there were only two left in the packet. She struck a match, lit one and settled into an easy-chair with the paper. A few minutes later the living room door opened and Linda walked in. Elsie registered the miserable expression on her daughter's face and decided against trying to talk her into a better mood. She set aside the paper, went to the foot of the stairs and yelled, 'Dennis, you up yet? You'd better be, because I'm not calling you again.'

She waited until he had grunted a reply, then turned back to discover that Linda had taken possession of chair and newspaper. 'Damn him,' she muttered, more to herself than to Linda, as she heard the unmistakable sound of bedsprings creaking upstairs. 'He's got back into bed. Dennis!' she screamed. 'I'm not calling you again.' Then she addressed Linda: 'What's the time?'

'Twenty past,' Linda replied, without looking up from the paper.

'Put kettle on, will you, love?'

As Linda disappeared into the back kitchen, Ivan opened the door, his clothes rumpled, hair ruffled from uneasy sleep.

'What's that thing doing here?' Linda demanded, when she returned from the kitchen.

'He didn't want to go back,' Elsie explained, 'so I told him he could sleep on the sofa in the front parlour.'

'I've left him. And no one – not you, not the Queen of England – will make me take him back.'

'Is it too much trouble for you to tell us why?' Elsie asked. 'This is the same Ivan I had to listen to you go on about for six months before you married him, isn't it?'

'I must have been mad.' Linda lifted the teapot from the stand on the table. 'He won't let me buy as much as a studio couch on the drip.' Oblivious to Elsie's confusion, Linda picked up the threads of an argument that had begun the day she'd left her husband. 'We can only have what we can pay for.'

'If it's a new winter coat you want, you can have one today,' Ivan interposed eagerly.

'That's a bit late.' Linda flounced into the kitchen.

'We've all got tempers—' Elsie began.

'I don't want to talk about it.' Linda returned with a bag of sugar, opened the canister and started to refill it.

'You've got to talk about whatever's wrong between you,' Elsie said.

'All right, then.' Linda looked up defiantly. 'Kids! He doesn't want one.'

'Of course I do,' Ivan contradicted. 'You've got it wrong, love. I want kids but when we can afford them—'

'I'm sick to death of hearing that word. Well, I wanted a bit more time to think things out, but seeing as how, between the two of you, I can't have that, here it is.' She went to the door, then turned back. 'I'm going to have a baby,' she shouted, and ran upstairs.

Hoping to cadge a cup of tea and half an hour's gossip, Martha Longhurst was disappointed to find Ena locking her front door behind her. 'Where you off to, Ena?'

Ena held up a letter. 'I've written to newspaper asking for advice on how to cope with Leonard Swindley.'

'You never have!' Martha gasped, shocked at the idea of anyone questioning the judgement of the chairman of the Glad Tidings Mission Hall Committee. 'Ooh, Ena!'

'And when I've finished with local paper, I'll start on Sundays,' Ena threatened. 'I can just see those headlines coming through the letterbox. "We accuse you, Leonard Swindley di-da-di-da-di-da."'

'You're not afraid of no one, are you, Ena?'

'No. And you want to know something else, Martha? After this,' Ena tapped her letter, 'is posted, you and me are going to Rovers. They're just about opening. I don't want one but I'll force meself.' She set her mouth in a grim line. 'Downright defiance, Martha, that's my motto from now on. Downright defiance.'

'Don't you dare touch me, Ivan Cheveski,' Linda warned, as he moved closer to her chair after Elsie had left for work.

Dennis held up a paperback he was flicking through. 'Mam must have been in a soppy mood when she bought this. "I will love you, darling, till my heart can no longer sing . . ." ' he chanted. 'Whoever wrote that should cop a load of you two.'

'Shut up,' Linda snarled.

'You don't live here any more,' Dennis sneered. 'You're only here on sufferance.'

'I'm paying my way,' Linda retorted.

'And I'm not, is that what you're getting at?'

'It's time you went down dole.' Linda left the table and cleared her plate and cup into the kitchen.

'I'll go in my own good time,' Dennis replied. 'What's it to you anyway? Just because you're in a bit of bother, don't go taking it out on me. God help that kid of yours!'

'What did you say?'

Dennis and Linda turned simultaneously to see Ivan standing in front of the fire, fists clenched, face grim and angry.

'Nothing.' Dennis leapt out of his chair and moved back, slamming his hip into the table as Ivan advanced on him.

'Oh, yes, you did. And it's not just her kid, it's mine too. And I want to make quite sure you know what you're up against before you say another word.'

Linda could see Ivan was on the verge of losing control, and shouted at her brother, 'Get out.'

Dennis didn't need any prompting. Seconds later, the front door closed behind him. Linda stared at Ivan then burst into tears. 'You don't want it.'

'Of course I want it.' Anger abated, Ivan stood in front of his wife, wondering whether he dared try to comfort her.

'But you said—'

'Now it's here, of course I want it.' He opened his arms and she fell into them. 'I'm dead pleased, Linda.'

'Really?' She looked into his dark eyes and saw only tenderness.

'Really.' He held her close. 'Dead pleased, love.'

There had been a time when Harry Hewitt had regarded a pint in the Rovers Return at the end of his shift a luxury before he went home for his tea. But that was before his wife died and he'd been forced to send his daughter to the orphanage. He'd even begun to refer to his home as 'the house' to his friends: it was no longer warm or welcoming, and the last place he wanted to go to after a day's work. At least in the Rovers he could rely on receiving a smile from Annie Walker when she served him. 'Pint please, Annie.' He looked around the pub. 'You putting up Christmas decorations this year?'

'Tomorrow night, Harry.' She lifted a pint mug down from one of the hooks that had been screwed into the shelf behind the bar and pulled his pint. 'You?'

'Not this year. Not without our Lucille.'

Sensing that he was depressed, she searched for something reassuring she could say to him. 'She'll have a marvellous Christmas in that orphanage, Harry. I know someone who rang up one year and tried to give them a cake. The matron didn't want it. She said they had enough cakes for Muldoon's picnic.'

Jack Walker walked behind the bar from the private rooms. 'Hello, Harry.'

'Hello, Jack.' As her husband joined them, Annie moved away. Harry knew from past experience that that meant the Walkers weren't talking.

'Ee, Harry.' Ena Sharples accosted him. 'There's a bobby knocking at your door.'

'Lend us five bob,' Dennis begged, as Elsie dropped the Christmas cards she'd bought on her way home from work on to the living room table.

'No.' Elsie sat down and unscrewed the top from her pen.

'Please.'

'No,' she reiterated decisively.

'You're stinking rotten awful, you are.'

'That's me.' Elsie remained unperturbed. 'What did they say down Labour today?'

'There was a job going on piecework, sorting parcels in Post Office.'

She narrowed her eyes as she looked up at him. 'And what did you say?'

'No . . . It were nights,' he protested, as she frowned.

'Do you mean to tell me that you've got the bare-faced cheek to sit there—'

'It were nights. I don't want to work nights. I can do better than that.'

'Yes, you're marvellous,' Elsie snapped. 'You can do anything, you're that bloody marvellous—'

'I'll walk into town now and get meself a job.' Dennis shouted her down.

'The last time you did that you ended up doing time. Well, I won't take you back again . . .' Elsie found herself screaming at a closed door. Turning back to the table she picked up the card she had been writing. The gilt message on the front glittered back at her, mocking and absurd.

Peace on earth and goodwill to all men.

'I got it,' Ena crowed to Martha and Minnie, as she set three bottles of milk stout on their table. 'That copper's come about the dog licences for Harry Hewitt's whippets. I bet he hasn't got them.'

All three looked up as the melodic strains of 'Good King Wenceslas' filled the bar.

'They're collecting for the aged and infirm,' Minnie revealed, with the authority of one who had been cornered and forced to give.

The snug door opened and a collecting-box was pushed in front of Ena's nose. She looked up to see the bespectacled eyes of Leonard Swindley peering down at her.

Harry left the policeman and ran up Coronation Street as fast as his legs would carry him. Esther Hayes was standing on her doorstep. 'Come in, Harry.' She opened her door wider.

Harry turned pale. 'Is she . . . is . . . ?'

'Lucille is fine,' Esther said, in response to his stricken look.

Harry entered Esther's living room to see Lucille calmly sitting on the sofa drinking a glass of milk. Not knowing whether to hug or thump her, he exhaled slowly and counted to ten before he trusted himself to speak. 'What are you doing here?' he asked at last.

'I walked home.' She smiled mischievously. 'I've a hole in my welly, look.' She lifted her boot.

'Walked it?' He looked at her sceptically. 'It's over twelve miles.'

'I didn't care how far it was, I wanted to come home for Christmas.'

'That's not until Sunday,' he remonstrated.

'All the ones who had somewhere to go went from the orphanage yesterday and I was left with the ones who hadn't anywhere. And they say that if you haven't got anywhere to go, no one wants you . . .' She choked back a tear.

'You silly billy.' Harry hugged her. 'I've sent all your presents there. I'd better phone the home and the police—'

'You'll not send me back?' Lucille begged, between sobs.

'I've got to let them know where you are, love.' He turned aside so Lucille wouldn't see the tears starting in his own eyes.

'I'll help, Harry,' Esther offered.

'But who's going to look after her when I'm at work?' Harry asked.

'We'll work out something.' Esther smiled at Lucille.

'Can I stay?' Lucille begged, scarcely daring to hope as she looked from Harry to Esther.

Harry relented. 'After Christmas you go straight back there.'

Lucille flung herself on him and locked her hands around his neck. 'I promise.'

'Promise,' he repeated sternly. 'No nonsense now.'

'No nonsense.' She crossed her fingers stealthily.

'It's a witch hunt, that's what it is,' Ena declared to Martha and Minnie, as Leonard led the Glad Tidings Mission Hall choir out of the Rovers Return. 'That lot are out for a poor old woman's blood. Have they ever come singing in here at Christmas before? Answer me that!'

'Well, come to think about it, no, they haven't,' Martha concurred.

'That rotten committee decided to come to seek me in my wantonness.'

'Your what?' Martha questioned, open-mouthed.

'Me wantonness,' Ena repeated crossly. 'That's how that lot talk. I can just hear them, "We shall go down to Sodom and Gomorrah – in this case the Rovers – and seek out Mrs Sharples – a poor woman who's never done any harm in her life." '

'Don't go upsetting yourself,' Martha advised, unnerved by Ena's strange language.

'I couldn't be more upset if I tried.' Ena swallowed half of her milk stout in a single gulp. 'When Leonard Swindley said something about me partaking of a little stimulant just now, I could have let him have this milk stout straight in his face.'

'But you didn't,' Martha retorted. 'You just said, "Good evening," and borrowed twopence from my change.'

''Ere, whose side are you on?' Ena demanded.

'There's no sides to it.'

'Isn't there?' Ena questioned angrily. 'All I know is I'm out of a home and a job.'

'What you going to do, Ena?' Minnie asked.

'One of my lousy daughters will just have to have me.'

'It won't come to that,' Martha assured her.

Ena pursed her lips. 'I wish I could think you were right, Martha Longhurst, I really do, but you didn't see the way Leonard Swindley was looking at me. Not like I did.'

'Why can't I sleep at home in my own bed?' Lucille nagged Harry.

'Because it's not aired,' Harry replied, 'and . . .' he looked over his shoulder to check that Esther wasn't in earshot . . . 'don't be so ungrateful.'

'Can I stop up just for once?'

'No,' Harry said sternly, 'you've had enough of your own way for one day.'

'Do you think I'll catch it when I go back?' she asked warily.

'They'll have had time to get over it by then so don't go spoiling your holiday worrying about that. But you'll have no presents,' he reminded her. 'I've sent them all there, except your granddad's.'

Esther bustled into the room holding a nightdress. 'It'll drown you, Lucille, but it's the best I can do.'

'Hey, Dad,' Lucille shouted after Harry, as he prepared to leave.

'What?' he asked, wondering what was coming next.

'Merry Christmas.' She gave him a wicked smile and took the nightie from Esther.

Ena Sharples stood with her ear pressed to the door between her private quarters and the Mission Hall. She was listening so hard her ears buzzed, but she didn't move until she heard footsteps. Then she burst into song. ' "My drink is water bright from the crystal stream . . ." '

She was well into the second verse when there was a knock at the door. She opened it to see Leonard Swindley. 'I wanted a word with you, Mrs Sharples.'

'Oh, you did, did you?'

Unable to meet her eyes he looked down at the well-scrubbed floor. 'About the social on Friday and the children's party.'

She crossed her arms over her ample bosom. 'Oh, aye? You think you'll get me to do all the dirty work and then, come the New Year, you'll get me out. Tonight you saw me in Sodom and Gomorrah . . .'

'Look, Mrs Sharples, perhaps I was a little overheated last night. Said one or two things I didn't really mean. And after all, this is the season of goodwill . . .'

'You're fond of pushing people around, aren't you?' she said. 'You even push that committee around.'

Leonard bristled. 'My dealings with the committee are hardly any business of yours, Mrs Sharples.'

'Oh, they aren't, aren't they? Not even when you put me out in the street? Put me out . . . out . . .' Ena stumbled. The room darkened. Shadows crowded in on her from the walls. '. . . put me out . . .' Her eyes felt strangely heavy, the floor loomed closer. The last thing that registered in her mind was the strength in Leonard Swindley's arms as he caught her. Then she was enveloped in blackness.

'Here's your tea.' Linda saw Ivan staring at her when she handed him his cup. 'Why do you keep looking at me? Have I got a smudge on my nose or something?'

'No, darling.' He grinned. 'Maybe I'm just happy.'

'You really are pleased about the baby?' She sought confirmation that their row was over.

'Of course I am.'

She sat on his lap and put her arms round his neck. 'You want it to be a boy or a girl?'

'I don't mind.'

'You must have some preference,' she persisted.

'All right, a girl, but as long as it's got two arms and two legs and they're waving about, I don't mind.'

'I must admit I like the idea of a girl. You can dress them up nice.' Linda reached for the packet of cigarettes on the mantelpiece, took out the last one and lit it. 'What will we call her?'

'Linda,' Ivan suggested.

'No, we will not,' Linda countered irritably. 'That's one thing I'll never forgive my Mam for. Linda's as common as muck.'

'Right, we won't call her Linda.' His smile broadened. 'You choose.'

'I fancy Dawn,' she mused. 'It's a bit unusual.'

He set aside his tea and wrapped his arms round her waist. 'We have to get a house. We can't have the baby in a flat.'

Linda returned his embrace. 'Oh, Ivan, you are good.' She kissed him. Moments later they were disturbed by a—

'Oh, heck!'

Linda looked up to see her mother standing in front of them. 'We're getting a house.'

'Well, I think you're doing the right thing.' Elsie winked

at Ivan. 'I suppose you're kipping on the settee again tonight . . .' As he turned bright red, Elsie said, 'It's all right, I've moved into the back bedroom and you can have my bed.'

'In that case I'll take my cocoa up.' Linda picked up her cup. ''Night, Mam. And I'd better say goodbye. Ivan and me will be off home first thing tomorrow morning. We've a lot of things to sort out. But if it's all right with you we'll be back for Christmas.'

'Of course it's all right, where else would you go on Christmas Day? 'Night, love,' Elsie called after her. 'So,' she looked at Ivan, 'someone's going to be a daddy and someone's going to be a grandma.'

'That's right.' Ivan grinned and followed Linda through the door.

'At last.' Elsie sighed as Dennis walked in, minutes after Ivan had climbed the stairs.

'Here I am.' Dennis dropped a bundle of banknotes on to the table.

Elsie picked up the money. 'Oh, God! Where did you get this?'

Tapping his nose, Dennis retrieved it, pushed it into his pocket and walked up the stairs, leaving Elsie gazing after him.

Martha Longhurst was on her way to the corner shop to buy a quarter of a pound of tea and a packet of soap flakes when she saw Leonard Swindley pinning a notice to the door of the Mission Hall. Wary of a rebuff, she sidled over to him. 'Have you heard anything about Ena, Mr Swindley?' she ventured timidly.

'Yes, Mrs Longhurst,' he replied briskly. 'Miss Nugent telephoned the hospital first thing this morning.'

'I've never learnt to use the phone myself,' she confided.

'The hospital said Mrs Sharples was comfortable.'

'They don't tell you much, do they?' She hitched her shopping bag higher on to her elbow.

'Oh, I don't know,' he countered. 'I thought the statement rather reassuring.'

'I'll go there meself and see about getting a visiting card.'

'You don't need one of those to visit a hospital any more, Mrs Longhurst. You can just go in during visiting times. It's seven until eight o'clock every evening. You will give Mrs Sharples our regards when you see her, won't you?'

'Yes, I'll do that,' Martha promised.

Leonard pushed the last drawing pin into the notice and dusted off his hands. 'If you'll excuse me, Mrs Longhurst, I'm trying to get as much done as possible. I've left my assistant in charge of the shop. This is one of those times when Mrs Sharples could really be of use.' He looked at her and hesitated. 'I don't suppose you'd consider being of help to us, Mrs Longhurst? Just on a temporary basis, that is, until Mrs Sharples comes back,' he added cautiously.

'I'd have to think about it.'

'I am sure that the committee would see that you didn't go . . . unrewarded,' he phrased carefully.

'How long would it be for, Mr Swindley?'

'That is for Mrs Sharples's doctors to say.'

'I see,' Martha said. 'And what exactly is it that you would you be wanting me to do for you, Mr Swindley?'

Chapter Four

The ward was Spartan; it was tidy, scrubbed pristine and reeked of the malodorous disinfectant unique to hospitals. Twelve beds, so neatly and tightly made that the patients looked like trespassers, were ranged at exact, neat intervals down one side of the long room, a corresponding twelve set along the parallel wall opposite them.

Ena Sharples was ensconced in a bed more or less in the centre. She sat up, rucking the tucked-in sheets, and glanced shiftily up and down. Having ensured that no nurses were in sight, she crouched at the foot of her bed and grabbed the clipboard that held her details. She was flicking through a series of incomprehensible graphs when a nurse snatched it from her hands. 'Mrs Sharples! You should be ashamed of yourself.'

Ena would not be intimidated by a slip of a girl: 'You frightened the life out of me,' she protested.

'This is private.' The nurse replaced the chart at the foot of the bed.

'Private!' Ena sneered. 'They are my particulars and I want to know what's wrong with me.'

'There's nothing for you to worry about, Mrs Sharples.' The nurse walked off, her rubber-soled shoes squeaking on the linoleum.

'That's it,' Ena muttered to herself. 'They always say that when you're dying. I'm on my way out. I'm going.' She fought back tears. 'And there's nowt that can be done about it.'

'Hello, Mam.'

Ena looked up from her Bible to see her daughter, Vera Lomax, hovering next to her bed. 'So you do come to see your mother sometimes, even if you do wait until she's at death's door.'

'I brought you this.' Her daughter held out a huge, leafy potted plant.

'That's a fool of a thing to bring me. How am I going to carry it when I go home?' Ena enquired ungratefully.

'Aren't they keeping you in, then?' Her daughter pulled up a chair and sat down.

'I don't know,' Ena said shortly. 'Where's that husband of yours?'

'He's got flu. I've had it too.' Her daughter sniffed loudly, as if Ena had asked her to prove that she really had been ill.

'I suppose that's why I've not seen hide nor hair of you

for two months.' Ena glanced up and down the ward at the visitors standing and sitting beside the other patients' beds. 'Where's your sister?'

'I don't know.'

'I suppose she knows which way my will goes.' Ena sighed theatrically. 'Well, I'm very sorry to disappoint the pair of you, but I won't be going just yet.'

Her daughter shuddered at the mention of death. 'Don't talk like that.'

'I had three doctors round me this afternoon and the food's terrible.' Ena shook her head. 'They're trying to make me eat boiled food.'

'You're very popular, Mrs Sharples.' A nurse approached her bed. 'You've another visitor.'

'Hello, Ena.' Martha walked up to her.

Taking advantage of the interruption, Vera rose to her feet. 'Well, I'm off, Mam.'

'You only just got here,' Ena grumbled.

'I know, but I want a fag and I can't smoke in here.' She offered Martha her chair. 'Besides, you've got Martha now.'

'Friends aren't like your own family,' Ena barked, as her daughter walked out.

'I'm sorry, Ena, I know I'm a bit late. I was delayed,' Martha gabbled. 'But you're in everyone's thoughts. Mr Swindley was only saying this afternoon—'

'Where did you see Leonard Swindley this afternoon?' Ena was instantly on the alert.

'When we were taking up tables, in Mission,' Martha divulged thoughtlessly.

'In Mission! Whatever were you doing there?' A knot of fear formed in Ena's stomach at the thought of Martha taking over her job and home.

'Helping out,' Martha answered, oblivious to Ena's mounting suspicions.

'You snake in the grass, Martha Longhurst! I'm out of it for five minutes and you move in—'

Martha looked heavenward and counted her blessings as a choir of children walked into the ward singing carols loud enough to drown out Ena.

After two sleepless night of worry over Dennis, Elsie was searching the mantelpiece for a cigarette next morning when he came in with the post he had collected from behind the front door.

'Cards.' He held them up to her.

'Leave them alone,' Elsie snapped.

'What's up?' he asked.

'You know as well as I do.'

'No, I don't.' He dropped the cards on to the table. 'Is there any tea?'

'In the pot.'

Dennis poured himself a cup then went to the overcoat he'd left hanging in the passage. He delved into the pockets. 'You take anything out of this yesterday?'

'Yes.'

'Where's my money?' he demanded.

'The other night you left here flat broke and you came back with twenty-five quid. I don't know where you got it—'

'You didn't give me a chance to tell you,' he interrupted. 'I—'

'And I'm keeping it safe so you'll have something to give back.'

'Who to?' he asked, returning to the living room.

'Whoever you nicked it off.' Elsie found a cigarette, then tore a piece off an old newspaper, twisted it into a makeshift spill and thrust it into the fire.

'I didn't knock it off,' he protested.

'We've been through this too many times before.' Elsie waited until the paper flared, lit her cigarette and dropped the spill on top of the coals. 'Where did it come from?'

'I met a fellow . . . Look, Mam, before I went inside I had quite a lot of money.'

'I know,' she agreed ironically.

'He lent me a fiver. I went to the dogs—'

'If you expect me to believe that, you haven't got the sense you were born with.'

'Then keep the twenty-five quid,' he snarled viciously.

Uncertain what to believe, Elsie watched him carefully. 'What's this fellow called?'

'Alf Whittle. But keep the money if you don't believe me.'

Wanting to believe him, Elsie murmured, 'Then all I can say is God bless Alf Whittle. Open me cards will you?'

Dennis thrust his thumb under the flap of the first one. 'It's from our Linda.'

'That was quick, she only left here yesterday. What does she say?'

' "Dear Mam," ' he read, ' "Ivan and me will be with you on Christmas Eve. We will be coming by bus, as trains will be crowded. Expect us when you see us. I have got you slippers, they look very nice. If you haven't got me anything yet, stockings would be very nice, size nine and a half." Here, she's sent you all this for the price of a card.'

'That's your sister.' As they both burst out laughing, Elsie suddenly realised that neither of them had done much laughing since Dennis had been released from gaol. 'We're going to have a good Christmas, kid. I just know it.' She smiled.

'And so do I.' He held out his hand for his twenty-five pounds.

Ida put down her knitting as Ken entered the living room. His hair was dripping raindrops, his duffel coat saturated and his shoes squelched as he made his way to the hearth.

'You're soaked through.' Ida helped him off with his coat. 'Have you finished your round?'

'Three more streets to go. I'm frozen stiff.' Ken dropped into the chair Ida had vacated. He drummed his feet on the floor in an effort to regain the feeling in his toes.

'Don't do that, your father's in bed,' Ida warned.

'What time is he on?' Ken was so cold even his jaw was stiff.

'Ten o'clock shift.' Ida opened the scullery door. 'I'll make a cup of tea, that'll warm you.'

'Thanks.' Ken crouched over the fire, siphoning its warmth into his frozen limbs. 'But as soon as I've drunk it, I'll have to go out again.'

'Not in that coat you won't. I'll get that old one of your father's.' Ida put the kettle on and returned to the living room. They heard a knock. 'Who can that be?' She went to the door.

Esther stood on the doorstep, tears mingling with the rain on her ashen face.

'Oh, Esther, whatever's the matter?' Ida stood back as Esther ran, panic-stricken, into the living room.

'Ken, have you finished your round?' Esther blurted breathlessly.

'Just about—'

'You didn't see Lucille Hewitt anywhere, did you?' she interrupted.

'No.'

Esther looked at Ida. 'I've looked everywhere, Ida. She's been so good the last two nights and yesterday, and no trouble at all today and then she went off – and I've been everywhere.'

Ida led her to a chair. 'Now don't you worry, Esther, she's probably only out playing. You know what kids are.'

'She's not. I've scoured the neighbourhood and asked all the other kids and no one's seen her.' Esther's voice pitched into hysteria.

'I think you've done enough looking for one day.' Ida pushed her gently into the chair. 'Our Ken will find her, won't you, Ken?'

Ken grabbed his father's old coat and headed for the front door.

'I only hope she turns up before Harry comes home,' Esther whispered hoarsely. 'I dread to think what he's going to say if he finds her gone.'

'I know you're only trying to take my mind off Lucille,' Esther accepted the cup of tea Ida handed her, 'but you read such terrible things in the papers. What if—?'

'What if nothing,' Frank interrupted, as he walked in fastening his collar stud to his shirt. 'The kid ran away from an orphanage to come home, so she's not likely to run away from home as soon as she gets here.'

Frank sat at the table and Ida went into the scullery.

She returned with a dinner plate heaped high with mince and potatoes, which she had been keeping warm in the oven, and set it before him. 'Come in,' she shouted, as someone knocked at the front door.

Footsteps came down the passage and Harry entered the living room.

'Have you found her?' Esther asked urgently.

Harry shook his head. 'I don't know what to do now, except contact the police,' he said despairingly.

The door opened again and Ken ushered in a very wet and sheepish Lucille.

'Where have you been?' Harry demanded.

'Shan't tell you.' Lucille grinned.

'Yes, you will, young lady.' Despite his relief at seeing her in one piece, Harry was in no mood for his daughter's mischief after the upset and trouble she'd caused to everyone, particularly Esther who had put herself out for them.

Lucille's bottom lip trembled as she looked at the assembled adults. 'You're not cross with me, are you?'

'Tell me where you've been,' Harry repeated, grim-faced.

'I had a card this afternoon from me gran with a pound in it, so I went Christmas shopping.'

'And what did you buy?' Harry asked.

'Presents,' Lucille whispered.

'Then let's be looking at them.' Harry stood waiting.

Lucille delved into her handbag and handed Esther a bottle of scent. 'It should be wrapped,' she murmured apologetically.

'Oh, love, that's just what I wanted,' Esther cried.

'I got you hair oil, Dad.' Lucille handed Harry a box. 'I wanted to get you whisky but the man said I had to come back when I was eighteen.'

'Hair oil's fine, love. Just don't disappear again will you?' He brushed his hand across his eyes, then hugged her.

'See that woman two beds along in a cross-stitch jacket?' Ena's voice rang out, high-pitched, audible to everyone in the ward as she talked to her daughter, Vera. 'If she rolls over once in the night, she rolls over twenty times. I wouldn't mind, but she's that hefty the bed creaks something awful. No sooner do I get off to sleep than she's waking me up.'

'You're all right in here, aren't you, Mam?' Vera asked.

'Oh, we've had some right goings-on. I said to the sister if that doctor thinks he's funny being a comic in the concert they put on for us—'

'I can't stay long, Mam,' she interrupted. 'The kids are waiting outside.'

Ena looked her daughter squarely in the eye. 'All right! How long have I got? Come on,' she prompted, as her daughter gaped at her open-mouthed. 'They must have told you how long I've got left. They talk to the relatives. Here,' Ena turned on Martha as she walked into the ward, 'I left strict instructions that you weren't to be let in.'

'That's a nice welcome,' Martha chided. 'I came to give you these, they're from the congregation at Glad Tidings.' She set a box of chocolates on Ena's locker.

'And you can take them back and tell them what to do with them an' all. And if you've any thoughts of moving into Mission Hall, forget it. I'm coming home to die in me own bed.'

Talking and laughing non stop, Linda and Ivan walked through the house into Elsie's living room. After kissing Elsie, and shaking Dennis's hand, Ivan set their suitcase the settee and made a beeline for the outside toilet.

Watching to make sure that Ivan had shut the door behind him, Linda opened the case and extracted a parcel. She thrust it at Dennis. 'Here, can you hide this for me? It's for Ivan,' she hissed.

Dennis pressed it, trying to guess what it was. 'I'll hide it upstairs.'

'Don't be daft,' Elsie reprimanded. 'He might come across it there – put it in the scullery cupboard.'

'This is for you, Mam.' Linda rummaged through the clothes and handed Elsie a bottle.

'You shouldn't be spending your money on me, you'll

be needing it in the months to come.' Elsie smiled. 'Besides, I've a bottle of that liquor you like for tomorrow.' She waited until Dennis went into the scullery, then asked, 'How are you and Ivan getting along now?'

'You wouldn't believe it.' Linda beamed. 'Ivan's really tickled pink about the baby. He spends all his time looking at second-hand prams.'

'He's a bit ahead of himself, isn't he?' Dennis closed the kitchen door behind him. 'You're not even showing yet.'

'Don't be so common,' Elsie rebuked him. 'And don't stand there watching fire go out. Get coal in.'

'All right, Mam.'

Linda and Elsie stared in amazement as Dennis picked up the scuttle and walked meekly out of the back door.

'Hey, did you see that?' Elsie asked Linda. 'He went to get coal without any backchat. I suppose that's his Christmas present to me.'

Ivan drew near to the fire as he joined them. 'I'll get that,' he offered when someone hammered on the front door.

'What else you got in there?' Elsie asked, as Linda closed the suitcase.

'That would be telling.' Linda looked up as Ivan returned with a frown on his face. 'What's up?'

'It's a copper.'

'What's he collecting for?' Elsie quipped.

'He's not collecting for anything,' Ivan said apprehensively. 'He said he wants a word with our Dennis.'

'Oh, hell.' Elsie sank down on a kitchen chair. 'Get him out of the coal house for me, will you, love?'

The perfect family holiday Elsie had hoped for didn't materialise. Between Christmas Eve and Boxing Day the police collected Dennis three times. Twice they took him to the police station for questioning, only to release him a few hours later without charge. But when he hadn't returned the third time by Boxing Day afternoon Elsie's nerves were in shreds and she couldn't stop her hands shaking as she lit her tenth cigarette of the day.

'The police haven't charged Dennis and that has to mean they haven't any evidence he's done anything wrong,' Ivan pointed out, as he, Elsie and Linda sat at the tea table.

'Did our Dennis say anything to you last night when he came home, Mam?' Linda asked.

'I tried to get him to talk but I couldn't get anything out of him,' Elsie muttered.

'Talking about me again?' Dennis walked in.

'They let you go again,' Elsie said more sharply than she'd intended, in an effort to sidestep his question. 'If you want tea you'll have to put the kettle on.'

'I won't bother, Mam. You know that old suitcase that used to be under my bed?'

'What about it?'

'Where is it?'

'I got shot of it months ago. What's this interest in suit-cases, all of a sudden?' Elsie knew the answer, but she wanted to hear it from Dennis.

'Haven't you heard? My friend Lord Muck's invited me to his yacht on the Riviera for the weekend.'

'There you go, making stupid remarks,' she snapped. 'I'm your mother and I have a right to know what's happening. You've been in and out of that police station—'

'If you want to know what's happening, ask them about it,' he said irritably. 'I haven't a clue what they're after.'

'You, little horror,' Linda lectured him. 'That's no way to talk to your mother.'

'Don't you butt in. That's all I need to make things worse.' Dennis strode out and seconds later the front door banged behind him.

'Don't worry, Mam.' Linda took her mother's arm and led her to the chair in front of the fire. 'You sit down and I'll make you a nice cup of tea.'

'Linda's right.' Ivan sat on the arm of Elsie's chair and put his arm round her. 'Don't worry.'

Elsie patted Ivan's hand but her thoughts remained with Dennis.

'What's the time?' Elsie spat on the iron, watched it sizzle, then smoothed it over the wide collar of her dress.

Linda looked up from the raffia-covered wine bottle she was helping Ivan turn into a lamp. 'Half past six.'

'Then he's not coming back tonight,' Elsie said despondently.

'All his things are still here,' Linda reminded her.

Ivan looked from his wife to his mother-in-law; it was difficult to decide who looked the most depressed. He reached for his coat. 'I'll look for him.'

'Stop prowling, Mam,' Linda ordered later, as Elsie opened the back door for the fifth time in as many minutes.

'He's gone to London, that's what he's done,' Elsie said wretchedly.

'How could he?' Linda asked. 'He's got no money.'

'Yes, he has. He's got the rest of that twenty-five quid.' Elsie closed the door and moved restlessly to the window. 'If it wasn't for him we'd be out enjoying ourselves, instead of sitting here like a load of wet lettuces. He can't keep his fingers to himself, that's his trouble.'

'He's not that bad,' Linda murmured.

At that moment, Ivan returned with Dennis. 'Where have you been?' Elsie turned on her son as he sat at the table.

'Having a drink in the Farriers, if you must know.' Dennis's head sank into his hands.

'Doesn't it ever occur to you that I worry about you?' Elsie asked, in a softer tone.

'I wanted a bit of peace and quiet.' He looked up at her. 'The coppers are coming back for me, do you know that?'

'Excuse me for being a bit dense,' Linda chimed in, 'but what is it you're supposed to have done this time?'

'There was a breaking-and-entering job last Wednesday—'

'The night you came home with twenty-five quid?' Elsie was horrified. 'You said you'd been to the dogs.'

'I had, and what's more I was there the time the job was pulled, but you're just like all the rest. Give a dog a bad name . . .'

'What makes them think it's you?' Ivan asked calmly.

'Two coppers in a patrol car are supposed to have seen me in the area, half an hour after it happened. They must have been off their heads, that's all I can say. If I'd pulled that job I would have been long gone by then.'

'Why haven't they been round here searching?' Ivan continued.

'Because all whoever-it-was took was a few sweets, and there's no point in searching for those because one box of sweets looks just like another so no one can prove whether they're nicked or not. But with my record, they pin it on me and I'll be sure to go down.'

'Who were you with at the dogs?' Elsie asked urgently.

'I was there on my tod.'

'Someone must have seen you,' Ivan insisted.

Elsie laid her hand on Dennis's shoulder. 'Look, love . . .'

'No, *you* look, Mam.' Dennis shrugged off her hand. 'You can't stay here arguing all night. You three go to the Rovers.'

'Only on condition you don't do anything stupid,' Ivan said.

'I'm not a kid,' Dennis replied truculently.

'I know you're not.' Ivan looked at Elsie and Linda. 'Believe him, he won't do anything stupid.'

Elsie saw that Dennis needed to be trusted and stood up. 'I'll get my coat.'

Ivan laid his hand on Linda's arm and hung back as Elsie walked into the Rovers. 'Do you think your Dennis did it?'

'I don't know what to think.' She walked into the bar and tapped her mother's shoulder. 'Here, Mam, Ivan's getting them in. What do you want?'

'Orange squash.'

'Whatever for?'

'If the worst comes to the worst, and the police do come, I'll not open the door with drink on my breath.' Elsie moved as a man pushed past. 'Hello, Harry.'

'Hello, Elsie.' His face broke into a smile. 'That was a tidy win your Dennis came up with last week.'

'He told you about that, did he?'

'I was there when he won it. I was standing in the same queue in the bookie's. I called out to him but he didn't see me.'

Elsie grabbed his arm. 'Would you tell the police that, Harry?'

'Of course I would if they asked me. Why?'

'They think he got the money somewhere else.' She waved to Ivan who was talking to Annie Walker. 'Forget the orange, I'll have a double Tia Maria, Ivan, love.'

Dennis was trying to wrap his clothes in a sheet of brown paper but as soon as he closed end of the parcel, everything dropped out the other. Muttering under his breath, he started as the door banged behind him. He looked up to see Ivan watching him. 'There's no use looking at me like that,' Dennis snapped. 'You can't talk me out of it. I'm getting out while the going's good.'

'It's all right, Dennis.' Ivan was relieved that he had caught him before he'd left. 'Harry saw you winning the money on the dogs and he's prepared to tell the police he did.'

Dennis threw the parcel on the table. 'You see? I told them!'

'Yes, you did,' Ivan agreed. 'Coming to the Rovers?'

'Ask a dull question.' Dennis reached the front door before his brother-in-law. He turned back and smiled. 'And seeing as how I've some of that twenty-five quid left, I'm buying.'

Chapter Five

The ward was hushed and silent. The night nurse checked the watch pinned to her apron. It was time for the last ward round, another half an hour and the day shift would be on duty. She screwed the top on to her fountain pen, piled up the patients' charts she had been updating and left the office. All the patients were sleeping peacefully with the exception of Mrs Sharples: she was crouched at the top of her bed in a most peculiar position. The nurse tiptoed over softly and peered into the gloom of the half-light that shrouded the room. Suspicious, she touched the sheet and blanket, then pulled them back. The pillow was tucked into the bed. She whirled around and opened the locker next to it. The shelves that should have been full of Mrs Sharples's personal possessions were empty.

The only evidence that remained to show Ena Sharples had been in the ward was an enormous, full-leafed potted plant.

★

'I've put you in the front bedroom, Alice. I hope you'll be comfortable.' Harry Hewitt carried his sister Alice Burgess's suitcase up the stairs. 'I'm sorry the place is in a bit of a mess, everything's been a bit neglected of late.'

'I'll say it has. To think of a brother of mine living in this mucky state.' Alice tutted disapprovingly as she ran her finger down the banister and examined it for dust.

'Aye, well.' Harry struggled to keep his irritation in check. Alice had been trying to boss him around since the day he'd been born. 'I'll leave you to unpack while I put kettle on to make you a nice cup of tea.'

'Make sure that the cups have been washed out properly before you pour it, Harry,' she warned him.

Harry dropped the suitcase at the foot of the bed and went downstairs.

Lucille was standing in the passage. 'What do we have to have her here for?' She stuck out her tongue in the direction of the stairs, turned her back and stomped into the living room.

Harry gritted his teeth. His sister had been the main reason why he'd left home as young as he had. But he dared not risk Lucille seeing that he resented Alice's presence in their house even more than she did. 'With your aunt Alice living here you won't have to go back to the orphanage, love.'

'You mean it?' Lucille's eyes shone bright, and suspiciously damp.

'Aye, love.' He wrapped his arm around her shoulders. 'It's been grand having you here over Christmas.'

'I really don't have to go back?'

'Not as long as your aunt Alice is here to look after you.' He winced when he heard his sister's heavy tread in the bedroom overhead. 'Promise me you'll be nice to her, love, and you'll help her in the house as much as you can.'

'I promise, Dad,' she repeated solemnly, and returned his hug.

'Right. you can start by finding the cleanest cup and saucer we have to serve her tea in.'

Leonard Swindley unlocked the door of the Glad Tidings Mission Hall, puffed out his chest and sailed into the vestry. Martha Longhurst followed, like a tugboat in his wake.

'Mrs Sharples!' Leonard dropped the bunch of keys he was holding. 'I had no idea—'

'I bet you didn't,' Ena cut in. 'Weren't expecting me, were you?' She glared from Leonard to Martha. 'You pair of snakes in the grass. Well, I've had the doctor round here looking at me first thing this morning and he told me I'm not on the way out, not yet any road. And seeing as how I told him straight that I'm not going back into that place with its bossy girls and boiled bad food, I'm back to stay.

And,' she pushed her nose very close to Leonard's, 'you two can like it or lump it.'

Elsie stood in front of the mirror in her living room. She hummed to herself as she brushed out her shoulder-length, thick curly auburn hair, then twisted it neatly and expertly into a French pleat. She was jabbing in the last hairclip when she realised she was humming, 'God Rest Ye Merry, Gentlemen'. Christmas had come and gone two months ago. Switching to 'Ain't She Sweet', she reflected that if it weren't for her new boyfriend, naval officer Bill Gregory, she'd be suffering from post-Christmas blues. As it was— She jumped at a knock at the door and called, 'I'm coming.' She took a few seconds to reapply her lipstick and dab scent behind her ears, then ran down the passage, opened the front door and stood stock still.

'Hello, Elsie.'

'What do you want?' she whispered, hoarse from shock.

'That's a fine way to greet your husband.'

'You haven't been that since you walked out of this door fifteen years ago.'

'Elsie,' he coaxed. 'Do we have to talk out here with half the street looking on?'

'I've nothing to say to you.' Elsie tried to shut the door in his face, but Arnold stuck his foot across the step.

'But I have something to say to you.' He stepped back and Elsie saw Ena standing outside the vestry door, hands on hips, staring at them. Grudgingly she opened the door wider and Arnold stepped inside. He closed the door and followed her into the living room.

'You look nice.' Arnold realised it was a stupid thing to say to a wife he hadn't seen for years the moment the words were out of his mouth.

Elsie didn't soften. 'You've got five minutes before I put you out of that door. And if you've come to ask me to take you back you've another think coming.' Elsie faced him.

'It's nothing like that.' Arnold took off his hat and twisted it in his hands. 'I've met a girl – well, a woman – her name's Norah Dawson. We're good together, Elsie. Really good.'

'I'm pleased for you.'

Arnold seemed to steel himself. 'I want a divorce, Elsie, so I can make an honest woman of her.'

'Forget it. There's absolutely no way that I'll give you a divorce.' Elsie's hand shook as she took a packet of cigarettes from the mantelpiece. 'I'm not having my name dragged through the courts.'

'We've lived apart long enough to arrange things quietly.'

'I said no.' Elsie struck a match, lit a cigarette and inhaled deeply.

'Refuse me, Elsie, and your name *will* be dragged through the courts, I promise you that,' he threatened. 'I've seen a solicitor. All I have to do is give him a list of the GIs you went out with during the war. Adultery – that's what it's called in case you've forgotten.'

'You wouldn't dare!' But despite her anger, Elsie remembered enough about Arnold Tanner to realise that he meant every word he'd said.

'Refuse me a divorce and watch me do just that, Elsie. I'm not here to play games. Norah's a good woman and I want to do right by her.'

'Then have your bloody divorce and be damned,' she retorted savagely.

'Thank you.'

Elsie stood leaning on the mantelpiece staring into the fire as Arnold went to the front door. She heard it open and close, and continued to stand immobile. She and Arnold had lived separate lives for far longer than the fifteen years that had passed since he'd walked out on her. Bloody war!

What difference would a divorce make now? Whatever there had once been between them was long gone. And even when they'd been together she'd never pretended to be faithful. Better to have a final break, even if it did mean that she'd be labelled a divorcee.

Wasn't it?

'Have I got something to tell you!' Ena set three open bottles of milk stout, half-pint glasses balanced on the tops, in the centre of the table in the Rovers' snug. She had a brand new piece of gossip but she was in no hurry to impart it to Martha and Minnie. She intended to sit back and relish the expressions on their faces.

'Is it serious, Ena?' Martha picked up her bottle and glass.

'What do you think?' Ena looked from Martha to Minnie. 'Madam Tanner has a new boyfriend. And it's not that sailor chap we've seen sniffing round her neither.'

'She never has!' Martha gasped.

'She has an' all. I saw him standing on her doorstep. But when she saw me looking, she invited him in, bold as brass, and in broad daylight. That woman's got no shame, that's what I've always said. No shame at all.'

'Ooh, Ena,' Martha and Minnie chorused.

'I warn you now, there's going to be trouble there. Two men in and out of that house at all hours of the day and night, you mark my words, sooner or later there's going to be fireworks, real fireworks, in number eleven. And it'll all be down to that brazen trollop.'

'You off out tonight, then, Ken?' Ida asked, as her son adjusted his tie in the mirror.

'I am,' he said briefly, glancing in the mirror at his father. Frank was sitting in his chair, apparently immersed in the newspaper, but Ken knew he was listening to every word.

'Susan Cunningham again?' Ida finished the row she

was knitting and held out the pullover sleeve, debating whether it was long enough for David's arm. She reached for the tape measure.

'No, not Susan. We haven't gone out in a while.' Ken picked up his sports coat from the back of a chair.

'I hope you didn't have a row.'

'Nothing like that. Just drifted apart when I met someone else.'

'You've a new girlfriend then?' His father laid the newspaper on his knee.

'Marion Lund.'

'Lund . . . Lund . . .' Ida's eyes rounded in alarm. 'Isn't she the librarian at the university? The one you introduced me to that time you helped me with the shopping after work?'

'That's the one.' Ken slung his college scarf round his neck. 'I may be late so there's no need to wait up for me.'

'What's up, Ida?' Frank asked, after Ken left. 'You look as though you've seen a ghost.'

'That Marion Lund, that's what's up,' she snapped. 'She's ten years older than our Ken if she's a day. What's a woman like that doing, going after a young lad like our Ken? It's downright wicked, that's what it is. Frank Barlow, how can you sit there with that stupid grin on your face?'

'A young lad never came to no harm having a fling with an older woman, Ida. I did the same thing when I was our Ken's age.' Frank flicked the paper open.

'A fling! I never heard such a thing in my life. Our Ken's a lad—'

'A lad wouldn't get an older woman like this Marion Lund to go out with him. Your "lad" is growing up fast. And what's up with you?' Frank asked, as David barged into the living room, still in his coat.

'You'll never guess.'

'No, we won't until you tell us.' Ida left her chair to fetch David's tea.

'I was playing football with the lads dinner time—'

'You'd think engineering apprentices would have better things to do than get all mucky playing football,' Ida interrupted , taking out her anger over Ken's new girlfriend on her younger son.

'A scout saw me.' David was crestfallen at his mother's attitude.

'A what?' She bustled in holding the steaming plate with a pair of oven gloves.

'Let the boy finish telling us what he's got to say, Mother,' Frank said.

'A football scout,' David explained, brightening when he saw that his father understood how important his news might be. 'He says I'm good enough to play professionally. He offered me a contract there and then with a London team. It's second division but he says I've the talent to go far and—'

'London!' Ida's jaw dropped.

'I'm moving up there. I start training with the club on Monday morning.'

'You can't! What about your apprenticeship?' Ida sank into her chair.

'They're offering me four times the money I'm getting in Ajax Engineering. And you don't have to worry, Mam. I'll be able to send home the same money I'm giving you now and you won't have the expense of keeping me.'

'I'm right proud of you, lad.' Frank left his chair and pumped David's hand enthusiastically up and down, as Ida burst into tears.

Dennis walked into the living room to see his mother sitting next to the fire. He knew she was preoccupied when he saw ugly red marks on her legs, the result of sitting too close to the flames. 'I've some news that might cheer you up.' He sat down opposite her.

'What?' Elsie gazed at him through faraway eyes.

'I've a job. A proper job,' he added, so there'd be no mistake.

'Doing what?' She raised her eyebrows cynically.

'Front-of-house manager in the Orinoco Club, starting Monday evening. And the wages are good, so I'll be able to pay my corner here.'

'The Orinoco – in town?' Elsie was surprised.

'That's the one. It has all sorts of acts, good ones too, top-liners. All the best comics and singers. I can make a real go of this, Mam. I'll be in the centre of everything. Showbiz here I come.' He took a packet of cigarettes from his shirt pocket and handed her one. 'What's up? You don't seem too pleased.'

'I am.' Elsie took the cigarette. 'I'm right pleased for you.'

'You don't look it.'

'Your dad was here.'

'What did he want?' Dennis struck a match and lit his mother's cigarette before his own.

'To divorce me.'

'Oh, aye?'

'Is that all you can say?' she shouted.

'What more is there to say? It's not as if you two have seen hide nor hair of each other in years.'

'I suppose not.'

'It was bound to happen sooner or later.' He saw that Elsie wasn't about to snap out of her mood, and added, 'One of me old mates has moved in round here. I'm going to call round and see him. You OK?'

Elsie glanced up at him. 'Fine, love, you go off and have a good time.'

He left his chair and hesitated.

'Clear off and leave me in peace, will you?'

'Whatever you say, Mam.'

'Cheeky blighter.'

He still waited for her to give him a smile before he left.

★

'Who's this new fellow in your life, then, Elsie?' Dot Greenhalgh, Elsie's co-worker at Miami Modes, exclusive dress shop, moved her umbrella so it covered both of them when Elsie joined her at the bus stop.

'What fellow?' Elsie was mystified.

'It's all over street. I heard it in the Rovers. There was a strange man on your doorstep and you invited him in. Is it over between you and Billy, then? I thought you and he were getting on well.'

'Who told you I had a new man?'

'I'm not sure.' Dot frowned with the effort of remembering. 'I think it was Martha Longhurst. Yes, that's right, it was Martha. She was on her way into the snug when she stopped me and asked who the fellow was.'

Elsie remembered Ena watching her and Arnold when they had been talking on her doorstep. Fifteen years had obviously been long enough for Ena to forget what Arnold looked like. 'I'll have the old busybody's guts for garters. Sticking her nose into my affairs! Old witch! I'll get her this time, you see if I don't.'

'Who?' Dot asked.

'Ena Sharples, that's who.' Elsie looked up as a bus pulled into the bay. 'The right number for once. Looks like we're going to be early.'

'That'll be a first.' Dot climbed on to the bus after Elsie

and sat in the seat alongside her. 'What you going to do to Ena Sharples, then, Elsie?'

'Go down to the local paper's offices in my lunch-hour and that's just for starters,' Elsie muttered.

'And what time of night do you call this to walk through the door, Harry Hewitt?' Alice Burgess stared at her watch as Harry joined her and Lucille in the living room.

'It's only half past seven.'

'Half past seven,' Alice repeated, before Harry could say another word, 'when you come off shift at six o'clock. And don't tell me it takes you an hour and a half to get home! A bus inspector, who knows the routes, can have the pick of the buses. You could be home in twenty minutes if you've a mind to. But, oh, no, not you. You leave me and your daughter wondering if you've been knocked down and killed in the street, and all the time there's your tea shrivelling to nothing in that oven.'

'All I did was call in Rovers for a pint after I finished work,' Harry remonstrated mildly.

'It seems to me that you spend more time in Rovers than you do in your own house. Well, Harry Hewitt, I've had it up to here.' Alice ran her finger across her throat. 'Enough's enough! I have my own life, you know. I came here out of the goodness of my heart to look after you and keep that daughter of yours out of the orphanage. I've worked my fingers to the bone ever since I stepped over the doorstep four months ago and all the thanks I get is sulks and temper tantrums from that madam,' she pointed at Lucille, 'and an off-hand manner and boozing from you. I'm going upstairs now, this minute, to pack.' She untied the pinny from round her waist and flung it at him. 'First thing tomorrow, I'm leaving.'

'Alice . . .' Harry made a half-hearted attempt to stop her but Alice brushed him aside and barged up the stairs.

'Let her go.' Lucille poked her tongue out at the door.

'And when the social services come round and say I can't look after you—'

'I'll tell them that *I* can look after *you,* Dad,' Lucille crowed. 'I can cook and clean as well as Auntie Alice, and we won't have to put up with her going on at us all the time.'

'I only hope they see it that way, love.' Harry's eyes darkened as he stroked her hair.

'Now, you sit at the table and I'll get your tea.' Lucille pulled out his chair for him. 'There's some extra gravy I can heat up, so it won't be as dried-up as Auntie Alice said it would. Although she had the oven on too high. I told her she did, but she wouldn't take any notice. She never does of anything I say.'

'You seen tonight's paper, Ena?' Martha Longhurst closed the door of the snug behind her and moved Ena's milk stout so she could set the paper down in front of her. 'She's got to mean you. I mean she has, hasn't she?'

'Sit down and stop blathering nonsense, Martha Longhurst,' Ena said impatiently.

Martha sat and folded the paper over. She pointed to a notice in the personal column. 'Just look at what it says. It's got to be you, Ena.'

Ena picked up the paper and read, in a slow, halting voice, '"Elsie Tanner of number eleven Coronation Street is aware of certain rumours being spread about her and she wants it be known that she will sue the perpetrators of the said rumours for slander in court if the talk continues." Well, of all the nerve! The brazen hussy, that's all I can say, when I saw her with my own eyes.'

'Saw what, Ena?' Minnie asked.

'Elsie Tanner, with that strange fellow on her doorstep. She can print all the denials she wants but he's her new man. That's what he is and there's no use in her denying it, not when I saw him.'

'Do you mean Arnold Tanner?'

'What?'

'Mrs Barlow said hello to him when he passed her house. I wouldn't have known him but Ida Barlow did. He asked after her and Frank and the boys and she said it was a long time since she'd seen him and he said, "About fifteen years." Was it him you saw, Ena, was it?'

Ena downed the last of her stout and made a face as if

it had been sour milk. She pushed her empty bottle towards Martha. 'It's your shout.'

Linda and Ivan burst into Elsie's living room less than ten minutes after she had come home from work.

'I wasn't expecting you two.' Elsie smiled at Linda's burgeoning figure. 'By gum, you're looking well and not long to go now.'

'Four weeks,' Linda said proudly, 'unless she's early.'

'Sit yourselves down and I'll make you a cup of tea.'

'You'll never guess what Ivan's gone and done, Mam.' Too excited to sit down, Linda hovered next to Elsie's chair.

'What *have* you gone and done?' Elsie looked at her son-in-law.

'You know how much I wanted to move into next door?' Linda said, before Ivan could answer.

'The landlord told you straight, he's not looking for tenants, he wants to sell.'

'And he has!' Linda screeched. 'To us! Ivan's gone and got a mortgage.'

'You never have.' Elsie gasped.

'I don't know how we're going to pay it,' he said.

'If it's extra you're after, there's a potman's job going down Rovers, working evenings. Jack asked me if our Dennis would be interested, the Lord only knows how Annie would have taken having him working behind the bar with her, but Dennis couldn't take it any road, seeing as how he spends every night in that club.'

'I'll go and see about the job now.' Ivan went to the door.

'You do that, love.' Linda held up the key to the house. 'Want to come and look round and see what needs doing, Mam?'

'Try and stop me.' Elsie hugged Linda, then went to get her coat.

'Mr Barlow?'

'Aye.' Frank stepped back into the hall and switched on the light. The young copper standing on the step looked serious.

'Mr Frank Barlow?'

'Aye. What's up? Is it . . . ?'

'It's bad news, I'm afraid, sir. Is anyone in the house with you?'

'My son, Ken. Our other son David's moved down south and my wife is out for the day . . . It's not David, is it?' Frank paled as he stepped back into the hall. 'Is he . . . ?'

'Your son is fine, Mr Barlow. Please, can I come in?'

'If it's not David, is it Ida?'

'Please, sir, can I come in,' the policeman reiterated.

'Ida – if she's hurt I have to go to her!' Frank grabbed his coat from the hook in the passage.

The policeman stepped inside the hall and closed the door behind him. 'Sir, please, can we sit down?'

Ken opened the door of the living room.

'It's your mother – she's hurt, I must go to her.' Frank continued to talk at speed as he buttoned his coat. Ken noticed that he'd missed a button at the bottom and it was lopsided. He looked from his father to the policeman.

'I'm sorry, Mr Barlow.' The officer gave up trying to get Frank into the living room. 'There was nothing anyone could do. Your wife stepped out in front of a bus. She was killed instantly. I am so sorry, sir.'

Ken grabbed his father's arm – Frank looked as if he was about to fall to the floor.

Chapter Six

The living room and parlour of the Barlow house was crowded with relatives and neighbours intent on paying their respects to Ida. Unable to stand the strain of polite conversation a moment longer, Ken walked into the scullery. Even there he couldn't be alone: it was full of women washing dishes and cutting sandwiches, all reminiscing about his mother as if she had been dead for years, not days. Turning up the collar of his black suit jacket against the cold, he stepped out into the back yard.

'Here you are, Ken.' Valerie Tatlock, Albert's pretty nineteen-year-old niece, followed him out and pressed a cup of tea into his hands.

'Thank you.' He forced a smile and glanced back at the house. 'I don't know what we'd have done without your help.'

'You'd have managed fine.' Valerie leant against the wall next to him.

Ken looked through the living-room window. 'He's hardly said a word since it happened.'

'It's not surprising he's lost without her. He and your mother were so close. She was a lovely woman.'

'My brother David couldn't even bring himself to come back here for the funeral.' Ken sipped the tea. It tasted like ashes.

'I saw your mother on the morning . . .' Valerie hesitated before continuing. 'She was so proud of you getting your degree. She told me that you'd applied for a job teaching in a public school down south.'

'I didn't get it,' he said, although the letter offering him the post had arrived the morning after his mother had been killed. He had sat looking at it for a long while, knowing that he had no choice but to turn it down. He couldn't leave his father, not with David living so far away. But he had yet to write his refusal.

'I'm sorry.'

'No matter,' he said. 'I've applied for a job closer to home. Assistant personnel officer at Amalgamated Steel.'

'So you can stay with your father?' Valerie asked.

Ken handed her his empty cup. 'As you said, he's lost without her.'

Elsie Tanner looked around at the friends who had gathered to celebrate her grandson's christening in the private party she had booked in the Rovers during Sunday afternoon closing time. Her life had changed completely in the three months since Linda and Ivan had moved next door to her. First, she had come to realise just how difficult it was to be a mother-in-law, mother and neighbour rolled into one, especially when Linda brought her troubles with Ivan around and expected tea and sympathy even when her rows with her husband were very obviously more her fault than his. And since the birth of the baby, she had rediscovered how sweet, wonderful – and demanding – babies could be.

She looked up as Jack Walker, chosen by Ivan to be Paul's godfather after he had been kind enough to give him the job as potman, banged on a glass with a teaspoon to attract everyone's attention.

'To my godson, Paul Cheveski. May he have a long, happy and charmed life.'

Everyone echoed Jack's toast and lifted their glass to Linda, who was proudly cradling her son.

'Hand him over.' Elsie finished her gin and orange before she took her grandson into her arms.

'Isn't he a little beauty?' Concepta Riley, the Walkers' Irish barmaid moved the shawl from Paul's face so she could get a better look at him.

'He's a little beauty with a mad father,' Elsie commented wryly, as Ivan picked up a salami he'd brought for the post-christening tea and jumped on to the bar. Leaping up and down he made a few movements with the salami that brought blushes to Annie Walker's cheeks, and sent Harry Hewitt and his friend Len Fairclough into gales of laughter.

'Ivan,' Linda remonstrated, as the other men proceeded to clap their hands in time to his dancing.

'It's a traditional Polish dance,' Ivan panted.

'Give me a hand to get him down, Mam,' Linda begged.

'Why? he seems to be enjoying himself.' Elsie glanced slyly at Annie, who was looking anywhere but at Ivan.

'Can I hold Paul for a moment, Elsie?' Concepta asked shyly. 'It's been a long while since I've cuddled a baby as small as him.'

'Course you can, love.' Elsie hated handing Paul over, but Linda was getting het up about the exhibition Ivan was making of himself so she deposited Paul in Concepta's arms and joined Linda in her attempts to get Ivan down.

'You like children, then?' Harry sidled over to Concepta as she cooed at Paul.

'I love them. I come from a large Irish family and I'm not ashamed to admit that I miss them all, especially on Sundays. When I was growing up we used to go to my grandmother's house for a big high tea. My mam, dad, brothers, sisters, uncles, aunts, cousins . . . Listen to me going on.' Concepta brushed a tear from her eye. 'Anyone would think I was homesick.'

'I like to hear you talk.' Harry smiled. 'And I've been meaning to ask you something. When's your evening off?'

'Friday. Why, Harry?'

'I was wondering if you'd like to go into town and see a film, or have a drink or something,' he said diffidently.

'Yes, I would.'

'Have a drink or see a film?' he asked.

'Either would be nice, as long as it's with you.'

His smile broadened. 'I'll pick you up here. Is seven o'clock all right?'

'Seven is fine, Harry. I'll look forward to it. But for now,' she looked at the queue forming at the bar, 'I'd better go and serve some drinks.'

'A double gin and orange for the proud grandmother.' Jack Walker handed Elsie a glass.

'Thank you, Jack, and cheers.'

'They look good together, a proper little family.' Jack nodded to where Linda and Ivan were putting Paul in his pram.

'That they are, yet it doesn't seem that long since our Linda was running around in short frocks,' Elsie said.

'You're going to miss them.' Jack cleared half a dozen empty glasses from the bar.

'What do you mean?'

'When they go to Canada.' He pushed a couple of empty beer bottles into a crate.

'What?'

Jack looked abashed. 'I'm sorry, Elsie, I thought you

knew. Ivan's been talking about nothing else since he started as potman here. And it stands to reason, doesn't it? By all accounts youngsters are better off in Canada than they are here. Lot more opportunities out there for them. And Ivan's a careful lad. He's really looked into it. He's even booked one of those cheap passages.'

Elsie slammed her glass down on the bar and stalked over to Linda.

'What's up, Mam?' Linda asked.

'Don't give me that butter-wouldn't-melt-in-my-mouth look, madam,' Elsie yelled. 'Canada! That's what's up.'

'Can we talk about this later, Mam?'

'No, we can't! We'll talk about it right here and right now! How is it that every Tom, Dick and Jack knows that you and Ivan are going to Canada except me – your own mother?'

'We've only just decided, Elsie,' Ivan interrupted, 'and we were going to tell you tonight after the christening.' When Elsie continued to glare at them, he went on. 'We're only thinking about Paul and what's best for him. It's a new country, a new start. They say you can really make a go of it out there if you're prepared to work hard. And you know there's no way that I can keep our Linda and Paul the way I'd like to keep them on the wages I'm getting at the steelworks.'

Elsie stared down at her grandson, sleeping contentedly in his pram in the christening shawl and gown that she had bought for him. 'Just don't expect me to give you my blessing, Ivan Cheveski, that's all I can say. Taking my daughter and grandson halfway around the world where I'll never see them again. Well, I never want to see you or her,' she pointed at Linda, 'ever again either.' She left the pub, banging the door shut behind her.

The carpets were thick and soft, the tables laid with crisply laundered white damask cloths. The waiters moved quietly, talking in hushed whispers more suited to a church than a hotel as Harry Hewitt and Concepta were shown to their table. But then, the restaurant at the Imperial had the reputation for being the best in the city and that was why Harry had chosen it.

It wasn't the kind of place Harry would normally have dreamt of eating in, and not only because of the exorbitant cost. But he intended to make this a special evening. One that he and Concepta Riley would remember for the rest of their lives. Ill at ease in his only suit, white shirt and stiff collar, Harry handed Concepta the menu as he unfolded and tucked a napkin – which was almost as thick as the towels he used at home – into his collar.

Concepta gasped. 'The prices here are ridiculous, Harry. You could feed a family of four for a week on what they're charging for one meal. It's downright ridiculous.'

'But it's a nice place, isn't it?' he asked anxiously.

'And so it should be. Considering what they're

charging, they can afford to gold-plate this room ten times over.'

'Order whatever you like,' he whispered, as a black-suited waiter, white cloth folded over his arm, approached their table.

'Would sir like to order anything from the wine cellar?' the waiter asked.

'We'll have a bottle of wine. What can you recommend?'

'Harry,' Concepta hissed, 'you know you prefer beer.'

'Make that champagne,' Harry said recklessly. 'Your best.'

'Certainly sir.' The waiter took the wine menu from him, folded it and walked away.

'Harry,' Concepta laid her hand over his across the table, 'we've been going out a whole month now. You know I like you, so you can stop trying to impress me.'

'I wanted this evening to be special.' Harry slipped his hand into his pocket and produced a ring box. He handed it to her. 'I hope you like it.'

Concepta opened it. An engagement ring set with three small diamonds lay on a bed of blue velvet. 'Oh, Harry!' She gazed from the ring into his eyes.

'I would be honoured if you would become my wife, Concepta . . . What's the matter?' He rose from his seat in alarm as tears started in her eyes. 'I know it's a bit sudden . . . If you need to think about it . . . Or you don't care about me the way I care about you . . .'

'It's not that, Harry.'

'Then what?' he demanded. 'I know it's only been a few weeks . . .'

'It's not the time. And I do care for you, Harry, you know that.'

Harry smiled in relief. 'I didn't, and it's good to hear you say that you do.'

'It's my family,' she confessed. 'They're conservative Catholic Irish, Harry. They'll be upset at the thought of me marrying not just an Englishman but out of the Catholic faith.'

'Are you saying you won't have me?' Harry's face fell.

'I didn't say that. I don't suppose . . . suppose . . .' she braced herself for rejection '. . . you'd consider converting?'

Harry stiffened awkwardly in his seat.

'One of my cousins married an English girl,' Concepta continued. 'She didn't convert, but she agreed that any children they had would be brought up in the faith.'

Harry leant across the table and grasped both of Concepta's hands. 'If that's all I have to agree to, then I'd like to see that ring on your finger. And I'd like another one to join it just as soon as we can get the banns called.'

Concepta saw the waiter approaching with an ice bucket containing a bottle of champagne and decided he could wait. 'Will you put the ring on for me please, Harry?'

Elsie sat alone in her living room, staring into space. During the month that had passed since Paul's christening she had stuck to her threat, and refused to see or talk to Linda or Ivan. And although she had gone as far as admitting to Dennis that she missed seeing little Paul she had blocked every attempt Dennis made to effect a reconciliation between her Linda and Ivan.

She knew, because Ena Sharples had gone out of her way to tell her, that every resident of Coronation Street who was at home would be standing outside their house that Saturday afternoon to see Ivan, Linda and Paul off. But then, she reflected, Ena was wrong because there was one resident who would be missing – her.

Dennis stood back with Linda and Ivan who were watching the last of their furniture being loaded into a van.

'Only the sideboard to go, missus,' a removal man called to Linda, as he stacked a couple of dining chairs and pushed them into the back.

Linda shifted Paul higher into her arms and turned her head to check that the two suitcases and the holdall in which she'd packed the essentials they'd need for the journey were still set aside in the hallway.

'Taxi'll be here in a minute.' Dennis put his arm round Linda and wrinkled his nose at Paul.

Linda looked at the door of number eleven. Her mother's front door was the only one closed in the street. 'She won't come out.' It wasn't a question.

'I'll go and see what I can do.' Dennis tickled his nephew's cheek.

'Don't put yourself out,' Linda said tersely. 'It's for her to make the first move.'

'Not when it comes to something like this, it's not.' Dennis fought his way through the crowd and walked into the house. 'Mam!' He found Elsie in the living room sitting at the table staring at a framed photograph of Linda and Paul. 'Aren't you going to come and see your daughter off?'

'I told her I didn't want to see her again. And before you put your oar in, I've washed my hands of the pair of them. Taking my grandson halfway across the world where I'll never see him again!'

'You're talking daft, Mam! Dennis tried to console her: 'Course you're going to see them again. Just think about them and what they're facing. Going off to a new life in a strange country they know nothing about. They must be frightened stiff.' Dennis crouched in front of her chair and took her hands his. 'Please, just go out there and wish our Linda and Ivan well. You know you'll hate yourself the minute they've gone if you don't.'

Elsie sniffed hard.

'Come on.' He helped his mother out of her chair and led her down the passage and into the street.

The last of the baggage had been loaded and Ivan was stowing the suitcases into a taxi that had just arrived. Elsie stared at her daughter. Linda looked back for a moment and broke down but it was Elsie who made the first move. She ran to her, hugged her and dropped a kiss on Paul's head. 'You take care out there, the three of you. And good luck.'

'Oh, Mam.' Linda buried her face in her mother's shoulder.

'And take care of my grandson.'

'We will, and thank you, Elsie.' Ivan helped his wife into the taxi and handed her his son, then kissed Elsie.

'Get off with you.'

The van drove down the street, the taxi followed it, the neighbours shouted, cheered and waved. But Elsie was the last to go indoors. And she waited a full five minutes after the taxi had turned the corner.

Annie Walker checked and double-checked the piles of coins and notes she'd taken from the till. Whichever way she added up the figures she was twenty pounds short. Frowning, she turned to a clean page in her notebook.

Jack struggled up from the cellar with a crate of milk stout. Reading the expression on her face, he asked, 'What's up, love?'

'You taken twenty pounds from the till?'

'No.'

'Well, there's twenty pounds missing.'

'You sure?' Jack heaved the crate on to the counter.

'I'm sure, but you can check the figures yourself if you don't believe me.'

At the note of hysteria in her voice, he murmured, 'Course I believe you, love.'

'It's that Dennis Tanner,' Annie pronounced. 'He's gone back to his thieving ways. I told you we should never have allowed him back in here when he came out of that place.'

'You can't go around accusing people, love,' Jack remonstrated mildly.

'He was alone in the bar when we opened tonight. He was the first one in. He must have waited until my back was turned, opened the till and taken it.'

'You don't know that for sure, love.'

'Who else can it be?' Annie demanded shrilly.

'Service!' Ena Sharples shouted, from the snug. 'Bottle of milk stout.' She pushed a two-shilling piece towards Annie. 'And don't go accusing Dennis Tanner of going near your till. I was here waiting for service, not that anyone took any notice of me, when he came in. And I've been stood here in plain sight of him and that till until he left. He didn't go near it.'

'Then if he didn't, who did?' Annie barked.

'Since I've been sat here, the only one that's gone near that till is you.' Ena stared Annie down.

'Twenty pounds doesn't just go missing like that, Mrs Sharples.'

'You accusing me now?' Ena questioned belligerently.

'All I'm saying is, money doesn't go missing unless someone takes it.'

'Keep your milk stout.' Ena left the snug as Martha and Minnie walked in. 'Come on, we're not staying in no pub where the landlady accuses us of stealing.'

'All I'm saying is that there's twenty pounds missing from this till and someone must have taken it,' Annie reiterated, refusing to back down.

'And just who do you think took it, Annie?' Harry Hewitt asked.

'I'm not accusing anyone but it's missing.'

'I wouldn't go in there if I were you, Dennis Tanner.' Ena's shrill tones echoed in from the street. 'Annie Walker thinks you took twenty pounds from her till.'

'I never!'

'I know you never,' Ena interrupted swiftly, 'but that hasn't stopped Madam in there of accusing you and everyone else in there of thieving it.'

'Atmosphere's a bit close in here, Harry.' Len Fairclough downed his pint. 'Shall we move over to the Flying Horse?'

'That's a good idea.'

Jack Walker stared in horror as, one by one, his regulars filed out to follow Ena, Martha and Minnie outside. When the door swung shut behind the last customer, he turned to his wife. 'Just look what you've done now, Annie.'

'The house hasn't looked this nice since mam died, Concepta,' Lucille said sincerely, when she walked in

111

from school to find a plate of homemade biscuits and a glass of milk set in front of her place at the table.

'That's nice of you to say so, pet.' Concepta stroked Lucille's hair as she sat down. She had never worked so hard in her life as she had in the three weeks that had elapsed since her and Harry's wedding. She had scrubbed, polished, washed and cleaned the house to perfection. But she still wasn't content. It didn't feel right for her and Harry to sleep in the same bed that he had shared with his first wife. But that was something she would have to tackle Harry about. She sighed as she glanced at the clock. And it was no use expecting him home early so they could talk about it. Marriage hadn't changed his habits. He still called into the Rovers for a pint every night after work. The problem was, nine times out of ten Len Fairclough was there too, and one pint became two and sometimes four . . . and while Harry drank, his dinner spoiled in the oven.

Already she felt as though she was turning into a nagging wife and she didn't like the sensation. Not one little bit.

Jack Walker stepped into the passage behind the bar. Listening intently, he heard the rattle of dishes in the kitchen in the private quarters and slipped surreptitiously through the connecting door into the public area. He took four five-pound notes from his back pocket and opened the till, wincing at the bell. He slipped them into the drawer, and jumped as Annie walked into the deserted bar behind him.

'Look what I've just found, love.' He pulled out the five-pound notes he'd just pushed in and held them up. 'They must have been here all along.'

Annie burst into tears.

'Whatever is the matter, love?'

'You've just put them in there.'

'I – I . . .' Lost for words Jack wrapped his arms round Annie's shoulders. 'How do you know, love?' he asked, as her tears soaked into his pullover and shirt.

'I don't know how you can ever forgive me, Jack. I found the money two days ago jammed at the back of the till.'

'And you didn't say a word!' he exclaimed indignantly.

Annie had never seen such anger on Jack's face. 'Where are you going?' she asked apprehensively, as he walked to the door.

'The Flying Horse, to explain to our customers. I only hope it's not too late to get them back.'

'What are you doing?' Frank Barlow asked Ken, as he lifted his typewriter on to the living-room table.

'You know that article I wrote for the *Survival* last week?' Ken wound a sheet of paper round the machine's roller. 'Well, they paid me for it and on the strength of that, I've been offered more money to write three articles for the *Banner* on life in a northern town.'

'Waste of bloody time if you ask me,' Frank said. 'That's no job for a young man. But, then, you couldn't cut it in the personnel department of the steelworks . . .'

'I told you, I hated having to reprimand and sack people. The job was getting me down and it's not as if I haven't a job to go to. I start teaching at the beginning of next term in Bessie Street School.' Ken fought to keep his temper. It was no use even trying to explain to his father that he'd earned the equivalent of six weeks' wages in the steelworks for a single article in *Survival* or that the money the *Banner* had offered him for three articles would keep him for three months. In his father's eyes, writing would never be a 'proper job'.

'If only your mother could see you now, hopping from job to job, sticking to nothing, not capable of getting or holding down a decent job like the one in that posh school down south you went for. I always said educating you would be a waste of money.' Oblivious to Ken's despair, Frank Barlow grabbed his coat and headed for the Rovers.

'New furniture?' Harry pushed his plate into the centre of the table. 'Whatever do you want new furniture for, Concepta? Is there something wrong with this?' He looked around their living room.

Concepta poured out two teas and sat beside him. 'Well, it's not as if we chose any of it together, is it, Harry?' she said, in her soft Irish brogue, too embarrassed to bring up the subject of the bed he had slept in with his first wife.

'No, I suppose not, love,' he agreed, comfortably full and tired after the three pints he had drunk in the Rovers and the lavish helping of meat and potato pie she had given him.

'We can afford new furniture, can't we, Harry?' she probed.

'Oh, aye.' He grabbed her waist and pulled her down on to his lap as she passed his chair. 'We'll see what can be done,' he murmured, after he'd kissed her.

Chapter Seven

As Frank Barlow drew close to the Rovers, he heard angry voices echoing from inside the bar. He recognised one of them as Len Fairclough's. The builder was holding forth and, as usual, shouting everyone else down.

'He might have more education than the rest of us put together, but swallowing a bloody dictionary doesn't give him the right to say the things he's said about us.' Len slammed his fist on the bar to emphasise his point, sending the pint pots rattling. He turned to see Frank standing in the doorway.

Conscious of the sudden silence and everyone watching him, Frank closed the door behind him and made his way to the bar.

'Pint?' Jack Walker asked, as he approached.

'Aye.' Frank felt in his pocket for change.

'Do you know what he called us?' Len's voice shattered the silence that had fallen over the room. ' "Lazy and ignorant", that's what he called us.'

'It was "lazy-minded and politically ignorant",' Annie Walker corrected primly.

'And I suppose you agree with him, Madam Hoity Toity . . .'

'That's enough of that, Len,' Jack ordered sharply.

'What's up?' Frank looked at Jack as he supped his pint.

'You don't know?' Len moved down the bar and poked his nose close to Frank's. 'Your bloody Ken, that's what's up.'

'Our Ken?'

'Calling us names,' Harry Hewitt chipped in.

'Our Ken hardly ever comes in here—'

'He doesn't have to come in here to insult us. Oh, no, not your Ken. He's too grand to lower himself to mix with the working classes.' Len finished his pint and slammed his mug on the bar. 'He writes articles for magazines and gets local paper to repeat them and print his slanders for him.' Len pulled a folded copy of the paper from his pocket and thrust it at Frank. 'It says in here that your Ken wrote an article for the *Banner* on life among the working classes. As if he'd bloody know what work is when he's never done a day in his life . . .'

'Language, Len,' Jack reprimanded.

'Sitting on his arse in university doing bugger-all for years. All he knows about is pen pushing,' Len sneered.

The regulars chorused angry agreement as Frank scanned the paper.

'That's no job for a grown man,' Len taunted him, 'writing lies about his neighbours. Rubbishing the class he comes from. And he hasn't even the guts to come in here and say owt to our faces. A bit of education and he thinks he's upper crust and so much better than the rest of us. He's no better than a bloody louse—'

'What did you say?' Frank spoke quietly but there was no mistaking the menace in his voice.

'I said he's a louse—'

Frank raised his fist and let it fly. It connected with Len's jaw, sending him soaring backwards. He would have crashed into a table if Harry Hewitt hadn't caught him.

'Talk about my son like that again and I'll give you another one, Len Fairclough,' Frank threatened.

Len fought free of Harry's restraining grip, catapulted back and caught Frank on the head. Staggering, they both raised their fists again.

'I'll have no fighting in this bar.' For all that both men were younger and fitter than him, Jack stepped between them and pushed them apart.

'He bloody started it!' Len yelled, his temper at boiling point.

'You started it when you said what you said about our Ken.' Frank rubbed his left eye, which was already red and swelling.

'And I said that's enough!' Jack reiterated sternly.

'Finish your drinks and get out of here, the pair of you, before I call in the police to take you down the station for affray.'

Frank picked up his pint. Eyeing Len, he sipped it slowly, deliberately eking it out. Len wasn't so fortunate: his glass was almost empty. Jack grabbed it when there was less than a quarter of inch of beer left. 'I haven't finished,' Len complained.

'Yes, you have, and the next time you come back in here, Len Fairclough, leave your temper at home.' Jack dumped the glass in the tray beneath the counter.

Frank stayed only as long as it took Len to walk out of the door, but as he followed him outside, he felt he had won a moral victory by remaining in the bar for thirty seconds longer.

Frank retraced his steps to his door. He opened it and stood in the passage, listening to the click of typewriter keys. He hung his coat on a peg, then walked into the living room and through the scullery, ignoring Ken who leapt to his feet. He soaked a teacloth under the tap and pressed it over his eye.

'What happened?' Ken asked.

'You don't know?'

'I wouldn't be asking if I did.'

His father pushed past him and sank into his chair next to the fire. 'Why didn't you say what you were writing about?' He gestured towards the typewriter. 'Comes to something when I have to hear it from neighbours.'

'Hear what?'

'Len Fairclough said you called him and everyone else round here ignorant, lazy beggars . . .'

'I said no such thing,' Ken protested. 'He's taken what I wrote in my article out of context.'

'Out of what?'

Ken hesitated. He was beginning to feel like an alien in his own back yard. 'I wrote an article about life in a typical working-class northern town for a magazine and the editor of another magazine saw it and asked me to write three more. I should have known that no one around here would understand what I was trying to do.'

'Too bloody royal, lad,' Frank raged. 'You can't expect people round here to understand, not when you call them names.' Frank looked pointedly at the papers piled neatly next to the typewriter. 'If you're intent on carrying on, I suggest you take whatever money they're paying you and use it to get yourself some boxing lessons.'

'I don't know why I even try.' Ken yanked the sheet of paper out of the typewriter, crumpled it into a ball and tossed it on to the fire.

Struggling with two heavy string bags, Concepta opened her front door and staggered into the passage. She felt sick, worn out . . . and worried. She hadn't expected marriage to Harry to be a bed of roses but neither had she been prepared for the roller-coaster ride of mainly downs that it had turned out to be. She dropped the bags and straightened her aching back. Voices and the most peculiar dragging noises were coming from the living room. Leaving the bags where they lay, she walked down the passage and pushed open the door.

'What's going on?'

Harry turned, saw her and dropped the end of the couch that he and Len Fairclough were manhandling through the scullery door.

'Bloody hell, Harry!'

'I'll have no swearing in my house, Len Fairclough,' Concepta chided.

'Sorry, love, but Harry's broken my toes.' Len hopped on his right foot, kicked off his left shoe and rubbed his foot.

Harry smiled sheepishly at his wife. 'I didn't expect you back so soon. It was meant to be a surprise.'

Concepta glanced at the gleaming new vinyl three-piece suite and highly polished dining suite in the living room and walked to the scullery door. The old furniture was piled outside in the back yard.

'You said you wanted new furniture,' Harry reminded her. 'Do you like it?'

'You big fool, Harry Hewitt. When I said I wanted new furniture, I meant for us to choose it together,' she scolded, in her soft Irish brogue.

'It's first-class stuff, love. The man in the shop gave me a real bargain, ten per cent off for cash . . . Don't you like it?' Harry held his breath.

Concepta walked to the table and ran her fingers over the surface. 'Whether I like it or not isn't the point, Harry.'

Sensing an argument coming, Len picked up his end of the sofa again. 'Give me a hand to get this out into the yard, Harry, and I'll be off. I'll be round first thing with the van to pick it up and get it to the saleroom.'

'Excuse me a minute, love.' He turned his back on Concepta, and tried to ignore the face Len was making at him as they heaved the sofa through the back door. 'Thanks, Len, I couldn't have managed without your help.' He waited until Len had walked out of the gate before he returned to the living room. Concepta was still staring at the furniture.

'I'm sorry, love, I thought you'd like the surprise . . . You still haven't answered me,' he pressed. 'Do you like it?'

'I'd have liked it a whole lot better if I'd chosen it,' she answered tartly. 'What's the new bedroom suite like?'

His face fell. 'I spent so much money on this, love, there wasn't any left over for a bedroom suite.'

Concepta's face crumpled from anger to dismay. She gripped the back of one of the new chairs for support.

Harry put an arm round her. 'I'm sorry, love, I didn't

think. But we'll start saving right away. It won't take us long—'

'It will take us months if not years,' she broke in. 'And the whole point of me wanting new furniture was a bedroom suite. Don't you understand, you big, clumsy fool? I hate sleeping in the same bed you slept in with your first wife. It's not right. If nothing else I deserve a new bed . . .' The end of her sentence dissolved into incomprehensible sobs.

'Then why didn't you say so, love? If you had, I'd have bought a bedroom suite first.'

'I thought you'd understand, Harry, but I should have known better than to expect anything from a great stupid man.' She collapsed on to the chair.

'I'll make it up to you,' Harry promised eagerly. 'I'll sell something – the dog . . . Or I'll borrow money. We'll get a new bedroom suite if that's what you want.'

'The last thing we can afford to do right now is borrow money.'

'We're not badly off, Concepta, with what I bring in and what you earn doing the odd shift in Rovers.'

'Which I won't be able to do much longer.' She looked up at him through tears. 'I never thought it could happen, Harry, not at my age. But it has. And I don't know what we are going to do.'

'Whatever it is, it can't be that bad, love,' he consoled clumsily.

'Yes, it can. I'm pregnant. We're going to have a baby,' she whispered, in an attempt to impress the seriousness of the situation on him.

'But that's wonderful.' He beamed.

'No, it's not. I fainted in the Rovers the other day and Annie guessed what was up. She said – she said I was far too old to be having my first at thirty-four. All sorts of things can go wrong with the baby and me. Everybody says so.'

'Don't you go listening to any old wives' tales, love. Nothing is going to go wrong, not with you or our baby,' Harry stated. 'First things first. You are going to give up your job at Rovers and we'll go out tomorrow and price bedroom suites. A lot of things are going to change around here. You've been doing too much. I can take over some things, and Lucille will help.'

'Lucille!' Concepta's eyes were round with alarm at the thought of telling her stepdaughter about her condition. 'Oh, Harry, what if she's jealous? What if she doesn't want the baby?'

'She'll be as pleased as punch, love,' Harry assured her, hugging her again. 'You mark my words.'

Too upset to contemplate the alternative, Concepta hoped he was right.

Elsie Tanner stopped in the doorway of the Rovers Return. She pulled her headscarf higher, covering all of her hair, and flicked down her umbrella. Opening the door, she dropped the umbrella into the stand behind it and walked to the bar. 'Gin and orange, please, Jack.' She rummaged in her handbag for her purse.

'We're seeing a lot more of you in here lately, Elsie.' Jack poured orange into a measure of gin. 'Not that I'm complaining. You brighten the place up.' He smiled, gaining a disparaging sniff from Annie, who disappeared to the snug end of the bar.

'I never thought I'd catch meself saying so, but I'm missing our Dennis. Since he left the Orinoco to work in Lenny Phillips's theatrical agency in London the week before last, the house has been like a morgue.' Elsie peeled off her headscarf and folded it into her pocket. 'It's so quiet without him thundering around the place, I can hear the sound of my own heartbeat.'

'You get used to peace and quiet, Elsie. After a while you even get to like it.' Len Fairclough pushed his empty glass across the counter. 'Another pint, please, Jack, one for yourself and one of whatever Elsie's drinking. I could write a book about living alone since Nellie packed her bags last month, took our Stanley and left. And do you know something? The best thing about it is I can do what I damn well please. The worst is a dirty house and no meal on the table.'

'If all you wanted your Nellie for, was to clear up your mess and cook your dinner, it's no wonder she left.' Elsie took the gin he'd bought her and poured it on top of the one in her glass. 'Cheers.'

'And cheers to you.' Len touched his glass to hers. 'We've come a long way from Bessie Street School, kid.'

'That we have.' Elsie laughed. 'You've stopped collecting worms and chasing girls with them.'

'That you know about.' Len winked at her.

'Ee, we had some fun in those days.' Elsie turned her mind back to her schooldays and decided that, for all the wild times she'd enjoyed during the war, they had been even more special – carefree and innocent . . . but then she'd had no idea what life had in store for her.

'Don't suppose you're looking for any extra work, Elsie?' Len hinted. 'Just a couple of hours a week tidying, cleaning and maybe cooking.'

'Now, why would I do that when I've just got rid of our Dennis and Linda mucking up my house?'

'Because women like things neat and tidy and there's lots of opportunity for a woman to practise tidying in my place.'

'You've more brass than a fender, Len Fairclough.' Elsie sipped her gin and orange and opened her handbag in search of a cigarette.

'Here, have one of mine.' Len took a packet from his shirt pocket and flicked it open. He pulled out his lighter and lit it for her.

'And there's no use in buttering me up neither,' she warned, her eyes glittering sternly as he smiled at her.

'I remember those cakes you used to make in cookery class. There wasn't a girl who could bake the way you did in them days, Elsie.'

'Lot of water's flowed down the canal since our school-days, Len. But I tell you what, I'll pick up a couple of pork chops on my way home from work tomorrow night. It's as easy to cook for two as one. Just you be sure that you've a clean pan and a couple of clean plates for us to put them on. Cooking is one thing, clearing up someone else's filthy kitchen quite another.'

'See you around half past six?'

'About then.'

He gave her a broad smile. 'Come on, then, drink up. Time for another.'

Martha Longhurst leant closer to Ena in the table in the snug. 'Elsie Tanner and Len Fairclough are getting awfully pally,' she whispered.

'That's hardly surprising,' Ena said, not caring who heard her. 'Now that Len's wife has finally packed her bags and drummed up enough courage to leave him, Madam Tanner's probably decided to move in. She never could live without a man for more than five minutes at a time, and it wouldn't bother her if he belonged to another woman. That one was born with the morals of an alley cat.' Ena pushed her empty glass towards Minnie. 'Your turn to get them in.'

Minnie turned vacantly to Ena. 'Sorry, Ena, I was miles away,' she apologised.

'I could see that, Cloth Ears. I said, it's your turn to get them in.'

'Yes, Ena.' Minnie collected the glasses and went to the bar. She considered herself to be the least important of her friends and had been overwhelmed and grateful for their interest in her since their schooldays. Ena had always been the decision-maker and leader, and Martha had always acted as Ena's lieutenant. But for once she felt that she had something really important to announce, and she had been plucking up courage all evening to break the news, hoping that neither Ena nor Martha would criticise the most momentous decision she had ever made, or put a dampener on the life-altering change she was about to make.

She took two half a crowns from her purse she handed them to Annie Walker. 'Three milk stouts, please, Mrs Walker.'

'I was sorry to hear about your mother, Mrs Caldwell. But ninety-two is a good age, not that's it's much consolation.'

'Yes, it is,' Minnie answered, wondering why people expected her to take comfort from her mother's age. Since the funeral she had been unbearably lonely in the house in Jubilee Street. And somehow it made it worse that she had lived there all her life. She only had to close her eyes to see her mother, father and husband rushing around in the morning, getting ready for the day ahead . . . 'How are you coping, Mrs Caldwell?' Annie asked sympathetically, as she took the tops from the bottles.

'As well as can be expected, but thank you for asking, Mrs Walker.'

'Don't forget your change, Mrs Caldwell.' Annie handed her a sixpence.

Minnie carried the bottles to the table. She sat back, watching Ena and Martha pour their stout, marvelling at the decision she had made. Her mother had been buried two weeks ago and she felt as though her whole life had been spent caring for other people. First her husband and then, after she'd been widowed, her mother, and now – now, finally, she had made a decision that was just for her.

'You're quiet, Minnie,' Martha commented.

'Cheers.' Ena raised her glass.

'I've something to tell both of you,' Minnie said suddenly.

'Out with it, then,' Ena said impatiently, glancing through the hatch to where Len and Elsie were still talking.

'I'm moving out of my house in Jubilee Street.'

'You never are!' Martha gasped. 'Not when you've lived there all your life?'

'That's why I thought it was time for a change.'

'That's just plain daft at your time of life, Minnie Caldwell,' Ena said dismissively.

'I saw Esther Hayes last week,' Minnie divulged, glad that she had made all her decisions and signed all the papers before consulting her friends. 'She was telling me as how she's decided to leave Coronation Street now that the last of her family have moved away. She said she didn't know why she'd stayed on so long in a house with no central heating and no proper bathroom or kitchen. She's put a deposit down on one of those new flats in Moor Lane.'

'What's that got to do with you?' Ena queried irritably. 'You can't afford a flat in Moor Lane.'

'No, I can't,' Minnie agreed, 'but I can afford to take on the tenancy of number five. I saw the landlord yesterday and me and my cat Bobby are moving in this Saturday.'

Martha and Ena couldn't have looked more shocked if Minnie had announced she was moving to Australia.

'And there's something else.'

'You've taken up fan dancing to pay rent,' Ena mocked.

'No,' Minnie said seriously. 'I've got a lodger to help pay the rent. He's a nice young man. His name's Jed Stone and he's a friend of Dennis Tanner.'

'A friend of Dennis Tanner! Minnie Caldwell, you've taken leave of your senses.'

'He seems a nice enough young man,' Minnie interposed defensively.

'I dare say so was Jack the Ripper.' Ena drank some of her stout. 'If he's a friend of Dennis Tanner you'd best watch out, that's all I can say. Did you think to ask just where they made friends?'

'No, Ena.'

'Then for all you know they could have been mates inside Walden Prison.'

'Ooh, Ena, you don't think that, do you?' Martha asked.

'I don't know what to think, except that she,' Ena jabbed her finger in Minnie's direction, 'is acting like a giddy young girl with no more sense than a hopping toad.'

'That was a grand meal, Elsie.' Len soaked up the last vestiges of gravy on his plate with a piece of bread, stuffed it into his mouth, loosened his belt and pushed his chair back from the table.

'Tea?' Elsie left the table.

'Aye, tea would be grand.' He gazed at the bones of the lamb cutlets Elsie had roasted. It was Friday night and Elsie had been doing his washing, ironing, housework and cooking for a week. The house had never run so smoothly, not even when Nellie had been living with him. But then Nellie always had spent more time crying and rowing with him than cleaning the place.

He had discovered that there was nothing like opening his wardrobe first thing in the morning to see rows of freshly washed and ironed shirts as opposed to dirty crumpled laundry piled high behind the scullery door, or walking into a clean and tidy kitchen to put the kettle on. But best of all was coming home after a day's work to a warm, welcoming living room, and a hot, home-cooked meal. He had never lived so well and he was grateful to Elsie for making it possible.

'There must be something I can do for you.' He offered Elsie a cigarette as he left the table for one of the easy-chairs set next to the fire.

'You're the one paying for the gas to cook the meal on every evening.' She cleared their plates into the scullery.

'I'd pay for the food an' all, you know that.'

'And have the whole street say I'm a kept woman as well as a brazen hussy for keeping house for you? No, thanks.' She handed him his cup of tea and sat opposite him.

'I'm surprised you pay heed to the gossips.'

'If I did that I wouldn't be here. But I have to live with meself. I set my own rules and they're a damn sight straighter than most people's.' She stirred her tea.

'They are that, love.' He racked his brains trying to think of something he could do for her. 'You still got that old range in your living room?'

'Asking the landlord to change it for a modern fireplace is like praying to the moon. He might look as though he's listening, but he'd rather slit his own throat than spend a penny on the house he collects rent from.'

'There's a modern fireplace in the yard at Birtwistle's Construction that's been sitting around for months.'

'I don't want you to get into any trouble or risk losing your job on my account.' Elsie hitched her skirt higher and stretched her legs in front of the fire to warm them.

'I won't. I'll ask the boss about it. If I can swing it, would you like it?'

'Would I heck as like!'

'Then I'll see what I can do.'

'I'll have to pay for it,' she warned him.

'You can pay whatever I pay for the grate, but I'll take the same for my time that you take for yours when you work here. Right?'

'Right.' She sighed with contentment. 'Want another cup of tea?'

'Want me to pour you one?'

'I thought you'd never ask.'

Chapter Eight

'I didn't know Mrs Tanner had called Birtwistle's in to do some work, Mr Fairclough,' Martha Longhurst said to Len, when she saw him heave a modern tiled fireplace off the back of the van he'd parked outside Elsie's house. 'Nice grate that. Expensive, was it?'

'It wasn't cheap,' Lean muttered distractedly, his back straining beneath the weight. He rested for a moment, then carried the fireplace past Martha, who was blatantly gawping, through Elsie's front door and into her living room.

He had already torn out the old range and it stood, black with the accumulated dirt of over eighty years' continuous use, in the back yard. Elsie had rolled back her rug and covered her furniture and as much of her linoleum as she could with old sheets but a thick layer of grey dust had settled on every surface and he suspected that it would take hours of scrubbing to restore the room to a state with which Elsie would be satisfied. He consoled himself with the thought that she'd find it a lot easier to clean a modern fireplace than the antiquated Victorian range.

'Want a cuppa?'

'Elsie?' He grinned at her as she walked in from the hall. 'What are you doing home this early?'

'Half day. Shops close midweek, even Miami Modes.' She stepped back into the hall, opened the door to the parlour and dumped her handbag and coat on the best sofa.

'So they do.' He shifted the grate into the cavity left by the range. 'And in answer to your question, I could murder a cuppa. This dust has got into my throat.'

'You've a bit of filling in to do there.' Elsie bustled past him into the kitchen.

'Won't take me long to brick this hold up and plaster over it,' he said.

Elsie went to the larder. The milk bottle was empty; she rinsed it under the tap, carried it to the front doorstep and exchanged it for the one the milkman had left that morning. She closed the door without noticing that the lace curtains in Ena Sharples's private quarters in the mission hall were twitching.

'It's downright disgusting, them two flaunting their affair like that,' Ena muttered to Martha as she rearranged the folds of lace. 'Elsie's nothing but a common tart. Spending all that time alone with Len Fairclough and him a married man. They should both be in work. And grates like that don't come cheap. I don't know where Elsie could have got the money to replace her old range.'

'Perhaps Len took it from Birtwistle's for her,' Martha suggested. 'After all she's been doing him a lot of favours lately . . .'

'I'll say she has,' Ena cut in abruptly.

'I meant in his house, his cooking and housework and the like,' Martha said.

'Well, if he is putting in that grate as a favour, I'd like to know if he paid for it or stole it from Birtwistle's.'

'Well, I just thought you should know about it.' Martha went to the door.

'You leaving?'

'I promised Minnie I'd pick up her pension for her. See you tonight, Ena?'

'You going past Birtwistle's yard?'

'I might.'

'You'll save me a trip if you do.' Ena closed the door behind her.

The thought that Len had bought the grate for Elsie bothered Martha more than the idea that he'd come by the fireplace dishonestly. He should be saving all his money for his legally wedded wife and son. Ena was right: Elsie and Len's behaviour was downright disgusting. She glanced back at the street as she walked around the corner. She couldn't stop thinking about Len and Elsie alone in the house. There was no saying what they were up to – and in broad daylight as well.

Was Len working for Birtwistle's or for Elsie? If Elsie, she doubted that Elsie was paying him – not in money any road. And if he was working on the side for Elsie when Birtwistle's were paying his wages . . .

Quickening her step, she headed for Birtwistle's yard. Someone there would know if Len Fairclough was working on a proper job that Elsie had paid for, or moon-lighting to please a woman brazen enough to consort with her lover in the middle of the day in a street full of respectable people. A woman so shameless she flaunted her adultery in the face of her neighbours as if it was something to be proud of.

Ken Barlow offered Valerie Tatlock his arm as they walked through the gates of the cemetery and down the main Tarmac path that led to the new graves. They passed ornate Victorian edifices of winged angels and monstrous chiselled urns draped with folds of marble. Gradually, the elaborate memorials of the late nineteenth century gave way to lower, smaller and neater headstones, marked simply with the names and dates of the deceased.

When Ken's mother had been buried, her grave had been on the edge of the vast burial ground, but although she had died only a few months ago, whole rows of gravestones had appeared behind hers. Ken realised that, very soon, her grave would be in the centre of a sea of them. He hated the thought: it was visible evidence of the way life moved on without his mother there to witness it, and an unwelcome reminder of how, sooner or later, every person alive, including himself, would be relegated to the obscurity of death.

'Do you bring flowers here every week?' Valerie broke the silence that had fallen between them.

'I try to.' He had grown close to Valerie during the months that had elapsed since his mother's death and he had reason to be grateful to her. Not least for calling in at odd moments of the evenings and weekends and frequently preventing his father blowing up in a tirade that invariably resulted in bitter arguments. Gradually, his gratitude had turned into love, almost without him being aware of what was happening until he found himself in a position where he simply couldn't imagine life without her. During the past week he had come to realise that Valerie knew and understood him better than anyone – apart from his mother.

'Valerie . . .' He hesitated, terrified of the answer she would give to the question he had been building up for days to ask her.

'Yes?' she murmured absently, reading the headstone of a girl who had died before her sixteenth birthday.

'Marry me,' he blurted.

She looked up at him in astonishment.

'Please.' He grasped both her hands in his. 'I love you, and I want nothing more than to settle down with you as my wife.'

She took his arm and they walked on in silence for a few minutes. Then, too afraid to pressure her for an answer, he busied himself with clearing the dead flowers from the urn on his mother's grave. He carried the urn and the flowers to a wastebasket and tap set close to the path twenty yards away, dumped the flowers, rinsed out the urn and filled it with fresh water. He replaced it on the grave, then crouched down and arranged the bunch of mixed daffodils and tulips he'd brought.

'You were very close to your mother,' Valerie murmured.

'She understood me better than anyone else in the family.' He rose to his feet. 'And, unlike my father, she also understood the value of education. I've a lot to be thankful to her for.'

She stared down at the flowers. 'Are you asking me to marry you just so you can have a woman in the house to come between you and your father?'

'No!' he exclaimed. 'And if you do agree to marry me, I'm not sure where we'll live, but it won't be with my dad.'

'Your mother has only just died, Ken. It's natural you're missing her . . .'

He looked her in the eye. 'I had a wonderful mother,

Valerie, and I'm the first to admit it's hard living without her. But I haven't asked you to marry me because she's gone. No one can ever replace her, and I wouldn't want them to. I don't want another mother, Valerie. I want you to be my wife. In every way possible.'

She smiled. 'Then the answer is yes.'

He reached out and took her hand in his. They stood looking at the grave for a few seconds then turned and retraced their steps.

Annie Walker brought in a tray of clean beer mugs and hung them on the hooks behind the bar as Concepta stacked dirty glasses on the trays beneath the counter. Annie considered gossip beneath her, but although both the bar and the snug were full, no customers were waiting to be served and all the regulars were engrossed in conversation. She couldn't resist trying to find out if Concepta knew any more than her about the latest gossip to rock Coronation Street.

'Have you and Harry seen anything of Len Fairclough?' she asked, with a casual air that didn't fool Concepta for a moment.

'Not much since Nellie walked out on him,' Concepta replied, tight-lipped.

'I'm not surprised she left, poor woman.' Annie shook her head sadly. 'The way Len treated her – and it's not as if he's grieving for her and Stanley. Not from what I've heard. A man like him doesn't deserve a wife—' Annie started. 'Len.' He had walked in wearing his best suit.

'Pint, Annie.' Len thrust his hand into the pocket of his trousers.

'You're dressed up, Len,' Annie observed.

'Had some business to see to.'

'Oh?'

'Man has to wear his best clothes when he goes begging for handouts.'

'Begging? Whatever do you mean, Len?' Annie pulled his pint.

'Haven't you heard?' He gave Annie a hard look. 'I've been sacked.'

'Whatever for?' Concepta asked.

'Not whatever, whoever,' he muttered, eyeing Ena, Minnie and Martha's table in the snug. 'I did a job for a neighbour as a favour and some bloody busybody from the street reported me to my boss.'

'Then it's your own fault,' Annie decreed. 'As an employer I don't hold with people doing jobs on the side that can harm the business that pays them a weekly wage.'

'I wasn't harming no one,' Len burst out. 'I was doing a friend a favour, a favour she – they wouldn't have been able to pay full whack for. And I was using materials that were going to waste. Everything would have worked out just fine if a nosy-parker hadn't seen fit to stick their nose in where it wasn't wanted and go tittle-tattling to my boss.

Seems to me there are some people in this street who need to learn to mind their own bloody business. And when I find the culprit they can look out.'

Innocent as she was, Annie sensed colour flooding into her cheeks. 'Mind the bar for me, dear,' she murmured to Concepta. 'I'll go and give Jack a hand in the cellar. He's obviously got problems or he would have been up by now.'

'What are you going to do, Len?' Concepta asked.

'Have a packet of crisps.' He pushed a threepenny bit and a penny across the bar.

'I mean about work.'

'Go on dole.'

Concepta pursed her lips in disapproval as she opened the till and dropped Len's money into it.

'For a week or two and then I'll set myself up in business,' he added, deciding it wasn't too soon to start advertising Fairclough Builders. 'Plenty of people round here want good jobs done at a fair price. And if I'm my own boss I'll only be answerable to meself. Then God help anybody who thinks they can have a go at taking me down a peg or two.' He took the crisps Concepta handed him and sipped his beer.

'The neighbours are only concerned with what's right, Len,' Concepta chided. 'This is a respectable area . . .'

'Heck as like. You'd be shocked at the goings-on behind some of the lace curtains in this street, Miss Prim and Proper.'

'People have been shocked,' Concepta retorted. 'You're a married man and it's high time you started behaving like one.'

'And what's that's supposed to mean?'

'Everyone knows that Elsie Tanner has been in and out of your house at all hours of the day and night—'

'Cooking and cleaning,' Len said heavily.

'That's Nellie's job.'

'Let me tell you something, love.' Len leant over the bar close to Concepta. 'She never did that, nor any of the other things wives are supposed to do very well, or,' he raised his eyebrows, 'willingly, if you get my meaning. And women are built to be comfort zones for men. Nothing more and nothing less.'

'Say that again, Len, and I'll clock you one.'

Len turned to see Harry standing behind him.

'That's my wife you're talking to, and when you're in her company, I'll thank you to keep a civil tongue in your head.'

Len moved away.

'I think you have something to say to Concepta,' Harry prompted sternly.

Len muttered, 'Sorry,' and went to a table. He sat with his back to the bar and opened his crisps. The door opened and Elsie walked in.

'What you having, love?' Len beamed, grateful for a friendly face.

'Gin and orange, but I'll get it meself.' Elsie looked around the crowded bar. People fell silent as she stared at her neighbours. 'I've been hearing some funny gossip lately,' she shouted in her clear voice, making sure everyone in the pub could hear her. 'I know this is going to disappoint some of you,' she glared over the partition to where Ena, Martha and Minnie were sitting, 'but just for the record, Len Fairclough and me are mates. Mates,' she repeated. 'Not lovers, not carrying on, just mates. Anyone want to say any different, they'll have me to contend with. Anyone want to argue?'

'You did say you wanted a gin and orange?' Concepta picked up a glass.

'Yes.' Elsie went to the bar. 'And there's something else you gossips should know. I'm off to Blackpool at the end of August for my holidays. Alone! Anyone object?'

No one dared speak until Elsie had paid for her gin and joined Len at his table.

Every resident of Coronation Street welcomed the birth of Christopher Hewitt on August 6th 1962. Despite the matrons' prophecies of doom, Concepta's age didn't create any problems. She was up and about inside ten days, running the house, looking after Harry, Lucille and the healthy, charming new baby and loving every minute of it. All the women in the street doted on Christopher and most of the men stopped to smile and tickle him whenever they saw Concepta wheeling him out in his pram. The only person who saw trouble on the horizon was Ena Sharples. Her sharp eyes hadn't failed to notice that since her stepbrother's arrival, Lucille had looked more miserable than she had ever seen her before.

Ena was leaving the Post Office about five weeks after Christopher's birth when she saw Concepta wheeling Christopher over to the draper's shop Leonard Swindley ran with Emily Nugent's assistance. Lucille was at Concepta's side, dragging her school satchel and looking bored.

'How's school going, Lucille?' Ena asked.

'Fine, Mrs Sharples,' Lucille muttered unconvincingly.

'And your young brother?' Ena questioned.

'He's lovely.' Lucille sounded even less convincing than she had done when Ena had asked her about school.

Concepta gave Ena a brittle smile. Outwardly they were a happy family but Lucille had changed since Christopher's arrival and, unlike Harry, Concepta couldn't help feeling that some of her complaints were justified. Christopher did cry a lot and always just when Lucille came home from school and wanted to concentrate on her homework.

She had tried to keep Christopher awake in the afternoon in the hope that he would sleep in the early evening when Lucille wanted the house to be quiet, but no matter what she did, the baby continued to cry every day between four and eight in the evening, just when she most wanted and needed him to be good.

Harry wasn't any help because he still carried on calling into the Rovers for a pint or two after work, leaving her to cope with a fretful Christopher while she tried to get his and Lucille's tea ready.

'If you'll excuse us, Mrs Sharples, I have to buy Christopher some new nightgowns,' Concepta explained. 'He's grown out of the first size already.'

'They're not bairns for long,' Ena agreed. 'Make the most of it while he's this size. Before long he'll be wanting more expensive things than a nightgown or two.'

'Yes, he will,' Concepta agreed politely. 'There's no need for you to hang about while I'm shopping, Lucille, love. Why don't you go on home and start your home-work?'

'Can I?' Lucille asked eagerly. 'I have a biology test tomorrow and I want to get good marks.'

'I'll test you after I've settled Christopher for the night if you like, love,' Concepta offered recklessly, conscious of Ena hovering. As Lucille ran off up the street, Concepta drew the pram close to the shop window and flicked on the foot brake.

'You want to wrap him up a bit warmer than that now autumn's here,' Ena criticised, fingering the hand-knitted blanket Concepta had tucked over her sleeping son.

'I'll bear that in mind, Mrs Sharples,' Concepta said, through gritted teeth, and walked into the shop. As the bell rang, Emily and Leonard walked out of the stockroom. Concepta hid a smile. She was certain that they hadn't been doing anything untoward in the back of the shop but Emily's adoration of her short, plump, balding, bespectacled boss was evident in every look she sent his way.

Concepta walked to the counter. 'I need two baby's nightdresses, please, Emily. Second size.'

'Your Christopher's growing quickly, Mrs Hewitt,' Emily ventured shyly. 'We have these, white flannel with blue rabbits embroidered on the front, or these, white with white flower embroidery and there's these. The embroidery is lemon so they're suitable for a boy or a girl.'

'But they look better for a girl,' Concepta said.

Leonard muttered, 'Excuse me,' and returned to the stockroom.

After settling on a plain white gown with white embroidery and another with blue rabbits, Concepta studied the knitted layettes on display under the glass counter as Emily wrapped her purchases and took her money. She tucked the parcel under her arm and left the shop.

She looked left then right. Oblivious to the traffic, she stepped out into the road and cried out.

'Is something the matter, Mrs Hewitt?' Emily ran out and grabbed her as a Post Office van drove past at speed.

'My baby.' Concepta looked frantically up and down the deserted street. 'My baby! I left him here . . .'

'Are you sure?'

'I'm absolutely sure. I parked the pram here. I put the brake on. I was talking to Mrs Sharples. Lucille had gone home—'

'Could Lucille have taken him?'

The words were no sooner out of Emily Nugent's mouth than Concepta ran off up the road to her house.

Detective Sergeant Sowman felt that he had seen it all in his twenty-odd years on the police force. And the one thing that he had learnt was when it came to most crimes against babies and young children, you didn't have to look far from home to find the culprit. Ignoring the whispers coming from the Hewitts' scullery where the women of Coronation Street had congregated in an attempt to help the family, he took the cup of tea Annie Walker handed him and sat back on the sofa in the living room. He looked across to where Lucille sat sobbing uncontrollably on the chair opposite.

'Lucille, love, don't take on so.' Annie patted her shoulder.

'I'd appreciate a word with young Lucille in private, Mrs Walker,' the detective sergeant said.

Annie Walker gave him a disdainful look but she returned to the scullery, where Valerie Tatlock and Emily Nugent were washing dishes.

'Come on now, love, you're not helping the situation,' Detective Sergeant Sowman said to Lucille. 'All I'm asking you to do is tell the truth.'

'But I've *told* you the truth,' Lucille said hysterically. 'Christopher was safe in his pram when I left him outside the shop. And I came straight home. I started my home-work right away—'

'And then?' he interrupted.

'And then Concepta ran in asking if I'd brought Christopher home . . . I . . . I—' She dissolved into tears.

'Come on now,' a note of impatience had crept into the officer's voice, 'this isn't getting us anywhere. Pull your-self together and we'll start from the beginning again. You were with your mam—'

'Concepta's my stepmam,' Lucille corrected him. After the officer's warnings it was of the utmost importance to tell him the truth about everything, no matter how trivial.

'Your stepmam, and then you met Mrs Sharples . . .'

Harry Hewitt heard his daughter crying as he walked down the stairs. She was only marginally less hysterical than Concepta had been when he had sent for the doctor half an hour earlier. The doctor had sedated Concepta and ordered her to stay in bed. He'd left her lying on the bed, staring blindly at the ceiling and he didn't know what was worse: the drug-induced torpor into which she had fallen, or the frenzy that had preceded it.

'Come on, Lucille. Tell me where you took Christopher. All we want is for him to be back where he belongs—' he heard the policeman say.

'An' that's all I want!' Lucille screamed. She jumped up as Harry entered the room and ran to him. Clutching him wildly, she pleaded, 'Tell them I didn't take Christopher, Dad. You know I wouldn't do anything like that. I might have complained that he was always crying but I loved him. You know I did.'

'I know, love.' Harry stroked her short dark hair. He nodded to the scullery door. 'Go and ask Mrs Walker if she'll sit with Concepta upstairs. And wash your face while you're there. Perhaps Valerie or Miss Nugent will make us some more tea.'

Lucille didn't need any second bidding, she ran out of the room.

Harry waited until she'd closed the door behind her. 'If Lucille said she didn't take Christopher, she didn't take him.' He sank down on to one of the chairs as if his legs wouldn't support him any longer.

'With all due respect, Mr Hewitt, half of my force and all the neighbours are out looking for your son. If he's anywhere to be found we'd have found him by now.'

'So, what are you suggesting?' Harry asked baldly.

'I've ordered the canal to be dragged. They'll have to break off when it gets dark but they'll start again first thing in the morning.'

'You think Christopher's dead?' The ghastly thought had crossed Harry's mind several times since he'd arrived home to hear the news that his son was missing, but it was the first time he'd forced himself to voice his fear.

'On your daughter's own admission she was jealous of the baby. Mrs Sharples told us that she found Lucille sheltering under the viaduct two nights back, and she was threatening to leave home because no one loved her. Mrs Sharples said she had to remind your wife that she had two children . . .'

'Ena Sharples is an interfering old busybody,' Harry snapped.

'That's as may be, Mr Hewitt,' Detective Sergeant Sowman replied calmly, 'but in my line of work, interfering old busybodies are heaven sent.'

'My God! You can't think that Lucille threw Christopher into the canal!'

'It has been known. A young girl used to getting her father's undivided attention suddenly having to share it with a new wife *and* a baby. In my experience jealousy can make people do funny things. Prompt a moment of madness.'

'If Lucille said she didn't touch Christopher after Concepta left him outside Swindley's shop, then she didn't,' Harry reiterated firmly.

'I'm going to the mobile headquarters we've set up on the corner of the street to see if anything new has come in.'

'You will let us know the minute you hear anything?' Harry hesitated. 'Either way.'

Detective Sergeant Sowman rose to his feet. 'I will, and I'll be back first thing in the morning. You can count on that.'

Chapter Nine

For three days and nights every adult resident of Coronation Street scoured the area looking for Christopher, while Concepta sank deeper into despair. Feuds and differences of opinion were forgotten as Ken Barlow and Len Fairclough joined forces to search every back lane and alleyway within a two-mile radius. Jack Walker and Frank Barlow knocked on doors and persuaded the most stubborn and anti-social of pensioners in the area to look in their coal- and wood-sheds and check their outhouses. The police dragged the canal and posted photographs of Christopher on lamp-posts and in the local paper, but all to no avail. No one had seen Christopher since Concepta had parked his pram outside Swindley's shop and no trace of him, his clothes or his pram had been found.

On the third night after Christopher's disappearance, Harry was woken by a loud knocking on the front door. His mouth dry with fear, his heart thundering in anticipation of the worst, he leapt out of bed, switched on the light and, to his horror, realised the bed beside him was empty. He checked the clock. It was three o'clock in the morning. Without stopping to grab his dressing-gown, he charged down the stairs in his pyjamas and opened the front door to see Detective Sergeant Sowman and Concepta outlined in the yellow light from the street-lamp.

'We found her wandering in Jubilee Terrace.' Holding Concepta by the arm, the officer helped her into the passage. 'The landlord of the local pub rang the station to complain that there was a madwoman screaming, "Christopher," over and over again at the top of voice in the street. The doctor's had a look at her, and given her something to make her sleep, but he told me to warn you to keep a close eye on her. Another bout like this and he'll have to admit her to the psychiatric hospital.'

'I'm sorry,' Harry murmured, shame-faced. 'She must have slipped out while I was asleep.'

'No need for apologies.' The detective sergeant opened the door and stepped back on to the pavement. 'We're all exhausted.'

Elsie Tanner allowed the young driver to help her from the back of his taxi. She took her purse from her handbag as he carried her suitcase to her front door.

'That will be two shillings and sixpence, madam.'

Elsie gave him half a crown and a sixpence.

'Thank you very much, madam.' He returned to his cab and tooted as he drove off.

'Elsie.' Ken Barlow ran up to her. 'I hope you don't mind but we – that is Jack Walker and me – searched your woodshed, coalhouse and outhouse while you were away.'

'If you found any coal, wood or other valuables you're welcome to keep them,' she quipped.

'We were looking for Christopher Hewitt,' Ken informed her.

'Something's happened to him?'

'He disappeared from outside Swindley's shop three days ago, and no one's seen him since.'

'Disappeared – oh, my God, you mean kidnapped!' Elsie dropped her keys in shock.

'The police say that if he'd been kidnapped the Hewitts would have had a ransom note by now. Besides, everyone knows that Harry hasn't any money – leastways none that would attract a kidnapper,' Ken said. 'Concepta's taken it hard. She's half out of her mind.'

'I bet she is,' Elsie concurred.

'If you see or hear anything . . .'

'I'll go straight round to the Hewitts, Ken,' Elsie promised.

'There's also a mobile headquarters parked at the end of the street. Jack and I are going out again now to Viaduct Street. We've searched it three times already but you never know, we might have missed something.'

'Good luck, Ken. If there's anything that I can do . . .'

'Someone will let you know,' Ken called back over his shoulder.

Elsie dropped her suitcase at the foot of the stairs. She opened the door to her living room and paused for a moment. She had bumped into an old schoolfriend of Linda's in the bus station, Joan Akers.

Joan's young man had gone down south to look for work before Linda had emigrated to Canada. Alone, penniless and pregnant, Joan had never heard from him again. She had been carrying a baby in the bus station, but unlike most young mothers she hadn't been anxious to show it off. She'd said he was sleeping but there was something else . . . Elsie searched her memory.

After Linda had left, Dot Greenhalgh had told her that Joan's baby had died and she'd moved into a bedsit close to where she was living.

Elsie picked up her keys and left her house. She went down Coronation Street and turned right into Rosamund Street. Ten minutes later she was in a street of large terraced houses. She walked up to one that had a row of seven bells beside the door. She went through the names until she came to Akers. She pressed the button next to it.

High heels clattered on an uncarpeted staircase, and a few seconds later the door opened and Joan peered out. 'Mrs Tanner, I didn't expect to see you.'

'Can I come in for a minute?' Elsie didn't wait for an

answer. She stepped into a bleak hall in need of painting and new linoleum.

'I'm a bit busy,' Joan prevaricated. 'The baby's fretful. He's teething.'

'Then I might be able to help. I've had two of me own and I haven't forgotten that much.'

Joan hesitated and Elsie was afraid that she'd order her to leave. Eventually Joan walked back up the stairs and Elsie followed her into a cramped bedsit hung about with soaking wet nappies and baby clothes.

'Oh, the poor mite.' Elsie walked over to a pram where a baby was kicking and crying feverishly. 'No wonder he's fretful. You can't keep a baby in a room this size with damp washing hanging everywhere.' She picked up the baby who was unmistakably Christopher Hewitt, set him against her shoulder and he fell silent.

'I know that,' Joan said guilty. 'That's why I'm looking for something bigger. But two rooms are so much more expensive than a bedsit.'

Elsie looked into the girl's terrified eyes. 'It's not just the washing, Joan, his mother is out of her mind with worry. You've got to give him back. You know that, don't you?'

A tear fell from Joan's eye as she nodded slowly.

Concepta sat on the sofa in her living room, holding Christopher as if she would never let him go again. 'I'll never, never be able to thank you enough, Elsie.' She brushed away a tear.

'There's nothing to thank me for. It was pure luck. I thought it odd when Joan didn't show off the baby to me when I saw them in the bus station, but that was before I knew that Christopher had been taken.' Elsie set the cup of tea Lucille had made for her in the hearth. 'I'm not making excuses for her, Concepta, but her own baby died just after it was born.'

'I'll never, never forgive her, never.' Concepta clutched Christopher closer. 'She's put us through hell for the last three days.' She looked up to see Harry and Lucille standing in the the scullery doorway. Lucille was pale, thin and even more tearful than her. 'Come here, love.' She set the baby down on her lap and opened her arms. Lucille ran to her.

'It's a change to see you doing something right,' Frank Barlow said to his son as Ken pushed a carnation into the buttonhole of the new grey suit he had bought for his wedding. 'You've had more luck than you deserve. That's all I can say. Valerie's a grand lass, out of much the same mould as your mother.'

'I know.' Ken glanced in the mirror and reached for the comb he'd stowed in the top pocket of his suit.

'Mind you, I think you've spent a scandalous amount of money on buying number nine in street. Five hundred and fifty pounds. You'll be paying it off when you're ninety. Your mother and me only gave a hundred and fifty for this house and it's been looked after since. Not like yours,' Frank added disparagingly.

'You and Mam bought this place in different times.' Ken reminded himself that he had spent his last night under his father's roof. He wanted to marry Valerie more than anything else in the world, but he was also looking forward to moving on and out of the house in which he'd grown up. Without Ida Frank's moods had grown even more unbearable to live with.

'And I think our David could have made an effort to come to his own brother's wedding. Seems to me he doesn't care twopence for the family now he's living high on the hog down south. Didn't come for your mother's funeral and now this.'

'He's playing an important match, Dad,' Ken reminded him.

'More important than his own brother's wedding?'

'I told him I understood,' Ken said patiently.

'Well, I don't,' Frank countered. 'What's more important than your own mother's funeral or your brother's wedding? Things that only happen once in a lifetime . . . That'll be your best man,' he added as the doorbell rang. 'College friend of yours, is he?'

'You know he is.' Ken finished tidying his hair and slipped the comb back into his pocket as the doorbell rang a second time. He glanced at his watch. 'We'd better get going if we want to be at St Mary's on time.'

'You're not inviting your posh pal in for a drink, then?' Frank shouted, as he walked down the passage.

Ken sighed. 'A quick one.'

'Right, then, get out a bottle of beer.'

Ken counted to ten under his breath, before going into the kitchen.

'You look beautiful,' Lucille Hewitt said wistfully, as Valerie Tatlock studied her headdress and veil in the mirror. 'I'll never look as gorgeous as you.'

'Yes, you will.' Valerie smiled at her bridesmaid. 'When the time comes you'll be stunning.'

'No one will want to marry me.'

'They'll be queuing up when you're old enough,' Valerie assured her.

'I don't know how you can stand there so calmly when you're about to be married. And honeymooning in London.' Lucille sighed theatrically. 'I'd give anything to go to London.'

'You will one day.'

'Send me a postcard?' Lucille pleaded. 'One of the Tower if you can. We've been reading about it in history. Ever so many people were killed there. It's supposed to be haunted.'

'If I see one, I'll send it to you,' Valerie promised.

'You look right gorgeous, love.' Albert Tatlock complimented his niece as he entered the living room. 'The
best-looking bride this street has ever seen.'

'I doubt that, Uncle Albert,' Valerie set aside the
mirror, 'but it's nice of you to say so.'

'Happy?' He offered her his arm.

'Very.'

'Then let's go.'

'I've come about the job.'

Len Fairclough looked the young lad up and down. He
was chunky, well built and had the right muscles for a
builder.

'The building apprenticeship that was advertised in
paper,' the boy elaborated. 'Have I come to the right
place?'

'You have,' Len replied.

'Name's Jerry Booth. I live round in Viaduct Street.'

'Didn't you work for old man Moffat who retired last
month?'

'Yes. He gave me a good reference.'

'Two weeks' trial suit you?'

'Yes.' Jerry beamed.

'Starting now.' Len pointed at the second-hand van
he'd bought that morning. 'You can clean and polish that,
inside and out.'

★

'I suppose this will be our normal life from now on,' Ken commented as Valerie cleared the breakfast dishes from the table into the kitchen. It was the first Monday morning in their new house and although they had returned from London the day before, they both felt as though they were still on honeymoon. 'It feels good doesn't it?'

'It does,' she agreed, marvelling at how effortlessly she and Ken had slipped into an easygoing intimacy.

'You don't mind me setting up my typewriter on the other half of the table, do you, love?' he asked as he set a couple of files and his portable typewriter on to the space she had just cleared.

'No.'

'A kiss from a rather wonderful, tolerant wife.' He smiled, the slow lazy smile that Valerie loved.

'No . . . not when you have to leave in a couple of minutes,' she giggled as she pulled his hand out from under the bodice of her dressing-gown. She picked up one of the files and opened it. 'When can I read your book?'

He removed the file from her hand. 'Not before it's finished and I've revised it.'

'I can't wait to read it.'

'It's just a novel about three lads growing up in a northern town. If I sell it, would you mind if I gave up teaching and wrote full time?'

'No, I wouldn't mind. In fact, I'd be really proud.'

He kissed her again. 'My father's right about one thing.'

'What's that?'

'I'm the luckiest man on earth.' He slipped on his sports coat. 'I wish we could have honeymooned for ever.'

Valerie walked to the front door with him. 'Some round here would say that two weeks in London is quite long enough.'

'I won't have enough with a lifetime of you.' He glanced at his watch. 'But Bessie Street School beckons. See you tonight?'

'I'll cook us something special to celebrate our second night in our new home.' She opened the door.

'Morning, Ken, Val.' Elsie Tanner pulled her nylon dressing-gown closer around herself as she dropped a milk bottle on to her doorstep.

'Morning, Elsie. Bye, love.' Ken walked quickly up the street.

'Have a good honeymoon?' Elsie smiled knowingly.

'Very good thank you, Mrs Tanner,' Valerie replied shyly. 'There's a lot to do in London.'

'I bet there is,' Elsie answered.

'Oh, Valerie, I'm really glad you and Ken have moved in,' Concepta said from the doorstep of number seven.

'That goes for me too,' Elsie chipped in. 'Since the house has been empty we've had nothing but teenagers trying to break in all hours of the day and night.'

'I hope you don't mind Mrs Tanner, Mrs Hewitt . . .'

'Elsie,' Elsie corrected her.

'Concepta.' Concepta grinned.

'I feel I should warn you that I'm closing down my hairdressing salon on Rosamund Street and moving my business into my front parlour. I hope you don't mind.'

'I don't mind,' Elsie said. 'In fact, I think you've got yourself a new customer.'

'And me,' Concepta enthused. 'It will be great just to slip next door to get my hair done. And I dare say you won't mind if I have Christopher on my lap while you do it.'

'Of course I won't mind. I love babies.'

'Oh aye?' Elsie lifted her eyebrows.

'I'll look forward to seeing both of you,' Valerie blushed. 'But, if you'll excuse me, I have the breakfast things to see to.'

Elsie rushed home from Miami Modes that evening, washed and changed in record time, and took extra care with her make-up. She checked the clock for the tenth time in as many minutes as she spat on her mascara block, rubbed her brush in the sticky mess and applied another coat to her lashes. Bill Gregory had sent her a letter three days ago telling her that he had a week's leave and she couldn't wait to see him.

The doorbell rang. She raced down the passage to

answer it. Bill was standing on the doorstep, dark and handsome in a navy blue suit.

'Oh, Bill.' Not caring if Ena Sharples and the entire complement of her neighbours were watching, she wrapped her arms round his neck and kissed him.

'Elsie, love.' He dropped his suitcase and returned her embrace. 'You ready?' he asked when she came up for air.

'For what?'

'I stopped off in the taxi on the way here. I've booked a table for us in that new Italian restaurant. We're going up town, love, to celebrate.'

'Celebrate what?'

'Our reunion.'

Jerry Booth was piling planks of sawn timber into the back of Len's van when he heard someone call his name. He looked around, and to his surprise, saw his uncle. 'Uncle Sam, what are you doing here?'

'I was made redundant last week so I thought I'd come down here to see if I could find work,' Sam Leach said diffidently.

'You're a long way from Newcastle and Auntie Maureen.'

'Aye, that I am, but there's nothing going round there.'

'I'm not sure there's much work round here either,' Jerry said. 'My boss has only just set up in business, so he won't be taking on anyone else. Not for a while.'

'He might change his mind and start firing and hiring

in earnest if he catches his apprentice gassing instead of loading the van as he ordered him to.'

Len appeared in the yard. 'This is my Uncle Sam, Mr Fairclough,' Jerry explained. 'He's come down from Newcastle to look for work.'

Len eyed the thin, slightly built man. He clearly wasn't up to hard work, not that he had any to give him. 'Well, I've nothing to offer you, Sam, but I've heard that the landlord of the Rovers Return round the corner is looking for a potman. You could try there.'

'Thank you, Mr Fairclough.' Sam picked up his case. 'Thank you very much. I'll try there right away.'

Ena Sharples pushed the stamp she had just bought at the counter of the Post Office into the compartment at the back of her purse. She was aware of the queue behind her, but she would not allow anyone to take her place until she was good and ready to relinquish it. She moved away only when her purse was securely back in her handbag. She turned to see Bill Gregory standing behind her.

'Sending a letter, Mr Gregory?'

'Yes.' He stuck the envelope he was holding into his pocket but not before Ena saw the name and address written on it. 'Mrs P. Gregory'.

'Writing to your mother?'

'That's right.' Bill flushed guiltily as he pushed past her and went to the counter. 'Stamp, please.'

Ena hitched her handbag on her arm and headed for Len Fairclough's yard in Mawdsley Street. He and Bill Gregory had been mates for years. If anyone would know whether Bill had a wife hidden away somewhere, it was Len Fairclough. She found him and Jerry Booth sitting outside the shed he called his office, drinking mugs of tea.

'Here, I want a word with you, Len Fairclough,' she shouted from the gate.

Len wandered over to her, mug in hand. 'What can I do for you, Mrs Sharples? Does the Mission roof need seeing to, or is there a window that needs repairing?'

'Nowt like that,' Ena retorted. 'You know this Bill Gregory Elsie Tanner's knocking round with, don't you?'

'Aye,' Len replied cautiously.

'Is he married?' Ena demanded bluntly.

'What makes you think so?'

'I just saw him send a letter in Post Office.'

'Since when has sending letters been a crime?'

'It was addressed to a Mrs P. Gregory.'

'Could be his mother.'

'And it could be that he's making a right fool of Elsie,' Ena snapped. 'And don't stand there looking all innocent and try to tell me Mrs P. Gregory is his mother. I can spot a liar a mile off, Len Fairclough, and you're a pretty poor specimen.'

'Not that it's any of your business but Bill's been

separated from his wife for years, Mrs Sharples.' Len realised it was pointless to try to pull the wool over Ena's eyes. As all the residents of Coronation Street knew.

'And Elsie doesn't know.' It wasn't a question. 'Don't try telling me she does.' Ena's voice rose. 'Elsie Tanner's many things but she'd never knowingly knock around with another woman's fellow.'

'There's no need to tell her, Mrs Sharples.'

'No need?' Ena spat out. 'I'm disgusted with you, Len Fairclough. And to think that you call yourself her friend. Well, you might not care about your neighbours, but I do. And I'll not stand idly by and see one of them made to look a proper fool. So there.'

'Trouble?' Jerry joined Len at the gate after Ena had walked off.

'Could be,' Len murmured. 'But for now let's go and lay that new hard standing in Victoria Street. If we don't finish that job today, I'll be losing money on it.'

Ena marched up to the door of number eleven Coronation Street and banged on it – hard.

Elsie opened it. 'Can I help you?' she asked Ena brusquely, guessing by the expression on Ena's face that she hadn't called round to give her good news.

'It's more like the other way round.' Ena crossed her arms. 'You got company?' She peered over Elsie's shoulder into the passage.

'What's it to you whether I have or not?'

'Bill Gregory?'

'Last I heard this is a free country and I'll invite who I damn please into my house, Mrs Sharples.'

'Even a married man?'

'What did you say?'

'Ask him about Mrs P. Gregory. Right, I've said all I came to say.' Ena set off back towards the Mission Hall, leaving Elsie staring open-mouthed after her.

'Who was it, love?' Bill asked, from the living room.

Elsie whirled around. 'Ena Sharples.'

'And what did that busybody want?'

'Are you married?' Elsie asked harshly.

'I don't think of myself as married. I've lived like a single bloke for years—'

'That's not what I asked,' Elsie cried. 'Are you or are you not married?' she repeated tersely.

'Phyllis and I have lived apart for years, Elsie. It's been over between us—'

'You divorced?'

'We never got round to it. But that's not to say we won't.'

'Get your bag, go upstairs, pack your traps and get out of here!'

'Elsie, love . . .'

'Don't you dare Elsie-love me!' she screamed. 'I may like a good time and I may have a soft heart but there's some things I've promised meself that I'll never stoop to doing. And one of them is playing around with a married man. Out!'

Chapter Ten

Annie Walker was leaning on the bar in the Rovers chatting to Harry Hewitt and Len Fairclough. 'I can't thank you enough for recommending Sam to us, Len. He's a proper gentleman, kind, considerate. I don't mind telling you that he's made a real difference around here. Does jobs before I even have to ask him. He sees what needs doing, goes ahead and does it. We've never had so many clean glasses in the place. He has them collected, washed and back in the bar in no time. Jack and I have given him the small bedroom and he keeps it like a new pin. '

Len stopped listening to Annie as Elsie walked in. He'd hoped she'd put in an appearance. He slipped his hand into his pocket. 'Gin and orange, Elsie?'

'Please, Len.' She joined him and Harry.

'That will be two refills for Harry and me, Annie love, and a gin and orange for Elsie.'

'You do look down in the mouth, Elsie.' Annie pulled

pints of beer into Len and Harry's mugs, then poured Elsie's gin.

'Bad day,' Elsie responded abruptly.

'Can I have a word with you, Elsie?' Len picked up his pint and her gin and orange. 'Over here might be a bit more private.' He led the way to an empty table.

'I warn you now, Len, if you're in a proposing mood, I'm not in a listening one.' Elsie's attempt at a joke had a sharp edge.

'Bill not with you,' he ventured.

'I would have thought that was obvious.' She took out a packet of cigarettes and offered him one.

'Ena told you, then.'

'Told me he was married.' She gave him a suspicious look as he flicked his lighter and lit her cigarette before his own. 'Damn you, Len Fairclough, you knew, didn't you? You knew he was married and you didn't say a word to me.'

'It's not as if he and Phyllis were living together. '

Elsie didn't wait to hear any more excuses. She picked up her glass and flung the contents into his face.

'There's a letter come for you, Ken,' Valerie Barlow announced, when Ken walked in from school on a cold, dark February evening. 'It was delivered second post this afternoon. From London.'

Ken hung his coat on the peg in the hall, dropped his briefcase on the stand and went into the living room.

Valerie had put the letter on the table. He picked it up, looked at the postmark and turned it over.

Valerie knew he had been on tenterhooks to hear the publisher's opinion of the novel he had sent off in such high hopes three weeks before. She thought it was brilliant but, conscious of the deficiencies in her education, she knew her opinions counted for little, even with Ken who loved her. 'Aren't you going to open it?'

Ken sat down, took the knife from the place setting Val had laid and slit the envelope. He removed the single sheet of paper it contained and read slowly.

'Is it a good news?' Valerie crossed her fingers behind her back.

He folded the letter and pushed it back into the envelope. 'They've rejected it. It doesn't quite fit their list.' He couldn't keep the bitterness from his voice. 'So, it looks like I'll be teaching in Bessie Street School for a few years yet.'

Valerie knew just how devastated he was. She racked her brains to think of something comforting to say but all she could come up with was, 'Are you ready for your tea?'

'As ready as I'll ever be, Val.' He couldn't meet her searching gaze.

'I'll get it, then.' She went into the scullery to fetch the plates from the oven, feeling as though the first rift had opened between them.

★

'Good evening, Mrs Walker.' Leonard Swindley addressed Annie formally as he entered the bar of the Rovers Return a few minutes after it had opened for the evening trade.

'And a good evening to you, Mr Swindley. We don't often see you in here. Can I get you a drink?' Annie replied.

'Yes, please, Mrs Walker, an orange juice.'

'My pleasure, Mr Swindley.' Annie reached for a bottle of orange juice, took off the cap, poured it into a glass and set it on the bar. She shook her head at the coins he offered her. 'This is on the house, Mr Swindley, it might persuade you to return to see us again some time.'

'This is an exceptional occasion, Mrs Walker. I do not as a rule frequent public bars. I am here to enquire after Sam Leach.'

'As I've said to our regulars, Mr Swindley, Mr Leach is a proper gentleman and a hard worker.'

'I am not surprised to hear it, Mrs Walker. Have you any idea of the difference he has been making to the lives of our neighbours? He has been doing the shopping for some of the housebound old folks.'

'I didn't know, but it doesn't surprise me to hear it, Mr Swindley. It is a pleasure to have him living and working in the Rovers Return.'

'He's even been helping some of the frailer congregation of the Glad Tidings Mission Hall with their heavy house-work. He carried in a whole load of coal for Mrs Shipley only last week. And when she told me, I thought I'd write a piece on him for the *Mission Gazette*. Something along the lines of how one good Samaritan can make an entire neighbourhood a better place to live in.'

'That is a wonderful idea, Mr Swindley.' Annie beamed.

'You don't think he would mind?' Leonard queried. 'He is such a modest, retiring individual.'

'I'm sure he wouldn't,' Annie said. 'I agree that he is not the sort of person to put himself forward, but he could hardly object to you writing good things about him. And I can't think of anyone more deserving of praise.'

'Thank you for your encouragement, Mrs Walker.' Leonard removed a notebook and pencil from his pocket. 'I would be grateful for any stories you have about his good deeds here that I could incorporate into the article.'

'Well . . .' Annie paused '. . . only last week he offered to mend Mrs Caldwell's broken back door for her. She's been waiting for the landlord to get round to it for over a month.'

'That is just the sort of information I need, Mrs Walker, thank you.'

Jack watched Annie talking nineteen to the dozen to Leonard Swindley, who was scribbling notes. He sighed as he went to deal with the queue forming at the bar. There were times when he wished his wife would pay more attention to the regulars who put money into the business and less to gossip.

★

Elsie Tanner switched off her alarm clock, grabbed her dressing-gown and went downstairs. There were three letters lying on the mat behind the front door. She stooped to pick them up. One was from Linda and she pushed it into her pocket to read it over her first cup of tea of the day. The second was from the gas board notifying her that they were putting up the price of gas, and the third was addressed to her in a hand she didn't recognise.

She went into the scullery, filled the kettle and put it on the gas then she opened the envelope.

Dear Mrs Tanner,
Due to the rising cost of living, your rent will be increased by five shillings a week from the first of next month.

Elsie read and reread it, and the more she looked at the words, the more incensed she became. 'Bloody landlord!' she cursed roundly. How dare he come to her with his hand out for more money when he never touched the house to make an improvement or repair any of the faults she had reported to him time and again? 'He wouldn't even put a bloody modern grate in when I asked him to. Instead I had to see to it meself.' She forgot conveniently that Len had done the job for nothing.

The kettle whistled, fraying her already ragged nerves.

She picked up the letter and the envelope, and tore both into shreds, then tossed them into the bin on top of last night's tealeaves.

Three weeks after her conversation with Leonard Swindley, Annie Walker was polishing the pumps in the bar when the first customers of the evening walked in: two men she had never seen before, both over six feet tall, well built with shoulders that filled the doorway and short haircuts that marked them out as soldiers – or policemen. Her curiosity roused, she walked over to serve them.

'Good evening, gentlemen, what can I get for you?'

'Are you're the landlady here?' the heavier of the two enquired officiously.

'Yes, I'm Annie Walker,' she replied, intimidated.

'And I'm Jack Walker, the landlord.' Jack rested his arm on Annie's shoulders to give her moral support. 'What can we do for you?'

'We're policemen.' The man who had spoken to Annie flashed his warrant card. 'We're looking for a Sam Leach.'

The second produced a copy of the *Mission Gazette* from his pocket. 'It says in here that Sam Leach works in this pub.'

'He does.' Jack could hardly lie to a policeman.

'Is he here?'

'It's his evening off,' Annie said shortly.

'Do you know where he is?'

She shook her head. 'He's free to do whatever he likes in his own time.'

'What time do you expect him back?'

'We have no idea,' Annie replied.

'Let us know the minute he returns?' The officer scribbled a telephone number on the back of a card and handed it to Jack. 'The minute,' he warned. 'Perverting the course of justice is a serious offence.' He gave Jack and Annie a stern look then followed his colleague out of the pub.

'Don't be daft, Mr Fairclough.' Jerry Booth would never have spoken to his boss like that if he hadn't been so upset. 'Uncle Sam would never kill my Auntie Maureen. You've seen him! He's so mild mannered he wouldn't say boo to a goose.'

'It's the quiet ones you have to watch, Jerry.' Len looked around for confirmation this and Harry Hewitt and Frank Barlow both nodded their heads.

'Len's right,' Frank endorsed. 'And Harry came in just before those coppers left. He heard them warn Jack and Annie that they'd be in trouble if they don't let them know the minute your uncle sets foot in here. It has to be something serious, doesn't it? And there's owt more serious than murder.'

Ena Sharples was just settling into her armchair with a cup of cocoa before bed when she heard a tap on the window. Leaving her cup on the table she went to the window, gearing herself up for a run-in with the teenagers who had been creating havoc in the street late at night recently. She moved the curtain aside and peered out. Sam Leach was standing in the shadows, a suitcase in his hand. She pointed to the side door of the Mission Hall and went through to the public area to let him in.

'I'm sorry, Mrs Sharples,' he apologised humbly, when she opened the door. 'I didn't know where else to go.'

'Come in, I've just made meself a cup of cocoa. You can join me.' Stifling her curiosity, she led the way to her private quarters. 'Leave your suitcase by the door and sit yourself down.' She went to the cupboard to get more milk.

Sam perched nervously on the edge of a chair. 'I suppose you've heard the police have been asking for me.'

Ena set the milk on to boil. 'Aye, I have. I should think the whole of Manchester has an' all by now.'

'You're not going to ask me what they want me for.'

'Folk in Rovers have already decided you murdered your wife.'

Sam almost fell off his chair. 'Me murder Maureen? No, Mrs Sharples, they've got it wrong there. I've not murdered her, but . . . I have left her.'

'That's desertion, that is.' Ena poured the boiling milk into a cup and mixed it with a couple of spoonfuls of cocoa and sugar. 'I take it the poor woman doesn't work.'

'No, she doesn't,' Sam admitted.

'Then how did you expect her to keep herself?'

'I didn't think. Truth be told, Mrs Sharples, I was so angry with her when I left I didn't care.' Sam took the cup from her and wrapped his frozen fingers round it. 'I couldn't take any more. She makes my life a misery . . . but you don't want to hear about my troubles.'

'Why not? I've nowt better to do.' Ena settled back into her chair.

'She's a bully, Mrs Sharples. Always tells me where to go, what to do, and who I can and can't talk to. If I try to do anything to please her, she shouts at me and tells me that I'm doing it all wrong . . . and she's always angry . . .' He looked up at Ena and gave her a diffident smile. 'These last few weeks round here have been wonderful. People have been so kind and friendly.'

'Only because you have been kind and friendly to them, Mr Leach,' she said firmly.

'I like helping folks out with their little problems. And Mr and Mrs Walker have been generous, letting me live with them and even insisting that I have my meals with them.'

'You do know that you have to go to the police?'

He finished his cocoa and set the cup and saucer on the table. 'Yes, Mrs Sharples.'

'And the sooner the better, before they come round asking any more questions and the residents make you out to be a mass murderer. Before you know it, that lot in Rovers will have you down as a Bluebeard.'

He rose to his feet. 'Please, Mrs Sharples, don't say owt to anyone. I don't want young Jerry to find out that I've deserted his auntie. Not yet any road. When I go back I'll write to him and try to explain.'

'I won't say anything, Mr Leach. You can count on me.' Ena reached for her coat.

'Where are you going, Mrs Sharples?'

'To police station with you. I expect you could do with a bit of moral support.'

'Aye, that I could. You're a rare diamond, Mrs Sharples. A rare diamond,' he repeated slowly. 'I don't know how to thank you.'

'You already have, Mr Leach. When you chopped the last lot of wood into sticks for my stove.'

Martha Longhurst glared at Ena in indignation. 'I don't know how you can sit there and drink that milk stout as if butter wouldn't melt in your mouth.'

'What would you have me do, Martha?' Ena asked calmly.

'Get down on your knees and beg forgiveness,' Martha retorted fiercely. 'I saw you with my own eyes at eleven o'clock at night marching Sam Leach in the direction of the police station. A nice man like that and you had to go shopping him to rozzers. I'll never understand how you could do it.'

'My conscience is clear.' Ena eyed the other regulars, who were watching her through the partition that separated the snug from the public bar.

'No one's talking to you in the whole of Coronation Street, you do know that?'

'I am,' Minnie Caldwell contradicted Martha in a small but resolute voice. 'I can't believe that our Ena would shop anyone to the police, Martha.'

'You denying what I saw with my own eyes, Minnie Caldwell?' Martha demanded heatedly. 'She took him to police station, I tell you.'

'That doesn't mean she shopped him,' Minnie repeated stubbornly.

'Then I'm not drinking with either of you.'

'Please yourself.' Ena sat back in her chair.

Martha took her milk stout and carried it over to the table set furthest from Minnie and Ena's.

'Mrs Sharples.' Annie Walker walked behind the bar of the snug. 'I owe you an apology. Mr Leach just telephoned Jack to say sorry for leaving without thanking us or saying goodbye to anyone. He said you'd been kind enough to listen to him and help him sort out his troubles. That he'd deserted his wife and you went along with him to the police station to give him moral support when he gave himself up. If you don't mind me saying so, that was a kind thing you did, Mrs Sharples.'

'No kinder than the things Sam Leach has been doing

for all of us round here,' Ena retorted, glaring at the regulars in the public bar.

'Your milk stouts will be on the house for the rest of the evening, Mrs Sharples,' Annie said magnanimously.

'Sorry, Ena.'

Ena rose to acknowledge the apologies of the others in the bar.

'Ena, why didn't you tell us?' Martha whined, when she returned to her seat.

'Because I promised Sam that I wouldn't tell anyone about his troubles until he'd had time to sort himself out.'

'Can I sit back at table?' Martha asked.

'You didn't ask my permission to leave.'

'Oh, Ena, can I?' Martha begged.

'It's a free country.' Ena finished the stout in her glass.

'My shout.' Martha went to the bar. 'Three bottles of milk stout, please, Mrs Walker.'

'Seeing as how mine is on the house, you can put one behind the bar for me to drink later, Martha,' said smartly.

Len stopped Elsie when she left her house to catch the morning bus to work. 'Isn't it a fine morning?'

Elsie eyed him suspiciously. 'It's freezing cold. You touched or after something?'

'I was hoping you'd go to the Federation of Master Builders Christmas dinner and dance next Saturday with me.'

'Posh do?'

'The poshest. Ballroom of the Imperial Hotel,' he answered warily, not sure how she'd react.

'Then it's going to be expensive.' She walked on.

'The tickets will be on me.' He ran after her.

'I'll need to wear my glad-rags.'

'Your gladdest.' He laid his hand on her arm to stop her hurrying away. 'You'll come? We'll take a taxi into town about six o'clock and have a few drinks in the bar first. Make a proper night of it.'

'All right, I'll go with you,' she agreed, tempted by the thought of an evening in town. It had been a long time since she'd been invited anywhere smart on a Saturday night.

'Elsie . . .'

'If I don't go now, I'll miss my bus.' Then turned back. 'But if I go with you, it will be as mates.'

'Course,' he called back. But nothing could still the worm of hope gnawing at the back of his mind. Nellie had petitioned for a divorce on the grounds of cruelty. Keen to be rid of a marriage that hadn't worked beyond the first few months, he hadn't bothered to contest it, or deny any of the outrageous allegations Nellie had made about his behaviour because he knew that cruelty was one of the grounds that guaranteed a quick decree nisi. His divorce from Nellie would be finalised next month. And who knew what a night out with Elsie in a posh hotel might lead to? Hopefully by the end of the evening, they'd be a lot more than just mates.

'Glad to see you pulling your weight for once, Jerry.' Pleased with the way his chat with Elsie had gone, Len grinned at his apprentice as he strode into his yard at the back of Mawdsley Street.

'I've almost finished loading up the van with all the bricks we need for that job in Viaduct Street, Mr Fairclough.'

'So, I see. Last night go well?' Len fished. Two weeks before Jerry Booth had met a typist, Myra Dickenson, at a dance in town and since then he hadn't been able to talk about anything else. No matter what the topic of conversation might be, it was Myra this, Myra that and Myra everything else.

'The meal was nice, Mr Fairclough. You were right about that café, it does lovely food. But the company was better. Myra's a great lass.'

'So you've led me to believe, Jerry,' Len said dryly.

'She's a really nice girl. And serious-minded, not like some I've taken out.'

'What do you mean, serious-minded?' Len heaved a brick cutter on to the van.

'Well, last night for instance. We were talking about weddings . . .'

'Weddings! Len exclaimed. 'You've only just met the girl and she's talking about weddings.'

'A relationship has to go somewhere, Mr Fairclough.'

'If every "relationship", as you put it, ended with me trotting up the aisle I'd have a bigger bloody harem than an Arab.'

'Like I said, Mr Fairclough, Myra's not like other girls,' Jerry defended her warmly.

'You be careful with a girl like that, lad,' Len warned him. 'Mark my words, you carry on with serious talk about marriage and she'll be leading you around by the nose like a prize bull. She'll be running your life for you, and before you realise what's happening, you won't have a minute to call your own.'

'You know something, Mr Fairclough?' Jerry replied earnestly. 'I really wouldn't mind.'

'Then you're a lost cause, Jerry me lad.' Len climbed into the van and turned the key. As he drove out of the yard he wondered if he had the right to chaff Jerry about Myra when he felt the way he did about Elsie. He wouldn't mind her leading him around by the nose like a prize bull if she allowed him to get his feet under her table.

He could think of far worse fates than waking up next to a woman like Elsie Tanner every morning for the rest of his life.

'A body could get used to these dinner dances.' Elsie sipped her sixth gin and tonic as she watched the couples waltzing around the dance-floor. Apart from one or two who looked like they'd wandered into the ballroom of the Imperial Hotel from *Come Dancing* most couples were content to hold each other close and just shuffle around.

'A body could,' Len agreed. He loosened the belt on the trousers of his best suit, and burped. The dinner of tomato soup, roast beef, four veg, Yorkshire pudding and gravy followed by Black Forest gateau had been good and substantial. He felt full, and satisfied with himself and the world. 'This is as good as it gets, kid.' He winked at Elsie.

To his amusement she returned his wink.

'I've had a good dinner, a few jars and I'm sitting next to a woman who has turned the head of every man in the room and the evening isn't over yet.'

'It soon will be.' Elsie took a cigarette from the silver case he offered her.

Len fell serious. 'It doesn't have to end, Elsie.' He laid his hand on top of hers on the table. 'We could have a whole lot more.'

'No, we couldn't, Len.'

'Just listen for a minute, Elsie. We've got on well since school days. We're real mates—'

'And that's one hell of a reason not to try to make it any more than it is,' Elsie interrupted.

'Why not? My divorce from Nellie will be through next month.'

'It wouldn't work, Len.'

'You won't even give it a chance?'

'No.' She squashed out her cigarette in the ashtray.

'Here, you've just lit that.'

'I want to dance.' She left her chair and stood in front of him. 'You coming, or do I have to ask someone else?'

Chapter Eleven

The Sunday after the dinner dance Elsie had a lie-in until midday. After a light breakfast of tea and toast she eyed her living room. It needed a good clean but her head was aching, probably from the number of gin-and-oranges she'd drunk the night before, and the last thing she felt like doing was housework.

Reluctantly she left her chair, cleared her breakfast things into the scullery and dumped them in the sink. She was opening the door of the cupboard where she kept her dusters and polish when she was interrupted by a knock at the door.

'Mrs Tanner!' a masculine voice shouted through her letterbox. 'Mrs Elsie Tanner, open the door, it's the bailiffs.'

Elsie crept silently down the passage and checked that the door was locked.

'I can hear you in there. You haven't paid your rent increase for six weeks.'

'I have paid my bloody rent – just not the increase,' Elsie

retorted. 'And the landlord owes me a lot more than thirty bob for all the jobs I've had to do round here that he won't touch.'

'Pay us the thirty bob now, love,' the bailiff coaxed, 'or we'll have to come in and take it from you in goods.'

'I'm not paying anything.' Elsie went into her parlour and dragged out a heavy chair. She pushed it against the front door.

'You can't stay in there for ever, Mrs Tanner.'

'Watch me!' Elsie yelled back.

'We're not going away.'

'Please yourself.' Elsie fetched the second easy-chair and pushed it behind the first.

'We'll get a court order and break down the door.'

'That'll take time, meanwhile you can ask the bloody landlord to start on the list of repairs I sent him months ago.'

'Mrs Tanner, 'please, be reasonable, we're only doing our job,' the bailiff begged.

'Enjoy your wait. It's going to be a long one. This is a matter of principle.' Elsie returned to her living room. She hadn't felt like doing housework earlier but she was damned if she was going to clean the place with bailiffs threatening to batter down the door. She put the kettle on again and flicked through the magazines she'd stuffed under a cushion.

She was immersed in an article about Princess

Margaret's hairdresser and halfway through her third cup of tea when she heard voices in the passage. She opened the door and saw Dennis shifting the easy-chairs so that two men behind him could walk into the house.

'What are you doing here? You should be in bloody London!'

'Didn't you hear them knock, Mam?' he asked innocently. 'They said they'd been waiting for you to open the door for ages.'

'They're bloody bailiffs, you daft bugger.' She clipped him round the ear.

'Ow! That hurt!'

'Good!'

'Hello, Mrs Tanner.' The leading bailiff smiled at her. 'That suite in the front room should fetch thirty bob at auction. We'll take it now.'

'You bloody won't.' Elsie picked up her handbag and took out her purse. She removed a pound note and four half crowns. 'Take your blood money and get out.'

'As I said, we're only doing our job, Mrs Tanner.' The man tipped his cap to her. 'Nothing personal. Oh, by the way,' he stopped in the doorway. 'I take it I can tell your landlord you'll be paying the extra five bob a week from now on. If you don't, we'll have to come back again. Not that I wouldn't like to see you again,' he grinned suggestively, 'just not in these circumstances.'

'Bloody cheeky . . .'

He held up his hands as if to ward off a blow. ''Bye, Mrs Tanner, nice meeting you.'

'You're a fine son.' Elsie turned on Dennis after the front door had slammed. 'Letting those bloodsuckers in.'

'How was I to know that they were bailiffs?' Dennis retorted.

'What you doing back here anyway?' Elsie filched a cigarette from the packet on the mantelpiece, lit it and sat in her easy-chair.

'Lenny Phillips at the agency sent me back up here to scout for the next pop star sensation – as soon as I find him or her we'll make a fortune.'

Elsie held out her hand. 'Right now I'll settle for the thirty bob you cost me to pay the bailiffs. And I'll thank you to pay the same every week from now on.'

'I'm your son,' Dennis protested.

'Exactly.' Elsie raised her hand higher. 'Thirty bob.'

Dennis dug into his pocket.

The bedroom was dark and silent but something had woken Concepta, and she lay tense and expectant, waiting for the sound to repeat itself. Then she heard it: Christopher's cough, racking and chesty just as it had been ever since autumn had turned into full-blown, cold wet winter.

She switched on the bedside light, sat on the edge of the bed and felt for her slippers with her toes. She slid her feet into them and went to the door.

'What's up, love?' Harry enquired sleepily.

'Christopher's coughing again.'

'It sounds bad.'

Concepta opened the door, and walked down the landing to Christopher's bedroom. He was standing, gripping the side of his cot, his face bright red in the subdued glow from the nightlight. 'You poor, poor boy.' She lifted him into her arms. His tiny body was burning, his face and head damp with perspiration. She leant him against her shoulder and rubbed his back as she carried him to her bedroom. There she propped herself up on pillows and nursed him.

'Can't you give him any more medicine?' Harry asked.

'He's had as much as I dare give him for one day. The instructions on the bottle said no more than six doses in twenty-four hours for a child between twelve and eighteen months. I gave him the last one at bedtime.'

'He just can't seem to shake it off, can he?'

'Nor will he while we carry on living here,' she said. 'This house is soaking with damp. There's no fresh air because we're hemmed in all sides by factories. If I could take Christopher back to Ireland, where there's plenty of fresh air and good farm food, he'd soon get over it.'

'Not that again,' Harry begged. 'Not at . . .' he squinted at the clock '. . . three in the morning.'

'You promised me you'd think about it, Harry.'

'And I have.'

'And?'

'I can't just up and leave. There's my job, the house, everything I've worked for all my life and Lucille's schooling. She's just coming up to her GCEs . . .'

'And you put those things before your son's health? You'd rather sit back and watch him suffer?'

'I said I'd think about it,' he said curtly. He turned his back on her and Christopher, and pulled the bedclothes over his head.

'And while you think about it, your son gets worse every single day. At this rate he'll soon be in a decline,' Concepta murmured, refusing to let the matter rest. She leant against the headboard. Christopher's small body blazed feverishly through the layers of his pyjamas and her nightdress. No matter what Harry did or didn't do, she knew she had no choice: she simply had to get away from Coronation Street. For Christopher's sake.

'I found him, Mam.' Dennis Tanner burst through the door of Elsie's living room followed by a tall, thin, gangly boy with more spots on his face than Elsie had seen currants in a currant bun.

'Found who?' She flicked ash into the tray on the centre of the table.

'The next pop sensation! Walter Potts, meet Elsie Tanner, my mother. He's going to be huge, Mam. You wait until you hear him sing.'

Elsie looked up at the boy. 'With a name like Walter Potts?'

'We're going to call him Brett Falcon. Can't you just see it up in lights? The great Brett Falcon, the newest and greatest singing sensation from the North, discovered by eagle-eyed talent scout, Dennis Tanner . . .'

'No, I can't.' Elsie smiled at the boy. 'Want a cup of tea, Walter?'

'I wouldn't say no, Mrs Tanner,' he answered shyly.

'What's that you got in your hand?' she asked suspiciously.

'It's his suitcase, Mam. His landlady didn't like him practising his singing in his room. She said he made too much noise, so I told him that he could move in with us, just until I get him on his feet.'

'Oh, you did, did you?'

'I'll pay you rent, Mrs Tanner,' Walter said eagerly. 'Just as soon as Dennis gets me a couple of jobs and the money starts rolling in.'

'I wouldn't hold my breath if I were you, not where our Dennis is concerned. You can have the spare room but I warn you now, it's only a box room. Turn right at the top of the stairs and it's the door at the end of the landing.'

'Thank you very much, Mrs Tanner.'

'Have your tea first.' Elsie said. 'Dennis was just about to make a fresh pot, weren't you, Dennis?'

★

Valerie Barlow set the vase of daisies she'd bought that morning in the centre of the table. She was waiting impatiently for the sound of Ken's key in the lock, half anticipating, half dreading his arrival. He had been so depressed since his novel had been rejected. And it wasn't just his novel. He had also been passed over for promotion. The authorities had appointed a deputy head from out of the area and Ken had not been consoled when one of his colleagues had told him it was usual to appoint from outside rather than within.

He had hardly spoken to her during the past month, and she had begun to feel more like Ken's housekeeper than his wife.

But today— She heard the door open and straightened the cutlery she had set out. She looked at him apprehensively as he walked through the door. 'How did it go?'

He smiled at her, reached out and swung her off her feet. 'I got it, love. Head of the English department at Granston Tech.'

'That's wonderful. You clever, clever husband.' She locked her arms round his neck and kissed him.

'I know I've been a right misery lately—'

'No, you haven't,' she lied stoutly.

'—But I won't be any longer. Things are going to change around here. We'll have more money for a start. And it's not just the money: it's a better job. I won't be so tired when I come home in the evening and we'll be able to do more together. Have fun once in a while.'

Valerie smiled, 'I hoped we'd have something to celebrate so I bought two steaks.'

'My favourite – and afterwards we'll go down the Rovers and have a couple of drinks.'

Ken looked so pleased with himself that Valerie almost told him the secret she'd been carrying for over a month but decided against overshadowing his good news. There'd be plenty of time to tell him later. She extricated herself from his arms, went into the kitchen and lit the gas under the frying-pan.

Emily Nugent folded a pile of babies' matinée jackets and stowed them neatly in one of the open drawers that slid into the glass-topped display counter. She opened the back and replaced the drawer as Leonard Swindley walked in. He removed his hat and unbuttoned his coat. 'Good morning, Miss Nugent. Early as usual I see.' He made the same comment every morning.

'Good morning, Mr Swindley.' Emily braced herself. She had been rehearsing what she was about to say for months rather than weeks. Truth be known, she had been thinking – dreaming – of nothing else for years. 'Mr Swindley?'

'Yes, Miss Nugent.'

'Do you know it is a leap year?' Her heart was thundering.

'I am aware of the fact.'

'And it's February 29th today.'

'Yes, Miss Nugent.' If he realised the significance of what she was saying, there was no outward sign of it.

'Will you marry me?' she blurted breathlessly.

He gazed at her as if she had taken leave of her senses. 'Can you possibly be serious, Miss Nugent?'

'Yes, Mr Swindley, I believe I am.' She sat abruptly on the stool behind the counter.

'You have honoured me, Miss Nugent, but the answer has to be no.' He went into the stockroom and closed the door behind him.

'And what time is this to roll up in the morning?' Len Fairclough demanded of Jerry Booth when he walked into the yard half an hour late on a fine June morning.

'I'm sorry, Mr Fairclough.' Jerry twisted his cap in his hand.

'I should bloody well think so, lad. Well, don't stand there looking gormless. Where's the bright eyed, bushy-tailed bridegroom of two months ago who couldn't wait to get up and out on the job first thing in the morning?'

'Mr Fairclough—'

'Are you or are you not going to get into that bloody van? Or do I need to put it in plain English? You're late and that means we're late to start on Mrs Halifax's wall!' Len shouted.

'I'm sorry, Mr Fairclough—'

'So you keep saying, but sorry isn't going to build that bloody wall! What's up, lad?' Len softened at the glum expression on Jerry's face. 'You look as if you've found sixpence and lost a pound.'

'The electricity was cut off in our house yesterday and the bailiffs were there when I got home. Myra told me she's behind with the mortgage and up to her neck in debt. She never said a word to me about it. And as if that's not bad enough she's borrowed off all the neighbours.'

'Look, lad, if it's just a couple of quid—'

'It's more than that, Mr Fairclough. And that's not all. Myra's pregnant. She telephoned her dad before I got home and told him everything.'

Len decided Mrs Halifax's wall could wait. 'What you going to do?'

'Her dad said he'd pay off all our debts but only if we live with him. He said there's plenty of building work round his way, so I should find something soon.' Jerry sat down on a pile of bricks.

'I might be able to raise your wages,' Len said hesitantly.

'It wouldn't help, Mr Fairclough. Besides, you're paying me the going rate for the job. No, there's nothing else for it, we're going to have to sell the house. I'm sorry, Mr Fairclough, I feel as if I'm letting you down.'

'Stop bloody apologising, lad.' Len lifted his cap and

scratched his head. 'I suppose you've a lot to be getting on with.'

'Yes,' Jerry mumbled miserably.

'You'll come and pick up the wages you're owed before you leave?'

'I will, Mr Fairclough. And thanks for everything you've taught me.'

'Looks like I should have taught you to stay away from spendthrift women, lad. What's that saying? "Marry in haste, repent at leisure"? Well, I suppose you've found that out the hard way. You know where to come if you want a reference. You're the best apprentice I've ever had.' Len gave Jerry a sideways look. 'But I wouldn't have told you that if you weren't going.'

'Can you imagine it, love? The nerve of the man!' Ken looked in the dressing-table mirror at Val who was brushing mascara on to her eyelashes. 'There I was standing in the middle of my classroom at break time with the butcher William Piggott pushing a hundred pounds into my hand on condition I made sure his son passed his exam.' He flicked through the ties in his wardrobe, chose one and hung it loosely around his neck.

'What did you do?' Valerie rose from the stool, picked up her dress from the bed, slipped it over her head and pulled on the sleeves.

'I took it, asked him to wait, then sent a boy to fetch the

headmaster and all the staff in the staff room to my class-room. When the head came, I handed the hundred pounds back to Mr Piggott, and told the headmaster exactly why he'd given it to me. I couldn't believe that anyone would think that a teacher could be bribed.'

'Zip me up, love, please.' Valerie turned her back to Ken.

Ken did so. 'Do you want me to fasten the hook?'

'Please. And it's a pity.'

'That I didn't take a bribe?'

'We could do with the money.'

'Val . . .'

'I was joking.' Valerie kissed her finger and planted it on his cheek. 'I went to the doctor today.'

'There's something wrong with you?' Ken asked in alarm.

'No . . . I'm pregnant.'

'That's wonderful.' Ken lifted her off her feet and kissed her.

'With twins.'

Ken sat abruptly on the bed. 'Twins? Are you sure?'

'The doctor is. Come on, lazybones,' she held out her hand and pulled him to his feet, 'we're late, and it's not every day that your father throws a party to celebrate winning five thousand pounds on the Premium Bonds.'

'It's an awful thing to say,' Ken murmured, as they walked down Coronation Street to the Rovers Return, 'but I'm not sorry my father used the money to buy that detached house in Bramhall. It's that much further away from us.'

'You won't say that to him, will you, love?' Val asked anxiously. 'It's his last night here and it would be awful if you two had another row before he went.'

'I won't say a word, but that's not to say *he* won't.' Ken opened the pub door. The Rovers was crowded with regulars and a few hangers-on who'd turned up after hearing that Frank was going to put twenty pounds behind the bar for drinks.

'I thought the least you could do was be on time,' was Frank's greeting when Ken and Valerie walked in.

'All I did was stop and change after work,' Ken protested.

'Why? It's not as if you work down a coal mine.'

'We have some good news—'

Frank thumped his glass on the bar and shouted, 'I want to thank all of you for coming here to say goodbye to me. I won't be back, or sorry to leave. Coronation Street's only fit for slum clearance—'

'What did you say?' Len Fairclough broke in angrily.

'I said the street's only fit for slum clearance. It should have been pulled down years ago,' Frank repeated.

'Think you're a nob now you've won some brass?' Len bellowed. 'Well, you're no bloody better than the rest of us!'

'Language,' Annie reprimanded.

'Come on now,' Jack Walker interposed quietly, 'this is supposed to be a party. A celebration.'

'I'm going to celebrate all right,' Len thrust his empty glass at Annie. 'I'm going to celebrate Frank's leaving. And good riddance to bad rubbish, that's what I say.'

'Mrs Walker,' Ena shouted urgently from the bar of the snug, 'can you telephone for an ambulance? Martha's collapsed!'

Annie ran to the telephone. Ken and Valerie, followed by Jack and most of the regulars, rushed to the snug. Martha was lying on the floor. Ken knelt beside her and checked her pulse. He looked up. Ena and Minnie were staring white-faced and wide-eyed at him. He glanced over his shoulder at his wife and shook his head.

Valerie went to Ena and Minnie and took their arms. 'Why don't you come into the public bar, Mrs Sharples, Mrs Caldwell? You look as though you could both do with a brandy.'

'But she was as right as rain a minute ago,' Ena said bewilderment. 'Telling us all about that new family that's moved into Rosamund Street . . .'

'Please, Mrs Sharples,' Valerie said.

'Don't tell me she's gone. Not just like that, without even saying goodbye. There has to be something you can do.' Ena pleaded, looking at Ken.

'I'm sorry, Mrs Sharples. Really sorry,' Ken said slowly.

'But there's nothing anyone can do. Not now.' Reaching out, he gently stroked Martha's eyelids, closing her eyes.

Elsie Tanner sat at the table and watched Dennis play with the food on his plate. He pushed the bangers and mash from one side to the other, burying the sausages beneath mounds of mash only to dig them out again.

'They won't taste any better for all that messing around, you know,' she informed him briskly.

'What?' He gazed across at her through dull, glazed eyes.

'The bangers and mash. I cooked them for you to eat, not mess with.'

'Oh.'

'Why so glum? You got Walter that recording contract, didn't you? And before he went off to Blackpool yesterday, the pair of you were over the moon when you saw that his record had reached number eight in the Hit Parade.'

'That was yesterday. Today Lenny Phillips telephoned the office and told me that he was putting my cards in the post. I've been sacked.' Dennis dropped his knife and fork on to his plate.

'Why would Lenny do that? He asked you to find the next pop sensation and you did just that. "Not Too Little Not Too Much" is on the radio every five minutes. I'm sick of hearing it.'

'Last night another agent signed Walter up in Blackpool.'

'But you discovered him.'

'And I only went and forgot to sign Walter to an exclusive contract, didn't I?' Dennis interrupted.

'You daft ha'porth.'

'That's me,' he muttered mournfully. 'I'm lucky Lenny didn't send his toughs after me. I thought Walter would have had more loyalty after me putting him up here . . .' He looked at Elsie. 'All right, you – but this is my house as well.'

'Found another job yet?' Elsie enquired.

'Give us a chance.'

'Start looking today,' Elsie warned, 'because I'm not keeping you.'

Chapter Twelve

'You met the new people in number thirteen yet?' Len Fairclough asked Harry Hewitt as they enjoyed a pint after work in the Rovers Return a week after Jerry and Myra had moved out just ahead of the bailiffs' arrival.

'No, Concepta and I were sorry to see Jerry and Myra Booth leave the way they did. Although there's some in the street who weren't – I think folk were fed up of Myra trying to borrow money.'

'Did she have some off you?' Len enquired curiously.

'Not me, and if Myra tried Concepta, she's not saying. You seen the new people?'

'I know them – leastways I know Stan Ogden. He used to deliver building materials to Birtwistle's when I worked there.' Len set his pint mug on the table and reached for his cigarettes. 'I met him in town with his wife and daughter once. Irma – that's the daughter.' Len grinned suggestively. 'She's a cracking little piece. Curves in all the right places, long brown hair, big brown eyes. When you see her old man and woman you'll wonder where she got it from.'

'Mrs and Miss Ogden came in here looking for work,' Annie interrupted from the bar where she was polishing glasses. 'Mrs Ogden's taken poor Mrs Longhurst's job as our cleaner and Irma is the new barmaid. And I'll thank you two gentlemen to keep your comments about her to yourselves and treat her respectfully.'

'We wouldn't dream of doing anything else, Annie, love. And thank you, it'll be nice to have a pretty face to look at in here for a change,' Len teased.

'You've the cheek of the devil, Len Fairclough.'

'I'll take that as a compliment, Annie.' He picked up his and Harry's glasses. 'Two more, please, love.'

Harry got up. 'Not for me. Concepta's none too happy these days and I'll not give her any more cause to go on at me than she already does.'

'See you tomorrow night?' Len handed Annie his glass.

'Hope so,' Harry replied, and went out.

'Concepta said anything to you about what's going on between her and Harry?' Len raised his eyebrows at Harry's retreating back.

'Do you really expect me to answer that, Len?' Annie asked.

'No, Annie,' Len murmured. 'I don't.'

★

Leonard Swindley double-checked the figures he'd written in the ledger against the takings, then bagged up the shop's takings ready for banking.

'Time to close the door, Miss Nugent.'

'Yes, Mr Swindley.' Emily turned the sign from 'OPEN' to 'CLOSED' and turned around warily. The atmosphere had been strained between her and Mr Swindley for months. And although neither of them had ever alluded to the proposal since she had made it in February, it had certainly affected their working relationship. 'May I leave now, Mr Swindley?' she asked hesitantly, heading for the stockroom where she kept her coat and handbag.

'I would appreciate a word with you first, Miss Nugent.'

'Yes, Mr Swindley.' She folded her hands and waited apprehensively.

'I have been thinking over your proposal that we marry, Miss Nugent.'

'I am sorry, Mr Swindley. I don't know what came over me, embarrassing both of us like that . . .'

'Then you didn't mean it.'

'Yes, yes, I did at the time . . .' she stammered.

'In that case I would be happy if you would do me the honour of becoming my wife.'

Emily couldn't believe what she was hearing.

He produced a jeweller's box and opened it. 'I hope you like the engagement ring I picked out, Miss Nugent.'

★

'Frank Barlow was right – the houses in this street are only fit for slum clearance.' Concepta Hewitt set Harry and Lucille's tea on the table, but didn't return to the scullery to fetch her own. Instead she stood behind her chair and faced Harry. 'I found another patch of damp mould this morning in Christopher's bedroom. It's no wonder he spends half the night coughing when there's water running down the inside of his bedroom walls.'

'I know this house isn't perfect, love—' Harry began.

'It's far from perfect and this,' she pulled a letter from her apron pocket, 'is a wonderful opportunity for all of us. My father needs someone to run his garage for him now he's too poorly to do it himself. You'd be earning more money than you do here, and we could rent a nice little bungalow in the village. We could be off before the end of the month, if you put your mind to it.'

'It's like I said, Concepta, I can't just up and go.'

'Why not?' she demanded.

'There's Lucille's schooling for a start.' Harry looked at his daughter.

'I spoke to Annie Walker this afternoon. She'd be happy for Lucille to move into the Rovers until she sits her exams and as soon as they're over, she can join us in Ireland.'

Lucille put down her knife and fork. 'Haven't I any say in this?'

'We've been talking about moving to Ireland for some time, Lucille,' Concepta reminded her. 'The damp in this house is aggravating Christopher's chest, and now there's an opportunity to build a better life too – for all of us.'

'Would you mind moving in with Annie, love?' Harry asked.

'Of course she wouldn't,' Concepta said. 'Annie would take good care of her—'

'I was asking Lucille, Concepta,' Harry interrupted.

'It would only be for a short while,' Concepta promised Lucille. 'In a few months you'll be able to leave school and join us in Ireland. And in the meantime we'll get everything ready for you. Decorate a bedroom just the way you'd like it, in your favourite colours. You'll love Ireland, Lucille – it's so green – and the village is beautiful and there are lots of teenagers the same age as you. You'll have a good time—'

'Lucille,' Harry broke in, giving Concepta a warning look.

'No one ever consults me about anything.' Pushing back her chair, Lucille left the table and flounced upstairs.

'That's settled, then.' Concepta tied a bib round Christopher's neck. 'I'll write to my father tonight and tell him we'll be with him just as soon as we arrange everything here. You'll hand your notice in tomorrow, Harry.' She made it clear that she wasn't asking him a question.

'It looks like you've left *me* no option either.'

Concepta returned to the scullery to fetch her own and Christopher's tea. She'd hated bullying Harry and Lucille but she was confident they'd thank her for it when they were settled in Ireland. Given time, they'd come to love it as much as she did. She was certain of it.

A couple of weeks before Christmas, David Barlow dropped his suitcase on the pavement and looked down the length of Coronation Street. He had left this place with such high hopes, and here he was back again after a couple of years – in disgrace – or something that felt very like it. Life was so unfair. He took a deep breath, picked up his case and walked past number three. He imagined knocking the door, shouting, 'Mam,' and seeing Ida run out of the living room in her flowered overall. Flustered by his sudden and unexpected return, she'd pat her short, curly hair into place . . .

He forced himself to remember that his mother was gone, dead and buried, and that he'd never see her again. He walked on to number nine and knocked at the door.

'Good Lord, David.' Valerie stepped back when she saw him on the doorstep. 'You should have written to say you were coming – not that you aren't very welcome,' she amended hastily. 'Come in.'

'It's not just you who's had a shock.' David nodded discreetly at her bloated figure. 'I'd no idea I was going to become an uncle so soon.'

'I'm not due for another two months, but I look further on than I am because it's twins.' She kissed David's cheek. 'This is a surprise. Are you hungry?'

'I had a sandwich at the bus station.'

'But you'll have a cup of tea?'

'Please, Val.' He dropped his case inside the door and followed her into the living room. 'You and Ken have it nice here.'

'Thank you.'

'And how is he?' He sat at the table.

'Fine, he'll be home from school in an hour.'

'Funny to think of our Ken teaching.'

'So,' Valerie set cups on the table, 'is this a holiday or are you back for good?'

'It isn't a holiday, not one that I wanted to take, any road, and I hope I'm not back for good.'

'That sounds mysterious.' She bustled into the scullery and put the kettle on.

'I've been suspended from professional football. Someone accused me of taking a bribe.'

'That's ridiculous! Anyone who knows you would realise you're incapable of doing anything like that,' she burst out indignantly.

'Thanks, Val. I could have done with someone who had your faith in me down South,' he said. 'The enquiries will take a few weeks, and until it's sorted one way or the other I thought I'd lie low here.'

'You're very welcome.' She picked up the teapot and poured hot water into it to warm it.

'I don't want to impose.'

'Nonsense, that's exactly what family's for, and you'll be company for Ken and me. There's the kettle whistling – you can tell me all about what's been happening to you while we drink our tea.'

The Saturday following David Barlow's return to Coronation Street, Emily Nugent sat in her wedding dress and veil in one of the upstairs rooms of the Rovers Return. Downstairs Annie Walker, with Hilda and Irma Ogden's help, had prepared and laid out a lavish reception buffet. The guests were already at the church. All she had to do was walk downstairs, get into the car, drive to the church, walk down the aisle, and she would become Mrs Leonard Swindley. Something she had dreamed of happening ever since she and Leonard had merged their shops before they had been taken over by the Gamma Garment chain.

But, as she looked at herself in the mirror, she knew she couldn't do it. It was so embarrassing, and not only for her, for poor Mr Swindley. She left her chair, opened the door and stepped out on to the landing.

'You look lovely,' Annie Walker gushed. 'A real bride . . .'

'Is Mr Walker here, Mrs Walker?' Emily asked urgently.

'Yes, love, why?'

'Do you think he'd mind very much if I asked him to go to the church and fetch Mr Swindley?'

'But Mr Swindley is at the church. Everyone is waiting. You'll see him in few minutes . . .'

'Not unless Mr Walker brings him here. I can't go through with it, Mrs Walker. I can't,' she repeated forcefully. 'I've just realised that I don't love Mr Swindley and it's wrong to marry someone if you don't love them, isn't it?' She sought reassurance.

'Yes, love, it is,' Annie agreed sadly. 'I'll send Jack to the church right away.'

The Monday morning after Emily and Leonard's wedding that wasn't, Ena Sharples strode into Gamma Garments to find it empty apart from Emily who was pinning a sweater on to a headless half-mannequin on the counter.

'Good morning, Mrs Sharples, can I help you?' Emily enquired, setting aside her box of pins and the mannequin.

'Aye, I'll have a pair of them support stockings. Size nine and a half.'

'Certainly, Mrs Sharples.' Emily pulled out the drawer and flicked through the contents, looking for the right size.

'You heard about Dennis Tanner?'

'No, Mrs Sharples.' Emily had been brought up to believe that if you had nothing nice to say about a person it was better to say nothing at all, and hated gossip. But

Mrs Sharples had the knack of making everyone listen to her tittle-tattle of the doings of her neighbours, whether they wanted to hear it or not.

'He's gone up to Newcastle again. He's in and out of Elsie Tanner's house like a yo-yo. And have you heard about them Ogdens who've moved into number thirteen? That Stan Ogden got Jack Walker into trouble with police. Stopping the clock in the Rovers so he could drink after stop-tap. But neither the police nor Jack saw the funny side. And Jack was nearly prosecuted for serving drinks after hours until Stan came clean. And the police weren't too happy about it then. So,' Ena crossed her arms across her ample bosom and looked significantly at the stock-room door, 'things awkward between you and Mr Swindley, then?'

'Not at all, Mrs Sharples,' Emily countered.

'You expect me to believe that?'

'We've always worked well together, Mrs Sharples,' Emily said quietly, wrapping the stockings in brown paper.

'He must be more forgiving than most men, that's all I can say. There's some I know who wouldn't take too kindly to being left looking like a proper Charlie at the altar.'

'That will be two shillings and elevenpence, please, Mrs Sharples.' Emily handed her the parcel.

'They've gone up sixpence!' Ena exclaimed indignantly.

'I am afraid they have, Mrs Sharples.'

'Scandalous.' Ena unzipped her shopping bag and removed her purse from the side pocket. She gave Emily half a crown and hesitated. Emily stood patiently, while Ena counted out fivepence more in halfpennies. 'Don't hold your breath waiting for me to come back here. It will be a while before I'll be able to afford to step through your door again.'

'Goodbye, Mrs Sharples.' Emily left the counter and opened the door for her.

'And goodbye to you, Miss Nugent.' Ena sniffed before she walked off down the street.

Leonard Swindley emerged from the stockroom after ten minutes' silence had convinced him Ena Sharples had gone.

'Mr Swindley, may I ask you a favour?' Emily ventured.

After Saturday's cancelled wedding, Leonard was wary of what Emily was about to say, but remembering that she hadn't been the only one to get cold feet about their marriage, and grateful to her for showing more courage than he had on the occasion, he answered her politely. 'Of course, Miss Nugent.'

'I've bought Annie . . .' She giggled. 'It's a car, a Morris Minor, actually. I've called it Annie.'

'I didn't know that you could drive, Miss Nugent.'

'I can't, Mr Swindley. I'm looking for someone to give me lessons. I know you can drive, so, I hoped . . . well, I hoped that you would be kind enough to take me out in it some time so I can practise for my test.'

'Do you have your provisional licence, Miss Nugent?'

'Yes, and I've tied L-plates to the car.'

'Then I would be delighted, Miss Nugent. Shall we venture out this evening, after work?'

'Oh, thank you very much, Mr Swindley. Would you like your afternoon cup of tea now?'

'I believe I would, Miss Nugent.'

Emily reflected that she'd meant what she'd said to Ena Sharples. It was early days but she and Mr Swindley seemed to be getting on better than they had done in months. And the atmosphere in the shop was certainly lighter. It was almost as if, in asserting herself, she'd made him see her in a new light. As a real person, and not simply part of the fixtures and fittings in the Rosamund Street branch of Gamma Garments.

'It doesn't seem the same without Harry calling in here every evening,' Annie Walker grumbled to Len Fairclough as she pulled him a pint.

'You missing him, then, Annie?' Len handed her the right money. He and Harry had been close friends since their schooldays but he would have thumped anyone who suggested he was lost without him.

'I don't mind saying I do, Len, but not as much as young Lucille does. She idolises her father.'

'How is she settling down?'

'She's no trouble,' Annie commented. 'She's a good girl and willing to help round the house. Does her homework every night without any prompting— Hello, Elsie, love.' Annie broke off to greet Elsie as she came in. 'Gin and orange?'

'Please, Annie.' Elsie leant on the bar, kicked off her left shoe and rubbed her foot. 'It's been a long day and I don't mind telling you I'm knackered after standing around for hours in Miami Modes. The shop might be high class and have thick carpets but after a couple of hours they feel just as hard as a concrete floor.'

'Let me get this.' Len paid for Elsie's drink.

'Only if I can get the next.' Elsie took her drink and hobbled over to a table as Annie relinquished the bar to Irma Ogden's care.

'I was wondering if you'd do me a favour.' Len sat next to her.

'That depends on what kind of a favour you're after,' Elsie replied warily.

'Without Jerry Booth to help me, I've ended up working all hours. The house is beginning to look a real mess. And I've no time to see to me washing or cooking . . .'

'Oh, no, I'm not falling for that a second time.' Elsie pushed a cigarette into her mouth and lit it, then passed the packet on to Len.

'I'd pay you.'

She shook her head. 'No, thanks. I'm not short now that Dennis has gone up to Newcastle.'

'I thought you'd be missing his lodging money.'

'He always borrowed more off me than he paid. The answer's no, Len. It's as much as I can do to look after my own place without taking on yours. If you need help, I suggest you advertise for a housekeeper.'

Annie Walker was collecting empty glasses from the table next to them. 'There's plenty of women would jump at the chance, Len,' she said. 'Job like that would suit a middle-aged or elderly widow down to the ground. Give them someone to fuss over.'

Len looked across to where Irma Ogden, a tight sweater stretched across her shapely breasts, was serving at the bar. He nodded agreement, but his mind was picturing a very different housekeeper from the respectable widow Annie Walker had in mind.

Emily Nugent steered slowly and carefully down the street. 'This road is ever so narrow, Mr Swindley.' She was conscious that she sounded almost critical and he was the one doing her the favour. But she was terrified of hitting something or someone. 'There's hardly any room for me to pass these cars, and – oh!' She slammed on the brakes, jerking them both forward as a policeman held up his hand and stepped in front of them. He glared at them then walked round to the passenger's side of the car.

Leonard would down the window. 'Can I help you, Officer?'

'You can begin by telling me why you instructed this lady to drive the wrong way up a one-way street, sir?'

'I didn't – I . . .' Acutely ashamed of himself for breaking the law, albeit inadvertently, Leonard was stuttering.

'You are a qualified driver, sir?'

Leonard found his voice. 'I am.'

'Then you are in charge of this car.'

'I am, Officer, but I assure you I didn't see any sign . . . Oh dear, I am so sorry.'

'Would you step out of the car and show me your driving licence, please, sir?' The policeman opened the door. Flushed, Leonard climbed out, reached for his wallet and removed his driving licence.

The officer studied it intently.

'I am a lay preacher . . .'

'And a fine example you're setting your flock, Mr Swindley.' The officer held up the driving licence. 'This expired six months ago.'

'Oh, no! I had absolutely no idea—'

'That makes two offences.'

Emily shrank back in the driving seat of the car. In all the years she had known Mr Swindley she had never seen him look so embarrassed or crushed.

★

David Barlow leant on the bar of the Rovers, propped his head on his hand and gazed intently at Irma Ogden.

Flattered by his admiration, Irma walked down the bar to serve him. 'Can I help you?'

'Any time.'

'Pardon?'

'I'll have a pint, and whatever you're drinking.'

'Thank you.' She lifted down a beer mug. His pulse raced even faster when he saw the swelling curve of her breast. 'I'll have a grapefruit juice.'

'You can have something stronger than that.' He reached into his pocket.

'No, I can't. I'm not allowed to drink alcohol when I'm working.'

'Ta.' David pushed the money at her as she served his pint. 'So, when did you move in around here?'

'How do you know I haven't always lived here?' she asked.

'Because I'd have remembered someone like you. In fact, I'd never have moved away if I'd seen you before I went.'

'Then you *are* from round here.'

'I used to be.' He held out his hand. 'I'm David Barlow.'

'Pleased to meet you.' Irma smiled. 'You must be Ken

Barlow's brother, the one who went down south to be a professional footballer.'

'That's the one.' He offered her a cigarette. 'So when's your night off?'

'You don't waste any time, do you?'

'Not when it comes to beautiful girls, no.'

'Friday night.'

'You're not free before then?' he asked, disappointed.

'Not in the evening, no.'

'But you are in the day?' When she nodded he continued, 'I'm at a bit of a loose end at the moment. What do you say we catch a bus into town tomorrow morning, look round the shops and have coffee?'

'That sounds like fun.'

'Then it's a date – tomorrow, ten o'clock at the bus stop.'

'That's a first, a morning date.'

'Let's hope it's the first of many.' To his surprise, he meant it.

Chapter Thirteen

Ena Sharples grabbed Len Fairclough's arm as he passed her in Coronation Street on his way home from the Rovers after work. 'I see you've an applicant for that job you've been advertising in paper.'

'You know more than me, Ena.' Len brushed off her arm and stepped back out of her reach.

'It's sitting on your doorstep waiting for you,' she announced, seeming inordinately pleased to be breaking the news.

'How did you know about the job?'

'I can read same as everyone else. You said housekeeper, but you didn't put down wages.'

'They're to be negotiated.' Len didn't bother to conceal his irritation with her for poking her nose into his affairs.

'If the money's right, I might apply for it meself.'

'Us? In the same house? It wouldn't work.'

'I'll have you know I can cook and keep house with the

best of them. Well, aren't you going to go and see who's waiting for you?'

'Aye, I suppose I'd better.' An image of a nubile young woman rose in Len's mind.

'When you see who it is, that smile will be wiped off your face.' Ena chuckled, and headed for the corner shop.

When Len rounded the corner into Mawdsley Street, Jerry Booth was sitting on a suitcase outside his front door.

'What you doing here?'

'I've come to apply for the job of housekeeper.' Jerry turned a miserable face to Len.

Len burst out laughing. 'You – a housekeeper?'

'I need a job, Mr Fairclough, and I need somewhere to live.'

'It didn't work out with you and Myra's dad, then?' Len asked sympathetically.

Jerry shook his head. 'It was hopeless from the day we moved in, Mr Fairclough. He not only wanted to run her life, he wanted to run mine as well. And then me and Myra started arguing and he always took her side. It felt as if the two of them were ganging up on me. And to cut a long story short I've left her. But I'd rather not talk about it, if you don't mind.'

'Bring your bags inside. You can start right away by finding us something for tea.' Len hung his coat on the peg in the hall. 'Is it just housekeeping you want to do, lad, or do you want your old job back?'

'I wouldn't say no to my old job, Mr Fairclough.' Jerry almost smiled.

'And I wouldn't say no to you getting it, but that's not to say I'll let you off cooking tea – whatever you make has to be better than what I'd serve up. You know where the kitchen is.'

'You off out?' Ken looked up when David breezed into the living room in a clean shirt. His brother smelt strongly of Old Spice aftershave.

'Only to Rovers.'

'For a drink or to see Irma Ogden?' Ken queried suspiciously.

'Seeing as how she's the barmaid, both.'

'It's not getting serious between you two, is it?' Ken asked, in a tone that suggested he hoped it wasn't.

'What's it to do with you?'

'Come on!' Ken snapped. 'You've only got to look at her family. Her father's more out of work than in it and her mother's a cleaner. They're common as muck.'

'And we're dukes?' David retorted.

'Of course not, kid.'

'And don't "kid" me. I grew up a long time ago,' David shouted.

'Whichever way you look at it, they're hardly our sort.'

'And who *is* our sort?'

'What's all the yelling in here?' Valerie asked, although

she had overheard the conversation from the scullery. She dried her hands on her apron.

'Nothing,' Ken answered.

'Noisy nothing.' She lowered her swollen body into an easy chair.

'You don't look well.' David passed her a cushion.

'It will all be over in a couple of weeks.' She sighed. 'And I, for one, will be glad when it is.'

'Anything I can do for you before I go?' David slipped on his jacket.

'No thanks. Have a good time.' Valerie liked Irma Ogden.

'Thanks, Val, I will.' David left, closing the door on the silence that had fallen over the living room.

'So, what do you think?' David whispered to Irma, when she'd finished serving Len and Jerry.

'I don't mind, but are you sure about it?' She paused awkwardly when Ken strode in holding a yellow envelope.

'A telegram came for you, David,' he said shortly, trying not to look at Irma as he handed it over.

David opened it and scanned the message. 'Irma, are Mr and Mrs Walker around?'

'What is it, David?' Jack Walker came out of the back

'Can I make a phone call from here please, Mr Walker? I'll pay for it.'

'You know where the phone is, David.'

'I wonder if it's good or bad news,' Irma speculated, as David went into the passage behind the bar.

'No doubt we'll find out soon enough. I'll have a pint.' Ken sorted through the coins in his pocket. He was finding it increasingly difficult to be civil to Irma Ogden now that she might become his sister-in-law.

Ken was on his second pint when David reappeared. 'Problems?' he asked.

'The telegram was from the manager of the club I was at down south. I've been cleared.'

'You didn't take the bribe?' Ken sounded amazed.

'You thought I was guilty!' David said furiously. 'You're my brother and you thought that I'd take money to throw a game?'

'No . . .' Ken tailed off. He couldn't think of anything else to say.

'Fine bloody brother you turned out to be.' David drew back his fist and slammed it into Ken's jaw. His brother hurtled backwards, cracked his skull on Len and Jerry's table and crashed to the floor.

Jack Walker reached him first. 'Call an ambulance, love,' he shouted to Annie. 'Ken Barlow's out cold.'

'I shouldn't have hit him.' David sank his head into his hands. 'Especially not with Val the way she is. If anything happens to either of them it will be my fault.'

'I saw Valerie today, and from the look of her, she was ready to go into labour at any moment,' Irma said soothingly. 'And as for Ken, you'd every right to hit him after what he thought of you.'

'He didn't deserve to be knocked out cold just as his wife went into labour.'

Irma gripped David's hand. 'Stop beating yourself up over it, love. They're both going to be all right.'

'Mr Barlow?' A young doctor walked down the corridor towards them.

'Yes.' David jumped eagerly to his feet.

'Your brother's come round. We've X-rayed his head and there's no serious damage, just a mild concussion. A week's rest and he'll be as good as new.'

'Thank you very much. Do you know how his wife is?'

'She's been taken up to the labour ward, Mr Barlow. Your brother has been asking to go there. Perhaps you could do the honours.'

'Yes, of course. Thank you,' David called after him, as he walked away.

'I told you it was going to be all right.' Irma hugged him.

'You did, didn't you?' Not caring who saw him, he kissed her. Then he went in search of Ken.

'Oh, Mr Swindley, such marvellous news,' Emily Nugent greeted him excitedly when he walked into the shop the following morning. 'Valerie Barlow had twins last night – a boy and a girl. They've named them Peter and Susan Ida, after Ken's poor mother. Ken called in this morning. They want me to be godmother and Ken's brother, David, is going to be the godfather . . . Is there anything wrong, Mr Swindley?' she asked, registering the serious expression on his face.

'Not entirely, Miss Nugent. That is very good news for the Barlows.'

'Yes, it is, Mr Swindley.'

'I have news of my own, some which I think you'll find very good, and some that is rather sad – but, I believe, only for myself. The good news, Miss Nugent, is that you have been promoted to manageress of the Rosamund Street branch of Gamma Garments.'

'Manageress, Mr Swindley? But what about you?'

'I've been promoted too, but I'm moving to head office.'

'In London?'

'Yes, Miss Nugent. And, unfortunately, right away. I hope you don't mind taking over as of now.'

Too choked to speak, Emily nodded.

'Good luck, Miss Nugent, not that you'll need it.' He shook her hand. 'You are the most efficient person I have ever had the privilege of working with. I will miss you and our daily chats.' His eyes misted and he fumbled for the door handle, then walked away quickly.

★

'You don't have to move out, David,' Valerie pleaded, when he came downstairs with his suitcase.

'Yes, I do,' he said. 'You need all the space you can get now with these two. I had no idea such tiny people needed so many things that take up so much room.'

'It's getting to look as though you can't swing a cat in here.' Valerie looked past the twins she was cradling in her arms, to the carrycots, plastic bath and nappy-filled clothes-horse that littered the room.

'And who'd want to swing a cat? Not you, lad, you're way too small, yet.' David stroked Peter's head.

'When will you be going back down south?'

'I won't. I had a talk with Sid Lambert yesterday. He offered me a job as manager-player for the local team and I took it. I've also been asked to write the football column for the local paper. And that brings me to my final bit of news. I'll only be Albert Tatlock's lodger for a couple of days. I'm renting one of those new flats in Sandy Lane.'

'They look lovely.'

'Wait until you see the inside and the furniture we've bought.'

'We've – then you and Irma . . .'

David tapped his nose. 'Not a word to our Ken.'

'I promise.'

'Or her family,' he warned. 'Irma's afraid that Hilda

and Stan will turn our wedding into a three-ring circus if we let them. She's leaving them a note so they won't worry about her and we'll ring the Rovers after the event so they'll have time to get used to the idea of having a son-in-law before we get back from honeymoon.'

'Then you're eloping.' Valerie smiled when he said nothing. 'She's a lovely girl, David. You're a lucky man.'

David picked up his suitcase. 'You know where to come if you need a babysitter, leastways for the next couple of days. After that I might be a bit busy for a week or so. Stay there, Val, I'll see myself out.'

Less than a week later, David Barlow found himself carrying his bride over the threshold of the flat in Sandy Lane. He had intended to take Irma up to London for a full week's honeymoon but, eager to start arranging the flat the way she wanted it, she had persuaded him to return to their new home after three days.

'Isn't it beautiful, David?' She smiled as she looked around the living room.

'Isn't it just?' He gazed into her eyes as he set her down.

'I'm sorry about my parents. So much for eloping to the local Register Office and marrying in peace and quiet. Trust my mother to turn the ceremony we planned into a right Macdoodle's picnic.'

'Couldn't be helped. Trust me to hire a taxi-driver with a loose mouth.'

Their private ceremony had been gatecrashed by Hilda and Stan Ogden, who'd insisted on throwing an impromptu reception in the Rovers. David had been glad to get away from everyone before stop-tap.

Irma wrapped her arms around David's neck. 'You sure you don't mind not moving back down south?'

'I'm sure. I have a great job, a newspaper column with my picture at the top and,' he kissed her, 'a beautiful wife. Want to see how the rest of the furniture we picked out looks in this place?'

'Can we start with the bedroom?'

'I think that's a very good idea, Mrs Barlow. Have I told you that I love you?'

'Not in the last five minutes.'

'We're going to be very happy, you know, in spite of what our families think or say to the contrary.'

'I know.' She looked around. 'I've forgotten. Which door do I open?

Prompted by Valerie, who was eager to build bridges between the Barlow brothers, and conscious that he hadn't made it easy for David to marry Irma, Ken arranged to call around the flat and take David out for a drink the night Irma went back to work in the Rovers after her honeymoon.

When David answered the door, Ken stepped inside and admired the clean, white walls and simple lines of the modern teak furniture.

'Very nice, our kid, you've done well for yourself,' he complimented. 'You ready for that drink?'

'A reporter rang the club this afternoon and asked if she could interview me for the paper. I said she could call round. You don't mind waiting, do you? We'll only be about ten minutes. Or, if you prefer, you can go on ahead to the Rovers.'

'I don't mind waiting.'

The bell rang as Ken spoke. 'That'll be her now.' David opened the door and returned with a glamorous brunette who sent Ken's pulse racing.

'I'm sorry, Mr Barlow,' she apologised. 'Am I interrupting something?'

'Not at all. This is my brother, Ken. Ken, this is Jackie Marsh, the reporter I was telling you about.'

'Pleased to meet you.' Ken rose from the sofa and shook her hand, holding on to it fractionally longer than necessary. 'I'll push off, if you two are going to be talking about anything personal.'

Jackie gave him a dazzling smile. 'It is the professional rather than the personal aspect of your brother's career that our readers are interested in, Mr Barlow.'

'Ken,' he corrected her. 'In that case, I'll just sit quietly and read the paper.'

'Please do. It's the one I work on. You'll find my column on page two.'

'I'll start with that, then.' Ken pretended to read the

paper, but he spent most of the time while Jackie was interviewing David watching her. He had never met a woman so pretty, poised and confident, and he wanted to see a whole lot more of her.

When Jackie had finished, she closed her notepad and returned it to her handbag. 'Thank you for your time, David. Ken, your brother is all yours.'

'Why don't you let me buy you a drink as a thank-you?' David suggested, oblivious of the admiring glances Ken had been sending Jackie's way. 'After all, every bit of advertising helps a professional footballer. Makes the public think we know what we're doing on a pitch even when we don't.'

'I'm sure *you* know, David,' she said mildly flirtatious.

'As it happens, David and I were just going for a drink.' Ken smiled. 'Why don't you join us?'

'Why not indeed?' Jackie gazed into Ken's eyes as he helped her on with her coat.

Emily Nugent was checking an order of baby layettes against an invoice when Valerie Barlow opened the door of the shop. She left the pram in the porch.

'Do you mind if I don't close the door, Emily? After what happened to Christopher Hewitt, I hate taking my eyes off the twins for a moment.'

'No, of course not.' Emily looked unusually flushed. 'I am so glad you're here, Valerie. I've been dying to tell someone my good news all morning and you're the first person to come into the shop. I have a friend who has a souvenir shop in Majorca.'

'Lucky friend.' Valerie sighed enviously.

'Lucky me.' Emily beamed. 'He's asked me to run it for him.'

'You are going to I hope?' Valerie was pleased: if anyone deserved good fortune it was Emily after all the thoughtful things she had done for family, friends and neighbours over the years.

'Yes. And I'm really looking forward to going. I've hardly been anywhere, apart from spending a weekend once in London and a summer holiday in Blackpool. I've never been abroad,' she confided, 'but I have heard that Majorca is beautiful. The weather's warm and sunny and there are lovely beaches and gardens.'

'You'll spare the occasional thought for us in the frozen North, I hope,' Valerie said, a little wistfully but without envy.

'I'm going to miss all of you.' Emily grabbed Valerie's hand. It was the most impetuous thing she had done since she'd asked Leonard Swindley to marry her. 'I telephoned my notice in to head office this morning.'

'When are you going?'

'A week Friday.'

Valerie hesitated. 'That doesn't give us much time to organise a leaving party.'

'I don't need a party,' Emily demurred.

'Yes, you do,' Valerie contradicted her. 'And as soon as I've bought the vests I came in to get for the twins, I'll go round to the Rovers to talk to Mrs Walker so we can start planning it.'

'That's very kind of you.' Emily was overwhelmed by the attention.

'Not at all. You deserve the very best send-off that everyone in Coronation Street can give you.'

David Barlow lay on a trolley in the hospital's casualty department. The pain in his knee was excruciating, but it paled into insignificance set against the anguish he felt from listening to the doctor's verdict on his injury. 'You can't be absolutely sure,' he argued.

'I'm afraid I am, Mr Barlow. I've spent some time studying your X-rays. You'll probably need at least one operation, possibly two, but there's no mistaking the severity of the damage to the joint. You will be lucky to walk with the aid of a stick. Running – and, I'm afraid, playing football – is absolutely out of the question.'

'David!' Irma rushed into the cubicle. 'Someone rang the Rovers to say that you were here. Are you all right?'

'No.' He gazed up at the doctor. 'Anything but.'

Shocked, Irma sank down on to the only chair in the cubicle. She tried to hold David's hand but he pulled it away.

'Your husband has just had some bad news, Mrs Barlow,' the doctor said.

'I'll never play football again.'

'Oh, no.' Irma covered her mouth with her hand.

David looked into her eyes. 'Do you realise what that means? I'm going to lose my job and probably the news-paper column. I have no idea how we're going to live.'

Annie Walker and Valerie Barlow were sitting in Annie and Jack's private living room behind the bar of the Rovers. Valerie had left the twins in their pram in the hall in the hope that they would remain quiet for five minutes so she could enjoy the coffee Annie had made for her. But Peter was making small waking sounds and she knew it was unlikely that the twins would sleep much longer.

'Of course we must organise a *bon voyage* party for Emily. Do you know when she's leaving?' Annie asked.

'The end of next week, Mrs Walker.'

'So soon,' Annie mused. 'We'll make it a joint party. Lucille heard yesterday that she passed her GCEs in science, English, French and geography,' she revealed proudly.

'Then she'll be leaving for Ireland, to join the Hewitts.'

'No! What do you think?' Annie's smile broadened. 'She's decided to remain here with Mr Walker and me and she's got herself a job at Marshall's Mill, working in the laboratories.'

'She's not going to Ireland?'

'No one was more surprised than Jack and me, but as Harry said to Jack after Lucille had spoken to him on the telephone last night, all her friends are round here. It's disappointing for Concepta and Harry, of course, but I don't mind telling you that we're delighted. Jack and I have really enjoyed having someone young around the place.'

'There goes Peter.' Valerie set aside her cup as her son began to wail. 'Two seconds and he'll wake Susan. I'm sorry, Mrs Walker, that was lovely coffee, but I have to go and feed them. If there's anything I can do to help with the party, you will let me know?' She went to the door.

'Don't you worry about the party, love. Irma and her mother will help me get everything in hand.' Annie nodded to the pram where, as Valerie had predicted, Peter had woken Susan. 'I think you have your hands full seeing to those two.'

'Yes, I do,' Valerie murmured, with a distinct lack of enthusiasm.

'Is anything the matter, love?' Annie enquired solicitously. 'You look worn out.'

'I feel worn out, Mrs Walker,' Valerie confessed. 'I never thought looking after two babies could be such hard work. As soon as they go to sleep and I think I can get my head down for a few minutes, one wakes and then it's only a matter of a few minutes before the other starts crying. I can't remember the last night I was able to sleep for more than an hour at a time.'

'Surely you can find a babysitter to give you a bit of a break, love?'

'To be honest, Mrs Walker, I think I need to get out more than I need to sleep. They're running evening classes in sociology at the local tech. I've persuaded Ken to babysit once a week so I can exercise my brain and talk to adults about something other than babies.'

'That's a very good idea, love, and I admire you for it, but I still don't think you should go without sleep. Perhaps Ken can take over from you when the twins wake at night on the weekend. Then he can have a sleep in when you get up with them in the morning.'

'Ken could sleep through an earthquake, Mrs Walker.'

'He wouldn't if you kicked him out of bed,' Annie retorted. 'And don't forget to get a babysitter so you can both come to the party.'

'I won't, Mrs Walker, and thank you for organising everything for Emily.'

Annie Walker stood on the doorstep and watched Valerie push the pram down the street. Rumours were circulating in the street about Ken Barlow. He had been seen in other pubs in the area in the company of an attractive young woman.

She hoped for Valerie and the twins' sake that it was no

more than idle gossip, that the lady in question was Ken's colleague, and they were discussing school and teaching matters.

Chapter Fourteen

'You sure you don't mind?' Valerie glanced at herself in the mirror over the fireplace to reassure herself that she looked passable. It had been such a long time since she had gone out alone in the evening that she was nervous, although loath to admit it to Ken.

'That's the tenth time you've asked me in the last five minutes, Val. No, I don't mind – and before you ask me, the twins will be fine with me.'

'You know where their bottles are, and the clean nappies?'

'I know.' He left his chair, took hold of her by the shoulders and marched her to the front door. 'Go, and have as good a time as anyone can in a sociology class.'

'Thank you.' She kissed his cheek. 'I will.'

Ken took a pile of marking from his briefcase, then returned to the living room and his chair, but he couldn't concentrate. Every time he looked at a page, an image of Jackie Marsh filled his mind. In an attempt to divert his attention away from her, he tried to think about his brother. Irma had cornered him in the Rovers two nights ago and confided that since his accident David had been acutely depressed. According to her, David spent his days lying in bed and his evenings drinking pints and whisky chasers in the Rovers, boring anyone who would listen with tales of what his career as a footballer might have been if it hadn't been cut short by his accident.

Ken felt sorry for him but his mind turned yet again to Jackie Marsh. He recalled the last evening they had spent together. She couldn't have made it clearer that she wanted more from him than just the odd hour or two of conversation in a pub. But was he prepared to give her more?

He looked around the untidy living room crammed with baby paraphernalia, toys scattered over the floor. Dust lay on the sideboard. The house was less and less a place where he could relax. He crept upstairs and opened the twins' bedroom door. They were lying on their sides in their cots sleeping peacefully. They weren't due to wake. He could go down the Rovers for a swift half, talk to the neighbours and forget his own and – if David wasn't there – his brother's problems for an hour. He'd be back before Valerie came home and she'd never find out he'd left.

He stole back down the stairs, picked up his coat, checked that his keys were in the pocket and went out.

Ken entered the Rovers to find everyone in the bar engrossed in a row between David and Irma. Irma was refusing to serve David any more beer or whisky. Unsurprisingly, since David was having trouble standing upright, Jack and Annie Walker were backing her to the hilt. He turned round, hoping to leave unnoticed, but David staggered towards him.

'Buy ush a drink.' He gripped Ken's shoulder in an effort to steady himself.

'I think you've had enough.'

'Go home and stop embarrassing everyone, David,' Irma ordered him crossly.

'I want another drink . . .' David allowed Ken to help him to a chair. He fell on to it and tried to focus on his brother. 'Jusht one more drink, then I'll go . . .'

'Try to reason with him, love,' Annie whispered to Irma. 'The last thing we need is any trouble tonight.'

Irma poured a glass of water and reluctantly joined Ken and David at the table.

'Yoush brrought a drink.' David's face fell when he saw it was water. He closed his eyes and dropped his head into his hands.

Irma pushed the water in front of him. 'Go home and sleep it off. When you're sober you can come round to me mam's and we'll talk. But until you snap out of feeling sorry for yourself and drinking yourself to death, I'm moving in with Mam and Dad.'

'Irma . . .' David slurred at her retreating back.

'Come on, our kid.' Ken gripped his brother's arm and

helped him from the chair. 'I'll see you home.' He exchanged glances with Irma as he steered David to the door. When he saw the gratitude in her eyes, he smiled at her.

Valerie's head was buzzing with the unfamiliar terms the sociology teacher had introduced to her and the rest of the class. And it wasn't just the words: some of the concepts about which he had spoken so matter-of-factly had seemed peculiar. No wonder Ken, with his advanced education, seemed like a stranger these days. What had he ever seen in her? She'd had to struggle to pass her hair-dresser's examinations and they were based on common sense, not philosophical ideas that demanded brains she'd never possessed.

She slid her key into the door, opened it and came face to face with a pall of thick, black smoke. She could hear Peter and Susan were screaming at the top of their tiny lungs. She charged into the house, straight through the blinding smoke, nose and lungs stinging and fought her way up the stairs.

The smoke was thinner in the bedroom than it had been downstairs and she could see babies thrashing wildly, their tiny faces screwed tightly as they continued to scream. She scooped both of them into her arms, ran back down the stairs and into the street, shouting for help.

Within seconds Elsie Tanner, Valerie's uncle Albert and the Ogdens were at her side. While Hilda and Elsie tried to soothe her and the babies, Stan Ogden and Albert ran to the house.

'Come into my place,' Elsie insisted. 'The babies will freeze out here in their nighties.'

'What's up?' Ken ran up the street from the direction of the Rovers.

Valerie had never been so angry in her life. 'You went out, leaving the twins in a blazing house!'

Ken saw the smoke billowing from the open front door and ran in, just as Albert and Stan emerged, coughing.

'A coal fell out of the fire on to the rug, love,' Albert spluttered. 'Apart from the smoke and the black smuts that have settled everywhere, there's no real damage.'

Valerie glared at Ken. 'No thanks to you.'

'Let's get the babies settled in my house for the night, love. Time to sort out what's what in your house in the morning.' Elsie wrapped her arm round Valerie's shoulders and led her away from Ken.

Jack Walker tapped a spoon against his glass until the crowd in the bar fell silent. 'To Emily and her new life in Majorca, and to Lucille,' he lifted his glass, 'for passing her examinations.'

As the toast was drunk, Emily recalled the bitter argument she'd had with her sister the day before. Her father had suffered a stroke four days ago and her sister had insisted that she give up her plans to go to Majorca to stay at home and nurse him, even though Emily had looked after her father single-handedly for the last six years. But when Emily had said it was *her* turn to build a life of her own, her sister had accused her being selfish and had threatened to put their father into a home.

Emily knew her sister well enough to realise that it was no idle threat. Feeling she had no choice, she had telephoned her friend in Majorca that morning to tell him that she would have to decline his offer of a job. Later, when she'd stopped crying, she had telephoned the airline to cancel her ticket, but when she looked round at the smiling faces of her friends and neighbours she couldn't bring herself to tell them the truth: that she wasn't going to Majorca but returning to her childhood home to nurse her sick father.

'Don't tell me,' Len joked, as Dennis Tanner walked in, 'you heard about Emily's leaving party and decided to make the trip from Newcastle rather than miss it.'

'Emily's leaving?' Dennis muttered absently.

'Want a drink?'

'Is me mam here?'

'Talking to Annie at the bar, last time I saw her.' Len frowned as Dennis left him. He had never known the boy refuse a free drink before.

As Dennis pushed his way through the crowd, Elsie caught sight of him and knew that something was seriously wrong. 'What's up?'

Conscious of the people around them, Dennis muttered, 'I came back.'

'I can see that. I can also see from that look on your face that something's wrong.'

'Anyone been in here looking for me?' Dennis glanced uneasily over his shoulder.

'You expecting anyone?' Elsie's voice was shrill with anxiety.

'I owe some people money.'

Elsie shivered, as if there was a chill in the air. 'What people?'

Dennis considered lying, but he knew he'd already said too much. 'I got heavies after me.'

'How much do you owe?'

'Ninety-four quid.'

'How the bloody hell—?'

'Please, Mam, not now. They know where you live, and they could have got here ahead of me.'

'Then we'd better go home. I'll try talking to them.' Elsie finished her drink.

'You got ninety-four quid?'

'You know I haven't.'

'That's the only kind of talking they'd be interested in.' Dennis was white with fear. Jack Walker leant over the bar. 'I couldn't help overhearing, Elsie. If we all go to your house with you, we'll soon send a couple of toughs packing.' He looked for support from the men in the bar but no one spoke. 'We can't let Dennis and Elsie face them alone. What if they won't listen to reason?'

'There's no use hiding in here, any road. Come on, whatever you've done, you're still my son.' Elsie took her son's arm and left the pub. Jack delayed only as long as it took him to roll down his sleeves and pick up his jacket.

'You're surely not going to go with them?' Annie protested.

'I got no choice, love.' He gave the men in the bar a scathing look. 'It doesn't appear that anyone else is willing to help.'

Valerie glared at Ken. She'd only moved back into their house from Elsie's two days before and they were barely on speaking terms. She wished he'd offered to go with Dennis. After all, Elsie had been the first to help her and the twins after the fire. It gave her one more reason to think that her marriage had fallen apart.

Elsie and Dennis turned up their collars against the rain and kept to the shadows as they walked along the street. Elsie glanced up and down it as she slid the key into the lock. She opened the door and they went in. Before she had time to close it, two men moved in behind them, seemingly from nowhere, and kicked it shut.

'Hello, Dennis.' The taller and heavier of the two pinned Dennis against the door.

Elsie ran down the passage, darted into the living room

and picked up the poker. She rushed back to the door just as Jack Walker strode in.

'For God's sake!' the second man exclaimed. 'We can't go hitting women and old men.'

His partner had no such scruples. After flooring Dennis, he grabbed Elsie's wrist and squeezed it so hard that she dropped the poker, which fell onto Dennis's leg. He cried out in pain.

'Ninety-four quid.' The man exerted pressure on Elsie's wrist, forcing her to her knees. 'If you give it to us now, we'll leave quietly. If you don't . . .' He pushed his face close to hers. 'You don't want to know what we'll do, if you don't.'

'Leave her alone.' Jack Walker flung himself onto the thug only to be shaken off into the wall.

'Here's your bloody ninety-four quid.' Len Fairclough appeared at the door and held out a bundle of banknotes. The man holding Elsie's wrist took it and flicked through, noting the denominations.

'It's all there! Take it and get out!' Len shouted.

The men backed out and Len ran to Elsie, who was still on her knees. 'You all right, love?' He helped her to her feet.

'Dennis?' She looked to her son.

'I'll live.' He limped towards her.

'Jack?' Len looked at the old man, who was rubbing his shoulder.

'I'm all right.'

'You,' Len poked his finger into Dennis's chest, 'start work first thing tomorrow morning as my labourer, and you don't stop until you've paid off every penny of that ninety-four quid. Understood?'

David Barlow knocked at the door of his in-laws' house at number thirteen Coronation Street. He stepped back, thrust his hands into his overcoat pockets and waited. A few seconds later Irma opened the door. She studied him for a few moments. He was pale and trembling, but he appeared to be sober.

'You been drinking?'

'Not for the last week,' he replied, shamefaced.

'Then you can come in.' She took him in into the musty, freezing cold front parlour. 'Sit down.'

David sat on the edge of one of the easy-chairs without taking off his coat.

'What have you got to say for yourself?'

David looked down at his shoes. 'I'm sorry, I know I've been difficult lately—'

'Difficult?' Irma exploded. 'You've been impossible. Wallowing in your own misery, thinking only of yourself and how your world has come to an end. Never sparing a thought for anyone else, least of all me. Lying in bed all day and drinking all night in Rovers . . .'

'I said I'm sorry,' he repeated defensively. 'What more can I say?'

'Nothing, but you can *do* one hell of a lot. Change your ways, David Barlow, or I warn you now, I won't be back.'

He pulled a creased envelope from his pocket. 'The club paid me compensation for my injury. There's a cheque for three hundred pounds in there.'

'What are you going to do with it?'

'I don't know,' he said slowly. 'That depends.'

'On what?' she enquired sharply.

'Whether you come back to me or not,' he answered.

'Do you want me to?'

'Of course I do,' he protested. 'I love you.'

'Enough to buy the corner shop? It's up for sale.'

'I didn't know.'

'It's a business we could both run, David. We could make a real go of it, a fresh start.'

'You make it sound as if we've married for years, not eight months.'

'Given what's happened in the last two months, I feel as if I've been married for years.'

'If you want to buy the corner shop, I'll find out what they're asking for it.'

'One thousand seven hundred and fifty pounds for the premises and two hundred for the stock.'

'That's almost two thousand pounds!'

'I can count, David. Can we afford it?'

'We'd have to take out a mortgage.'

'Then do it. I've worked in shops and I'm sure I can

run it. Building up the business is something we can do together.'

'You mean it?' He dared to reach for her hand.

'I mean it – but there are conditions. You'll get out of bed every morning and you'll stop drinking – the way you have been.' She realised it might be a bit much to expect him to give up visiting the Rovers altogether.

'I'll do anything to get you back.' Then he had to ask, 'You coming home with me now?'

'I suppose the flat is a tip.'

'I cleaned it before I came out.'

She gave him a small smile. 'I'll get my coat. It'll be interesting to see what your idea of cleaning is.'

Ken Barlow walked out of the school gates at lunchtime and jumped on to a bus. Five minutes later, he got off and walked into a café. Jackie Marsh was sitting at a table in the back corner, staring into a cup of coffee. He sat down opposite her and she looked up.

'Everything all set for tonight?' She reached for his hand under cover of the table.

'It is.'

'What have you told your wife?' She caressed his fingers.

'That I'm attending a teachers' union conference.'

'And she believed you?'

Ken hung his head. When he had started seeing Jackie the subterfuge and half-truths he had told Valerie had been just a small part of the glamorous, exciting other life he lived with Jackie. But tonight their affair was heading into dangerous uncharted territory. He wasn't sure how he'd feel waking up beside her in the morning.

'You've booked the hotel?' she pressed.

'Mr and Mrs Ken Jones are booked into the Grand Hotel in Llandudno tonight and tomorrow night.'

'I'll meet you on the six o'clock train.'

'On the train,' he agreed, 'not the platform, someone might see us.'

She glanced around the café. All the other customers appeared to be engrossed in their own affairs, so she risked kissing his lips. 'That's on account,' she whispered, 'until tonight.'

'Until tonight.' He glanced at his watch. 'I'd better get back to school.'

Ken left the café without buying anything. He glanced at his watch and realised he had ten minutes to waste until the next bus came along. He was looking in a bookshop window when he felt a sharp tap on his shoulder.

'You mad or just plain stupid, Ken Barlow?'

He whirled round to see Elsie Tanner standing behind him. 'What do you mean?' His heart began to race. Elsie was notoriously blunt. If she had seen him with Jackie . . .

'Kissing other women in broad daylight. Risking your marriage, your wife's happiness *and* that of your children.'

She shook her head. 'And you are supposed to be educated. Well, in my opinion you want your head examined.'

'I don't know what you're talking about, Elsie.' The blood rushed to his cheeks.

'Then I suppose it wasn't you I saw kissing the brunette in the café just now.'

'Elsie, I . . . You won't tell, Val, will you?' he begged.

'That depends.'

'On what?' he asked warily.

'Whether I ever see you with that woman again.' She turned on her heel and walked away.

Elsie had only just come home from work when she heard a taxi pull up outside. There was a knock at the door and she opened it to see Linda on the doorstep, two suitcases at her feet, Paul – who had grown into a sturdy toddler she never would have recognised – sleeping in her arms.

'What are you doing here? You should have written.' Elsie took Paul from Linda's arms and carried him into the living room. She laid him gently on the sofa and covered him with her coat, then poked the fire, which blazed warmth into the room. 'Sit down, love.' She took the cases from Linda and dropped them at the foot of the stairs. 'I'll make you a cup of tea, you look worn out and frozen.'

'It's been a long journey.' Linda stretched out her hands to the fire. 'Paul was horribly seasick for the first couple of days. He'd hardly got over it before we docked at six o'clock this morning, and since then we've spent all day changing trains and waiting in stations.'

'Well, you're here now. How long can you stay?' Linda didn't answer. She took off her coat and sat on one of the easy-chairs next to the fire. 'I've left Ivan, Mam. I've fallen in love with a Mountie.'

'I see.' Elsie set the guard in front of the fire for Paul's sake, straightened up and searched the mantelpiece for a cigarette but all she found were two empty packets. She pulled back the guard and tossed them on to the fire, then faced her daughter. 'Your brother's home too. It never rains but it pours.'

'Is that you, Ken?' Valerie was holding a bowl of mashed potatoes and creamed chicken when Ken walked in after school. 'I'll carry on feeding the twins, if you don't mind, love, but I've packed your clothes for the NUT conference. The suitcase is upstairs on the bed. I know you're only going for two days but I gave you three clean shirts, three sets of underclothes and three pairs of socks. It never hurts to have extra in case you get caught in a rainstorm or something. And I picked up your brown suit from the cleaner's. I left it hanging on the wardrobe door because I wasn't sure if you'd want to wear it or pack it. I put in your red and green ties and your brown shoes. Oh, and don't forget to pick up the chicken sandwiches and the flask of coffee I made you for the journey. They're in the kitchen.'

'Thank you, love.' Ken walked up the stairs and into the bedroom. Just as Valerie had said, his suitcase was neatly packed. Slowly, deliberately, he lifted out the shirts and replaced them in his side of the wardrobe. Then he did the same with his underclothes. After he had put away his suit, he closed the door and stowed away the case.

'You're going to have to make a move, Ken, if you want to get to the station in time to catch the train.' Valerie was wiping potato off Peter's face.

'I'm not going, love.' He slipped off his jacket, hung it on the back of his chair and sat at the table.

'What do you mean? You said the conference was really important.'

'Not as important as you and the twins. Let's have a family weekend, just you, me and the children. No, you sit there,' he said, as she rose from her chair. 'I'll go and get those sandwiches you made and a couple of plates. We'll share them.'

Chapter Fifteen

D ot Greenhalgh waved madly at Elsie as she walked towards the crowded bus stop on a fine spring morning. 'I've wonderful news. I can't wait to tell you . . .'

'Your Walt's found himself a job?' Elsie interrupted.

'No. What's up with you? You look a right misery-guts this morning.'

'All the more reason for you to give me some wonderful news.' Elsie unwrapped the cellophane from a packet of cigarettes she had just bought in the corner shop from David Barlow, who didn't look at all happy serving behind a counter for all that he and Irma had been running the shop now for six months.

'The Yanks are back.'

Elsie snapped the head off a match she was about to strike. 'You serious?'

'Would I lie to you about something like that? They're holding a twenty-two-year VE Day reunion. Gregg Flint came round last night.' Her face broke into an enormous smile. 'He hasn't changed a bit. We're going out this evening to catch up on old times.'

'And what does Walt think of that?' Elsie asked, referring to Dot's husband.

'He can think what he likes. He doesn't own me,' Dot retorted. 'Anyway, Gregg has this friend, Gary Strauss. He's a bit young but he wants to take you out with us.'

'What do you call a bit young?' Elsie questioned warily.

'Probably somewhere about your Dennis's age.'

'You expect me to go out with a lad the same age as our Dennis?'

'It's not really *going-out* going out,' Dot qualified. 'Just having a bit of a laugh. You'll like Gary, Elsie. And Gregg can't wait to see you again. Say you'll come, please.'

The last thing Elsie wanted to do was go out with a boy the same age as her son, but neither did she fancy an evening with Linda wittering on about her Mountie the way she had every night after she had put Paul to bed.

'I'll come, but if I feel stupid or I don't like Gary, I'll be off.'

'That's grand, Elsie.' Dot linked her arm in Elsie's as the bus pulled around the corner. 'We'll have a great time. You'll see.'

'I don't believe the arrogance of it – sheer bureaucratic arrogance born of ignorance!' Ken Barlow slammed the front door behind him.

'Don't believe what, love?' Valerie asked placidly, as she lifted Peter out of his high-chair.

'The council has refused permission for our students to hold an anti-Vietnam war meeting in the town hall.'

'Oh.' Valerie wasn't sure what else to say.

'The city fathers are afraid to voice any opinion except the official line because the Government hasn't allowed them to think for themselves for years. Well, we're holding our meeting outside the hall, on the steps, and I'll be there.'

'Won't that be asking for trouble, love?'

'Yes!' he snapped. 'Don't bother with tea, I want to get there early.' He dropped his briefcase in the hall and left.

Valerie took Susan from her high-chair and she and Peter toddled off to the 'play' corner where she kept their toys. She had thought that things had become easier between her and Ken after he'd cancelled his weekend 'conference' months ago, but now she realised that for all her hopes, Ken hadn't changed. Their marriage was just as strained as it had ever been.

'When I heard the Yanks were back, I thought it wouldn't be long before I'd see you two all dolled-up.' Ena looked Elsie and Dot up and down as they walked, arm in arm, down Coronation Street.

'What's life for, if not for having a good time, Ena?' Elsie called back, as they headed for the car parked at the end of the street.

'Elsie, sweetheart, as young and beautiful as ever.' Gregg opened the door of the car and climbed out. He swept Elsie off her feet, hugged her and swung her round in his arms. 'It's great to see you again.' He kissed her cheek, then kissed Dot's lips and helped them both into the back of the car.

'It's good to see you, Gregg.' Elsie smiled. 'And Dot's right, you haven't changed a bit.'

'That's just what a man needs to hear after twenty-two years in the wilderness.' He turned to his companion. 'Gary Strauss, meet Elsie Tanner.'

'Pleased to make you acquaintance, ma'am.' Gary turned round in his seat and offered Elsie his hand. To her amusement, he looked even younger than Dennis.

'Right! Good time, here we come.' Greg turned the ignition key.

'Nice car,' Elsie said.

'It's rented.' He drove away from the street. 'Do you know that Steve's back in town, Elsie?'

'Steve Tanner?' Elsie tried to sound nonchalant but her hand shook as she opened her handbag and rummaged for cigarettes.

'Never could get over you guys having the same surname. Did you ever wonder if you were related way back, hundreds of years ago?'

'It would have been Steve and my ex-husband, not me. And the answer to your question is no, I didn't.' Elsie offered her cigarettes around.

'He wants to see you.'

'Twenty-two years is a long time, Gregg. Some things are best left alone,' Elsie said.

Gregg turned round and smiled at her. 'Not that long.' He winked at Dot. 'I think we've already proved that, haven't we, angel?'

'I wondered how long it would be before you turned up.' Elsie let a crumpled, unshaven Ivan into her house the following morning.

'I would have been here sooner, but Linda left in such a hurry I had things to clear up, like selling the house and packing up the furniture.'

'Well, your wife is in the kitchen giving your son his breakfast, before taking him to school. He went up a class last week,' she said proudly. 'Our Dennis is in one bedroom, Paul and Linda in the other and I'm in the third, but you know where the sofa is in the front room. I'm off to work.' Elsie stepped past him and ran quickly down the street lest he try to delay her. Some reunions – especially fraught ones between estranged husbands and wives – were best left private.

As usual, Dot was at the bus stop before her. 'Last night was fun.'

'It was,' Elsie agreed, still surprised by how much she had enjoyed the evening and Gary's company.

'Gregg and me had a talk when he took me home. He was saying how much Steve wants to see you.'

'So he said when I was there.' Elsie knew which way the conversation was headed and tried to end it before it began.

'Won't you even think about meeting him?'

'I'll think about it.' The bus pulled into the bay; Elsie jumped on, found a seat and opened her handbag to look for her purse. The last person she wanted to discuss was Steve Tanner, especially with Dot. Her friend was far too astute: she might guess that she'd been thinking of nothing and no one else ever since Gregg had told her that Steve was back in town.

'That will be one and six.' David Barlow put the three sixpenny biros his brother wanted into a paper bag and handed them over.

Ken gave him two shillings. 'I suppose you heard what happened last night.'

'Irma called round your house. Val told her that you'd gone to some banned demonstration or other.'

'It was an anti-Vietnam war demonstration. Don't you care about anything that happens outside this narrow little street with its petty politics and squabbling?'

'I have better things to worry about,' David answered absently, dropping sixpence into his brother's hand.

'Like?' Ken challenged.

'Like my own problems,' David snapped.

'I was arrested.'

'Why?'

'I've just told you, for taking part in a banned demonstration,' Ken said testily. 'The police charged me with disturbance of the peace too. I'm on in court next week.'

'Neither offence is particularly serious. You've a clean record, you'll probably be bound over, or get off with a fine.'

'I'm not paying a fine, not for a matter of principle. The way I see it, the local authority is the lawbreaker – not me. Someone has to stand up and be counted when it comes to the stupid decisions politicians make in our name. And there's none stupider than waging war on innocent civilians in a Third World country . . .'

'This is a shop, not a soapbox,' David reminded him. 'And should you be fined, and refuse to pay, you'll go to prison.'

'Yes, I will. And gladly for a matter of principle.' Ken's eyes held a fanatical gleam.

'And what are your wife and children supposed to do while you serve time for a matter of principle?' David enquired.

'You just don't understand, do you?'

'No,' David agreed. 'I never have.'

'For all that you or anyone else around here cares about the serious matters in life, you may as well be dead,' Ken announced, and stalked out of the shop.

As there were no other customers, David left the shop

and put the kettle on, then made a cup of tea and carried it upstairs. Irma was lying in bed, her face as white as the pillows.

'You feeling any better, love?' David asked.

'Not really.'

'I've made you some tea.' He set the cup on the bedside cabinet. 'I think I should go downstairs and call the doctor.'

'Yes,' she agreed hoarsely, 'I think you'd better.'

Usually Irma played down illness. Worried sick, not just for her but the baby they hadn't yet told anyone else that she was carrying, David ran down the stairs and picked up the telephone.

'Hello, Elsie, long time no see.' Steve Tanner waylaid her as she left Miami Modes to take her lunch break. She could barely see him behind the enormous bunch of cream and yellow roses he was carrying but her heart did a back flip. He might be wearing civilian clothes but he was every inch the Yank officer with whom she had fallen head over heels in love over twenty years before. 'You don't have anything to say after twenty-two years?' he prompted.

'Like Gregg, you haven't changed a bit,' she said, when she finally found her voice.

'I could say the same about you, Elsie.'

'Could you now?' Elsie had no idea what she was

saying. She only had to look into his deep blue eyes to feel the years rolling away. Once again she was in the Palais, gazing across the dance floor at an American officer standing at the bar with his buddies. An officer she had believed too handsome to notice the likes of her. But, to her surprise, he had asked her to dance, then stayed with her until the last waltz. Then he had walked her home. Before morning she had lost her heart and, looking at him now, she realised she had never reclaimed it.

'Dot said you get a break about this time of day.'

Elsie broke free from her reverie. 'An hour for dinner.'

'I saw a Chinese restaurant round the corner. Shall we experiment with their menu?'

'Love to.'

'By the way, these are for you.' He handed her the roses.

'Thank you, my favourite colours.'

'I remembered.'

'They smell gorgeous.' She buried her face in the blooms and breathed in their heady scent.

'Shall we go?' He offered her his arm. She took it, feeling as though she were floating on air.

'Elsie?' He looked down at her.

'Yes?'

'This is just the beginning, you do know that?'

She took a deep breath. 'For now, let's just enjoy remembering the good old days.'

'And have a few good new days?' he suggested.

'We'll see,' she replied cautiously.

A week after his arrest, Ken stood upright in the dock of the magistrates' court and glared contemptuously at the three people who were looking down at him.

'Twenty-five pounds' fine or seven days in prison.' The leading magistrate narrowed his eyes and glowered at Ken.

'I refuse to pay a fine to any court that is not representative of the people and their rights,' Ken said truculently, aware that the reporter of the local paper was sitting on the public bench, taking notes.

'Then seven days in prison it is. Constable, take the prisoner down,' the magistrate ordered.

David squeezed Valerie's hand reassuringly then jumped to his feet. 'I'll pay the fine.'

'No, you will not,' Ken shouted. 'I refuse to allow you to. I told you, both of you,' he looked from David to Valerie, 'this is a matter of principle.'

'The prisoner may meet with his family privately to reconsider his decision for ten minutes before he is transferred to Strangeways.'

Following the magistrate's directive a police constable led Ken out of the court and into a private room. A few minutes later David and Valerie joined them.

'Before either of you start, you are not going to change my mind about this,' Ken said firmly.

'Then you're a bloody fool,' David retorted angrily.

'Language,' the constable reprimanded.

'Neither of you understands the first thing about principles—' Ken began warmly.

'No, we don't.' David helped Valerie to a chair. 'But we understand families and our responsibilities towards them. What are Val and the twins supposed to do without you for a week? You're prepared to let them suffer—'

'People are suffering and dying in Vietnam.'

'I don't doubt it. People always suffer and die in a war. But I fail to see how you going to prison when Val needs you at home can help them.' David clenched his fists.

'Someone has to make a stand!'

'Do you think anyone in Vietnam gives a damn whether a teacher in Manchester goes to prison for a week or not?' David challenged.

'You'd give a damn if the whole world outside your fiddling little corner shop and Coronation Street were wiped off the map tonight.'

'Like you wouldn't give a damn if Val cracks up trying to cope with the twins on her own?

'No more of a damn than you gave when you worried Irma sick after your accident, and disappeared into a whisky bottle for a couple of months.'

David stared at his brother scornfully. 'Those problems have long been sorted. We have different ones now.' If he hadn't been so furious with Ken he would never have said so much.

'Like what?' Ken snapped

'Like Irma has lost the baby she was carrying. But no matter, that's small fry compared to what's happening in Vietnam,' he said sarcastically. 'Come on, Val, love, I'll take you home before Hilda has a breakdown trying to cope with the twins.'

Valerie shook her head. 'Would you mind waiting outside for a minute, David? I've something to say to Ken.'

David went outside and closed the door behind him.

'This is a matter of principle,' Ken reiterated, in a softer, gentler voice.

'I don't expect you to sacrifice your principles for me or the twins,' Valerie said shortly. 'But I want to tell you that we won't be waiting for you when you get out of prison.'

'But . . .'

'I've put up with a lot from you, Ken.'

'Like what?'

'Your affair with Jackie Marsh for a start.' Silence closed in on them, thick and suffocating. Eventually she added, quietly, 'I knew about it all along.'

'Nothing happened,' he protested.

'Nothing, Ken?' She raised her eyebrows.

'I suppose Elsie Tanner told you she saw me kissing

Jackie in a café. But that's all it was, Val, a couple of drinks and a few stolen kisses. It never went any further.'

'Elsie didn't tell me anything. I found out for myself. And it would have gone a whole lot further that weekend you were supposed to be going on a teachers' conference.'

'But that's just it! I didn't go, love! I couldn't go through with it. You and I spent that weekend together. Made it a family weekend . . .'

'It doesn't matter now. I'm going up to Scotland to spend some time with my parents.'

'You'll be home when I come out.' He tried to grab her hand but she walked to the door.

'I honestly don't know, Ken.' She left. He heard her talking to David, then there was silence.

'Ready?' the constable asked.

'For what?' Ken looked at him quizzically.

'Strangeways. You did say you wanted to go to prison.'

Elsie tried to visualise the clothes in her wardrobe as she travelled home from work. She needed something spec-tacular for her fourth date with Steve. There was her best frock, a black lace that was truly stunning, but what if he decided to take her for a quiet drink in a back-street pub and picked up fish and chips on the way home? She smiled wryly. She was panicking over nothing. Steve had hinted that he was going to take her somewhere special tonight and none of their other dates had exactly been mundane. She would wear her black lace and get Linda to help her pin her long hair into curls on the crown of her head.

She rounded the corner of Coronation Street to see a police car outside her house and a group of neighbours standing outside.

'It's your Paul,' Ena announced, as Elsie rushed to her door. 'He didn't come home from school. And Linda and Ivan can't find him anywhere . . .'

'He's been gone for two hours,' Hilda Ogden chipped in. 'Your Ivan and Dennis have searched everywhere and the police and neighbours are out looking now.'

'The police are knocking doors.' Ena had to have the last word.

Ignoring her neighbours, Elsie opened the door and darted inside. Linda was sitting on the sofa in the living room with a policewoman. There was no sign of Dennis or Ivan.

'Oh, Mam.' Linda jumped up and flung her arms around Elsie's neck, clinging to her the way she had done when she'd been a child. 'I should have never let Paul come home from school by himself. But since they moved him up a class he's been begging me to let him find his own way. He said none of the other mothers of the kids in his class met them at the gates. Dennis and Ivan have looked everywhere but there's no sign of him anywhere. I know something's happened to him. I just know!'

'Calm down, love, they'll find him.' Elsie helped her back to the sofa.

'Might I make another cup of tea, Mrs Tanner?' The policewoman piled her and Linda's cups on to a tray she'd found in the kitchen. 'You look as though you could do with one.'

'I could, thank you,' Elsie said quietly, and gripped Linda's hand.

The following four hours were the longest of Elsie's life. She drew some comfort from the knowledge that every available able-bodied man in the neighbourhood was out looking for Paul. Then, just after darkness had fallen and Linda was in danger of becoming hysterical, a second police car pulled up outside the house. The policewoman showed a sergeant into the living room. He sat in the chair opposite Elsie and Linda.

'We've found him, Mrs Cheveski.'

Linda jumped to her feet.

'Please sit down,' he ordered authoritatively.

To Elsie's amazement, Linda did as he asked.

'Your husband and brother are with him. They're travelling in the ambulance with him to the hospital.'

'Oh, my God!' Linda sobbed. 'What's happened to him?'

'He was pulled from the canal. He was unconscious, cold and wet, but he was breathing. It's too early to say what, if anything, is wrong with him, but if you and your mother would like to go to the hospital . . .'

'Of course we would.' Elsie rose to her feet.

'I'll take you in the patrol car.'

Steve Tanner brushed his hair, splashed a little more after-shave on to his cheeks and glanced at himself in the full-length mirror of his hotel room. He picked up his keys, dropped them into his pocket, left the room and walked down the corridor to reception. He'd parked his rented car outside, and hummed softly to himself as he drove the two miles to Coronation Street. He smiled when he realised the tune was one of his wartime favourites, 'Don't Sit Under the Apple Tree With Anyone Else But Me'.

The street was deserted. He parked a few doors down from Elsie's house, left his car, felt a sharp pain in the back of his head and tumbled into total blackness.

'He's a strong boy, Mr and Mrs Cheveski,' the doctor looked grave as he spoke to Linda and Ivan, 'but the last thing I want is to give you false hope. He has pneumonia and it's very serious. At best I can only give him a thirty per cent chance of surviving.'

Forgetting that he and Linda had separated, Ivan put his arm round her shoulders. 'Can we see him, Doctor?'

He needs absolute quiet.'

'*Please* – we won't say a word,' Linda begged.

'Then you can sit with him for a few minutes. I'm sorry, Mrs Tanner,' he apologised to Elsie, 'I know you're Paul's grandmother but we can only allow two visitors to a bed.'

'That's all right. I'll go to the canteen and get myself a coffee. It will help keep me awake. I've a feeling that this is going to be a long night.'

'Rest assured,' the doctor said, 'that absolutely everything that can be done to save your Paul is being done.'

'Thank you, Doctor,' Linda whispered. She glanced back at Elsie as the doctor led the way into the intensive-care ward.

Chapter Sixteen

Elsie was sitting in the hospital canteen, smoking a cigarette and ostensibly drinking a cup of coffee, when Dot and Gregg walked in.

'Elsie, you heard.' Dot ran over to her table and Gregg followed.

It's serious, Dot,' Elsie murmured, desolate. 'He only has a thirty per cent chance of surviving.'

'You can't say that, Elsie, not until after he's been X-rayed.' Gregg pulled out a chair and sat at her table.

'X-ray?' Elsie repeated, bewildered. 'There's no point in X-raying someone with pneumonia.' She pushed her coffee aside. It was cold and had a peculiar metallic tang.

'How do you know he has pneumonia?' Dot asked.

'The doctors told us.'

'You've seen a doctor already. They wouldn't talk to us.'

'I'm not surprised, Gregg. You're hardly family.'

'Neither are you.'

'I'm Paul's grandmother.'

'Your Paul, something's happened to him?' Dot moved her chair closer to Elsie's.

'He fell in the canal and they brought him in with pneumonia. He's on the intensive-care ward. Linda and Ivan are with him now. The doctors are doing all they can . . .' She stared from Dot to Gregg. 'If you didn't know about Paul . . .'

'We came in after I received a call about Steve,' Gregg said. 'We went to your house but there was no one in.'

'What's happened to Steve?' Elsie gripped the table hard. She felt as though her entire world was falling apart.

'Ena Sharples found him lying unconscious beside his car in Coronation Street.' Gregg reached for Elsie's hand. 'Someone hit him over the head, but we won't find out the extent of the damage until he's been X-rayed.'

'What do you mean, "someone"?' Dot questioned angrily. 'It was Walt. He even had the gall to boast about it to me, Elsie. He thought Steve was Gregg and had a go at him because I told him straight that Gregg's given me the first good time I've had since the war.'

Elsie pushed back her chair, slopping the coffee into her saucer.

'Where are you going?' Gregg asked.

'Upstairs to check if there's any change in our Paul and to tell Linda where I'll be. Then I'm going down to

X-Ray to wait until they've finished with Steve.' She ran out of the canteen.

'Your husband's come round, Mrs Tanner.' The doctor pulled the curtain behind him as he left a cubicle.

Elsie didn't bother to correct him. She wanted to know everything there was to know about Steve's condition and, as his wife, she stood to learn more than if she told the doctor she was a friend. 'Is he badly hurt?' she asked anxiously.

'The X-ray is clear so there's no serious damage, but he has concussion. We'll be keeping him overnight but it's only a precaution. I'm not expecting him to develop any other symptoms and if he doesn't he'll be discharged in the morning.'

'Can I see him?'

'He's been asking for you. You can go in now, if you like.'

'Thank you.' Elsie might have breathed easier if she hadn't been worried sick about Paul. But there had been no change in his condition and the nurses had made it clear that grandmothers were considered a nuisance on the intensive-care ward. It had been as much as she could do to extract a promise from them to telephone Casualty if there was any change in Paul's condition.

Steve was sitting up on a trolley. Dried blood matted his hair, his face was unusually pale and he looked tired, but she was relieved to see him in one piece. 'Elsie, they said you were here.' He smiled at her. 'I didn't expect you to come.'

She sat on the chair beside his bed and reached for his hand. 'I was here before you arrived. My grandson Paul is in intensive care. He has pneumonia.'

'I'm sorry, sweetheart. That sounds serious.'

'It is,' she confirmed succinctly.

He squeezed her hand. 'And there was me thinking that I was going to give you an evening you'd remember for the rest of your life.'

'I've had one of those, all right,' she said dryly.

'You must want to sit with Paul.'

'I can't. They only allow two to a bed and my daughter Linda and her husband are with him.' She tried to return his smile. 'So it's just as well that I have you to talk to – if you're up to it, that is. You look sick as a pig.'

'I feel as sick as a pig, whatever that means. I'm sorry. I didn't even make it to your front door tonight. The last thing I remember is getting out of my car – then *bam*.'

'I wouldn't have been in if you *had* made it. We've been here for hours.'

'There'll be other evenings for us,' he said philosophically. 'Won't there?' He gazed into her eyes.

'I hope so,' she whispered.

'And for the moment, even here, with me like this and your grandson in intensive care, there's no one I'd rather be with than you.' He lifted her hand to his lips and tenderly kissed her fingertips. 'It has taken me twenty-two years to realise that I love you. I don't want to wait another twenty-two before you marry me.'

'Marry . . .'

'You said you were divorced.'

'I am.'

'I know the timing isn't great and I'm offering you a battered body but it will heal. And, in the meantime, perhaps we can pass the time by making plans for a future – together. The future to start when Paul recovers and I'm out of here.' He looked directly into her eyes. 'Paul *will* recover, Elsie, I'm sure of it.'

Elsie believed him. But, more than that, she realised she was no longer alone.

'So, soon-to-be Mrs Steve Tanner, how do you feel about living in the States?'

'Can I let you know after I've had time to think about it?'

'Yes, as long as we spend the time between now and then discussing what kind of house or apartment you'd like and how you intend to furnish it. We have a wide choice in America. There's city living and country living and condominiums . . .'

'What are those when they're at home?'

'They'll take a bit of explaining.'

Elsie only half listened to what he was saying but she

was intensely grateful to him for trying to take her mind off what was happening upstairs.

Steve finally fell asleep at four o'clock in the morning. Elsie stole quietly from his cubicle and took the lift to the intensive care ward. She glanced through the glass panel into the waiting room. Linda was standing close to Ivan, her head on his shoulder, and even from that distance Elsie could see that her daughter was trembling and Ivan's eyes were wet with tears.

A chill claw of fear closed around Elsie's heart but she forced herself to put one foot in front of the other. Terrified of what she was about to hear, she opened the door.

Ivan saw her first. 'They told us a minute ago, Elsie.' His voice was clotted, thick with emotion. 'Paul's going to be all right. He's just come round. He's going to be all right,' he repeated, as if he'd only just begun to believe it. 'Our Paul is going to recover.'

Linda pulled away from Ivan and ran to her.

A nurse appeared. 'The doctor said that you can see Paul again for a few minutes, Mr and Mrs Cheveski.' She smiled at Elsie. 'Mrs Tanner, I'm sure the doctor wouldn't mind if his grandmother peeped around the door as well.'

Two weeks after his night in hospital, Steve Tanner pulled up in front of a small family saloon car parked outside number nine Coronation Street. He turned off the ignition of his rented car, picked up Elsie's left hand and fingered the solitaire diamond ring he had given her earlier that afternoon.

'It's beautiful, Steve,' Elsie murmured huskily. 'I never thought I'd ever wear a ring like this.'

'It's no more than you deserve.' He slid closer to her, cupped her face in his hands and kissed her gently. 'I had no idea that so much could be arranged in the space of one short afternoon. Church, flowers, cars, reception – this time next week we'll be Mr and Mrs Tanner, on a plane and on our way to a new life in America.'

'A new life. I only wish—'

'No more wishes.' He grinned. 'No more regrets over twenty-two wasted years when we could and should have been together, and—' he kissed her again '—absolutely no doubts. We're heading for a new beginning and I think we should go inside and tell Dennis, Linda and Ivan they're acquiring a stepdad and Paul a step-grandfather.'

'You're right.' Elsie smiled determinedly.

He left the car and walked round to open her door for her. The door of number nine opened and Ken Barlow stepped out.

'Ken,' Elsie stopped him, 'I'd like to introduce my fiancé, Steve Tanner. Steve, meet my neighbour, Ken Barlow.'

'Congratulations,' Ken said sincerely, as he shook Steve's hand. 'You're a lucky man.'

'You don't know how lucky,' Steve replied. 'We're getting married next week.'

'You, Val and the twins will be invited, of course.' Elsie was blatantly fishing for information. Valerie had left Coronation Street over a month ago, the day after Ken had started his week's jail sentence, and hadn't returned.

'We'd love to.' He nodded to the saloon car parked outside his door. 'I'm driving up to Scotland now, to fetch her and the twins home.'

'Then this car is yours?' Elsie asked.

'I picked it up this morning. I've been a bit of a fool,' Ken said awkwardly, 'but then you'd know all about that, Elsie.'

'It wasn't me who told Val about that reporter.'

'I know. And I'm grateful you had the courage to tackle me about my behaviour. It stopped me from making an even bigger idiot of myself than I did.'

'She wants to come back?' Elsie asked.

'She wrote to me last week. When I got her letter I went out and bought the car so we could have some outings. Do more things as a family.'

'I'm sure Val will be delighted.'

'I hope so.' He hesitated for a moment. 'I've done something else too, something Valerie might not be too pleased about.'

'Then perhaps you should keep quiet about it,' Elsie advised.

'You've heard they're knocking down the Mission Hall.'

'Yes.' She gave a wry smile. 'Ena will be homeless.'

'They're building maisonettes on the site. I've put a deposit on one for Valerie, me and the twins. I thought all the mod cons would make it easier for Valerie to cope with the housework.'

'I'm sure it will. I can't see any problem there.'

'Hopefully Valerie will like it, but I'm not too sure how she'll react to our new neighbour. Ena has been given the one next door.'

Elsie had the grace not to laugh until Ken had driven away.

'Mam, I've never seen you in anything that suited you so well. You look really glamorous. Like a film star. Steve's going to be knocked out when you walk up the aisle.' Linda pulled out the lace trimmings on Elsie's white bridal suit. 'This is going to be one day the street will talk about for years.'

'I can't believe so many people are making the effort to come at such short notice.' Elsie glanced slyly at her daughter in the mirror. 'Concepta and Harry from Ireland, and . . . your Ivan is still here.'

'We had a long talk last night and we've decided to give our marriage another go for Paul's sake. Seeing him at death's door made both of us realise what's important in life.'

'I'm glad to hear it, love. I'm only sorry you had to find it out the hard way.' Elsie pushed a curl into place on the crown of her head and sprayed it with lacquer.

'Ivan's heard of a job going in Birmingham. He's sure of getting it because one of his mates is in charge of the hiring. He's going on ahead tomorrow and Paul and me will follow as soon as he's sorted somewhere for us to live. But I am going to miss you, Mam. Since I married Ivan, all we seem to have done is say goodbye.'

'America isn't Mars any more than Canada was.' Elsie fought to suppress her tears.

'Dennis!' Linda shouted, hearing his heavy tread on the stairs. 'Haven't you finished dressing yet?'

'Just about.' He walked in carrying his suit jacket, waistcoat and cufflinks. 'I can't get these damned things into my shirt.'

'Come here, you're hopeless.' Elsie hugged him, then slipped the cufflinks through the double buttonholes in his shirt cuffs. 'How will you manage when I've gone?'

'Perfectly,' he assured her, with a confidence that fooled neither of them. 'Don't you worry about me, I'll be fine.'

'I'll put your buttonhole in for you.' Linda grabbed his jacket. 'And remember, everyone will be watching you when you give the bride away.'

'They'll be too busy looking at Mam to give me a second glance.'

'I hope so,' Linda said seriously. 'Because, knowing you, you're bound to do something daft.'

Gregg pushed Steve's buttonhole into his lapel and fastened it with a pin. 'You sure you're not rushing into this?'

'I've know Elsie for twenty-four years,' Steve reminded him.

'And for twenty-two of those you never set eyes on her.'

'That doesn't mean I didn't think about her.' Steve glanced in the mirror and picked up his hairbrush.

'It must have been a lot of thought to make you give her diamond the size of a bird's egg.'

'I know you, Gregg, you're trying to tell me something. Out with it, whatever it is.' Steve brushed his hair then carried his brushes to a small case that lay open on the bed.

'She's not quite your class.'

'What?' Steve glared at his friend. 'Say that again and I'll punch you into next week.'

'Perhaps "class" is the wrong word, Steve,' Gregg amended hastily. 'What I'm trying to say is, there are a lot of differences between you.'

'Of course there are, and that's what makes being with Elsie such fun.' There was a steely glare in Steve's eyes that dared Gregg to say another word on the subject.

Gregg went to Steve's case. 'Is there anything more to go in here?'

Steve glanced round the hotel room. 'No, that's it.'

'Then I'll put it in the car with the others.' Relieved at getting off so easily, Gregg opened the door and left.

'See you all in the Rovers.' Elsie ducked into the bridal car as Annie, Concepta, Valerie, Irma, Lucille and Linda showered her with confetti. Steve grabbed her arm as he climbed in beside her and she burst out laughing. If anything his hair was covered with even more blue and pink paper petals than hers.

'Happy, Mrs Tanner?' Steve fingered the gold band he had slipped above her diamond engagement ring.

'Blissfully, Mr Tanner. You?'

'Happier than any man has a right to be.' He bent his head to hers and kissed her. 'I believe the fairytale term is "and they lived happily ever after". And this is the fairy tale come true.'

'Take Christopher and go on ahead in the car with Annie and Lucille, love,' Harry Hewitt said to Concepta, as Elsie and Steve drove off to the accompaniment of the combined cheers of their guests. 'I'll travel back to the Rovers with Len in his van.'

'You sure, love?' Concepta asked.

'I know what the inside of Len's van will be like, and it wouldn't be fair to ask any of you women to sit in it wearing your glad-rags.' Harry saw his wife off in the hired car and walked to Len's van, which he'd parked at a suitably discreet distance from the Methodist Church whose minister had agreed to marry Elsie although she was a divorcee. The van looked like what it was: the runabout of a jobbing builder who wasn't too particular about maintaining his vehicle.

'You could have cleaned it for the wedding,' Harry grumbled, clearing the mess of crumpled cigarette packets and sweet papers from the passenger seat and pushing them into the glove compartment.

'You sound like my ex-wife. What's the point, when it will only get in the same state again next week?' Len sat behind the wheel and started the engine. They had only driven a few yards when he noticed the van veering oddly.

'You got a flat tyre?' Harry asked.

'Not that I noticed when I got in, but it would just be my bloody luck when we're both wearing our best suits.' Len pulled in to the side of the road. He left the van and inspected the front. 'It's not the tyre but something's not right. The wheel's at an odd angle.'

Harry climbed out of the passenger seat and examined the nearside front wheel. 'If you've got a jack I'll take a look at it.'

'We might be better off leaving it and looking for a taxi.' Len glanced around the deserted street. There wasn't even a telephone box in sight.

'And of course there's going to be dozens of those passing here at this time of day,' Harry commented caustically.

Len opened the boot, lifted out the jack and fixed it into the jacking point. 'How do you like life in Ireland?'

'It's just what Concepta said it would be, lots of fresh air and good farm food. Her family are great, the business is doing fine and Christopher's thriving. No more chesty coughs and he's started school.'

'But?' Len pressed, as he fitted the handle into the jack and began to turn it.

'But it's not where I grew up,' Harry said softly.

'That bad?' Len lifted his eyebrows.

'I never said it was bad. Just different.'

'So you've given up your roots because Concepta wanted to go back to hers. You won't catch me giving up my life for a woman.'

'You've jacked the car up high enough,' Harry broke in testily, resenting Len's implication that he was henpecked. 'I'll take a look.' He peered under the van, then stuck his head close to the inside of the wheel. 'Lift it an inch higher, Len.'

Len turned the handle on the jack. He heard the groan of straining metal and the car shuddered.

'Harry! Get out!'

The jack wavered – then collapsed with an almighty crash.

'Harry!' Len ran to the front of the van. 'Harry!' He strained to lift the van, but failed to shift it an inch. The street was still deserted. He ran as fast as his legs would carry him to the nearest house.

'Where on earth could Harry have got to?' Concepta asked, as she took a sausage roll from the plate Annie offered her.

'He'll be along in his own good time. You know what men are like. He and Len probably stopped off for a pint on the way,' Annie replied. Four large sherries on an empty stomach had relaxed her to the point where she felt inordinately pleased with herself and the world in general. She offered the sausage rolls to Gregg, with a coy smile. 'Tell me, Gregg – I may call you Gregg?'

'You sure may, Annie.'

To Jack Walker's annoyance the American had slipped an arm around his wife's waist. 'Annie's well away,' he complained to Ken as he pulled pints for him and his brother.

'She's just enjoying herself.'

'Mark my words, her next move will be embarrassing

and not just for her – for those who have to watch it as well.'

Lucille joined them. 'Do you think Uncle Len's van could have broken down? He and Dad seem to be taking for ever to get here.'

'Here they are now.' Ken jerked his head at the door, where Len stood, looking round the room, a policeman behind him. Lucille ran towards him.

Len gripped her shoulders. 'Where are Concepta and Christopher, love?'

'They were talking to Annie at the bar . . .' Lucille glanced from Len to the constable. 'Where's my dad?'

Len's face creased in pain.

'Something's happened to him, hasn't it?' Her voice rose.

'I need to talk to Concepta, love.'

Lucille's eyes widened as the worst scenario she could think of filled her mind. 'He's dead, isn't he?'

Len hugged her to him and beckoned to the Barlow brothers. 'Ken, David, find Concepta and Christopher and take them to the snug, please, quickly, before Elsie and Steve leave. I'll bring Lucille.'

'Harry?' Ken mouthed in shock.

Len nodded assent.

Linda, Annie, Valerie, Hilda and the other women in the street were shouting good wishes and showering Elsie and Steve with confetti when Ken closed the door to the snug. He heard Concepta's animal cry of pain as Steve led Elsie out of the pub on the first leg of the journey that was take them on their honeymoon.

Chapter Seventeen

David Barlow opened the door of the shop as quietly as he could, slipped off his shoes and tiptoed into the back storeroom. He hid the holdall he was carrying behind a box of tinned beans. When he heard Irma call downstairs he knew he hadn't been as quiet as he'd hoped.

'David?'

'Be up in a minute, love.' He locked the door, hung his coat on the rack, set his shoes beneath it and ran up the stairs. Irma was sitting on the sofa, flicking through a magazine.

'Did you enjoy your drink with Ken?'

Something in her voice set alarm bells ringing. 'No, love, because I didn't go for a drink with him.'

'I know. I saw Val this morning. She happened to mention that Ken's been busy every Wednesday for the last two months holding rehearsals for the college play he's directing.'

'I didn't want to lie to you—'

'Then why did you?' she demanded. 'I suppose you've another woman hidden away somewhere.'

'It's nothing like that,' he assured her.

'Is it too much to ask where you've been?'

He realised she was hurt as well as furious. 'I've been playing football again. And after the way I behaved when I was injured I thought you'd be angry.'

He'd expected her to fly off the handle and start throwing things, but she set down her magazine and looked intently at him. 'The doctor told you that you'd never play again.'

'He was wrong, love. I realised a couple of months ago that the pain had gone. I went to the doctor's, he checked out my knee and sent me to the hospital for another X-ray. No one knows why or how, but apparently it's healed itself.'

'So you thought you'd start playing again?'

'Football was my life, love.'

'I know. And there's no need to look at me like that. I might feel like killing you, but I won't. Not this time, any road. But I am bloody furious with you for telling me a pack of lies about your Wednesday nights out.'

'I'm sorry, love, but I thought you'd stop me going.' He sat down beside her.

'I might have tried. But I'm pleased for you.' She moved closer to him then hesitated. 'You're not thinking of going back to play professionally?'

'Yes,' he replied baldly. 'Do you mind?'

'Not if the money's good and we keep the shop. I'll have to get someone in to help . . . What's up?' she asked, as he moved back to his chair.

'We'd have to give up the shop, love.'

'Why? It brings in good money.'

'A letter offering me a contract with a football team came this morning.'

'And you didn't even tell me that you'd applied for the job!'

He sensed her temper rising but now that he had gone this far he wanted to get everything out in the open between them. 'I needed time to think out the offer myself, love. I needed to be absolutely sure that it was what I wanted to do. And then I had to get the job. I told you, I only heard this morning.'

'You're going to take it?'

'Yes,' he answered decisively.

'And if you have another accident like last time? I warn you now, David, I couldn't take that all over again – the self-pity, the drinking . . .'

'I promise you it won't happen again, love. If I'm unlucky enough to have another accident I'll be better prepared for it. And after running one shop we could always buy another. A bigger one, because I'd be earning good money. Enough for us to set aside a good sum every week.'

'Looks like you've thought everything out.' There was a hint of resentment in her voice.

'I have, love.' He ignored her bitterness. 'And taking the contract does mean that we'd have to move away from here. But you agreed, football is my life. It's the only thing I've ever been good at.'

'I wish we didn't have to sell the shop.'

'We'll get enough to give ourselves a new start and buy a nice house.'

'There's no guarantee I'd find another job quickly,' she warned.

'Perhaps you wouldn't have to. We could start trying for a baby again. You did say you wanted to,' he added, when her eyes grew suspiciously damp.

'I know.' She fought back her tears. 'But suppose I lost that one too?'

'Nothing will happen next time, love. It won't. I promise you.' He moved close to her and put his arms round her.

'You can't be sure.'

'It's your decision, love.'

She looked up at him. 'It wouldn't hurt to try. Anyway, even if we do move away I can come back here any time I want to visit Mam and Dad, can't I?'

'No, love.' David braced himself. 'The job is in Australia.'

*

On Saturday afternoon Dickie Flemming walked along Coronation Street and stopped outside number nine. The front door was nicely painted and in first-rate condition, as were the windows. His heart sank. He had a feeling that the inside of the house was going to be in the same excellent condition as the outside and that meant the asking price would be more than his savings. Nevertheless, he knocked at the door. Ken Barlow opened it.

'I saw your advert in the paper and I've come about the house. My name is Dickie Flemming.' He held out his hand.

Ken shook it, taken aback by the boy's youthful appearance. He looked as though he should be kicking a ball in the street, not buying a house. 'Would you like to see round it now?'

'Yes, please, if it's convenient.'

'Come in, I'm Ken Barlow.' Fortunately Valerie had tidied the house before she had taken the children to the park. Ken didn't attempt to sell it to Dickie, he just showed him round. When they finished he took the boy back to the living room.

'Would you like a cup of tea?'

'Yes, please, Mr Barlow.'

'Sit down, make yourself at home.' Ken went into the scullery and returned a few minutes later with a tray of tea and biscuits.

Dickie was sitting on the edge of the sofa looking uncomfortable. 'There wasn't a price in the paper, Mr Barlow,' Dickie said tentatively, when Ken handed him his cup.

'No, there wasn't, but now you've seen the place for yourself, you'll understand that I can't let it go for less than a thousand pounds.'

'I'm sorry, Mr Barlow, I've wasted your time. I agree it's a fair price but way out of my league.'

'How much can you afford?'

'Only five hundred, Mr Barlow. That's all my savings. I'm halfway through my engineering apprenticeship and no building society will give me a mortgage. My girlfriend . . . We're getting married soon,' he explained quickly, in case he gave Ken the wrong impression, 'and she works but we'll be hard put to meet all the household bills. What I'm looking for is a cheaper house, one that needs a bit doing to it.'

'If that's what you're after, my father's house might suit you at number three.' Ken flicked through his keys. 'It's been empty for the last four years, and it's in need of some love, care and decoration, but it's basically sound. The asking price is four hundred pounds.'

Dickie beamed. 'I could afford that, Mr Barlow.'

'Would you like to look it over when we've had our tea?'

Dickie set down his cup. 'Can we go right away, please, Mr Barlow?'

★

Ken was saying goodbye to Dickie Flemming when Len Fairclough pulled up in his van. 'Can I have a word, Ken?'

'Now?'

'You're not busy, are you?' Len climbed out of the driving seat.

'No – want to come in for a cup of tea?'

'It might be better to talk inside than on the street.' Len gave Ena Sharples a hard look as she watched them from the doorstep of the Mission Hall. 'You heard that Jerry and me got the contract to build the maisonettes that are going up on the Mission Hall site?'

'I hadn't, but congratulations,' Ken said, glad to see the work going to a local man.

'I need a bigger yard and an office. Now that Emily Nugent's come back after looking after her father – not Majorca, poor thing – I've taken her on as my secretary. So, to cut a long story short, given the state of my house in Mawdsley Street I thought I'd pull it down, extend the yard, build an office there and buy another house. A thousand for this seems fair.'

'It's my asking price,' Ken agreed.

'We'll call it a done deal, then.' Len offered Ken his hand.

Ken shook it, feeling that he'd never had such a profitable afternoon.

★

Hilda Ogden crossed her arms and leant against the scullery door. She was livid with her husband, Stan, but she also knew how stubborn he could be when he was in one of his moods. She'd never succeed in talking him round to her way of thinking about Irma and David emigrating – not now that he'd lost his temper. But that didn't stop her from trying.

'I can't see why we can't go to Australia with our Irma and David,' she said peevishly. 'It will be a new start for all of us.'

'You and me are way too old for a new start. And there's no way I'm leaving Weatherfield. I was born here, I grew up here, I'll die here and be buried here.' Stan slammed his fist on the table, sending it rocking.

'But she'll be far away from us. Right on the other side of the world. I'll miss her.' Hilda whined.

'You can write to her, can't you?'

'And we can visit them?' Hilda suggested hopefully.

'Last time I looked they weren't taking buttons instead of money to pay ship's passage that far.' Stan's attempt at a joke infuriated Hilda all the more and he knew it. 'If she wants to see us, she can visit us,' he said flatly.

'But I told her we'd go with her.'

'You'll just have to tell her different the next time you see her, won't you?' he shouted. At that moment the front door opened and Irma walked in with David.

'Your father won't go to Australia.' Hilda tossed her head and turned her back on Stan.

'We came to give you some good news,' David began, 'but if it's not the right time perhaps we should come back another time.'

'You've changed your minds about going to Australia,' Stan asked hopefully.

David shook his head. 'The shop's been sold. The new people, the Cleggs, will be moving in there when we leave in a fortnight. You'll like them, Hilda.'

'Not as much as I like my own daughter,' Hilda said acidly, 'But I suppose I should congratulate you on the sale,' she conceded.

'You should congratulate us on something else too, Mam.' Irma beamed. 'I'm pregnant.'

The time between David and Irma selling their shop and sailing to Australia passed in a whirlwind of parties and activities, not just for them but also Ken and Valerie. And it wasn't until a month after they'd left that Ken really began to miss not only his brother but, to his surprise, Irma as well. He hadn't realised just how much his sister-in-law's lively common sense and humour had lifted the atmosphere of family meals and parties until she was no longer there.

'I never thought I'd miss our kid and Irma so much.' Ken admitted to Valerie as he fastened his shirt collar and pushed up his tie.

'I miss them too.' Valerie cleared the dishes from the table on to a tray. 'But one thing I don't miss is the old house. This maisonette is much easier to keep clean.'

'And so much more peaceful since you persuaded Ena Sharples to restrict her prayer meetings and harmonium playing to two hours in the morning and from six till eight in the evening.' He checked the clock as the strains of 'Jesus Wants Me For A Sunbeam' wafted from next door. Ena had ten minutes left to Val's curfew and she was making the most of them.

'She's not as bad as I thought she'd be,' Valerie took the tray into the kitchen. 'She even offered to babysit the twins if we wanted an evening out.'

'We should take her up on that – go to the pictures and have a meal in town next week, perhaps?' he asked.

'I'd like that. Any day in particular?' She knew that if she left it open, Ken would forget all about it as soon as he stepped out of the door.

'Friday would be good. Do you have anything planned for this evening?'

'There's a pile of mending in the basket and a play on the radio I'm looking forward to listening to.'

'Not television?'

'Doesn't go with mending.'

'Right.' He picked up his jacket and his keys. 'The college's production of *The Country Wife* will be staged two weeks tonight, but if the cast don't do any better than they did last week, it won't be worth seeing. None of them knew their lines. 'Bye, love.' He kissed Val's cheek.

When she had finished washing the dishes and putting them away, Valerie brought out the mending basket and tuned the radio to the play. She'd just started stitching up the hem on Ken's trousers when she heard a noise in the kitchen. She set down her sewing and walked in to check if anything was wrong. A strange man holding a carving knife blocked her path. She started to scream, but he clasped his hand over her mouth, gagging her, then dragged her back into the living room.

'One word and you're a goner.' He threw her on to a chair and stood facing her. 'Is anyone else in the house with you? The truth.' He lifted the knife to her throat.

'Only my children, they're upstairs sleeping. Please don't hurt them,' she begged in a whisper, praying the twins wouldn't wake.

'Go into the kitchen, make me something to eat and I might not hurt them – or you. Any tricks, and . . .' He ran his fingers along the blade.

Too terrified to move, Valerie continued to stare at him.

'Kitchen, woman.' Trembling with fear, she stood up and backed towards the kitchen door.

Ken Barlow into Coronation Street and saw half a dozen police cars parked outside the maisonettes.

'You can't park here,' a policeman informed him officiously as he pulled up and jumped out.

'I live there.' Ken pointed at his maisonette.

'You'd be Mr Barlow, then.'

'Yes – what's going on?'

The policeman moved away to talk to a superior officer, and Len Fairclough walked up with his new lodger Ray Langton, who worked with Len and Jerry in the building business. 'Len, what's going on?' Ken appealed urgently.

'Ena called the police half an hour ago—'

'Mr Barlow.' An inspector drew Ken aside. 'It appears that your wife is being held hostage by an escaped prisoner in your maisonette.'

'Hostage!' Ken stared at the policeman in horror.

Ena joined them. 'I heard your Val tapping out SOS on the heating pipes, so I called the police.'

'Is she all right?' Ken's blood ran cold at the thought of what the man might be doing to her.

'She must have been all right to bang on the pipes,' Ena said reassuringly.

'I've got to go to her.'

'That's the last thing you can do, sir. You'd get in the way of our operation.'

'Damn your operation! That's my wife in there!' Ken roared.

'All the more reason for you to stand back, sir.' The

inspector nodded to two constables, who moved in and grasped Ken's arms.

'Val!' Ken screamed, at the top of his voice. He watched two police officers batter down the door of his maisonette. As soon as it shattered open, four officers rushed inside. For the longest five minutes of his life Ken stood and watched in silence. Finally, three policemen emerged, dragging a man between them. Another came out a few moments later, holding Valerie who was sobbing.

'Please, let me go to her,' Ken pleaded. The police officers relaxed their grip on him and he rushed across to take Valerie in his arms.

'She's a bit shocked but she'll be OK,' the police officer said gently.

'Did he . . . ?' Ken could hardly bring himself to ask the question uppermost in his mind. 'Did he . . . ?'

'I didn't lay a finger on her,' the prisoner yelled, as the police fought to push him into the back of a police van. 'You tell them, missus,' he bawled at Valerie. 'I didn't lay a finger on you.'

Ken looked at Valerie. 'He didn't touch me,' she sobbed. 'But he had a knife . . .'

Ken held her close. He had been a pacifist all his life but for the first time he felt an uncontrollable rage that he sensed could lead to violence – even murder – if he were left alone with the man who had threatened his wife with a knife. As he stroked the back of Valerie's head he wondered how a pacifist should react when his own family was threatened.

'I think your wife should go to the hospital, sir,' the inspector suggested. 'She's in shock and it might be as well she's checked over. We'll take her in the patrol car.'

'You go with her, Ken,' Ena said. 'I'll sit with the twins, and make sure the police do a reasonable job of securing your door for the night.'

Ken didn't argue. He took off his coat, slipped it over Valerie's shoulders and followed the police officer to the patrol car.

Elsie thanked the taxi-driver for carrying her suitcases to her door, paid him and stared at her front door. It seemed odd to knock on it, but she had left her keys with Dennis, assuming that she would never need them again. She rapped hard. A pretty girl opened it.

'Can I help you?' she sang out cheerfully.

'I'll say you can,' Elsie retorted. 'You can start by telling me just who you are and what you're doing in my house.' She heaved the first of her cases through the door.

'I'm Jenny, Dennis's girlfriend.'

Elsie looked her up and down. 'And where is his lordship?'

Dennis appeared in the living-room doorway. 'Mam, you're back!' he exclaimed, in astonishment.

'I see your intelligence hasn't improved.' Elsie dumped the last of her bags at the foot of the stairs.

'That's a lot of luggage for a holiday,' Dennis remarked.

'It is,' Elsie agreed.

'Steve with you?'

'No. How long has she,' Elsie jerked her head towards Jenny, 'been living here?'

'A couple of days. Is Steve coming?'

'I hope not. Six months of him was as much as I could take. I hope Miss Girlfriend's got her own room.' Elsie saw by the look on Dennis's face that Jenny hadn't. 'Right. Now I'm home, she sleeps in the spare room and you sleep in yours. Understood?'

'You bloody hypocrite!' Dennis gasped.

'This is my house. You don't like the way I run things, you can move out. Well, come on, make yourself useful. Carry my cases up to my room.'

Dennis picked up the largest suitcase. He gestured for Jenny to follow him and led the way upstairs. 'She's in one of her moods,' he whispered, when they were both on the landing. 'Best do as she says, and move your things into the spare room. It will only be for tonight.'

'You *are* going to tell her . . .'

'Bad mood or not, that's one thing I *am* going to do. Right now.' Leaving Jenny to ferry her things out of his room he ran back down the stairs and went into the living room. Elsie was sitting in her easy-chair, smoking a cigarette.

'You didn't give Jenny or me a chance to tell you that we're getting married in the register office tomorrow. Our Linda and Ivan are our witnesses and you'll be welcome too, if you want to come.'

'Married? When did all this happen? You didn't even know the girl when I went to America.'

'We've been working together for four months. I wrote to you last week.'

'I wouldn't have got it.'

'I asked you what you wanted done with the house. Jenny and me are moving to Bristol. The hotel we're working in is one of a chain and they're opening up a new place.'

'Dennis, don't you think this is all a bit sudden—?'

'No, Mam,' he interrupted firmly. 'I love Jenny and she loves me.'

Elsie thought of her shattered marriage, begun with so much promise and ending in a welter of arguments. Why hadn't she realised that she'd be a fish out of water in Steve's world and her working-class ways would embarrass not only his friends – but him? Then she remembered the beginning of the marriage Steve had told her would have a fairy tale ending. 'Happily ever after.'

If Dennis and Jenny felt as strongly about each other as she and Steve had felt about one another on their wedding day, who was she to spoil it for them?

'In that case, all that's left for me to say is what do you want as a wedding present?'

'I saw your Dennis and the love of his life down Rovers,' Len said, as Elsie showed him into her living room. 'He said you'd come back for a visit. Good timing, arriving the day before his wedding.'

Elsie offered Len a cigarette. 'It's not a holiday, Len. I'm back for good.'

'It didn't work out between you and Steve, then?' He flicked his lighter and lit both their cigarettes.

'No.'

'You didn't like America?' Len probed.

'America was fine. It was Steve. I didn't fit into his world, no more than he fitted into Coronation Street. We gave it a go, but it was hopeless from the start,' she said briskly, trying to put a brave face on it.

But Len knew her too well. 'It must have broken your heart to leave him.'

'Love isn't enough when you have nothing else in common,' she murmured slowly, as if she hadn't heard him.

'I'm sorry, love.'

'Yes, well.' She gave him a forced smile. 'I'm back for good. How about taking a separated woman down Rovers for a drink?'

'I thought you'd never ask. Go and get your coat.'

'Thanks, Len.'

'For the drink? I haven't bought it yet, woman,' he joked.

'For being a bloody good friend and always there when I need someone.'

'As long as there's breath in my body I'll always be there for you, love.'

Chapter Eighteen

'If you're after Elsie Tanner she won't be home from work for another half-hour,' Len Fairclough's lodger, Ray Langton, informed the stranger knocking at the door of number eleven. The plumbing job Len had sent him on had gone quicker than he had anticipated and he'd arrived home an hour earlier than usual.

'Elsie's working?' Gregg Flint asked.

'In the florist's round the corner in Rosamund Street.' Ray pointed Gregg in the right direction. 'The Pink Posy Bowl.' He knew Len had been none too pleased when Elsie had started working for bookie Dave Smith who owned the shop. Len regarded Dave as a rival for Elsie now that she was separated from her husband, although Elsie had shown little inclination to go out with either of them

'Thanks. I'll catch up with her there.' Gregg walked round the corner and waited while Elsie wrapped a bunch of carnations for a young girl. When the shop was empty, he crossed the road and went inside.

'Hello, Elsie.'

'You here to buy flowers?' Elsie snapped.

'What's on offer?' He risked a smile.

'What you see.' She waved her hand indicating the aluminium buckets filled with carnations, irises, tulips and forced hot-house roses.

'What do you recommend?'

'That depends on who you're buying for,' she replied warily.

'Let's say a lady with good taste who's difficult to please.'

'Roses always go down well – mind, they're the most expensive flowers in the shop,' she warned.

'Roses it is.' He glanced at the array in the buckets. 'I'll take a dozen red.'

'That'll cost you a pound.'

'You know how to charge.' Gregg pulled a roll of banknotes from his pocket and peeled off a pound note.

'My boss does.' Elsie lifted the bucket of long-stemmed red roses on to the counter and spread out a sheet of paper.

'Can I talk to you?'

'You are,' Elsie reminded him dryly, choosing a perfect rosebud and setting it diagonally on the paper.

'Steve is missing you.'

'Then he should have taken more notice of me when I was around.' She picked out another two blooms.

'He was devastated when you left. He's hoping to persuade you to come back and give your marriage a second chance.'

'Then why didn't he come to see me himself?' Elsie wondered aloud.

'He's here.'

'In Weatherfield!' Elsie accidentally snapped the head off a rose. She dropped it and the stem into the waste-bin behind her.

'He wasn't sure you'd talk to him if he turned up and knocked on your door. But he's staying in the same hotel as before. He'd like to see you, Elsie. All you have to do is name the time and place,' he added persuasively.

'I'll think about it. I won't say any more than that,' she muttered, taken aback that Steve had followed her to Britain.

'I'll tell him you'll be getting in touch with him, then.'

'You can tell him what you like, Gregg. I said I'll think about it, and I will.' She handed him the bunch of roses.

'They're for you.' Before she could protest, he had left the shop.

Elsie thought about Steve when she cleared the shop and closed it for the night. She continued to think about him as she walked round the corner, along Coronation Street and into her house. When she sat down with a cup of tea and her first cigarette of the evening she realised that she been thinking about nothing and no one else but Steve ever since she had boarded the plane in America and there was no point in continuing to think about him. It was staring her in the face. After what had happened – or, more accurately, not happened – between them in the States, she wanted a divorce. There was absolutely no point in remaining married to a man who was ashamed of her and her ways and who felt he had to apologise for marrying her to his toffee-nosed friends. And then there had been their last few vicious fights . . .

She crushed her cigarette in an ashtray, slipped on her coat and walked down to the Rovers. She asked Jack if she could use the telephone and booked a taxi to pick her up from her house and take her to Steve's hotel.

'Drink, Elsie?' Len asked, as she walked back through the bar.

'Thanks for offering, love. but I haven't time.'

'Going somewhere nice?' he fished.

'To talk to Steve.'

'You're going back to America?'

Elsie gave a caustic laugh. 'He's in Weatherfield, staying in the same hotel as last time he was here.'

'Then it's back on between you two.' Len's face fell and Elsie realised that he had never quite relinquished the torch he'd carried for her.

'I'm going to ask him for a divorce. See you later, Len.

Thanks, Jack.' Her high heels rang out on the flagstones as she left the pub.

Elsie's hand shook as she lit the second cigarette since the taxi had picked her up. The decision to see Steve had been difficult enough, but now that barely half a mile separated them her mind was a blank. It had seemed so simple when she had telephoned the taxi company from the Rovers. She would see Steve and ask him for a divorce. But now that she was within minutes of that reunion she doubted that she could find the courage to knock on his door and say, 'Hello, Steve, I want a divorce.' And if she did, what would his reaction be?

The radio in the front of the cab crackled noisily and a woman's voice echoed over the speaker. Elsie caught the words 'Mr Fairclough . . . nine Coronation Street . . . to be taken to . . .'

She froze, furious with herself for telling Len that she was going to see Steve and mentioning the hotel. There were times when Len carried friendship too far. Afraid the situation might become unbearable – or even violent, if both she and Len confronted Steve – she tapped the driver's shoulder.

'I've changed my mind. Return to Coronation Street, please.'

'You sure, missus?'

'I'm sure.'

★

The following morning Elsie was arranging a mixed bouquet when a policeman walked into the shop. There had been a time when Dennis was at home when she had dreaded a police officer approaching her. But not any more. Dennis and Jenny were doing well in Bristol and she had high hopes that her son had finally settled down.

'Can I help you, Officer?' she asked.

'Mrs Elsie Tanner?'

'That's me.'

'I'm afraid I have some bad news for you, Mrs Tanner. There's no easy way to say this. Your husband has been found dead.'

Stunned, she sank down on to the stool behind her. 'Dead?' she repeated numbly. 'Are you sure?'

'Mr Steve Tanner.'

She nodded bleakly. 'How . . . when . . . ?'

'He was staying in a hotel. The staff found him at the foot of a staircase last night. We're not sure how he died yet but there will be a post-mortem. We'll find out more then.'

The weeks following Steve's death passed in a nightmare kaleidoscope of surreal images and bizarre events for Elsie. The police turned up on her doorstep at all hours of the day and evening to question her and they continued to do so even after they had checked her alibi with the taxi firm.

Both she and Len felt themselves to be under suspicion, especially after they were forced to confirm that they had been close friends for years.

Len was hauled unceremoniously down to the station whenever it suited the police. And every time he told the same story. That he had taken a taxi to the hotel, confronted Steve and tackled him about the way he had treated Elsie in America. He freely admitted that he had visited Steve to thump him but maintained that he had hit the wall instead. The bruises on his knuckles and blood on the wall of Steve's room bore out his version of events but that hadn't stopped the police forcing him to take part in an identity parade.

It wasn't until the coroner's court returned an open verdict that Elsie felt herself free and exonerated. She buried Steve, found the courage to face his mother and his friends, and returned to Coronation Street to pick up the threads of her life. But it wasn't easy, especially after Dave Smith closed the Pink Posy Bowl and she found herself out of a job.

'I'm sorry, Elsie,' Dave apologised, when he called to give her her cards along with her severance pay, 'but the Posy Bowl was losing money hand over fist. It was one drain too many on the bookie's. But there is a silver lining.'

'I wish I could see it from where I'm standing,' she muttered, counting the notes he'd given her.

'I've sold the shop to Alan Howard.'

'Who?'

'Alan Howard, big businessman round here.'

'So big I've never heard of him,' Elsie snapped.

'He's refitting the shop as a hair salon. Taken on a friend of yours, Valerie Barlow, as head stylist.'

'And that's supposed to make me jump for joy?'

'You don't give a fellow a chance to get a word in edge-wise. I put in a good word for you and he's prepared to offer you the job of manageress. He'll pay you ten bob a week more than I did, and there's commission.' He eyed her as she handed him a cup of tea. 'If you're interested, here's the address of his office. He said you can call round any time between ten and twelve in the morning.'

Elsie took the card Dave handed her and turned it over.

'You'll like Alan, Elsie. He's your type.'

'Oh, aye, and what *is* my type?' she enquired acidly.

'Flash and good-looking with money to burn.' He laughed.

'Handel Gartside. Now there's a name from the past. What does 'e want?' Ena placed two fresh bottles of milk stout on the table and joined Minnie in the snug at the Rovers. She was suspicious of people, especially when it came to Minnie. Her friend had always been vague and out of touch. If she was getting herself embroiled in some-thing, Ena needed to know the details as she would inevitably be the one to sort things out.

'He says he's still got feelings for me.' Minnie's voice had acquired a slower, even more dreamlike quality than usual.

'Rubbish!' Ena spluttered. 'He's after something, you mark my words.' She brushed off her mac and wagged a finger. 'Minnie Caldwell, you should be ashamed of yourself. A woman of your age.'

'He turned up one evening without warning. He said he'd always had a crush on me and asked if he could see me again.'

Ena folded her arms across her chest. 'I wouldn't give him houseroom. Cheeky monkey. It must be thirty years since 'e lived in the street. What's he sniffing round here for anyway?'

'Like I said, Ena, he came 'specially to see me.'

'A likely story,' Ena sneered.

'He said he wants to take me to tea. To a fancy restaurant.'

Ena sipped her stout. The last thing she wanted was for her friend to be taken in by Handel Gartside and possibly let down. But she couldn't suppress the selfish thought that if Minnie went off with Handel she would lose her companionship.

'So, where's this fancy place he wants to take you?'

'It's in town, Ena. You can come too.'

'Me?'

'Yes, Ena. Handel and I would be very pleased if you would join us.'

Ena finished her stout and set her empty glass on the table. 'D'you want another or what?'

'No, thank you, Ena. I'm fine.'

'Please yourself.'

Minnie lifted her glass to her lips and took a ladylike sip. 'It's thirty-*three* years since Handel was in the street, Ena.'

'The smell of hair lacquer always takes me back to the time I did my apprenticeship.' Valerie Barlow breathed in the scent as she and Elsie set up the salon in readiness for the day's trade. 'And it reminds me of the Saturday nights before I met Ken when I used to go dancing at the Palais.'

'Ancient history.' Elsie smiled.

'Feels like it.'

'You say some daft things.' Elsie was in no mood for Val's reminiscences. The diary was full and their first customer was expected any minute. 'Now, turn the sign round to "Open" and stack the dry towels.'

As head stylist Val resented being ordered about by Elsie, but she didn't want to start the day on a sour note and she could see that Elsie had something on her mind. In fact Elsie had been in a mood since the salon had opened, which was hardly surprising considering what she had been through over the last couple of months.

Elsie busied herself in the stock cupboard. Anything to take her mind off Alan Howard. The last couple of weeks, he had taken to calling in at the salon to check on his new investment. It was understandable from a business point of view but, suspecting that he had an ulterior motive, she had told him more than once that his presence flustered the staff, which wasn't good for custom.

'I wonder if Alan will put in an appearance today.' Val set out plastic bottles of spray on the shiny black console.

'Let's hope he finds something better to do.' Elsie checked the diary.

'It must be lovely to have all that money, not have to worry about a thing.'

'I can't disagree with you there, love.' Elsie left the desk and pulled armfuls of pink nylon capes from the cupboard. Since Steve had died and left her an inheritance she wasn't badly off, so she had little interest in Alan's money. But he was good-looking. Too good-looking – she had been attracted to him from the first time they'd met, but emphatically denied it to everyone, including herself. It was obvious he had the same effect on the other girls at the salon, but it was always her eyes he looked into and her arm he brushed against.

Mid-morning brought an unexpected and welcome lull. Only two customers were under the dryers, both engrossed in the serials in *Woman's Own* and the *People's Friend*. Elsie sank down on to one of the low, vinyl uphol-stered chairs in the waiting area and slipped off her shoes. She was rubbing her ankles when Alan popped his head round the door. 'Morning, ladies.' He scanned the salon, then closed the door and sat down beside Elsie.

Elsie jumped up, put on her shoes, straightened her dress and stood behind the half-moon desk.

Alan patted the seat beside him. 'I'm not here with a whip. Take the weight off.'

'There's work needs doing.' Elsie rubbed out an entry in the diary and blew the bits in his direction.

Valerie appeared with a tray of tea. 'Sorry, Alan, I didn't hear you come in. Fancy a cuppa?'

'No, thanks, just wanted to go through a few things with Elsie here.' He turned to Elsie. 'So, how are the bookings coming along?'

'See for yourself.' She handed him the diary.

'I'm racing on Saturday and it's a sad driver who hasn't a girlfriend to cheer him on at the finish. If I win, we'll have our picture in paper. The winner with his girl in one hand and a bottle of champagne in the other. How about it?' He gave her his most charming smile. 'You, me and the winner's cup.'

'You're my boss and I'm not your girlfriend.'

'But you could be.' Alan leant on the desk and gazed up at her.

'I'm busy,' Elsie lied.

Annie Walker stood in the bar but her mind was obviously miles away. The new barmaid, Betty Turpin, who had recently moved into the corner shop with her sister Maggie Clegg, suspected it was in the cemetery where Annie had buried her husband Jack the week before. His death had come as a shock to all the regulars. He'd had a heart attack while visiting his daughter in Derby. And poor Annie had been left to organise a funeral for a husband who had never had a day's illness in his life.

Annie's increasingly frequent periods of remoteness made it difficult for the staff to run the Rovers. The bar was full and the barmaids were hard pushed to serve the queues of impatient customers, but Betty knew there was no point in asking Annie to help. Since Annie's daughter had broken the news of Jack's death over the telephone, Annie had taken to neglecting the bar and staring into space at the most inopportune moments.

'Excuse me, Mrs Walker, we've run out of salt and vinegar crisps. Shall I fetch some more?' Betty tapped Annie's shoulder.

'Pardon, dear?' Annie enquired distantly.

'Crisps. salt and vinegar. We've run out, shall I get some more?'

'Yes, dear.'

Betty fetched a new box from the back storeroom, and bumped into Emily Nugent who'd returned to the street and taken up lodgings in the Rovers as a stopgap measure that seemed to have become a permanent arrangement. 'Sorry, love,' Betty apologised.

'That's all right, Betty. It's busy tonight.'

'I haven't had time for a fag yet,' Betty complained, as she stacked crisps on the shelf behind her.

Annie snapped out of her reverie. 'Cigarette, dear,' she corrected. 'My Jack agreed with me that abbreviations are unacceptable in commercial premises.'

'What is she on about?' Betty looked at Emily.

'Who's next?' Emily asked tactfully, ignoring Betty. She turned to see Willie Piggott staring at her.

'Watch the birdie.' Willie was hinting at Ernest Bishop's photographic business. Ernest was Emily's latest boyfriend.

'Mr Piggott, what can I get you?' Emily enquired stiffly.

'Pint of mild and a quiet chat.' He leered. 'What time do you get off here?'

'That's none of your business.' If word got back to Ernest that Willie Piggott had been chatting her up Emily would be mortified. She pulled a pint and put the coins Willie gave her into the till.

'I'll be waiting outside at closing time.' He moved to a table in the corner.

'What did he want?' Betty asked, noticing that Emily was upset.

'He was just being silly.' Emily served the next customer, but she couldn't concentrate. She made mistakes with people's change, and Betty reprimanded her more than once for being slow. She glanced at the clock above the bar.

In ten minutes they would close the Rovers and she would have to talk to Willie Piggott. He had threatened to withdraw the lease on her boyfriend Ernest's camera shop if she didn't spy on her employer, Len Fairclough, and pass on confidential details of the price Len was tendering for a council contract to build a student hostel in the town.

The tea rooms Handel Gartside had chosen were at the posh end of the high street, and as Ena and Minnie rode there on the bus, Ena told Minnie – again – that she didn't trust Handel, or like him inviting another gentleman to make up a foursome.

Minnie sat silently, letting Ena drone on. She didn't care what Ena said. She was meeting Handel and, with luck, Ena would hit it off with Handel's friend and would leave her to enjoy her tea with Handel in peace.

'George Mulliner! Of all people!' Ena spotted him sitting with Handel at the table furthest from the door of the tea rooms.

'Shh, they'll hear us, Ena,' Minnie admonished.

'Don't care if they do.' Ena sniffed. But she allowed George to help her off with her coat, and while Handel hung them on a wooden coat-stand, George handed round the menus.

'May I say, Mrs Sharples, that you look a picture of loveliness.' George sounded as if he had been practising his compliment all week.

'I don't need words dripping with honey, George Mulliner, and I'll thank you to remember it,' Ena said dismissively. 'Order me an Eccles cake and a pot of tea. I'm parched!'

'I'll have a Chelsea bun, with a pat of butter, please.' Minnie whispered to Handel.

The waitress, who had a voice to match Ena's, took their order and went to the counter where she asked the staff to make up her order double quick, as one of the ladies at her table was noisy and annoying other customers.

The minute Ena had eaten her cake and drunk her tea she was anxious to leave. She had seen enough of George for one afternoon and hoped that Minnie had seen enough of Handel. 'Ready?' she barked at Minnie.

'Not yet, Ena.' Somehow Minnie found the courage to defy her friend.

'Have another cake and some more tea, Ena,' Handel pressed her.

'Please do,' George coaxed.

It was the last thing Ena wanted, but Minnie appeared impervious to her authority. 'Seems I've no choice,' she muttered ungraciously.

Chapter Nineteen

'An accident! What kind of accident?' Elsie interrupted as Valerie told her the news.

'Alan's car crashed during the race. That's all I know.' Valerie was upset, but Elsie was distraught. 'I only just heard. Ken said someone in the Rovers was at the track and saw it happen. What's going to happen to the salon?'

Elsie ran out of her door without bothering to put on her coat, and charged down to the Rovers. If Alan was dead . . . She tried to put the thought from her mind as she sidestepped a group of children playing pitch and toss, and was just about to enter the Rovers when a man blocked her path.

'Where's the fire, Elsie?' Bill Gregory smiled at her.

'I have to go.' Elsie pushed him aside and disappeared through the smoked-glass doors into the pub.

Bill decided against following her. There would be plenty of time to catch up with Elsie. He pushed his hands into his pockets and strolled down the street, absorbing the familiar scene. A new life beckoned. Now that his wife had died, he planned a fresh start. And he wanted Elsie to be part of it.

Valerie set Ken's breakfast in front of him. 'A man came round the salon yesterday when Elsie was doing the banking. Apparently what Elsie heard in the Rovers is right. Alan is expected to make a full recovery from his injuries, although he's going to be in hospital for a fair few weeks yet. He also mentioned that Alan has decided to sell the salon. Alan's asking four hundred pounds, but he was only going to offer three hundred and fifty, so, if we came up with four hundred I could be my own boss,' Ken knew she was attempting to convince him that buying the salon would be an investment that would secure their future. 'I know four hundred pounds is a lot of money . . .'

'You're telling me it's a lot of money.' Ken would have liked nothing better than to buy the salon for his wife, but four hundred pounds was beyond his means. He left the table. 'I have to go. I'll be late for school. But we'll talk about it later.' He smiled at her. 'All right?'

'Fine.' Valerie returned his smile.

Perhaps they could borrow the money – if they could think of someone flush enough to lend them that much, Ken thought. Before he reached the end of the street he decided to call in on Dave Smith on his way home from work. If anyone had the money, the bookie would – but would he be prepared to lend it?

When Valerie opened the door of the salon she was imagining what she would call the business if it belonged to her.

'You're late,' Elsie complained. 'The phone hasn't stopped since half past eight, and I've had to take in the deliveries.'

Valerie slipped off her coat. If she owned the business she'd be the one to give the orders, and she'd have quiet music playing in the background, not Radio One blaring day in, day out.

'Val? Are you with us?' Elsie snapped.

'Will you be putting in an offer?'

'An offer for what?' Elsie asked as Valerie hung her coat over her handbag in the back room.

'This place. Ken and I are thinking of putting in a bid. I thought I should tell you, seeing as how we're friends.'

The doorbell heralded a customer. It was as much as Elsie could do to make the usual pleasantries. She had had no idea that Alan was selling the place but, then, she hadn't wanted to set the gossips going by visiting him in hospital. Perhaps he would have told her if she'd gone out with him . . . Perhaps he was moving away . . .

'Are you thinking of putting in a bid?' Valerie

repeated, after she had washed and set the hair of their first customer.

'I haven't had time to think about it.' Elsie settled their second customer into a chair and handed her a magazine. The phone rang and she went to answer it.

The more Valerie thought about it, the more she was convinced that she and Ken would find the money somehow. She knew Ken. Although he'd been taken aback by the amount, he liked the idea of her owning the business.

As she walked home she imagined the changes she would make after they had bought it, but she stopped when she saw Ken walking purposefully away from their house towards the bookie's. Surely he couldn't be hoping to win the money they'd need?

'Auntie Annie, I'm joining the Salvation Army.' Lucille Hewitt bounded up to the bar where Annie was arranging cork beer mats around the pumps.

'You're what, dear?' Annie murmured, only half listening.

'I'm joining the Salvation Army!' Lucille repeated.

That time Annie understood her. 'Are sure it's something you want to do?' she asked, concerned that Lucille hadn't thought through the implications of her decision.

'Mrs Sharples says she knows someone in the Army who'll put in a good word for me if I'm serious. But I'd have to prove to them that I can be trusted.' Lucille jumped up on to a bar stool and piled the beer mats into a tower.

'Who needs to be trusted?' Annie's son, Billy, who'd returned home to help out his mother after his father's death, strolled in wearing jeans and a vest. He was a good-looking lad in his mid-twenties, who used his looks with women every chance he got. And although Annie was blind to many of his faults, she wasn't blind to his womanising.

'Put a shirt on, Billy,' she reproved.

'In a minute. Who was saying what, about needing to be trusted?'

'Me, I'm joining the Sally Army. And I'm joining right now. 'Bye.' Lucille jumped off the stool, unlocked the door and left.

Annie gave Billy a worried look.

'I can't see Lucille in the Sally Army,' Billy muttered.

'Who knows? They might teach her a sense of responsibility. And talking of responsibility,' Annie removed the cloths from the pumps, 'as soon as you're dressed you can fill out those forms. The brewery won't wait for ever.'

'I'll look at them after I've washed and changed.' Billy retreated from the bar. He had come home to help his mother, but Annie had assumed that he meant to take over the tenancy of the Rovers. He had yet to find the courage to tell her that he was happy as a mechanic. He was in the process of buying the Canal Street garage, but he'd decided it was best to wait a bit before telling her that bit of news. In a few weeks she would be strong enough to accept his decision not to take on the pub – or so he hoped.

'You're as young as you feel.' Bet Lynch, the new manageress of the laundrette that had opened on Rosamund Street, thrust out her chest, giving Frank Bradley, one of Len's casual labourers on his building site, an eyeful of her best asset.

'So, do I get a feel?' Frank's hand was around Bet's waist in an instant and would have ventured further if Bet hadn't removed it.

'You're a quick worker.' Bet glanced round the bar to check if anyone had seen Frank move in on her. She fancied Frank, but he was only nineteen, almost half her age, and she knew from hints dropped by Len Fairclough and Ray Langton, who employed him, that he had already been in serious trouble. But he was the first man she'd found attractive in years and, as far as she could tell, he appeared to feel the same way about her.

'Another drink?' Frank slurred.

'No, love, I'm fine.' She had to be at work early in the morning. In two short months her life had altered out of all recognition. She'd moved into a flat above the corner shop, taken a new job and here she was on a date with Frank.

'So, what shall we do later?' Frank returned with his drink and, under cover of the table, rested his hand on her knee. 'Your place.'

'You're not backward in coming forward, I'll say that for you, love.' Bet had thought that Frank was set for a night out at a club with his mates and she was flattered that he should suggest they go to her place. 'But why not?'

Frank downed his pint in one. 'Ready when you are.'

'Are you always this fast?'

'No point in hangin' about. Time and tide . . .'

'I get poetry too.' She giggled.

Frank held out his arm. She hesitated for a split second, then took it.

Len Fairclough leant across the bar and whispered into the barmaid's ear. 'Ooh, that tickles,' she complained, pulling at his moustache.

'Do you like it?' Len was fishing for compliments, and this particular barmaid was always full of them.

'I think a moustache makes a man look mature.'

That wasn't what Len wanted to hear. He had grown a moustache in the hope that it made him look younger and he had let his hair grow long for the same reason.

The barmaid moved on to serve the next customer and he was beset by an overwhelming sense of loneliness. He was not short of admirers. Maggie Clegg had made it obvious that she was available. But he needed someone who would make him feel young again. And the barmaid did just that.

'You doing anything Monday night?' he asked, as she walked back up the bar.

'I might be,' she teased.

'Right, that's a date. Give me your address and I'll pick you up outside your place. Seven o'clock all right?'

She reached into her bosom for a pen. 'I'll write down me address for you.'

Hilda was clearing the table after Stan's tea when there was a knock on the front door. Stan answered it.

After a little while, when he hadn't returned, she shouted, 'Stan? Are you going to be there all night?'

Her husband walked in, flanked by two police officers.

'Oh, my God! What have you done now, Stan?' Hilda sank on to a chair before she fell down.

'I'm sorry, Mrs Ogden.' An officer approached her while his colleague helped Stan on to a chair. 'There's been a car accident. In Australia.'

'Irma . . . David . . . little Darren – he's only just four months old . . . It can't be little Darren . . .' She turned a shell-shocked face to the constable.

'Your son-in-law David and grandson Darren were killed outright, Mrs Ogden. Your daughter has been seriously injured. I'm sorry.'

'Darren.' She stared uncomprehendingly at the officer. 'He can't be dead. I haven't even seen him. He can't be dead,' she repeated numbly. 'He can't be.'

Stan heard Hilda's words but he couldn't decipher their meaning. His whole world had fallen apart.

'Portugal? you want me to go to Portugal with you?' Elsie asked Bill Gregory incredulously.

Half of the regulars in the Rovers turned and stared in the direction of their table.

He lowered his voice to a whisper. 'I'm buying a wine-bar there, and I want you to come with me.'

'As what?' Elsie enquired suspiciously.

He looked into her eyes. 'I know this is neither the time nor the place, but will you marry me, Elsie Tanner?'

Elsie was more tempted than she had ever been in her life to say yes to a man. But after Steve she had to be sure that it was the man she was accepting, not the lifestyle he offered. 'Can I think about it?'

'You can have all the time you want until next Friday.' He picked up their glasses.

'Why next Friday?'

'Because I'm leaving for Portugal on Saturday. Meet you here, seven o'clock, Friday night.'

'If it's yes I'll be here,' she promised.

'And if it's no?'

'I think you already know the answer to that.'

Elsie watched Bill go to the bar. Just the word 'Portugal' conjured images of long, sunny days, colourful scenery without a tinge of the grey that drained northern landscapes. And a wine-bar meant a holiday atmosphere every night of the year. It was very, very tempting. And Bill? She looked at him again and realised that she had some hard thinking to do before Friday.

Unable to sleep, Ken tossed and turned in bed. His mother was dead. He was estranged from his father, and now David had gone. He knew he had shocked the neighbours by refusing to fly out to Australia for David's funeral, but David and the tiny nephew he had never seen weren't really in an Australian cemetery. David was instilled in his memory. He would be part of Ken for as long as he lived. Besides, what good would it do to go all that way to stand at a graveside when Valerie and he needed four hundred pounds? Or, rather, *had* needed four hundred pounds, he reminded himself angrily.

His approach to Dave Smith for a loan had backfired. He had alerted Dave to the fact that the salon was on the market, which had prompted the bookie to make an offer for the place himself. Ken had cashed in all of his and Valerie's insurance policies the following day in the hope of outbidding Dave, but it had been useless: the contract had already been signed between him and Alan Howard.

And Valerie – he rested his arm lightly around his wife's waist. She was exhausted by the news of David and Darren's death and the stress of losing a salon that had never been hers. Hearing moaning in the next room, he left the bed and woke Valerie.

'I think Susan is having a nightmare. I'll see to her.' He padded out of the room and into the children's where he saw Susan writhing in agony. 'Val!' he shouted.

Ten minutes later the doctor arrived. Susan's temperature was dangerously high and the pain was even worse.

'It's a stomach bug.' The doctor packed his stethoscope into his bag. 'Give her a couple of aspirins and if she's still like this in the morning bring her along to the surgery.'

'She is only four years old and this is more than a stomach bug!' Ken contradicted furiously. 'Look at her, she is in absolute agony.'

'You're a doctor, Mr Barlow?' the doctor enquired sarcastically.

'Get a blanket, Val,' Ken ordered his wife. 'Wrap Susan in it. I'll ask Albert to sit with Peter then I'll start the car. We're taking Susan to Casualty.' Ignoring the doctor, he left the room, ran into his own bedroom and pulled his trousers over his pyjamas.

Casualty was crowded, but Susan was whisked away from them as soon as they arrived.

'Sit down, love. They'll tell us as soon as they know anything.' Ken led Valerie to a plastic chair.

'I can't.' Valerie paced uneasily, looking at the doors at the far end of the corridor through which they had wheeled Susan. 'Why don't they tell us what's happening? Oh, Ken, if anything happens to her . . .'

'Susan will be fine, love,' he insisted unconvincingly. 'They know what they are doing. Please, sit down.'

Val finally made her way to a plastic seat and sipped the hot sweet tea Ken had fetched from the machine.

Once Valerie settled, Ken's thoughts turned to David. After losing his mother and brother he didn't know what he would do if something happened to his daughter. It was obviously something serious or they would have allowed them to stay with her.

'Mr and Mrs Barlow?'

'Is Susan all right?' Valerie demanded of the absurdly young doctor.

'It's appendicitis. Susan has been taken straight to theatre.'

'Oh, my God! She could die!'

'Calm down, Val, nothing is going to happen to her. She will be OK, won't she?' Close to panic, Ken looked to the doctor for reassurance.

'There is every chance that the operation will go smoothly, Mr Barlow. Thanks to you getting your daughter to us when you did.'

'Then if we hadn't brought her in . . .' Val faltered.

'The delay might have cost you your daughter's life,' the doctor informed them baldly.

By the time Susan was safely out of the theatre, Ken had made a decision. From that moment on, he would put family first. He said this to a tearful Valerie and a drugged, sleepy Susan who barely listened to what he was saying and certainly didn't appreciate the importance of his announcement. But then they didn't know about the sabbatical he had been offered in New York, and now would never tell them about.

'What's all this?' Alan asked, as he stepped into Elsie's hall to see suitcases piled behind the door.

'I'm going to Portugal with Bill tomorrow. He's bought a wine-bar there.' Elsie wished that her heart wasn't turning somersaults at the sight of Alan in her house.

'You can't go, Elsie,' Alan said flatly.

'And why not?'

'Because I love you.'

Silence closed in on them, dense and overpowering.

Elsie stared into Alan's eyes. He seemed as stunned by his admission as she was. 'Bill's offering me a life in the sun in a holiday paradise. It's a chance to get away from here and I'm taking it.'

'I need you.' Alan grasped her shoulders and gazed into her eyes. 'I need you,' he repeated forcefully.

'Do you?' she asked, in wonder.

'How can you doubt it, Elsie?' He kissed her gently on the lips then, as she responded, with urgency and passion. 'I've never been very good with words . . .'

'You don't need them,' she murmured. 'Not now and not any more.'

'Mr Noblett, you are impossible,' Lucille shouted through Arthur Noblett's letterbox as she knocked at his door for the fourth time. She had been allocated Mr Noblett by Mrs Sharples's Salvation Army friend who had decided that he needed looking after. She was supposed to clean for him and generally help out, but he had made it clear that he didn't want anyone fussing around his home, least of all a slip of girl like her.

'Mr Noblett, are you going to let me in or do I call Mrs Sharples?'

Very slowly the front door opened a crack. An old man peered out, straining to focus through dirty, smudged spectacles. 'You can come in on condition you don't touch nowt,' he mumbled, through toothless gums.

Lucille smiled at her triumph. She was finally able to venture into the pensioner's house and do her duty as a possible new Salvation Army recruit. She stepped inside and reeled back at the stench. The wallpaper in the passageway was hanging off the walls, the smell of damp was overpowering. A thin tabby cat scurried past her legs and made its escape as she closed the door behind her. She picked her way through the piles of newspapers, unopened letters and circulars littered across the threadbare runner.

'I don't want anyone fussing me.' Arthur led the way into a back kitchen. It was dark and dingy, an old rag shut out any daylight that might have filtered through the unwashed windowpanes.

Lucille had never seen such squalor. Arthur settled himself into his old chair and folded his arms across his chest.

'So . . .' Lucille tried to think of something to say and came up with, 'Have you got a telly?' She looked around the heavy oak furniture.

'Nah. I did 'ave me radio, but it broke. I'm lost without it.'

'Where is it? Maybe I could have it mended.' Lucille was glad of an excuse to leave. She began searching through the litter of papers and rags that covered every surface and eventually found an old wireless set on top of a table in the corner. The wooden housing was heavy, but she managed to lift it and was trying to carry it out of the room when Arthur stopped her.

'You can't take that. Leave it alone.'

'I can have it mended for you. Mrs Walker's son Billy is good with his hands. He'll do it, I'm sure.'

'I don't want anyone touching it.' Arthur tried to

wrestle with Lucille but she was determined to take it and, in so doing, carry out her mission to help her charge.

'I'm trying to help,' Lucille protested.

'An' I told you I don't want no help.'

Her back straining beneath the weight, Lucille darted past him and out through the door.

As Elsie lay with Alan in her bed, she realised darkness had fallen. She glanced at the clock on the bedside cabinet. She had missed her date with Bill, so by now he would know what her answer was. She was staying in Coronation Street. But she had a reason.

Alan looked lovingly into her eyes. 'And I thought racing was exciting.'

'Thank God you weren't killed in that crash before we'd a chance to get wed.'

Alan rolled over to pick up his clothes from the floor. Elsie sensed the change in him, reached for a cigarette and lit it. 'What's the rush?'

'I promised to meet Dave Smith in the Rovers. Business,' he replied shortly.

'Are you coming back here? Or shall I come round to your place?'

Alan sat on the bed and caressed her legs. 'Why not come round to my place? And bring more than just an overnight bag.'

'On what basis?' she enquired.

'I think we should move in together. That way we can be together every night . . .'

'You mean live in sin.'

'No one thinks like that these days,' he said.

Elsie reached for her dressing-gown. 'If you think I'll live with you as your tart, you've another think coming.' Her eyes blazed. 'If you can't be bothered to marry me, you can get out, now!' She knew she was shouting, but she didn't care who heard her. She had turned down marriage to Bill and a life in Portugal for Alan, and all the while he had only wanted her as a mistress.

Alan left. On his way to the Rovers he decided that as soon as the sale of the salon went through he would leave the street and return to Newcastle. After all, there was nothing left in Weatherfield to keep him from going. Not now.

Elsie sat on the floor and cried her heart out. Why did she always opt for the wrong man? It was as if every time Fate gave her a chance, she took it with both hands and threw it away.

Chapter Twenty

Emily waited nervously in the lane behind Len's yard. What she was about to do went against every one of her moral principles but she had no choice. She'd tried to talk to Mr Fairclough about Willie Piggott's attempt to blackmail her, but he hadn't picked up on any of her hints, which was unusual for him.

'You got what I want.' Willie Piggott's voice came from behind her.

Emily thrust an envelope at him. 'Now will you leave me and the lease of Ernest's shop alone?'

'A promise is a promise, love.' He walked away. Emily reached for her handkerchief and blotted her tears.

Len watched their encounter from the window of the office he had built in his yard and rubbed his hands in glee. He turned to the man beside him.

'What did I tell you? That tender I left in the filing cabinet for Emily to copy is way too high. Roscoe and Co. are bound to get the council contract to build that new student hostel.'

'And we'd buy all the materials for the job from you.' The man held out his hand. 'It's a pleasure to do business with you, Len.'

'And with you, Mr Roscoe.' Len shook his hand firmly.

'I can't believe that this time next week we'll be in Jamaica.' Valerie looked around her bedroom. Every room in the maisonette was full of cardboard boxes and wooden tea chests packed with all their worldly possessions, earmarked for storage or the move. But it wasn't simply a move. It was emigration and the whole thing seemed like a dream. She felt as though she was caught up in a whirl-wind and a small part of her was already homesick.

Ken pushed a cufflink into his shirt and fastened it. 'Are you nearly ready?'

'No,' Valerie replied honestly. 'You go on ahead, love.'

'Are you sure?' he asked.

'Yes. Do you think the twins will be all right with Uncle Albert?'

'They will. I'm not too confident about him, though,' he joked. 'See you in the Rovers.' He kissed her cheek and left.

Valerie walked around the maisonette one last time. She couldn't suppress the feeling that she had forgotten something. There had been so much to do since Ken had accepted the teaching post in Jamaica. She tightened the belt on her dressing-gown, took the towel off her hair and draped it around her shoulders. She would take extra care with her appearance tonight. The entire street would be at the Rovers for the biggest farewell do in years.

She reached for her hairdryer. The plug was hanging by a thread, even though she had asked Ken to fix it several times. She glanced at the clock and realised she was running late. She had no other means of drying her wet hair, so she would have to risk using it. She plugged it in. The shock that surged through her body paralysed her. She tried to drop the hairdryer but it remained glued to her hand. She toppled to the floor unable to prevent herself knocking the electric fire into a packing case. The last thing she saw before she was plunged into total darkness were the flames, flaring high as they spurted from the box.

A passer-by heard the Barlows' bedroom window shatter and saw fire bursting through the broken glass, sending shards crashing to the ground. He ran into the Rovers. While Annie rang 999 the regulars streamed out to see what they could do. It wasn't much. They helped Ena from her maisonette, and salvaged a few of her possessions before the flames burst through the walls into her home.

Len Fairclough, Stan Ogden, Billy Walker and Dickie Flemming had to throw their full weight against Ken Barlow to stop him running into the blazing building.

They stood back and watched. Within minutes, the fire

engines arrived. Firemen pulled out their hoses and trained them on the inferno that the maisonettes had become. When the entire block had been reduced to smoking, blackened ruins four firemen went in and carried Valerie Barlow's blanket-shrouded remains from her gutted home. But by then Ken was unconscious, lying heavily sedated in Albert Tatlock's spare room.

'Alan, you sold this business weeks ago, remember?' Elsie handed change to the final customer of the day. 'Goodbye, Mrs Malone. See you next week.'

'I came to see you.' Alan opened the door for Mrs Malone and watched her leave.

'Happen I don't want to see you.' Elsie opened the till and bagged the takings.

'I heard what happened to Valerie Barlow. I'm sorry.'

Elsie's eyes misted over. 'It were a real tragedy.'

'How's her husband taken it?'

'He's a broken man,' she said shortly.

'But Dave's found another stylist.'

'Yes. She's nowhere near as good as Val, though,' Elsie said loyally.

Alan abruptly changed the subject. 'Elsie, I'm sorry. Walking away from you the last time I saw you was the stupidest thing I've ever done in my life – and I've done some crazy things. If you're still willing, I'll marry you tomorrow.'

Elsie's head told her to tell him to go to hell. But she had never been much of one for listening to her head. 'Tomorrow's a bit short notice.'

'Next week, then?' he asked hopefully.

'If it can be arranged.'

He opened his arms and she went to him.

'Stand back!' The duty constable yelled at the crowd pushing against the barriers. There hadn't been such excitement in Coronation Street since the night the maisonettes had burnt down. Then, morbid curiosity had drawn people but today they were hoping that the shell of the building might need dynamiting. However, the demolition crew had only brought a crane and wrecking-ball.

'Who are you pushing, Hetty Thorpe?' Ena demanded of the woman next to her.

'Excuse me for breathing!' the dour-looking woman retorted.

The officer stepped in. 'Come along now, ladies. If there's anything to see, you'll both get a good view of it.'

'Some of us have more right to be 'ere than others,' Ena said. She was thinking of Valerie Barlow and, despite her outwardly tough shell, she was close to breaking point: it was tragic for such a young life to have been taken.

'It's a good job them flats are coming down. They should never have been built in the first place, if you ask me,' Hetty commented.

The concrete ball thudded against the outer wall of the building and Ena winced. 'Good riddance to bad rubbish,' she whispered, thinking of Valerie and trying to forget the possessions she had lost in the blaze as chunks of masonry tilted menacingly, then crashed to the ground.

After the first two walls had been reduced to rubble, most of the onlookers dispersed. Ena was one of the last to leave. She wiped a tear from her eye, and pretended it was caused by grit.

'Are you going to join our protest, Mrs Sharples?' Emily Nugent stopped her as she walked down the street to her temporary lodgings in Minnie's house.

'What protest?'

'The council have announced that they're going to build a warehouse and a community centre on this site.'

'What's wrong with a community centre?' Ena asked.

'It's not so much the community centre, Mrs Sharples, it's the warehouse. Some of us think that the whole area is getting too industrialised.' Emily didn't wait for Ena to reply. She needed to get as many signatures as possible while there were still people in the street.

Ena wasn't concerned about the warehouse – it would be clean enough, apart from extra traffic. But a community centre would need a caretaker. And as caretakers went, she was up there with the most experienced. She quickened her pace.

'Mrs Sharples!' Emily caught up with her and handed

her a slip of paper. 'That's the date and time of the protest meeting. We'd be very pleased if you would join us. You're well respected in Coronation Street.'

'No, thank you,' Ena replied. 'And don't think you can get round me like that. I'll not be joining no protest.'

Surprised at Ena's reaction, Emily approached Hetty Thorpe. But Hetty was in no mood for protests either. She, too, knew a thing or two about being a caretaker, and a brand-new centre with all the latest equipment was something that needed looking after, as only she knew how.

Two months after the maisonettes had burnt down and a week after her register office wedding to Alan Howard, Elsie Howard steeled herself against the jolt of the plane as it touched down on a grey, foggy, north of England morning. She felt as if the bump had brought her sharply back to reality. Her wedding to Alan had been smaller than the one to Steve but no less perfect. And the honeymoon in Paris had been wonderful, until last night when Alan had dropped the bombshell that he was bankrupt. Instead of looking forward to an easy life she would have to get another job – and quickly.

'Penny for them?' Alan looked at her in the loving way she had found endearing before he had broken his news and now found irritating.

'That's one thing you haven't got, sunshine. A penny,' she reminded him bitterly.

'We'll be fine, Elsie. It's just a matter of sorting a few things out.'

'I agree. How about we start with divorce?'

They continued their journey in silence. That night while Alan tossed restlessly on the parlour sofa, Elsie cried herself to sleep in her bed. Would she ever be lucky in love? Or was she destined to fall in love with the wrong men until they screwed down her coffin lid?

Annie Walker hadn't left her bedroom. Not since she had received an official visit from the brewery after a spot check had revealed that the gin in her optics was watered. To the disgust of the regulars, who believed Annie's protestations of innocence, the Rovers was closed 'pending further investigations' and the Flying Horse had acquired a new crowd of regulars.

Len Fairclough was annoyed at the brewery's refusal to believe Annie, but he didn't mind transferring his custom to the Flying Horse. His first date with the young barmaid, Anita, had led to others and a proposal of marriage she had been 'thinking over' for a fortnight.

'So, will I get my answer tonight?' Len pressed, as she served him a pint of bitter.

'Wait and see.' She swung her hips as she went to serve another customer.

Len decided there and then that he'd make her give up work as soon as they were married. He wouldn't trust a wife of his in a job where she was free to flirt with all and sundry. He took his pint and pushed his way through the crowd to the only free seat, next to the door that led to the toilets. He was sitting, supping his pint and gazing at Anita, when a boy on his way back from the gents fell over his feet.

'Sorry, mate,' he mumbled.

'No harm done,' Len said easily.

'Home for you. You've had enough.' The boy's companion laid a steadying hand on his shoulder.

'I'm a bloomin' genius . . .'

'Yeh, we all know that.'

'I can see the headlines now. Landlady done for diddlin' . . .' The boy hiccuped and fell on Len's lap.

'You know anything about problems at Rovers?' Len asked casually, as he helped the boy to his feet.

'What's it to do with you?'

'Nowt.' Len smiled. 'Just curious, that's all.'

'It's tit for tat, that's what I say.'

'Drop it,' his friend warned.

'I had a good deal going there,' the boy swayed on his feet, 'till that ugly son of hers stuck his oar in, and put a stop to it.'

'Stop to what?' Len enquired innocently,

'Me fiddling. I work on deliveries from brewery see, and all I had to do was get a couple of empty barrels into every delivery and pass them off as full ones at the back of the cellar. No one was any the wiser and it weren't doing no one no harm and she was that dozy she would have never rumbled me. I made a bit of bunce selling those barrels on to . . . well, never mind on to who. But then that Billy Walker had to come along and tell the brewery that he thought I was fiddling a couple of barrels on every delivery. Not that they could prove it – not for sure, any road. But they put a bloke on my lorry who started double-checking every barrel as it came off. And that was that.'

'Tough,' Len commented.

'It wasn't as if it was costing Billy or his ma more than they could afford. But I was that mad I got some empty bottles of gin and poured in half in half. Half water, half gin. I figured if I couldn't have it one way I'd have it another. But then I thought, what the hell, they screwed me, I'd screw them, so I called the inspectors in on the Rovers.'

'Come on, lad.' Len rose to his feet and clamped his hand on the boy's elbow,

'Where?' The boy looked at Len in alarm.

'You and me are taking a little walk down the police station.'

'Oh, no.'

'Oh, yes. And get a move on. I want to be back here before closing time.'

★

'We're closed,' Anita shouted, when Len tried the door of the Flying Horse. He cursed loudly. It had taken an eternity for the police to take statements and the boy had found himself charged with drunk and disorderly behaviour as well as fraud. But the time he'd spent had been well recompensed by the smile on Annie Walker's face when he had called in at the Rovers on his way back to the Flying Horse to tell her she'd been exonerated.

'I didn't know it was you, Len.' Anita saw him through the window and opened the door. 'Fancy a drink while I finish up the glasses?'

'No. And shouldn't you be knocking off now?' Len looked at his watch. He wanted her to himself, and he wanted to hear her answer.

'You sound just like my father.' Anita returned to the bar.

'Do I get my answer?'

'Yes.'

'Yes?' he repeated, staring at her in wonder.

'Yes.' She pouted her lips, inviting a kiss and giggling when he reached over the bar and gave her one. 'But I warn you now, that moustache has to go.'

'Why?'

'It makes you look like my father.'

'So, I sound like your father and now I look like your father.'

'You're practically the same age.' Anita poured herself a drink.

'Am I?' Len was alarmed by the thought.

'Don't look so hangdog. I like older men.'

'Why?'

'They've more brass,' she replied honestly. 'What's that saying?' She frowned. '"Better to be an old man's darling than a young man's slave." '

'Better find yourself another old man, love.'

'What?' Anita's eyes rounded.

'This old geezer's just woken up. Goodnight.' Len turned his back on her and left the pub.

It hadn't taken Elsie Howard long to find a job. A prefabricated warehouse had been erected on the site of the maisonettes and made ready for occupancy within two months of the rubble being cleared. She had applied for, and got, the position of checking supervisor with responsibility for hiring and firing junior staff. But it was taking all the tact and diplomacy she possessed to tell Hilda Ogden that she wasn't suited to the job she'd applied for.

'I'm sorry, Hilda, but you're simply not suited to the position.'

'Not suited!' Hilda screeched. 'You're a fine one to talk.'

Dennis Maxwell, the warehouse manager, joined them. 'I could hear you three offices away, Mrs Howard. What's the problem?'

'It's 'er! Telling me I can't 'ave a job,' Hilda shouted.

'Mr Maxwell, I have explained to Mrs Ogden that she is simply not suitable,' Elsie said calmly.

'And she's a fine one to talk,' Hilda said archly.

'What do you mean, Mrs Ogden?' Dennis asked.

'She,' Hilda pointed at Elsie although only the three of them were in the room, 'was accused of shoplifting.'

'Accused, not charged, Mrs Ogden,' Elsie protested. 'I was innocent.'

'Is this true, Mrs Howard?' Dennis asked.

'It is true that I was accused of shoplifting by previous employers, but charges were never brought.'

'Then I am afraid that I must suspend you pending further investigation,' Dennis said firmly.

'I'll get my coat.' Elsie tried and failed to ignore Hilda gloating as she went to the cloakroom.

'And I will have to ask you leave, Mrs Ogden. As Mrs Howard said, you are clearly an unsuitable candidate for the vacancies we have here.'

Hilda didn't look quite so smug as she walked out of the warehouse.

Dennis returned to his office. He'd already decided to reinstate Elsie after a week or so. With her leanings and his know-how, they could clean up in the warehouse and the company would be none the wiser.

Ernest Bishop paced up and down Emily Nugent's living room with his hands tightly clasped behind his back.

'Is anything the matter, Ernest?' Emily asked.

'Well, dear.' He sat at the table only to shoot up as though he had sat on a pincushion.

'Shall I make some tea?' she offered.

'Yes. No. Why not?' Suddenly Ernest craved a few minutes alone. Was he ready for marriage? Modesty aside, he was aware that he was a competent lay preacher. He had considered himself wedded to the cause, but his superiors on the Mission committee wanted more. They demanded respectability, and they had warned him that if he wished to remain a preacher, he must marry. But what if Emily turned him down? The committee would have no qualms about pressing him to resign.

He knew that he should have other motives for wishing to marry Emily. He closed his eyes, intent on asking the Almighty for guidance, but Emily disturbed him by bringing in a tray.

'Ernest, if there's something bothering you, if you need to talk . . .' Emily could no longer imagine life without Ernest. And she had sacrificed so much for him, even succumbing to blackmail so Mr Piggott wouldn't cancel the lease on the photography shop. She had long since decided she would never tell him. But if ever he needed proof that she loved him . . .

The kettle whistled in the kitchen and Emily left the room without receiving an answer. Ernest started pacing again, rehearsing what he was about to say. 'The thing is, dear, the committee says I must marry, and you are the perfect candidate.'

'Candidate.' Emily reappeared with the teapot and milk jug. 'Are you thinking of standing for an election, Ernest?'

'On the contrary. Although I do feel that I am about to put myself forward for a vote of confidence. Think carefully, Emily, do you feel that you can rely on me?'

'Of course, Ernest.' Emily felt she had to face facts no matter how unpleasant. 'If there is a problem, please tell me. If you no longer want to see me . . .' The notion was so unbearable her voice failed her.

To her astonishment, Ernest knelt before her. He took her hand and gazed into her eyes. 'Emily, will you consent to be my wife?'

Emily felt as though her heart were soaring from her body. 'Yes, Ernest,' she breathed softly.

'I am so happy . . .' Ernest rushed from the room, leaving Emily bewildered, but happier than she had ever been in her life before.

'You're useless, Stan Ogden, that's what you are,' Hilda complained as she watched the bailiffs carry their colour television out through the door. 'First you leave lorry driving to take a job as a night watchman because it will give you more time at home. Then you get the sack for sleeping on the job. And now you're standing back and allowing the bailiffs carry our possessions out the house without lifting a finger . . .'

'Be reasonable, love, what can I do?' Stan asked.

'You're inhuman, that's what you are,' Hilda screamed after the bailiffs, as they drove away.

The postman handed Hilda her mail and walked on quickly before she turned on him.

Hilda sifted through the envelopes as she closed the front door and returned to the kitchen. One was unfamiliar. She peered at the postmark then opened it. 'Five hundred pounds,' she whispered, falling back into a chair.

'I've said I'm sorry, Hilda.' Stan looked at her in despair.

'It's the Premium Bonds.' Her hand shook as she held out the envelope to him. 'We've won.'

Stan took the letter from her, read it and sank into his chair.

'I'll make a pot of tea.' Hilda headed for the scullery where she took comfort in the mundane task.

'We could move house,' she suggested, as she poured out two cups.

'We should pay off Dave Smith,' Stan said.

'It's not like you to be the sensible one, but I suppose you're right. Will there be anything left over?'

'I should think so.' Stan smiled. 'We could do this place up a bit. We could 'ave one of them cocktail bars.'

'Ooh, I've always wanted one of them, with little stools in front and opticals on the wall.'

'And we could throw a party,' Stan added. 'Have a proper celebration, like.'

Annie Walker shook her head despairingly as Lucille wandered into the bar of the Rovers, sat on a stool and played with the beer mats. The girl's constant presence around the pub all day and evening was beginning to worry her.

'Lucille, love, isn't there something else you could be doing instead of wasting your time like this?' she suggested tactfully. 'Perhaps you could look for a job. It's weeks now since the factory closed.'

'There's nothing about, Auntie Annie.' Lucille wrote her initials with a finger in the highly polished surface of the bar.

'Don't do that, dear.' Mrs Annie wiped the smudges with a bar cloth. 'Why not go along to the newsagent's and get a copy of tonight's paper? There may be something there for you.'

'I got an early edition. There was nowt in it.'

'What about your charitable work?'

'I gave that up when your Billy wrecked Mr Noblett's radio. It cost Mrs Sharples a pound to replace it. I don't think I'm cut out for the Sally Army.'

'Perhaps not, love, but you must be cut out for something and the sooner you find it the better,' Annie said sternly. 'If I were you I'd go and take another look at the paper.'

Lucille left the stool and went into the private quarters at the back of the pub to do as Annie asked.

Chapter Twenty-One

'Have you done much of this type of work before?' The manager of the Aquarius Club looked Lucille up and down with the eye of a professional accustomed to hiring and firing girls.

'Not much. But I'm ever so good at it,' she replied, with more confidence than she felt. Lucille thought the manager looked about the same age as her Uncle Len, but he was dressed like a teenager and she couldn't help noticing that his hair was greasy. She had told her auntie Annie that she was visiting a friend, and she knew Annie would be horrified if she could see her now dressed in her shortest skirt, with make-up plastered thickly over her face. She had changed in the toilets at the bus station, and had earned herself a few wolf-whistles after her transformation.

'Strut your stuff, then. And remember, only the best is good enough for the Aquarius.'

Suddenly shy, Lucille unbuttoned her coat. 'Have you got any music?'

The manager shouted to someone, who put on the latest Bee Gees hit. 'Up on stage, love, so I can see you.'

Lucille climbed the steps and started to dance, slowly and clumsily at first, then she forgot where she was and gyrated and swirled just as she did when she listened to records in her bedroom.

'You start tomorrow night,' the manager yelled, before the record ended. 'Be here at seven.'

'I will. Thank you, sir.'

'Help yourself to another Fondant Fancy, Hetty,' Ena offered graciously. The hospitality she had laid on for Hetty Thorpe was lavish, but she had recalled an old saying of her mother's, 'Sugar catches more flies than vinegar', and hoped it would work in Hetty's case.

'Don't mind if I do.' Hetty took a green one decorated with a walnut.

Ena refilled their teacups and sat back in her rocking chair. 'So, tell me, what are the facilities like in this new community centre?'

'Well, as I said, the committee showed me round after they appointed me caretaker.' Hetty couldn't resist crowing at her triumph. 'And as community centres go, it's pretty much up to scratch. There are one or two small problems that need sorting but, as you know, caretakers can always find something to do.' Hetty bit off the creamy top of the cake and stared at the bare sponge beneath it.

'Good facilities are half the battle when it comes to attracting people into a centre. Of course, the windows will be well protected. Strong glass, and plenty of mesh on the outside. They'll need it round here,' Ena said. She knew there was no mesh: she had walked round the centre four times after dark when there was no one around to see her.

'There's no need for mesh on the windows. Not on a new place,' Hetty declared authoritatively. 'The locals will be proud of it and they'll want to look after it.'

'You're probably right,' Ena acquiesced meekly. 'But, then, you're not from round here, are you?'

'As I said at my interview, that's a good thing. It doesn't do to be too familiar with folks when you have to be strict with them about abiding to council and committee rules.'

Ena bit into her chocolate cake. 'Well, I'll say it again, Hetty, congratulations on getting the job.'

'Thank you. And I'm sorry you were unsuccessful,' Hetty lied, licking crumbs off her lips. 'But, as they say, all's fair in love and war.'

And this is war, Ena mused. She picked up the teapot. 'Shall I make fresh tea?'

'Only if you're having some, Mrs Sharples.'

'Call me Ena, Hetty.' Ena stood up, bent her knee, rubbed it and grimaced.

'Are you all right, Ena?'

'Just an old injury that aches from time to time. I don't have to tell you about the unpleasant side of being a caretaker. My knee's never been the same since the Jackson kids caught it with a brick.'

'What?' Hetty's eyes widened in alarm. 'Kids round here threw a brick at you?'

'It was because I banned them from the Mission Hall for . . . Well, you don't want to know what for,' Ena murmured. 'Let's just say some messes are more unpleasant than others to clear up.'

'Oh, they never . . . Kids today! I don't know what the world's coming to.' Hetty was shrill with indignation. 'They don't still live around here, do they?'

'Yes – terrible family, everyone says so. No one can do a thing with them, the coppers, the school, rent's never paid, but even bailiffs won't venture too close to them. But, being a caretaker, you'd know the sort.' Ena nodded sagely. 'And the council must have thought you can take care of yourself, or you wouldn't have been given job in first place. Didn't they warn you to call the police the minute the Jacksons put in an appearance?'

'No.'

'And then there's the Mooneys. The council would have warned you about *them*. If anything, they're even worse.'

'There's an alarm system in the new centre.' Hetty finished her Fondant Fancy in two bites. 'Top notch, latest thing. It'll be linked up to my flat so I can deal with any problems straight away.'

'You'll need it. The Jacksons once cut the telephone wire into the Mission Hall.'

Hetty gasped. 'They never did.'

'You must have impressed the council with your dedication.' Ena rubbed her knee again, picked up the teapot and made her way to the stove. 'Being on call day and night is no joke, I know. And those alarms are so sensitive they go off when a cat piddles within fifty yards of them.'

Hetty reached for another fondant. Evidently, being a caretaker in Weatherfield was not the same as being a caretaker in the parts of Greater Manchester she was used to.

'That's right, make yourself at home.' Ena was finding it increasingly difficult to be polite. She had hoped there'd be one or two Fancies left for her tea tomorrow.

'They sound a right rough lot around here, Ena.' Hetty took the tea Ena handed her.

'They are, oh, they're that, all right,' Ena agreed. 'But it's different when you know them. You know who to trust and who not, and it saves a lot of bother. Years back when I was in hospital, Leonard Swindley – he used to manage the old Mission of Glad Tidings Hall before it was pulled down – well, he appointed a relief caretaker. She let wrong sort in and they tried to burn the place down.' Ena shook her head sadly as she took the last Fondant Fancy before it disappeared on to Hetty's plate. 'Sad case.'

'What happened to her?' Hetty whispered.

'Last I heard she was in one of them special hospitals for life.'

'It'll be getting dark soon.' Hetty glanced at the empty plate that had held the cakes, set her cup down and left her chair. 'Can I have my coat, Ena? I like to be home before daylight fades.'

'Course, Hetty.' Ena fetched it and helped her on with it. 'You don't want to be waiting at no bus stop round here in the dark.'

Ena saw her visitor out. As she closed the door behind her she couldn't suppress a smile. The caretaker's job in the community centre would be hers for the asking, just as soon as Hetty had posted her letter of resignation.

'I found a job this morning, Auntie Annie,' Lucille announced at the lunch table the following day.

'What kind of a job, dear?' Annie asked.

'Receptionist, YMCA. There's only one snag. I'll be working the evening shift.' Lucille reached for the bread and butter Annie had cut to go with their ham salad.

'I didn't know the YMCA had evening receptionists.'

'It's their busiest time. That's why they have a day receptionist and me in the evenings. But they'll pay for a taxi home.'

'Well, that's not so bad. I'm proud of you, Lucille,' Annie said. 'Well done, dear. I'm so glad our little talk yesterday in the bar prompted you to do something for yourself. As you'll be working late and you were up early for the interview you should have an afternoon nap. Don't worry about the dishes. Mrs Ogden will do them.'

'Thanks, Auntie Annie.' Lucille ran upstairs, and studied herself in the dressing-table mirror as she swung her hips from side to side. 'Who'd have thought it?' She grinned. 'Me, a go-go dancer!'

Annie Walker had taken a night off from the Rovers to attend a Licensed Victuallers' Association meeting, and the customers and staff were making the most of her absence. Even Ernest Bishop had succumbed: although drinking was against his principles he felt he could indulge himself in a sherry or two – or three – on this very special occasion. A solitaire engagement ring was safely tucked away in his top pocket and he planned to present it to Emily just as soon as she joined him.

'Have you seen it, Len?' He opened the box and displayed the ring to Len Fairclough – everyone else in the bar had seen it at least twice. 'I chose it because the salesman told me ladies prefer a single diamond. One stone – one true love. It's more tasteful. It cost six months' wages but you only get engaged once, don't you?'

'Not if you're our Len.' Stan Ogden leered. 'I've seen more women in and out of his house lately than I've had hot dinners.'

'Lay off, Stan,' Len warned. He had realised that Ernest was drunk.

'Why shouldn't he know the truth?' Stan argued. 'We court them because they make us believe we can't live without them, then the minute they've a ring on their finger, wham! We find ourselves in the dog-house – and worse off than the dogs. At least they've kennels to crawl into so they don't have to listen to women wittering on at them for the rest of their lives.'

'My Emily isn't like that,' Ernest slurred.

'Saint, is she?' Stan waved his pint in the air, slopping it.

'Emily.' Ernest rose to his feet and swayed as she walked into the bar. 'Do I have news for you!' He led her into a secluded corner.

'Bless them, they're pretty to watch,' Len said condescendingly. He pushed his empty glass towards his lodger and employee, Ray Langton. 'Your shout.'

'Round the world?' Emily couldn't believe what Ernest was telling her. She was also shocked: it was the first time she had seen him the worse for drink. 'You're going round the world,' she repeated.

'That's right, my darling. The travel company want me to take all the photographs for their new brochures. Aren't you pleased for me?'

Emily was more stunned than pleased. She'd assumed that Ernest had asked her to meet him to make plans for their wedding but instead he was telling her that he was about to take a contract that would take him away from her. And he was pleased.

She sipped her lime cordial and looked around the room. People were staring at her. Some, like the terrifying Mr Ogden, were even giving her sly winks. She would have liked to leave but forced herself to remain. She loved Ernest. She should want the best for him, even if it took him away from her. After all, it was a marvellous chance . . .

Conscious that everyone was still watching her, Emily gave Ernest an insincere smile. 'That's wonderful news, Ernest. I'm pleased for you, and very proud.'

'I knew you would be.' To her embarrassment he kissed her cheek. 'All I need now is someone to run the studio in my absence.'

'I will, Ernest. It's the least I can do. I'll hand in my notice at the warehouse first thing on Monday morning.'

Music blared loudly and Emily saw Lucille fiddle with a portable radio behind the bar. When she found Radio Luxembourg, she turned up the volume full blast and, egged on by the customers, began to dance to the music.

Ernest fumbled in his pocket. 'Emily, my darling,' he shouted, above the din, 'I have something for you.'

To his chagrin he realised that Emily wasn't looking at him. Like everyone else she was watching Lucille who had climbed on to the bar and was dancing. Ray Langton left his seat and started whooping and clapping. Seeing Lucille, who he had always regarded as his niece, in a whole new light, Len felt too embarrassed to watch her until Bet Lynch joined her. Focusing on Bet he whistled appreciatively.

Ernest shouted in an attempt to be heard over the music. 'Here.' He pushed a black ring box into Emily's hand. 'Please accept this token of my true love and esteem for you.'

The music stopped. Annie Walker was standing in the doorway glaring from her ward to the customers.

'Ernest . . .' Emily stared down at the box. 'This is empty.'

'You found Emily Nugent's engagement ring in your turn-up?' Len threw back his head and laughed.

'Serves that silly bugger Ernest Bishop right for flashing it round the pub,' Stan said. 'Look,' he glanced furtively over his shoulder, 'Hilda's been on at me to find a job. Don't suppose you've anything going here?'

Len looked doubtfully at Ray. 'We do need someone in the yard,' Ray said.

'OK, we'll give you a month's trial,' Len conceded.

'You won't live to regret it, Len,' Stan promised.

'I'd bloody well better not,' Len warned.

'You know it makes sense, Ken,' Valerie's mother, Edith Tatlock, said to him as he sat slumped in the easy-chair in the living room of his rented house.

'Damned gossips round here told you I've been drinking, didn't they?' he snarled.

'No,' Edith replied evenly, 'and even if they had, I wouldn't have listened to them.'

'Well, I have,' Ken said defiantly.

'Did it help?' Edith asked gently.

'No.' Ken sank his head in his hands.

'Albert wrote and told me about the women you've had in and out of this house to look after the twins since Valerie died. He said none of them worked out.'

'I tried . . .'

'I know you did, love, and I'm not blaming you or them. It's not surprising none of them could cope with Peter and Susan. They're missing their mother.'

'I'm missing her.' Ken lifted a tearful, defiant face, and stared at her.

'I know you are, love, and that's why the twins will be better off with me in Scotland, if only for a little while until you come to terms with what's happened. You can't help them while you remain in this state.'

'Come to terms . . . You make it sound as if I've lost a job or a dog. I lost my home, everything I owned and,' his voice dropped to a whisper, 'everything I loved. My life ended the day Val died.'

'No, it didn't, Ken.' Edith moved closer to him on the sofa and took his hand in hers. 'It didn't because you're here and you have to go on. You have no choice, for the sake of the twins and . . .' she hesitated, '. . . yourself. I'm not saying this is going to be a permanent arrangement,' she said briskly, 'just until you sort out something better than this rented house. Perhaps you should move on.'

'Out of Coronation Street?' Ken stared at her in horror. He couldn't leave the street now. It would be like leaving Valerie behind. Like admitting that his life with her had meant nothing.

'Please, at least think about allowing the twins to come to Scotland with me,' Edith murmured.

'They can go,' Ken said miserably. 'At least they'll have a settled life with you and Val's dad in Glasgow. That's more than I can give them.'

'Only for now, Ken.' Edith left the sofa. 'If it's all right with you I'll pack their things and take them first thing in the morning. And remember, you'll be welcome any time. Nothing can ever alter the fact that you are their dad, and always will be,' she added softly as she left him in the living room, alone with his memories.

'It's your bloody fault,' Len hissed at Ray. 'You were the one who said we needed help in the yard.'

'And you were the one who told him he could start,' Ray reminded him.

'I didn't know then that Stan Ogden was such a lazy feckless sod.'

'SODU,' Stan greeted them, as he joined them in the cabin for his tea break.

'Watch your mouth, Stan,' Ray said, from behind the copy of the *Sun* he'd picked up as soon as Stan appeared.

'That's what I'm going to call it.'

'Call what?' Len asked irritably, spooning sugar into his mug of tea and stirring it.

'The Stan Ogden District Union.' Stan poured himself a mug of tea from the battered tin teapot.

'What did you say about a union?' Len demanded, opening a packet of chocolate digestives.

'Looks like Stan's decided to start a union.' Ray turned to page three of the *Sun* and held it sideways.

'That right?' Len asked Stan.

'That's right,' Stan confirmed.

'Oh, aye. I'd like to see you try,' Len said, a note of challenge in his voice.

'There's nothing stopping me. The law's on my side in matters such as these.' Stan sipped his tea and filched one of Len's biscuits. 'And for your information, I've already done something about it.'

'Like what?'

'Wait and all will be revealed,' Stan teased.

Ray realised that Len was seconds away from thumping Stan. He folded his paper and threw it on to the table. 'Go on, then, tell us. What exactly have you done, Chairman Stan?'

'I invited a union representative, a Mr Charlie Dickinson, to call round this yard this morning, so you'd all better be prepared.'

Ray and Len exchanged a glance as Stan smirked and snatched the *Sun* from Len.

When Charlie Dickinson arrived, Len was taking a delivery of sand.

'Mr Fairclough?'

'Aye.' Len took one look at Charlie's briefcase and burst out laughing.

'I would like to check that you have all the relevant documents, licences and brochures displayed on these premises.'

'You what?' Len chortled.

'I would like you to show me your noticeboard.' Charlie's temper rose when he saw that Len had no intention of taking him seriously.

'Ray!' Len shouted across the yard to where Ray was loading the van. 'Show this union man our noticeboard.'

'Our what?' Ray asked in confusion.

'You heard. Take him into the cabin.'

Ray saw that Len had no intention of dealing with the man, so he walked up to him and led him away. Len left them alone in the cabin for half an hour, then joined them. He walked in on a lecture and wished he'd stayed longer in the yard.

'You have been lax, Mr Langton, very lax in your

working practices. No noticeboard, no brochures advising employees of their rights and, worst of all, Mr Langton, you will be breaking the code if you refuse to pay Mr Ogden the going rate. In view of the standards of safety and facilities – or, more to the point, the shortcomings in both areas – I strongly suggest that you pay an extra pound a week to compensate Mr Ogden for the conditions you have forced him to tolerate. These are my findings.' Charlie handed a piece of paper to Ray. 'I will expect your answer by midday tomorrow.' He snapped his briefcase lock to emphasise his point.

Ray glanced at the paper. 'You can have our answer now, Mr Dickenson. Mr Fairclough and I agree to all your conditions.'

'What?' Len snatched the paper from Ray.

'You agree, Mr Fairclough,' Charlie asked.

'Absolutely!' Len nodded agreement. 'One hundred per cent. My partners and I have seen the error of our ways and agree to these terms and conditions.' Len offered his hand and Charlie shook it.

'I will inform Mr Ogden of the good news.' Charlie left the cabin somewhat deflated. He enjoyed a good argument and this encounter had gone too well for his liking.

Len emptied the teapot into the bin and set about making some fresh tea.

Stan stuck his head round the door. 'I suppose I should say thank you, but I'll simply say, I told you so!'

'Tea when you've finished shovelling all that sand into the bins, not before. By the book, remember,' Len ordered.

'Bloody slave driver.' Stan shambled off.

'Who's going to tell Stan he'll get a pound a week less in his wages from now on because we've been paying him two pounds a week more than union rate?' Ray asked.

'How about we let him find out for himself at the end of the week?' Len suggested.

'Who is she, Alan?' Elsie demanded.

'This is ridiculous,' Alan countered irritably. 'I've told you twice, Elsie, she was just a woman who was buying a car. She asked to see the manager. I went to discuss the details with her.'

'You expect me to believe that?' Elsie stood, hands on hips, in front of him.

'Yes, because it's the truth.' Alan was relieved that Elsie was quizzing him about a customer. She might have asked him about Janet Reid. He turned to the mirror and tightened the knot of his tie.

'I've been hearing rumours as well.' Elsie stood behind him and studied his face in the mirror. 'About you and Janet Reid.'

The look of guilt was fleeting but it sent Elsie into a rage. 'So there *is* something in it.'

Alan smiled at her. 'You have a wild imagination, darling.'

Elsie didn't say another word. She grabbed her coat, left the house and slammed the front door behind her. She went straight to the Rovers and used the telephone to book a taxi.

Chapter Twenty-Two

After she had paid off the cabbie, Elsie knocked on Janet Reid's door loud enough for the whole street to hear. When Janet answered, Elsie walked straight inside. 'What have you been up to with my husband?' she demanded bluntly.

'It were nothing, Mrs Howard. Just a fling, a one-night stand, that's all,' Janet muttered.

Elsie leant against the wall for support. It hadn't crossed her mind that Alan might have spent a whole night with another woman. 'Where and when?'

'Mrs Howard, you don't really want to know,' Janet mumbled.

'Damn right I do. I wouldn't be asking if I didn't.'

'A hotel in Leeds. We were supposed to be at a conference.'

Sickened by the thought of Alan and Janet taking off their clothes and cavorting naked together, Elsie didn't wait to hear any more. She left Janet's house wishing she'd never set eyes on Alan Howard.

She walked home in a daze and sat up waiting for Alan to put in an appearance. When dawn broke, she went to bed. At midday she drew back her bedroom curtains and looked down to see Alan carrying his suitcase down the street. She turned her back on him and reached for her dressing-gown.

She hadn't even had to throw him out. And perhaps that was just as well. Good riddance to bad rubbish – wasn't it?

'Clear off. Haven't you lot got homes to go to?' Ena was tired and more irritable than usual. She had turned off the lights in the main hall, only to realise that she had forgotten to switch off the electric heaters. And while she had walked round the community centre a second time, a gang of teenagers had starting throwing stones at the windows. Ena had had just about as much as she could take. Youth-club nights always meant more work: things were never put away properly, and she couldn't bear the thought of being reprimanded for not keeping the centre tidy. She paused to catch her breath before she stacked the plastic chairs. If only the kids would tidy up after themselves. An hour later, Ena switched off the last light. She fumbled for her keys and pulled the reinforced main door closed. All she could think of was getting back to the flat and her bed.

*

The following morning, Ena was woken by a loud knock at her front door. She pulled on her dressing-gown and went to answer it. 'Who is it?'

'Mrs Sharples, I am here on behalf of the committee.'

Ena opened the door. 'Would you mind waiting in my sitting room while I get dressed?'

'Not at all, Mrs Sharples.'

Ena joined the official ten minutes later with a tray of tea. 'I'm sorry I slept late, but I was up half the night clearing the mess left by the youth club.'

'I'm sorry, too, Mrs Sharples, but I haven't come here to discuss that. There was a break-in at the centre last night and the new colour television was stolen.'

'That's impossible. I was there myself last night. I locked up—'

'It appears that not only were the doors left unlocked but the alarm had not been set.'

'But . . .' Ena recalled closing the doors but she couldn't remember locking them. She was mortified. She had failed in her duty and was terrified of the consequences. 'I . . .' She fell silent, not knowing what else to say in her defence.

'We had an emergency meeting this morning and came to the conclusion that this job is too onerous for one person, especially a woman. In short, Mrs Sharples, we have decided to appoint an assistant caretaker.'

'An *assistant*?' For Ena it was the ultimate humiliation. The committee were dissatisfied with her and the thought was unbearable.

Ena's heart was beating at twice the normal rate when she showed the official out of her flat. She considered visiting her doctor but dismissed the idea. She slipped on her coat and walked to the police station to report the teenagers who had thrown stones at the centre's windows the night before. She couldn't be sure they were the ones who had broken in, but they deserved a fright anyway.

'We go back a long way.' Len put his arm round Elsie's shoulders as they sat in the bus shelter.

'I know I can always rely on you, Len, and I'm grateful. How did I get myself into this mess?' she murmured absently.

'By marrying Alan Howard.'

'Aye.'

Len wanted to kiss her, but refrained, sensing that if he did, it would bring Elsie more problems than she could handle. 'Shall we walk? If we don't we might find ourselves sitting here all night.' He offered her his arm.

'Thank you.' They fell companionably into step. 'It's good to know that you'll always be my friend, no matter what.'

'Aye.' Len had wanted to be more than a friend to Elsie for so many years. He wondered if she would ever see him as the lover he longed to be. He suddenly realised that while he remained her friend, a willing shoulder for her to cry on between boyfriends and husbands, she would never see him as anything more. Or, perhaps more importantly from his point of view, free him to find a life of his own.

'See you in Rovers tomorrow night?' Elsie asked, as he left her outside her house.

'I may be busy for the next few days.'

'Whenever, then.' Upset by his offhand dismissal, Elsie opened her door and noticed the light was on. She dumped her coat on the banister and went into the living room. The scullery door was open and Alan was standing at the stove beating eggs in a bowl.

'What the hell do you think you're doing?' Elsie dropped her handbag on the table. 'Who said you could come waltzing back in here?'

Alan turned off the stove and faced her.

'I asked you a question.' Elsie made for the scullery door.

'Please, listen to me, Elsie.' Alan moved towards her but she retreated.

'I can listen from here.' She collapsed into her easy-chair.

'I can't live without you, it's as simple as that.'

'You should have thought of that before you slept with Janet Reid.'

'I'm sorry, I made a mistake, love. I wish I could undo

it, but I can't. Please, let me make it up to you. Please, Elsie. We were good together, you know that.'

Elsie's heartbeat quickened. She had been lonely, very lonely, and they were still married, but the pain of his betrayal was raw. 'What makes you think things will be any different?'

'I've bought the Canal Street garage from Billy Walker.'

'With what? Chocolate money?' Elsie enquired.

'I borrowed the money from my first wife.'

'And that's supposed to make me feel better?' Elsie sneered.

'I did it for us, Elsie. Half the trouble between us was to do with money, can't you see that?'

'And you think you can cure that problem by borrowing?'

'I've run garages before. I'll soon pay every penny of the loan back, and make enough money to get us out of this street.'

'It's not so bad,' Elsie said defensively.

'That depends on who's in it.' His eyes met hers and they stared at one another for what seemed like an eternity.

Elsie made the first move. She kicked off her shoes, put on her slippers and lifted her apron from the clothes rack in front of the fire.

'Do you want anything in this omelette you're making? There's a bit of cheese left.'

Alan moved behind her and put his arms round her waist. 'I love you, Elsie Howard.' He dropped a kiss on the nape of her neck.

'You know where the cutlery is. And there's a new bottle of HP in the cupboard.' She couldn't stand it but she had some – just in case.

Annie Walker ran cold water into the washbasin in her bathroom for a few minutes, then filled the tumbler and returned to her bedroom. She gazed at the photograph of Jack that had pride of place on her dressing-table. 'Don't look at me like that, Jack,' she addressed the photograph gravely. 'I know I should be pulling myself together, but these things take time.' She tried to imagine what her husband would say to her if he could see her.

'Things will be a lot better now our Billy is working at the Rovers.' She continued her one-sided conversation with him as she turned back the bedclothes and climbed into bed. She took the sleeping tablets from the bedside drawer, placed one tablet on her tongue and washed it down with a mouthful of water.

She reached for the cord and turned out the light. 'I did tell you that our Billy has sold the garage, dear, didn't I? To Elsie's new husband, Alan Howard. But, then, you never met Alan Howard, did you, Jack? Goodnight, my love.'

★

The next morning, Annie woke feeling less tired but oddly disembodied, as if she wasn't in the Rovers – or anywhere *real*, for that matter. She dressed and made her way downstairs, where Billy was sorting out stock behind the bar.

'Good morning, lazybones,' Billy joked, pushing a crate of empty Mackeson bottles to the end of the bar closest to the cellar.

'That's no way to speak to your mother, Billy. I have been resting.'

Billy tried to make amends. 'I've brewed tea. What would you like for breakfast?'

'I'll just have tea, thank you, Billy.' Annie knew that she hadn't eaten properly for days but she simply wasn't hungry.

'I'm worried about you. Is there something wrong?' he asked.

Annie heard his question but couldn't explain why she felt as she did. All she knew was that although she had just left her bed she couldn't wait to get back there. 'I'm just tired. I think I'll go back to bed for an hour. Can you look after things here?'

'I'll manage. Are you sure that's all it is – tiredness?'

'I'm sure, love.' Annie made her way upstairs and closed her bedroom door.

The doctor didn't arrive until four o'clock. Billy took him upstairs and tapped on his mother's bedroom door, then opened it and peered in.

'Mum? I have the doctor with me.'

The doctor followed him into Annie's room, took her pulse, saw the empty bottle of pills on her bedside cabinet and called an ambulance.

'You're sure she's taken an overdose?' Billy asked in disbelief, when the doctor replaced the telephone on its cradle.

'I'm sure.' The doctor folded his stethoscope into his bag and snapped it shut. 'Good job you called me when you did. Let's hope it's not too late to pump her stomach.'

'So you can see the position I'm in, can't you, Councillor Fairclough?' Rita Bates gave Len what she hoped was a pathetic, yet appealing smile.

'Of course, Mrs Bates.' Len returned Rita's smile. She was an attractive woman, in need of his help. It made his position as a local councillor seem worthwhile for once.

'Someone said you were on the housing committee, so I thought I would mention my problem.'

Len cut her short. 'I'll do my best. But the housing shortage being what it is, everyone wants a new council house these days.'

'I understand. Thank you for listening to me, Councillor Fairclough.' Rita coyly lowered her eyes.

'Len,' he corrected. 'I'll try to do something for you before your house is demolished.'

'I couldn't ask for more . . . Len.'

'We should meet again to discuss this. Do you know the Rovers Return?'

'The pub on the corner of Coronation Street?'

'That's the one. Shall we meet there at seven o'clock next Tuesday?'

'I'll be there.' She gave Len her hand and allowed him to hold on to it a fraction longer than necessary. Len Fairclough was an attractive man. Much more so than Harry, the man she called her husband.

Annie woke in unfamiliar, antiseptic-smelling surroundings. She tried to sit up and fell back weakly on to a hard pillow.

'Hello, Mrs Walker. How are you feeling?' A nurse helped her to sit up, and held a glass of water to her lips.

'My throat is sore,' Annie complained.

'That will be from the tubes they had to pass down to pump your stomach. Do you remember taking too many sleeping pills?'

'I overdosed?'

'I'm sure it was just an accident.'

Mortified, Annie lay back on her pillow and cried. 'I'm sorry, I'm so sorry.'

'There's no need to upset yourself, Mrs Walker. Accidents happen.'

'That's what it must have been.' Annie clutched at the straw of dignity the nurse had offered.

'You need to rest now, Mrs Walker, and if you need anything, anything at all, I'm on duty all night.'

'Thank you, Nurse.'

Annie lay back and watched the nurse walk down the ward. She plumped up pillows, smoothed bedcovers and had a kind word for each of her patients. Annie thought of Jack and how devastated he would have been to see her now. She *had* to pull herself together, for his sake if not her own. She couldn't bear the thought of sullying the name she bore – his name. And that meant doing without sleeping tablets, even if she never slept again.

Furious with Elsie, who'd more or less ignored him since taking Alan back into her life and house, Len arrived at the Rovers half an hour early for his date with Rita. He was sitting supping his second pint when she walked in with a man.

'Len,' she gave him a smile as she joined him, 'this is my husband, Harry Bates. Harry, this is Len Fairclough, the councillor I was telling you about. '

Len was annoyed with himself for misinterpreting Rita's flirting as anything other than self-interest. He offered the man his hand.

'Rita said you can help us with a house,' Harry said gruffly, sitting at Len's table without offering to buy either Len or Rita a drink.

'As I explained to your wife, due to the housing

shortage there is a heavy demand for new council housing. But we've been building them as fast as we can for the last two years and we've made inroads on the waiting list. At the end of 1970 there were five thousand families waiting to be rehoused. Now, only halfway through 1972, it is down to just under three thousand and the council has pledged to do its utmost to clear it in the next five years. I don't see any problem with you jumping to the head of the queue, provided you can prove that your house is being demolished. Oh, and you'll need to show us your marriage certificate.'

Rita glanced at Harry. 'That would be difficult, Len. You see, we're not actually married, just common-law husband and wife.'

'That throws a different light on the matter.'

'Why?' Harry demanded belligerently.

'Put yourself in the position of a legally married couple on the housing list, Harry,' Len said flatly. 'How would you feel if you found out that an unmarried couple had been rehoused ahead of you?'

Hilda adjusted the scarf she'd tied to cover the rollers in her hair, wiped the perspiration from her forehead with the back of her hand, dunked her mop in the sudsy water, lifted it into the draining well at the top of the aluminium bucket and rested her weight on the handle to squeeze it dry.

'Is that you, Mrs Walker?' she called when she heard someone walking down the back staircase.

'Yes, good morning, Hilda.'

Hilda breathed in the light, floral scent of Annie's perfume and wished she could afford to buy expensive colognes and make-up. Annie Walker always looked so well groomed. She always felt grubby and down at heel in comparison, dressed in her faded cotton print overalls with her dirty hands and broken fingernails. 'How are you feeling, Mrs Walker?'

'Fine, thank you, Hilda.' Annie abruptly changed the subject. 'Have you nearly finished?'

'Apart from this last bit of floor.' After two hours of solid cleaning, Hilda was exhausted. She glanced at the clock above the bar. Ten past eight. She had twenty minutes to finish up, put everything away and get over to the betting shop.

'I have a hair appointment this morning and I need to lock up before I go.' Annie reached for her coat.

Hilda gazed enviously at Annie's pale blonde hair, which as usual was immaculately curled, and wondered why Annie was off to the hairdresser's. There were days when she was too tired to even take the curlers from her hair in the evening because she'd only have to put them back in to go to bed.

Hilda mopped the last few inches of lino. 'That's me done in here. I'll empty this out back and I'll be off.' She picked up the bucket and went into the yard to empty the water down the drain.

Ten minutes later Hilda unlocked the door of the betting shop. She could have cried at the sight that met her. The floor was carpeted with crumpled betting slips and every ashtray was full to overflowing. Newspapers and crushed cigarette packets had been thrown everywhere and all four waste-bins had been knocked over. The glass partitions that separated the bookies from the punters were smeared and, as if that wasn't enough, one of the fluorescent tubes in the ceiling was flickering.

'Bloody hell!' She took off her coat and hung it with her handbag on the coat peg, next to a discarded anorak. She retied the strings of her wrap-around overall for the second time that morning and waded through the debris to the store cupboard, where she lifted out a brush and a yellow plastic bucket full of cleaning equipment. A minute later she was hard at work.

She left the toilets until last. She cleaned other people's more often than she did her own, and while she was resigned to her station, it didn't stop her wishing she was rich enough to pay someone to do her housework.

The next job was Benny Lewis's flat. She walked in and, for the first time since she had left her bed at half past five, she put her feet up. Ten minutes later she switched on the radio and sang along to Jimmy Young's selection on Radio Two as she dusted and vacuumed the living room.

She hated doing Benny's bedroom, and that day was no exception. She gathered his dirty underclothes, shirt and socks from the floor and pushed them into the Ali Baba basket in the corner. She emptied the ashtray down the toilet, and washed the whisky rings from his glass-topped bedside cabinet.

When Benny's flat was spick and span, Hilda pulled on her coat, slammed the door and walked to the Capricorn Club, stopping to pick up some chips on the way. The club stank of stale smoke and beer, but Hilda didn't care. She cleared the dirty glasses from a table, sat down and opened the newspaper-wrapped parcel of chips. Then she pushed two chairs together so that she could put her feet up while she ate her dinner.

She felt more like sleeping than cleaning when she had eaten the last chip, but she started by collecting glasses from the tables. The club had a decent vacuum cleaner and, taking pride in her work, Hilda sang along to the noise of the machine.

Two hours later, she put on her coat and made her way into the street, her hands swollen from her day's work. She caught sight of herself in the shop windows as she walked past and wasn't pleased at the sight of the drab she had become, but she was bringing in a decent sum every week, and, as Stan said, if she didn't work, what else would she do with her time?

At seven o'clock she was back at the Capricorn washing dishes in the kitchen. Baskets holding the remains of chicken and chip meals were piled higher than her head on the draining board and the dishes that had held slices of Black Forest gateau were balanced on a trolley behind her. Hilda thought of the supper she would have with Stan when she got home. That was the best perk of this job, taking home the kitchen leftovers.

'There was cream left over tonight as well, Stan, so I brought some home in that little jug. Help yourself.' Hilda beamed.

'I love a slap-up meal especially when it's free.' Stan shovelled gateau into his mouth. 'Just think what this would have cost us in the club – not that we could afford to go. You're a right little treasure, love.'

Unused to compliments, especially from Stan, Hilda forgot for a moment that she was worn out. 'It's nice to be appreciated, Stan.'

'In fact, with your five jobs, there's no point in me working, is there, love?'

Hilda assumed he was joking and laughed. She wiped her mouth on a paper napkin from the club and poured cream over her piece of gateau.

'I've some news for you.' Stan sat back in his chair,

loosened his belt and burped. 'I handed in me notice today. From now on, I'll stay at home, and you can go out to work.'

Hilda almost choked.

'You are now the official Ogden household bread-winner.' He held up his glass of beer. 'God bless you, love. The best day's work I ever did in me life was marrying you.'

The night after Len had met Rita and Harry in the Rovers, he was on his way to bed when he heard a quiet tap at the front door. He opened it and looked up and down the street.

'I'm here.'

He glanced down to see Rita sitting on his doorstep. Her face was bloody and her dress torn. 'Did Harry do this to you?' He helped her into the hall and closed the door.

'He thought I fancied you. But, then, he thinks I fancy every man I talk to,' she muttered.

'And do you?' Len led her into his living room.

'Of course not.' She sat down and watched Len walk into the scullery and fill a bowl with cold water.

'What about me?' He bathed her face, relieved to see that her injuries were nowhere near as bad as they had looked. 'Do you fancy me, Rita Bates?'

'I suppose I do,' she whispered, clamping her hand over

his as he held a cloth to her cheekbone. 'But Bates isn't my real name. It's Littlewood, Rita Littlewood.' She winced as Len touched a gash on her nose.

'Well, Rita Littlewood,' Len smiled, 'welcome to Coronation Street.'

Chapter Twenty-Three

'I thought it was the bride, not the groom, who was supposed to be late for the wedding,' Alan commented, as he and Elsie undressed for bed.

'I'm amazed Emily managed to get Ernie Bishop near an altar long enough to exchange their vows. He's more mouse than man – and an indecisive mouse at that.' Elsie unhooked her bra and slipped on a sheer black nylon négligé.

'Very nice,' he murmured appreciatively, as she lifted her arms to unpin her hair. 'I always knew marriage had some benefits.'

'Oh, aye?' Elsie gave him a teasing look.

'By the way, now that the garage is doing well and I've finally managed to persuade Billy Walker to stop calling in every five minutes to see if I'm making a better job of running it than he did . . .'

'I'm surprised Annie got her own way there.' Elsie ran her fingers over her scalp to make sure she had removed all the hairpins. 'Billy didn't seem at all keen to give up the garage to take on the tenancy.'

'Anyway, I've decided to go into partnership with Jim Frazer.'

Elsie gazed back at Alan in her dressing-table mirror. 'Go into partnership doing what?'

'Selling used cars. I've arranged to meet Jim and a friend of his down the Rovers tomorrow night to talk things through.'

Elsie watched as he sat on the bed and peeled off his socks and trousers. 'I presume this friend of Jim's has money to burn, because as far as I know that garage of yours is just ticking over. And you need money to buy used cars, especially when you can't be sure of selling them on for a few weeks or even months.'

'The garage is doing a bit better than just ticking over, love,' he said archly. 'And Jim's the one with the money, not his friend. Knowing him, she's more likely to be one of his floozies than an investor. Her name's Hunt – Deirdre Hunt. You heard of her?'

Elsie shook her head. 'No one of that name lives round here. By the way I've a piece of news myself. I wasn't expecting it after I was suspended for a week a couple of months back, but I've been offered promotion in the warehouse.' She picked up her perfume and dabbed some behind her ears. 'There's just one snag. It's in head office in Solihull.'

'And I suppose Dennis Maxwell is moving there too,' Alan said flatly.

'Happens he is. Why?'

'You're not going and that's final.'

'Alan . . .'

'Have you ever wondered why he reinstated you after that row over Hilda?'

Elsie hesitated. 'Because he found out that I'd never been charged with anything?'

'Charged had nothing to do with it. He's as bent as a five-bob note, and now that he knows something about you that head office doesn't, and he's given you cause to be grateful to him, he's out to use you. And knowing that villain as I do, when trouble comes – and it will – you'll be the one left carrying the can.'

Elsie would have bitten Alan's head off for suggesting such a thing if Dennis Maxwell hadn't bought her lunch the day before, and dropped a casual suggestion in the middle of their seven-ounce sirloin steaks and chips that her past misdemeanours, while not amounting to anything serious, would be better remaining their 'little secret'.

Alan stood behind her in his Y-fronts. He rested his hands on her shoulders. 'I love you, Mrs Howard, and perhaps it's time I reminded Dennis Maxwell that he's messing with my wife.'

'I can look after myself,' Elsie countered brusquely, annoyed with herself for being taken in by her boss.

'I never said you couldn't, love.' He kissed the back of her neck, stepped out of his pants, tossed them into the linen bin and climbed into bed. 'I'm lonely,' he complained plaintively.

'I'm here.' Elsie laughed.

He patted the empty half of the bed. 'Not where you should be, Mrs Howard.'

'Window-cleaning. That's how I started and I should never have moved on to anything else.'

'From what Hilda told me, you wouldn't have gone back to it if she hadn't had a go at you when you told her that you'd decided to give up work.'

'I was just joking.'

'Hilda didn't see it that way.' Annie held out her hand.

'She doesn't always understand me.' Stan pulled a handful of coins from his pocket and paid Annie for the pint she'd pulled him. 'I'm cut out to be my own boss. No one on my back telling me what to do, or when to do it.'

'And you can give yourself a two-hour lunch break,' Annie Walker commented.

'I haven't been in here that long.'

'Oh, yes, you have,' Annie contradicted him. She might make her living out of the likes of Stan Ogden, but she couldn't help feeling angry when she thought of Hilda slaving away to keep her husband in beer money when he was too idle to put in a day's work.

'My, doesn't time fly when you're having fun.' Stan tried to focus on the clock above the bar. He was tired, so tired he felt he could sleep for a week. 'Can't keep my customers waiting.'

'If you do, they won't be your customers for much longer.' Annie watched him down his fifth pint since he had walked in at twelve o'clock.

'See you tonight, Annie.' He set his glass on the bar, went outside and picked up his ladders.

'You all right up there, Stan?' Len shouted, as he passed Stan who was perched, motionless, at the top of his ladder in Rosamund Street.

'Why shouldn't I be?' Stan shook out his chamois and polished the panes of the bedroom window. Then he climbed down the ladder. The world was wavering around him and he felt peculiar – very peculiar indeed. He sat on the pavement and leant back against the wall. When he looked up minutes – or maybe hours – later a crowd had gathered around him.

'There he is.'

'You dirty old man, you should be ashamed of yourself.'

'It's disgusting, that's what it is.'

'What's disgusting?' Stan mumbled, wondering if he were dreaming.

'Can I ask what you're doing here, sir?' A policeman peered down at him.

'Having a rest,' Stan slurred. 'No law against that, is there?'

'I think you'd better come down the station with me, sir. For your own protection,' the officer added, as a woman moved in on them wielding a rolled umbrella.

'Disgusting.'

'Peeping Tom.'

Stan finally twigged what was happening. 'Me? A peeping Tom? I'm a window-cleaner!'

'A likely story.'

'But I am,' he protested.

'Whatever you say, sir.' The officer tightened his grip on Stan's arm. 'We'll sort it all out at the station. Excuse me, ladies, gents, let us pass, please.'

Hilda paced furiously around her living room. Stan – her Stan – being charged with breaching the peace! It was ludicrous. No one who knew Stan could possibly believe he was a peeping Tom. There was no denying that he did stupid things now and again. She glanced at the bar he'd built when they'd won the Premium Bonds, thought of the party they'd never had because he'd drunk all the booze before she'd had time to invite anyone. But this was different: he was obviously ill. Even now, in the middle of prime evening drinking time, he was tucked up in bed fast asleep. She'd show them.

She picked up her key and charged out of the house to

the Rovers. The bar was packed but everyone fell silent when she walked in.

'I had no idea my neighbours were such morons,' she shouted. One or two customers looked away, a few stared at their drinks. 'This is what I think of you lot!' She spat on the floor.

'Hilda,' Annie reprimanded her.

'And that goes for you and all,' Hilda yelled. Amid her rage she knew that in the morning she'd regret screaming at Annie. Turning on her heel, she held her head high as she stalked out of the pub.

Before she'd married, Emily would never have dreamed of querying Ernest's judgement but, then, she'd never expected him to disregard her abilities as well as her opinion. 'Ernest, are you sure you're doing the right thing in employing Rita Littlewood as a roving photographer?' she asked.

'She has experience, Emily, and she gets on well with people. I need to expand the business. Now that I am a married man with responsibilities, I have to consider and cater for public taste, even when it isn't my own.' Ernest was anxious to please his new wife but he also wanted to make it clear that she had no say in his business decisions.

'I know she gets on well with people,' Emily said, not wanting to carry the conversation into the murky area of

Rita's morals, 'but I'm certain that I could have done the job just as well, if not better than her.' She reached for her handkerchief and blew her nose. 'The least you could have done was ask me.'

'It never even crossed my mind, Emily. Business is business, dear. Now, if you'll excuse me, I'm expecting important clients. Staff portraits for a firm's in-house magazine, which could lead to more much-needed work.'

Emily left the studio humiliated and resentful. She was confident that she was as good, if not better, a photographer than Rita Littlewood. But Ernest couldn't have made it clearer that he didn't trust her to be anything other than his wife and skivvy. He preferred to employ a singer at the Capricorn Club rather than his own wife . . .

A blue poster pasted to a lamp-post boasting the headline 'STRIPPERS' caught her attention. She couldn't understand how any woman could take off her clothes in front of a crowd of men. Ernest would be horrified if she were even to contemplate doing such a thing. Yet these shows were popular and Ernest had said he had to cater for public taste . . . There had to be a market for photographs of strippers. Possibly the girls would buy them to hand out to their 'special' gentlemen friends . . .

Checking over her shoulder to make sure no one was watching, Emily tore the poster from the lamp-post. She was just as capable of being a roving photographer as

Rita. And she would sell her photographs, which was more than Ernest had done lately.

'What's wrong with the way we run things now?' Len Fairclough emptied his tea slops into the sink and turned his grimy *A Present from Blackpool* mug upside down on the draining-board. 'We manage.'

'Is that what you call it?' Ray mocked. 'I'm telling you, Len, we could run this business ten times more efficiently with a secretary. Remember that job you lost because no one was around to take the call when it came in? We missed out on five hundred pounds' profit there.'

'We can't afford to pay out any more in wages.' Len pulled an invoice from his pocket and handed it to Ray.

'This is exactly what I mean.' Ray waved it in the air as he followed Len out of the cabin. 'If we had a secretary, I could hand this over and forget about it.'

'A secretary would mess things up. As it is, we know where everything is.'

'Turn round.'

'Why?'

'Just do it.'

Len looked back through the open door into the cabin.

'Now, tell me that mess doesn't need sorting,' Ray said.

'Hello, Ray.' A girl in three-inch stiletto heels picked her way daintily through the rubble around the gates.

'And hello to you.' Len eyed her bust outlined beneath

a skintight sweater. Her skirt was short and she had one of the finest pairs of legs he had whistled at.

'Deirdre Hunt, Len Fairclough.' Ray effected the introductions.

She held out her hand. 'Ray has told me all about you.'

'He didn't tell *me* about *you*,' Len retorted.

'Deirdre's our new secretary,' Ray informed him.

'Well, I'm off.'

'Where to?' Ray called after him.

'Price the job down Canal Street.'

Ray knew full well Len wasn't off to price any job. He was angry with him for employing Deirdre without his permission and intended to spend a long lunch hour in the pub.

'What are you rummaging for?' Alan asked when he arrived home to find Elsie on her hands and knees in front of the sideboard.

'Sherry. I was sure we had a bottle here somewhere. Have you seen it?'

'Not me.' He kicked off his shoes and sat at the table. 'What's for tea?'

'Pork chop and chips.'

'Great. Fancy a drink down Rovers afterwards?' He pulled her on to his lap as she rose to her feet.

'I fancy something else more.' She cupped his face in her hands and kissed him.

'That would be nicer after a drink – or two,' he whispered, nibbling her ear.

'Have it your own way.' Elsie was put out, but made an effort not to show it. 'I'll get the tea.'

Len arrived for work the following morning, stood on the step of the cabin and peered inside. 'Bleeding hell!'

Deirdre was sitting behind a desk, complete with typewriter and phone. The filing cabinet had been moved next to her chair. As he watched, the telephone rang and Deirdre answered it. 'Good morning, Fairclough and Langton, builders.'

Ray appeared and stood beside him. 'Recognise the place?'

Len went inside. Even the sink had been scrubbed clean. 'Where's my mug?'

'Here, Mr Fairclough.' Deirdre hung up the telephone and handed Len a strange mug.

'That's not mine.'

'I washed it.' She smiled. 'Shall I put kettle on and make tea, or would you prefer coffee?'

Once Len realised that he didn't have to run to the cabin every time the phone rang, or deal with any of the paperwork, he conceded that hiring Deirdre was one of the better decisions Ray had made. Business boomed: before the end of the week, orders were high and the yard was running efficiently.

'You know the best thing about having a decent secretary?' Len murmured, as he and Ray made their way to the Rovers on Friday after work.

'What? Ray asked.

'The chocolate biscuits.' Len grinned. 'She always gets us chocolate biscuits.'

Emily braced herself. She needed to prove herself to Ernest, and she would. Head high, she walked up to the door of the strip club. 'I'm Emily Bishop.'

'You look more like a nun than a freelance photographer. Sure you'll cope, love?'

Emily couldn't have been more affronted if the doorman had patted her on the head. 'I'm an experienced professional,' she lied.

'Whatever you say.' He jerked his head at the door. 'Go on in, it's all yours. But be careful not to upset the punters. You do, and the boss will have you thrown out pronto. Most don't like their picture taken, in case the missus finds out what they get up to on their boys' nights out.'

'I won't upset anyone,' Emily assured him. 'Will it be all right if I start backstage?'

'Please yourself,' he said laconically. 'Take the door on the left-hand side.'

Emily walked through the dimly lit bar area, then made

her way down a dingy corridor into a communal changing room, where girls were donning 'costumes' too brief to warrant the name.

'You're new.' A girl in four-inch heels, a turquoise G-string and an artificial snake smiled at her.

'I'm a photographer.'

'Can you do portfolio shots?' At the mention of the word 'portfolio' all the girls crowded in on Emily.

'Of course.' Taking shots of schoolchildren couldn't be *that* different from portfolio shots of 'artistes', could it?

'We need all the help we can get to get out of this joint and into a better class of club.'

Emily looked around for a backdrop. 'How about in front of that mirror?' She pointed to a full-length mirror bordered by naked light-bulbs. 'That way you'll get two views for the price of one.'

'Suits me – and me first.' The girl who had greeted her stood in front of the mirror and struck a provocative pose.

Emily had never found photography so easy: accustomed to playing to an audience, the girls twisted, turned and smiled directly at the lens with the minimum of prompting. After a while Emily didn't even blush when they stripped off what little they were wearing and stood in front of her stark naked.

When she collected their names and addresses and totted up the value of the invoices to be sent out, she realised she had succeeded. Never again would Ernest question her professional capability. Not once he'd seen how much money she had brought into the business in just one night.

Elsie heard scratching at the door and winced. Alan was having trouble getting his key into the lock – again. She had tried to ignore his drinking, but it was impossible. She couldn't even do her job in the warehouse properly for worrying about where he was and what he was up to.

He was invariably bad-tempered and hungover when he woke in the morning; he returned from work stinking of whisky and their sex life had been non-existent since he had taken to falling asleep on the settee every night. Worst of all, he had let himself go: once smart, he now looked as though he habitually slept in his clothes and hadn't changed them for months.

She had tried talking to him, but it only led to ferocious arguments. Only that morning he had denied he had a problem and accused her of being neurotic.

'Hello, love, what's for tea?' He fell backwards, hit the wall and slid to the floor.

'Nothing.' Elsie grabbed her coat and handbag. 'I'm going out.'

Alan watched her leave. Slowly, deliberately, he reached into the inside pocket of his overcoat for the half-bottle he'd bought earlier. He unscrewed the top, took a swig and fumbled for a cigarette. He crawled into the scullery, pulled himself up on the gas stove, turned on a jet and tried to light his cigarette from it. At the third try he succeeded. He pulled off his tie and overcoat, then tossed them aside. He was tired. He'd lie down, just for a little while, and when he woke he'd think of a way to sweet-talk Elsie. When he woke . . .

'Another gin and orange, Elsie?' Len asked, as he walked into the Rovers with Ray to find her staring at an empty glass.

'No, I have to get home, but thanks for offering, Len.' She picked up her coat and walked home, dreading what she'd find waiting for her.

She opened the door and smelt burning. Without stopping to think what she was doing, she ran inside. The living room was full of smoke, the scullery door open. She grabbed a teacloth, wrung it under the tap, threw it over the smoke and flames coming from the cooker and turned off the gas.

Alan lay snoring on the scullery floor, oblivious to the fire that might have burnt down the house and him with it. Elsie stared at him in disgust. She had reached breaking-point. If he didn't pull himself together and get help, she would throw him out. It was either that or lose her sanity because she couldn't take one more day of what he was doing to her – and himself.

'Twenty-three points! We got twenty-three points!' Bet Lynch danced round the bar with Len Fairclough while the others in the football-pools syndicate, Stan, Ray and Alan, ordered drinks all round.

'Seventy five quid! I've never had so much money in my life. Keep the vodkas coming,' she said to Ray, downing the one he handed her in a single swallow.

'What you going to do with it, love?' Len asked.

'Have a bloody good holiday, and get blotto every night.' Bet glanced at the men in the room. Since Frank had thrown her over for a younger woman there hadn't been anyone special. And what good was a holiday when she had no one to share it with – no one to care whether she lived or died?

'That's a great idea,' Ray enthused.

Alan sipped lemonade as if it was poison. He had no option: stay on the wagon or lose Elsie and his home.

Stan grimaced. At Hilda's insistence he had handed over most of his winnings to her, and the couple of quid she had allowed him to keep to celebrate had almost gone.

'I want another vodka.' Bet banged her glass on the bar, earning herself a disapproving look from Annie Walker.

'How about saving it until tomorrow, Bet, love?' Len suggested mildly.

'I want a drink now.' Bet made a face at Annie.

'Come on, love, Len and me will get you a taxi.' Ray staggered over to help her. They were all unsteady on their feet but Bet was far and away the worst for wear.

'Go away.' Bet swung a punch at Ray, missed and fell

back on a chair. Len shook his head at Ray, only to receive a thump from Bet, which landed behind his ear.

'That hurt,' he complained.

'It was meant to.' Bet stuck her tongue out at him. 'And I'll see meself home.'

'Bet . . .'

'I said I'd see meself home,' she bellowed.

'You can see yourself out of the Rovers,' Annie ordered sharply. 'It's past closing.'

'Come on, Bet.' Len took one arm, Ray the other, and they helped her outside.

As soon as the fresh air hit her, Bet became violent again: she swung her handbag and hit both of them in the face. 'You don't go the same way as me, and there's no way I'm giving either of you what you're after, not tonight,' she slurred.

Ray burst out laughing.

'Gerroff!' Beth screeched. 'Gerroff and get lost, the pair of you!'

'Think she'll be all right?' Ray asked Len, as they lurched back to Len's house.

'She hasn't far to go.'

Bet watched them go, then turned and set off for home, dragging her coat by the sleeve. After she had walked a few steps she realised she was cold. She picked up her coat and tried to put it on but it had taken on a life of its own. The simple task turned into a wrestling match. She lost. She dropped the coat and moved on.

The wall came out to meet her and she grazed her arm. Then she fell sideways into a shop doorway and landed on two empty milk bottles. 'All this money,' she muttered, 'and it's all mine.'

A shadowy figure stopped in front of her.

'Don't I know you? Weren't you there the night of the—?'

Bet never finished her sentence. The man caught her by the elbow and shoved her into an alleyway. She tried to scream, but a dull booming filled her ears and blotted all coherent thought from her mind. She fell into a deep dark pit. A pit lined with thick cushions of sensuous black velvet that closed around her, warming her chilled body.

Stan was the last to leave the Rovers. He sang an old Elvis Presley hit, 'Are You Lonesome Tonight', to himself as he meandered down the street. The he tripped. He kicked the obstacle towards the light and saw it was a coat. It didn't look too bad. The thought crossed his mind that Hilda might like it.

He picked it up and groaned. He should have visited the gents' before he left the Rovers. Carrying the coat, he dived into the alleyway to relieve himself and tripped a second time.

He crouched down, and peered into the gloom. Even in

the darkness he could see the congealed blood on Bet's face. He ran back to the Rovers and, yelling for help, he pounded on the door.

Chapter Twenty-Four

'It wasn't a mugging.' The police officer met Len and Ray in the waiting room outside Bet's hospital ward. 'Her handbag wasn't touched and there was over seventy pounds in it.'

'Then it was . . .'

'It wasn't rape either, Mr Langton,' the constable interposed. 'I've spoken to the lady and she knew the man who attacked her. She gave evidence against him in court before she came to Weatherfield. Apparently he tried to blackmail a friend of hers.'

'Woman with a past, our Bet,' Len mused.

'Off the record, sir, I'd say she could do with all the friends she can get right now.'

Ray pushed open the door to the ward. Bet was lying in the bed nearest the door; her face was black and blue, her forehead creased in pain.

'Thanks,' she whispered hoarsely when Ray laid a bunch of anemones on her locker and Len presented her with a box of chocolates. 'Some holiday.' She looked disparagingly around the ward. 'Who'd be here instead of Spain?'

'At least you're alive, love.' Len pulled up a chair and sat next to her bed.

'Who do you know in Scarborough?' Alan asked Elsie.

'An old schoolfriend.' Elsie dropped her make-up into her handbag.

'When will you be back?'

'I'll be home tonight. I'm only going for the day. See you.' She kissed his cheek and left the house before he could interrogate her any further.

She caught the London train. The old schoolfriend was a figment of her imagination. If she hadn't been so bitterly ashamed, she would have told Alan the truth: her son, Dennis, was back in prison serving a three-year sentence for fraud.

She took a taxi across London. The prison was different to the one Dennis had been in before, but the same old sick feeling filled her stomach as she paid the driver. Nothing had changed since the last time she had stood outside high wooden gates waiting to see her son. And, just like the last time, there was a crowd waiting with her. At two o'clock precisely a small door opened in the massive gates, and a warder ushered the visitors through. Elsie took a last drag on her cigarette and threw the butt end on to the floor.

★

'Mam, you didn't have to come.' Dennis looked thinner, older and more drawn.

'Yes, I did. When all's said and done, you're still my son. How's Jenny?'

'She left me.'

'Then I'm all you've got.'

Tears welled in Dennis's eyes.

'You got over this before, you'll get over it again,' she told him, with more confidence than she felt.

Elsie left the prison preoccupied by thoughts of the beautiful baby and mischievous toddler Dennis had been. Where had it all gone wrong? Was it her fault?

Racked by guilt she didn't see the taxi as she stepped into the road. Or feel the pain as she was thrown back on to the pavement from the force of the impact. She was blissfully unconscious.

Ken spotted Janet Reid standing behind the reception desk of the council offices and felt like an awkward teenager about to ask a girl out for the first time. He knew that she was single, and he knew that she dated men because he had seen her out with colleagues from his school. He also knew that she had a certain integrity because she had been quick enough to throw Alan Howard over, once Elsie had confronted her and told her to leave her husband alone.

But he still hesitated. It wasn't as if he hadn't been out with other women since Valerie's death. There had been a brief fling with Rita Littlewood before he'd realised he didn't care for her any more than she did him. She had been using him to get back at Len, who was quite happy to sleep with her provided she didn't ask for a more permanent arrangement. His problem was that he was a one-woman man, but his woman was dead and she had left him with two children who needed a mother. It had been very hard to leave them last weekend in Scotland and, on the train home, he had decided that their needs held priority over his. He walked up to the desk.

'Hello – Janet, isn't it?'

'It is.' Janet glanced up from the appointment book.

'I'm Ken Barlow. You deal with my expenses. From Bessie Street School,' he elaborated. 'I recently moved there from teaching in the college.'

'We've spoken on the phone.' Janet patted her hair into place.

'I wondered if you'd like to have dinner with me one evening.'

Janet smiled. Why not?' she replied.

'Does Friday suit you?'

'Perfectly. Where were you thinking of going?'

'The Green Dragon Chinese on the high street. Shall we say eight o'clock?'

'I'll be there.'

'I'll book us a table.'

Every unattached girl who worked for the council knew Ken Barlow's tragic story; they also knew he was after a wife and that he had children who didn't live with him. Janet gazed down at her ring finger and looked forward to her date.

'It's been two weeks since I last saw my wife . . .' Alan knew he was shouting, and was also aware that he wasn't helping the situation. Officers were trained to ignore people who made scenes in police stations. But he was convinced that Elsie hadn't left him of her own accord. He reined in his temper and lowered his voice. 'I know what you're thinking . . .'

'You do, sir?' the young constable enquired, with a smirk that Alan longed to wipe off his face.

'Most people who disappear want to. But if my wife had intended to leave me she would have taken her things. She left with only the clothes she stood up in and about ten pounds.'

'You are the Mr Alan Howard who was cautioned for being drunk and disorderly on more than one occasion in the last six months, sir?'

'Yes,' Alan conceded, 'and I'm the first to admit that I've been a less than perfect husband, but if Elsie had wanted to leave she would have told me so to my face, not sneaked away.'

'Your wife might be involved with someone else, sir,' the constable suggested.

'She would have told me.' Alan fought the urge to pick up the cocky lad and shake him.

'Mr Howard.'

'Yes,' Alan turned to the sergeant who walked towards them holding a piece of paper.

'There's a woman in a London hospital with concussion. She was knocked down in the street. She had no identification on her but the description matches your wife.'

Alan snatched the paper from the sergeant. He saw 'St Thomas's Hospital' and ran to the door.

'It might not be her, Mr Howard,' the sergeant shouted.

'And it might be!' Alan yelled back.

'Nellie Harvey said she saw you coming out of the Aquarius Club at eleven o'clock at night with thick make-up all over your face.' Annie confronted Lucille at the lunch table. 'You lied to me. All the time I thought you were in the YWCA you were dancing in that club. I'm ashamed of you, and your father would be, if he were alive.'

'No, he wouldn't,' Lucille retorted. 'He'd be proud of me for finding work. I know he would. And go-go dancing is better paid than any receptionist's job.'

'Goodness only knows who you've been mixing with.'

'Nice people, that's who,' Lucille interrupted. Her pride wouldn't allow her to tell Annie the truth. That she had embarked on an affair with the love of her life, Danny Burrows, only to find out from the other girls that he was married with a baby. She'd sent him packing and written to her stepmother, Concepta, hoping that she could get away from everything and everyone in Weatherfield and live with her in Ireland for a while. But she had sent her letter two weeks ago and was still waiting for a reply. What if Concepta didn't want her?

'I don't understand you at all, Lucille. In my day, girls wanted to be well thought of by people and considered ladylike. A go-go dancer!'

'Letter for you, Lucille.' Recognising that his mother was about to launch into one of her lectures on morality, Billy tossed it to Lucille as he joined them for breakfast.

Lucille tore it open and scanned it eagerly. 'You don't have to worry about me any longer, Auntie Annie. I'm going to Ireland.' The she remembered her manners. 'But thank you for everything you've done for me.'

'We'll miss you, Lucille, won't we, Billy?' Annie turned to her son so that Lucille wouldn't see the tears in her eyes. But she couldn't help feeling that part of her would be relieved when Lucille Hewitt was someone else's responsibility.

Elsie opened her eyes to see Alan sitting beside her, a frown creasing his broad, handsome forehead.

'So,' he joked, 'how was Scarborough?'

'Alan . . .'

'I know, love. I know everything. The sister told me you came round this morning, asked after your Dennis and begged her not to worry him by telling him you were in here. Why didn't you ask them to contact me?'

'Because I was ashamed.'

'Of what?' he asked in bewilderment.

'Of lying to you. Of Dennis . . .'

'I've a proposition to make to you, Mrs Howard. Our marriage hasn't exactly run smoothly. You've put up with my bankruptcy, moods and drinking, and I've done precious little for you in return. How about I sell the garage, take the money and carry you off back to my old stomping ground in Newcastle? We'll begin again in a fresh place with new people, and leave our ghosts and the gossips behind.' He blotted her tears with her handkerchief.

'I'd like that, love,' Elsie murmured softly. 'In fact I'd like it very much indeed.'

'I can't sleep, Doctor,' Hilda complained. 'I wake at four every morning and I find meself crying all the time.' She fumbled in her sleeve for her handkerchief.

'I heard about your husband being charged with disturbing the peace.'

'When they thought he was a peeping Tom.' Hilda shook her head. 'That's all been sorted. The police caught another man and everyone apologised to Stan and me.

Ever so nice they were. Mind, it were horrible to think the neighbours could believe Stan would do such a thing.'

'Do you get out much, Mrs Ogden?'

'The truth is, Doctor, I don't want to go out at all. Most days,' she fought back her tears, 'I just want to curl up and hide.'

'It sounds as if you are suffering from depression, Mrs Ogden,' the doctor diagnosed. 'It's common enough and we're seeing more and more of it these days. In my opinion the best cure is a change of scenery.'

Hilda wiped her eyes and blew her nose. 'Isn't there anything you can give me? Pills or something?'

'I'd rather not prescribe anything at this stage,' he said. 'Why don't you talk to Stan?'

'He doesn't care.' She sniffed.

'Come back and see me in a week's time. We'll talk about it again then.'

Hilda left the surgery, feeling hurt and resentful. She had hoped the doctor would give her sleeping tablets, or the Valium so many of her friends were taking and talked about down the Rovers as a miracle cure.

When she got home, she pulled the evening paper out of her letterbox and crawled into bed. She turned to the 'Deaths' column and saw an advert on the opposite page. 'The Monte Umber Cruise Liner seeks staff for voyage to Caribbean. Stewards, caterers and cleaners required. Apply . . .'

Could she – dare she –? She crept downstairs, took a writing pad from the sideboard drawer and carried it back upstairs. Her teacher in junior school had spent a long time teaching them to write nice letters, and she took extra care over every word she penned.

'I never expected to succumb to a whirlwind courtship.' Janet held up her left hand and admired the diamond ring and wide gold wedding band Ken had slipped on her finger in a register office, eight weeks to the day since their first date.

'I know you and the twins didn't get on all that well this weekend, and I'm the first to agree that my mother-in-law can be difficult, but I'm sure you'll all be fine with one another, given time.' Ken was trying to reassure himself as much as Janet as they travelled back to Manchester from Glasgow on the train.

'It might be as well if we don't see too much of them,' Janet said.

'Are you talking about my mother-in-law or the twins?' Ken asked in alarm.

'Both, darling.'

'Are you saying you don't want the twins to come and live with us?'

'No,' Janet answered. 'Just that they shouldn't come just yet. Let's face it, Ken, there isn't enough room for the four of us in the poky house you rent. And it wouldn't be fair to expect the twins to come back to less than their grandparents can give them in Glasgow.'

'I hadn't thought about that, Jan. You're right.' The house *was* too small for him, Janet and two growing children. They would have to find somewhere larger, even if it meant leaving Coronation Street – but that would be a small sacrifice, he thought, if he could finally bring his family together.

'Half past six, outside gate six,' Ray muttered absently, from behind the *Daily Mirror* when Deirdre pressed him about the arrangements for their night out. He was on his tea break and wanted five minutes' peace and quiet, not a load of hassle from his girlfriend.

'I'll come round to your house.'

'No you won't.' Ray dropped the newspaper. 'You'll meet me at the football ground.'

'Why?'

'Because I have to get there early to pick up the tickets, that's why.'

'Give me one good reason why I can't call round your place so we can walk there together?' Deirdre demanded. Ray had come up with excuses all week as to why she couldn't visit him at his house.

'If you're not outside the grounds at half past six I'm going in without you.' Furious, Ray delivered his ultimatum. He was feeling increasingly hemmed in by Deirdre: he worked with her during the day and went out with her practically every evening, and claustrophobia was beginning to set in.

'I won't be there.'

'Deirdre . . .' Ray found himself shouting at a closed door. Cursing, he crumpled his paper and tossed it on to the floor instead of the bin. The cabin was so bloody tidy it was getting on his nerves. Just like Deirdre.

Billy Walker was clearing glasses from the tables in the Rovers at seven o'clock in the evening the night of the football match when he glanced at the clock and realised that Deirdre Hunt had been sitting alone at the bar for an hour. 'No Ray tonight?' he asked lightly.

'Don't ask.' Deirdre finished her gin and tonic.

'Like that, is it?' Billy dumped the dirty glasses in the tray beneath the bar.

'Let's just say a difference of opinion,' Deirdre replied shortly.

'You heard about Alison, then.'

'Who?' She stared at Billy.

'Sorry, I thought you'd found out.'

'You can't leave it there.' Her stomach turned somersaults and she felt sick.

'I had no business saying anything. Let me get you another drink. Same again?' Billy picked up her glass.

Deirdre hesitated.

'I'm only offering you a drink.'

'First, you tell me what you know,' she said quietly. 'After saying what you just did, you owe me that much.' When he remained silent, she added, 'How would you feel if it was you?'

'All I know is that this girl Alison turned up on Ray's doorstep last week and he let her stay. She has a baby with her.'

'And everyone in the street knew this except me?' Suddenly everything fell into place: Ray's refusal to allow her to call round at his place, his irritability and short temper . . .

'It might be nothing, Deirdre.' Billy delivered the platitude in a monotone. He didn't believe what he was saying and he didn't expect her to either.

'Keep your drink.' Deirdre buttoned her coat and walked out.

Janet waited until she'd cleared her own and Ken's tea dishes into the scullery before she opened the sideboard drawer and lifted out a pile of estate agents' brochures. After only a few weeks she was finding her marriage stale. She wanted more – much more than Coronation Street could offer – and she had a feeling that if she didn't start prodding Ken to make a move, they'd both remain in his rented house in the street until they died.

'I made some enquiries today, Ken.' She set them down on the table beside him.

Ken flicked through them. 'These are way out of our price range.'

'Not really, darling.' Janet sat beside him and pulled the details of one of the properties towards her. 'Look at this one.'

Ken studied the photograph. 'This is huge! You must be joking.'

'If you don't want your family to be comfortable . . .'

'This isn't a question of comfortable. This is a question of bankruptcy.'

'Then you won't even put in an offer.' She moved away from him.

'Absolutely not.'

Her tone changed. 'Well, I'm not having your children here and that's final.' She flounced up the stairs. Ken stared after her. It was time to face facts. She hadn't married *him*, she had married what she had mistakenly thought was a ticket to middle-class suburban Manchester. She had no intention of living with his children – in Coronation Street or anywhere else.

'So, do you fancy doing something tonight?' Ray ventured. Deirdre hadn't spoken to him for a week and he suspected that if he didn't make the first move, she wasn't going to.

'I'm busy. You have your hands full anyway, with all those nappies to wash.' She folded the plastic cover over her typewriter.

'You've heard.'

'I've heard,' she snapped.

'Deirdre, let me explain—'

'You don't have to. Billy Walker's done it for you. He's taking me out tonight.' Deirdre picked up handbag, left the cabin and walked across the yard.

Ray watched her go and wondered why he hadn't he taken the trouble to explain to her that Alison had turned to him when her boyfriend had thrown her out. And, despite what everyone thought, the baby wasn't his.

Six weeks after Hilda had sent off her letter, she waited impatiently for Stan to come home from his window-cleaning round.

When he walked in, he eyed the plate of steak, chips and peas she had set in front of him, and asked, 'What's all this in aid of?'

'We're celebrating.' Hilda opened a bottle of beer and stood it next to his glass.

'What?' Stan asked. Hilda hadn't cooked or cleaned in weeks. In fact, she'd barely left her bed. He gave her a sideways look. Her hair was out of curlers, she had make-up on and, to his surprise, she didn't look half bad for a change.

'I'm off to the Caribbean for six weeks.'

'You what?' Stan put down his knife and fork.

'On a cruise.' She beamed.

'Doctor been giving you funny tablets, or what?'

'I got a job on a ship as a cleaner. And I'm going.' There was a tone in her voice that warned Stan not to try to talk her out of it.

'Six weeks?' he whispered faintly.

'That's right.'

'I might as well move in above the chippy.'

'Whatever suits you, Stan.'

'Elsie and Alan's house is much bigger than ours, Janet,' Ken argued in an attempt to find a compromise solution to the problem of finding a home large enough for all his family. 'If we rented it, there'd be plenty of room for the twins to come and live with us.'

'You promised we'd buy a house of our own. A big house, away from this street.' Janet bit her bottom lip, which was trembling.

'It's only until we can find the right place. Renting the Howards' house is a stopgap until we find a place at a price we can afford.'

'Promise?' Janet pressed.

'I promise, love,' he assured her. 'I'll find us a house of our own as soon as I can.'

Janet sat next to him on the sofa and rested her head on his shoulder, watching as he flicked through the new set of brochures she had collected from the estate agent.

'What's this?' He narrowed his eyes.

'Nothing.' Janet tried to snatch it from him. How could

she have been so stupid as to mix that one in with the others? He held it out of her reach.

'This isn't a house, it's a boarding school.' He opened the pamphlet and found a letter.

' "Thank you for your enquiry. If you need further details . . ." You thought you could get rid of my children, is that it?' Ken was angrier than Janet had ever seen him before. He grabbed the pile of leaflets and threw them at her. 'I've been worrying myself sick wondering how the hell I was going to afford a mortgage on the kind of house you wanted and all along you were planning to send my kids away. You never had any intention of allowing them to live with us, did you?'

'I was trying to do the sensible thing—'

'Sensible!'

'Ken, please, I want what's best for all of us.' She ran after him as he went to the front door.

'Get away from me.' He glared contemptuously at her. 'I wish I'd never set eyes on you, much less married you.'

'What did you want, Ken?' Janet taunted. 'A wife, or a mother for your children?'

'If you're trying to tell me that you're not the only one to blame, you're right,' he said. 'But let's call it a day, shall we? Before we say anything we'll regret later.'

'Deirdre Hunt.' Annie Walker sat down suddenly. 'Billy, you're telling me you're engaged to Deirdre Hunt?'

'Aren't you pleased for me?' Billy asked his mother.

Annie couldn't give him the answer he wanted. She was mortified to think that her son was engaged to a tart like Deirdre. She had hoped he would make a better choice. 'It's your life, Billy,' she said wearily. 'It's your life.'

Chapter Twenty-Five

Ken let himself into his empty house, went into the scullery and opened a tin of beans. He took the crust from the sliced loaf he'd bought in the corner shop and stuck it in the toaster. Janet had packed her bags and left the day after their row. He hardly missed her. In fact it was just as well she'd gone because it irritated him even to think of her. He ate his meal in the scullery, returned to the living room and dumped a mammoth pile of marking on the table.

An hour later he was at breaking-point. He couldn't concentrate for more than a couple of minutes at a time for the din of lorry engines, the hiss of brakes and the shouts of the warehousemen as they loaded and unloaded the lorries going in and out of the warehouse yard, opposite the house. He slammed down his pen, went outside and barged his way through the goods entrance of the yard into the warehouse office.

'I've had it up to here.' He drew an imaginary line

across his forehead as he stood in front of the owner Julius Berlin's desk. 'Everyone has a breaking point and you've just pushed me to mine.'

Julius gazed coolly back at him. 'Won't you sit down, Mr . . . ?'

'Barlow, Ken Barlow, an extremely irate resident of Coronation Street.' Ken stood behind the chair Julius offered him.

'What seems to be the problem?'

'Your bloody lorries!' Ken's fury waned in the face of the man's composure. 'In and out of the street at all hours of the day and night, never giving us poor residents a minute's peace.'

'What do you suggest I do about it?'

'Limit the hours you take deliveries.'

'To what?'

'Normal working hours, nine till five.'

'That sounds entirely reasonable to me, Mr Barlow. Won't you please sit down?'

'Why should I?'

'Because I'd like to offer you a job.'

Ken stared at the man for a moment, then burst out laughing.

'I assure you, I'm not joking, Mr Barlow. Honest, direct people who speak their minds without giving a damn for the consequences are in short supply. I know, because I'm always looking to employ them.'

Half an hour later Ken left the warehouse, having accepted a post as Northern Executive Administration Assistant at Berlin Warehousing on twice the salary he was earning at Bessie Street School – and, perhaps even more important, with half of the responsibility. Without trying, he had revolutionised his entire life.

Half an hour before closing time at the Rovers, Bet was attempting a tango on the bar. If Annie Walker had been sober she would have stopped her, but Annie had enjoyed one too many sherries that evening. She, along with Bet and half a dozen other women from the street, had won an all-expenses-paid holiday to Majorca, playing 'Spot the Ball' in the local paper. As Bet had been the one to send in the coupon, none of them was prepared to tell her now that she was making a fool of herself.

'Is that Bet Lynch?' a young soldier asked Len, as they waited at the bar for Annie to serve them.

'That's our Bet.' Len laughed as Bet lifted her skirt to her waist, giving the men an eyeful of her lace-trimmed pink nylon knickers.

The squaddie carried the two pints of beer Annie handed him to a back table and sat next to his mate.

'Is it her?' His friend stuck two cigarettes on the table.

'Yes.' The boy turned his back to Bet and drank his beer.

Bet slipped, screamed and giggled drunkenly when Len caught her.

'She would have broken her neck if that bloke hadn't grabbed her.'

The soldier who'd bought the beer turned to see Bet giving Len a great big wet kiss. 'Pity he bothered.' His disgust was evident on his face.

Bet saw him watching her and yelled, 'What's up with you two misery-gutses? Never seen anyone enjoy themselves before?'

Annie stepped in. 'Why don't you go out back, Bet, and wash the glasses?'

'You just want to get rid of me!'

'No, love, Annie's just fixing it so we can be alone together.' Len winked at her, picked up the tray of glasses and carried it out the back.

Bet glanced at the boys before she left the bar. They didn't look old enough to drink.

Suddenly, for no apparent reason, she remembered a day seventeen years before when she had handed over her six-week-old son for adoption. It hadn't been easy but then she'd had no choice. He would be about their age now . . .

'Bet, where are you?' Len shouted.

'Coming, love.' Swishing her skirt, she tangoed her way into the kitchen.

★

'I'm only here for Christmas, Minnie.' Ena heaved her suitcase on to Minnie's spare bed in her rented house at number five Coronation Street.

'I know, Ena. But you may as well put your things away properly while you're here.' Minnie had been looking forward to having company over Christmas and had cleared out a chest of drawers for her friend.

'I suppose I could put me smalls in there,' Ena capitulated.

'I'll put kettle on so we can have a nice cup of tea. See you downstairs in a minute?'

'I'll be right behind you.'

Ten minutes later, in a comfortable armchair in front of a roaring blaze, Ena was more content than she had been in months. Minnie was lucky to have her own place and she was grateful to her friend for inviting her. She only wished she still had a flat or house to call her own, but since she had been forced to give up her caretaker's job through ill health she had resigned herself to living in the noisy, overcrowded old folks' home that her daughters had found for her.

'Would you like a date?' Minnie offered her a long cardboard box. 'Or a chocolate brazil?'

'How could you afford this lot on your pension, Minnie Caldwell? There's even a bottle of sherry on that sideboard.'

'And I've a turkey in the larder,' Minnie said proudly.

'You know how it is, Ena, I've been saving. A little here, a little there, it's surprising how it mounts up.'

'A turkey just for the two of us,' Ena admonished. 'A chicken would have done.'

'My old lodger, Jed Stone, you remember him?'

'That friend of Dennis Tanner's who went back to prison? Don't tell me you're expecting him?' Ena exclaimed.

'He's a reformed man. He wrote and told me he got parole, so I said he could come here for Christmas.' Minnie stared defiantly at Ena.

'I didn't expect to be eating my Christmas dinner with a criminal, even though the good Lord Himself was full of forgiveness. I'm going to lock up my jewellery, and I suggest you do the same.' Before Ena left the room, there was a knock at the door.

'That'll be him now.' Minnie rose stiffly from her chair.

'It's dark out there. Ask who it is before you open that door,' Ena warned.

'Who is it?' Minnie shouted through the letterbox.

'Eddie Yeats.'

'And who's Eddie Yeats when he's at home?' Ena called back.

'A friend of Jed Stone. He lost his parole and he said that as I was coming out and had nowhere to go for Christmas, you wouldn't mind if I had his Christmas dinner instead of him.'

'Of all the barefaced cheek!' Ena exploded.

Minnie didn't hesitate. She opened the door.

'Good evening, ladies.' Eddie grinned and bowed. 'I brought you these as a present.' He handed Minnie a box of candles.

'Come in, Mr Yeats. I prepared a room for Jed, and if he said you could have it, you're welcome in my house,' Minnie offered, bravely ignoring Ena's stern looks.

'And a merry Christmas to both you, ladies. I've come prepared to work. Here are my credentials.' He handed Minnie a Christmas card. 'That's from Jed. He'll testify to what a first-class cook I am. Tomorrow,' he smiled at Minnie and turned to Ena, 'neither of you two charming beauties will lift a finger.'

'Ooh, that's nice, isn't it, Ena?' Minnie returned Eddie's smile.

'Otitis media? What the hell is that when it's at home?' Stan asked the doctor. Hilda had no sooner come home from her cruise than he had started having giddy spells. And when he had fallen from his ladder twice the day before, even she had had to accept that they could no longer be put down to his poor diet while she'd been away.

'It means your balance is disturbed, Mr Ogden,' the consultant explained. 'You won't be climbing ladders again for a while.'

'But I'm a window-cleaner . . .' Stan was talking to

himself; the consultant had already moved along the ward to the next patient.

'How are we going to manage?' Hilda wailed.

'I'll have to sign on the dole.' Stan slid down in the bed and lay back on the pillows. 'We won't live in luxury but we'll live.'

'You did pay your stamp like I asked you to before I went away?' Hilda knew that Stan wouldn't be entitled to dole if he hadn't. 'There was six months owing.'

'All you ever do is nag, woman. I need my rest.'

'Don't tell you haven't . . . Stan, how could you?' Hilda burst into tears. The money she'd made on the cruise ship wouldn't last more than a couple of weeks if she had to use it for housekeeping. And she had been hoping to buy herself a new coat.

'Stop whining.' Guilt made Stan irritable. 'It'll sort itself out.'

The following morning, Hilda pushed the exercise book that held Stan's scribbled lists of customers into the pocket of her mac, went into the back yard, shouldered his ladders and picked up his chamois and bucket.

It took her all morning, but she cleaned the windows of twenty houses and was amazed when she made half a week's housekeeping. At this rate she and Stan would have no worries about holding their heads above water.

She was eating her sandwiches on the bench in the

Rosamund Street bus shelter when a man of much the same stamp and build as Stan, but with ginger hair, approached her.

'Mrs Ogden, this is your lucky day.'

'Do I know you?' She moved further along the bench to get away from him.

'I was chatting to your Stan just before he fell off his ladder. I'm Eddie Yeats.' He held out his hand. 'Minnie Caldwell's new lodger. I didn't know you were in the window-cleaning business as well as Stan.'

'I'm not, but with Stan in hospital I'd no choice but to take over his round.'

'How about I help you out, just for this afternoon?' Eddie needed a job. Without one, he'd soon be headed straight back inside – no one could survive on what the social paid out.

'Just for this afternoon?' Hilda looked at him quizzically. 'What's in it for you?'

'A couple of quid and, who knows, if we get on, we could possibly expand. Take on enough clients to keep both Stan and myself occupied when he comes out of hospital. Climbing ladders is no job for a lady like yourself, Mrs Ogden.'

It had been a long time since anyone had called Hilda a lady. 'We'll give it a try, but just for this afternoon, Mr Yeats,' she cautioned.

'Eddie, please. And I wouldn't have it any other way.

Here.' He took the bucket from her as she pushed the empty paper bag that had contained her sandwiches into her pocket. 'Let me carry the ladder and bucket. What say you do the downstairs and I do the upstairs? That way we'll have the round finished in half the time. Shall I borrow my landlady's bucket on the way so we can have one each?'

'I sneaked an afternoon off,' Len said, as Bet opened her door to him. 'You going to let me in?'

'Why?'

'This is why.' Len stepped into her hallway, took her into his arms, kicked the front door shut and kissed her. He slid his hands beneath her sweater.

'Hold on.' Bet caught them and moved them away from her.

'Sorry,' Len said. 'You're enough to drive a monk wild. Why don't we go upstairs?'

'It's the middle of the afternoon,' Bet protested, not at all sure she wanted Len in her bed.

'Day or night, what's the difference?'

She looked into his eyes. She couldn't deny that he was attractive – and it had been a long time. 'I suppose we could always close the curtains,' she murmured.

'If you're tired, Mrs Ogden, it's because you're doing too much. I saw you cleaning windows in Viaduct Street yesterday,' the doctor admonished her.

'I've got help now with that. Mr Yeats does all the upstairs ones,' she protested.

The doctor sat back in his chair and looked her over with a professional eye. 'Why don't you give up cleaning windows altogether and let Stan take over?'

'Because he hasn't been signed fit for work yet. He's only been out of hospital a month.'

'I told him he was fit to go back a week after the hospital discharged him.'

'You what?' Hilda's jaw dropped.

'Mrs Ogden, you said you weren't well,' the doctor remonstrated, as Hilda gathered up her handbag and went to the door.

'I'll be better, just as soon as I've seen Stan,' she assured him.

'We'll have to make a habit of this.' Len stroked Bet's hair and kissed her, then swung his legs out of her bed.

'We will.' She smiled lazily and stretched. 'It's good to have a man I can trust.'

'You'll always be able to do that, love. I'm not much of one for gossip.' Len reached for his clothes.

She watched him pull on his underpants and trousers. 'So, when you moving in?'

Len zipped his trousers. 'I'm not.'

'But—'

'This just a bit of fun.' Len slipped on his shirt. 'Love

in the afternoon and all that. It'll give us both something to look forward to.'

'Look forward . . . A bit of fun . . . Is that all I am to you?' she demanded.

'Come on, don't tell me that a girl like you takes it seriously.' He tucked his shirt into his trousers and buckled his belt.

Bet went white with anger. 'A girl like me? And what's one of those, Len?'

'Don't go looking for something that's not there.'

'You're just like every man I've ever met. You used me.' Bet picked up her pillow and flung it at him.

'From where I was lying ten minutes ago it felt like the other way round, love.' Len laughed.

'You swine!'

'Be realistic, Bet, Romeo and Juliet this isn't.' He backed towards the door. 'Thanks for the afternoon. Sorry we won't be doing it again.' Len closed the door a split second before Bet flung the lamp at him. He heard the sound of the glass shade splintering on the door panel and ran down the stairs before she could come after him.

'Hard afternoon?' Hilda asked, as Stan wandered in smelling of beer an hour after their usual tea-time.

'Not too bad, love. I had a nice chat with Annie and some of the regulars. What's for tea?'

'This.' Hilda dumped a bucket of the wash leathers they used for cleaning windows on the table.

'You will have your little joke.'

'This isn't a joke.' Hilda crossed her arms and stared at her husband. 'You're fit for work.'

'How do you . . . ?' Stan took one look at her face and realised she knew the truth. 'So the doctor says, love, but I'm still not well.' He adopted a pained expression.

'You're well enough to take my money and go boozing down Rovers all day.'

'I thought you enjoyed working with Eddie.'

'I'll tell you something about me and Eddie,' she shouted. 'The round has brought in ten times the money since we took over. You're a lazy toad, Stan Ogden, but tomorrow you start work again. I'll ask Eddie to collect all the money and hold on to it until he can give it to me and you'll get no food in this house or beer money until you do the windows of ten more houses a day than Eddie. And that's final.'

'Miss Lynch?'

Bet pulled her dressing-gown around her and nodded.

'Sign here.' The postman pushed a form and a pen into her hand.

Bet scribbled her signature, took the recorded delivery envelope and ran back up the stairs. She sat at the table, opened it and looked at the letter heading. 'Ministry of Defence'. Mystified, she read on.

★

'I heard someone scream as I passed your door and as it was open . . . You all right, Bet?' Eddie Yeats took one look at Bet slumped over her kitchen table and realised she was anything but all right. 'Shall I call a doctor?'

'No,' Bet croaked. 'Go away.'

'Not until I know you're OK.' Eddie saw the letter lying on the table and picked it up. 'Is this what upset you?'

Bet nodded.

'Can I read it?'

She waved her hand in a gesture of defeat. He scanned the letter and sat on the chair beside her.

'Bet, love,' he laid his hand over hers, 'I am so sorry. I had no idea you had a son. And to get killed at seventeen in Northern Ireland . . . I don't know what to say.'

'He found out that I was his mother and he came looking for me a few weeks ago. I never saw him, but he saw me. He wrote to me afterwards to tell me that he'd seen me in Rovers – drunk and dancing around . . .'

'I'm so, so sorry, love.'

Eddie's sympathy, coming on top of everything else, was more than Bet could bear. She began to sob.

'Come on, love.' Eddie helped her to her feet. 'Let's get you into bed. Then I'll call the doctor.'

She shook her head fiercely.

'No arguments, love. I'll manage without Hilda today. She'll sit with you until the doctor comes.'

Too broken to fight him, Bet allowed Eddie to lead her into her bedroom.

To Eddie's surprise it was Stan who opened the Ogdens' door at his knock.

'You're late,' Stan complained.

'What's it to you? You fit to start again?' Eddie asked, in surprise, as Stan put his coat on.

'Seems so.' Hilda was standing behind him in the passage, and Stan turned and gave her a scathing look.

'It might be as well. Bet Lynch is ill. I called in Rovers and telephoned the doctor. He's calling round some time this morning. Don't suppose you'll sit with her until he arrives, Hilda?' Eddie looked at her over Stan's shoulder.

'I'd be glad to, Eddie.' Hilda picked up her mac. 'A morning sitting down talking to someone is just what I need.'

Ken read the notice pinned on the board in the corridor with a growing sense of disbelief. 'How can they make twenty per cent of the warehouse staff redundant?'

'There'll be no bugger left soon,' Edna Gee muttered, standing alongside him.

Ken walked down the corridor, knocked on Julius

Berlin's door and walked in without waiting for an answer.

'I've been expecting you,' Julius said uneasily. 'You don't have to worry. You'll get redundancy and with your qualifications you'll soon pick up another teaching post.'

'I'm not here for me,' Ken said hotly, 'but for the work-force. This is 1975. You just can't throw everyone out of work when jobs are hard to come by . . .'

'Jobs always are hard to come by in a recession,' Julius agreed. 'Do you think I'm enjoying having to do this? I haven't enough work to keep everyone occupied. We're losing money.'

'There has to be another answer besides cutting staff.'

'Tell me what it is and I'll do it, Ken.' Julius faced him head-on.

'What happens when things pick up and you have no staff to call on?'

'I'll hire again. You can tell everyone that there'll be a full list of redundancies posted before the end of the day. I'm compiling it now.' Julius held up a clipboard. 'It's on a last-in, first-out basis. I thought that was fairest – and, Ken,' he added as Ken opened the door.

'What?'

'I'm sorry I persuaded you to give up teaching.'

'As I said, I'm not concerned about myself. I'll find something else soon enough. It's the others I'm worried about.'

★

'She's slept all afternoon,' Hilda whispered, when she let Eddie into Bet's flat. 'I think the doctor gave her something. Nice flowers.'

'I thought so.' Eddie sniffed the bunch of freesias he'd bought for Bet. 'Small, but they smell nice.'

'I'll be off, then.' Hilda folded her coat over her arm.

'You look better for a day off, love,' Eddie remarked.

'To be honest, it was nice to put my feet up for once and . . .' Hilda gave him a sheepish smile '. . . Bet wasn't the only one who slept.'

Eddie saw her out and went into the kitchen in search of a vase. There was a box of painkillers on the draining board. He flipped it open. It was empty.

He dashed into Bet's bedroom. She was sitting on the floor at the side of the bed holding a handful of pills.

'That's not going to help anyone, love.' He closed his hand over hers.

'The only decent thing I ever did has gone. I've made a right mess of my life. Who would care if I died?'

'More people than you think, love.' He took the pills from her hand.

'You don't know how I feel.'

'Yes, I do, love. I've been inside and served time. You can't make more of a mess of your life than that.' He helped her back into bed. 'Now, let's talk this out.'

Chapter Twenty-Six

Bet woke at dawn. The sun was streaming through the open curtains and Eddie was standing next to her bed with a cup of tea.

'Ready for breakfast?'

'You don't have to bother.'

'No bother,' Eddie assured her. 'It'll be on the table in five minutes. Scrambled eggs on toast with beans all right?'

'It's more than I usually eat in the morning.' Bet was relieved that it was the first time a man had spent the night with her and not slept in her bed. She drank the tea, went into the bathroom, washed her hands and face and wandered into the kitchen to find Eddie rinsing out her tights. 'What are you doing?'

Colour flooded into his cheeks. 'I'm sorry, it's nothing kinky. I didn't mean to offend you. Force of habit. Comes of doing time. You learn to look after yourself when you're inside.'

'You're the first person to do my washing since me Mam died. Thanks, Eddie.' She paused for a moment. 'Thanks for everything.'

Eddie fumbled awkwardly for his keys. 'Got to go to work. But I'll see you tonight, in Rovers.'

'I'll be there,' Bet declared.

'Bet . . .'

'You don't have to worry, Eddie, I won't do anything daft.'

'Promise?'

'I promise,' she answered.

Ken applied for, and took, the first job he saw advertised, driving a taxi. He looked on it as a stopgap but, to his surprise, he discovered he enjoyed ferrying strangers around the town. It wasn't stressful, he met people from all strata of society and brought in enough to cover his bills. After teaching and all the problems he'd had to deal with in Berlin's warehouse it made a welcome change.

'Where to?' he questioned a woman, who flagged him down on an exceptionally foul and filthy night.

'Is that you, Ken? Whatever are you doing driving a cab?'

'Janet, you're looking well,' he said, as she climbed into the back. He meant it. She was wearing a beige caped mac and her hair had been cut short in a new, flattering style.

'I could say the same about you.' She turned to the

man who sat beside her. 'This is Vince. Vince, meet Ken. My husband.'

'Hello.'

Vince broke the silence that followed Ken's greeting. 'If we don't get a move on, the restaurant will let our table go.'

'Which restaurant?' Ken pushed the car into gear.

'The new Italian on the high street.'

'I know it.' Ken headed into town.

'Why don't you join us, Ken?' Janet offered.

'I hardly think that would be appropriate.'

'Oh, I don't know. Vince and I are living together, and you're obviously managing perfectly well without me.'

'I am.' Ken smiled.

'I told you Ken's and my marriage was a disaster, didn't I, Vince?'

'You did.'

Ken started to laugh, and Janet and Vince joined in.

'Janet's right, mate,' Vince said. 'You should join us.'

'Not to talk about old times,' Janet added. 'We can toast separate lives.'

'If that's the toast, Jan, count me in.' Ken pulled up outside the restaurant and switched off the ignition.

'I don't want a long engagement, Billy.' Deirdre played with her empty glass as she sat on a bar stool in the Rovers and watched him work.

'We haven't enough money saved to get married.' Billy handed Len a pint and took his money.

'I don't care about money.'

'What we going to live on?' Billy enquired tersely. 'Fresh air?'

'We're both living all right now, aren't we?' Deirdre said pointedly. 'I don't see either of us starving and they say two can live as cheaply as one.'

'And what exactly do you propose we live in? A cardboard box out back?'

'Your bedroom might be better.' Deirdre winked.

'You want to live with my mother?' he whispered. Annie was standing at the other end of the bar, close to the snug.

'Better that than live apart.' Deirdre took out her diary. 'How about the twenty-fourth of May? It should be warm, and perhaps we could go away for a few days. To the Lake District or the seaside.'

'You're going away?' Annie walked back up the bar and looked at Billy.

'On honeymoon, Mrs Walker.' Deirdre was aware that her future mother-in-law couldn't stand her but she forced a smile. 'Billy and I have just fixed the date for the twenty-fourth of May. Have you thought what you're going to wear?'

'Not yet, dear.'

'Mother of the groom,' Deirdre reminded her.

'Everyone will be looking at your outfit. If you like I could help you choose it.'

Annie gritted her teeth. 'I think I'll wait until the latest spring fashions are in the shops.'

Ken was sleeping after a late night shift when a siren woke him. Leaping out of bed, he pulled back his curtain to see smoke and flames pouring out of the warehouse windows. He dressed hurriedly and ran downstairs.

'Ken,' Julian stopped him as he charged out of his house, 'Edna Gee's been killed. The police have sent someone round to tell her husband Fred.'

'What happened?' Ken stepped back as firemen raced back and forth, running hoses out from their engine.

'We had a break-in last night, the police called me and I checked round. I thought everything was all right but they must have left something burning in the stockroom. Edna was first in as usual. She opened the stockroom door and there was an explosion . . . There weren't many of us in and we managed to get out, but poor Edna . . .'

'We have to evacuate the street, because of the toxic fumes.' The fireman pulled his helmet from his head and wiped his forehead with the back of his hand. 'Could you two gentlemen help us to get everyone to the community centre? The police have called in the Salvation Army to help with tea and blankets.'

'Bloody kids,' Albert Tatlock grumbled, as he walked

alongside Ken to the centre. 'This wouldn't have happened in my day. We were too afraid of coppers and the birch to put a foot wrong.'

'How do you know it was kids?' Ken asked.

'I saw them running away from the warehouse last night. It was me who called the police.'

'It's not the kids' fault, Uncle Albert, I've taught most of them round here. They're not a bad lot but there's nothing round here for them to do except get into trouble at night,' Ken said.

'What sort of things do you think they should be doing, then, Ken?' Councillor Alf Roberts asked from behind them.

Ken turned to face him. A tall, large man, with dark hair, wearing a well-cut wool suit, Alf looked brisk and businesslike. Ken knew the man both by name and reputation as someone who was good at effecting change and persuading others – particularly bureaucrats with entrenched opinions – to his point of view. 'A youth club would help to channel their energies into useful activities. Offer them classes in things they want to do, like art and pop music. You could run a couple of dances—'

'That's right,' Albert broke in testily. 'Use the ratepayers' money to mollycoddle delinquents. They should do National Service. That would sort them out.'

Ken took two mugs of tea from a volunteer and handed one to Albert. 'They need someone to set them a good example, Uncle Albert, not a sergeant major to drill them. That would only make them even angrier and more resentful than they already are.'

'Do you really think if there was a youth club for the kids to go to, there'd be less vandalism round here?' Alf asked Ken.

'Yes, I do,' Ken reiterated firmly. 'I really believe it's as basic as that.'

'What do you think, Mam?' Deirdre walked out of the changing room in a satin wedding gown trimmed with layers of lace and pearl buttons.

'A proper fairy-tale gown,' Blanche Hunt gushed. 'Do you think this is too much?' She looked in the mirror and studied the pale blue and lemon dress with bolero jacket she'd chosen.

'Very nice.'

'Your wedding gown fits perfectly now it's been altered, Miss Hunt,' the shop assistant assured Deirdre.

Blanche looked critically at the dress. 'You've done a fine job considering how little time she gave you to take it in.'

'What do you mean, "little time"?' Deirdre demanded.

'Well, you're positively galloping up the aisle.'

'I'm not pregnant, Mam.'

'I never said you were.' Blanche checked the outfit she was wearing one last time in the mirror.

'It looks good on you, madam,' the assistant complimented her.

'I'll take it,' Blanche finally decided.

'Billy and I love each other, Mam, it's only natural that we want to get married as soon as possible. We've no reason to wait.' Suddenly Deirdre had the oddest feeling that she was trying to convince herself, not her mother, that Billy was the one for her. She busied herself unfastening the long row of pearl buttons on the front of her dress.

'You've gone quiet, love.' Blanche emerged from the cubicle and handed the assistant her wedding outfit.

'I'm fine, Mam.'

All brides got cold feet before their wedding, or so everyone said. She was seeing Billy tonight. He'd soon get rid of her doubts. Wouldn't he?

'Nineteen days from now you'll be Mrs Billy Walker.' Billy poured Deirdre a gin and set it together with a bottle of tonic water on the bar in front of her. Deirdre picked up the gin and absently downed it in one.

'It's not your hen night yet.' Billy was glad that his mother hadn't seen what Deirdre had done.

'Are you thinking what I'm thinking?'

'You want to call off the wedding?' Billy ventured.

Deirdre nodded.

'Deirdre, I'm so glad you're here, dear.' Annie walked

in wearing a new outfit. 'What do you think of this for your wedding?'

Deirdre had difficulty keeping a straight face. 'It's the same outfit me Mam chose earlier today.'

'Oh, dear.'

'But it looks good on you,' Billy said.

'I can hardly wear the same outfit as Blanche.'

'You won't have to, Mrs Walker.' Deirdre took a deep breath and braced herself but Billy broke the news for her.

'We've just agreed to call off the wedding, Mam.'

'I'm sorry to turn up on your doorstep without warning, Ken,' Alf Roberts said apologetically, 'but it's urgent.'

'As you see, I'm just off to work.' Ken pocketed his cab keys.

'Can you spare me five minutes?' Alf asked.

'As long as it *is* only five minutes. Come in.' Ken opened the door to his living room.

'I remembered what you said the day we had to evacuate the street,' Alf began. Ken looked bemused. 'About the local kids needing a youth club,' he reminded Ken. 'You did mean it?'

'Of course, but I fail to see what I can do to help you.' Ken glanced at his watch.

'I raised the topic at a meeting of the leisure committee yesterday and they decided to offer you the position of community officer in charge of, and solely responsible for, the day-to-day running of the community centre with a free hand to hire whatever part-time staff you need to put your ideas into operation. Within the limits of a budget, of course.' He handed Ken a folder. 'The decision to offer you the appointment was unanimous. Unfortunately it will be temporary, but only until the full council passes the budget and, believe you me, that will be no more than rubber-stamping. We were hoping you could start right away.'

'I'm flattered, but I'm not sure.'

'You don't have to give me your answer now. All we ask is that you give our offer serious consideration. A man with your ideas who knows the area and the local kids could make a real difference, Ken. My telephone number is on the outside of the folder. I would appreciate it if you could call me some time over the next few days.'

'I will.' Ken walked Alf out, locked his front door and stepped into his taxi. He had no doubt that the job would prove to be a challenge. And it would be a chance to put some of his socialist principles into action. An opportunity like this came once in a lifetime. He had to take the post, if only to find out if he was up to the job.

'I heard Billy Walker's taken a job in Jersey.' Ray Langton sat on the edge of Deirdre's desk and helped himself to a biscuit from the open packet on top of the filing cabinet.

'That's right.' Deirdre didn't look up from the invoice she was typing.

'That's a strange thing for someone who's getting married the week after next to do.'

'We called it off.'

'We called it off?' Ray enquired sceptically. 'Or Billy jilted you?'

'We called it off,' Deirdre snapped.

'So that's why you went dancing last night.'

'I went dancing because I felt like it.' Deirdre fought to control her temper.

'I'm not surprised Billy went off and left you. There's no way I'd allow my fiancée to go out dancing without me.'

'Then it's a good job I'm not your fiancée, isn't it?' She finished the document, pulled it from the machine and inserted another.

'You've got a nerve.'

'I've got a nerve? What about you?'

'You never gave me a chance to explain why Alison and her baby were living with me. You just went off with Billy.'

'I went off with Billy because I didn't want to be just one more body in your harem,' she yelled furiously. 'It wasn't enough that you were living with a girl, you wanted another to go out with in the evening.'

'Alison is a friend, and that's all she is. A friend,' he repeated firmly. 'We go way back. She used to live next door to me when we were kids. Her boyfriend threw her and the baby out, she had no money and nowhere to go so she came to me. I could hardly let them sleep on the street, now, could I? And for your information she left yesterday to move in with her sister in Scotland.' They stared at each other for a few moments. 'Have you and Billy really called off the wedding?' he asked quietly.

'Yes.'

'Then you're a free agent.'

'I suppose I am.'

Ray leant towards her and, very slowly and very gently, kissed her. 'I love you, Deirdre. It took a bloody stupid row, Billy Walker and your broken engagement to make me realise how much. Please, give me another chance?'

'Yes, Ray.' She moved even closer to him. 'I believe I will.'

The two boys stood on the toilet seat, bracing themselves against the walls of the cubicle. They listened to Bet Lynch and Annie Walker chatting as they cleared the bar. Someone came in and switched off the light in the gents'. In the darkness both boys breathed a little easier. The chances of them getting caught now were minimal. Ten minutes later they heard the bang of the outside door and the rattle of chains as Annie Walker fastened the lock. A few moments later the stairs creaked as she climbed them.

Les jumped from the seat and switched on his torch.

'Don't make so much noise.' Neil switched on his own

torch as he stepped down beside his friend. He slid the bolt back on the cubicle door and crept into the bar. 'Fancy a drink?'

Les nodded as Neil gingerly lifted the counter and stepped behind the bar.

'I'll have a short,' Les whispered. 'But hurry up, we haven't got all night.'

After four vodkas apiece, they left the bar and made their way by torchlight to Annie Walker's private living room at the back of the pub.

Neil held up Annie's handbag. 'This is a piece of luck.' He emptied it on the table. Discarding the handkerchief, make-up bag and comb, he grabbed Annie's purse. Opening it, he stuffed the coins in his trouser pocket and folded the banknotes into his shirt.

'How much you got there?' Les asked.

'Twenty quid or so, we'll share it later.'

'Even Stevens, or I'll thump you.' Les rummaged through Annie's prized china cabinet. 'She must have more money hidden around here somewhere. There's tonight's takings for a start.'

Neil pulled the drawer from the sideboard and tipped it upside down on the floor. He found nothing of interest so he did the same with the other three drawers, then yanked out the contents of the two cupboards. 'You're making a bloody din,' he warned, as Les smashed one of Annie's Royal Doulton figurines.

'Her fault for having nothing worth nicking.'

Neil went into the kitchen and rummaged through the cupboards, emptying the sugar and flour canisters over the floor.

'What you do that for?' Les asked,

'Mess the snobby bitch's place up.'

'Did you hear that?' Les asked in alarm.

'It's a car door slamming in street. You know what would be worth having? Her jewellery. Second-hand shops pay a mint for good pieces like she wears. My brother flogged a bracelet he found in my mother's drawer and he got ten quid for it. Just think what we'd get for some of the rings she wears.'

'Where would she keep them?' Les shone his torch around the kitchen, which was covered in sugar, flour and a bottle of ketchup Neil had poured over the mess.

'Not in here, stupid. They'd be in her bedroom.' Neil led the way up the stairs. 'I'll wait here with the torch, and shine it in from here when you go in,' he whispered to Les, when they reached the landing.

'Why do I have to go in? She might be awake,' Les complained.

'She won't, stupid. All you got to do is find her jewellery box and run out with it. Now, go.' Neil turned the knob of the door closest to him and pushed Les in. He shone in his torch and illuminated a stripped bed.

'Wrong room,' Les said, relieved.

'Tell you what, we'll stand outside all the doors and listen hard for her breathing.'

A few minutes later, Neil shoved Les into Annie's bedroom. Both boys held their breath as she turned over in her sleep. When she settled back, Les tiptoed over to her dressing-table. An ornate wooden box stood in front of the mirror. Les looked back at Neil.

'Hurry up,' Neil mouthed.

Les lifted the lid of the box and the lilting strains of the 'Blue Danube' waltz filled the air.

'Who's there?' Annie sat up, reached for the light switch, pressed it and stared at Les. 'What are you doing here?' She looked around frantically for something with which she could defend herself but there was nothing. She pulled the bedclothes to her chin and crouched in the bed.

'Where's the money?' Neil demanded.

'Money? You're only lads. I'm calling the police.'

Neil picked up a silver photo frame and hurled it at Annie. It hit the headboard, missing her temple by an inch.

Annie jumped out of bed and Neil blocked her path. She screamed. Suddenly Len Fairclough and Ray Langton were in the doorway.

'Right pair of bloody hoodlums, aren't you?' Len caught hold of them by their ears. 'We saw the mess you made downstairs.'

'We saw torchlight bobbing about through the pub

windows,' Ray explained to Annie. 'There's no power cut so we guessed someone was up to no good.'

'How did you get in?'

'Went round and borrowed Bet's keys. We left her calling the police from the shop. They'll want to talk to you,' Len warned. 'Why don't you get dressed, Annie, love, while we take Al Capone and his mate here downstairs to wait for them?' Len tightened his grip on their ears until both boys squealed like stuck pigs. 'Come on, lads, time for you to face the music.'

Annie heard the police knock at the door. She tried to hurry but her fingers had lost their dexterity. She was still trying to fasten the button on the waistband of her skirt when she went downstairs. Halfway down, she began to think of what might have happened if Len and Ray hadn't turned up when they did.

As the shock hit her, she fainted and fell headlong into the hall.

Chapter Twenty-Seven

'Someone obviously thinks a great deal of you, Mrs Walker.' A nurse carried an enormous bouquet of hothouse flowers over to Annie's bed.

Annie struggled to open her eyes. Her head hurt abominably. The doctor told her that she'd hit it when she fell down the stairs but the pain wasn't her only problem. She had been lying in bed worrying about the brewery's reaction to the break-in at the Rovers. She was convinced that they would decide that an elderly widow wasn't a suitable licensee and if they forced her to retire she had no idea what she would do with herself, or where she could go. The Rovers had been her home since the day Jack had carried her over the threshold when she'd been a young bride.

'I'll put them in water for you.' The nurse handed Annie the small envelope that contained the card.

Annie opened it and narrowed her eyes to decipher the message. It was difficult without her reading glasses. 'It's from the brewery. They say they're looking forward to me returning to the Rovers.'

'It's good to know that your work is appreciated.' The nurse took the card from Annie. 'I'll fasten it to the bow and tie it on to the vase.'

'Thank you, and you're right. It is nice to be appreciated,' Annie agreed. All of a sudden her headache didn't seem quite so bad.

The enthusiasm Ken Barlow had brought to his new post of community officer was waning. To his cost, he'd discovered that organising activities was one thing, getting everything to run smoothly, according to the plans he made, quite another.

'No, Uncle Albert, you won't have to take your clothes off,' he told Val's uncle patiently. 'We want an artists' model, not a nude. All you have to do is sit still while the students sketch you.'

'What they want to draw me for?' Albert enquired suspiciously.

'Because you have an interesting face.'

'I don't think I have.'

'That's because you see yourself in the mirror every morning when you shave. Can I help you?' Ken asked.

A young woman had stepped into the hall and was looking around as if she wasn't at all sure she was in the right place. 'Are you Mr Barlow?'

'Yes. You must be . . .' Ken stared at her and his mind went blank. He'd engaged a tutor to run literary appreciation sessions but he couldn't remember her name.

'Wendy Nightingale,' she introduced herself.

Ken shook her hand. 'Welcome to the centre. I'll show you round. This, as you will have gathered, is the hall. Uncle Albert, you go on into the art class, I'll see you later.' Ken pointed Albert in the direction of the studio, then turned back to Wendy. 'The kitchen, with tea and coffee-making facilities, is down this corridor,' he indicated the door, 'and this is your room.' He paused outside and peered through the eye-level glass panel. 'Some of your students have already arrived. I have to get back to the art class, but perhaps we can get together at break-time?'

'I'll look forward to it.' Wendy gave him a shy smile.

'If you need a lift home, perhaps we could talk about your class on the way,' Ken suggested.

'I have my own car, but thank you for the offer.'

Ken glanced back at Wendy as he walked to the art room. He had sensed a rapport between them. Something he hadn't experienced since Valerie had died.

Blanche Hunt dropped the frying-pan back on to the stove, and turned off the gas before the bacon burnt to a crisp. 'The sixth of June? That's madness, Deirdre. You were supposed to marry Billy on the twenty-fourth of May.'

'I know, Mam,' Deirdre agreed.

'All that money spent on the dress, ordering the flowers and the cake, booking the church . . .'

Ray squeezed Deirdre's hand and stepped forward. 'Deirdre and I had a stupid misunderstanding and it was no wonder she turned to Billy Walker. But . . .' he glanced at Deirdre and drew courage from her smile '. . . I love her, she loves me, and there's no reason why we should delay our wedding.'

'You want a big do?' Blanche asked, in a tone that suggested *she* didn't.

'A small one in the register office. You're welcome to come.'

'That's big of you,' Blanche snapped.

'The only other people we've invited are Len and Rita. We've asked them to be witnesses,' Ray added smoothly.

'There's something else, Mam,' Deirdre said hesitantly. 'We haven't much money so we were hoping we could move in here. Just until we get enough together to put a deposit on a house.'

Blanche looked dubious. 'This place is big enough. But I don't know, love. Two women sharing one kitchen never works. I know – I tried it with my mother-in-law.'

'I'm a builder, Blanche. I could divide the house into two flats at no cost to yourself,' Ray offered. 'We'd pay rent obviously, and we could live upstairs or down, whichever you'd prefer.'

'Upstairs,' Blanche said firmly. 'I only hope you're doing the right thing.'

'I know we are, Mam.' Deirdre put her arm round Ray's waist. 'This time I haven't a single solitary doubt. Not even a niggle.'

Wendy turned her back to Ken and slid to the side of the bed. He moved behind her and slipped his arm round her waist.

'What's the matter, Wendy, love?'

'Guilt,' she replied. 'I hate cheating on Roger and I hate the way this makes me feel.'

'Then tell Roger you don't love him any more and move in with me,' Ken begged. 'We love one another.'

'That doesn't give us the right to hurt other people or wreck their lives. I stood up in church and promised before God to love, honour and obey Roger until death do us part, and here I am lying naked in your bed.'

'I can't be sorry about that.'

She turned to face him. 'Neither can I – when I am with you,' she said. 'But when we're apart it eats me alive.'

'Then don't leave me.'

'If it were only that simple,' she murmured wistfully.

'It's not complicated. Go home, tell Roger you don't love him any more, pack your bags and come back here.'

'Have you ever asked yourself how you'd feel if you had a wife?'

'I have a wife,' he broke in wryly, thinking of Janet. They had lived apart for so long, it was difficult to remember the brief time they had spent together.

'I meant one you live with.'

'I'd better go and see who that is before they hammer down the door.' Ken left the bed and slipped on his dressing-gown. He ran down the stairs and opened the door.

'That's for messing with my wife.'

Ken reeled back as a fist connected with his jaw.

'Ken!' Naked, apart from a sheet she'd grabbed from Ken's bed, Wendy ran down the stairs and rushed to his aid. 'How could you?' She turned on her husband.

'You expect me to stand back and do nothing while you climb into another man's bed?' Roger glared contemptuously at Ken.

'No,' she said quietly. 'I'm sorry, I should have told you about Ken and me.'

'Get dressed,' Roger ordered. 'You're coming home with me right now.'

'No, I'm not,' Wendy told him softly. 'Not now and not ever again, Roger. I'm sorry that I didn't have the courage to tell you about Ken and me before this happened. But I love him and I'm staying.'

'Then there's nothing more to be said.' Roger turned on his heel and walked away. As Wendy closed the door she and Ken heard the sound of a car engine.

'Did you just say what I thought you did?' Ken asked.

'Do you mind if I move in this afternoon?'

'It's what I've been hoping for since I first set eyes on you, love.' He winced as he tried to smile.

'That bruise needs seeing to.'

'You could try kissing it better,' he suggested.

'Only after we've tried more orthodox treatment. Come into the kitchen.'

'I didn't realise you were bossy.'

'There are a whole lot of things you don't about me, Ken Barlow.'

He folded his arms round her and kissed her lips. 'And it's going to be a whole lot of fun finding out what they are.'

'Come on Ernie, it's Ray's stag night,' Len coaxed. 'We're here to celebrate and that means sending him off in style.'

'Does that mean we have to go into a place like this?' Ernest Bishop paled as he glanced at the explicit posters pasted outside the strip club and was extremely glad that he had avoided holding a stag night of his own. At Emily's insistence his wedding to her in Mawdsley Street Chapel had been a quiet one.

'Cor, look at that.' Ray peered so closely at the poster he hit it with his nose.

Blushing, Ernest turned aside.

'Your Emily took photographs in here,' Len reminded him.

'She's a woman.'

'So are they.' Len propelled Ernest through the door. Alf Roberts and Ray Langton followed them into the darkened room.

'Oh dear.' Ernie retreated when he saw a girl dancing on stage. She was naked apart from a purple G-string, two purple and gold tassels pasted over her nipples and purple high heels. 'I have to go.'

'Go where, love?' A hostess wearing a white bikini trimmed with gold fringes hooked her fingers into Ernest's collar and pulled him towards her. Ernest tried to stand his ground but between the hostess's pulling and Alf, Ray and Len pushing him, he didn't stand a chance. Before he realised what was happening he was standing on the stage and the purple and gold tassels were whirling an inch from his face.

'Go for it, Ernie,' Len shouted.

The music faded, the stripper bowed. When she stood upright she was holding both tassels. The audience went wild, and switched to laughter when she took the tassels and stuck them on the end of Ernest's nose. Moments later something dropped on his head. He grabbed it. And was left holding the G-string.

'What you waiting for, Ernie?' Len yelled. 'Chase after her.'

★

'We're here to make a delivery. One husband, only slightly the worse for wear.' Len tried and failed to focus on Emily, who was standing in the doorway of her house dressed in a quilted nylon dressing-gown and pink slippers ornamented with huge pink pom-poms.

Ernest lifted his head and hand and wiggled his fingers in a parody of a wave at his wife, then slumped back on Ray's shoulder.

Emily clenched her fists. It was bad enough that Ernest had forgotten their wedding anniversary and instead gone out with Ray, Alf and Len to celebrate Ray's stag night. But to return to her in this state – unable even to stand on his own feet!

'I'm not taking the delivery, Len.'

'He's your husband,' Len shouted, as she slammed the door in their faces.

'Not when he's in that condition he's not,' Emily countered primly, from the other side of the door.

'What we supposed to do with him?' Ray slurred.

'Leave him in the gutter for the police to find, for all I care,' Emily answered.

Len heard her running up the stairs, and solemnly whispered, 'I think she means it.'

'We'll have to take him home with us.' Ray was tired, and all he wanted was his bed, preferably with Deirdre in it, but he suspected she wouldn't treat him any more kindly than Emily had treated Ernest, if he turned up on her doorstep now.

'Drag him home with us, you mean.' Len eased Ernie's dead weight on to his shoulder. 'One puff and he'll fall down.'

Ray puffed, and he and Alf dissolved into laughter.

'Ssh!' Len held his fingers to his lips. 'We'll wake the street.'

'I think it's already awake.' Ray saw the light flicker on in Deirdre's bedroom. Tomorrow night, that was what he was looking forward to. And all the nights after that.

'Someone's got to say it, and it may as well be me,' Albert Tatlock confronted Ken. 'It's a bloody disgrace, that's what it is. An affront to all the decent people in the street and our Val's memory. Both of you wed to other people and flaunting your sin by living openly together. I don't know what you're thinking of. You hold a position where people look up to you—'

'Wendy and I are in love,' Ken interrupted tersely.

'Is that what you call it?' Albert sneered.

'We made the mistake of marrying the wrong people,' Ken said. 'When we divorce them, we'll get married.'

'And in the meantime?'

'We have no choice but to carry on as we are.'

'Living in sin.' Albert declared flatly. 'And what does your wife think of that?'

'Janet is living with a man called Vince.'

'Degenerates.' Albert shook his head disparagingly. 'The lot of you are bloody degenerates. Well, you'll get your comeuppance, that's all I can say. And it's coming sooner than you think,' he added darkly.

'What do you mean?' Ken dropped his pen on to his desk, sat back in his chair and looked at Albert.

'Your lifestyle has come to the notice of the committee. They've had complaints.'

'From you?' Ken asked dryly.

'Not me,' Albert said angrily.

'What I do in my private life is none of *your*,' Ken pointed his finger at Albert, 'or the committee's damn business.'

'We'll see about that.' Albert went to the door. 'I've said my bit and not for your sake. Val left you two young ones to think about, not that you've been doing much of that lately.'

'And what do you mean by that? I support them, don't I?' Ken said indignantly, smarting because there was more than a grain of truth in what Albert had said.

'From a distance,' was Albert's parting shot before he walked out of the door.

'I've made my mind up so there's no use in either of you trying to talk me out of it.' Blanche set the teapot on the table, and reached for Ray and Deirdre's cups. 'The offer for my corsetry shop is a good one and when an old friend asked me to help him run a country club in Kenilworth, it seemed too good an opportunity to pass up. All I would like from you two is a promise that you'll look after the house for me. I'd rather not sell it. Not until I know for sure that running a country club is for me.'

Ray put his hand over Deirdre's. 'You make it sound as if we're doing you the favour, Blanche.'

'You are.' Blanche handed him his tea.

'We'll be happy to look after the house until we can buy one of our own,' Deirdre agreed.

'Perhaps this one in a few months,' Ray suggested.

'I'm not living in Coronation Street.' Deirdre recalled the visit she had made to the doctor that morning. In seven months she and Ray would become parents, but she hadn't told him the good news yet because she was unsure how he'd react when he discovered that she'd become pregnant on their honeymoon. 'And I'm not bringing up any child of mine here, neither,' she burst out, to Ray's and her mother's astonishment.

'You'll not get an answer, love,' Hilda warned Ena Sharples, when she saw her knocking on Minnie Caldwell's door. 'Minnie moved to Whaley Bridge a month ago to be near Handel Gartside.'

'Whaley Bridge?' Ena dropped her suitcase in shock.

'Didn't she tell you?'

'She couldn't have, because she didn't know I was

coming.' That morning Ena had stormed out of St Anne's nursing home after one argument too many with the matron. She'd been relying on Minnie to put her up until she could sort something out for herself. 'I'll just have to get a room in Rovers.'

'Annie Walker doesn't rent rooms,' Hilda said.

'We'll see about that.' Ena picked up her suitcase and headed to the end of the street. There was half an hour to go before afternoon closing time and Annie was behind the bar chatting to Bet Lynch.

'Mrs Sharples, nice to see you back,' Annie greeted her. 'Would you like me to serve you a milk stout in the snug?'

'I want a room.' Ena dropped her case to the floor.

'We don't let rooms, Mrs Sharples,' Annie informed her politely.

'That sign outside says "Rovers Return Inn". An inn is where people stay and I want a room,' Ena reiterated.

'I know Mrs Caldwell has locked up her house and that must make it awkward for you, Mrs Sharples, but I don't let rooms. The Rovers hasn't been an inn for years.'

Ena pulled up a bar stool and sat down. 'That sign outside says "Inn". If you don't give me a room, I'll sue under the trade descriptions act.'

'But we don't let rooms.' Annie repeated, her patience dwindling.

'I'd make it worth your while,' Ena offered. 'I could even clean for you.'

'I have Mrs Ogden.'

'Big place like this, there must be things that want doing all the time.'

Annie capitulated. 'We could give it a try, Mrs Sharples. Just for a week. If it doesn't work out . . .'

'A week's all I need to sort myself out with something permanent.' Ena picked up her case and headed for the snug. 'I'll have that milk stout now.'

'I heard what you've been up to, Ernest Bishop,' Ena teased, as she dusted the chapel. It hadn't taken her long to pick up the threads of her old life or to notice that the chapel hadn't had a good going-over since she'd left Coronation Street.

'What exactly have you heard about me, Mrs Sharples?' Ernest enquired, in trepidation.

'Going into one of them strip-tease clubs with Len Fairclough, Alf Roberts and Ray Langton.'

'I didn't want to,' he protested. 'They made me.'

'Dragged you in there kicking and screaming, did they?'

'Not exactly,' he confessed uneasily. He wondered just how much Ena Sharples had heard. He couldn't bear the thought of people discussing his ultimate humiliation – the tassels and the G-string. And then Emily throwing him out of the house. How could he have forgotten their anniversary?

'The Mission superintendent asked me to tell you that

he wants to see you. They're holding a special committee meeting here tonight.'

'I'll never be able to preach again.' Ernest sank down on the pew Ena had just finished polishing.

'You will, if you tell them that you only went into the club to study degenerate behaviour and obscenity so you could fight Satan with his own weapons.'

'They'd never believe that, Mrs Sharples.'

'Why wouldn't they when it's the truth, Mr Bishop?' Ena rammed the lid back on to the round tin of lavender-scented wax polish.

'The truth,' he repeated wonderingly.

'It is, isn't it?' She smiled disingenuously.

Elsie Howard shifted her suitcase into her other hand as she stood and gazed down Coronation Street. Nothing had changed since the day she'd left. In fact, now she was back, she felt as though she had never been away. She walked slowly down the pavement, hesitating for a moment outside number nine. So many years . . . so many wasted years . . .

She took another step and rapped on the door of number eleven.

Len opened it. 'My God, look what's the wind's blown in.' He gave her a broad smile.

Despite the misery gnawing at her, Elsie smiled back. 'Long time no see, Len.'

'Want a cup of tea, kid?'

'Aye, I could murder one.'

Len stepped outside in his socks, took her suitcase from her and carried it inside. He left it at the foot of the stairs. 'You know where the living room is.' He helped her off with her coat and hung it on the newel post.

'This place is tidier than I remember.' Elsie looked around as she sat at the table.

'I'm getting better at housekeeping.'

'More like you've found yourself a daft woman to do it for you.' Elsie watched as he went into the scullery to fill the kettle.

'You back for good?' Len asked.

'Alan and I decided to call it a day.'

'I'm sorry.' He padded into the living room and set cups and a sugar bowl on the table.

'There's no point in flogging a dead horse. Any lodgings going round here?'

'I think there's a room empty in the corner shop. Oh, and I heard there's a job going. Manageress in a lingerie shop where Gamma Garments used to be.'

'I'll get on to it.'

'Not until you've drunk your tea.' He went out and poured boiling water into the teapot. 'Well, this is cosy, isn't it?' He sat next to her.

'Like I've never been gone, except for the grey hairs I've grown since I left.' Elsie smiled mischievously. 'And the ones that have appeared on your head.'

'Speak for yourself, Elsie Howard.'

'Not for much longer. I'm going back to Tanner.'

'Wise move.'

'What's a wise move?' Rita Littlewood flung back the door and glared at Len and Elsie sitting companiably at the table.

'Me changing my name back to Tanner,' Elsie explained.

'And moving in with Len?' Rita asked acidly.

'I'm not moving in with Len,' Elsie protested. 'I called to find out if there were any lodgings or a job going round here.'

'I bet you did an' all,' Rita retorted.

'It's the truth, love. Len and I are just good friends. Have been for years.'

'That's right,' Len chipped in.

'You expect me to believe that, Len Fairclough?' Rita asked.

'Please yourself, Rita,' he said casually. 'I couldn't give a damn whether you believe me or not.'

'You—' Rita ran out in tears.

'Someone's in love,' Elsie sipped her tea.

'Not me.' Len pushed the sugar bowl towards her. 'Help yourself to more if you want it.'

Chapter Twenty-Eight

'**H**ilda, love, can we have a little chat?'

Hilda saw Eddie Yeats staring at the teapot on her and Stan's breakfast table but she refused to take the hint. Stan and Eddie should have left on their round ten minutes ago if they wanted to put in a full day's work before dark.

'You can have as much chat as you can get in before Stan's ready.' She opened the door to the scullery. 'Get a move on, Eddie's waiting,' she yelled at her husband.

'Just cleaning my shoes, love.'

'Tip the used water over them after you've finished washing your first set of windows,' she advised.

'Hilda, love—'

'Just hurry up.' She closed the scullery door and looked expectantly as Eddie.

'You know Minnie Caldwell's gone to live in Whaley Bridge, to be near Handel Gartside?'

'I think it's ever so romantic to have a gentleman friend at her age.' Hilda brushed a tear from her eye.

Eddie sneezed loudly, which jolted Hilda back to unromantic reality. 'It's left me without a landlady and I was hoping you and Stan would consider having me as your paying guest.'

'That's a good idea, Eddie.' Stan joined them from the scullery. He and Eddie had discussed the idea the day before and he had already earmarked Eddie's money as an addition to the beer allowance Hilda made him. 'We've two spare bedrooms,' he reminded Hilda, who was scowling.

'I'll have two of you to run round after. Two lots of laundry, double the bed-making, extra food to buy and cook—'

'I'd pay you, Hilda,' Eddie interrupted.

'Me, not him.' Hilda pointed at Stan and his face fell. 'You handy round the house?'

'In what way?' Eddie asked warily.

'This place needs decorating.'

'Then I'm your man,' Eddie boasted. 'I can decorate with the best of them.'

'You can help him.' Hilda handed Stan the bag of sandwiches she'd cut for his break. 'Start with this room, work your way round the downstairs, then move on to the upstairs. Right?'

'Right,' Stan reiterated gloomily. 'Let's go, Eddie,' he murmured, anxious to leave before Hilda made any more plans for their free time.

'I'll air the spare bed.' Hilda followed them into the passage. 'You can move in tonight, Eddie.'

'Thank you, love. I knew you'd come up trumps. I'll pay you the first week in advance tonight. See you then.'

Alf Roberts saw Ena Sharples walk out of the corner shop and ran to catch up with her. The council had advertised twice in the past month for a caretaker for the community centre and no one had applied. He'd heard Ena was back in Weatherfield and also that Annie Walker had been driven to the end of her tether by Ena's inter-ference in the routine of the Rovers. For all Ena's shortcomings, Alf knew that the leisure committee would be prepared to hire her in preference to having no caretaker at all.

'Mrs Sharples,' he gasped, when he caught up with her.

'Not very fit, are you, Alf Roberts?' Ena commented, eyeing his red face.

'I've been running to catch with you,' he explained superfluously.

'And now you've got me, what do you want wi' me?'

'How would you like your old flat and job back?'

'I take it no one else wants it,' she retorted caustically.

'The council has the vacancy and I happened to mention to the committee that you had returned to the area. They asked me to approach you,' Alf lied.

Ena fought her initial impulse to dance in the street.

She could leave the Rovers, move back into her own place – her own place! 'I'll take it,' she snapped. 'But only as a special favour to you and the committee.'

'Thank you, Mrs Sharples. I'll get the keys and meet you there in an hour.'

'An hour would suit me fine.' Ena turned back to the Rovers. It was good to know she'd spent her last night under Annie Walker's roof.

Elsie Tanner heard the bell ring as the shop door opened. She looked round from the stock she was arranging on the back shelf. A tall, good-looking man was standing at the counter. Good-looking men were at a premium in Coronation Street and doubly so in Sylvia Matthew's lingerie and separates shop.

She gave him a smile. 'Can I help you?'

'I certainly hope so,' he said in a South London accent as he extended his hand. 'I'm Mike Baldwin.'

'The Mike Baldwin who bought the warehouse in Coronation Street?'

'The same,' he answered.

'You've made a difference round here. Jobs were scarce until you took on a lot of the local women as machinists. We're hoping their pay packets will boost our trade.'

'Did Sylvia tell you she was considering selling the shop?' he asked bluntly.

'Last week.' Elsie crossed her fingers under the counter.

Sylvia had told her that she was hoping to sell it as a going concern and Elsie had been concerned that the new owner might not keep her on as manageress.

'I made her an offer for the place yesterday and she accepted.' Mike studied the stock on the shelves. 'I'm turning it into an outlet for the jeans and denim coats I manufacture.'

'So, you'll be changing the stock.' Elsie had a feeling that wasn't all that Mike Baldwin would be changing. Youngsters, not middle-aged women, bought jeans, and they wouldn't want someone like her serving them.

'It's nothing personal, Mrs Tanner, but the sort of trendy gear I manufacture would benefit from someone younger fronting the shop. I've given the job of manageress to Gail Potter.'

'My assistant.' Elsie struggled to keep her voice even. Good jobs were hard to come by especially for someone her age.

Mike leant on the counter and smiled at her. 'I've been talking to a few people about you. You have quite a reputation around here.'

'I do.' Elsie prepared to defend herself.

'Mature, experienced in sales and handling people. I could put you to better use elsewhere in my organisation. How does the offer of sewing-room supervisor in charge of all the machinists sound?'

'Like a lot of hard work,' Elsie retorted, without thinking.

A job – this man was offering her a job and she was practically turning it down!

'It will be,' he agreed dryly. 'But I'll make it worth your while. Shall we say a twenty per cent increase on what Sylvia's been paying you to run this place?'

'I'll consider it.'

'Twenty-five per cent.'

Elsie hadn't intended bargaining, but for a pay-rise of that magnitude she'd consider working for the devil himself. 'Consider it taken.'

'You can put a sale notice in the window right away and slash the price of all the stock by fifty per cent. I'd appreciate it if you'd work the week out here and start in the factory first thing Monday morning. See you then.' Mike winked at her and left.

Elsie watched him walk away and decided that, whatever else he was, Mike Baldwin fancied himself as a lady-killer. She pitied the girls he had working for him. She held no illusions about herself. Men like Mike Baldwin chased young skirt, not mature women.

'Overripe like an old Cheddar that's been in the fridge too long,' she muttered, opening the drawer that held the sale tickets.

Mike was sitting in his office, feeling pleased with himself and the world in general. He had just taken on another three girls as machinists. Two had excellent experience and the third was quick-witted enough to be a fast learner. The man he'd employed as his wages clerk, Ernest Bishop, was as sober and humourless as his name, but he was efficient and he didn't have to see much of him. And from Monday he'd have Elsie Tanner to see that the girls spent less time gossiping and more time sewing. With her in charge he expected to see production rates rocket.

'Come in,' he shouted, at a knock on his door. Two women walked in together. He recognised both as barmaids from his new local, the Rovers Return. 'And what can I do for you, ladies?'

'I'm Bet Lynch and this,' Bet pointed at her companion, 'is Betty Turpin. We're here to see about a job.' Without waiting to be asked, they sat on the chairs in front of his desk. They'd heard the factory girls talking in the Rovers, and Mike was paying his workers two shillings an hour more than Annie Walker was paying them.

'I've hired all the girls I need for the moment.' Mike propped himself on his elbows and stared at Bet. Unabashed, she hitched her mini-skirt higher to show several more inches of thigh.

'Couldn't you put us on a waiting list?' Betty Turpin suggested.

'Have either of you ladies any experience?'

'Plenty as a barmaid and in shop work,' Betty answered proudly.

'That won't help you machine a straight seam.' Mike was still staring at Bet. 'What about you?'

'The same but I pick up things fast.' Bet licked her lips.

'I bet you do. Perhaps we could discuss another opening I may have,' Mike murmured. 'You work at the Rovers, don't you?'

'That's the last place where I'd want to talk about changing jobs.'

'We'll have to fix up a meeting somewhere else, then, won't we?' Mike scribbled a telephone number on a piece of paper and handed it to Bet. 'Give me a ring. I'm busy this week, but next week is clear.'

Bet managed to show several more inches of thigh as she stood up. 'I'll let you know when and where.'

Nine months almost to the day after they were married, Ray Langton cradled his baby in his arms. 'She's beautiful, Deirdre. I never thought I'd have a daughter who looked like this. Her eyes are so blue . . .'

'All babies have blue eyes. They may change.' Deirdre sat up in the hospital bed and held out her arms. Ray gave her the baby.

'Less than a day old and she's already got me hooked around her little finger.' He gently disentangled her tiny hand from his.

'I told you my contractions were real yesterday.'

'You can't blame me for not believing you after what

happened last week,' Ray reminded her. 'You insisted they were real then.'

'They *felt* real,' she countered defensively.

Ray was too happy to argue. He stroked the baby's cheek with the back of his finger.

'You'll register her as Lynette Langton,' Deirdre said, 'like we agreed?'

Ray nodded without looking up from the baby.

'And you'll see the vicar about the christening, and ask Ken, Emily and Betty to be godparents?' she said, as the bell rang, signalling the end of visiting time.

'I will.'

Ray patted the breast pocket of his jacket as he left the ward. The paper inside crinkled. He had already registered their daughter as Tracy Lynette but he'd held off telling Deirdre. There was no use in starting a row. Deirdre would come round to the idea of calling their daughter Tracy when she saw he had no intention of calling her anything else.

He glanced at his watch. It was almost eight o'clock. Len, Alf, Ken and half of the street were waiting in the Rovers to wet the baby's head with him. It promised to be a good night.

'Thank you, Mr Baldwin.' Bet Lynch took the vodka and tonic he handed her.

'Not a bad pub, this.' He looked around the Flying Horse as he sat beside her.

'The Rovers is better,' Bet said tartly.

'The voice of the loyal barmaid.'

'What's this job, then, that you think I can do?' Bet asked.

'You know I bought a house in the street.'

'Everyone in Weatherfield knows you bought number five and, thanks to Len and Ray, they also know you spent a small fortune modernising it.'

'I have to have somewhere comfortable to stay when I'm up here from London. I hate hotels.'

'You have a house in London?' Bet asked.

'I do.' He tasted his whisky.

'A bigger one than number five?' she questioned in an offhand manner that didn't fool Mike.

'It's detached in an acre of garden with five bedrooms and three bathrooms.'

'That must be nice.' She unbuttoned the second and third buttons of her blouse and leant forward, giving him an eyeful of her best asset.

'My wife lives in it.'

'Oh.' She turned aside and opened her handbag lest he see the disappointment on her face.

'But she's in London and you're here.' He fondled Bet's knee. 'How about you share number five with me?'

'And why would I do that?' she asked bluntly.

'Because I need a housekeeper to see to my home comforts and you'd live rent- and bill-free in a modern, easy-to-run house.'

'I already have a job in Rovers.'

'And you'd keep it and all your wages for pin money.' Under cover of the table he slid his hand higher up her thigh. 'And you'd not find me ungrateful.'

'I might give it a try.' She moved back as his fingers reached her knickers.

'Tonight, after another couple of these.' He picked up her empty glass.

'Make it a double.'

'Why not a triple?' He raised his eyebrows. 'It would save time.'

'Come on, Elsie, don't be mean,' Susie Birchall, one of the machinists in Mike's factory, coaxed. 'Gail Potter says I can share her room in your house. You'll be getting twice the rent.'

'And twice the lodgers,' Elsie complained. Gail Potter, who'd been her assistant in the lingerie shop and had been promoted to manageress by Mike when she had taken the post as supervisor in his factory, had persuaded her to take her in as a lodger a couple of weeks before. But much as she liked Gail and enjoyed her company around the house, she wasn't in a hurry to take on a second young girl. 'That means twice the mess.'

'I'll do my own cooking, washing and cleaning like Gail.'

Elsie made a face. Suzie Birchall was a handful; she was only seventeen, brash, bright, breezy and full of self-confidence. Ready to make everyone dance to her tune. She reminded Elsie of herself at that age, convinced that she could take on the world and win.

'All right,' she finally conceded. 'You can stop your nagging and move in, but you put one foot wrong and you're out.'

'Thanks, Elsie, you're an old brick.'

'Less of the old. What's up with you three?' Elsie demanded as three of Mike's older machinists, Ivy Tilsley, Vera Duckworth and Marie Stanton stalked in and slammed the workroom door behind them.

'Ernest bloody Bishop, that's what's up with us,' Ivy raged. 'He's only gone and shifted payday to Friday, hasn't he? We told him Thursday's late-night shopping around here and we need to get groceries in for weekend but he wouldn't listen. "Mr Baldwin said that Friday is the new pay night and I'm here to implement his decisions."' Ivy mimicked Ernest's voice.

'And we can like it or lump it,' Vera Duckworth added.

'He said that to you?' Elsie asked quietly.

'No,' Vera admitted, 'but he might as well have.'

'I'll have a word.' Elsie left her seat.

'You won't get anywhere with Ernie,' Ivy warned. 'He's a born yes man. I swear he'd walk into a fire if Mr Baldwin asked him to.'

'I'm not going to see Ernie.' Elsie opened the door. 'I'm going to the horse, not the horse's mouth, and I suggest you all keep your heads down and those machines running while I'm gone.'

The pile of finished jeans had grown considerably by the time Elsie returned.

'Well?' Ivy asked in exasperation, when Elsie sat down without volunteering any information.

'You'll get paid on Thursday, as usual.' Elsie picked up a pair of jeans and checked the stitching.

'Hello, Emily.' A woman stepped out of the shadows as Emily walked up Coronation Street from the Mission Hall.

Emily peered into the shadows. 'Janet, Janet Barlow?' she repeated hesitantly as Janet stepped under a street-lamp. Her old neighbour was thinner, her hair shorter and curlier than the last time she had seen her.

'How are you, Emily?'

'I'm fine, how are you?'

'Fine,' Janet repeated mechanically.

'I didn't know you'd moved back into the street.'

'I haven't. I don't suppose you've time for a chat?'

'I'm sorry.' Emily shook her head. 'But Ernest and I have been at a Mission Hall meeting all evening. He stayed behind to talk to some of the committee and I have to get his supper on the table. He doesn't like eating after ten and it's gone that already. Perhaps—'

'It *is* late,' Janet broke in, before Emily could make any more protestations.

'We could get together some other time.'

'Yes,' Janet said softly, 'some other time. Goodbye, Emily.'

'Goodbye.' Emily ran off up the street.

Janet walked on down to number one. She knocked at the door and stood back, uncertain of the reception she'd receive. 'Hello, Ken,' she greeted him as he opened it.

'Janet, this is a surprise.'

'Can I come in?'

'Yes.' He stepped back so she could join him in the hallway. 'What brings you here so late?' He helped her off with her coat and hung it on a peg.

'I wanted to talk to you.'

'And I know what about.' He ushered into the living room and offered her a seat.

'You do?'

'You want me to divorce you so you can marry Vince,' he suggested.

'No, not that.' Janet shook her head. 'Could you do me a favour?'

'That depends on the favour,' he answered warily.

'Can I stay here, just for tonight?'

'You've quarrelled with Vince?' He didn't want to refuse Janet if she was really in trouble, but Wendy had walked out on him two weeks ago after a series of increasingly bitter quarrels. Although Wendy had insisted that she wouldn't return, he hadn't entirely gave up hope that she would change her mind. And the last person he wanted her to see if by some miracle she should walk through the door was his estranged wife.

'No, it's nothing like that,' Janet prevaricated. 'I'm going away tomorrow – to London. And I just need somewhere to stay for the one night.'

'And Vince?'

'I'll be meeting him in London. He moved down there a couple of weeks ago. I wasn't sure I wanted to go there with him but I've decided to give it a try. Can I stay, Ken?'

'This is Val's uncle's house. He has one bedroom, I have the other. There's only the boxroom.'

'That will do fine, Ken. As I said, it's only for the one night.'

'I'll make a hot-water bottle to air the bed and get some bedclothes.'

'If you give me the bedclothes I'll make it up. I really appreciate this, Ken.'

'Sure you don't want to talk?' He set the kettle on to boil and rummaged in the alcove cupboard for one of Albert's rubber hot-water bottles.

'I'm sure.'

'I have plenty of books here you could read.'

'I'll be leaving early in the morning so I'll get straight to sleep, but thank you all the same.'

Ken filled the hot-water bottle, picked up Janet's bag, then led the way upstairs and along the landing to the boxroom. He set the bag down, opened the airing cupboard and took out a set of sheets, a couple of pillows and two blankets. 'There's an eiderdown.'

'These will do, Ken. It's not cold.' She took the bundle of linen from him.

'I'll go downstairs and make us some tea.'

'Not for me, Ken, I really would rather just go to sleep.'

'Then I'll see you in the morning.' He backed down the landing.

'I'll be off at the crack of dawn. My train leaves at six. Thank you again for putting me up. I really appreciate it.'

'You are all right, Janet, aren't you?'

'Never better.' She went into the boxroom and closed the door, leaving him no option but to return downstairs.

Behind the closed door, Janet opened her bag and extracted a bottle of pills. She looked round the tiny room. There was no glass so she opened the door and went to the bathroom. She took a toothbrush out of a plastic mug, rinsed it under the tap and filled it with cold water, then returned to the boxroom.

The next day Ken came home for lunch. The old-age pensioners club weekly meeting was being held in the centre that afternoon and the youth club in the evening. Both tended to be gruelling sessions and he had been trying, without success, to persuade one of the groups to shift their day. In the meantime he needed sustenance to see him through to the evening.

He went into the living room to find Albert sitting at the table reading the newspaper over the remains of his tea and toast.

'I had a late breakfast,' Albert informed him.

'I was about to offer you an early lunch. How do you fancy scrambled eggs on toast?'

'I think I'll give my tea and toast a chance to go down first.' Albert folded the paper and sat back in his chair. 'Whose coat is that in the hall?'

'What coat?' Ken asked absently, as he opened the scullery door.

'The woman's coat.'

'Woman . . . Janet must have left it. She came round late last night after you'd gone to bed and asked if she could stay the night before going to London. I told her she could. You don't mind, do you?' As the lodger, Ken felt guilty that he hadn't asked Albert sooner. After all, it was his house.

'She's still your wife, isn't she?'

'In name I suppose she is.' Ken closed the scullery door and returned to the hall. Albert was right. Janet's coat was still hanging there . . .

He ran up the stairs two at a time, walked along the landing and tapped on the boxroom door. 'Janet?' He opened the door. Janet was lying on the bed fully dressed, her fist clenched around an empty pill bottle. Her hand was cold when he touched it and half a dozen pills tumbled out on to the blanket beneath her. She was dead.

Chapter Twenty-Nine

Emily Bishop was lying on the sofa in her living room with a blanket over her. Ernest handed her a cup of tea and tucked another cushion beneath her head before he answered the door. A few moments later he returned with Ken Barlow.

Emily took one look at Ken and burst into tears. 'I'm so, dreadfully, awfully sorry,' she sobbed.

'You have nothing to be sorry about, Emily.' Ken sat in the chair opposite the sofa and took her hand.

'Can I get you anything, Ken?' Ernest hovered uncertainly behind him. 'A cup of tea? I've just made a fresh pot. Or coffee, perhaps?'

'Nothing, thank you, Ernest,' Ken said. 'I've been in the police station all day and they drink enough tea there to flood Weatherfield and float a Cunard liner.' His bad joke fell awkwardly into the strained atmosphere. 'I bumped into Elsie Tanner on my way back and she told me that Emily fainted in the street when she heard about Janet.'

'I met Janet in the street last night on my way home from the Mission Hall.' Emily blew her nose into the handkerchief Ernest handed her. 'She wanted to talk but I told her I was busy—' She broke down again.

'Which you undoubtedly were,' Ken reminded her gently.

'She must have thought that I didn't care about her!'

'She wouldn't have thought any such thing.' Ken patted her hand. 'You were kind to her when she lived here and you can't blame yourself for not having time to talk to her last night.'

'But if I had just taken a few minutes, it might have made a difference. She might not have swallowed those pills.'

Ken shook his head. 'It wouldn't have made any difference. I saw Janet's boyfriend, Vince, at the police station. She left him a couple of weeks ago when she was diagnosed with depression. Her doctors discharged her from hospital yesterday afternoon because she'd convinced them she could look after herself. She fooled the professionals,' his mouth set in a grim line, 'and she fooled me. I had no inkling there was anything wrong with her when she asked if she could stay the night at Uncle Albert's house. She told me she was tired and needed somewhere for a night before moving on to London. So if anyone's to blame it's me. I could have pressed her instead of respecting her privacy. But I didn't.'

'I've heard that people who are really determined to kill themselves never cry wolf,' Ernest muttered in the silence that followed. 'Neither of you could possibly have known what was going on in her mind.'

'Thank you for saying so, Ernest.' Ken rose to his feet. 'But Janet had been – and still was in name – my wife. She came to me and I can't help thinking that in itself was a cry for help. Only I wasn't listening.' Ken had visited the Bishops to set Emily's mind at rest, but instead he was pouring out his own guilt over Janet's death.

'Depression is an illness, Ken,' Ernest reminded him.

'We're both so sorry.' Emily wiped her tears. 'It was good of you to call in.'

'It's the least I could do.' Ken walked to the door. 'And thank you again, Emily, for being such a good friend to Janet.' He smiled at her and opened the door. The house was beautifully decorated and cosy, and he couldn't help feeling a pang of envy. Ernest and Emily had a comfortable home, a strong marriage, and were clearly devoted to each other. It was the kind of relationship he had forged with Valerie and had been searching for since her death. But now, after what Janet had done not only to herself but to him, he doubted that he would ever again experience that closeness with a woman.

'Thank you for calling.' Ernest stood on his doorstep and watched Ken walk down the street to Albert Tatlock's house; he looked solitary – and desperately lonely. As he closed the door he was suddenly grateful for all of his blessings, most of all Emily.

'I saw Hilda Ogden leaving as I walked across from the factory. What was she doing here?' Mike Baldwin questioned Bet, as he walked into his living room.

'Cleaning.' Bet pursed her lips and gazed at herself in the mirror as she backcombed her hair.

'*Cleaning?*' Mike exploded. 'You're supposed to be my bloody housekeeper.'

Bet dropped her comb on to the cluttered mantelpiece and picked up her lipstick. 'Only as far as the likes of Annie Walker and the more "respectable" people in this street are concerned.' She managed to make 'respectable' sound like an insult. 'We both know what I am, Mike, and it's not your housekeeper.'

He watched her dispassionately as she applied a gleaming coat of Scarlet Passion to her lips. 'I warned you that I like my home comforts but you take no bloody notice of anything I say. There's never a meal ready when I come home—'

'And there won't be,' she broke in tartly, 'not while you insist on coming home ten minutes before I'm due to start my shift in Rovers. Now, if I could give up my job . . .'

'To do what?' Mike dropped on to the sofa and propped his feet on one of the dining chairs.

'More housekeeping.' She sat astride him and loosened his belt.

He grabbed her hands and pushed her away. 'You'll have to move out this weekend.'

'The hell I will!'

'The hell you won't!' he contradicted her. 'My wife's coming down from London.'

'You told me this was *my* house.' She climbed off him.

'As long as it suited, and it doesn't, not any more. And just for the record,' he gave her a cold, empty smile, 'it's my house and you are about to move out.'

'Where do you expect me to go?'

'That's your problem, Bet,' he snapped.

'You'd put me out on the street?'

'If you're too idle to find anywhere else to go.' He refused to rise to her bait.

'I can't afford to move out.'

'Pull the other one – you haven't paid a penny in rent or bills for months. But who knows? You might find yourself another sucker to keep you in exchange for . . .' he gave her a salacious grin ' ". . . housekeeping" duties.'

'You bastard!' She picked up a cushion and flung it at him.

'That's me.' He retrieved it and pushed it behind his head.

'I'll ask Renee Bradshaw if I can move into her spare bedroom in the flat above her corner shop for the weekend, but I'll be back first thing Monday morning.' She left the room.

'No, you won't, sweetheart, not Monday and not any time,' Mike muttered to himself, as Bet closed the front door on her way to the Rovers.

'We have to do something to commemorate the Queen's Silver Jubilee,' Annie Walker declared from behind the bar as she served the regulars in the Rovers Return. 'It only seems like yesterday that we were celebrating Her Majesty's coronation.'

'Nineteen fifty-two wasn't yesterday, Annie.' Alf Roberts set an empty mug on the bar.

'And here we are, in 1977.' Annie pulled him a pint.

'Weatherfield Council is organising a carnival.' Alf paid Annie for his own and Len's pints.

'That's it! We'll have a street float,' Annie suggested eagerly.

'Queens through the ages would be an appropriate theme for our Queen's Jubilee,' Emily murmured shyly, as Ernest set two fresh glasses of sherry on their table.

'That's a good idea.' Ever ready to support Emily, Ernest nodded enthusiastically. 'It's fitting we do something historical on such an auspicious occasion. You'd make a marvellous Elizabeth the First, Emily.'

'I think I'd make a better one,' Annie chipped in, never slow at putting herself forward. Ernest was about to object when Annie added, 'Of course, we'll need a lorry, and I just might be able to persuade the brewery to lend us one of theirs.'

'I'm sorry, love.' Ernest squeezed Emily's hand as Annie moved on to serve Ken Barlow and Albert Tatlock.

'Thank you.' She smiled, not too disappointed. Unlike some husbands – she glanced at Stan Ogden and Ray Langton who'd left their wives at home as usual – Ernest always tried his best to make her happy.

Rita Littlewood cleared the kitchen and the tables of the café that Len had opened in the back room of the newsagent's he had bought at number ten Coronation Street and called the Kabin. She had no illusions about the role she played in Len's life. He had only given her the job as manageress because he wanted to keep her close to him – or more accurately his bed in number nine.

She opened the till, bagged the day's takings, locked the door and walked down Coronation Street to number nine. She knocked on the door, and, when Len opened it, handed him the bag.

'And you can have the keys to go with it.' She pressed them into his palm.

'What's this in aid of, Rita?' Len stepped out on to the pavement and looked at her in confusion as she backed away.

'I've been offered a four-month singing contract in Tenerife,' she crowed. 'And I'm taking it.'

His eyes rounded in disbelief. 'You're leaving Weatherfield?'

'Quick off the mark, aren't you?'

'But who's going to run the Kabin for me?'

'Mavis Riley.'

'She's not up to it.'

'She's been under my feet long enough. If she can't manage the place on her own by now, she never will.' Rita turned her back to Len and wiggled her fingers in the air. ''Bye, and think of me sunning meself on the beach while you're slaving away here.'

He ran in front of her, forcing her to face him. 'You can't just walk away like this, Rita.'

'Yes, I can.'

'There has to be something I can do!'

'Drive me to the airport tomorrow,' she interrupted. 'My plane leaves at midday and I need to get there a couple of hours before.'

Len needed time to think, and one night was all she was offering, so he agreed. 'I'll pick you up at eight-thirty. All right?'

'All right,' she answered, as if she was the one bestowing the favour. 'But if you're one minute late I'll call a taxi.'

'Not a bad place, this.' Mike Baldwin glanced around Renee Bradshaw's flat above her shop.

'Fat lot you care what it's like,' Bet retorted, 'as long as I'm out of your hair.'

'Don't be like that.' He nuzzled the back of her neck. 'You've cost me a lot of aggro. My wife found a bottle of your perfume in the bathroom and your blonde hair blocking the plugholes. I had the full interrogation treatment.'

'She's not your wife.'

'What did you say?'

'You heard me – she's not your wife.'

'Who says so?' Mike demanded.

'She came in the shop when Renee asked me to mind it for an hour. We got chatting and she told me you two aren't legally married. She's only your common-law wife, and that makes her no better than me.'

'That depends on who's making the comparison.' Mike moved closer and slid his hands beneath her sweater.

'You bastard . . .'

'Absolutely, but that's why you love me, isn't it, Bet?' He pulled her round to face him, pressed his lips to hers then pulled up her sweater and bra. Bet hated herself for succumbing, but once she'd kissed him back, there was no stopping either of them.

'I'm going to enjoy calling in on you here from time to time.' Mike threw back the bedclothes and climbed out of Bet's bed.

'Don't bother.'

'Don't try telling me you didn't enjoy that.' He smirked.

'I can't afford to stay here. Renee wants eight pounds a week rent. I can't afford that.'

'Beat her down.'

'I've tried, she won't budge.'

Mike hesitated. He'd never been a one-woman man and he had no intention of changing his ways at his time of life. A live-in common-law wife and a mistress in the same street appealed to him. It gave him choice with little effort on his part and both women were willing and eager – once he pushed the right buttons.

Bet looked up at him. 'I suppose you're going home now to climb into *her* bed.'

'Since when have you joined a Sunday school?'

'I don't like the way you use me.'

'Come on, sweetheart, we use each other. You're just as much of a free spirit as I am.'

'Free spirit? I'm more of a bloody fool for putting up with you.'

'Do you want me to have a word with Renee?' He belted his trousers over his shirt.

'It wouldn't do any good.' Bet turned over in the bed.

'We'll see about that.' He pulled back the eiderdown and kissed her naked shoulder. 'See you soon.'

Whistling 'Hound Dog', Mike ran down the stairs into the shop where Renee was serving Ena Sharples.

'Visiting upstairs?' Ena enquired sharply.

'Just making sure that my ex-housekeeper has settled in, Mrs Sharples.' He gave her an insincere smile.

'Do you want anything else, Mrs Sharples?' Renee asked.

'I do, but don't mind me. I can't make up me mind whether to buy a tin of peaches or apricots for my Sunday tea.'

'Why don't you splash out and take both?' Mike asked, after Ena had gazed intently at the shelf of tinned fruit for five tense, silent minutes.

'Because, unlike you, I'm not made of money,' Ena bit back. 'I've only me pension.'

'Then take both on me.' Mike lifted the tins down and added them to Ena's modest pile of shopping.

'I'll not take charity from the likes of you,' Ena snapped. 'I'll have the peaches, Renee.'

'Right, Mrs Sharples.' Renee totted up Ena's purchases. 'I'll add them to your account.'

'I'll settle up on Tuesday as usual.' Ena stuffed her shopping into her bag, gave Mike a scathing look and left the shop.

'If looks could kill . . .'

'. . . I'd be dead,' Mike finished. 'Bet told me you're charging her eight pounds a week rent.'

'It's the going rate,' Renee insisted.

'I'm not arguing.' Mike pulled a ten-pound note from

his back pocket. 'Charge her six and this will cover the difference for the next five weeks. I'll give you another tenner then. OK?'

'OK.' Renee stuffed the note into her overall pocket.

Mike tapped his nose. 'Our little secret.'

'If anyone hears about it, it won't be from me,' she assured him.

Len pretended to concentrate on his driving as he headed out of the city towards the airport. Rita was sitting beside him, two large suitcases and a small bag stowed in the boot of his car. She had mentioned that her singing contract was for four months but, judging by the amount of luggage she was taking, she wasn't expecting to return to Weatherfield in the near future and he suddenly realised how much he would miss her – and not just between the sheets.

His eyes fixed on the road, he said, 'Please don't go.'

'Give me one good reason why I should stay,' she answered softly.

'Me.'

'So you can carry on treating me like dirt? A toy to play with when you've nothing better to do – and drop when you have?'

He braced himself. 'Marry me.'

'If this is one of your jokes . . .'

'No joke.' He glanced at her, upright and rigid, poised

on the edge of the seat beside him.

'You're proposing to me?'

'Trying to.'

'You're three years too late,' she informed him. 'I'm off to a new life, doing the job I've always wanted to do and in the sun.'

'Won't you at least think about it, Rita?' he begged.

'We're here.' She changed the subject as he drove up to the terminal building. 'Find a space in the short-stay car park – I'll pay. It'll be worth the extra not to have to lug the cases.'

Len found a space, left the car and fetched a trolley. Opening the boot, he piled Rita's suitcases and bag on to it.

'Thank you for driving me to the airport.' She waited for him to kiss her cheek.

'I'll see you inside.' As he pushed the trolley, he ventured, 'I wish you'd reconsider.'

'So you can get me back to Weatherfield to run your precious Kabin for you, while you spend the next year or two making excuses as to why we can't fix a date? No, thank you, Len Fairclough. I know you too well,' she said.

'I'll marry you the minute we can arrange it. Tomorrow, if possible. It can't come soon enough for me.'

She stared at him in astonishment. 'You mean it, don't you?'

'I've never been more serious in my life.'

Rita looked away from him to the board logging the

departures. Her flight to Tenerife was due to depart in two hours and five minutes.

'Rita?'

She whirled round to face him. 'Why, Len?' she demanded. 'Why ask me to marry you now, of all times, when I have everything I've ever wanted within my grasp?'

'I'm sorry, Rita love. I know I haven't treated you well but I'll change – I'll do anything I can to make you happy. We could make it work between us, I know we could.'

'What makes you so damned sure?'

'Because I love you, and I've only just realised how much.'

'I never thought my life would come down to this – a decision made on the spur of the moment at an airport. Have you any idea what you're asking me to do? Give up the best career break I've ever had, or am likely to get, to live with you in Coronation Street and help you run your business?'

'I love you,' he repeated simply.

'You don't deserve me.'

'I know I don't,' he agreed. 'But that doesn't stopped me hoping you'll come home with me.'

'You've got cheek, I'll give you that, Len Fairclough.' She turned back to the board. The flight was leaving in one hour and fifty-eight minutes. 'Can we honeymoon in Tenerife?'

'Wherever you want, love.' He swept her into his arms. 'The sooner I put a ring on that finger,' he kissed the fingertips of her left hand, 'the sooner I'll be happy. Can I put your cases back in the car?'

'Yes,' she whispered. 'Yes, you can.'

Elsie Tanner studied the brand-new cream and brown outfit hanging on the back of her living-room door. The matching hat, gloves and handbag lay abandoned on the sideboard. Len and Rita had invited her to their wedding in St Mary's but she hadn't been able to bring herself to go. She picked up the letter that had arrived that morning from Alan. She opened it out and read it again. The last three lines burnt into her, stirring emotions that tore her apart.

> Please, Elsie, accept as I have had to that our marriage
> is over and divorce me so I can marry the woman I love,
> Elaine Dennett. I hope that you, too, will find happiness
> with someone else. Best wishes, Alan.

After everything they had been to one another. *Best wishes* – was every relationship she embarked on doomed to failure? Was she cursed in some way? First Arnold, then Steve, now Alan. Had all her marriage break-ups been her fault?

Now she felt as though her whole world was falling apart. As well as her husband she was losing her best friend. She closed her eyes and recalled the blackest moments in her life. All the bad times Len had seen her through. He'd been there, holding her hand in court when Dennis had been tried and imprisoned the first time for burglary, when Arnold had walked out on her, leaving her to bring up the children alone. When she had returned from America with her marriage to Steve in tatters.

Was it coincidence that this letter had come from Alan on the day Len was marrying Rita? She left her chair and untied the belt of her robe. Her world might be falling apart but, whatever else, Len's friendship had never been selfish. The least she could do was go to his wedding reception in the Greenvale Hotel and wish him and Rita well. It wouldn't be easy, but she owed him that much.

The reception was well under way when Elsie reached the private room where the management had laid on a buffet and a DJ. To everyone's amusement, Len's best man, Alf Roberts, was attempting to jive with Rita's bridesmaid, Mavis Riley. He wasn't built for dancing and his stomach wobbled with every step he took, but Elsie applauded along with everyone else.

Rita eyed Elsie as she made her way across the room towards her and Len. She knew all about her husband's crush on Elsie, which she suspected he'd never entirely get over for all his protestations that he loved her, not Elsie. Sometimes she thought she could have borne it more easily if he and Elsie had been lovers – if they had, he might have got Elsie out of his system. But she had never forgotten the wistfulness in his voice when once, rather the worse for drink, he had confessed that Elsie had never allowed him into her bed, insisting that it would ruin their friendship.

'Elsie, sorry you couldn't make it to the church,' Rita said, as Elsie kissed her cheek.

'Something came up.' Elsie moved to Len. 'I wish both of you the very best.'

'Thank you, Elsie.' Len accepted her chaste kiss.

'Our song, Len,' Rita said, when the DJ put 'Secret Love' on the turntable.

Before they moved to the dance floor, a tall, imposing man joined them.

'Introduce me to your friend, Len,' he asked.

'Ted Brownlow, Elsie Tanner.'

'Dance, Elsie?' Ted asked.

'I never thought the day would come when I'd dance at Len's wedding,' Elsie laughed, 'but I'm glad it has.'

'What do you think of the hotel?' Ted asked, as he took Elsie on to the floor.

'Very swish.'

'I own it.'

'Do you now?'

'I'll show you round after this dance, if you like.'

'I'd like that very much indeed.'

*

Len saw Elsie smile at Ted and felt as though someone was twisting a knife in his guts.

'Thanks for the introduction.' Ted handed Len the drinks he had bought for him and Rita after the dance. 'Elsie seems like a nice woman.'

'She is, very nice,' Len said, and added, 'So nice, she's been living apart from her third husband for months.' He walked away, leaving Ted staring at his back.

Chapter Thirty

As he walked towards the warehouse from the bank, Ernest Bishop mulled over Coronation Street's disastrous attempt to enter a float in the carnival Weatherfield Council had organised to celebrate the Queen's Silver Jubilee. Annie Walker's Queen Elizabeth the First costume had been perfect, although in his opinion, Ena Sharples had made a better Queen Victoria than Annie had made Queen Elizabeth. And Bet Lynch as a flimsily clad Britannia had earned more wolf whistles and admiring looks from the Rovers' regulars. But the Rovers was as far as any of them had got. After he had taken the time and trouble to dress up as Walter Raleigh, Ken as Sir Edmund Hilary and Albert Tatlock as Sherpa Tenzing they had never climbed on the lorry because Stan Ogden had left the lorry lights on all night and the battery was flat.

So, they had remained in the Rovers, set up a kangaroo court and sentenced Stan to buy drinks all round. It had been a good evening and both he and Emily had enjoyed it, even it hadn't turned out quite as they'd expected.

He walked into the wages office, opened his briefcase and removed two bulging bags full of cash that he had picked up from the bank. He lifted a tray of empty wage packets on to his desk, tipped the money out of the bags, then slowly and methodically began to arrange the money into piles. First the ten-pound notes, which he secured beneath a brass paperweight, then the pound notes, which he slipped beneath his stapler. He piled the fifty-pence coins into four neat little towers and the twenty-pence coins into half a dozen similar towers alongside them. He had just started on the ten-pence coins when the door to his office burst open and two men rushed in, wearing black Balaclavas that hid their faces.

He jumped out of his chair and slammed against the wall as a shotgun was pushed into his chest.

'Bag the cash.' The man with the gun picked up one of the empty bags Ernest had brought from the bank and flung it at him. It fell to the floor.

'I couldn't possibly—' Ernest stammered.

'Bag it, Grandpa.' The man grabbed the second bag and hit Ernest with it.

'I – I—' Terrified, Ernest gibbered.

'If you know what's good for you, you'll do it. *Now!*' The boy pushed the barrel of the shotgun into Ernest's chest. '*Now!*' he yelled, at the top of his voice.

Trembling, Ernest reached for the bag and started transferring the fifty-pence coins into it.

'The tenners first.'

'I protest.' Ernest was scarcely aware of what he was saying. 'This isn't your money. The girls have worked hard for their wages. Mr Baldwin, sir—'

Both men turned to see Mike standing in the doorway behind them. He held up his hands.

'Drop the gun,' he murmured, deliberately keeping his voice soft and low. 'Come on, lads, there's no harm done yet and there won't be if you drop it.'

Even as Mike spoke, the man with the gun tightened his trigger finger. There was an explosion and Ernest was blown off his feet. He landed awkwardly on his side on the floor, a crimson stain spreading outwards over his chest, soaking the grey pullover Emily had knitted for him.

'You bloody morons—' Mike, too, crashed to the floor, felled by a blow to his head. He was vaguely aware of the men running off, but he had to help Ernest. He crawled towards him and heard the ragged, rasping sound of his breathing. At least he was alive.

'I've phoned 999, Mike, the ambulance and police are on their way.' Alerted by the commotion, Elsie had run in from the factory floor in time to see the men make their escape. She looked down at Ernest. 'Oh my God . . .'

Mike heard Elsie, but he concentrated on Ernest. 'You fool,' he whispered, as he tried to support him in his arms.

'You sweet, loyal fool, you should have given them what they wanted. Nothing is worth this.'

Stan Ogden and Eddie Yeats had spent the morning cleaning the inside of the stained-glass windows in St Margaret's Church. After they had eaten the sandwiches Hilda had cut for their break and emptied their flasks of tea, they moved on to the outside, which were thick with grime and green mould.

'I swear these haven't seen soap and water since the war,' Stan grumbled, tipping away the third bucket of water he had used on one of the larger windows.

'All the more reason for them to give us the contract to clean them regularly, so they never get in this state again,' Eddie said optimistically. 'Stop your moaning, Stan, and put some real elbow grease into it.'

Stan glanced across the road as an ambulance raced down the street, bell ringing and blue light flashing. 'Something's going on. One of us should go down there and see what it is.' He dropped his cloth into his bucket.

'Keep polishing, the vicar's coming,' Eddie hissed.

The ambulance raced off before the vicar reached them. 'You've done a wonderful job, Mr Ogden, Mr Yeats,' he complimented them. 'I haven't seen the windows so clean for years. In fact, I never knew the colours in them were so vivid. That beautiful deep royal blue and shimmering, translucent green, for instance.'

'They were very dirty.' Eddie climbed down his ladder and poured his water down a storm drain at the corner of the church.

'It is heartening to know there are still good charitable people like your kind selves out in the community,' the vicar gushed. 'Prepared to give your time and your expertise to keep the church clean.'

'Charitable?' Stan spluttered.

'No false modesty, Mr Ogden, you *are* charitable, and God will bless you for the work you have done this day.'

'What about when the windows need cleaning next time?' Eddie called after the vicar, as he walked away.

The vicar turned. 'God will provide and we were rather hoping that you would return.'

'Then you will give us a contract to clean the church?'

'Dear me, no, Mr Yeats. We haven't the funds. That is why we are so grateful for your help now.'

'Charity!' Stan gripped his ladder hard as he stared at Eddie. 'I've worked all bloody day for charity!'

'Don't swear, you're in a churchyard,' Eddie admonished him.

'Not for long.' Stan picked up his ladder, bucket and wash-leathers and walked down the path to the gate. Eddie watched him go, eyed the last two unfinished windows and followed suit.

When they reached the gate of Mike Baldwin's factory they saw a crowd.

'What's happening?' Stan asked.

'Haven't you heard?' Ena Sharples stepped forward, relishing her role as harbinger of bad news. 'Two men tried to rob the wages department. They shot Ernest Bishop.'

'Is he going to be all right?' Eddie asked in alarm.

'No one knows. They've taken him away in the ambulance. Emily's gone with him, although in my opinion she wasn't in a fit state to go anywhere. She won't be any help to Ernest or anyone else in the hospital. And the police have taken Mike Baldwin away. He's a witness.'

'Poor Emily,' Eddie murmured, watching the crowd disperse.

Annie Walker slipped her arm round Emily's shoulders and led her down the main corridor towards the hospital entrance. She wished there was something she could say to help comfort her friend, but she remembered how she'd felt when Jack had died, and she knew that no words could possibly comfort Emily as she faced the bleak, lonely journey to the home she and Ernest had shared, and he would never enter again.

She helped Emily into the taxi she had ordered, and held her hand as the driver took them to Coronation Street. Emily's eyes were blank, her hand clammy and trembling from shock. Annie had only to look at her to experience again the horror that had beset her for months after Jack's death.

'What number Coronation Street?' the driver asked.

'Three,' Annie answered. She helped Emily out of the car and inside the house. Within minutes of their arrival people were knocking at the door. Annie knew it was useless to try to keep the well-meaning neighbours at bay, so she showed them into Emily's living room. They brought flowers, cards and their heartfelt, sincere sympathy, but nothing penetrated the trance that Emily had fallen into.

Annie set about making tea and welcoming the visitors, hoping it was what Emily would have wanted her to do if she had been capable of deciding for herself. The small rituals associated with death had begun: people felt that they had to try to be of some use. And although Emily was oblivious to their attentions, Annie hoped that some day she might remember that after Ernest had died she had been surrounded by people who cared for her, and in time come to draw comfort from their concern and presence.

'It seems wrong to pin something like that on the board the day after Ernest Bishop was buried.' Concerned for Emily's feelings, Annie Walker had closed the Rovers for Ernest's funeral.

'I feel sorry for Emily, but life has to go on.' Bet Lynch pushed the final drawing-pin into the notice. The brewery was offering a free drink every day for life to its longest-standing customer and Bet had heard on the grapevine that several of the street's older residents intended to apply for the prize.

'It's going to be odd not seeing Ernest walking back and forth to work, or calling in here with Emily for a sherry. Good evening, Mr Tatlock,' Annie greeted Albert as he walked in. 'The usual?'

'Please.' He stood at the bar while Annie pulled him a pint of mild.

'Terrible about Ernest Bishop,' he began.

'Terrible,' Annie concurred. 'I hope the police catch the thugs who killed him and, when they do, string them up.'

'So, you thinking of trying for the free drink every day for life, Mr Tatlock?' Bet deliberately changed the subject because she knew that if she didn't Ernest's murder would be the sole topic of conversation in the pub all night.

'I heard about it. It's right, is it? A free drink every day for life for the longest-standing customer.'

'That's right,' Bet said, 'and you must have been coming in here for quite a while.'

'I have that,' Albert said proudly. 'I had my first drink in here during a Whit Week Walk in 1919.'

'Then you should win, no argument.' Bet reached under the counter. 'All you have to do is fill in one of these forms and we'll send it off to the brewery for you.'

'And I'll have one of those forms an' all, Bet Lynch.' Ena walked through the bar on her way to the snug. 'If they're the forms for the free drink every day for life.'

'They are.' Annie handed her one.

'And you can forget all about winning,' Ena said to Albert. 'I had my first drink in here on Christmas Eve in 1918 when you were still at the front in France, and I can produce witnesses to prove it. So,' Ena looked at Annie, 'how long do I have to wait for my free drinks after filling in this form?'

'As soon as the brewery have had a chance to look at all the forms and choose the winner.'

'I'll expect my free daily milk stout at the end of the week, then. I'll take this,' Ena held up her form, 'into the snug and I'll have my usual while I fill it in.'

The police officer sat awkwardly on the upright chair Ken Barlow had set in front of the sofa where Emily sat, sunk deep in misery.

'I know it's little consolation, Mrs Bishop, but we caught them,' he revealed.

'Who?' In the space of a few days Emily had become painfully thin. Her face was lined and drawn, her eyes hollow. She was steeped in a despair that was unbearable to contemplate.

'The two villains who shot your husband,' he answered gently. 'And I assure you that they will be punished for what they did. They will be tried for murder and, considering that we have overwhelming evidence against them, I don't doubt they'll both get life imprisonment.'

'Can I go to the trial?' Emily asked, in a remote voice.

'You can, Mrs Bishop.'

Ken held her hand. 'I will go with you, Emily.'

'Thank you,' she whispered.

'I just wanted to let you know we'd caught them before you read it in the newspapers.' The officer set the teacup Ken had given him on the table and stood up.

'I'll see you out.' Ken opened the door.

'Constable?'

'Yes?' The police officer turned back to Emily.

'Thank you for coming.'

He nodded and followed Ken into the passage. 'She has taken it very badly,' he said, as Ken handed him his helmet.

Ken wanted to ask him how else he would have expected Emily to take the news of her husband's brutal murder but, suspecting the officer meant well, he refrained. 'She has a lot of friends and neighbours prepared to rally round.' He opened the door to reveal Annie Walker, Elsie Tanner and Deirdre Langton, holding her daughter Tracy, on the doorstep.

'We heard they caught the men who killed Ernest,' Annie explained.

'Would it help if we saw her, Ken?' Elsie asked.

'It certainly won't do any harm.' He stepped back. 'Please, all of you, come in.'

The following evening, Emily was sitting in her living room with Tracy Langton on her lap. Tracy was turning the pages of a picture book and demanding an explanation to accompany each illustration, and Emily was more animated than either Elsie or Deirdre had seen her since Ernest had been killed.

Elsie rose to her feet when she heard a knock at the door. 'I'll get that.'

'If you're all right with Tracy, Emily, I'll make us a fresh pot of tea.' Deirdre picked up the teapot.

'Tracy seems happy enough.' Emily rested her chin against the little girl's soft blonde hair and breathed in the scent of baby soap and shampoo.

'She knows her godmother,' Deirdre told her.

Elsie ushered Ivy Tilsley into the living room. Before she had a chance to say a word Ivy was in full flow.

'I've come round with a petition, one I know you'll want to sign, Emily.'

'What kind of petition?' Emily looked annoyed at the interruption to her and Tracy's reading.

'I heard they caught the murderers who killed your Ernie and I decided to do something about them. This,' Ivy pushed a thick writing pad at Emily, 'is a petition to bring back hanging. When I have enough signatures I'm going to send it to our MP.'

'I don't want to sign it.' Emily stroked Tracy's curls and looked down at the picture book.

'*What?*' Ivy exclaimed incredulously.

'I don't believe in capital punishment, Ivy. Please, take it away.'

'I can't believe you've asked me to do something like this and, what's more, I can't believe I'm doing it. You use me unmercifully, Mike Baldwin,' Bet Lynch complained.

'I use you!' He lifted his eyebrows in amusement. 'Face it, sunshine, it's not as if I'm asking you to dig ditches or clean toilets.' He handed her fifty pounds in ten-pound notes. 'All you have to do is take out a prospective buyer and show him a good time at my expense. The two of you will enjoy the best restaurant, the best meal, the best wine . . .'

'And me?' she demanded. 'Am I part of the package you promised him?'

'There isn't a man alive who wouldn't enjoy an evening all the more for having a pretty girl on his arm. Now remember,' Mike tugged down the front of the black silk dress Bet was wearing, exposing her cleavage, 'have a good time, wear him out, get drunk, do whatever you have to, but don't forget for one minute that your job is to pull in the order he's placing.'

'And if I get you the order?'

'I'll let you keep the change from the fifty quid.'

'Forget it.' Bet dropped the money on to his desk.

'I was joking. You'll have as much again.'

'Promise?'

'When have I ever let you down?' He gave her a croco-dile smile.

'All the time.' Despite her misgivings, Bet picked up her jacket, left the factory and minced, in her three-inch stiletto heels, to the Jaguar parked in the street outside the gates.

The man in the driver's seat opened his window and eyed Bet as if she were a piece of livestock.

'Are you, George Livesley?' she snapped. She didn't like the look of him and she resented Mike for talking her into doing this.

'If you're Bet Lynch I am.' He reached over and opened the passenger door. 'I know just the place to take a girl like you.'

Bet tried and failed to smile. 'I can't wait to get there,' she lied.

Rita Fairclough set Len's tea of lamb chops, mashed pota-toes and peas in front of him. 'I can't believe you've taken out a bank loan using the Kabin as security.'

'It was either that or this house, love.' Len took the small jug of mint sauce she handed him. 'I need three thousand pounds' worth of materials to do this job.'

'What I can't understand is, if it's such a massive contract for such a big firm why they can't pay you up-front for the materials.' She opened a bottle of beer and set it next to his glass.

'Because that's not the way big firms operate,' he explained. 'They lay out thousands on land and property, buy in expert architects to oversee the project, employ top-notch builders and pay on completion of the job.'

'And you and Ray will be converting this big old house into an hotel.'

'A first-class, five-star hotel,' Len informed her proudly.

'How long is it going to take for the loan to come through?'

'It already has. The materials were delivered to Clayton's warehouse this afternoon. Ray and I checked them in.'

'Why not have them delivered to the yard?'

'Three thousand quid's worth?' Len shook his head. 'You have to be joking. We wanted somewhere secure. Clayton's warehouse is roofed and he employs guards.'

'I still don't like you using the Kabin as security. We could lose it.'

'We won't. This job is going to put Fairclough and Langton on the map, love. It will lead to bigger and better jobs. We're expanding and moving into the big time.' Len rubbed his hands together. 'Money, here we come. And now I'm a married man,' he watched Rita's hips as she headed for the scullery to fetch her own meal, 'it's time to move on. We don't want to live in Coronation Street for ever, do we, kid?'

'I suppose not.' Rita kissed him as she returned with her plate. Despite Len's enthusiasm and promises of great things to come, she couldn't quell a nagging doubt. What if he and Ray lost money on the job? What if the hotel fell through? How would they ever repay three thousand pounds out of what he was bringing home from the small jobs he and Ray were doing now?

'It's going to be great, love,' Len promised. 'Next year we'll have money to burn. We'll take a holiday somewhere warm and exotic – and I don't mean Tenerife. How do you fancy the Caribbean?'

'Let's talk about it then, Len.'

'You don't think this is going to work out, do you?' He threw down his knife and fork.

'I'm just more cautious than you. Do you want another beer, love?' she asked, knowing how to divert him.

He drained his glass and handed it to her. 'Please.'

'We've had two bottles of wine already, George,' Bet reminded him as the waiter brought a third bottle to their table. George had drunk the lion's share of both. She had only had half a glass all evening. She had decided that as Mike was footing the bill and owed her for this favour, she might as well drink her favourite vodka and tonic.

'This stuff goes down like lemonade,' George boasted.

'Fill my glass,' he told the waiter, the second he had removed the cork. 'And bring two large brandies with our coffee and dessert. What you going to have, Bet?' He pinched her knee.

Irritated by George's passes, she murmured, 'Just coffee for me, George.'

'And brandy,' he insisted, 'and I'll have a piece of that peach gateau over there with a scoop of rum and raisin ice cream and . . .' he looked at the illuminated shelves of the dessert cabinet '. . . some cheese.'

'May I remind you that we are closing in ten minutes, sir?' the waiter ventured.

'Remind me all you like.' George laughed. 'I'm not going till I've eaten my fill. Good job, this,' he bragged to Bet, after the waiter had left. 'I can get any clothes manufacturer to foot my meal and hotel bills – in first-class establishments, mind – because every damned one of them is chasing my orders. The biggest and the best they're likely to get in today's diminishing market.'

Bet glanced at the clock as the waiter brought George's dessert, cheese, their coffee and brandy. 'I'll have the bill, please, and . . .' she glanced at George who was getting more expansive and flushed by the minute '. . . perhaps you'd call us a taxi.'

'A taxi? What do you want a bloody taxi for?' George banged the table with his fist. 'You forgetting we came in my Jag? My bloody expensive Jag.'

'I haven't forgotten, but I thought that after all you've drunk—'

'I can take it, not like some I could mention. You drinking that?' He pointed to her brandy.

'Not on top of vodka.'

'"Not on top of vodka",' he mimicked. 'I never thought old Mike would fix me up with a temperance school-marm.'

'Finish your drink,' Bet snapped, as he scraped up the last of his gateau and ice cream.

As the waiters moved in on their table, George tipped Bet's brandy into his own, swirled it round once and drank it in a single mouthful. He rose unsteadily to his feet, leaving the coffee and cheese untouched on the table.

Bet went to the till and paid the bill. When she stepped outside George was trying to slide his key into the lock of his car. He opened the door at the third attempt.

As he slid behind the wheel, Bet remained resolutely on the pavement. 'I wish you'd let me call a taxi.'

'Don't be daft, woman. Get in.'

A crowd was gathering around them, so Bet reluctantly climbed in beside him. George turned the ignition key and sped off, weaving in and out of the traffic on the high street. He turned towards Weatherfield just as a dark figure stepped on to a zebra crossing.

'You hit someone!' Bet screamed, but he put his foot down and raced away from the scene.

'Stupid bugger wasn't looking where he was going,' George slurred.

'You've got to stop!' she begged hysterically.

'So some wet-nosed copper can put me in the slammer? Not bloody likely.' He headed for Coronation Street.

Chapter Thirty-One

The following morning, Len was whistling as he strolled into the yard to see Ray Langton sitting on a pile of blocks with a grim expression on his face. 'Trouble with Deirdre?' he enquired. Once he had persuaded Rita to give up her singing career in favour of a life as a housewife, his marriage had become everything he'd hoped it would be – especially in the mornings before he and Rita got up.

'You obviously haven't heard.' Ray lit a cigarette. 'Clayton's warehouse burnt to the ground last night and all our materials with it.'

'Bloody hell!' Len sank down beside him. He filched a cigarette from Ray's open packet. 'That'll set us back a bit. How long will it take for the insurance to pay out so we can replace everything?'

'Never.' Ray inhaled deeply.

Len's face darkened. 'That's not funny.'

'It's not meant to be. I spoke to Clayton this morning. The contents of the warehouse weren't insured.'

'Then we'll sue him – we'll—'

'Even if we had the money to hire a solicitor, Clayton's nothing left to give us, Len. Face it, we're broke, he's broke, we're all bloody broke.' Ray took a final drag of his cigarette and threw it away.

'Whoever George hit could be seriously injured – or worse.' Bet shuddered at the thought that she'd been a passenger in a car that had killed someone. 'You have to call the police, Mike.'

Before Mike could answer her, George snapped, 'That's the last thing he should do, you stupid tart!'

'You shut your mouth, George Livesley,' Bet hissed, rounding on him. She'd left the flat above the shop and run to the warehouse first thing to tell Mike what George had done, only to find George sitting coolly in the visitor's chair in Mike's office as if nothing had happened.

'Call the police, Mike, and you'll never see another order from me,' George threatened.

Face impassive, Mike glanced at Bet. 'Go home.'

'He could have killed someone!' Bet shouted.

'Go home,' Mike interrupted, in a harsher tone. 'I'll call in to see you some time this afternoon, and until then, you do nothing. Understand?'

'I'm not your bloody pet, Mike Baldwin.' Bet was furious at being ordered about. 'If you don't call the police, I will.'

'You'll do no such thing,' Mike spoke in a quiet tone that held more menace than any shouting.

'I – I—' Bet picked up her coat and handbag and flounced out. Mike left his chair and closed the door behind her.

'I'm glad you see sense, even if your tart doesn't, Mike.' George leant back in his chair for the first time since he'd entered the office.

'So, when I am going to see these orders of yours?' Mike returned to his chair.

'Soon.'

'Very soon.' Mike leant across his desk towards George. 'Or I'll put in a telephone call to your wife and tell her about your evening out. The three bottles of wine, the brandy, not to mention the blonde bimbo and your little "accident" on the way home.'

George narrowed his eyes. 'You wouldn't dare.'

'Try me,' Mike murmured. 'If the order isn't on my desk by midday, you won't have to wait long to find out exactly what I'm capable of.'

'And the police?'

'Chances are they'll track you down. I noticed the dent in your car on my way in to work this morning and, as sure as hens lay eggs, someone else has already seen it. If I were you I'd visit the police station before they visit you.'

'We're desperate, love,' Ray coaxed Deirdre. 'The business is in real trouble. Len's already mortgaged the

Kabin. He's seeing the bank manager now about raising more money on his house.'

'I don't care,' Deirdre said. 'You are not mortgaging our house to put the money into the business when you've already lost three thousand pounds. It would be throwing good money after bad. This house is all we've got and it's mortgaged to the hilt. It's Tracy's future, and you're not gambling with it.'

'You don't understand business, love. We've lost the materials for the job. We can't do the work without them. We stand to lose all our profit, and if Len and I manage to raise the money to replace the materials, even after we've made good our losses we'll make a fortune,' he pleaded.

'The answer is no, Ray, and that's my final word.'

'I can't ask Len to find all the money himself.'

'You're going to have to, and if he questions it, ask him whose bright idea it was to store the materials in the warehouse in the first place.' Deirdre went into the kitchen and started washing up.

'Fairclough and Langton could go bust,' Ray warned her from the doorway.

'Better that than we lose the roof over our heads.'

'I'll have no work.'

'There are plenty of other builders who'll employ you.'

'And if they don't?' He had raised the spectre of unemployment to frighten her.

'Then I'll have to bring in a wage. And you can stay at home and look after Tracy.'

Gail Potter carried four outfits down the stairs and into her landlady Elsie Tanner's living room. 'You know how it is, Elsie,' she said, continuing their conversation. 'You meet this boy, and you know, you simply *know*,' she repeated, 'that he's the right one for you.'

'I think I can just about remember feeling like that a couple of centuries ago,' Elsie said wryly, as she looked up from the evening paper. 'And where exactly did this momentous meeting take place?'

'At a party Suzie took me to. Brian – that's his name – Brian gazed into my eyes and said, "How would you like to spend the rest of your life with me?"'

'Spare me the syrup,' Elsie pleaded.

'Then he asked me to go to the cinema with him tonight – the big one in town. I'm meeting him at seven.' Gail picked up two of the outfits and held each in turn in front of her. 'What do you think? My black mini-skirt and grey sweater,' she swung a black skirt and figure-hugging angora sweater in Elsie's direction, 'or this blue one?'

'Too dressy for the cinema,' Elsie advised.

Gail looked critically at the dress. 'You're right. And then there's my pink sweater and grey skirt or—'

'They look good on you. They're fashionable and casual enough – go with those.'

'Thanks, Elsie, you're an absolute darling. I must put my face on.' Gail gathered up all four outfits and raced up the stairs.

Elsie returned to her paper. It had been a long time since she had prepared for a date with a man she was convinced would change her life. But that didn't stop her remembering the rush of excitement, or knowing exactly how Gail was feeling.

'In the bedroom, love,' Rita called down, when she heard the front door close. She checked her reflection in the full-length mirror. Was it her imagination or had she put on weight? The figure-hugging blue sequined dress seemed tighter than when she had last worn it. She reached down behind her back and struggled to pull up the zip.

It was strange how things turned out. Len had been adamant when they'd married that she should give up her singing career but now that he'd lost three thousand pounds' worth of building materials, he was begging her to go back. However, after her long break all she could get were engagements in second-rate working-men's clubs and she hated going into them.

'Do me a favour, love?' she asked, as Len appeared in the doorway. 'Do my zip up and fasten the hook at the top.' After he'd done as she asked, she twirled around in front of him. 'How do I look?'

'Stunning.'

'You could sound a little more enthusiastic.'

Len sank down on the edge of the bed and buried his face in his hands. 'Sorry, love, I can't. The hotel developers have gone bust.'

'Bust? You mean there won't be a hotel?'

'Not one built by Fairclough and Langton, there won't.'

'But you replaced all the materials!'

'And we're stuck with them. We'll use some – in time – but it's going to take us years to go through everything and in the meantime the firm's six grand in the red.'

A lump formed in Rita's throat. 'What are we going to do, Len? I can't keep us on what I bring in.'

'You won't have to. Ray and I went to the bank this afternoon. They asked us to pay back our debt at the rate of sixty quid a week over two years and we jumped at it. We had no choice – it was either that or go bankrupt.'

'You'll never pay it.'

'Yes, we will,' he countered. 'Ray and I signed up to work for an emergency cover service this afternoon. We'll both be working all the hours God sends for the next two years but it can't be helped. I'm so sorry, love.' He dropped his hands and looked up at her. 'This isn't the life I promised you when we got married.'

'No, it isn't.' She sat beside him on the bed. 'But two years isn't for ever. We'll weather it, Len.'

'Even when I make you sing in crummy working-men's clubs?'

'It doesn't matter.' She tried to believe what she was saying as she slipped her high-heeled sandals on to her feet. 'It really doesn't matter.'

Gail looked up and down the street. She tried to recall every sentence of the conversation she'd had with Brian Tilsley at the party, but the more she tried the more her memory was fudged by the kisses they'd shared. But for all that, she was sure he had promised to meet her at seven o'clock on Friday outside the cinema.

She glanced at her watch. There was no sign of him, and even if he turned up now, how desperate would he think she was, waiting twenty minutes past their agreed meeting time?

She pushed her hands into her pockets, flicked her long, light brown hair behind her ears and walked up the road towards the bus stop. No one else was waiting and she presumed she'd just missed one. Wonderful evening this was turning out to be. Five minutes later a man moved in behind her. She turned round and stared at him.

'You've a nerve!'

'Pardon?' Brian Tilsley ran his hand through his thick brown curly hair and looked at her in confusion.

'I've just waited twenty minutes for you to turn up outside the cinema.'

'We had a date?'

'You don't remember? Party, last Wednesday . . .'

'I was so drunk I was out of my mind last Wednesday. It was a good party, so good I can't remember a thing after nine o'clock, but it's comforting to know I've excellent taste in women even when I'm totally out of it.' He held out his hand. 'Nice to meet you. I'm Brian Tilsley.'

'I know – I wasn't drunk or out of my mind.' Gail looked at his hand for a moment, then shook it. 'Gail Potter.'

'I'm sorry.' He gave her a disarming smile. 'As there's no bus, do you fancy going for drink so I can make it up to you?'

She hesitated. 'Just a quick one.'

'You in a hurry?'

'Sort of,' she lied.

'Why? I thought you'd cleared the evening to go to the cinema with me.'

'Clever clogs, aren't you?' She smiled as she took his arm.

'And what's wrong with the food in the Kabin all of a sudden?' Len complained as Ray headed for the café the baker Joe Dawson had opened in the unit next to Len's Kabin, incidentally poaching more than half of the Kabin's trade. And to add insult to injury Joe had persuaded Len's old secretary, Emily Bishop to manage it for him.

'I fancy pasty and chips,' Ray called back.

'I sell pasties in the Kabin.'

'Mavis didn't have any this morning.' Ray pulled up his

coat collar against the rain and slouched off. His relationship with Len had been strained ever since they had lost
the big contract they had pinned so many hopes on. And
being called out three times in the night on plumbing
emergencies, the last time at four in the morning by a
stupid woman who wouldn't have had a problem if she'd
used her common sense, hadn't helped.

He stepped into Dawson's café, nodded to Emily, who
was manning the till, and walked into the back. The waitress, Janice Stubbs, was clearing a table. He pulled her
into a corner out of sight of the till and kissed her. A
movement in the doorway disturbed them so he sat at a
table and picked up a menu.

'Can I take your order, sir?' Janice asked loudly.

He watched the doorway as he slipped his hand up
Janice's skirt and fondled her thigh. 'You certainly can.'
Lowering his voice, he whispered, 'Your place, five o'clock.'

Janice nodded as Emily carried a tray into the back.

'Pasty and chips, sir?' Janice scribbled on her notepad.

'That will do nicely.' Ray winked at her.

'Who is this girl you've been seeing?' Ivy Tilsley
demanded, standing behind Brian as he splashed after-
shave on to his face.

'Gail Potter,' he answered, 'as if you didn't know.'

'She works for Mike Baldwin but not in the warehouse
with the rest of us – she manages his shop.'

'So she told me.'

'And what else has she told you? Anything about me?' Ivy demanded, instantly on the defensive.

'No, she just said she knows that you work in Mike Baldwin's factory.'

'She's not a Catholic.' Ivy crossed her arms across her chest and glared at her son.

'Strangely enough, religion's not something that has come up in conversation between us.'

'I'm not having you bringing any girl into this house who isn't a Catholic,' Ivy warned, as Brian went to the door.

His only answer was to close the door behind him.

Ivy's husband, Bert, put down the evening paper. 'You can't live the boy's life for him, Ivy.'

'So, what do you expect me to do?'

'Be tolerant,' he suggested mildly. 'Because if you try putting Brian off Gail, you might risk losing him altogether.'

'Rubbish!' she snapped. 'I brought Brian up a Catholic. He is a Catholic, he's staying a Catholic and he's not marrying out of the faith.'

Bert had long since realised that arguing with his wife was futile. He shook out his paper and turned to the sports page.

Emily Bishop left Dawson's café and walked slowly down Coronation Street. The days when she was at work weren't too bad: there were people to serve, things to do, and when she was busy, although she could never forget Ernest or the ghastly way he had died, she managed somehow to put the pain of losing him to the back of her mind.

The most difficult time for her was when she finished work for the day. She had always looked forward to her evenings with Ernest. Not that they'd ever done anything special, just shared a meal, an occasional sherry in the Rovers, watched a television programme or visited the cinema, but the time had been theirs, and she missed him then, with a pain that was almost physical. She smiled with pleasure when she saw Deirdre and her little daughter, Tracy standing outside her front door.

'What a lovely surprise to see you. How kind of you to call round.' She opened the door and went straight through to the scullery. 'I'll put the kettle on.' She returned with a bag of Tracy's favourite iced gems.

'We don't want to be a bother,' Deirdre said.

'How could my goddaughter and closest friend be a bother? To be honest, I was dreading coming back to an empty house, and instead I find two of my favourite people here.' She gave Tracy a hug along with the biscuits.

'You spoil her,' Deirdre said.

'What's a goddaughter for, if not to spoil?' Emily asked.

'I wanted to talk to you,' Deirdre took a deep breath and looked into Emily's eyes. 'Tell me, truthfully, how long has Ray been having an affair with Janice Stubbs?'

Emily sat down abruptly.

'I know it's going on,' Deirdre said, 'so, please, just tell me the truth.'

'Shouldn't you be asking Ray that question?' Emily hedged.

'You're my friend, or at least you say you are, so I'm asking you.'

'I've noticed that Ray always sits in the back of the café and he and Janice spend a lot of time whispering to each other whenever he comes in.'

'And that's all?'

'I hoped it was nothing, just an infatuation, but . . .'

'But?' Deirdre pressed.

'It might be nothing, but when I came back early today from doing the banking, Janice had closed the café and they were both in the stockroom.'

'That's all I needed to know.' Deirdre scooped Tracy into her arms and headed for the door.

'It might be nothing.' Emily ran after her.

'It's not nothing,' Deirdre said vehemently. 'And it's high time Ray and I did some serious talking.'

'Do you want to leave Tracy here?' Emily asked, frightened by the look on Deirdre's face.

Deirdre turned and handed her over.

'Don't worry, I'll give her tea.' Emily smoothed the child's hair back from her face. 'We'll be company for each other.'

★

Elsie Tanner and Gail Potter heard the screaming coming from number five as they left the factory. All the residents of Coronation Street were used to arguments but this was different. Both of them had been waiting for weeks for Deirdre to find out about Ray's affair with Janice. For all that Ray had thought they were being discreet, it was no secret, and the last person in the street to find out about it had been Deirdre

'How could you do it?' Deirdre shrieked. 'Not just to me, but Tracy! What kind of marriage is it when the husband goes off and sleeps with another woman?'

'Just look at yourself! The way you're ranting and raving, the way you've let yourself go since Tracy was born!' he added viciously. 'Always going on at me about money—'

'If I didn't, you'd have mortgaged this house to save the business and we'd have lost everything.'

'Always have to be bloody right, don't you?' he taunted. 'Is it any wonder I strayed, given the way you behave? You're more like a bloody prison warder than a wife.'

Incensed, Deirdre lifted her hand, intending to slap Ray, but he caught her wrist and hit her instead. She cried out and reeled across the room. 'Get out!'

'Get out.' He laughed mirthlessly. 'This is more my house than yours, but not for much longer. I'm leaving. I've been offered a job in Amsterdam.'

'Offered or applied for?' She rubbed her cheek where his blow had landed.

'What's the difference?' he sneered.

'Going there with your Janice?' she taunted.

Ray paused. He was suddenly viewing the ugly scene with an objective clarity that horrified him. How had things come to this pass between him and Deirdre? He loved her, they had a beautiful daughter . . . 'Come with me,' he pleaded.

'When hell freezes over.'

'Not even for Tracy's sake?'

'It's Tracy I'm thinking of,' she retorted. 'Do you think for one minute that I'll ever trust you again after the way you've betrayed me with that tart?'

Furious at her rejection, his temper escalated again. 'Then you'd better hurry up and find somewhere else to live because I'm selling this house.'

'If it wasn't for me we would have lost it.'

'You'll never let me forget that, will you?'

'It's also Tracy's house,' she pointed out, refusing to be sidetracked.

'If she has nowhere to live it will be your fault for not coming with me. I'm offering for the last time.' He held his breath hoping, even now, that she'd change her mind.

'The answer's no.'

'Then start packing, because the house will be on the market tomorrow.'

'You'd put your own daughter on the street?'

'You're doing that, Deirdre,' he said firmly, needing to believe it. 'Not me.'

Emily enveloped Deirdre in her arms and held her close for a few minutes. Then she helped her to a chair. Tracy was sitting wide-eyed on the sofa, watching her mother cry.

'It's all right, Tracy,' Emily soothed her. 'Your mam's upset but she'll soon be fine.'

'How can I be when Ray's selling the house? I have no money, no job, nowhere to go, Tracy to look after.' Deirdre burst into tears again. 'What's going to become of us?'

'You'll be fine,' Emily assured her, feeling guilty for confirming Deirdre's suspicions about Ray's affair.

'But—'

'No buts.' Emily lifted her goddaughter on to her lap. 'You and Tracy can move in with me.'

'But I've no money. I won't be able to pay you anything. And with Tracy I won't find it easy to get a job. How will we manage?'

'We'll cross that bridge when we come to it.'

'Emily, I'll never be able to repay you.' Deirdre saw that she was frightening Tracy and made a valiant effort to dry her tears.

Emily looked from Deirdre to Tracy. 'I think I'll be

getting the best of the bargain.' She dropped a kiss on Tracy's head. 'It will be nice to have someone to come home to again.'

Chapter Thirty-Two

'Gail, we get on, don't we?' Brian Tilsley began diffidently, one evening, as he and Gail walked up Coronation Street from the Rovers Return.

'I suppose we do,' Gail answered warily. Since the night she had thought that Brian had stood her up, only to meet him at the bus stop later, they hadn't spent an evening apart. But Ivy had made a point of coming into the shop every chance she got, and she hadn't missed an opportunity to let her know that no matter what Gail thought of Brian, or how much she hoped they might have a future together, the Tilsleys – or to be more accurate, Ivy – would never tolerate a non-Catholic as a daughter-in-law.

And much as Gail loved Brian and hoped he felt the same way about her, she couldn't escape the fact that he had never told her he loved her. If he was about to tell her that he wanted to finish with her, she wouldn't be able to bear it.

'Supposing we got married.'

'Married!' She halted, unable to take in what Brian had said. She had been expecting a brush-off, and he was asking her to marry him.

He turned and blocked her path. He cupped her face with his hands and gazed intently into her eyes. 'I love you.'

'You've never said that before,' she murmured, in wonderment.

'Come on, you know I fell in love with you the first moment I saw you.'

'Was that when you were too drunk to remember me, or at the bus stop after you'd stood me up?' she teased gently.

'Even when I was drunk I had enough sense to know that I'd met the girl I wanted to spend the rest of my life with.'

'But marriage is such a huge step.'

'Not for me,' he countered. 'I've had enough of sneaking around. I want to go to bed with you every night, wake up beside you every morning and spend every minute I can with you. What do you say, Gail? Let's tie the knot as soon as it can be arranged.'

'Your mother will never accept me.'

'I don't care. Whatever she says or does won't make any difference to the way I feel about you.'

Gail was amazed to think he would brave his mother's disapproval for her, but her mind turned to practical matters. 'I have hardly any savings.'

'That makes two of us.'

'Where would we live?'

'What would it matter as long as we were together? And before you come up with any more problems, we'll find somewhere.' He kissed her, and the embrace he had intended to be tender ended in a passionate clinch that sent their senses reeling.

'So, what do you say?' he murmured, when he released her.

'Yes.'

Rita Fairclough waved to the taxi-driver, who had been paid by the club she'd worked in, then slipped her key into her front door. She was exhausted, her throat was sore, her feet ached, it was after one in the morning and, as if that wasn't enough, the club had been the roughest and noisiest she'd sung in for years. The manager suffered from a common male complaint – which a fellow artiste had christened 'desert disease' – palms, *and* fingers, that wandered over every eligible female's bosom and thighs.

She opened the door and stepped inside, but before she could switch on the light, she tripped over a pile of rubble in the hall. Swearing, she limped into the living room and gazed at the mess around her. The house looked like a building site. A month ago she'd given Len a list of the improvements she wanted him to make, starting with knocking the parlour and living room into one to make a single decent-sized room. Then the kitchen would be redecorated and fitted with cupboards and a washing-machine, and a proper bathroom put in upstairs in the smallest bedroom so she wouldn't have to wash in the cold, draughty, makeshift one he had cobbled together in the old scullery.

He had begun enthusiastically enough, tearing down walls and stripping the plaster back to the brickwork on those that were to remain, but for the last two weeks he had made no progress whatsoever.

She hobbled into the kitchen, soaked a tea-towel under the cold tap in the old Belfast sink, wrapped it round her ankle and limped back to the dusty sofa.

'I thought I heard you come in.' Wearing Y-fronts and nothing else, Len stood in the hall looking through the gap that had been a wall.

Rita sniffed and recognised the unmistakable smell of beer. The thought that he had left this mess to go drinking in the Rovers all evening while she had been facing a restless, unappreciative audience was more than she could stand.

'Yes, it's me,' she said furiously. 'A burglar wouldn't come into this bomb site.'

'Something up, love?'

'You! That's what's up!' she yelled. 'I twisted my bloody ankle coming in this – this – pigsty's too good a word for it. You go out drinking night after night while I work all the hours God sends—'

'Ray and I went out on an evening call. We stopped off for one on the way home, that's all,' he protested, somewhat inaccurately.

'You're a lying toad, Len Fairclough, and I'm sick of you – just as I'm sick of you expecting me to run your bloody Kabin and go out singing to bring in money to pay off your debts when you can't even pull your finger out long enough to build us a decent place to live. Out of my way!' She pushed him aside and climbed on to the first stair.

'Let me help you, love—'

'Don't you dare touch me – ever again!' Wincing with every step, Rita made her way into their bedroom, pulled a suitcase from the top of the wardrobe, opened it and flung in the contents of her underwear drawer.

'You can't go anywhere at this time of night.' Len stood over her. He looked ridiculous with his stomach bulging over his underpants, but Rita wasn't in a mood to laugh.

'Oh, yes, I can.' She threw in an armful of dresses and took a coat from her wardrobe. Draping the coat over her shoulders, she closed the case and staggered down the stairs.

By the time Len had pulled on a pair of trousers she had called a taxi.

'Where are you going?'

'What do you care? Anywhere has to be better than this hole.' She buttoned her coat.

'You're being ridiculous.' He laid his hand on her arm. Whirling around, she slapped his face, hard.

'I won't let you go.' He clutched his cheek, which was stinging from the force of her blow.

'You can't stop me.' She raised her hand again and, instinctively, he stepped back. They stared at one another for a moment. Then a horn sounded in the street. She wrenched open the door, heaved her suitcase after her and climbed into the back of the cab.

Len watched the taxi move on up the street. The half-dozen pints he had downed in the Rovers on top of a full day's work had exhausted him. He wanted to go after her – but to where? Besides, he was in no fit state to drive and, given his present state of finances, he didn't dare risk losing his licence.

He went back into the house, closed the door and gazed at the mess. Rita was right, it was worse than a pigsty and it was time he did something about it – but not now. He flopped down on the sofa to think about Rita and how he could get her back. Two minutes later he was fast asleep.

'I hope you and Tracy will be comfortable here,' Emily said, as she helped Deirdre to carry Tracy's clothes and toys into her spare bedroom.

'I'm sure we will, but I don't know how I'm ever going to pay you back, or even keep Tracy and myself in food and clothes.' Deirdre forced back an overwhelming wave of emotion. Although she had refused Ray's offer of reconciliation, it had been hard and horribly final to see him pile his suitcases into the taxi and leave the street.

'I've been thinking about that.' Emily pulled open the curtains and set Tracy's bags on the bed. 'It's not going to be easy for you to work and look after Tracy. Perhaps it might help if I gave up working in the Kabin so we can set up a business we can run from the house.'

'What kind of business?'

'Secretarial. You ran Fairclough and Langton's office before you had Tracy, and I did all the bookkeeping when I managed Gamma Garments. You could take in typing and I could do bookkeeping. I already have a telephone, so we will be able to offer a message service as well. That way we could supply a complete office service for small businesses and jobbing tradesmen and look after Tracy between us at the same time.'

'Do you really think we'll make enough money to keep ourselves?' Deirdre asked hesitantly.

'If we don't, it won't be for want of trying. I've drafted an advertisement we can put in some of the local shops.' Emily pulled a piece of paper from her pocket and read,

' "Coronation Street Secretarial Bureau. We cater for all the needs of the small business. Typing, bookkeeping and telephone-answering service by arrangement. Reasonable fees. For further information contact . . ."

And then I put our names, this address and telephone number.'

'We've nothing to lose by trying.' Deirdre spirits lifted at Emily's professional approach.

'And while we try, we can set up a playpen and keep an eye on Tracy.'

'Let's put the advertisement in the shops tomorrow.' Deirdre smiled for the first time since Ray had left for Holland.

Gail walked back slowly from Mike Baldwin's shop in Rosamund Street. She hated to act the martyr but she felt that she had made a lot more sacrifices for Brian since their wedding two months ago than he had made for her. She had taken instruction and converted to the Catholic faith to please his mother. She had even agreed to move in with Ivy and Bert, Brian's father, until they had saved enough for a deposit on a house of their own, although she suspected that Ivy just wanted to hold on to her son as long as she could. But the biggest problem wasn't Ivy: it was Brian.

He had proved he loved her by marrying her, but the minute they'd returned from their honeymoon on the Isle of Man and moved in with his parents, he'd continued to behave as if they were single. He wanted to go out some-where every night, if only for a drink in the Rovers, instead of saving towards a deposit on their own place.

She didn't like sitting with Bert and Ivy in their living room night after night any more than he did, but if they didn't start saving seriously soon, they'd never move out.

'Brian's bought the new Elton John LP,' Ivy told Gail, before she'd had time to take off her coat.

'We're supposed to be saving for our own house.' When she saw the triumphant smile on Ivy's face, Gail wished she'd waited to say that until she and Brian were alone.

'You said you liked it.' Brian sat back as Ivy set a plate of fish and chips in front of him.

'What are you doing?'

Brian speared a forkful of chips and ferried them to his mouth. 'Eating me tea,' he mumbled, through a full mouth.

'I bought sausages. I was going to make us sausage and mash.'

'A man's hungry when he comes home from work, Gail,' Ivy lectured. 'It's not fair to ask him to wait. And you're late,' she added, unable to resist sticking in a pin.

'I went to the shop to buy Brian's tea,' Gail raised her voice, 'and I come back to find you giving him fish and chips and—' She fought back tears when she looked at the LP.

'It's only one record, Gail.' Realising how upset she was, Brian pushed aside his plate.

'Everyone's entitled to a treat now and again,' Ivy chipped in.

'This is between me and Brian, Ivy.' Gail finally took off her coat.

'I won't be spoken to like that in my own house.' Ivy bristled.

'Then it might be as well if I leave now, because it's obvious that we're not going from here to our own house. Not while Brian wastes our money on things like this.' Gail grabbed the record from the table and flung it at his head.

'Well, all I can say is I never treated my husband the way you treat our Brian.' Ivy folded her arms and glared disapprovingly at Gail.

'Don't tell me you didn't enjoy that, Ivy!' Gail exclaimed. 'You're doing exactly what you set out to do – drive us apart.'

'Mam,' Brian remonstrated, when Ivy opened her mouth as Gail ran out of the room and up the stairs.

'That's right,' Ivy burst out, 'take her side.'

'There's no side to take, Mam.' Brian left the table. 'Gail's my wife.'

'What about your tea?' Ivy demanded indignantly.

'Give it to Dad.' Brian raced up the stairs, taking them three at a time. He found Gail lying face down on the bed, crying into the pillow.

'Go away,' she mumbled brokenly.

'I'm sorry about the record, love. I'll take it back.'

'No shop exchanges records.'

'It won't happen again. I promise,' he said. 'From now on I'll save every penny I can towards our own place.'

'You mean it?' She sat up and looked at him, aware her face was red and blotched. She knew she always looked horrible when she cried.

'I mean it.'

She hugged him, burying her face in his shoulder so she wouldn't have to look into his eyes when she gave him the momentous news. 'I'm glad, love. You see, I'm pregnant.'

'Is this the Coronation Street Secretarial Bureau?'

Emily looked at the middle-aged man standing on her doorstep and, to her discomfort, saw that he was rather attractive. Feeling disloyal to Ernest's memory, she replied, 'Yes it is. Can I help you?'

'I'm Arnold Swain. I own the pet shop in Rosamund Street. I saw your advertisement in the corner shop and I was hoping that you could keep my accounts for me.'

'I would be delighted, Mr Swain. Won't you come in?' Emily led him into her living room. Since business had expanded, she and Deirdre had invested in two desks and a filing cabinet. Despite the playpen and the television the house looked more and more like an office.

'I have all my paperwork and bank books with me.' Arnold opened his briefcase.

'Then if you'll sit down, Mr Swain . . .'

'Arnold, please.' He gave Emily a dazzling smile.

'Arnold.' Shyly, Emily returned his smile. 'Let's see what we can do for you.'

'Here you are.' Bert Tilsley was even gruffer than usual when he handed Brian a cheque.

'What's this?' Brian asked suspiciously.

'Open it and see, lad.' Bert reached for his cigarettes.

Brian unfolded the cheque and stared at it in amazement. 'Three hundred pounds!'

'It was your mother's and my holiday money for Benidorm. I decided it would be put to better use if you and Gail borrowed it and put a deposit on that place in Buxton Close. I know Gail's got her heart set on it, even though you've a little one coming and it's only got one bedroom. But, then, we all have to start out somewhere.'

'I don't know what to say, Dad.' Brian stood awkwardly in front of his father, then shook his hand.

'It's only a loan,' Bert warned. 'We'll be wanting to go to Benidorm next year.'

'I'll pay you back,' Brian promised. 'Every penny.'

'See that you do, lad.' Bert lit a cigarette. 'It's not working out with your mam and Gail in the same house and kitchen. That's not to say that either of them are wrong,' he added diplomatically, 'just that it's not working out.'

'I can't wait to see Gail's face when I tell her about this.' Brian looked at the cheque again.

'Then go and find her, lad.'

Brian hesitated for a fraction of a second. Then, as emotion took precedence over reticence, he hugged his father and raced up the stairs in search of Gail.

Deirdre Langton was taking her time over washing the dishes in Emily's kitchen. She had deliberately left the door ajar, not because she expected Tracy to cry – once she put her daughter to bed at seven o'clock in the evening she slept a full twelve hours – but because Emily and Arnold were alone – again – in the living room. Feeling as though she was prying, she listened to the soft murmur of their voices.

Arnold had long since given up the pretence of visiting purely to discuss business. It was obvious that he was attracted to Emily and she to him. There was no denying that, superficially, they made an eminently suitable couple. They were both attractive, middle-aged, intelligent people, and Deirdre was the first to admit that if anyone deserved to find happiness it was Emily after the appalling tragedy of Ernest's early death.

But she couldn't dispel the feeling that, for all his charm, manners and outward suitability, there was something not quite right about Arnold Swain and when she heard the word 'money', she eavesdropped all the more.

'Of course, it's not for me to pry, Emily,' Arnold continued, 'but your late husband did leave you reasonably well provided-for, didn't he? I mean, you're not totally reliant on what the business brings in, are you?'

Suspicions roused, Deirdre crept closer to the door.

'Like most people, I have to work, Arnold,' Emily answered evasively, leading Deirdre to believe that Emily resented Arnold questioning her on such a personal matter. Somehow, it was all too easy, the plausible, good-looking businessman and the eligible and reasonably well-provided-for widow.

'But supposing you didn't have to work. Wouldn't you enjoy a well-deserved retirement in a nice house, somewhere in the country?'

'That is simply not an option, Arnold,' Emily replied evasively.

'But would you consider retiring the country if you could?' he persisted.

'If circumstances changed and it were possible, I might think about it.'

Either Arnold or Emily put a tape into the music centre and Deirdre could no longer hear them for the strains of Tchaikovsky's piano concerto. She stepped back to the sink and forced herself to examine her doubts. Did she dislike Arnold because if he married Emily and moved in she and Tracy would have to find somewhere else to live? Or was it something more? Despite her misgivings about her motives, Deirdre decided to ask questions about Arnold Swain in Weatherfield the very next morning.

*

'Hello, Dad, Uncle Albert let us in. Long time no see.'

Ken Barlow looked up from the *New Statesman* to see his sixteen-year-old daughter Susan bound into the living room with a tall, thin, spotty young man in tow.

'This is a surprise! Why didn't you say you were coming?' He set down his paper, left his chair and hugged his daughter.

'This is my boyfriend, Duncan Craig,' Susan announced blithely, returning Ken's hug and kissing his cheek.

'Hello, Mr Barlow.'

Ken shook hands with the boy and watched as Susan wrapped her arm round Duncan's waist.

'We decided to call in and spend a night with you before we go camping in the Lake District.' Susan picked a couple of apples out of the fruit bowl and handed one to Duncan, then bit into the other.

'Camping,' Ken echoed faintly. 'Does your grand-mother know?'

'Course. We've got a tent and everything.'

'One tent.' Ken tried not to sound as horrified as he felt.

'No sense in carrying two when we've enough other stuff to haul around. You got anything to eat, Dad? We 're starving.'

Ken tried desperately to gather his senses. He felt as though he had lost his little girl: there was little resemblance between his Susan and the confident young woman standing before him. And, even worse, she was obviously heading for what had been known colloquially in his day as a 'dirty weekend' with a boy he knew absolutely nothing about.

'Food, Dad,' Susan reminded him, reducing her apple to a core.

Ken realised he'd been staring at them. 'What do you fancy?'

'What have you got?' Susan asked.

Ken considered the deficiencies of the larder he and Albert Tatlock kept. The old man did most of the shopping and he bought the same food he had lived on for years. 'I could cook you an old-fashioned breakfast, eggs, bacon, black pudding, beans, tinned tomatoes and toast.'

'That sounds good, apart from the black pudding.' Susan looked at Duncan, who nodded.

'You can settle in while I make it. You'll find bedclothes in the airing cupboard. You can have the boxroom, Duncan, and you can have my room, Susan. I'll sleep on the sofa in the parlour.'

'I can sleep there, Mr Barlow,' Duncan offered.

'I wouldn't hear of it. There's a very comfortable sofa bed,' Ken lied. All the floorboards in the house creaked so he'd be better placed in the front room to hear anyone creeping about upstairs. But, then, what was the point when Susan would be off with Duncan to sleep in the same small tent tomorrow?

'OK, Dad, we'll be down in a couple of minutes.' Susan grabbed Duncan's arm and steered him upstairs.

Ken went into the scullery and took eggs, bacon, lard and butter from the fridge. He continued to think about Susan while he melted fat in the frying pan and laid strips of bacon under the grill. It had been easier when Susan and Peter were small and he had caught the train to Glasgow every other weekend to take them on outings to a park or the zoo. As a visiting, rather than hands-on, father he had found it comparatively easy to shower them with presents and talk to them, if not on a profoundly deep level then at least one that had convinced him that he was connecting with them.

Now his beautiful little daughter had disappeared and in her place was a young woman with more poise and self-assurance than Valerie had ever possessed.

And he had no idea how to talk to her, let alone be the father she deserved.

Chapter Thirty-Three

Deirdre was pleased for Emily when all she discovered from her meticulous, and occasionally less than discreet, enquiries into Arnold Swain's business and private life was that he was not only solvent but very comfortably off. She put her feelings of disquiet about Arnold down to the difference Emily's good fortune at finding another man she could love would make to her own and Tracy's future. And she was angry with herself for being so dog in the manger after everything Emily had done for her and Tracy. Not that she had ever taken Emily's love, support and generosity for granted, far from it, she was simply nervous about moving to a new home with only her three-year-old daughter for companionship.

Slowly, gradually, over Arnold's six months' courtship of Emily, she realised, along with all of Emily's other friends, that she hadn't seen her friend so happy since Ernest Bishop's death. And when Emily and Arnold set their wedding date for September 10, 1980, she offered to help them organise the day into one the whole street would remember.

She shopped with Emily for her outfit – a stunning blue silk designer dress, with a lighter blue pillbox hat, decorated with a veil. And she bought herself and Tracy blue silk bridesmaids' dresses to complement the bride's. And in between helping Emily to organise her wedding, reception and buy clothes for her honeymoon on the Isle of Wight, she made plans for a new and – now she wouldn't always be able to count on Emily being there for them – independent life for herself and Tracy.

'It's good to see Emily smiling again,' Ken Barlow said to Deirdre, as they waved off the taxi taking the newly-wed Mr and Mrs Arnold Swain from the Rovers Return to the station on the first leg of their honeymoon.

'I only hope she'll always be this happy.' Deirdre picked up Tracy, who was still waving at the empty street, and held her close.

Ken noticed Deirdre frown. 'You're not convinced.'

'I'm worried about her.' Deirdre glanced at him. 'Not because Tracy and I have had to move out of her house,' she explained defensively. 'Alf Roberts has been very generous. He'll pay me a good wage to manage the shop, and is renting me the flat above it for less than I was paying Emily. To be honest, I'm looking forward to working there. I enjoyed running the secretarial bureau with Emily but it's time to move on now Tracy is older and not so demanding, and I'm looking forward to seeing a lot more people. It's just that . . .' She tailed off. If she said any more she would be disloyal to Emily who had been a true friend to her and Tracy when they had most needed one.

'It's just that?' Ken prompted.

'I've said enough.'

'If you were about to say that Arnold's a bit glib and too good to be true, I'd agree with you.'

'You sense it too.' Deirdre's relief was evident in her voice.

'With my track record I'm the last person to give out any advice on relationships, so let's hope our instinct about Arnold Swain is wrong.'

'I'll settle for that.' Deirdre crossed her fingers and made a secret wish that Emily would always be as happy as she had looked when Arnold had slipped the wedding ring on to her finger in the register office. 'You know, you're very easy to talk to, Ken.'

'Nice of you to say so.' Ken walked Deirdre and Tracy slowly up the street to Emily's door. 'If you need any help with moving into the flat, I've a strong back.'

'Thank you, but Alf's already taken most of our stuff in his car. There's only these bridesmaids' dresses to pack,' Deirdre fluffed out a frill on Tracy's, 'and our ordinary clothes to put on, and we'll be on our way to our new home.'

Ken watched her slip the key into Emily's door. 'Do you fancy seeing a film with me one evening?'

'I can't leave Tracy.'

'I understand.' Assuming she'd given him the brush-off, he walked away.

Then Deirdre shouted after him, 'Could I change my mind if I get a babysitter?'

Ken's smile broadened as he turned back to her. 'Let me know the evening and I'll clear it.'

'Our very first home.' Brian Tilsley swept Gail into his arms and carried her, playfully protesting, from the living room of their new house into the bedroom. He dropped her, laughing, on to their unmade bed.

'If we're going to eat and sleep between sheets tonight, I have to straighten this place out.' Gail returned his kiss as he lay beside her.

There was a knock at the door. 'Damn,' Brian complained. 'Who can that be?'

'Go and find out.' Gail pushed him off the bed.

'You're a hard-hearted wife.' Tucking in his shirt, Brian went to the door and opened it to see his mother-in-law standing in the street with a suitcase and bags piled around her feet.

'My boyfriend threw me out. Bring me bags in.' Audrey

Potter pushed past Brian and walked into the living room. 'This could be made to look quite nice. You've landed on your feet here, love,' she said to Gail, when her daughter emerged from the bedroom.

Gail saw the amount of luggage Brian was carrying in. 'What are you doing here, Mam?'

'That's a fine greeting from a daughter to a mother, I must say!' Audrey complained. 'As I was just telling Brian, me boyfriend threw me out.'

'You can't stay here.' Gail looked at Brian for support, but he was still bringing in her mother's bags. 'We've only the one bedroom.'

'You've a sofa, haven't you?' Audrey bounced up and down on it, testing the springs. 'You wouldn't see your mother out on the street, now, would you?' She parried Gail's scowl.

'No, I wouldn't, but you can't stay for more than a couple of nights,' Gail informed her bluntly. 'This place is too small for me and Brian, let alone visitors.'

'Then you should have got yourselves a bigger house, especially with a baby coming.'

'We can barely afford this place as it is.' Brian took Audrey's comment as a criticism.

A couple of nights is all I need,' Audrey said confidently. 'I'll soon find myself somewhere else.' Seemingly oblivious to Gail and Brian's reluctance to take her in, Audrey picked up one of her bags. 'You won't mind if I hang a couple of things in your wardrobe, will you, love? It would be a pity if they got creased.' Without waiting for Gail to reply, she sailed into the bedroom, leaving her daughter and son-in-law to exchange troubled glances.

Albert Tatlock filled the kettle, slammed it down on the stove and lit the gas. As the temperature of the water rose, so did his temper. Ken had gone out for the evening with Deirdre Langton, and he found it impossible to understand why an educated, intelligent man like Ken, who'd had the sense to marry a wonderful girl like Valerie, a niece he had loved as if she'd been his own daughter, would waste his time on a divorced woman who wore short skirts and far too much make-up. The more he pictured Deirdre and Ken together, the angrier he became. There was only one word to describe a woman like her – tart!

He heard the front door open, warmed the teapot, tipped out the water, spooned in tealeaves and poured on boiling water. He took the pot into the living room and thumped it down on the table as Ken walked in.

'Evening, Uncle Albert.' Ken took off his coat and hung it in the passage.

'And what time do you call this to come home?' Albert grumbled, as if Ken were a teenager.

'The film didn't finish until half past ten. It was one of

those new long ones.' Ken sensed Albert's anger but chose to ignore it.

'It's a quarter to twelve. It only takes twenty minutes to drive from town to here in that new Jerry car of yours.'

'Deirdre invited me in for a quick cup of tea.' Ken overlooked the gibe at his new car.

'And tea is all you went into her flat for?'

'Yes,' Ken snapped. 'Come on, out with it. What's bothering you?' he asked.

'Deirdre Langton, that's what's the matter. Our Val would turn in her grave if she could see you now, taking a woman like that out.'

'A woman like what?' Ken bristled.

'Divorced from her husband,' Albert said scathingly, 'trying to bring up a little girl on her own—'

'Everyone is entitled to make a mistake,' Ken interrupted. He had decided that the old man had said more than enough about Deirdre.

'She's nowhere near good enough for you. And don't you go forgetting that any woman you take up with is going to be Susan and Peter's stepmother.'

'For pity's sake, I took the woman to the pictures. We're hardly trotting up the aisle.'

'All the same, she's not the sort of woman a decent man should want to keep company with. I don't know what's come over you lately. Buying enemy cars—'

'The Germans aren't our enemy any more. They buy

our goods, we buy theirs, and the trade is good for both our countries.'

'It is a Jerry car, isn't it?'

'It's a Volkswagen.' Ken agreed, weary of arguing.

'Whatever fancy name you use, there's no way I'm having it parked outside my house. I telephoned the police today and told them just that. I'm not putting up with it. It's an insult to all the lads who died fighting for this country in two world wars. They didn't make the ultimate sacrifice for folk like you to go round buying a Jerry car.'

'Both wars have been over a long time, Uncle Albert.'

'Not in my book. I only have to close my eyes to see lads who died alongside me in the trenches. I can still hear their screams at night when I go to bed . . .'

Ken tried to close his mind to what Albert was saying because experience had taught him that it was impossible to reason with the old man when he was in one of his moods. When Albert finished ranting, he murmured, 'If you feel that strongly about me parking the car outside the house, I'll rent a garage in Viaduct Street.'

'You do just that.' Abandoning the tea he'd made, Albert left the living room and climbed up the stairs. As a final indication of how he felt, he slammed his bedroom door.

Emily draped half a dozen of Arnold's newly ironed shirts over hangers and put them into the wardrobe. It was a simple domestic task but she was enjoying looking after a man again. After Ernest had been murdered she'd never thought she'd find happiness with anyone else, but her honeymoon on the Isle of Wight had been romantic – and perfect. Arnold had selected a four-star hotel with its own section of beach and he'd spared no expense. They'd eaten in the best restaurants on the island and he'd insisted on buying her a beautiful gold bracelet as a memento. But much as she loved him, she couldn't help feeling uneasy at his suggestion that they sell his business and her house and buy a place in Derbyshire.

He had driven her out to the village he had picked out for them to live in. She had been forced to admit that it was prettier than anything Weatherfield or Coronation Street had to offer, but she was loath to give up her home and move away from her friends, especially Deirdre and little Tracy. She couldn't have loved her goddaughter more if she had been a blood relation.

Disturbed by a knock at the door, she hung away the last shirt and ran down the stairs. A man in a smart suit, white shirt and red tie, holding a briefcase, was standing on her doorstep.

He gave her a practised smile. 'Mrs Swain?'

'Yes, can I help you?'

'If you are Mrs Margaret Swain, you certainly can.'

Emily looked at him in confusion. 'I think there must be some mistake. I am Mrs Emily Swain.'

'I'm sorry to disturb you, Mrs Swain.' He stepped back. 'I was looking for the wife of Mr Arnold Swain.'

'My husband is Mr Arnold Swain. We've been married three weeks.'

'Then possibly your husband is related to Mrs Margaret Swain. This is my card.' He pulled out his wallet from his inside pocket, removed a card and handed it to her. 'The office telephone number is on there. We're holding a policy Mrs Margaret Swain took out fifteen years ago. It has matured and she has yet to claim it. If you could ask her to get in touch with us I would be grateful. The we can send her a cheque.'

'I'll ask my husband if he knows a Mrs Margaret Swain.' Emily watched the man walk down the street and climb into his car. As he drove round the corner, Arnold tapped her shoulder.

'Who was that you were talking to?'

'Oh, Arnold, I didn't see you there. It was an insurance man asking after a Mrs Margaret Swain.'

'Margaret!' Arnold paled.

Emily looked at him uneasily.

'I think we had better go inside,' he murmured.

Emily sat very still and silent on her sofa, struggling to take in the enormity of what Arnold was telling her.

'I was very young and our marriage didn't last as long as the honeymoon. We were in Blackpool. She went off and left me after we'd been there four days.'

'You're divorced and you didn't think to tell me you had been married before!' Emily went to the mantelpiece to reposition her carriage clock and china figurines so that she wouldn't have to look Arnold in the eye.

'We're not divorced, Emily.' Arnold grabbed a cushion and clutched it to his chest, as if he were trying to shield himself.

Emily stared at Arnold in bewilderment. 'Are you saying that you are still married to her?'

'I suppose I am,' he whispered, as if he couldn't believe it himself.

'You never divorced her?'

'I will now,' he assured her.

Too shocked to speak, Emily tried to think through the implications of Arnold's confession. Her husband was legally married to another woman, in which case he couldn't possibly be married to her. Their wedding, their honeymoon, all his assertions that he loved her, even the ring he had given her – all were meaningless. He had another wife.

'Get out!' she commanded hoarsely when she had regained her composure.

'Emily—'

Unable to bear Arnold's pleading after what he had done to her – the fool he had made of her – she repeated, 'Get out! And take every single thing that belongs to you, because if you don't, I'll burn them as soon as you've gone.'

Arnold went upstairs. A few minutes later, the front door closed behind him.

'Emily, what are you doing?' Deirdre stood in Emily's living room, watching Emily, who was on her hands and knees, dip a scrubbing brush into a bucket that smelt strongly of disinfectant and begin to scour the hearthrug.

'Cleaning the house.' Emily didn't look up.

'You're going to ruin your rug.'

'I have to clean everything. I don't want any trace left.'

Deirdre couldn't make sense of what Emily was saying. 'Ken said he saw Arnold walking down the street with a suitcase.'

Emily looked up. 'I threw Arnold out. He's married to another woman and . . .' tears rolled down her cheeks '. . . they're not divorced.'

'Oh, Emily, I'm so sorry.' Deirdre sank down on the sofa.

'Don't!' Emily shouted. 'I haven't disinfected that yet. And I haven't washed the cushions!' She leapt to her feet and began to tear the covers off them.

Deirdre went to her friend and hugged her. 'Hilda's

taken Tracy for a walk. I'll help you finish cleaning, then I'll go to the police station with you to report Arnold.'

'Not long to go now.' Audrey winked at Gail as she helped her to lay the tea-table.

'I'm beginning to feel the baby's never going to come.' Gail patted her enormous bump then went into the kitchen to check on the pork chops she was frying.

'It was a good night out last night.' Audrey followed her and took the salt and pepper out of a cupboard. 'If Brian borrows a car from work again tonight, we could go back to that pub.'

'I told you last night, Brian risked his job borrowing that car. Don't ever ask him to do anything like that again.'

'I didn't twist his arm, did I?' Audrey countered huffily.

'He wouldn't have borrowed it if you hadn't nagged him day and night about it for the last week.'

'He enjoyed his evening as much as I did and no wonder, the way you two live, staying in night after night, watching the telly so you can scrimp and save. It's not natural for kids your age. You behave more like OAPs than newly-weds.'

'Our baby is going to be born any day.'

'So you keep reminding me. The trouble with you, Gail, is that you always have been a bit of a stick-in-the-mud. Hello, Brian.' Audrey beamed at her son-in-law as he walked through the door. 'Did you manage to borrow the car again for tonight?'

'No.' Brian shrugged off his coat and flung it on to a chair. Sensitive to her husband's moods, Gail realised that something was wrong.

'Come on, Gail,' Audrey chivvied, 'the worker's entitled to his tea as soon as he comes home.'

'I'm not a worker any more.' Brian sat at the table. 'The boss saw me driving the car around town last night so he gave me my cards and a week's wages.'

Gail dropped the glass she had been about to put on the table. It shattered. 'What are we going to do?' she asked. 'It was bad enough when I had to give up work and we were down to one wage. We'll never manage on what the dole pays out.'

'Something will come up,' Audrey said blithely. 'Brian's a good mechanic.'

'Without any references,' Brian interposed gloomily.

'This is all your fault, Mam.' Gail turned on Audrey. 'Never giving a thought for the future or saving, always wanting to go out and have a good time. Well, Brian and I have our baby to think of and from now on we're going to put him or her first. And that means I want you out of this house, right now.'

'Now? But tea's cooking, those chops will burn—'

'Let them.' Gail raised her voice to emphasise that she meant what she'd said. 'Pack your things and get out.'

'To where?'

'I don't care.'

'Gail, don't be hasty. You're about to have a baby, you don't know what you're saying, your hormones are playing up—'

'This has nothing to do with hormones or being hasty, Mam.' Gail sat at the table next to Brian and laid her hand over his. 'I'm doing what I should have done over six months ago when you turned up on the doorstep. Throwing you out.'

Ken walked into the corner shop on his way to work and handed a shopping list to Deirdre. 'Can you put this up for me, please, love? I'll pick it up on my way home tonight.'

'No problem.' Deirdre scanned the list then clipped it to a peg above the till.

'Any chance of you getting a babysitter this week so we can go for a drink – or the cinema, if you prefer?' he asked.

'Not this week.' She averted her eyes. 'One of Ray's colleagues is over from Holland and he's invited me out for dinner tonight. I don't like leaving Tracy with babysitters more than one night a week.'

'Some other time perhaps.' Ken left the shop. Since Val's and Janet's deaths he had become a past master at concealing his feelings. He made a mental note to ask Albert to pick up the shopping as he strode towards his car.

★

Brian Tilsley fought his way from the crowded bar in the Rovers to the table where Gail was sitting with his parents. He handed her an orange juice, his mother a Tia Maria and his father a pint.

'As soon as the baby's born we'll celebrate with champagne.' He lifted his pint glass and touched it to Gail's. 'Happy New Year.'

'I feel that it *is* going to be a happy one now that Ron Sykes thought better of sacking you and my mother's moved back in with her boyfriend.' Gail grimaced, Brian jumped to his feet.

'You all right?'

'It's obvious she's not.' Determined to take charge, Ivy shouted above the noise in the pub. 'Bert, call an ambulance. Brian, go home and get Gail's case for the hospital. Elsie,' she waved across the room to Elsie Tanner, 'we need woman's help here.'

'No, we don't.' Gail exercised her new-found authority. 'I need to go to the hospital, and the only person I want to come with me is Brian.' She reached out and gripped his hand – hard. So hard that Brian wondered whether she was trying to break his fingers.

'So what you think of my flat?' Mike Baldwin asked Deirdre, as she mixed drinks for his guests in the kitchen he'd had crafted from antique oak.

'Nice.'

'*Nice?* It's a luxury penthouse.'

'So you've said.' Deirdre was bored with Mike's boasting. She'd only accepted his offer to act as hostess for his New Year's party because Ken hadn't asked her out for six weeks – not since she'd told him she was having dinner with one of Ray's colleagues. She had wondered whether or not to explain that Ray had asked her to meet him so she could tell him about Tracy and the progress she'd made since he'd left.

She liked Ken and had hoped they could have a future together, but she couldn't help wondering if he saw her merely as a diversion, someone to go out with now and again. She had no illusions about Mike Baldwin. She knew that was *exactly* how he thought of her, a bit of fun, a girl on the side, one of several women he saw casually. But Ken had seemed different, and it had taken his absence from her life to make her understand just how comfortable and content she felt when she was with him.

The doorbell rang again and Mike went to answer it. She put the drinks on to a tray and carried them into the living room. She almost dropped it when she saw Mike usher in Ken and a glamorous girl. She recognised her as a beautician who worked on the cosmetics counter of the largest department store in town.

'Your sherry, Emily.' She handed a glass to Emily, then turned back to look at Ken, but Mike had taken him and his date into the master bedroom to show them the spectacular view.

Emily was watching Mike, and when he left the group he was talking to and went over to attend to his music centre, she joined him.

'Can I have a word with you, please, Mr Baldwin?'

'Which word would you like?' he joked, as he flicked through his record collection. He hadn't exchanged more than a dozen words with Emily since Ernest had been murdered in his factory because, although he would never have admitted it, he felt uneasy in her presence. If he'd been the sort of person to analyse his feelings he might have grasped that he felt guilty for not having done more to save Ernest.

'Please, Mr Baldwin, you can have any woman you want . . .' Emily plucked up courage to continue. 'But I beg you, stay away from Deirdre.'

'And why should I do that?' he queried, amused.

'Because little Tracy has too many uncles in her life as it is. And because you're the sort of man who hurts people without realising it . . . or meaning to,' she added.

Mike glanced into the kitchen and saw Deirdre hand in hand and deep in conversation with Ken Barlow.

'Emily, something tells me that even if I wanted to continue seeing Deirdre she wouldn't want to see me.'

Then he spotted the girl who'd come with Ken standing alone, looking out of the window. 'Do you happen to know her name?' he asked.

Chapter Thirty-Four

'I almost didn't go to Mike's party tonight,' Ken said, as he walked Deirdre back to the corner shop. He reached for her hand. 'I'm glad I did.'

'So am I,' she murmured.

At that moment, the door of the Rovers burst open. Ivy Tilsley and Audrey Potter ran out arm in arm. 'It's a boy,' they sang in unison. 'It's a boy! Ken, Deirdre, we have a grandson! Nicholas Paul Tilsley! It's a boy!' they shouted to a crowd of New Year revellers on the other side of the road.

'Congratulations and happy 1980,' the revellers slurred.

'Wonderful news,' Ken shouted to Ivy and Audrey, as they danced up the street with Bert in tow. He walked Deirdre to her door. 'Who's babysitting Tracy?'

'Mike paid Hilda. He needed a drink-pourer and glass-washer that much.'

Ken bent his head to hers and kissed her. 'See you tomorrow?'

'Yes, please.'

'And all our tomorrows after that?'

'What?' Her heart was racing. Logic told her that she and Ken had nothing in common, but as she gazed into Ken's eyes under the light of the street-lamps, sense was overwhelmed by a greater emotion.

'Marry me.'

'There's Tracy, your children . . .'

'We could be a family, Deirdre.'

'I believe we could.' She wanted to believe him. A family – her, Tracy and Ken, his children and, soon, more children of their own.

'I'm waiting for my answer.'

'Yes.' She kissed him. 'Would you like to come in so we can start the New Year the way we mean to go on?'

'I was hoping you'd say that.' He followed her inside and up the stairs to her flat.

'Of course we want you to live with us, Uncle Albert.' Ken was exasperated by the old man's obstinacy.

'There's no "of course" about it,' Albert shouted. 'My own daughter doesn't want me.'

'Deirdre and I aren't Beatrice.'

'And this is your house, Uncle Albert,' Deirdre pointed out.

'You've enough money to buy any house in Coronation Street, or anywhere in or out of Weatherfield, come to that,' Albert snapped at Ken.

'So you don't want us living with you, is that what you're saying?'

'Course not.'

'Good. Because for once in your life you're going to listen to what someone else has to say.' Ken sat back on the sofa and slipped his arm round Deirdre's shoulders. 'The doctor told me there's no way you should be living on your own, and Deirdre's agreed that we'll forgo our plans to buy a modern house with a garden for Tracy so that we can live here with you.'

Ken saw that the old man was fighting back tears. 'I'll not be treated as a charity case.'

'No one is treating you as a charity case,' Ken told him firmly.

'All we're asking is that you allow us to turn your front parlour into a bedroom for you. That way you won't have to climb the stairs at night and Tracy can sleep upstairs, next door to us,' Deirdre interposed.

'It's the most rational solution to find the space we'll need when Deirdre and Tracy move in.'

'You really want to live here, in my house, with me, Deirdre?' Albert asked.

'If you're prepared to allow Tracy and me to move in, yes.'

'Then you're welcome,' he muttered gruffly.

'What did you say?' Ken teased him.

Deirdre dug her elbow into Ken's ribs to silence him.

'And you don't mind us moving your bedroom down-stairs?'

'If that's what you and Ken want.'

'You'll have to let me know what your favourite colours are. Perhaps I could get a wallpaper pattern book.'

'Decorating is women's work,' Albert dismissed the idea, 'but you can change whatever you want. Knowing what women are like, you will any road. I'm off to Rovers.' He stomped into the hall, picked up his coat and cap and left the house.

Ken looked at Deirdre as the front door closed. 'You're a miracle-worker. I was dreading that, but it didn't go too badly.'

'He's a sweetie when you get to know him, isn't he?'

'Is he?' They burst out laughing. When they recovered, Ken asked, 'So, do we have everything sorted for the wedding, soon-to-be Mrs Barlow?'

'The church is booked, thanks to you finding a vicar prepared to marry a divorcee, Alf Roberts has agreed to give me away, Emily's matron of honour, Len's promised to shake the mothballs out of his best suit to be our best man and our daughters are bridesmaids. I wouldn't dare interfere in Annie Walker's ideas on catering for the reception, and Ray's given us his blessing.'

'So everything's in hand.'

'I'm looking forward to two weeks of sun, sand, sea and

having you all to myself in Corfu more than the wedding,' Deirdre moved closer to him.

'You're not worried about leaving Tracy with Emily?'

Deirdre shook her head. 'She'll be fine. Emily's as good with her as I am.'

'Fancy practising for the honeymoon?' He lifted his eyebrows.

She wrapped her arms round his neck and kissed him. 'Race you upstairs.'

Len Fairclough halted outside the brightly lit windows of the Blackpool laundrette and shaded his eyes against the glow. Dressed in a brown, flowered overall, Rita was loading washing from a plastic basket into a machine. He opened the door, walked up behind her and tapped her shoulder. She spun round and stared at him, open-mouthed. He had been rehearsing this moment every day and night throughout all the months he had been searching for her, but now it had finally come, all he could say was, 'Hello, love.'

She continued to gaze at him, speechless.

'Please, come home.' There was a begging note in his voice. 'I miss you.'

Much as Rita wanted to throw herself into Len's arms, she held back. She had forged an independent life for herself. Even she had to grant it wasn't much: a bedsit in a cockroach-infested Victorian house in dire need of renovation, a job as manageress of a laundrette in just about the seediest area of the seaside town, hardly any friends, and long, lonely hours spent watching television or walking on the beach or promenade when she wasn't working. But she wasn't about to admit the deficiencies of her new life to Len.

'If you come home with me now, I'll do anything you want. I looked at a semi-detached house in Handforth last week. If you like it, I'll sell the Kabin and the house in Coronation Street and we'll move in there. These last few months without you have made me realise that you're the only thing in my life that means anything. Please, Rita, say something,' he pleaded, 'even if it's only, "Go to hell."'

'All I wanted was for you to modernise our house in Coronation Street.'

'And if I do?'

'I'll come back.'

'And if I promise to start tomorrow?'

'Come round to my place. You can carry my suitcase after I've packed it.'

He hugged her, lifted her off her feet and held her close. 'I'll never let you go. Not a second time.'

'Then keep your promise about the house,' she warned, starting as she meant to go on.

'Mr Baldwin, this is a surprise. Can I help you?' Emily was flustered at the sight of him on her doorstep. She couldn't begin to imagine what he wanted with her. His reputation as a ladies' man, coupled with the scandal he attracted, unnerved her. Looking at him, suave and confident in his bespoke three-piece brown suit, cream linen shirt and silk tie, she was amazed that she'd ever had the temerity to tackle him about Deirdre.

'I know you work from home and you must be busy, Emily, so I'll get straight to the point. I'd like you to take over the factory accounts and put up the girls' wages at the end of every week for me.'

'That's far too big a job for me to run from home,' she protested.

'That's why I want you to come and work full time for me in the factory. I'm offering a good salary and asking nicely.' He gave her a charming smile. 'I did the wages myself last week and gave all the girls an extra four pounds. They thought it was manna from heaven. Can you imagine the job I'm having getting that money back?'

Emily sensed that they were both thinking of Ernest. Could she work in the office where he had been shot? Was Mike Baldwin offering her the job out of guilt because he had heard that the secretarial business had fallen off since Deirdre had left to marry Ken last month?

'Perhaps it was a bad idea . . .'

'No – no, it's not,' she interrupted.

'You can think about it if you like.'

'I don't need to.' She considered the half-dozen bookkeeping accounts that remained. She could easily do them in the evenings. 'Thank you for thinking of me. I'll take the job, Mr Baldwin.'

'Can you start immediately?'

'Nine tomorrow morning?' she suggested.

'That will do nicely.' He winked at her. 'We'll discuss wages when you come in – I promise you'll not find me ungrateful.

'Ron Sykes has sold the garage,' Brian announced, as Gail set his tea of pie, mash and mushy peas on the table.

'Who's bought it?' she demanded, alarmed.

'Does it matter?'

'It matters if they don't keep you on.'

'Ron sold it because he's taken a job in Qatar.' Brian picked up his knife and fork. 'He's landed a six-month contract to service the government's fleet of vehicles. It's fantastic money. He asked if I wanted to go with him.'

'Pity you can't.' Gail set the sauce bottle, salt and pepper on the table and sat opposite him.

'Why can't I?'

'Because you have me and Nicky to think of,' she retorted.

'This is my big chance to earn some real money and our chance to save some, Gail. I'd be a fool to turn it down.'

'You can't leave me alone with the baby for six months!'

'Come on, love, six months will soon go. Now that your mother's left her boyfriend for good and lodging with Elsie Tanner, you have her and my mother just down the road if you need help with Nicky. Both of them grab every chance you give them to babysit. And when I come back with the money, we'll be able to buy a bigger house and Nicky can have his own bedroom. He can't keep sleeping in ours. We'll even be able to put some money aside for his future.'

As Brian built castles in the air, painting pictures of the fabulous future that the money he would make in Qatar would secure, all Gail could think about was spending six long, lonely months on her own with a small baby and her mother-in-law watching every move she made.

Rita Fairclough looked at the house Len had almost finished building in the gap between numbers five and nine Coronation Street after he had demolished what little was left of number seven.

'So, what do you think?' He glanced at her over his shoulder as he scooped up another pile of freshly mixed plaster.

'I'm impressed. Everything looks clean, fresh and modern. I'm going to enjoy living here.'

'We're not moving in, love,' he said quickly. 'I've already had a pile of enquiries and the money I make on this will pay for all the improvements you want doing on number nine.'

'There's no comparison between this place and number nine. Everything here is perfect and sparkling new, the floors, the ceilings, the woodwork. No amount of improving our place would get this finish. The plaster's old and cracked so we'll have to carry on wallpapering instead of painting. The skirting-boards and doors are old and chipped.' She left the large living and dining room and walked into the empty kitchen. 'Put a nice fitted kitchen in here with those new real wood doors and those tiles I saw advertised in last Sunday's colour supplement, and it would be every woman's idea of a dream kitchen. And I've seen just the bathroom suite I want for upstairs, the one they have in the plumbing shop in the high street with a shower and a bidet. We'd be in heaven. Our dream home come true.' She returned to the living room and smiled at him.

'Sorry, love.' He carried on plastering without looking at her. 'We need the money, and as soon as this house is finished I'm selling.'

She didn't argue with him. She climbed the staircase he had fixed into place the day before. The three bedrooms and the bathroom were finished, apart from the plastering. She went to the window and looked down on the street. It wasn't time to try to change Len's mind about selling the house – not yet.

'You look very smart,' Hilda commented, as Eddie Yeats entered the living room in his best grey pinstripe suit.

He picked up a bottle of aftershave and splashed a double helping on to his cheeks. 'I've a date.'

'Anyone I know?' She set the paper aside.

'You know I've been on the CB radio a lot lately.'

'Calling yourself – using the handle "Slim Jim".' Hilda was attempting to show him that she had been listening to him when he'd been rabbiting on about his new hobby.

'Slim what?' Stan Ogden looked up from the football match he was watching on television.

'Slim Jim is my CB name,' Eddie explained. Stan turned back to stare at the screen and Eddie added, 'I've hooked up with a girl called Stardust Lil and we've arranged an eyeball—'

'A what?' Hilda asked, a custard cream poised in front of her mouth.

'An eyeball – in CB terms, that's a meeting,' Eddie clarified. 'And it's tonight.'

Stan started to laugh. 'If you've only talked to her on that radio thing of yours, she could be ninety-five and as ugly as sin.'

'And she might turn out to be the lady of my dreams.' Eddie lifted his jacket from the chair and put it on. 'See you later.'

'Good luck,' Hilda called after him, as he went to the door.

'You'll need it,' Stan called after him.

Eddie walked down the street. Stan's scepticism had

rekindled his own. Stardust Lil had sounded brilliant over the radio and they had enjoyed conversations that had lasted until the early hours of the morning. When she was talking he felt he could listen to her for ever but what was she going to be like in the flesh? Old? Fat? Ugly as sin, as Stan had suggested?

He jumped on the bus and went into town. He had arranged to meet Stardust Lil outside a high-class pub, the kind of place he would never normally go into because the drinks were double the price they were in the Rovers. He left the bus, almost crossed the road to the pub, then stopped. Two women were standing outside, one an attractive lady with thick, glossy chestnut hair, the other an enormously fat middle-aged frump.

'Just my luck,' he murmured disconsolately. A few seconds later another woman joined the fat one and they walked off up the street together. He took a deep breath, braced himself and crossed the road. 'Stardust Lil?' he murmured hopefully.

She gave him a shy smile. 'My name's Marion – Marion Willis.' She held out her hand. 'I'm pleased to meet you.'

'And I'm very pleased to meet you. Slim Jim – or, rather,' he returned her smile, 'Eddie Yeats. Would you like a drink?'

'I hoped you two could give me some advice.' Emily Bishop accepted Ken's invitation to join him and Deirdre in their living room. She smiled self-consciously when she walked in, embarrassed at interrupting them so soon after they had returned from honeymoon.

'You don't need an excuse to call, Emily, you're welcome any time.' Deirdre went into the scullery and put the kettle on.

'How's the job going in the warehouse?' Ken asked.

'You know about that?'

'Uncle Albert heard about it in the Rovers. There's not much that gets past anyone in Coronation Street, Emily, I thought you would have known that after all the years you've lived here,' Ken said.

'The job is fine.'

'I'm glad to hear it.'

'It's not that, Ken.' She took the cup of tea Deirdre handed her. 'Thank you. It's just that I had a letter yesterday from Arnold's solicitor. Apparently Arnold had a heart attack shortly after . . . well, shortly after . . .'

'He left the street,' Deirdre supplied helpfully, setting her own and Ken's tea down on the table.

'Yes, and then he had a nervous breakdown. Anyway, Arnold died last month in a psychiatric hospital.'

'I'm sorry,' Ken murmured.

'That's not why I called,' Emily broke in. She'd never forgiven Arnold for lying and making a laughing stock of her. The last thing she wanted to talk about was Arnold or their disastrous marriage – it hadn't even *been* a marriage.

'It's just that he's left me some money, rather a large amount. I don't want it, so I telephoned the solicitor and told him just that.' She knotted her fingers nervously together as she looked at Ken. 'But he said I have to take it and if I don't want it I can give it away.'

'If you don't feel comfortable taking it, Emily, why don't you do just that?' Ken suggested.

'Set up some kind of memorial in Arnold's name, you mean?' She asked dubiously, not wanting to glorify Arnold.

'It doesn't have to be in his name.' Ken took the tea Deirdre had made him, spooned sugar into it and stirred it. 'I saw something in the paper the other day. The local hospital is looking for people to endow beds. You could endow one for Ernie, he died there and I can't think of a more fitting memorial for a man like him. And if there's any money left over, the community centre's always looking for equipment.'

'That's a very a good idea, Ken, thank you. I'll contact the hospital and the community centre first thing tomorrow.'

'I don't know why you had to take a job in Jim Dawson's café,' Ivy railed at Gail. 'It's not as if you need the money. I know Brian's sending more than enough for you and Nicky to live on in comfort.' Ivy was fishing: she had assumed her son was sending Gail money every week, but if he was, Gail had yet to tell her the amount.

'I took the job waitressing at Jim's Café three days a week because I was going mad staying at home seeing no one and doing nothing except looking after Nicky!' Gail shouted.

'That's not what I've heard.' Ivy crossed her arms in triumph. 'You were seen going into a cinema in town with a lorry driver.'

'I went out with one of the customers from the café,' Gail snapped. 'So what?'

'You're a married woman, that's what, and don't expect me to keep quiet when Brian comes home,' Ivy retorted. 'I'm not going to sit back and not say a word to my own son about the way his wife's carrying on behind his back. My grandson deserves a better mother than you're turning out to be, Gail.' With that, she stalked out of the house.

Gail lifted Nicky from his baby-walker and cuddled him. She had no doubt that her mother-in-law would carry out her threat. Why, oh why couldn't Ivy see just how lonely she was without Brian?

Rita Fairclough straightened the cutlery she'd set out on her best white damask tablecloth. 'Your tea's ready Len. It's your favourite, steak, chips, green peas and bread and butter.' She poured him a glass of beer and sat beside him.

'What are we celebrating?' he asked suspiciously.

'I found a buyer for the house.' She picked up the vinegar and sprinkled it liberally over her chips.

'The new house?'

'Oh, no.' She glanced around the living room; she had nagged Len into papering it with beige mock silk paper in a palm-tree design. The buyer had loved it.

Len set down his knife and fork. 'What have you done?'

She broadened her smile in an attempt to defuse his temper. 'Sold this place. I got talking to the binman, Chalkie Whitely, this morning. He happened to mention he was looking for a place, I told him we were thinking of selling this and he offered me ten thousand for it. I thought it was good price, so I took it. We have a gentleman and lady's agreement.'

'Ten thousand,' Len repeated cautiously.

'I know it's not as much as you would have got for the new one,' she relaxed now that she knew he wasn't going to shout at her, 'but, then, you've put so much work into the place, I thought we should enjoy it, not some stranger who wouldn't appreciate it. We'll be very happy there, don't you think?'

Len cut a large piece of steak and nodded as he put it into his mouth. He had recalled what his life had been like when Rita had run off to Blackpool.

'This is your place?' Marion Willis gazed round-eyed at the living room of Mike Baldwin's penthouse. The four-piece suite in the open-plan living area was of pale cream leather and deeply upholstered. The coffee table, made from a single circular piece of wood, was bare and the pictures on the wall, prints of single plants, she found rather dull. There was no clutter, none of the small homely touches she thought so essential to a house.

Desperately trying to act as if he was at home, Eddie looked around, wondering where Mike kept his drink. 'Would you like a drink – or tea or coffee?

'What drink do you have?' Marion sat on the edge of one of two sofas without taking off her coat.

'I'm not sure. My cleaner does my shopping for me.' On their first date, Eddie had told Marion that he was a successful businessman. Since then his lies had taken on a life of their own, growing more elaborate and expansive every time he saw her. When she had asked to see where he lived, he'd put her off. But when Hilda had casually mentioned that morning that Mike was staying overnight in London, he'd filched the keys to the penthouse from her handbag before meeting Marion.

There was no risk: he'd return them to Hilda's bag before morning, but that didn't make him feel any more comfortable now.

'Have you a gin and tonic?' Marion asked shyly.

'I'm sure I have somewhere.' He opened a cupboard door to reveal a vast record collection. He pulled back the door alongside it. It held a stack of videos, some with alarming titles, but he stopped reading them after *Naughty Schoolgirls in Paris*. The third cupboard held a drinks tray, with gin, whisky and brandy.

'I'll see if there's any tonic in the fridge.' He opened three doors before he found the kitchen. The fridge was stacked with beer, wine, Perrier and tonic water. He managed to find two glasses, poured himself a beer and Marion a tonic so she could add gin in the living room.

Wondering how he had got himself into this mess, and trying not to think of how much Marion meant to him, or how she'd react if she discovered that he was not only a fraud but a window-cleaner who lived in lodgings, Eddie returned to the living room.

Chapter Thirty-Five

'I hope I've come to the right house, Mrs . . . Emily. I'm Mrs Swain, Mrs Margaret Swain. Arnold's wife.'

Emily had imagined Arnold's wife a hundred times but she had never expected her to look so down-at-heel, badly dressed and unkempt. If she had seen her in the street she would have mistaken her for a vagrant.

'You'd better come in.' Emily showed her into the living room. The woman looked even worse in the neat, comfortable surroundings of Emily's home. 'Please, sit down.'

'Thank you.' Margaret removed her coat and sat on one of the chintz-covered chairs next to the gas fire. 'I had a letter yesterday from Arnold's solicitor telling me that he left everything he owned to you. I can't understand why.' Tears started in her eyes and she pulled a grubby handkerchief from her sleeve. 'I'm his legal wife. We never divorced but he didn't look after me. Never gave me a single penny in all the years we were married.'

'He told me you left him on your honeymoon.' Emily felt it was tactless of her to bring up the subject but she had to know if everything Arnold had told her was a lie.

'You must have known what he was like, but was that any reason for him to leave his entire estate to you and nothing to me? Do you think that's right when I'm his legally married wife?' She clutched her handkerchief to her nose again. 'Arnold's money may not seem a lot to you.' She glanced around the cosy living room with its expensive china ornaments, made-to-measure curtains and neutral silk wallpaper.

Emily thought of the cheques that she sent that morning to the hospital and the community centre. She'd done exactly as Ken had suggested. She had endowed a bed in the hospital in her beloved Ernest's name and, at the suggestion of the youth leader, she had purchased a trampoline for the youth club.

'I don't want to be any trouble,' Margaret whined, 'but I've been ill and I haven't been able to work . . .' Her tears escalated into sobs and she covered her face with her hands.

Emily reached for her handbag. She opened it, took out her cheque book and wrote a cheque for the same sum of money that Arnold had left her. Margaret's sobs subsided as she handed it to her.

'Arnold didn't treat either of us very well, did he?' Margaret said, as Emily showed her out.

'No, he didn't,' Emily agreed, and hoped she'd never hear Arnold Swain's name again as long as she lived.

Brian opened his front door, dropped his bag in the living room and shouted for Gail.

'Brian! Why didn't you let me know you were coming home?' Gail ran out of the kitchen to greet him, arms outstretched, but she stopped in her tracks when she saw the thunderous expression on his face.

'I had a letter from my mother.'

'I bet you did,' she snapped. It wasn't the way she'd dreamed of greeting Brian on his return after six months away, but her joy at seeing him was tempered by Ivy's revelation last week that he had written to tell her that he'd spent his last leave in Cairo rather than come home to his family.

'You've been going out with other men while I've been away, and don't try to deny it! I've already been round to my mother's. She said you were seen in the town with a lorry driver.'

'I—'

'Well, you're not the only one who's had an affair,' he interrupted furiously, without giving her a chance to defend herself. 'I went out with a nurse when I was abroad and she was a damned sight prettier than you. And a lot more willing and able in the bedroom.'

'The only way I've been unfaithful to you is in your

mother's evil mind,' Gail screamed. 'And if you find other women more attractive, then you should go back where you came from. Right now!'

'Perhaps I'll do just that.'

'I won't stop you . . .'

Ivy Tilsley stood outside Gail and Brian's front door and listened to them yelling at each other. When little Nicky started crying at the noise his parents were making, she rang the doorbell.

Her grandson was upset, and who better to look after him than his grandmother?

Deirdre Barlow left the corner shop and walked the few yards to number one. She unlocked the door and stepped inside. Ken had picked up Tracy from the child-minder and she was sitting on the rug, playing with her dolls.

'Hello, love,' Ken murmured absently, from behind the evening paper.

'You heard what happened to Betty Turpin, the barmaid from the Rovers?' she asked.

'Mmm, yes, someone did say something about it in the community centre today. I wasn't sure how much of what they said to believe. You know how people exaggerate.'

'They couldn't be exaggerating by much when she's still in hospital,' she said pointedly. 'And it's all everyone's been talking about in the shop today. Betty was mugged last night when she was walking home from the pub. By all accounts, two lads snatched her handbag, pushed her to the ground, broke her arm and left her lying in the street in agony. It's disgraceful. I don't know what's happening to this place. It's come to something when it's not safe for a woman to walk along this street late at night.'

'According to this,' Ken shook his paper, 'there's been a spate of muggings around Manchester lately.'

'Don't you think the Community Council should be doing something about it?'

'What do you suggest, love?'

'Something – anything,' she snapped, irritated by his attitude. 'The police came round the shop asking if I'd heard anything. So I told them about Raymond Attwood.'

'What about Raymond Attwood?' Ken enquired frostily.

Deirdre knew from the chill in his voice that he was angry with her for mentioning the local boy's name, but he had always had a soft spot for kids who came from poor or uncaring homes.

'Raymond's been spending a lot of money on sweets in the shop lately, and he's been trying to get the older boys to buy beer and spirits for him. I twigged what he was up to so I refused to serve them. And when I asked Raymond why he was so flush, he wouldn't give me an answer.' She stooped down to give Tracy a hug and a kiss.

'That's hardly surprising,' Ken told her. 'You can't go

accusing people just because they're spending more money than usual.'

'But I'm sure it's him.'

'Can you prove it?'

'You know I can't.'

Ken glanced at his watch. 'What time's tea? I've a Community Council meeting tonight.'

'You're always out at meetings,' Deirdre complained.

'I was in last night,' he reminded her.

'For the first time in two weeks. All I ever seem to do is work in the shop, cook and clean here and look at the same four walls every night. Perhaps if we had another baby—'

'Not that again.' Ken cut her short. 'I'm Tracy's step-father and father to my own two. That's more than enough for me. We don't want any more.'

'You mean *you* don't want any more,' she said angrily.

'Too right. It's just too much responsibility. Three children are more than enough for any family.'

'Your children don't even live with us. And when you married me, you promised we could be a family and in my book that meant having children of our own.'

'I'm not prepared to discuss the subject.' He returned to his paper.

'We live more like a couple who've been married for forty years than newly-weds,' Deirdre raged. 'This isn't the kind of life I expected when I agreed to marry you.'

'What were you expecting?' The frost in his voice thickened.

'More fun, more excitement, more pleasure . . .'

'And I thought you were grown-up enough to accept the life we have,' he said.

Deirdre went into the kitchen, took a tin of beans and another of sausages from the cupboard. She lifted a saucepan from the rack and banged it down on the stove in an attempt to vent her anger. Mike Baldwin had called in at the shop that afternoon when she had been alone. After a certain amount of the flirting every woman in the street had come to expect from him he had suddenly invited her to go to the pictures with him next Tuesday. Evidently he knew that Ken attended Community Council meetings on the first Tuesday of every month, and she decided that maybe, just this once, she would take Mike up on his offer. It might teach Ken a lesson.

'Deirdre.' Ken knocked on the kitchen door.

'I'm busy,' she shouted, cursing Albert's antiquated gas cooker as she tried to light it.

'The police are here. They want a word with you.'

Deirdre shut off the gas, set the tins down on the kitchen table and opened the door.

'Mrs Barlow.' The same young constable who had come into the shop that afternoon stood in the middle of the cramped living room, which was filled with Albert's old-fashioned furniture. 'The sergeant asked if I'd call to thank you for the information you gave us earlier today.' The officer toyed with his helmet, which he'd taken off as soon as he'd entered the house. 'We brought Raymond Attwood in for questioning after we spoke to you. He confessed to mugging Mrs Turpin and a dozen others.'

'Thank you very much for calling in, Officer.' She glanced at Ken, who avoided her eye. 'Would you like a cup of tea?'

'I haven't time, Mrs Barlow, but thank you for offering,' the constable replied politely.

'Stay there, Ken, I'll see the officer out.' She was angrier than ever now with Ken for criticising her for giving the police Raymond Attwood's name. She turned on her heel and showed the constable to the door.

Annie Walker shook her head as Mike Baldwin shouted at Eddie Yeats in the bar of the Rovers. 'Keep it down, please,' she called out. 'I keep an orderly house here. 'No breeding, that's that man's trouble,' she whispered to Bet Lynch as she walked past her behind the bar.

Bet propped herself on her elbows and watched Eddie squirm as Mike dropped his voice but continued to harangue him.

'It's no use you denying it,' Mike hissed. 'One of my neighbours saw you leaving with a girl.'

'She could have been mistaken.' Eddie's colour heightened and he shifted guiltily from one foot to the other.

Mike looked at Eddie with contempt. 'My neighbour gave me an accurate description, one that fits only one man in Weatherfield, and, as it happens, the only man apart from Stan Ogden who has access to Hilda's keys. That *is* how you got in, isn't it? You "borrowed" Hilda's keys to my penthouse.'

'Hilda didn't know I'd taken them,' Eddie said swiftly, terrified that Hilda might lose her job.

'So, you admit you stole the keys from Hilda's handbag and broke into the flat! I've a good mind to go to the police.'

'We didn't do anything – I just wanted to show her what a penthouse looked like . . .'

'To pass off my home as yours?'

'We didn't do any damage – we only had a couple of drinks and I'll pay for them,' Eddie offered.

'You know what you are, Eddie Yeats? You're bloody pathetic. Simply not worth bothering with. But I warn you now, you ever do anything like that again and I *will* go to the police. I'll get them to book you for illegal entry, trespass, thieving and anything else they can think of.'

As Mike stormed off, Eddie looked uneasily around the bar – half of his neighbours had heard what Mike had said. And he was dreading confessing the truth to Marion. But he had no choice: if he didn't, he had a feeling that, sooner rather than later, she would find out for herself that he wasn't a successful businessman but a window-cleaner who lived in lodgings. He left his half-finished pint and walked out to look for her.

'You can't blame Gail for going out occasionally with other people – even men.' Bert Tilsley was defending his daughter-in-law to his son as they sat in Brian's living room drinking tea. 'Think about it, lad. She's had no life at all since you left, and I'm telling you now, not many wives would put up with their husband living and working thousands of miles away.'

'It's not as if I didn't support her,' Brian protested. 'I sent her money every week.'

'No amount of money can make up for a husband and father not being there for his wife and son. Your business is to stay at home with your family. Their needs should come first, no matter how much money you can make abroad.' He had called in to see his son at a time when he had known Gail would be working in the café.

'Dad,' Brian looked his father in the eye, 'did Gail have an affair while I was away?'

'The only affair Gail had was in your mother's imagination,' Bert said flatly. He paused for a moment. 'Did you make as much money as you hoped to abroad?'

'I made a fair bit. Enough to buy a forty per cent share in a new garage Ron's setting up in Weatherfield.'

'Is that what you intend to do with it?'

'I'm thinking about it.'

'Things still not right between you and Gail?' Bert asked.

'Not really.'

'Then I suggest you do all you can to put them right, for your own as well as her and Nicky's sake. You couldn't wait to marry the girl – you were that besotted with her.'

'I didn't expect married life to be so bloody boring.'

'Welcome to the real world, lad.' The front door opened and Bert left his chair.

'Stay.'

'Not likely. You'll think about what I've said?'

Brian nodded. He heard his father exchange a few words with Gail in the passage, then got up and went into the kitchen. Gail had made a pie the night before for their tea and he put it into the oven to warm, then returned to the living room. Gail was crouching in front of the gas fire unbuttoning Nicky's coat.

Anxious to stave off a repeat of the shouting match of the previous evening, Brian cleared his throat. 'I was just telling my father that Ron's offered me a partnership in a new garage. If I bought into it, it would take just about every penny I've saved over the last few months.'

'A garage in Qatar?' Gail asked, in a small voice.

'No, in Weatherfield. My father thinks I should take it.'

'Do you want to?' She took Nicky's coat and hung it with her own in the hall. She had hoped that Brian coming home would make everything right again, but the last two days had been worse than when she'd lived alone. Their constant arguments had made her long for the time when there had only been her and Nicky in the house.

'I think so,' he said, when she returned. 'My father also said something else.' He looked her in the eye. 'He said you hadn't had an affair, just a couple of nights out with people.'

'He's right. I didn't. But you did,' she said accusingly.

'I'm sorry. Can you forgive me?'

'I'd just like life to go back to the way it was, Brian, without all the arguing and you jumping to conclusions every time your mother tries to make trouble between us. I'm not the only one in the street who thinks Ivy Tilsley's taken over from where Ena Sharples left off when she left Coronation Street to go into the nursing home in St Anne's.'

'I'll try to make it up to you.' He picked up Nicky and held him close. 'Both of you.'

'I suppose that's all I can ask you to do,' she said.

'I'll lay the table for tea, shall I?'

'Please.'

As Brian went into the kitchen Gail hoped that they could make a fresh start. But she knew it would be an uphill struggle. Ivy had done a great deal of damage to their marriage by planting suspicion in Brian's mind.

Eddie squirmed uncomfortably on Marion Willis's sofa. He'd told her the whole story but she hadn't said a word. Deciding that she wanted nothing more to do with him, he rose awkwardly to his feet.

'I'm sorry for lying to you, Marion,' he muttered, wishing she'd say something. 'I guess you won't be wanting to see me any more, so I'll be off . . .'

Marion rose and stood beside him. 'Why on earth did you think you had to impress me, Eddie?'

'Because I was afraid of losing you.' He'd always been embarrassed by emotion and there was no way he could put his feelings for her into stronger words than he had already used. 'Which is strange, really, as I've ended up doing just that.'

'I care about you, Eddie.'

'After the way I tried to fool you into thinking I was something I wasn't?' He stared at her in amazement.

'Yes, because you told those lies to try to hang on to me.'

'I care for you.'

'I know.' She smiled. 'And I care about you. Enough to marry you, Eddie Yeats.'

Eddie was astonished by her declaration, and it took him a few moments to recover. When he did, he said exactly what she had been hoping to hear. 'I'll buy you an engagement ring tomorrow, love.'

'Can I choose it?'

'Any one you want in the shop,' he offered generously, then made a mental note to check his savings balance first thing in the morning.

★

Deirdre leant against the door of Mike Baldwin's penthouse. She didn't move or attempt to take off her coat until he had closed all the blinds in his spacious living room.

'Do you know something, Deirdre? After only four dates I'm tired of sneaking around like this.' He helped her off with her coat, dropped it on to a chair and kissed her.

'So am I,' she whispered, when he allowed her to come up for air.

'Then leave Ken and live with me.'

'You really mean that, don't you?' She gazed into his eyes as he slid his hands beneath her sweater.

'Yes.' He unhooked her bra and caressed her breasts.

'It wouldn't work out between us.'

'Why not?' He tried to kiss her again, but she slipped from his grasp.

'Because of the kind of man you are. If I did move in with you, it wouldn't be long before you were bored with me, and then you'd look round for another woman to have an affair with.'

'You're very cynical, my love.'

'I'd call it realistic, given your track record with women.' Despite her pronouncement she allowed him to pull her sweater over her head and led her into his bedroom.

'If I remember rightly you're hardly a saint yourself. Ray Langton and Billy Walker aside, let's face it, you wouldn't even be here if you were. You'd be stuck at home with your safe, boring husband.'

'Leave Ken out of this,' she snapped.

'I rather think you've done that for both of us.' He unbuttoned his shirt. 'We're alike, Deirdre. Kindred spirits who are suited to each other. Live with me and I'll promise you a roller-coaster ride to life.'

'And Tracy?' she asked. 'You'll give her a roller-coaster ride as well?'

'The best – it'll be fun all the way, and I'll prove myself a better father to Tracy than Ken could ever be.' He unzipped her skirt and pulled her back on to the bed alongside him. 'You'll move in with me?'

'I'll think about it,' she compromised.

'How about me calling round your house after you come home from the shop tomorrow so I can pick up your and Tracy's things and bring them back here?'

His offer was tempting, so very, very tempting, given the state of her and Ken's marriage, and there was Mike's lifestyle to consider. He had promised her a roller-coaster ride to life and she knew that was a promise he would live up to. The problem was, roller-coaster rides had their downs as well as ups.

'I'll give you and Tracy all the things Ken can't. And we'll have children together. Lots of them.'

That swayed her. 'I'd have to tell Ken I was leaving him.'

'I'll give you half an hour after work before I drive over to your place to pick you up. How's that?'

She hesitated for a split second then nodded.

He folded back the bedclothes. 'I love you, Deirdre.'

'And I love you.' She meant it . . . so why was she having such trouble erasing Ken's face from her mind?

Chapter Thirty-Six

Brian proudly showed his father around the garage he and Ron Sykes had bought and which he was managing for Ron, who had opted to stay in Qatar.

'Very nice.' Bert was impressed by all the tools and machinery although he didn't have a clue what half of them were for. 'And you own forty per cent of the place.'

'And manage it on a day-to-day basis and make all the decisions about how it should be run, so you can say it's as much mine as Ron's.' The day before Ivy had tackled Brian about the depression his father had succumbed to since being made redundant. Brian wasn't certain that her solution to his father's problems was the right one but he decided to broach the subject anyway. 'And I'd like you to come and work for me, Dad.'

'Doing what?' Bert asked suspiciously.

'There's dozens of things you could help out with. For a start, there's answering the phone and making the bookings for services and repairs when I'm busy, besides the masses of small things that need doing.'

'I'm no mechanic,' Bert growled.

'You don't need to be a mechanic to check oil and water levels in engines and radiators, or set tyre pressures.'

'You really think I could be of some help?' For the last couple of years, Bert hadn't found it easy to get a job that had lasted more than a week or two, but he hated the thought of his son offering him charity.

'You could be a real help to me here, Dad,' Brian assured him, concealing his doubts. 'I've taken on an apprentice, Kevin Webster, and you'll be doing me a favour by keeping an eye on him.'

'If you think I really could . . .'

'I wouldn't have asked you if I didn't.'

Bert's face broke into a smile and Brian realised that his mother had been right. All his father needed was something to make him feel useful again.

'No, don't call round tonight,' Deirdre warned Mike, as she served him cigarettes in the shop.

'But we agreed I would come half an hour after you got home. You'll need help to get your and Tracy's things to the penthouse. If I come round with the car at, say, half past five—'

'I need to tell Ken why I'm leaving him. We haven't

even been married a year yet. I owe him an explanation, Mike, and I can't rush it. It wouldn't be fair.'

'You're leaving the man because he treats you the same way he treats the furniture, and you want to be fair to him?' Mike exclaimed.

'Ssh,' she whispered. 'Someone might hear you upstairs.'

'Deirdre . . .'

'I said I'd leave Ken and I will. But I'll call a taxi. I don't want you to come face to face with him. The last thing I want is to cause an argument between you two.' She handed Mike his cigarettes, took the five-pound note he handed her and rang open the till.

'I think you caused an argument between me and Ken Barlow the day you first agreed to come out with me, love,' Mike said dryly.

'Ken has the right to hear why I'm leaving him from me, without interference from you,' she insisted. 'And my reasons for leaving him are nothing to do with you.'

'Do you really believe that?'

'No,' she answered in a small voice.

'I'd rather be there, in case there's trouble between you.'

'There's bound to be trouble.' She didn't want to think what Ken's reaction might be.

'And if he asks you to stay with him?'

'I won't change my mind.'

'Promise.'

'I promise.'

He leant over the counter and kissed her, unaware that Emily Bishop was watching them through the shop window.

Emily turned and pretended to walk up the street to her house as Mike left the shop. Soon after she had started working in his factory she had become aware of the number of visits he made every day to the corner shop, far more than his consumption of cigarettes or the occasional bar of chocolate warranted. And from the number of evenings she had babysat for Deirdre lately, and the corresponding number of evenings Mike's answering-machine had been left switched on – even though he knew she was in the middle of sorting out the factory's tax return – she'd suspected that something was going on between them.

She went into her house, made herself a cup of tea and left it standing on the table. Then she retraced her steps to the shop and waited until it was empty before going inside and closing the door behind her.

'Emily, how nice to see you.' Deirdre smiled. 'What can I do for you?'

'You can think about what you're doing to Ken and Tracy, for your sake as much as theirs,' Emily said.

'I don't know what you're talking about.'

'Yes, you do,' Emily contradicted her. 'I saw Mike

Baldwin kissing you earlier. I know you've been seeing him behind Ken's back. Deirdre, Ken is a good man, please don't throw your marriage away.'

'Ken ignores me the same way he ignores everything that isn't connected to his bloody Community Council! We never do anything, or go anywhere!'

'And Mike Baldwin is much more exciting?' Emily suggested mildly.

'Yes, he is,' Deirdre said emphatically. 'We do things together, go to interesting places, meet interesting people. He treats me like a lady, not part of the furniture.'

'Mike Baldwin's had plenty of practice in treating women like ladies. He's had more girlfriends than Ken's had hot dinners.' Then Emily introduced the subject uppermost in her mind. 'Have you thought what kind of a father he's going to make for Tracy?'

'A good one. He has money—'

'Money isn't everything, Deirdre.'

'I know it's not,' Deirdre faltered defensively. 'I'm not a gold-digger, Emily.'

'I know, and I also know that you're a wonderful friend and mother who is about to make the most terrible mistake of her life if someone doesn't stop you.'

'I can't stand living with Ken a moment longer.'

'Have you told him how you feel?' Emily asked. Seeing Deirdre was close to tears, she handed her a handkerchief. The shop bell rang.

'Something wrong, Deirdre?' Ivy Tilsley probed.

'Something in my eye.' Deirdre blew her nose. 'What was it you said you wanted again, Emily?'

'A packet of mints, please.' Emily took a roll from the display and handed Deirdre a fifty-pence piece. When Elsie Tanner and half a dozen factory girls came in, she left, hoping that she'd at least given Deirdre cause to think seriously about what she was doing.

'You happy here, Marion?' Eddie Yeats asked, as he glanced around Elsie Tanner's living room, with its cosy gas fire, comfy three-piece suite and clutter of make-up and hairbrushes adorning the mantelpiece.

'Yes. Elsie's a great landlady and fun to live with.'

'It's nice of her to allow you to bring a friend round when she's out.' He took the cup of tea she handed him.

'She's knows you're more than a friend, Eddie, and I asked if you could visit me this afternoon because I have something to tell you.'

'Something good, I hope?' Eddie said apprehensively. He hadn't been able to believe his luck since Marion had told him she wanted to marry him. 'You haven't changed your mind about the wedding, have you?'

'No, but I'd like to bring it forward.'

'We haven't saved enough money,' he began. 'Another couple of months . . .'

'We haven't another couple of months, Eddie.' She sat

beside him on the sofa. 'Whatever money we've saved will have to do. I'm pregnant.' His shocked expression prompted her to clarify what she'd said. 'I'm going to have a baby and I dare not tell my mother, she'd be furious. She created such a fuss when I said we wanted a quiet register office wedding and she's already talked to the vicar of All Saints. If we don't grab the first date he has free I'll begin to show.'

'You're pregnant,' Eddie repeated slowly.

'Yes.'

'But . . .'

'Are you pleased?' she asked anxiously.

'Pleased?' He grasped her hand and gazed into her eyes. 'Oh, love, this is wonderful! Who would have thought it? Me, a father. Of course we'll get married just as soon as we can arrange it.'

'Hello, love.' Ken walked in and pecked Deirdre on the cheek. He picked Tracy up from the floor where she was crayoning in a colouring book, tossed her in the air and caught her, making her giggle. 'Have a good day?' he asked, suddenly conscious that Deirdre was unusually silent.

Deirdre couldn't bring herself to answer him. Her own and Tracy's suitcases were packed and standing upstairs in the bedrooms but now that the moment to leave Ken had arrived, she knew she couldn't go through with it.

'Something wrong, love?' Ken's sudden, and in view

of the chill that had fallen between them last few weeks, uncharacteristic tenderness was more than she could bear.

'Yes,' she croaked hoarsely.

'What?'

Whatever else, she knew she had to tell him the truth before he heard it from someone else. 'I've been having an affair with Mike Baldwin. I packed Tracy's and my cases earlier so we could move in with him. He's expecting us. But now . . . now . . . I don't want to leave . . .' Tears fell on to her cheeks.

The blood drained from Ken's face. His expression registered disbelief, then disgust and contempt. 'Get out!'

'Ken, please, listen to me . . . You've been so distant lately, so wrapped up in the Community Council and everything else that you haven't had time for Tracy or me. I even began to wonder why you bothered to marry me—'

'Get out!'

'Please, Ken, this isn't only my fault. Think what the last few months have been like for me. Work in the shop, housework here, never going anywhere, never doing anything, and most of the time you're too tired to talk to me.'

'So, I drove you into Baldwin's bed? Is that what you're saying?' His features contorted with pain.

'No . . . I'm not making excuses, just trying to explain why it happened,' she pleaded. Upset by the shouting, Tracy began to cry. Ken picked up the child and buried her face in his shoulder to shield her from the sight of her mother's tears. The gesture tore at Deirdre's heartstrings.

'Ken, please, can you ever forgive me?'

'After you slept in Baldwin's bed?' he challenged.

'It's you I love. I'm sorry it's taken me this long to realise it – I know that I've hurt you—'

'*Hurt* me? Believe me, Deirdre, you have absolutely no idea how I'm feeling right now.'

'I love you but I wanted more . . . excitement, life! We never seem to do anything, go anywhere—'

'And life and sex with Baldwin was exciting?'

'I love you. Please, don't tell me to get out again.' Sobbing hysterically, she sank to the floor. There was a knock at the door and Ken tried to ignore it, but at the fourth bang, still carrying Tracy, he went to answer it.

Mike Baldwin was standing on the doorstep. 'I've brought my car round to pick up Deirdre and Tracy.'

If Ken hadn't been holding Tracy he would have hit him. 'Deirdre's told me about you two. They're staying.'

'I want to see Deirdre.'

'My wife no longer wants to see you.' Ken tried to close the door but Mike wedged his foot in the doorway.

'I want to hear that from her, not you.'

'It's true, Mike.' Deirdre appeared briefly in the living-room doorway.

Ken kicked aside Mike's foot and slammed the door in his face.

Tracy's arms tightened around his neck as he leant back against it. He closed his eyes against his pain. Whatever else, Deirdre loved him enough to send Mike Baldwin packing, and enough to tell him to his face about her affair. She loved him almost – but not quite – as much as he loved her. Because, no matter what, he would never betray her.

'Dad . . .'

'It's all right, Tracy.' He hitched the child higher in his arms. 'Let's go and find your mam and make you some tea, shall we?'

'What's going on?' Eddie walked into the Ogdens' living room to find Hilda sitting at the table in tears and Stan standing by the kitchen door with his head in his hands.

'Ask Stan.' Hilda brushed away her tears with the back of her hand and went into the kitchen.

'Stan?' Eddie looked at his mate.

'I borrowed some money from a moneylender,' Stan revealed. 'He's threatened to take us to court unless I repay him.'

'How much did you borrow?' Eddie pulled a chair out from the table and sat down.

'It's two hundred quid now.'

'Two hundred quid?'

'I haven't been able to do all of my window-cleaning round lately. I'm not up to climbing ladders any more, but I was too ashamed to tell Hilda so I borrowed enough to give her housekeeping. I hoped to make it up later but I never did. I didn't think it would come to this. It just mounted up.'

Eddie thought rapidly. He and Marion needed financial stability now with a baby on the way. He couldn't help but smile every time he thought of the baby . . .

'That's right, laugh at me. Stupid old Stan, always in trouble.'

'I wasn't laughing at you, Stan, honest. I was thinking about something else. Look, suppose I bought the round off you. It's got to be worth a couple of hundred quid and I have that in savings.'

'What do you want to do that for?'

'I'll have a wife to support soon, and I can keep you on, just to do the downstairs windows. What do you say?'

'He says, "Yes, and thank you very much." I don't know what we'd do without you, Eddie. Between the lodging money you pay and all the other things you do for us, we wouldn't be able to manage without you.' Hilda bustled in from the kitchen with the teapot. She set it on the table, then wrapped her arms around Eddie's neck, hugging him with such force that he felt she was trying to strangle him.

'Hey, Hilda, no need to throttle me.' Embarrassed, Eddie peeled her off him. 'I'll withdraw the money from the bank tomorrow.'

'Thanks, Eddie, I don't know how I'll ever repay you.' Subdued, Stan sat alongside him at the table.

'You can start by being my best man. I'm going to be needing one, and a lot sooner than I thought.'

'Then you and Marion . . .' Hilda beamed as she looked at him.

'Just as soon as we can arrange it, Hilda.'

Brian Tilsley sat with his arm round his mother's shoulders outside the hospital ward. Ivy hadn't stirred or said a word in over an hour, and the only sound was Nicky's footsteps as he ran from one end of the long corridor to the other with Gail at his heels.

A doctor left the ward and Brian jumped to his feet.

'Is there any news?' he asked. His father had been inflating tyres at the garage when – as far as Brian and his apprentice Kevin had worked out – he had over-inflated one. It had exploded, knocking him unconscious, and although Brian had called an ambulance right away, Bert had been in a coma for over a week. But that hadn't stopped Ivy hoping that the doctor had called them in that morning to tell them Bert was about to make a miraculous recovery.

'I'm sorry, Mrs Tilsley, Mr Tilsley.' The doctor stood in

front of them. 'There is no doubt that Mr Tilsley has extensive brain damage.'

Brian blanched.

'Can I see him?' Ivy asked.

The doctor nodded. 'We've taken him off the life-support system and he is breathing on his own, but we can't give you any idea how long he'll be in his present condition, or even if he'll ever regain consciousness.'

'I understand.' Ivy turned back to Gail. 'Take Nicky home, Gail. Brian and I will be back in an hour or so.'

Feeling shut out, Gail watched her husband and mother-in-law disappear into the ward.

'The bride and groom.' Stan proposed the toast, which was taken up by Annie Walker and all the guests who had been invited to Eddie Yeats and Marion Willis's wedding.

Eddie held Marion's hand, rose to his feet and began, 'On behalf of my wife and I . . .' Then, ignoring the roars of laughter, he continued, 'I would like to thank you all for coming here today to wish us well.'

Annie sent Bet Lynch round to pick up drinks orders and Elsie walked over to Eddie and Marion.

'You've been a perfect lodger,' Elsie said to Marion, 'and it will be lovely to have you as a neighbour in number eleven.'

'I'm afraid we won't be moving in,' Marion said quietly.

'Eddie and I didn't want to tell anyone before the wedding but my mother's had a stroke and we'll be moving into her house in Bury to take care of her. She needs me and, with a baby coming, it would too difficult to try to live here and look after her. We'd be forever on the road.'

'I'm sorry to be losing you,' Elsie said.

'We're sorry to be leaving.' Eddie made a face that said a great deal about what he thought of his mother-in-law. 'But at least Marion's cousin's offered to look after her mother so we can have our honeymoon in Benidorm.'

'Benidorm.' Elsie sighed wistfully. 'Spain will be wonderful at this time of year, all that sunshine. I'd give anything to live there.'

'Wouldn't we all?' Marion agreed.

Eddie squeezed his bride's hand. 'Two weeks is better than nothing, love.'

'Yes, it is.' Marion smiled bravely. Eddie wasn't the only one who was dreading living with her mother.

Deirdre left the living room as soon as Albert came home from the Rovers. She smiled at him when she saw him in the hall.

'It was a nice wedding.'

'That it was.' He took off his cap and muffler. 'You going to bed?'

'Yes.'

'Bit early, isn't it?'

'I'm tired out,' she explained. 'I'll be up early in the morning with Tracy and I've a full day in the shop tomorrow.'

'I'll say goodnight, then.'

'And goodnight to you, Uncle Albert.'

He watched her walk up the stairs then went into the living room where Ken was watching a documentary on the First World War. 'Don't know how you can watch that, it was bad enough living it,' he grumbled, as he sat in his chair.

'It's the only way my generation can find out what it was like.' Ken looked across at him. 'Like a cup of tea?'

'No, but I would like a word.'

'About what?' Ken didn't know why he'd asked. He already knew the answer to his question.

'You and Deirdre.'

'I know the atmosphere's been a bit strained between us lately . . .'

'Strained?' the old man echoed. 'I was thinking of bottling it and selling it as fog.'

'Nothing passes you by, Uncle Albert,' Ken observed ruefully.

'Nowt can, considering the three of us are living in the same house.' Albert stretched out his legs in front of the gas fire. 'Has Deirdre going to bed early anything to do with me coming in?'

'It's more to do with what we said to one another before you came in,' Ken told him.

'But my living with you doesn't help.'

'It's not you, Uncle Albert, it's us,' Ken said. 'We're going through a rough patch. And after talking to Deirdre tonight, I think it might be an idea if we moved to a bigger house to make a fresh start. But, of course, we want you to come with us,' he added.

Albert shook his head. 'I'm too old to go gallivanting around changing houses.'

'The one thing Deirdre and agree on, Uncle Albert, is that you should carry on living with us.'

'I've been thinking, would it make it any easier if I gave you and Deirdre this house? That way you wouldn't feel guilty about any improvements you made. You're going to get it any road when I'm gone.'

'I couldn't possibly accept the house for nothing.'

'Then you don't want it.'

'Maybe, if you let me pay the going price,' Ken suggested.

'Please yourself. You'll get it either way. There's no one else I want to leave my bits and bobs to.'

'You've a daughter,' Ken reminded him.

'Who couldn't give a damn about me.' Albert rose stiffly from his chair. 'I'm off to bed. It was a good wedding but a long evening. Goodnight.'

'Goodnight, Uncle Albert, and thank you for trying to

help. Don't worry, Deirdre and I will sort our problems –
somehow.'

'I hope you will, lad. I hope you will.'

Chapter Thirty-Seven

Brian reached across the scarred, chipped table in the Rovers Return and gripped Gail's hand. 'Come on, love,' he coaxed persuasively, 'it makes sense. Ron is going to sell his sixty per cent share of the garage no matter what. Think how I'd feel if some stranger came strutting in, throwing his weight around when I've built that place up from a customer base hardly worth having to what it is now. If we sell the house, we'll raise enough to buy Ron out.'

'And we'll have to move in with your mother,' she said flatly.

'The way business has picked up at the garage, it won't take me long to make enough to put down a deposit on another place. Besides, now that Dad is going into a nursing home he'll never come back here to live. My mother's going to need company.'

'And that company has to be you.'

'And you and Nicky,' he added. 'Gail, she's my mother . . .'

'So I've discovered, since I married you.' Gail allowed her bitterness to surface.

'You don't want me to buy Ron out?'

'Buy Ron out,' she said, weary of argument. 'Put our house on the market and we'll move in with your mother.'

'I knew you'd see it my way.' He beamed triumphantly.

'Did you?'

'Another drink?' He picked up her empty lager glass.

'Why not?' she said miserably. Ivy's constant carping and criticism would be even harder to take when they were both under the same roof. She had created havoc between her and Brian when they'd been living in their own place – Gail dreaded to think what her mother-in-law could accomplish once they were all in number five Coronation Street.

When Ken went into the Rovers and saw Gail sitting alone at a table, he noticed that there was more hubbub than usual coming from the crowd centred around Annie Walker at the bar. He slipped his hand into his pocket, pulled out some change and walked up to Annie, who was deep in conversation with Stan and Hilda Ogden, Brian Tilsley and Elsie Tanner.

'Have you heard about the decision the council's made, Ken?'

Ken didn't have to ask Annie to explain what she meant. The residents had organised a protest group in an effort to stop Mike Baldwin and his business partner, Alec Gilroy, turning the warehouse on the corner of Coronation and Rosamund streets into a nightclub. 'I've heard,' he confirmed.

'And Alf Roberts, of all people, having the gall to call himself our councillor and representative, supporting Mike Baldwin's application for planning permission! I dread to think what's coming here.' Annie shook her head. 'Cars and noise at all hours of the night. Loud music, drugs, drunks . . . When I think of all the work we put into gathering signatures on our petition against that club, my blood boils. All that effort wasted! Mike was in here earlier crowing, telling us that there's nothing we can do now to stop him.'

'He's right, there's nothing you can do now the decision's been taken,' Stan agreed, a Job's comforter.

'There's one thing left that we can do about it and I've already done it.' Ken nodded to Annie when she held up a pint mug. 'I've written a letter to the *Gazette* suggesting that our esteemed councillor, Alf Roberts, is more interested in business than the voters around here who elected him.'

'Good for you, Ken,' Annie approvingly. 'Pint, or half?'

'Does this look all right?' Deirdre zipped up her brown trousers and checked that her gold silk blouse was buttoned straight.

Ken was knotting his tie. 'You look very nice.'

'I wish I could believe you.' She sat at her dressing-table and applied another coat of mascara and lipstick.

'I mean it.' He rose from the bed, rested his hands on her shoulders and kissed the back of her neck. 'You said you wanted more excitement in your life, well, I can't think of a more exciting evening,' he teased. 'Uncle Albert's eighty-eighth birthday party combined with the Ogdens' fortieth wedding anniversary. The Rovers Return will rock tonight.'

She gazed at him in the mirror and he smiled. Tentatively she smiled back and he stroked her cheek with a finger. Was it his imagination, or was the strain between them lessening? Had their marriage weathered the storms it had been through?

'I'm not sure about the babysitter . . .'

'She's going to be fine,' Ken assured her. For once it had been impossible to get a sitter Tracy knew because every resident of Coronation Street had been invited to the double party. 'Every woman who works in the Community Centre uses her and they all swear by her. Besides, can you even remember the last time Tracy woke after we put her to bed?'

'No,' Deirdre conceded.

'And if she does, we can be back here in two minutes. I've left the number of the Rovers next to the phone.'

'Thought of everything, haven't you?'

'Not quite.' He held out his hand. 'Ready?'

'Just about.'

Ken opened the bedroom door and shouted. 'Uncle Albert?'

'I've been waiting for you two for ten minutes,' he called from downstairs. 'The babysitter's been here a quarter of an hour.'

Ken ran downstairs and lifted Deirdre's coat from the rack. He helped her on with it when she returned from giving the babysitter some unnecessary last-minute instructions.

They were halfway down Coronation Street when Albert froze.

'What's up?' Deirdre asked.

'Her, that's what's up,' the old man muttered, staring at a square-built, grey-haired, middle-aged woman standing outside the Rovers.

'You haven't met Beattie Pearson, Uncle Albert's daughter, have you, Deirdre?' Ken forced himself to be polite, although he suspected from previous encounters that Beattie had only turned up at her father's birthday party to make a scene. 'Beattie, this is my wife, Deirdre. Deirdre, Beattie.'

'Pleased to meet you.' Deirdre held out her hand but Beattie ignored it.

'You've come to wish your father a happy birthday?' Ken suggested forcefully.

'I've come to see him, and you.' She blocked Ken's

path and poked a finger into his chest. 'You bought my father's house at a knockdown price, depriving me of my rightful inheritance.'

'I paid him the full estate agent's valuation,' Ken protested.

'You swindled me.' She raised her voice when she saw other residents leaving their houses to make their way to the Rovers. 'That house is mine by right!'

'It was mine,' Albert intervened. 'I sold it, which I had every right to do. And I'll thank you to remember that I can do what I like with my own things, as long as I'm here. No matter how much you'd like to put me in a box, I'm not gone yet. The house was mine and the money Ken paid me for it is mine. And I'll give it to whoever I like – and I'm telling you now, it won't be you.'

'I'm your daughter, your own flesh and blood.' Beattie jerked her chin towards Ken. 'He's nothing to you.'

'He's been looking after me ever since our Val died and he's been a damned sight better to me than you have. More like a son than a nephew-in-law.' Albert gave Beattie a scathing look. 'I wish I'd had a lad of my own instead of a useless, selfish daughter who never thinks of anyone except herself. I'd have been better off without you. Clear off, you're no child of mine.' He went into the Rovers and Deirdre followed.

'Are you coming? It is Uncle Albert's birthday,' Ken reminded Beattie.

'After what he just said to me?' Beattie turned her back and walked away.

'I've never seen the Rovers so full,' Ken said to Annie, as she poured the drinks he'd ordered and set them on a tray.

'It's not every day we have a fortieth wedding anniversary *and* an eighty-eighth birthday in the street. Although,' Annie lowered her voice, 'Albert doesn't look at all well to me.'

'He had words with his daughter before he came in.'

'I saw her hanging around outside earlier. I hoped she'd come to give Albert a present.'

'She gave him that all right,' Ken said. 'A load of lip.'

'Oh, while I think of it,' Annie searched under the counter, 'a reporter from the local paper, the *Recorder*, was in here this afternoon looking for you. She gave me her card to give to you.'

'Did she say what she wanted?'

'She said she was impressed by the letter you wrote to the paper about Alf Roberts being more interested in business than the people who elected him.' Annie found the business card and handed it to Ken, who glanced at it and pushed it into his pocket. 'She said to tell you that any time you want to use her paper to sound off about any local happenings you're more than welcome.'

'I might just do that.' Ken had been incensed by reports that the council were planning to close all the local youth clubs. He'd spoken to a youth worker who'd uncovered evidence that council employees were massaging the attendance figures to prove that the clubs weren't used.

'Careful, Ken,' Annie warned. 'You don't want to make any more enemies than you have already.'

He picked up the tray. 'You're a fine one to warn me about that, Annie. Who backed me every step of the way over the nightclub? We might have lost one battle but there's others that need fighting.'

'Perhaps you're right,' Annie agreed, 'but I'm getting too old to help you fight them any more. Just be careful, that's all I ask.'

'I will.' He returned to the table where Deirdre, Albert and the Ogdens were waiting for their drinks.

'I bet you're missing Len,' Ivy Tilsley said to Rita, as she, Rita and Elsie Tanner sat at a table drinking gin and tonic. Rita and Elsie knew that Ivy hadn't made a throwaway remark. Every time a husband or wife spent a night away from the street, Ivy saw it as a portent of divorce or, at the very least, an affair that would lead to separation.

'I *am* missing Len,' Rita agreed, 'but the contract in Ashton was too good for him to miss. And he was home the weekend before last.'

'Judging by the smile I saw on his face when he was here, he was enjoying a second honeymoon,' Elsie chipped in, attempting to put Ivy in her place.

Rita gave Elsie a wary smile of gratitude. She hadn't forgotten Len's crush on Elsie, although they'd managed to develop a healthy respect for one another since they'd been neighbours.

'Deirdre and Ken Barlow don't look too happy. And, judging by Albert Tatlock's colour, he won't be seeing an eighty-ninth birthday.' Ivy glanced up from her prophecies of doom just as Annie Walker beckoned to Ken. 'I wonder what she wants him for now. They spend hours talking to each other, you know. And the minute anyone gets close enough to hear what they're saying, they shut up.'

'Perhaps they're planning to elope,' Rita suggested flippantly.

'Or Annie's short of a washer-upper, and Ken doesn't want to know anyone he moonlights in the Rovers kitchen,' Elsie joked. She picked up her empty glass and Rita's. 'Same again, ladies?'

'Please.' Ivy finished her gin and tonic.

Elsie picked up Ivy's glass and walked over to Stan and Hilda. 'Can I buy the happy couple a drink?'

As Stan struggled to focus on her, Elsie realised he'd had more than enough to drink. 'Mine's a pint please, Elsie, love.'

'And I'll have one of those Tia Marias, please, Elsie.' Hilda giggled. 'Ken bought me one, and I really liked it.'

'So I see.' Elsie moved to the bar where Ken and Annie were still deep in serious conversation. 'When you two have finished putting the world to rights, I'd like three gin and tonics, a Tia Maria and a pint of whatever Stan's drinking, please.'

'Elsie.' Ken caught her hand and pulled her close to him and Annie. 'Annie's just had a telephone call from the police. They were at Len's house. Our babysitter heard them knocking and went out to see what the noise was about. She told them that practically the whole street was in here so they telephoned Annie.'

Annie sniffed back her tears. 'It's Len, Elsie, he's dead.'

'He fell asleep at the wheel of his car and crashed into a bridge a couple of hours ago,' Ken explained. 'The officer I spoke to said he was killed outright.'

'Len,' Elsie whispered. She would have fallen if Ken hadn't slipped his arm round her waist. He realised that Rita wasn't the only one who would be devastated by Len's death.

'So much for a street celebration,' Ken said, as he closed the bedroom door in the small hours of the morning. Deirdre was propped up in bed staring into space. He sat down beside her and unlaced his shoes.

'It was an awful end to the evening,' she agreed. 'Poor Rita. How is she?'

'Shell-shocked. The doctor gave her something to help her sleep. She's staying in one of the spare bedrooms at the Rovers tonight. I can't think of anyone better than

Annie to look after her. She knows all there is to know about losing a husband. She and Jack were very close, and I don't think she ever recovered from his death.'

'Albert didn't look well either. Everyone said so.'

'Is it any wonder after the scene Beattie made outside the Rovers?' Before he took off his jacket Ken felt in his pockets. His hand closed round the card the reporter had left for him in the Rovers. He glanced at the name: Pam Mitchell. He made a mental note to ring her the next day, then set the card under his keys on his bedside table, where he'd be sure to pick it up in the morning.

'This is set to be a right miserable Christmas.' Elsie Tanner blotted a tear as she sat beside Annie Walker in the church. Rita was in the front pew, staring ahead at Len's coffin, covered with flowers, on a dais in front of the altar.

'It's a tragedy,' Annie agreed. 'And to think that he and Rita were so happy just a couple of weeks ago, moving into the new house, his business taking off after all the hard work he's put in over the years . . .'

As the vicar asked the mourners to rise to sing the first hymn, hands closed on Elsie's shoulders and a familiar voice whispered in her ear, 'Remember me?'

Elsie glanced over her shoulder. Her old boyfriend, Bill Gregory, was sitting in the pew behind her. 'Bill.'

'I couldn't believe it when they told me you were still living in Coronation Street. See you after the funeral?'

Elsie nodded, then turned back. Annie had opened her hymnal at the right page and she began to sing.

Bill! She had forgotten what close friends Len and Bill had been. So close, Bill had asked Len to help him arrange his wife's funeral shortly before he left to open his wine bar in Portugal. Of course Bill would make the effort to come to Len's funeral, even if he was still living in Portugal. She recalled the night Bill had asked her to go with him. The same night that Alan Howard had turned up on her doorstep. If he hadn't . . . would Portugal have been her home too?

'I *am* asking you, Deirdre,' Ken said patiently as they walked through the park towards the children's playground on a cold, grey December afternoon so Tracy could play on the swings. Sunday afternoon outings had become part of their routine since Deirdre had confessed to her affair, and they had decided to make a concerted effort to save their marriage.

'You're not asking me,' she contradicted him. 'You're telling me what you've decided and there's a difference. First you leak a confidential report to that journalist about the council closing youth clubs, then you get the sack, and now you're telling me you're using our savings to buy a share in the *Recorder* when you know nothing about newspapers.'

'What is there to know, Deirdre?' Ken deliberately kept

his voice light. 'I've written enough articles for them in my time, and sold them. I do have an English degree. Perhaps it's time I put it to some use.'

'Do you really think you can pay the bills and keep us and your children on the profit from your share of the *Recorder*?'

'I do.'

'Then go ahead and try,' she challenged. She didn't like the idea of Ken putting their savings into a venture that might fail, but since he had forgiven her for her affair with Mike Baldwin, she felt she had no choice but to support him in whatever he wanted to do. It was almost as if she had a lifelong obligation to make up for the hurt she had caused him.

'I can't believe it.' Annie Walker poured Elsie Tanner a gin and tonic on the house. 'You really are leaving the street?'

'On January the fourth. Roll on 1984, that's what I say.' Elsie raised her glass to Annie. 'Cheers.'

'The street won't be the same without you.'

'It'll soon recover,' Elsie said philosophically. 'Years ago, before I married Alan Howard – and what a disaster that turned out to be – Bill Gregory asked me to help him run his wine-bar in Portugal. I turned him down then, but I'm not fool enough to turn him down a second time.'

'What about your house?' Alf Roberts asked.

'I've put it on the market and told our Linda to get

what she can for it. Nothing's going to stop me this time, not houses, possessions, family ties, nothing. Sun, sea, sand and sangria, here I come.'

'Isn't sangria a Spanish drink?' Alf asked.

'Possibly,' Elsie replied carelessly. 'Spain Portugal – it's all the same to me – hot and Mediterranean. Happy New Year to both of you. Annie, the next round is on me.'

'This is the yard.' Rita Fairclough was showing Bill Webster, who had bought Elsie's house a week after Linda had put it on the market, around Len's yard. Bill was a local builder with two children, Kevin and Debbie, and they had moved into number eleven. Kevin was Brian Tilsley's apprentice and apparently a steady enough lad, but Rita had heard that Bill's sixteen-year-old daughter Debbie was a flighty girl with an eye for the boys.

'It must be hard seeing another man in your husband's yard,' Bill said.

'It is,' she said shortly, 'but I have to be practical. If you pay me the rent I'm asking and buy the stock at valuation, it's yours. You have seen the estimate?'

'Yes, and it's more than fair, Mrs Fairclough.'

'And the rent?'

'You'll get it on the nail, the first of every month.'

Rita held out her hand. 'Then we're going to get on well, Mr Webster.'

'I hope so, Mrs Fairclough. I've already secured my first job – repairing the roof of Mawdsley Street chapel.'

Rita swallowed hard. Mawdsley Street chapel was the last job for which Len had tendered before taking the contract in Ashton. She dropped the keys into Bill's hand. 'Good luck, Mr Webster.'

'And to you, Mrs Fairclough.' She left the yard and he let out a satisfied sigh. At last he had all the space he needed to expand his business and make a proper home for Debbie and Kevin. Hopefully, life would be plain sailing from now on.

Gail put Nicky to bed in the tiny boxroom of Ivy's house. She read him two stories, then went downstairs in time to see Ivy leaving the house for her customary night out in the Rovers.

'I won't be long, Gail.' It was what Ivy said every evening before she went out, and she was never home before stop-tap.

'Enjoy yourself,' Gail murmured automatically, then went into the living room. Brian was sitting in front of the television, watching a sitcom. She sat beside him and he wrapped his arm absently round her shoulders.

Encouraged by his unusual display of affection Gail decided to broach the subject uppermost on her mind. 'Alma Sedgwick mentioned today that she's decided to live in Spain with her boyfriend.'

'Oh aye?' Brian muttered, immersed in the sitcom.

'You know her husband bought the café from Jim and she owns it now? Well, she asked how I felt about taking over as manageress.'

She had succeeded in attracting Brian's attention. 'You can't do that. You've Nicky to look after,' he said indignantly.

'That's what I told you when you said you wanted to go to Qatar, but it didn't stop you going.'

'That's different. I'm a man.'

'And I'm a woman. We both work to bring money into the house.' She managed to keep her temper – just. 'Think about it for a minute, Brian. It'll mean extra money. We'll be able to save all the more for a deposit to buy a house of our own, away from here.'

'We're doing that anyway. Business at the garage is picking up.'

'I know, but extra money will make it happen all the sooner. You know how much I want my own place.'

'You just want to get away from my mother. And you still haven't answered me – what about Nicky?' He turned down the television and sat facing her.

'Nicky's fine with the child-minder, and we need our own place. We can't live here much longer. When we moved in it was just a temporary arrangement until we saved enough for a deposit on our own place again.'

'And to keep my mother company because my father was ill,' he reminded her.

'Brian, face facts. Your father's been dead a month now, and I'm very sorry for your mother but it's not as if she's elderly or infirm. She's perfectly capable of looking after herself. It's time she got used to being on her own. And she will, just as soon as we move out. Can I take the job?'

'Yes,' he said, turning up the television because he wasn't prepared to discuss moving out of his mother's house any more than he had already.

Chapter Thirty-Eight

'First Ena, then Elsie, now you.' Ken shook his head sadly. 'It seems as though all the mainstays of Coronation Street are leaving. Nothing will ever be the same again.'

'It's kind of you to say so, Ken.' Annie handed him a porcelain plate of cream cakes. 'But I'm too old to run the Rovers on my own. The responsibility has been getting me down lately, and when my sister suggested I should retire to live with her in Derby, it seemed the right thing to do. It'll give me the chance of a bit of peace and quiet for a change.'

'There's no doubt you deserve it. It's just me being selfish. I'm going to miss you,' he said.

'Thank you.'

'Do you know who the brewers are putting in here to replace you?' He switched to a practical subject before they both became too maudlin.

'Fred Gee, the casual barman. He's been working on and off around her for a few months now . . .'

Ken knew the man and his peculiar ideas only too well. 'Fred, run the Rovers!' he exclaimed incredulously.

'He's willing.' Annie smiled.

'And that's about all he is.'

'The appointment is only temporary,' she reassured him.

'For the sake of the Rovers, I'm glad to hear it.' Ken left his chair. 'Take care of yourself, Annie, I'm going to miss you.'

'And I'm going to miss you.' Annie hugged him. After he'd gone Annie sat quietly for a while before going upstairs to pack.

Ken walked out through the bar.

Fred was standing next to a glass case. He pointed to the pies it contained as Ken passed. 'Now the Rovers is under new management, we're going into catering in a big way. How would our local reporter like to taste one of our pies and a side salad, and give the Rovers Return's new cuisine a write-up in the *Recorder*?'

'On the house?' Ken asked.

Fred's face fell. 'Of course.'

'Then I'll try it.'

Brian Tilsley pushed the sports bag that contained his squash kit and racket under the coat rack in the hall and looked into the living room. Gail was alone, sitting on the sofa reading the paper.

'My mother gone to bed?'

'Hours ago.' Gail stared, stony-faced, at the clock.

'It's not that late.'

'It's after midnight and we've both got work tomorrow,' she reminded him.

'What's that supposed to mean?'

She folded the newspaper and set it aside. 'That you're out until this time every night, spending money we can't afford with your new friends who have pound notes to burn. The fees you paid to join that squash club alone would have kept us in groceries for two months. We're never going to be able to afford our own place at the rate you're going.'

'They're good friends, Gail. You should come out with me more often so you can get to know them. They're going off to Spain next month for two weeks. If I cleared the bookings in the garage we could leave Nicky with my mother and go.'

'Leave Nicky with your mother for two weeks and go off on holiday?' she gasped incredulously. 'What kind of father are you?'

'The sort that wants a good time. There has to be more to life than running a garage and shouldering family responsibilities, Gail. I want to have some fun before I get old.'

'No one forced you to marry me. And, if I remember

rightly, you said you wanted Nicky as much as I did before he was born. Can't you see how ridiculous you're being? And I don't just mean spending money we haven't got with these so-called new friends of yours. Can't you see they don't give a toss about you?'

'You don't even know them.' He ran up the stairs, undressed, climbed into bed and turned his back to her side of the bed.

'You've a nerve showing your face in here,' Fred Gee shouted angrily, as Ken walked into the Rovers.

'I take it you didn't like the article I wrote about your "cuisine", Fred?'

'Like it? Why, you—'

'I told the truth. I've never seen anything like that pie served up as food before.' Ken leant on the bar. 'I'll have a half of bitter, please.'

'I'll get it for you, Ken,' Bet Lynch offered.

'You're going to have to do more than bring in disgusting pies if you want to be made permanent licensee of the Rovers.'

'The brewery found out about those pies without your help, Ken.' Billy Walker walked in and joined them from the private quarters behind the bar. 'And Fred's not temporary manager any more. The brewery called me and asked if I could come in to sort out the mess he's made since my mother left a month ago.'

'Good to see you.' Ken shook Billy's hand before taking the glass Bet handed him. 'I'm glad to see someone sensible in charge.'

'I won't be here long,' Billy warned him, 'just until the place is back on its feet and the brewery have had time to appoint a full-time licensee.' He looked at Fred, then down at the overflowing slop trays beneath the beer pumps. Fred didn't need a second glance: he reached for the bucket kept beneath the bar.

One fine spring afternoon in April Deirdre returned with Tracy from a visit to the shops in town to find Beattie Pearson sitting in the living room with Ken. The fact that Beattie had called was an event in itself, but Deirdre only had to look at their faces to realise that something was terribly wrong.

'Albert . . .'

'The first visit he made to me in years,' Beattie dabbed her red nose with her handkerchief, 'and he had to go and die in my armchair while I was in the kitchen making us a cup of tea.'

Stunned, Deirdre almost collapsed on to the sofa beside Ken. Ken lifted Tracy on to his lap and unbuttoned her coat.

'I'm so sorry, Beattie.' Even as Deirdre offered Albert's daughter her condolences, she hoped that the woman hadn't called to make a scene about Albert selling them the house.

As if she'd read Deirdre's thoughts, Beattie opened her handbag. 'I came to give Ken this.' She pulled out a long flat box and handed it Ken. 'It's Dad's medal that he won in the First World War. He was that proud of it, he never went anywhere without it. He would have wanted you to have it, Ken. He always looked on you as the son he never had.'

'I'd never have had the cheek to apply for the job of licensee if you hadn't put me up to it.' Bet Lynch was sitting on a stool behind the bar of the Rovers. She crossed her legs, showing yards of thigh, just as Billy Walker joined her.

'The trouble with you, Bet, is you're always too quick to put yourself down. Well,' Billy looked at the assembled regulars, 'my bags are packed, so I'll be on my way.'

'One for the road. On the house?' Bet nudged him.

'Why not?'

'Back to Jersey?' Ken asked.

'After I've visited Mam in Derby.' Billy lifted the pint Bet handed him. 'Cheers, and here's to the new land-lady. May she last as long and do as good a job as the last one.'

'I'll drink to that.' Ken lifted his own glass. 'I'm all for promoting from the ranks. Bet made a first-class barmaid and she has the makings of a first-class licensee. Just what the Rovers needs.'

'To the first unmarried manageress in the brewery chain,' Betty Turpin toasted, 'the first but not the last.'

'I didn't know you were into women's liberation, Betty,' Ken joked.

'You thinking of making many changes round here, Bet?' Kevin Webster asked.

'A few,' Bet replied guardedly, 'but slowly. I think Fred Gee proved that quick fixes don't work.'

Everybody laughed at her reference to the Rovers 'cuisine' that Fred had tried to introduce, and Bet looked around the bar. The pub might be dingy and old-fashioned, especially when she considered that most of the popular pubs in town had long since knocked all their small rooms into one big bar, but for all its shabbiness and failings the Rovers Return was hers. And she intended to make the brewery proud that they'd chosen her as its licensee.

'The girls are horrid to me at school,' Tracy complained to Ken and Deirdre, as they sat round the tea-table one Friday night. 'No one else in my class has a different name to their mam and dad. So why am I Tracy Langton?'

'I've explained that to you dozens of times, Tracy, love,' Deirdre said patiently. 'Ken's not your real dad. I married your father a long time before I married Ken. He lives in Amsterdam. You know he does because

663

he sends you lovely presents for your birthday and Christmas.'

'I can't remember seeing him,' Tracy said with immutable childish logic. She looked at Ken. 'You told me that you're my dad.'

'I am,' he said firmly. 'Your stepdad, but still your dad.'

'Then I want the same name as you, and I want a dog as well.'

'A dog is out of the question.' Ken picked the easier option Tracy had offered for discussion. 'We can't have a dog, love. What would it do when your mam and me are at work and you're at school?'

'Sleep in the house.'

'But a dog wouldn't sleep. He'd get bored and lonely and start chewing everything. The furniture—'

'Your clothes and toys,' Deirdre interrupted, as opposed to the idea as Ken was.

'I don't care.' Tracy wriggled down from the table and stamped her foot. 'I'm the only girl in my class without a dog and without the same name as their mam and dad.' Closer to a temper tantrum than tears, she ran out of the room.

'Come back here, Tracy, you haven't finished your tea,' Deirdre shouted after her.

'No,' came a muffled yell from upstairs.

'Leave her, love,' Ken suggested mildly. 'I'm the first

to admit that I don't want a dog but she's right about her surname. I know Ray refused to allow me to adopt her when we were first married, but that was over three years ago, and he hasn't seen Tracy since. He's good when it comes to sending Tracy presents on special occasions but it might be worth writing to ask him again. Perhaps you could tactfully remind him that Tracy's no longer a baby but a sensitive seven-year-old.'

'I'll write to him tonight.'

'I think you should.' Ken left the table and picked up Tracy's plate. 'She's hardly touched her tea. I'll take this up to her and try to explain why we can't have a dog.'

Brian tried to quell the queasy feeling in his stomach as he pulled out his keys and unlocked the front door of his mother's house. He hated having to admit that Gail had been right about his new friends. Squash nights had given way to evenings at the casino and he had been horrified to discover that he'd lost over eight hundred pounds. That was more than a full month's takings from the garage before the overheads had been paid. It was only a matter of time before Gail checked their savings account and realised the money was gone.

He dumped his coat in the hall and went into the living room. Gail was waiting for him, a thunderous expression on her face. She threw their savings book on to the table.

In the hope that she'd forgive him sooner if he confessed everything, he said, 'You were right about my friends. I didn't fit in. They . . . well, they started going to the casino,' he went on, unnerved by the expression on her face. 'They had so much more money than me. We all enjoyed ourselves at first, and I started to win but then . . . well, I didn't notice how much I'd lost until it was too late.'

'You've lost practically all of our savings. The money I waited on tables to earn. The money we were going to use as a deposit for a house. And you had the nerve to tell me last week that I should give up work to look after Nicky, when you're making less in the garage than I do in the café.'

'Love, I'm sorry.' He moved towards her but she retreated.

'I'm tired of sharing a house with your mother, Brian. And I'm tired of putting up with you and your extravagant ways, of never knowing where we are with money. Nicky and I deserve better. I've rented a bedsit for us and we're moving into it as soon as the taxi I've called arrives.'

'If that's the way you feel, then bloody well go,' he shouted, his temper roused.

'I am.'

'Over a few lousy quid!'

'It's much more than a few quid, Brian.' She turned

back to face him. 'All I want is a bit of peace and quiet and my own space to live my life the way I want to with Nicky.'

'And you're going to find that in a bedsit?' he sneered.

'If that's all you've left me with, yes. I'll do my job, I'll bring up Nicky, and I'll live alone because the one thing I'm sure of is that I don't want to spend the rest of my days living with your mother.'

'It's all down to you, Deirdre,' Alf Roberts said as they stood by side surveying the corner shop. 'You won the election fair and square, ousted me as councillor . . .'

'Only by seven votes,' Deirdre said magnanimously.

Angry when Ken turned down the local Labour Party's request that he stand as their candidate because it might conflict with articles he printed in the paper, and outraged when a child was knocked down on Rosamund Street, she'd fought for a public crossing in the street. When she was successful one of her supporters offered to help if she stood as a local independent candidate in the council elections. She'd accepted the challenge in the face of Ken's scepticism and to her own and everyone else's amazement won the seat.

'I wouldn't have got those seven votes if you hadn't pushed the planning permission for Mike Baldwin's and Alec Gilroy's nightclub through the planning committee.'

'Well, it's all water under the bridge now, and since

I've lost my seat on the council I'll have time to concentrate on the business. I'll have to anyway, now that you've given notice. When I took a long, hard look at all the other corner shops around Weatherfield, it made sense to turn this one into a mini-market. Expand the shop-floor area, increase the stock and wait for the turnover to double.'

'You're probably right,' Deirdre agreed. 'I'm always getting asked for things we don't have.'

'I hope you're used to it, because that'll happen a lot when the voters make demands on you, Councillor Barlow,' Alf said wryly.

'You getting Bill Webster in to do the alterations?'

'He's starting next week. He's promised to have everything finished in two weeks and then I'm inviting everyone in Coronation Street to come to the grand opening ceremony. Bet Lynch is opening it.'

'Bet Lynch?' Deirdre wondered if there was more to Bet and Alf's relationship than she knew about.

'She was Miss Weatherfield 1955.' He held out his hand to Deirdre. 'Come to the party?'

'We've been friends and neighbours too long to have any hard feelings.' Deirdre shook it. 'Ken, Tracy and I will be there.'

As soon as Deirdre walked into the house Ken charged downstairs in panic. 'Tracy's gone! I came home from work and she wasn't here. I've been up and down the street and searched the area, then came home and stripped her bed. I found this under her pillow.' He thrust a folded piece of paper at Deirdre.

'You read it,' she begged, her heart pounding.

'"I've emptied my moneybox and taken a train to Newcastle to visit Susan, she'll let me have a dog. Tracy."'

Trembling, Deirdre sat on the bottom stair. 'I'll get the first train to Newcastle. You stay here in case she comes back – and we should tell the police. She's only nine years old – anything could happen!'

The phone rang and Deirdre ran to answer it. Ken followed and she balanced the receiver between them.

'She's safe, Dad, she's with me.'

Ken had never been so glad to hear his daughter Susan's voice.

'If it's all right with you and Deirdre I'll keep her here with me tonight and bring her back tomorrow on the train. I could stay for a few days.'

'We'd love to have you,' Deirdre broke in fervently, then buried her head in her hands.

Ken took the receiver from her. 'Yes, Susan, love, of course it's all right for you to stay. It'll be wonderful to have both my daughters home where they belong.'

'I tried to explain to Tracy that it wouldn't be fair to expect a dog to live with you, but perhaps a kitten or a budgie would be all right.'

'We'll talk about it when you get here,' Ken said quietly. 'Safe journey.'

In her bedsit, Gail latched the security chain on the door before she opened it. It was Brian. 'What are you doing here?'

'I wanted to see you. Can I come in?'

'No, it's late and Nicky's asleep.'

'My mother threw me out.'

'She came round to the café to tell me that you were running around with other women.'

'I wouldn't have if you hadn't left me,' he said. 'Look, Gail, we can't talk through the door like this. Let me in.'

'Wait a moment.'

Brian half expected Gail to shut the door in his face, but she picked up her keys, unfastened the chain, stepped outside and closed the door quietly behind her.

'I had a word with Deirdre Barlow, she's our councillor now.'

'I keep up with the news in the café,' Gail informed him.

Undeterred, he continued, 'Deirdre pulled a few strings with the council. She's got us a three-bedroom council house in Hammond Road. I know it won't be as good as having our own place, but please,' he held out his hand to her, 'come back, Gail, if only for Nicky's sake.'

'And your friends?'

Her face was blank and he couldn't read anything in her eyes. 'I haven't seen them since you left. If you come back, I promise I'll never see them again. I'll work hard, pay the rent and save enough for a deposit on a new house. Please, Gail, I miss you and Nicky. I need both of you – I love you.'

'Let me know when you get the keys to the house.' She opened the door of the bedsit and slipped back inside, leaving him standing on the doormat.

'So,' Audrey Potter swung her shapely leg back and forth as she sat on a bar stool and eyed Alf Roberts, 'he's the man with the money.'

'I don't know about money.' Gail offered Ivy and her mother her packet of crisps. 'Alf's just turned the corner shop into a mini-market and he paid for the food for this party but that doesn't make him Rockefeller.'

'Depends who you're comparing him with.' Ivy glanced at Mike Baldwin, who was standing at the bar with Alec Gilroy, the manager of the Graffiti Club. 'I wonder what those two are cooking up. It'll be no good, I know.'

'Drinks, ladies.'

Before Brian could set the tray down on their table, Audrey had picked up her whisky and orange.

'I think I'll go and get acquainted with one or two of

your neighbours.' She left the table and, swinging her hips, made her way over to where Alf Roberts was talking to Bet.

She stood back for moment and watched them: from the way Bet was flirting with half of the male customers in the bar she knew she was no threat. Bet wasn't treating Alf any differently from her other customers. True, he wasn't much to look at: overweight, with the features of a doughboy, but he was well groomed and expensively dressed and she was tired of grafting for a living and even more so of lodging in other people's houses.

When Bet went to serve a customer Audrey made her move. She sat on the stool next to Alf's and said, 'Hello, I'm Audrey Potter.'

'Pleased to meet you.' He held out his hand. 'Alf Roberts.'

'I know.' She took his hand and held it without shaking it. 'Tell me, are you interested in anything besides mini-markets?'

'Your mother's on a hiding to nothing there,' Ivy pronounced scornfully. 'It's disgusting. No woman should fling herself at a man the way she is throwing herself at Alf Roberts.'

'Audrey's just having a bit of fun, Mam.' Brian knew that Gail was sensitive about the way her mother carried on. He glanced at his wife as she continued to watch Audrey chat up Alf.

'It's obvious he can see right through Audrey's act,' Ivy snapped. 'She's making a right fool of herself.'

Gail shook her head. 'I'm not so sure, Ivy, but time will tell.'

'You look peaky, Hilda,' Ivy said tactlessly as they both shopped in the mini-market one Saturday morning.

'It's probably the strain of looking after Stan,' Hilda replied. Even her voice sounded tired.

'How is he?' Alf asked, although he, like the rest of the residents of Coronation Street, thought that whatever was wrong with Stan had to be trivial. The man had moaned about non-existent ailments for most of his life in an attempt to get out of working. Still – he hadn't seen him down the Rovers lately and that was unusual.

'He's really bad, Alf. Stan hasn't got out of bed to come downstairs in weeks.' Hilda looked along the shelf and wavered between a tin of tuna and one of salmon for their tea. Tuna was so much cheaper, but Stan loved salmon and he hadn't been eating lately. Perhaps it would be worth the extra expense to tempt his appetite.

'Hello, Hilda.' Deirdre breezed in with Tracy. 'One packet of sweets and one comic, mind,' she warned her daughter as Tracy made a beeline for the magazine stand.

'Hello, Deirdre . . .' Hilda's face turned from pale to

ashen. Without warning she slumped to the floor. Deirdre caught her just in time to prevent her head from hitting the freezer.

Chapter Thirty-Nine

Hilda woke to see Eddie Yeats sitting next to her. 'Where am I?' she mumbled, staring up at an unfamiliar ceiling.

'In hospital.' Eddie leant over her. 'They sent for me to see if I could talk some sense into you. It's bad enough Stan being ill without you wearing yourself to a frazzle trying to look after him. When you collapsed in the corner shop two days ago, Deirdre Barlow had to send for two ambulances to bring you both into hospital. The doctors told me you're suffering from complete mental and physical exhaustion and you have to rest. If you don't . . .' Eddie shook his head, unable to come up with any punishment dire enough if Hilda dared to defy her medical advisers.

'Stan?' she croaked hoarsely. 'How is Stan?'

Eddie had been dreading her asking. Stan had been ill for weeks, but even when he'd read Hilda's accounts of Stan's illness in Hilda's letters he hadn't thought his friend's illness was serious. Stan was always looking for – and finding – aches and pains that prevented him from working, but never from drinking in the Rovers.

'I'm sorry, Hilda,' he reached for her hand, 'he died last night. It was peaceful. He just went to sleep and never woke up.'

Hilda didn't burst into hysteria as he expected her to. Instead she continued to stare at him as tears trickled down her cheeks. 'I want him buried properly. In a real grave with a place for me beside him when the time comes.' She struggled to compose herself. 'It won't be too long now.'

'Cremation would be a lot cheaper,' Eddie said tactfully, wishing he could think of some comforting words to say.

'I don't care how much it costs. I'll sell the house if I have to. I want my Stan to be buried properly, and I don't want no stinting on the funeral neither.' She glared at Eddie. 'I mean it.'

He patted her hand. 'If that's what you want, love, I'll help you organise it.'

'You promise me. I know you, Eddie, if you promise to do something you will. And it's for Stan as much as me.' Hilda struggled to sit up in the bed.

'I promise, but only if *you* promise *me* that you'll stay where you are for the moment.' He pushed her gently back on to the pillows. Unable to face her grief any longer, he shifted his gaze to the window behind her bed. 'But it's going to be a cold, grey funeral,' he muttered, as the first snowflakes of November fluttered down from the night sky.

'Susan's idea of getting Tracy a kitten was a good one,' Deirdre said to Ken, as she made a newspaper ball and tossed it to the newest member of the Barlow household. Tracy had insisted that Susan put her to bed and the pair had gone upstairs.

'She's turned into quite the diplomat.' Ken still found it amazing that he had a grown-up daughter. 'You get on well with her, don't you?'

'Of course I do.' Deirdre glanced up from Tracy's skirt which she was lengthening. 'Why do you ask?'

'I took Susan in to work with me today. She seemed really interested in what we're trying to do with the *Recorder*. I've been thinking of taking on a new reporter anyway.'

'You offered her a job?'

'No, love. I wouldn't do that without discussing it with you first. It just occurred to me that if she came to work on the paper she could live here with us.'

'I'd like nothing better,' Deirdre said. 'But you'd have to ask Susan how she feels about it. It would have to be her decision.'

'What would be Susan's decision?' Susan walked into the room.

'I wondered if you'd like to work on the paper with me. We're thinking of taking on a junior reporter anyway,' Ken explained. 'And if you took the job, Deirdre and I would like you to live here with us.'

'I'd have to go back to Newcastle to clear my bedsit first and that would take about ten minutes, plus the train time to get there and back, but as soon as that's done I'm all yours.' She smiled as she looked from Deirdre to Ken. 'Anyone like a cup of tea?'

'I'd love one,' Deirdre said. 'Ken would see a body die of thirst before he offered, no offence, darling.'

'None taken,' Ken muttered mechanically. He had suddenly seen the downside of living in a houseful of women.

'So, as I was saying, Alf and me have decided to get married two days before Christmas,' Audrey chattered, as she and Ivy helped Gail clean her new council house. 'That way we can spend Christmas in Paris.' Audrey unwrapped Gail's best china from the newspaper and put it in the sink.

'You sure you're not rushing into this, Mam?' Gail asked.

'Not at all. Alf and I have just fallen head over heels in love. You should remember how that feels. I've not forgotten what you were like when you were courting Brian even if you have. My life is *perfect*. I can't believe how miserable I was only a few weeks ago.' Audrey sighed, then looked at Ivy, who was cleaning the inside of the kitchen windows while Brian cleaned the outside. 'You remember what it's like to be in love, Ivy, don't you?'

'I remember, all right,' Ivy snapped, 'but I didn't go rushing into anything. My Bert and me were engaged a full two years before we married, not five weeks.'

'It must have been hard to wait that long.'

Ivy gave Audrey an old-fashioned look. 'Not that hard.'

'Well, Alf and me are both mature people.' Audrey turned Ivy's disapproval to her advantage. 'And we've nothing to worry about or wait for. Alf's promised to look for a really nice detached house in an upmarket area when we come back from honeymoon.' She glanced around her daughter's new council house. 'And you'll be most welcome to visit us any time you want to, Gail love. And you can bring Nicky.'

'My landlady's really nice,' Kevin Webster said to Sally Seddon, as he drove her down Coronation Street in his van. 'She offered to take me in as a lodger when my dad took a building contract in Germany and left with my sister. I didn't even have to ask if I could move in with her. She knew that I couldn't go with them because I have an apprenticeship at Brian Tilsley's garage. And she's gone out of her way to make me feel at home. She's only just lost her husband – perhaps you know her? Hilda – Hilda Ogden.'

'I've heard the name.' Sally dabbed ineffectually at her muddy tights with her handkerchief.

'I'm sorry, I didn't mean to soak you as I drove past the bus stop,' Kevin said ruefully.

'It wasn't your fault. There was a hole in the road.'

'That doesn't make me feel any better about making you miss a job interview. I know how hard jobs are to come by round here. It took me ages to find an apprenticeship. I'd just about given up hope of finding one when Brian Tilsley took me on.' He stopped the van outside Hilda's house and turned off the engine. Then he got out and walked round to help Sally out of the passenger seat.

Hilda had been glad to take in Kevin as a lodger. After Stan died the house had seemed unnaturally quiet, but when she walked out of the kitchen and saw Sally Seddon, covered with mud, standing in front of her fire she was incensed. She knew the Seddon family by reputation. But, then, everyone in Weatherfield did.

'What are you doing here at this time of day?' she asked Kevin coldly.

'I drove through a puddle and soaked Sally at the bus stop.' Kevin explained. 'I told her you wouldn't mind me bringing her here to get cleaned up before I drive her home. I could hardly leave her on the street the way she was.'

'I suppose not.' Hilda sniffed.

'Well, I'll leave you two ladies to it.' Kevin realised that there was no way Sally could take off her tights if he remained in the living room, so he went into the kitchen. 'I'll make us all a cup of tea, shall I?' He closed the door behind him.

'I can see what you're up to, young lady.' Hilda gave Sally a stern look.

'I'm not up to anything,' Sally protested. 'Kevin soaked me and he offered to bring me back here so I could clean up my tights.'

'That's because Kevin is a nice, innocent boy,' Hilda said, 'and that's why I want you to stay well away from him. Understand?'

'No, Mrs Ogden, I don't,' Sally said. 'I'm a nice girl, honest. Just give me a chance to prove it.'

'A sackload of letters came into the *Recorder* office today about that story you wrote on the hostel for the home-less, Susan,' Ken said, as they were having tea at the end of the day. Susan had been out all day doing interviews for features while he had been wrestling with manage-ment meetings. He envied her the reporter's life.

'You have a well-developed social conscience, like

your father.' Deirdre passed Susan a slice of apple tart and the jug of custard.

'From the reception your articles are getting in the paper, and the friends you're making round here, I think we can safely say that you're settled in Weatherfield.' Ken took the jug from his daughter and poured custard over his own and Tracy's tart.

'My life's taken a definite turn for the better since I've been here,' Susan agreed blithely. 'I've even found myself a boyfriend.' She glanced at her watch. 'And as I'm meeting him in twenty minutes for our fourth date, I'd better get a move on.'

'Why haven't we heard about this boyfriend before?' Ken asked suspiciously.

'Because three dates mean nothing, but after the third there's a chance it could get serious. Am I right?' Deirdre gave Susan a conspiratorial glance.

'You are.'

'And,' Deirdre continued, 'given that you're the over-bearing, interfering father—'

'I am not,' Ken protested.

'Deirdre was only talking about fathers in general. Really, Dad, you've nothing to worry about.' Susan spooned the last of her pudding into her mouth. 'Mike's wonderful. A real gentleman'

'Mike?' Ken's throat went dry.

'Mike Baldwin. You probably know him – he owns a factory around here.' Oblivious to Ken and Deirdre's horror, Susan left the table. 'Don't wait up for me. I might be late. 'Bye, Dad, Deirdre, Tracy sweetheart.' She kissed them, then hurried upstairs.

'Can I go upstairs and watch Susan put her make-up on?' Tracy asked.

Deirdre nodded, too terrified to look at Ken. They sat in silence for ten minutes until they heard the front door bang behind Susan.

Ken pushed back his chair. 'I'll go after her.'

'You'll do nothing of the kind,' Deirdre said.

'She's a child – she knows nothing about men. She's an innocent—'

'She's a grown woman, Ken.'

'Mike Baldwin doesn't give a fig about Susan!' Ken shouted. 'He's using her to hurt me because you stayed with me and rejected him!'

Deirdre winced at the painful reminder of her past. 'He could really be fond of her.'

'Like he was fond of you?' Ken sneered. 'I know him. I know his type. He uses people like chess players use pawns – I'm going after them.' He left the table.

'Please, Ken, don't,' Deirdre begged, 'not tonight. If you go after them now, you and Mike will end up brawling in the street, and what will that accomplish?

You need to think about it first, to talk to Susan sensibly. If you don't you'll lose her.'

'I'll think about it, but only until tomorrow morning.'

'You sure you know what you're doing down there?' Bet Lynch asked Jack Duckworth as he attempted to change a fuse in the cellar of the Rovers.

'I know exactly what I'm doing,' he called back testily. No sooner had he spoken than lights flooded on in the bar to the cheers of the regulars.

'I think that's earned me a pint on the house,' Jack said, as he climbed back up the stairs.

'Only one, mind,' Bet lifted down a mug. 'Enjoy your honeymoon, Audrey?' she asked, as the new Mrs Roberts walked back into the bar from the ladies'.

'Paris was wonderful,' Audrey gushed.

'I bet it was, and cold over Christmas, I should think,' Bet sniped.

'Not that I noticed.'

'I heard your Alf has bought number eleven.' Bet, like all the women in Coronation Street, had been subjected to Audrey's tales of the 'superior' detached house he was going to buy in an upmarket area. And, like the other women, she wasn't above reminding Audrey that she was no better than the rest of them.

Audrey fought to conceal her disappointment that Alf had bought such an ordinary house and, what was worse, expected her to turn their front parlour into a hairdressing salon. But she still tried to put Bet down. 'Alf and I have great plans for number eleven.'

'He's bought your drinks and a packet of your favourite smoky bacon crisps – it's not champagne and caviar but, then, they say a change is as good as a rest,' Bet said as Audrey swept over to the table Alf had commandeered.

'You shouldn't complain about Hilda,' Sally reprimanded Kevin as they drove back from a pop concert at five o'clock in the morning. 'She's been very good to you – and me. Allowing me to move in and sending my mam packing when she came round to collect my dole money for my dad.'

'I've every right to complain when she makes me sleep on the sofa downstairs and sits up half the night listening for creaks on the landing.'

'We've always the back of the van, like tonight, haven't we?' Sally moved over and rested her head on Kevin's shoulder.

'That's not the same as snuggling up all night together,' he complained. 'And I care for you, I really do, Sally. The only person left in my life is you, now that my father and the rest of my family have gone to Germany. I want to marry you.'

'On what?' she laughed. 'We haven't a bean between us.'

'A register-office wedding can't cost much, and if we

were married Hilda would let us sleep together. What do you say?'

'I say that Hilda might not like the idea of having a married couple as lodgers. Oh, my God, look at that smoke coming from the Rovers.'

Kevin slammed on the brakes, jumped out of the van and ran towards the pub. 'I'll get Bet out, you phone nine-nine-nine,' he yelled.

Sally rushed to the telephone box while Kevin smashed his way through a ground-floor window and climbed into the pub.

As soon as her call had been logged, Sally ran up and down the street banging on doors and screaming, 'Fire!'

She was trying to run into the Rovers when Ken Barlow came out into the street in his dressing-gown. He ran up to her and gripped her firmly by the waist. Several of the residents were streaming out of their houses to find out what was going on.

'Let me go!' Hysterical, Sally tried to fight free. 'Kevin's inside.'

'You called the fire brigade?' Alf Roberts asked.

'Yes, but Kevin's inside – he went in to get Bet!'

'Hold her, Alf.' Ken passed Sally to him.

'You can't go in there, Ken.' Alan Bradley, Rita Fairclough's new live-in lover, grabbed his arm. 'Can't you see those flames have reached the upstairs? You wouldn't be able to do a thing to save yourself or anyone else if you went in there.'

Deirdre crept close to Ken. She knew from his stricken expression that he was thinking of his first wife, Valerie.

A fire engine hurtled around the corner and halted with a screech of brakes outside the pub.

'Everyone back,' an officer shouted, forcing the residents to the pavement on the opposite side of the road. 'Leave it to the experts, love,' he said to Sally who was trying to escape Alf's grip to run into the pub. 'I take it there are people inside?'

'Two,' Ken told him. 'The pub landlady and a young man who went in to rescue her.'

'Do any of you know which is her bedroom?'

'There.' Hilda pointed it out.

'Why don't they go inside?' Sally whispered, as men swarmed round the engine, running out hoses and putting on protective clothing.

'They will, love, soon, I promise you.' Ken wondered if help had, again, come too late.

Everyone watched as the flames licked higher through the building, breaking through the roof as smoke clouded out of every window. The air was filled with the sound of shattering glass, and they could feel the heat even from across the road. Hilda moved close to Sally, who clutched her arm so hard that Hilda thought it might break.

'He'll be all right, love,' Hilda murmured, needing to

believe it herself. Kevin was so young, so bright, so full of life . . .

Three firemen with breathing apparatus climbed the engine's ladder while another directed it towards the window of Bet's bedroom. To the terrified onlookers, they moved with irritating slowness. Sally began to scream even louder.

'*Kevin!*'

Two firemen entered through the broken window. A few moments later, one emerged with a figure slumped over his shoulder.

'He's moving, love,' Ken said, as Kevin was handed to the fireman on the ladder.

A few seconds later the second fireman emerged with Bet.

The officer who had taken control of the proceedings walked over to the engine. He returned a few moments later.

'Both rescued and rescuers are fine, but we've called an ambulance. It might be as well to get them checked over to make sure. Hey, where are you going, young lady?' he shouted to Sally, as she broke free from Alf.

'To tell Kevin I love him and I'll marry him. He asked me tonight,' she called back.

The next morning, exhausted from his broken night, Ken left his house and walked into Mike Baldwin's factory, going straight to Mike's office.

Mike grinned when he saw him. 'Good morning, Ken,' he greeted him expansively. 'To what do I owe the pleasure of this visit?'

'As if you didn't know.' Ken drew back his fist and punched Mike as hard as he could, to the delight of Ivy Tilsley who was standing behind him. 'Stay away from my daughter,' he growled.

Mike toppled from his chair, then rose slowly to his feet, rubbing his chin. 'And if I don't want to?'

'I'll tell her exactly what you're like. And that you seduced Deirdre.'

'If I remember rightly, Deirdre didn't mind being seduced by me at all. It made a nice change from her boring existence with you.'

Ken clenched his fists.

'Go on, hit me again, Ken – you know you want to.'

Not trusting himself to remain there a moment longer, Ken left the factory and drove straight to the office of the *Recorder*. He grabbed Susan's hand, pulled her into his office and closed the door.

'Dad, what on earth is the matter?' she asked in bewilderment.

'Mike Baldwin,' he answered flatly. 'You can't see him any more.'

'Why ever not?'

'Because he's no good. He hasn't an ounce of integrity in his entire body. He makes money by skating just this side of the law. And he's a womaniser who seduces every girl he comes across who takes his fancy. Whether they're married or not. And I should know. Your stepmother was one of them,' he revealed harshly.

'Deirdre . . . Mike had an affair with Deirdre?' She reeled back against the wall.

'He did.' Ken sank down into the chair behind his desk.

'If Mike had an affair with Deirdre . . .'

'I just told you he did.'

'Then she must be as much to blame as him,' Susan said hotly. 'And you can't stop me seeing the man I love just because he slept with your wife.'

'Susan!'

'You've never been much of a father to Peter or me. Don't think you can start getting heavy-handed with us now.'

'Susan . . .' Ken looked up and saw that he was talking to the door.

'Yes, I had an affair with your stepmother,' Mike confessed to Susan, as they sat at one of the back tables in the Graffiti Club. As the brewery had decided to take advantage of the fire damage to remodel the Rovers, the manager of the Graffiti, Alec Gilroy, had suggested that the residents of Coronation Street use his club as a temporary local.

'When?' she asked baldly.

'It happened the year after she married your father.

They were going through a rough patch and I fell in love with her.'

'Are you still in love with her?'

'No,' he replied emphatically. 'But when we were sleeping together, I thought enough of her to ask her to come and live with me. She promised she would, but she changed her mind and stayed with your father. Whatever your father has told you, it wasn't a casual fling between Deirdre and me.' Mike turned his chair to face Susan and took both her hands in his. 'I thought I loved her but now I wonder if I ever knew what love was before I met you. Marry me. I know you're younger than me, young and fresh and unspoiled, and I'm a cynical, conniving bastard, but no other woman has ever made me feel the way I feel about you. What do you say? Could you consider marrying an old fogey like me?'

'My father wouldn't like it.'

'I'm not asking your father to marry me.'

'I couldn't carry on living with him if I said yes to you now.'

'Then I'll drive you to Coronation Street, you can pick up your things and move in with me right now. What do you say?'

'I say yes.' Susan finished her drink and left her chair.

'Susan may have moved out of the house but you'll see her at work tomorrow,' Deirdre reminded Ken. 'And I warn you, if you carry on opposing her relationship with Mike, you'll risk losing her. And for ever this time.'

'You're right,' Ken agreed reluctantly. 'I should never have hit him but I lost my temper. It was his arrogance that did it. He sat there goading me, full of himself, reminding me that he'd had Susan . . . and you.'

Deirdre wondered if Ken had ever really forgiven her for her affair with Mike, but he was too wrapped up in his own pain to consider hers.

'If I hadn't called to see him this morning, I wouldn't have hit him, and I wouldn't have spoken to Susan about him and she wouldn't have moved out of the house and in with him . . .'

'You can't keep torturing yourself with might-have-beens, Ken.'

'I've never been much of a father to her or Peter.'

'None of this is your fault.' Deirdre went to him but he seemed oblivious to her touch. 'You did what you thought was best at the time for your children. And Susan and Peter had a stable, happy upbringing with their grandparents. They've both said that.'

'Yes, they have, haven't they?' Ken replied, prepared to clutch at the straws Deirdre offered.

'Look, you'll be seeing Susan tomorrow. The twins' twenty-first birthday is in a couple of weeks. Why don't you offer to forget your differences and throw them a party? You have to keep talking to her, Ken.'

'If I do that, there's hope she'll see sense.' He looked at Deirdre, but she couldn't reassure him. She herself had come under Mike Baldwin's spell once and she had been neither as young nor as naïve as Susan. If Susan was really in love with him then nothing would stop her doing what she wanted. Deirdre knew that, but she couldn't face telling Ken the unpalatable truth.

Chapter Forty

'You still managing to talk to Susan?' Deirdre asked Ken, after she'd put Tracy to bed.

'Just about. At least, I talk to her about work and the kind of birthday party she and Peter want in April.'

'Not Mike?' Deirdre asked warily.

'No.'

'Well, we did have some good news today.' Deirdre held up an envelope that had come in the post that morning. 'Tracy's adoption came through. As from now, she is no longer Tracy Langton but Tracy Barlow.'

'That *is* good news.' Ken smiled for the first time in days.

'Tracy was that excited when I told her. When she comes back from Brownies, she'll want to thank you herself. She's even drawn a picture in honour of the occasion.'

'They've done a good job of renovating the Rovers. I would never have known it was the same place I drank in the last time I was here,' Peter Barlow said to Ken, as they picked up their drinks from the bar, which had been transformed. With its stained-glass panels, brocade wall-paper and new dark wood seating and tables it was unrecognisable as the shabby, rather down-at-heel pub Bet Lynch had taken over a few months before.

'They've done a good job, but they took their time over it. The place was closed for eight weeks.' Ken had to shout above the band he'd hired to play at the twins' twenty-first. For all that the room was packed with guests doing their utmost to have a good time, he was finding it difficult to ignore the way Mike Baldwin had clung to Susan all evening.

He was glad he'd opted to follow Deirdre's suggestion of a party for the twins, although his present of a party seemed trivial in comparison to the brand-new car Mike had given Susan – along with an engagement ring. When Deirdre had warned him not to spoil the evening by creating a scene when Susan had shown him the ring, he had tried to delay Susan's wedding by telling her that he couldn't afford to pay for it for at least a year after funding the party. But his plan had backfired when Mike had offered to pay for both wedding and reception. Mike had even given Susan a date, having already booked the church, a reception in the biggest hotel in Manchester and flights to a luxury hotel in the Caribbean for their honeymoon. Susan had been delighted, but already Ken was dreading what May 14 would bring.

As he continued to watch Susan, he thought back to the day she and Peter had been born. It didn't seem very long ago, and he felt as though he was losing her before he'd even had her.

'Alec Gilroy seems very interested in you, Bet,' Ivy Tilsley commented as Bet poured sherry for her, Hilda Ogden, Vera Duckworth and Rita Fairclough.

'He's just out for a good time, same as everyone else,' Bet said dismissively but she narrowed her eyes as she looked back at Alec over her shoulder. After the brewery had paid a fortune to remodel the Rovers, it had closed the Graffiti Club in the hope of killing all opposing trade. Alec had been made redundant and one of the draymen had told her that the brewery had warned Alec there was no chance of him taking over another pub or club in the near future as there were no vacancies. Alec hadn't seemed too bothered about losing his job: since the Graffiti had closed he had taken to hanging around the Rovers. Bet was beginning to wonder if he was interested in her or the pub she ran.

'What's a nice boy like Kevin Webster doing with a tart like Sally Seddon?' Ivy asked Hilda, knowing that Hilda had grown close to the girl since she had moved in with her and Kevin.

'They're a nice young couple,' Hilda retorted defensively.

'I don't know how you can call any Seddon nice,' Ivy carped.

'The poor girl never had a chance. The first week she moved in with me, her mother came round to get her dole money to give to her father. They've taken every penny she's ever earned.'

'Earned!' Ivy exclaimed. 'She's on the dole.'

'She was good enough to take over my cleaning jobs for me the other week when I was ill,' Hilda retorted hotly, 'and if you ask me, she's every bit good enough for Kevin. They suit each other.'

'They really intend to get married?' Rita asked, in an attempt to defuse the mounting tension between Ivy and Hilda.

'I think they will,' Hilda said.

Ivy looked at Mike and Susan. 'Well, they're better suited in age than some, that's all I can say. Talk about May and December – Mike Baldwin's got himself a right little gold-digger there. But, then,' she gave a theatrical sigh, 'Susan Barlow'll end up in clover, not like the rest of us who have to graft in Mike's factory for next to nothing every day.'

'That's a terrible thing to say, Ivy,' Emily Bishop reprimanded her as she passed their table. 'I happen to know that Susan is very much in love with Mr Baldwin and we should be wishing them well.' Then she made a beeline for Ken and Deirdre's table. If anyone needed her support for the rest of the evening, they did.

'No, Susan,' Ken said firmly. 'If you want to marry Mike Baldwin in three weeks' time, go ahead. You're of age and you can do it without my blessing. I won't give you away and I won't be there. Those are my final words on the subject.'

Peter saw his sister run to Mike in tears. He left his date and went to his father. 'What have you said to upset Susan?'

'That I won't go to her wedding.' Ken picked up his beer and drank half of it. It left a peculiar taste in his mouth. 'I refuse to stand back and watch her throw her life away on a man like that.'

'Susan doesn't see it that way,' Peter argued. 'She's in love with him.'

'More fool her. And you approve?' Ken challenged his son.

'It's not for me to approve or disapprove,' Peter said coldly. 'We're talking about Susan's happiness.'

'And you think she'll be happy with a man like that?'

'I don't think she'll be happy full stop if you carry on the way you have been about her and Mike. You've never been a great father to either of us, we hardly saw you when we growing up—'

'I did—'

'I know,' Peter cut in ruthlessly. 'You did what you

thought was best after Mam died. And Gran and Granddad did a great job of bringing us up and you didn't have to see us too often.'

The criticism was justified, and Ken had the grace to remain silent.

'But this should be the happiest time of Susan's life,' Peter continued. 'And all you can go on about is some stupid feud between you and Baldwin. Tell me, is whatever it is that's between you and him really more important than the way Susan will feel on her wedding day?'

Deirdre stood watching in the background as Peter tackled his father. She knew her husband, and could see that he had taken to heart everything Peter had said. And when he crossed the bar to talk to Susan she knew that the whole family would be attending Susan's wedding. She only wished it could be as a happy one.

'My cousin Ian called in the garage today to say goodbye,' Brian said casually to Gail as he came home from work. 'He's off back to Australia tomorrow. I thought he might have stayed longer, but it's probably just as well he's going back. All he could talk about was Australia and what a great place it is. You know something? After talking to him, I think we should consider emigrating to Perth.'

'I could never emigrate.' Gail's hands shook as she laid the table.

'Why not?' Brian asked, mystified. 'It's not as if we've much here besides the garage, and I could sell that for a good price tomorrow. We live in a council house, you've a job managing a café but you could pick up as good a job, if not better, in Australia.'

'I'm not going, and that's final.'

'I don't understand.'

'It's not just Australia.' Gail gripped a knife so hard it cut into her palm. 'It's Ian.'

'My cousin. For pity's sake, what's wrong with Ian?'

'Please, Brian, let me finish.'

Ivy had called in on her way home from work to tell Gail that she knew about her brief affair with Brian's cousin. Someone – Ivy didn't say who – had seen Ian pulling the bedroom curtains one night when Brian had been working away on a repair job for one of the big haulage companies. It had been useless for Gail to protest that it had been more of a one-night impulse fling than a full-blown affair: Ivy hadn't been in a mood to listen. But Gail didn't doubt Ivy would tell Brian the little she knew at the first opportunity she got, which was why she'd decided to confess. But there was something else – something Brian's mother didn't know.

'You've always said you want to live further away from my mother,' Brian said when she fell silent. 'Well, I can't think of anywhere further than Perth.'

'I said it's not just your mother.' Gail paced to the

window, pushed back the curtains and looked out at the garden in the gathering twilight. 'I had an affair – a fling,' she corrected herself, 'with Ian.'

'You what?'

'And I'm pregnant. I don't know if you or Ian is the father.'

'Ian,' he repeated slowly. 'You had an affair with my cousin?'

'Not an affair, a fling. It didn't mean anything.'

'You slept with my cousin and now you tell me it didn't mean anything!' he roared.

'You had an affair when you went abroad after Nicky was born.'

'And you did this to get back at me. Is that it?' he questioned furiously.

'No. I made a mistake, Brian, and I'm admitting it. I'm sorry. I can't undo what's been done. But Ian has gone back—'

'And left you carrying his bastard.'

'The baby might be yours.'

'And it might not be.' He ran his hands through his hair. 'I can't take this. I'm leaving. If Nicky wants me, I'll be at my mother's.' He left the room and ran up the stairs. She heard the bedroom door open, the scrape of a suitcase being taken down from the top of the wardrobe and pulled along the floor.

She crouched on the sofa and buried her head in her

hands. If everything had been right between her and Brian, she would never have slept with Ian. She began to wonder if things had been right between them since Nicky had been born – in retrospect, even before then, they'd always seemed to be lurching from one crisis to another.

'I've heard that the Paul Getty of Weatherfield has been sacking his employees again,' Ken crowed to Susan as they sat in the *Recorder* office. 'Two in one day. It must be a record. George Wardle for clocking in Pauline Walsh when she wasn't there, and Vera Duckworth for sneaking off to do some shopping. Perhaps we should run an article on the modern-day Scrooge.'

'That's it!' Susan dropped a pencil on to her desk, picked up her coat and put it on.

'What's "it"?'

'That's one remark too many. I can't stand you going on about my husband any longer. I'm leaving.'

'Susan . . .'

She picked up her handbag and went to the door.

'Don't be hasty.' Ken recognised his own stubbornness in his daughter. 'You will come and see us at the weekend?'

'If you can manage to have me in your house for five minutes without mentioning Mike's name, I'll think about visiting Tracy and Deirdre. They accept my marriage.'

Susan left the office, walked to her car and drove straight to Mike's factory. She knew she wouldn't get any sympathy from her husband for walking out of her job on the *Recorder*. Mike had been nagging her for weeks to start a family. He didn't understand that she wanted a job more than she wanted children because she felt that there'd be plenty of time to have them later, when she'd done everything she wanted to with her life.

'This is a pleasant surprise.' Mike caught Susan's hand and pulled her round his desk on to his lap. 'Tell me, what is my gorgeous and glamorous wife doing visiting me at this time of day?'

'She has just walked out of her job.'

'Wonderful.' He smiled gleefully. 'Let's get pregnant – now, this minute.'

'Slow down, lover-boy.' She pushed his hands away as he tried to unbutton her blouse. 'I've been thinking.'

'You don't need to do that to get pregnant.' He kissed the soft skin below her ear.

'Be serious.'

'Why?'

'I want to start a company to make children's clothes.'

'You want to design clothes?'

'Why not? I was good at art and needlework at school. I think I'd be good at it. I know it would take money . . .'

'Yes, it would. A lot of money.' He hugged her close.

703

'Tell you what, I'll give you the money and you can set up your company as a subsidiary of mine. Making all those tiny clothes for tiny beings might give you some ideas about us having a family of our own.'

Ian Latimer looked through the window of the café, searching for Gail. The place was crowded. A rather clumsy waitress moved awkwardly between the tables. Then, suddenly, he saw her standing behind the till talking to an elderly gentleman as she took his money and presented him with a receipt. Of choice, he would have preferred to confront Gail in private, but having travelled halfway round the world in response to the letter he had received from Audrey Roberts, he had no intention of leaving without seeing her. He pushed open the door, walked past the man Gail had served and went to the counter.

'Hello, Gail.'

Gail couldn't believe her eyes. 'You're in Australia.'

'I was in Australia, until your mother wrote and told me you were having my baby.' He eyed her waistline. 'You're pregnant.'

'The baby might be Brian's.'

'Is it?'

'I don't know,' she admitted, shattered by his unexpected arrival and the admission he had wrung out of her.

'Look, Gail—'

'Do you mind, young man?' A woman pushed past Ian

to the till. 'I want to pay my bill. One tea and a toasted cheese sandwich.'

Aware of Ian standing, watching her, Gail she took the money the woman offered and handed over her change.

'Is there somewhere quiet we can go?' Ian asked, when the woman had left.

'It's the lunch-hour rush. I can't leave Mavis to cope on her own.'

'Then I suppose I'll have to say what I came to say right here and now. Marry me, Gail.'

'I'm still married.'

'Your mother told me in her letter that Brian offered to take you back if you had an abortion.'

'I couldn't do that to my baby.'

'So she told me. She also told me that Brian's divorcing you and it will be finalised next month. Marry me, Gail. Bring Nicky and the baby and come to Australia with me. We can start a new life. You have no idea what it's like out there. It's a new, clean, fresh country and it's beautiful . . .'

'You make it sound so easy,' she murmured wistfully.

'It is.'

'I can't just up and leave. All my family are here and Nicky's started school—'

'We have schools in Australia, good ones too,' he interrupted.

Another voice spoke behind them. 'My mother said

she'd seen you sniffing around. I should have known I'd find you here.'

Gail and Ian turned to see Brian with his fists clenched in the doorway of the café.

He walked towards Ian and Gail shouted as Brian lashed out. Her warning came too late: Brian hit Ian on the side of the face. He reeled backwards, crashing into a table and startling three old ladies who'd been exchanging gossip over cups of tea. Their crockery went flying and all three jumped to their feet and screamed in terror as Ian staggered upright.

'Brian, no!' Gail yelled, as he followed his first punch with another.

'I should have done that the last time he was here. To think I let you into my house, introduced you to my wife . . .' Brian cornered Ian as he backed towards the door. Gail fell to her knees and moaned.

Mavis ran up to her. She took one look at Gail, who was clutching her stomach, and shouted to Brian and Ian. 'Stop it! Can't you see she's ill? Call an ambulance, quickly.'

Audrey and Ivy sat side by side in the hospital waiting area, watching Ian and Brian eye each other from opposite sides of the room.

'The baby can't possibly survive,' Ivy said authoritatively, 'not when Gail's only five months gone.'

'Please, Ivy, for once stop prophesying doom. Can't

you see we're all worried sick about Gail?' Audrey broke in abruptly.

'I'm only trying to be practical. We have to face facts—'

'Not until they are facts.' Unable to stand the tension in the room a moment longer, Ian reached for his cigarettes, stepped outside and lit up. When he turned, Brian was standing behind him.

'Come to hit me again?'

'I suppose you came back for Gail.'

'I've had a blood test. If this baby's mine I'll do everything I can to persuade Gail to return to Australia with me. From what I've seen, you're not a fit husband or father,' Ian said contemptuously.

'I'll never let you take Nicky out of Britain.'

'That's up to the courts to decide, and in cases like this the mother always gets custody of children.'

'In cases like what?' Brian challenged.

'Cases where the father's living with another woman. Gail's mother wrote and told me you're living with a woman called Liz Turnbull.'

'Is it any surprise I'm living with another woman when my wife slept with you and is in there now . . .' Brian pointed back towards the ward '. . . having your baby? When I think of the way you moved in on Gail while I was away, I could knock your block off.'

Ian fingered the bruise on the side of his face. 'Like to try your chances when I can see what's coming?'

'Stop it, both of you.' Audrey had appeared and pushed herself between them. 'The doctor's just been to see us. Gail's had a baby girl.'

'The baby's alive?' Ian whispered hoarsely.

'She is at the moment. And the doctor's told us that Gail will be fine, and hopefully, in time, so will the baby. She's a fighter.'

'Which is more than her dad is,' Brian said scornfully to Ian. He threw his jacket over his shoulder and walked off.

'Have you taken me out to dinner because you're interested in me or the Rovers Return?' Bet Lynch asked Alec Gilroy as they sat at a table in the plush, chandelier-illuminated dining room of Manchester's most expensive hotel.

'That's a cynical question for an attractive woman like yourself to be asking, Bet,' he reproached her.

'Charm doesn't work on me.' She picked up the menu and studied it.

'No?' he enquired sceptically.

'We both know that the brewery's determined to sell off the tenancy of the Rovers, and we both know you want it every bit as much as I do.'

'A little bird told me you have three thousand pounds saved towards buying it.' He glanced over his shoulder and saw the wine waiter making his way to their table with the champagne he'd ordered.

'I'm getting a bank loan for the rest.' Bet tried to sound casual, but that morning the bank had offered her five thousand pounds less than she'd asked for.

'Twelve thousand pounds is a lot of money to borrow.'

'Tell me about it, but under my management the Rovers is doing better than it ever has before.' Bet looked at him coolly as the waiter set the ice bucket on their table and proceeded to open the champagne.

'So you've already raised all the money you need?'

'Not quite.'

'If you're short I could lend you some.'

She laughed. 'So you can foreclose on me, move in and ask the brewery to let you take over the tenancy when I go bankrupt? Thanks, but no thanks, Alec. I wasn't born yesterday. Everyone who works for the brewery knows you're next in line for a manager's job as soon as a tenancy falls vacant.'

'You don't trust me an inch, do you, Bet?' He tasted the champagne the waiter had poured, then nodded to him to fill their glasses.

'No.' Bet lifted her full glass and touched his. 'Cheers. Here's to mutual distrust.'

'If you wanted to borrow, say . . . for a figure . . . five thousand pounds . . .'

Bet almost dropped her glass when Alec mentioned the exact amount she was short.

'I'd have papers drawn up, all legal. You could pay me

back at two per cent above base bank rate. That would be fair to me and you. Purely a business deal, and nothing whatsoever to do with the Rovers.'

'You mean it?' Bet struggled to suppress her misgivings. She knew no one else apart from Mike Baldwin who had the kind of money she needed, and after the way he had used her over the years, he was the last person she wanted to crawl to for a loan.

'I mean it. Have you chosen from the menu yet?' he asked, as another waiter approached. Alec gave the man an ingratiating smile. 'We need a few more moments.' Then he said, 'So, Bet, do you want my loan or not?'

'Only as long as it's legal and above board and the papers are properly drawn up by a solicitor,' she said, trying to ensure that nothing could wrong.

'I wouldn't have it any other way. Now, let's look at the food. What do you think of *pâté de foie* as a starter?'

Chapter Forty-One

'Ian's left for Australia.' Audrey watched Gail carefully as she gave her the news.

'Has he?' Gail murmured as she tucked the six-week-old baby she'd named Sarah Louise into the cot that had been Nicky's.

'He told me the blood test proved that he wasn't Sarah Louise's father, and although he was still prepared to marry you, you sent him packing.'

'He was just complicating things.' Gail didn't want to talk about the situation between her, Ian and Brian.

'Ivy told me Brian flatly refuses to see the baby.'

'It's his choice.' Gail picked up Sarah's bottle, carried it to the sink and rinsed it out.

'But she's his daughter.'

'Brian doesn't think so.' Gail ran the tap and proceeded to fill the sink with hot, soapy water.

'Then it is over between you and Brian?' Audrey pressed. 'Ivy said he's living with this woman, Liz

Turnbull, and he's left you here on your own to bring up the children.'

'I wish I *was* left on my own,' Gail snapped. 'Brian's round here every five minutes, wanting to see Nicky and take him places. And when he brings Nicky back, all Nicky can talk about is Auntie Liz this and Auntie Liz that. I can't bear the thought of that – of Brian's floozy being near him,' she said. 'I just wish that Brian had the sense to see the damage he's doing to Nicky. He's a child. He should feel secure with his parents. Instead, Brian uses him to score points. "Nicky's happier with us than he is with you,"' she mimicked, in a fair approximation of Brian's voice. 'As if any child wouldn't be happy being bought toys and taken on outings. The trouble is, Brian's giving me so little money that until I go back to work I have practically nothing spare to spend on Nicky.'

'Feel better for that rant?' Audrey asked.

'Oh, Mam.' Gail leant heavily over the sink. 'I've made a real mess of my life, haven't I?'

'No more than I made of mine,' Audrey said philosophically. 'You know you can ask me for help whenever you like, don't you?'

'I know.' Gail thought of the new man in her life. Jeff Singleton was a plumber employed by the council. He had called to fix the heating when it had broken down and had ended up staying, first for coffee and then for a meal. Nicky liked him, and Jeff liked the baby. It would be the easiest thing in the world to lean on him and allow him to look after her and her children. If it hadn't been for Nicky and the way he adored his father, she would have been so very tempted to allow him to do just that.

Alec Gilroy sat down in the office of brewery boss Cecil Newton. 'I'm not at all surprised that Bet Lynch disappeared without saying a word to anyone. She owes money everywhere and her creditors were moving in.' Alec offered Cecil a cigar. 'It's not just the bank and her suppliers she defaulted on. She borrowed money to buy the tenancy of the Rovers Return from me as well.'

'She told us that she took out a bank loan to top up her savings,' Cecil said indignantly.

'She did. She borrowed seven thousand from the bank, five thousand from me and put in three thousand of her own. When I looked at the figures I couldn't see how the Rovers' turnover would sustain the repayment of such large loans. Not long term, any road. I tried to tell her, but . . .' Alec shrugged '. . . you can't tell some women anything. Their heads aren't right for business.'

'If we'd known she'd borrowed that much we would never have sold her the tenancy.'

'That's what I thought. And that's why I came round to see you as soon as I heard she'd disappeared.'

'So, you free to take over the tenancy?' Cecil asked Alec bluntly.

It was the question Alec had been waiting for. 'That depends on the terms you're offering.'

'The same as we offered Bet Lynch.'

'Less five thousand pounds. I did give it to her,' Alec demurred, 'and now she's done a bunk I'm never likely to see a penny of it again.'

'Very well,' Cecil capitulated. 'Less five thousand pounds. You have ten thousand pounds?'

'I'll write you a cheque now.' Alec reached into his inside pocket. 'You drive a hard bargain, Cecil.'

'You think so?' Cecil asked, in a tone that suggested he knew more than he was letting on.

Jeff Singleton set down a bottle of wine and a rented video on Gail's table as she nursed Sarah. 'I thought we'd have a night in tonight after Brian's brought Nicky back and you've put him to bed.'

'Sounds nice,' she murmured.

'Are you sure? You don't seem very pleased.'

Gail looked anxiously at the clock. 'Brian should have brought Nicky back half an hour ago.'

'Perhaps they're held up in traffic, or Brian's taken him somewhere and they're enjoying themselves so much he's forgotten the time.'

'I suppose so,' Gail said doubtfully. The phone rang and she picked it up.

'Gail—'

'Brian, thank heavens you phoned. I've been worried sick about Nicky. You're late. Is he all right?'

'Nicky's fine and so am I, thank you for asking,' he said caustically. 'I just wanted to let you know that you'll never see Nicky again.'

'Brian—'

'Just listen,' he ordered sharply. 'I don't want my son brought up by another man. I saw you and Jeff Singleton with Nicky in the park yesterday and Nicky told me he's round the house at all hours of the day and night. So I've decided to take Nicky and leave the country because it's the only way I'll get to bring him up the way I want to, and the only way he'll know who his father is.'

'Brian, please, you don't know what you're doing. Nicky needs me—'

'He needs his father, Gail, and don't worry, I know how to look after him. You'll never see him again.'

There was a click followed by the buzzing sound of the dialling tone. Gail fell sobbing to her knees, as Jeff crouched beside her, uncertain what to do.

Bet sat back in the chair of the beach café enjoying the warm Spanish sunshine. To her astonishment she looked up to see Alec Gilroy walking towards her with a tray holding two glasses and a jug of sangria.

'Nice here, isn't it?' He poured two glasses and handed her one.

'How did you find me?' she asked.

'It wasn't difficult.'

'I don't recall sending any postcards back to Weatherfield.'

'I have a friend who works in a travel agency. He remembered an attractive blonde who bought a one-way ticket to the Costa del Sol. And because the management of the hotel you're staying in offers free rooms to travel agents for recommending it to their clients, I knew exactly where you'd be staying.' He took the chair opposite hers. 'I don't know if you've heard, but I've taken over the tenancy of the Rovers.'

'I didn't need to hear it.' Bet sipped her drink and opened her eyes wide at the amount of alcohol it contained. 'You've been after it ever since the Graffiti Club closed.'

'I'm here to ask you to come back with me.'

'As what? Your barmaid?' she sneered.

'No.' Alec laid his hand over hers. 'As my wife.'

Bet was an expert at concealing her feelings but Alec's unexpected proposal threw her. 'You've got to be joking.'

'I've never been more serious in my life.'

'I don't believe you.'

'Why not? As I've said many times, you're a very attractive woman, Bet. Why is it so difficult for you to believe that a man like me could fall in love with you?'

'Because I never believed in fairy-tales. Not even when I was little.'

'Perhaps this will help.' He opened a box and took out a sapphire and diamond engagement ring. 'I brought this with me, just in case.'

'It might not fit.' She itched to try it on, but she still suspected that he was having some bizarre joke at her expense.

'And it might.' He took her hand and slipped the ring on to her finger. 'Perfect. So, what do you say?'

The sangria had gone straight to her head and Bet couldn't make up her mind if she was caught up in a dream or a nightmare. 'Yes, Alec.'

He looked around. 'It is nice here, but make the most of it. We have to fly back tomorrow. We have a pub to run and a name to change from Lynch to Gilroy.' He rested his hand on hers and raised his glass. 'To us.'

Jeff Singleton showed Rita Fairclough's live-in lover, Alan Bradley, into Gail's living room. Alan was shocked by Gail's frail, drawn appearance. In the two weeks since Nicky had gone missing and the police had instigated a nationwide – and fruitless – search for him she had aged ten years.

'Alan's called in to say that Brian telephoned him.' Jeff eyed Audrey and Ivy, silently appealing for their help as he broke the news to Gail as gently as he knew how.

'Did he say anything about Nicky?' Gail asked urgently. She turned a wide-eyed, frantic face to Alan. 'The police were here earlier. They still haven't found him. I told them that Brian has probably already taken him out of the country . . .'

'Please, Gail, listen to what Alan has to say,' Jeff pleaded.

'Brian telephoned me this morning. He told me I could buy the garage from him if I paid him two thousand pounds in cash today as an immediate down-payment. I've arranged to meet him in the motorway service station this afternoon. I thought you'd want to come with me.'

'Will Nicky be with him?' Gail leapt to her feet.

'With everyone in the country searching for him, there's no way Brian would risk leaving him with anyone,' Audrey said logically.

'I'll get my coat.' Gail went into the hall.

'I'm coming with you,' Audrey called after her.

'And me, I'm his mother.' Not prepared to be left out, Ivy jumped to her feet.

Jeff left his chair.

'Brian has taken Nicky because he doesn't want another man in his life, Jeff,' Alan warned him. 'If he sees you, he'll run. And this is between husband and wife, ladies,' he said to Audrey and Ivy. 'I think it's best they sort it out between themselves, don't you?'

'You're right,' Jeff agreed reluctantly.

'I'm ready.' Gail was out of the door before Alan.

★

The drive to the service station was the longest ten miles Gail had travelled in her life. Alan tried to pass the time by making small talk, but after a quarter of an hour of monosyllabic replies he gave up.

'Stay in the car,' he ordered Gail, as he followed the signs to the services. 'If Brian sees you he might drive off.' He parked the car, left it and walked to where he could view the car park. Gail watched him carefully, and when he focused on a van in the middle ranks, she followed his line of vision and saw a blond head through the windscreen. Unable to sit still a moment longer, she left the car and ran towards the van.

'Brian – please!'

'Stay back!' Brian shouted at Gail, as he climbed out of the driver's seat. He turned to Alan. 'I told you to come alone.'

'Please—' Oblivious to the traffic, Gail ran in front of a car. The driver missed her by inches. Unaware of the havoc she was creating, Gail raced up to Brian's van and hammered on the windscreen.

Nicky looked up from the front seat. 'Mam!' His voice was muffled by the closed windows.

'Brian, Nicky needs me,' she begged.

'He has me,' he said coldly.

'Please,' she pleaded. 'Let him go, please, Brian, you can't separate us like this. When he's older he'll never forgive you.'

As Nicky fought with the childproof lock on the door, Brian leant on the bonnet with tears in his eyes.

'Please, unlock the door so Nicky can get out, Brian,' Gail begged.

Alan and two policemen were walking towards them and Gail realised that Audrey, Ivy or Jeff must have called them. Brian looked from her to Nicky, crying hysterically in the van.

'If I open the door, it's only because I don't want my son to see me being arrested,' Brian said to her.

'Whatever you say, Brian.'

Finally he opened the door of the van. 'Do you want to see your mother?'

Nicky didn't answer. He ran headlong and flung himself into Gail's arms.

'I suppose you're going to tell the police to throw the book at me?' Brian challenged.

'No.' Gail swallowed her tears as she held Nicky close. 'Our son needs both his parents. Thank you for giving him back.' She turned aside so that Nicky wouldn't see the policemen closing in on his father.

'I'm a businessman, Susan,' Mike said, as they both prepared for bed, 'and I agree that the quality and design of the clothes your company, Hopscotch, produced was great. So was the advertising – but, then, it should have been for the price I paid the agency you picked out to handle the campaign. But when it comes down to it, Hopscotch is losing money – a lot more than I'm prepared to throw away. I know you gave it all you've got, but so did I. My company subsidised it every week of its six months' life but no more. Hopscotch ceased trading as of this afternoon.'

'And what am I supposed to do now?' Susan demanded.

'You can run the factory shop I'm opening in the loading bay until . . .' he gave her a bright smile '. . . you get pregnant.'

'No.'

'No to the factory shop or no to getting pregnant?'

'No one will want to buy anything in a factory shop in Coronation Street,' she grumbled. 'It's hardly an area you'd expect to find designer clothes for sale.'

'Then you don't want the job?'

'No.'

'In that case it's wonderful to know that you want to give up work and start a family.'

'I didn't say that.'

He grabbed her arm before she could slip on her nightdress and pulled her down on to the bed. 'I'm not prepared to wait any longer. I want children before I'm too old to enjoy playing with them. I don't want to take my kids to the playground and be mistaken for their grandfather.'

'You're hurting me,' she struggled to fight him off, 'and I'm not ready to have a baby.'

'The subject isn't up for discussion, Susan. Not any longer. You knew I wanted children when we married. You said then that you wanted them too.'

'I do – just not yet.'

'You've run out of time. If you want to stay married to me, you get pregnant.' He rolled her on to her back and climbed on top of her. She reached to her bedside cabinet for her birth-control pills, but he was too quick for her. He crushed the packet in his hand, then stuffed it beneath his side of the mattress.

Furious that Mike had dared give her an ultimatum, Susan retrieved the pills as soon as she could be sure that he was asleep. She went into the bathroom, ran the cold tap, filled a glass with water and swallowed one. After washing her face and hands, she crept back through the bedroom, where Mike was still sleeping, into her dressing room, packed a case and waited for dawn.

Shortly after it broke, she stole out of the house and into the garage, climbed into her car and headed for her father's house.

'Deirdre's already left on council business, and Tracy and I are having breakfast,' Ken said, as he opened the door to her. 'Like a cup of tea?'

'I wouldn't say no.' She dropped her case in the hall, followed him into the living room, took off her coat and sat next to Tracy at the table.

'Bit early for a visit, isn't it?' Ken asked, after he'd despatched Tracy upstairs to clean her teeth.

'I suppose it is.'

'Did you call for any reason in particular?' he asked warily, not wanting to get involved in an argument between Susan and Mike. Much as he wanted Susan to divorce Mike, he was aware that if he encouraged her to leave him, a future reconciliation might result in him losing his daughter, possibly for good, which he wanted to avoid at all cost.

'Mike wants children and I don't,' Susan said flatly.

'That sounds like an argument that should stay strictly between husband and wife,' Ken said flatly.

'Are you telling me I can't come back here?' Susan demanded.

'If you make a sensible, considered decision to leave him and if the two of you have discussed it in a calm, reasonable manner and you've agreed that your marriage is at an end, then you're more than welcome to come back here. But if you've had a spat and left him on the spur of the moment in the hope that he'll come crawling here to get you, you can pick up your case and go right back to him. Because I'm not having your differences with him played out in front of Tracy.'

Susan left the table. She picked up her case and went out to her car. Dropping the case into the boot, she climbed behind the wheel and drove away. Her father was right. She couldn't expect him to sort out her problems with Mike. And she did love her husband. The only question was whether she loved him enough to have his baby.

She glanced at her watch. If she stopped off at the baker's on the way home, she could tell Mike that she went out early to fetch fresh rolls for breakfast and he need never find out just how close she had come to leaving him. Because the one thing that she could be sure about was that her father would never ever tell him about this.

'The police told me you didn't want to press charges so I called round to say thank you. Now that I've said it, I'll be on my way.' Brian turned up his collar against the rain and stepped away from Gail's door.

'Come in.' She opened the front door wider and turned her head. 'Nicky, your father's here to see you.'

'I didn't think you'd let me see him, or allow me in the house,' Brian said, as she helped him out of his wet coat and hung it over the newel post at the foot of the stairs.

'I told you in the car park, Nicky needs both of us.'

'And Sarah?'

She held his look for a second, then turned away.

'Audrey told me that Sarah Louise is my baby. Nicky!' he shouted, as their son came racing down the stairs. He reached into the coat that Gail had hung up and extracted a small parcel. 'I brought you a present. Unwrap it in the living room and I'll come and show you how it works.' He waited until Nicky had raced off then said, 'I know I have no right to ask you this, Gail, but do you think that, given time, you could ever forgive me? As you said, Nicky needs both of us and when Sarah Louise is older she will too. I know I've behaved like an idiot and I've hurt Nicky as well as you, but I'll do anything you ask of me and I'll try to get on with Jeff.'

'Jeff doesn't call around any more,' she interrupted him.

'He doesn't?'

'He wasn't my boyfriend,' she said, 'just a friend, a shoulder to cry on – God only knew, I needed one. But, then, you always were one to jump to conclusions, Brian.'

'Would you ever,' he had difficulty swallowing the lump in his throat, 'consider taking me back? For Nicky and Sarah's sake,' he added.

She nodded. 'For Nicky and Sarah's sake.'

'And this time, I swear, I'll make it up to you. I promise.'

'No, Brian. No swearing and no promises you can't keep. Just try to make the children happy. That's the least both of us can do, even if we can't be happy ourselves.'

'To our son or daughter, and make the most of it because it's the last drink you'll have for eight months.' Mike handed Susan a glass of the champagne he'd poured and checked the results of the pregnancy test for the tenth time in as many minutes. 'Happy?' he asked, as she sipped her drink.

Susan nodded, but even as she forced herself to return his smile she wondered how she had allowed herself to be painted into this corner. She had married Mike because she loved him, and he had offered her everything she'd craved: excitement, a lavish, luxurious lifestyle. But most of all she had thought that he'd accepted her need to forge an independent career and life for herself.

But now that had gone with the demise of Hopscotch, all of a sudden the trappings of her life with Mike, the rambling mansion he had bought to replace the penthouse flat, the expensive his and hers sports cars, the designer furniture, clothes and jewellery, seemed like prison shackles. She looked at him in mounting horror as he started talking about the nursery they would decorate, the private schools they would view, the musical and other talents they would nurture in their child.

Suddenly she realised she couldn't go through with it.

She couldn't carry on living with Mike and there was no way that she was ready to have his baby – or anyone else's.

Chapter Forty-Two

Mike Baldwin's face contorted with anger and another emotion Susan couldn't decipher. 'You're a murderer,' he said savagely. 'You didn't have a miscarriage. You had an abortion. You killed our child!'

'I didn't,' Susan cried unconvincingly. She hadn't really expected him to believe her story of a miscarriage, but she was prepared to argue rather than plunge into motherhood.

'Murderer!' he hissed.

'I'm not a thing you've bought, Mike, like the furniture, this mansion, your cars, your employees. I'm a person in my own right. I have my own ideas—'

'Murdering ideas.' Insane with rage he brushed his arm across her dressing-table, sending her perfume bottles, make-up and ornaments crashing to the floor. 'Get out of my house! I never want to see you again as long as I live!'

Terrified by his rage she ran downstairs, picked up her coat, handbag and car keys and fled. When she was safely locked into her car she checked her purse to see if she had enough money for a one-way ticket back to Newcastle. She knew there was no point in going to see her father. Not after the last time she had asked for his help after quarrelling with Mike. And she couldn't take the car because, although Mike had given it to her, he had been careful to register it in his name.

Once she was certain she had enough money she drove to the station. She would abandon the car in the street outside. Sooner or later the police would tell Mike where it was.

Hilda wrapped the last of her china ornaments in newspaper and looked around the living room. Like the house, it was full of memories, most of them happy for all that it was number thirteen Coronation Street. She brushed aside a tear as they flooded back. The day her daughter, Irma, had brought her young man, David Barlow, home for the first time. The rows she'd had with Stan – and the making up afterwards. The parties when they'd had the neighbours round. The laughs she and Stan had shared with Eddie Yeats.

'This the last case, missus?' the removal man asked.

'Yes.' Hilda dropped the newspaper parcel on top of the others in the tea chest and watched the man screw down the lid. He picked it up, heaved it on to his shoulder and carried it out.

Kevin Webster allowed him to pass, then joined Hilda. 'Sally and I will miss you. It's not every landlady who'll take a married couple as lodgers, you know.'

'It's not many landladies who are lucky enough to get lodgers like you and Sally.' Hilda dabbed at her eyes with her handkerchief. 'I never thought I'd leave this house but, then, I never thought I'd get an offer like the one Dr Lowther has made me. Housekeeper to just one retired man in a house in the country. It's too good to turn down at my time of life. Doing all those cleaning jobs every day was beginning to get me down.'

'You'd be very welcome to come back to this house any time. Sally and I can't thank you enough for selling it to us.'

'It's not as if I've given it to you,' Hilda retorted, emotion making her brusque. 'You'll be paying off that mortgage for a long time.'

'Everyone in the street is waiting outside to give you a good send-off,' Kevin told her.

'I thought I'd had enough of a send-off last night in Rovers!'

'You know people round here.' Kevin steered her gently to the door. 'You're one of them and they're not anxious to let you go.'

'Get on with you.'

'No more?' The removal man poked his head round the door and glanced into the room.

'No more,' Hilda echoed.

Kevin held out her coat and hat. Hilda allowed him to help her on with her coat, then looked in the hall mirror for the last time. There had been no point in packing it or some of her other things. Dr Lowther's house was fully furnished and it was senseless to take things she'd have no room for when Kevin and Sally could use them. Unable to resist one last quick peek into the living room, she dried her eyes and followed him to the door.

'It's nice to have a family get-together.' Audrey pushed one of Gail's fairy cakes into her mouth, 'particularly at this time of year. I hate January and February – they're so cold and dark. Christmas has gone and spring still seems so far away, there's nothing to look forward to.'

'Well, there will be from now on. Our Sarah Louise's birthday.' Ivy lifted her one-year-old granddaughter out of her high chair and on to her lap, giving her a cuddle and the stuffed toy panda she had chosen for her present.

Brian saw the two grandmothers vying for the position of top dog with Nicky and Sarah, and said, 'Time to cut the birthday cake, Gail. Do you know where you put the candle?'

Gail followed him into the kitchen. 'I told you, it's in the box.'

He closed the door behind her. 'I've been thinking.'

'That's a dangerous occupation for you.' She looked at him, and it seemed as though she was seeing him for the first time. She had fallen in love with him, married him and they'd had two children together. Love had long since gone, yet she had allowed him back into her life for the children's sake. And for the first time since she had known him, he hadn't let her down. He had done everything he had said he would do, and more, to prove himself a good father to Nicky and Sarah. But whatever spark there had once been between them had died somewhere between the rows and reconciliations.

'Marry me, Gail.'

'I did once and it was a disaster,' she answered flippantly, taking the cake out of the box. 'And you were the one to divorce me – remember.'

'I was angry after Sarah Louise was born because I thought she wasn't mine.'

Gail resisted the impulse to remind him that at the time he had also told her that he wanted to marry Liz Turnbull.

'It won't be a disaster the second time round, I promise you. Nicky and Sarah need security. Please, marry me?'

'A big church wedding with all the trimmings?' She couldn't believe he was serious.

He shook his head. 'A quiet do in a register office as soon as we can arrange it.'

Nicky chose that moment to run into the kitchen demanding cake.

Gail looked from her son to Brian. 'If I marry you again it will only be for the children's sake.'

'Isn't that reason enough?'

'It will have to be,' she whispered.

'I told you, I'm far too busy to take time off for a honeymoon right now,' Alec Gilroy told Bet, as again she brought up a subject he refused to discuss.

'So you said.' Bet slapped two airline tickets down on the bar.

'You bought tickets anyway?' Alec's temper rose.

'Yes, but they're not for you. They're for me and Stella Rigby.'

'Stella – nymphomaniac Stella?' Alec went white.

'We'll have a great time together.' Bet tickled Alec under the chin. 'Don't go overworking yourself while I'm away.'

'Stella will be after every man in trousers . . .'

'And shorts and swimming trunks.'

'Bet, how could you do this? You know what she's like.'

'Yes, I do,' Bet answered sweetly. 'She's great fun. That's why I asked her to come with me. But don't worry, Alec, we're only going for a week. It could be worse – we might have booked a fortnight.'

Ivy Tilsley had expected Brian and Gail to be overjoyed at her news and couldn't help feeling shocked and let down by their lukewarm attitude to her announcement.

'I know Don Brennan's a taxi-driver,' Brian said. 'I've been servicing his taxi for the last couple of years.'

'He may be a nice man, Ivy,' Gail interposed, 'but isn't this decision of yours to marry him a bit spur of the moment?'

'Hardly that,' Ivy countered. 'The wedding isn't until the thirteenth of June and it will be in St Luke's Catholic Church. And we've booked our honeymoon. We're going to Corfu, so with all the preparations we've made you can hardly call it a hole-in-the-corner affair, like some people around here have had.'

Gail and Brian both knew that she wasn't referring to their quiet register-office remarriage, but to Audrey's wedding to Alf Roberts.

'I've decided to get married in white, but a suit—'

'I'll get that.' Brian left to answer the door.

'Mam, nice of you to call in,' Gail greeted Audrey as Brian showed her into the living room. 'Ivy's just called round to tell us she's getting married—'

'In June,' Ivy interrupted, unable to contain herself a moment longer. 'To Don Brennan, the taxi-driver. We're getting married in St Luke's, he's moving into my house and we're honeymooning in Corfu. I do hope you'll be able to come—'

'I won't.' Audrey shook her head as Brian brought in an extra cup from the kitchen and picked up the teapot. 'I've had a phone call to say that my son's had a car crash in Canada. He's seriously ill and I have to go out there. I'm on my way to the travel agent's now to book a seat on the first plane I can get.'

'Your son!' Gail stared at her mother in disbelief.

'I wanted to tell you and Alf about Stephen, but somehow it never seemed to be the right time. The last thing I wanted was for you two to find about him this way. I had him when I was sixteen. In those days there was no question of an unmarried girl being able to keep a baby and I had to give him up for adoption but it was a private one because I wanted to keep in touch . . . Look, love, I can't stop to explain now. I have to book a flight. Good luck, Ivy,' she added as an afterthought as she rushed out, leaving Gail, Brian and Ivy thunderstruck.

Alf Roberts sought refuge behind the counter when he saw Shirley Armitage walk into his mini-market. He'd been trying to let the flat above the shop for over a month and when Shirley had come in the week before, asking if she could have it, he'd promised it to her. If he'd known that Kevin Webster's friend, Curly Watts, would ask the same question the following day, he would never have told Shirley that she could have it.

There was no contest as to which of the two he would prefer to have as a tenant.

He decided to tell Shirley that Audrey had promised the flat to Curly without his knowledge and he had given Curly the go-ahead to move in.

'Mr Roberts?'

'Yes.' Consumed by guilt, he pretended to check the figures in the ledger he had totalled the night before.

'I met Kevin Webster and Curly Watts just now in the street. Curly said he's moving in here.'

'That's right.'

'But last week you promised *I* could move in tomorrow. I've given my landlady notice.'

'That's not my fault.'

'Yes, it is,' she remonstrated. 'We had an agreement. You said I could move into the flat and now you've given it to someone else.'

'Look, love,' Alf pushed the ledger aside, 'it's not me. You know what people are like round here.' He looked into her eyes and Shirley knew exactly what he meant. She had been fighting racial prejudice all her life, and Alf, like the 'people around here' who might or might not exist, didn't like the colour of her skin. 'You just wouldn't fit in.'

'And I would, is that it?'

'Curly,' Alf greeted him, as he stepped forward, 'I didn't see you there.'

'I bet you didn't. Shirley says you promised her the flat the day before you told me I could have it. What are you playing at?'

'It doesn't matter, Curly,' Shirley said, all fight ebbing from her. She was used to racism, and she wasn't prepared to become any else's 'cause'.

'I'm not taking the flat, Mr Roberts,' Curly said, 'not after you promised it to Shirley.'

'It's fine, Curly.' Shirley backed away from the counter. 'I don't mind looking for somewhere else.'

'Well, I do. Alf promised you the flat so it's yours by right.'

Alf looked from Curly to Shirley. 'When you two have finished, it's my flat and I'll say who can and can't live in it.'

'You're a bloody racist, Alf Roberts, that's what you are,' Curly declared. 'I'm disgusted with you. You might not know it but there are laws against people like you.'

Shirley shrugged. 'It happens all the time, it's no big deal.'

'It is to me.' Curly looked at Shirley. 'Unless . . . The flat has two bedrooms. Why don't we move in together?'

'As friends?' Shirley asked cautiously.

'Of course as mates, what else would it be?' Curly held out his hand and Shirley shook it.

Mike Baldwin was sitting behind his desk staring at the grey, overcast early January sky and evaluating his lot in life. Nineteen eighty-nine didn't promise to be any more auspicious for him than the previous year. He and Susan were in the throes of a divorce. The factory was what could be best described as ticking over: it wasn't losing money, but it wasn't making much either. There didn't seem to be much going for him at all. Bored, he leant back in his chair and propped his feet on his desk.

Emily Bishop knocked the door. 'Mr Baldwin, there's a Mr Maurice Jones to see you.'

'Show him in,' Mike muttered disinterestedly. He'd heard of Maurice Jones – he was the property developer who had already bought the community centre and all the land behind the factory – and wondered what he wanted. Lifting his feet from his desk, he got up and faced the door.

'Mr Baldwin?'

'Yes.' Mike shook the middle-aged man's hand. 'What can I do for you?'

'Sell me your factory.'

'You come straight to the point, don't you?'

'Always,' Maurice replied succinctly.

'You're a property developer, my factory's a going concern.'

'And I'd give you a price that would reflect that.' Maurice handed Mike an envelope.

Mike opened it and pulled out a sheet of paper bearing a final figure that was more than double what the factory was worth.' He smiled. 'You've got yourself a deal, Mr Jones.'

Emily left her house and shivered as she locked the door. She hated freezing, dark winter mornings. She crossed the street to the factory and was surprised to see Ivy Brennan, Vera Duckworth and the rest of the girls gathered outside the gates.

'What's going on?'

'It's all locked up,' Ivy replied.

On hearing the sound of an engine labouring, Emily and the women peered through the gates and made out the shape of a bulldozer bearing down inexorably on the factory from the direction of the cleared site where the community centre had stood. As they watched, the bulldozer continued to move forward and flattened the factory wall.

'They're demolishing the building!' Vera exclaimed indignantly.

Ivy was so angry she screamed.

'Mr Baldwin said he'd sold the factory as a going concern.' Emily clung to the gates, unable to believe what she was witnessing.

'What kind of going concern,' Vera sneered, 'when we've nowhere to work?'

'I'm going to see about this.' Emily ran across the road to the Barlows' house. She knocked at the door, and Deirdre opened it. 'Can I see you?' Emily asked breathlessly. 'As my local councillor?'

'Come on, Deirdre, be reasonable,' Mike said smoothly, as he handed her a cup of Blue Mountain coffee. 'I sold my factory to Maurice Jones as a going concern.'

'You can prove that?'

'We had a gentleman's agreement,' he said dismissively.

'It's hardly my fault if he flattened the building and reneged on his promise to keep the workers on.'

'Those women worked for you for years. They gave you their time and their loyalty, and they weren't always well paid for it.'

'That's market forces for you.' He shrugged his shoulders.

She ignored his cavalier attitude. 'And now, without so much as a by-your-leave, they're out of a job with no redundancy pay to cushion their unemployment. Nothing!'

'Deirdre, Deirdre . . .' He gave her a disingenuous smile that reminded her of their affair. A memory she'd rather forget. 'Life is hard. If anyone tries to tell you different . . .'

'I know, they're trying to sell you something.' Instinctively, she pulled her skirt down another inch – ridiculous when she recalled that she had been his step-mother-in-law.

'Legally, I don't owe those girls a penny.' He sat back in his leather chair and swung his feet on to a matching buttoned footstool. 'When I sold the factory they were all employed, the building was standing, and Maurice Jones told me he intended to run the place.'

'I don't care about the legalities. You know as well as I do that you would never have sold the factory if you hadn't done nicely out of the deal. Morally, you owe all those girls redundancy payments.'

'I work within the letter of law, Deirdre.'

She rose to her feet. 'Fine, if that's the way you want to play it, let's see what damage a round-the-clock picket can do to the site. I think I can safely guarantee that Maurice Jones won't be building anything in the near or distant future.'

'You wouldn't . . .'

'*I* wouldn't, but the girls have already got it organised. And then, of course, there are the people I know who work on the local papers. Not to mention the friends I have in the radio and television stations. Your name will sound good on the evening news.' She picked up her coat and handbag. 'Good evening, Mike. Thank you for the coffee.'

He reached inside his jacket pocket. 'Exactly how much redundancy payment would you consider fair?'

'The girls and I have made a few notes.' Deirdre opened her handbag and extracted an exercise book. 'You're welcome to look at them.'

'Brian, I don't want an argument. I know it's an awful thing to say, but I don't care enough about you to argue any more,' Gail said wearily, when she came downstairs after putting the children to bed. 'We've been leading separate lives for months now. I told you when you asked me to forgive you last year that we wouldn't make one another happy. I don't even think we're making the children happy, and they were the excuse for us getting back together.'

Brian shook his head in despair.

'There has to be more in life for both of us,' Gail said quietly.

'So you think we should split up again?'

'Yes. And I think the logical solution would be for me to keep the children and this house. They're used to living here, and the hours I work in the café are more flexible than the ones you work in the garage. You never know when you're going to be called out on emergency in the middle of the night.'

'I suppose I could always move in with my mother and Don until I find a place of my own.'

'Do you mind?'

'Splitting up?' He thought about it for a moment. 'It's admitting defeat, but in a way I'm relieved. We've spent the last year trying too hard. And it's been exhausting for both of us.'

'We've been through a lot together, you and I.'

'We have, but . . .' he gave her a tight smile '. . . at least we're not screaming and shouting at each other this time. I'll go and pack my things.'

'Brian?'

'Yes?' He turned back.

'You can see the children any time you want to. There's no need to fix special days or times.'

'Thank you.' Brian walked up the stairs.

'I fancied you the minute I first saw you,' Curly confessed to Shirley, as they lay together in his bed.

'So much for us moving in together as friends.' She sat up and threw the bedclothes back.

'Don't go, not yet.' He pulled her down beside him. 'Living with you has been just about the best time in my life, and I want you to know that I've never been so happy. I realise I haven't been easy to live with, what with all the studying I've had to do and everything, but when I get this HND in business studies, I'll get a really good job and then . . .'

'And then?'

He squeezed her. 'I want to carry on living with you, Shirley. And we'll have good time, lots of them.'

She tried to conceal her disappointment as she returned his embrace. It wouldn't hurt if once, just once, he said he loved her.

Brian Tilsley looked around the disco and wondered what he was doing there. He'd enjoyed going to dances to pick up girls when he'd been younger and single, but now everyone in the room looked like a kid. And the clothes the girls were wearing and the music were so different from what he remembered that he'd have had no difficulty in believing he'd landed on another planet.

'On your own?' A young girl joined him in his booth; she was pretty with dark eyes and long brown hair.

'Yes.'

'Enjoying yourself?'

He smiled at her. 'I wasn't until now,' he said. 'Want a drink?'

'Please. Vodka and orange.' He picked up his empty lager glass and tried to leave the booth. A crowd of boys blocked his path.

'You've got yourself a right slapper there, mate.' One of the boys pushed his face close to Brian's.

Brian tried to sidestep him but another lad stepped in front of him and leant towards the girl.

'What do you want with him?'

The girl turned her back.

'I asked you a question.' The boy grabbed the neck of her dress.

'Leave her alone.' Brian hit the boy's hand away.

'Push off, we're just talking,' the girl shouted at the boys.

'Just talking,' the boys mocked.

'She told you to push off.' Brian shoved the closest boy who careered into the crowd behind him.

'You push off, mate.' The boys moved forward aggressively.

'Let's get out of here.' The girl grabbed Brian's hand and led the way through the crowd towards the exit.

Suddenly Brian felt a sharp pain in his chest, but the girl continued to pull him towards the door.

'Slow down,' he gasped, as they got outside.

'You all right?'

'No.' Brian reeled under the neon sign above the door and clutched his chest. When he pulled away his hand it was covered with blood. He slumped to the ground. The last thing he saw was the girl he'd picked up leaning over him and screaming for help.

Chapter Forty-Three

'My daddy is dead. He won't be back, not ever again.' Nicky looked up at Gail, who was struggling to contain her tears.

'No, he won't, Nicky, not ever again. He's gone to be with the angels, or at least he would be with the angels if your mother had given him a good Catholic burial.' Ivy was too immersed in her own grief to be concerned about her small grandson's misery, but her husband wasn't. Don Brennan lifted Nicky from Gail's lap and tried to distract the boy by carrying him off to the buffet table.

'I can't believe that you didn't give Brian a full Catholic burial,' Ivy ranted. The other mourners who had returned to Gail's house for the post-funeral tea of ham sandwiches and Madeira cake moved away in embarrassment as Ivy continued to yell at her daughter-in-law.

'Brian wasn't a practising Catholic.' Gail forced herself to curb her temper because Nicky was still within earshot.

'He was still a Catholic. But you were never a wife to

Brian,' Ivy hissed venomously. 'In fact, you were never much of anything to him. You weren't good enough to wipe his boots. Why he had to pick a cheap tart like you to marry, I'll never know.' With that parting shot, Ivy stormed out of the house.

'Gail, we – I mean me and the lads – we're going to push off now.' Martin Platt, Kevin Webster and Curly Watts's friend hovered awkwardly in front of her. 'But if you ever need help for anything, you know where to come.'

'Yes,' Gail murmured mechanically. She had been inundated with offers of help since Brian's murder but none had registered. All she wanted was for Brian to walk through the door, and she was having difficulty coming to terms with the fact that he would never again visit the children.

'Martin's right. Any time you want a fuse mended, or anything mechanical seeing to, shout for us.' Kevin followed Curly to the door.

'Thank you.' Gail thought that the three looked so absurdly young that they were the last people she'd ever call on for help.

'We'll be off, then. See you around, mate.' Kevin chucked Nicky under the chin.

Audrey joined her daughter as the three boys filed out. 'Ivy had a nerve, saying those things to you.'

'She's upset, Mam, she's just lost her son. I'll take Nicky and Sarah Louise upstairs. All these people in the house are unsettling them.' She collected Nicky from Don Brennan, then turned her back on the crowd in her living room and walked away, feeling more alone than she had ever felt in her life. Even during the times Brian had left her.

'Everything looks great, Shirley,' Sally Webster said.

'I only hope Curly thinks so.' Shirley smiled when she saw Martin and Kevin rearrange a plate of tuna vol-au-vents so it looked as though it hadn't been touched. She had spent the last couple of weeks organising a surprise party for Curly to celebrate their first year of living together. The food and drink had accounted for a sizable chunk of her savings and it had been a nightmare to invite all of Curly's friends without arousing his suspicions.

'Quiet, everyone,' she hissed. 'I can hear him coming. Hide!' She switched off the lights and people scuttled behind the furniture.

Curly opened the door, walked in and switched on the lights.

'Surprise!' Everyone leapt to their feet.

As Curly looked around, Shirley saw that he was more angry than surprised. 'What's this?'

'Surprise party,' she stammered.

'I can't party tonight. I have to revise for an exam tomorrow so, if you don't mind . . .' He opened the door, leaving the guests no choice but to file out.

Shirley watched them leave. She glanced at the food and drink she'd taken such pains to prepare. Without a word, she picked up a roll of cling film and went to the buffet table.

'I'm sorry,' Curly said. 'Tonight's just not the right night. Perhaps tomorrow after the exam . . .'

'No, Curly. It will never be the right night.'

'I've said I'm sorry, Shirley.' Guilt made him more than usually irritable.

'It's not just this. It's you, working for your HND in business studies. We're poles apart, and we always will be. I'll never be a proper match for you. You want some bright young girl who's as ambitious as you are.'

'That's rubbish, Shirley.'

'No, it isn't, but it doesn't matter. I'll sleep in my own bedroom tonight and move in with my sister tomorrow until I find somewhere else to live.'

'I love you.' To his surprise he discovered that he meant it. 'I was hoping we get could get married.'

She wanted to tell him that it was too little, too late. What she actually said was, 'It would be an absolute disaster, Curly. Goodnight.'

Rita Fairclough sat drumming her fingers on the arm of her chair as she waited for Alan Bradley to come home. The postman had brought her a letter from the building society that morning, asking for a repayment on the loan

Alan had taken out against her house. Several women in the street had tried to warn her that Alan was only after her money, and she'd ignored them. But now that she had the evidence, she had been forced to face facts.

Unable to sit still, she walked down the passage, opened the front door, stepped outside and saw Alan coming down the street. Returning to the living room, she stood next to the fireplace and waited for him to arrive.

'Hello, love.' Alan breezed in.

'I want to know what this is.' She held up the letter from the building society.

'I borrowed some money against our house.'

'It's not our house,' she informed him coldly. 'It's mine.'

'I'm living with you, aren't I? You told me when I moved in that I could be your common-law husband.'

'That didn't mean you could claim ownership of my possessions.'

He slammed the door and moved towards her. 'But it's all right for me to live with you. And it's all right for me to contribute towards the bills. I just can't have anything that's yours. Is that what you're saying, Rita?'

'People tried to warn me about you.' She shrank back in fear, as he continued to move towards her. 'They said you were after my money but I wouldn't listen . . .'

She faltered as Alan's face contorted in rage. His features changed and she felt as though she were looking at a stranger. He closed his hands around her throat and tightened them. She tried to scream, to fight him off, but it was hopeless. He was too strong for her. The ceiling grew faint and distant above her head, then she could no longer see it, only a suffocating greyness that blotted all else from view.

'Breathe deeply. Come on, Rita, you can do it. Breathe in deeply.'

Rita opened her eyes and looked up into the face of a uniformed paramedic.

Jenny Bradley was eyeing her anxiously from over his shoulder. 'I came in just as Dad was trying to strangle you. I called the police. They've taken him away.'

'The ambulance is here,' the paramedic said. 'You seem to be OK, Rita, but we'll run you into hospital so they can check you over. It's just a precaution.'

Rita turned on her side and curled into a small, tight ball. She closed her eyes, unable to believe that she'd been fool enough to trust Alan enough to take him into her house and her bed.

Ken glanced at his watch as he drove into Coronation Street. It was half an hour after midnight and he'd promised Deirdre and Tracy that he would be back early. He'd taken his secretary out to dinner and, as usual when he and Wendy went out together, one thing had led to another and finally to her flat and her bed.

Much as he hated to admit it, since Deirdre had become immersed in council business, he had become closer to Wendy Crozier than he was to his own wife. In the office it felt as though he and Wendy were the married couple and Deirdre the outsider. But that didn't stop him feeling guilty about letting Deirdre and Tracy down on such an important night.

He switched off the car headlights and killed the engine. Then he locked it and went into the house. Deirdre was up and waiting for him. She glanced at the clock when he walked in.

'And what time is this to come home on New Year's Eve?' she enquired frostily.

'I'm sorry, I lost all track of time, love.'

'As lies go, that's not a very good one. How much longer do expect me to carry on believing the fairy stories you're feeding me?' she asked bluntly.

'I said, I'm sorry.'

'For having an affair?'

Ken felt as though he had been punched in the stomach.

'What's her name, Ken?'

He flung himself into a chair.

'I asked you a question. The obvious answer is Wendy Crozier, your secretary,' she continued. 'You've been spending every minute you can with her lately.'

'I'm sorry, Deirdre.'

'You've already said that.'

'I don't know what else to say.'

'Forget the apologies, Ken. You know where the suit-cases are, and which wardrobe and drawers hold your clothes.'

'You just said forget the apologies!'

'I don't want them, only your absence from this house.'

'For God's sake, where do you expect me to go? It's after midnight on New Year's Eve.'

Deirdre glanced at the clock. 'No, it's not, Ken. It's the early hours of New Year's Day and I'm starting the new year as I intend to go on. This is going to be a happy 1990 for me once you are out of the house. Goodbye.'

Ken unwrapped the bottle of whisky that he'd bought in the mini-market, and set it on the kitchen table of the flat. Since Deirdre had thrown him out three months ago on New Year's Eve, he felt as though his entire world had collapsed. He'd left Coronation Street that night and driven back to Wendy Crozier's flat. She had welcomed him with open arms and, for a week or two, they had managed to fool themselves that they were happy. But as the days passed they had realised that day-to-day living was mundane in comparison with the heady excitement of the snatched, exhilarating moments of an illicit affair.

Romance died beneath a mound of dirty laundry, tedious shopping trips and domestic problems. Wendy's flat wasn't big enough for both of them and, used to her own space, she had complained when he covered her kitchen table with papers and stacked piles of books at his side of the bed.

Deirdre's lawyer had fought hard for the rights of his client, and things had come to a head when, having virtually no savings because he had sunk them into the *Recorder*, he had been forced to sell his newspaper to the *Weatherfield Gazette* to raise enough cash to pay Deirdre the settlement along with the house.

Used to being his own boss, he'd found it impossible to work under the strictures imposed on him by the editor of the *Gazette*, who'd insisted on changing the *Recorder* from the pioneering investigative paper he had built up into a bland gossip-shop. The sale had also hastened the demise of his relationship with Wendy, when the editor of the *Gazette* had appointed her editor in his place.

He went to the cupboard, took out a glass and poured himself a measure of whisky. As he held it to the light, it looked more like a quadruple than a single measure but he was past caring. He opened a can of Coca-Cola and poured some into the whisky, filling the glass to the brim. He was drinking the best part of a bottle of whisky a day and he didn't like the taste, only the oblivion and the dreamless sleep it brought when he passed out.

Not knowing what else to do after he had lost the editorship of the paper, he had returned to teaching, asking Alf

Roberts to let the flat above the shop to him when Curly Watts moved into lodgings with the Duckworths. It was only after he'd moved in he'd realised he could have gone anywhere in the country – or the world – yet he had returned to Coronation Street to lick his wounds like an injured animal returning to its lair.

He lay on the sofa and balanced the glass of whisky and Coke on his chest. Perhaps there had been more to his subconscious reasoning than simply licking his wounds. There was Deirdre. How could he have been stupid enough to let her go? At least while he remained in Coronation Street he could monitor her comings and goings – or, more importantly, the comings and goings of the new friends she'd made. After she had kicked him out, it hadn't been long before men were paying court to her.

The first had been an electrician, Dave Barton, who had saved Tracy and put out a fire she had started while trying to cook chips. Initially Ken had assumed Dave had returned to number one to sort out the electrical damage, but when he had seen him returning to visit Deirdre night after night, he grasped that there had to be more to it than that.

Because Dave finished work later than him, it had been easy to follow Dave home. And once he knew where he lived, he monitored every visit Dave paid to Deirdre. Then, suddenly, Dave's visits had ceased, and Phil Jennings's began. Ken hadn't liked Dave Barton, but he loathed Phil Jennings. The man owned a string of amusement arcades in Weatherfield and that was enough for Ken to bracket Phil in the same class as Mike Baldwin.

He'd heard that Phil Jennings was a self-styled businessman without integrity, who didn't care where or how he made money as long as he made it, and he'd seen nothing in the man's behaviour to contradict that opinion.

He glanced at his watch and wondered if Phil was still with Deirdre. He had seen him going into the house at half past eight and neither Phil, Deirdre nor Tracy had emerged before he'd left his vantage point to return to the flat at eleven o'clock because his hip flask had run dry.

He don't know what he would have done if Alf hadn't allowed him to take what he wanted from the shop and put it on a tab that he paid off at the end of every month. He swallowed his drink down in one. His head buzzed and the room swam hazily around him as he set his feet on the floor.

It took an enormous effort to focus on his watch. Half past eleven. Long past closing time in the Rovers, so the stragglers would all be at home, and past the time when Deirdre's boyfriend should be in his own house. Moving slowly and deliberately, Ken set his glass on the coffee table, rose to his feet and felt in his pocket for his keys. He staggered to the door, hitting the wall and doorpost on his way out.

The fresh air made him reel. He grabbed a lamp-post for support as he stood opposite the house that had been his home for so many years. There were no lights on that he could see. Had Deirdre gone to bed? The master bedroom was at the back of the house, Tracy's at the front, and Deirdre saw to it that Tracy's light was out no later than half past eight on school nights. Deirdre might be in the kitchen or the living room. Was Phil still with her, and if he was, were they making love?

As his imagination went into overdrive he pictured Phil and Deirdre naked, stretched out in front of the gas fire in the living room, a spot he and Deirdre had often chosen when they were first married. Phil might be unbuttoning her shirt, unzipping her skirt and peeling off her underwear at this very minute.

Or perhaps they weren't in the living room after all. Ken's heart raced at the thought of Deirdre and Phil lying together in the bed that he had shared with her.

The images were too much for him to bear. Lurching across the road he put his shoulder against the front door and burst into the house.

'Deirdre.' His voice fell thick, unrecognisable into the darkened hall as he tripped over something. Light flooded out of the living room and Phil and Deirdre were staring at him as he lay sprawled on the floor.

'What the hell do you think you're doing, breaking my door down at this time of night?' Deirdre yelled.

'I . . .' As his drink-fuddled mind strove to come up with an excuse that sounded even half-plausible, Ken got to his feet.

'And you're drunk,' Deirdre pronounced in disgust.

'Deirdre, I'm sorry. I love you, I . . .'

Phil grabbed him and frogmarched him to the open door.

'Deirdre, please . . .' Ken could feel tears running down his cheeks.

'You can't keep hounding me like this.' Deirdre's anger escalated as a door opened upstairs and Tracy appeared on the landing.

'What's happening, Mam?'

'Nothing!' Deirdre softened her voice. 'It's nothing, love, go back to bed. I'll tell you about it in the morning.'

'We're divorced, Ken,' she reminded him after Tracy had closed her bedroom door, 'and it's high time you accepted it.'

Phil twisted Ken's arm behind his back. 'Come round here again terrorising Deirdre and Tracy and I'll break your bloody legs.' He flung Ken out into the street. Moments later the door closed, and Ken heard the rattle of chains and the sound of bolts being pushed home.

He continued to lie on the pavement, staring at the litter of sweet wrappers in the gutter, wondering how he had sunk so low.

'Alma, are you sure you know what you're doing?' Emily Bishop asked Alma Sedgewick as they sat in the café sharing a pot of coffee.

Alma pushed her dark hair back from her face, and reached for the sugar. 'Of course I know Mike Baldwin's reputation, the same as everyone else. But since he sold his business to Maurice Jones and lost most of his money in that Spanish property deal, he's changed. Honestly, Emily, you wouldn't know him as the same man you worked for. He wants to wipe the slate clean and make a fresh start in business just as he has in his private life with me.'

Emily nodded, although privately she felt that it was more likely that crocodiles would stop eating fresh meat than Mike Baldwin change his womanising ways or drop his sharp business practices.

'He's taken a job for Peter Ingram, making travel-bags for one of his customers.'

'I didn't know Mike had set up another factory.' Emily was still smarting at the way she and the other girls had been thrown out of work when Mike had sold the factory without consulting them.

'He hasn't got a factory. He's running the business from our flat, the one he bought in the Docklands when he sold the mansion after divorcing Susan. All he has is one machine, he's doing the job himself.'

'Mike's sewing bags?' Emily enquired faintly, unable to believe what Alma was telling her.

'You find that strange?' Alma stirred her coffee.

'Incredible.'

'I think it's proof that he really has turned over a new leaf. Starting at the bottom again can do that to a man,' Alma said. 'You must come round some time.'

'I'd like to.' But the last thing Emily wanted to do was come face to face with Mike Baldwin not now – and not for a very long time.

Barely able to contain her excitement, Sally Webster left the doctor's surgery and danced her way into the chemist's. There, she bumped into Gail Tilsley, who was waiting for a prescription at the counter.

'You look happy,' Gail commented. The assistant called her name and she stepped forward to pick up her prescription.

'I am.' Sally waited until Gail had pushed the bag the assistant had given her into her pocket. 'I'm going to explode if I don't tell someone soon. I'm pregnant.'

Not even the huge smile on Sally's face could lift Gail's spirits.

'Aren't you happy for me?' Sally was dismayed that Gail had heard her epic news with so little enthusiasm.

'Yes, of course I am.' Gail made an effort to pull herself together. 'I'm really happy for you and Kevin, Sally. You must be delighted.'

'We've been trying for a couple of months, but one of my friends has been trying for years . . . What's the matter, Gail?' Sally couldn't ignore Gail's misery a moment longer: she was so ecstatically happy that she wanted the entire world to share her joy.

Gail had kept her secret and worried about it for so long that Sally's concern was more than she could bear. She felt tears start into her eyes and she turned aside. But not quickly enough: Sally had seen that she was crying.

'Come on back to our house, Gail,' she said. 'I'll make you a nice cup of tea.'

'I feel awful about burdening you with this, Sally.' Gail and Sally sat side by side on the sofa in Sally and Kevin's living room. The pale, coffee-coloured floral wallpaper and fresh white gloss paint had transformed the room and Gail thought Hilda Ogden would never have recognised her home.

'What are friends for?' Sally leant forward and poured two cups of tea. She handed Gail one and pushed the sugar bowl towards her.

'I've been so lonely since Brian died. Not that there was anything left between us, but he was always *there*, if you know what I mean. Coming round to see the kids, helping with the shopping and doing any odd jobs I wasn't up to tackling around the house. And when Martin—'

'Martin Platt?' Sally interrupted.

Gail saw the shocked look on Sally's face and guessed what she was thinking. 'I know he's just a kid . . .'

'Eighteen isn't a kid, Gail.'

'He's ten years younger than me so you can't blame me for thinking he's a kid. Well, he kept on coming round and I thought it was great. Nicky's been a bit of a handful since Brian died and he adores Martin. They played games together in the garden, football, cricket – Martin even brought round a game machine so he and Nicky could play on it together. And it all seemed so innocent, like I had two boys in the house. Then in the evenings after I'd put the kids to bed, I started making supper for both of us. Martin started . . . Well . . .' Gail made a valiant effort to pull herself together. After telling Sally as much as she had, she could hardly stop now. 'I'm pregnant,' she announced baldly.

'But that's wonderful,' Sally began enthusiastically.

'For you, maybe, but not for me. No one should be a father at eighteen.'

'Since Martin was man enough to make you pregnant, he's man enough to take responsibility for a baby,' Sally said decisively. 'You can't possibly be thinking of having an abortion.' Her hands closed protectively over her own abdomen.

'What else can I do?' Gail asked. 'It's far too much responsibility to put on a boy of Martin's age. And it's not even as if it's just this baby. There's Nicky and Sarah to think about. They've not long lost their father.'

'You just admitted that Martin practically lives in your house.'

'As a friend. The kids don't know we're lovers.' Gail saw the joy radiating from Sally and remembered how she had felt when she had discovered she was pregnant with Nicky.

She and Brian had made such a mess of their marriage. She couldn't even be pleased when she discovered she was pregnant with Sarah because she hadn't known whether Brian or Ian was the father. She wondered if she would ever be pregnant with a child that both she and the father wanted.

Chapter Forty-Four

'I can't see why you need my old flat above the café,' Alma Sedgewick grumbled to Mike Baldwin as they walked from his flat in the Docklands to the newest, smartest restaurant that had opened alongside the canal. It was a fine summer evening. The air was soft and balmy, almost Mediterranean, and Alma had taken advantage of the warmth to wear one of her best outfits: a thin-strapped blue silk top and matching trousers.

'I told you,' Mike said impatiently. 'I've bypassed Peter Ingram and gone direct to his customers. I've undercut his prices and snatched orders for the denim bags he was making from under his nose. I can't keep up with them, the way they're flooding in, so I need to employ girls who can. And I need somewhere for them to work. There isn't room in my flat here for more than one machine and seeing as how you've moved in with me and aren't using your place, it makes sense to put them in there.' He rubbed his hands together gleefully as he looked out over the expanse of water. 'I'm back in business, love.'

'But my flat above the café is too small to turn into a factory,' Alma pointed out logically.

'I know that. It's just a start. I'll probably only want it for a week or two, a month at the most. I contacted some of my old workforce this morning and they're raring to get back to it.'

'I'm not surprised. Most of them haven't found anything else since the factory closed down.'

'I managed to lay my hands on a dozen industrial sewing machines in a bankruptcy sale. I can have them moved in tomorrow, and the girls can start the day after. As soon as they've cleared the orders I've taken and the money comes in, I'll be able to rent somewhere more suitable for them to work. All I need is the key.'

Alma thought she detected a hard note in his voice as he mentioned the key – again. He opened the door of the restaurant and waited for her to walk in ahead of him.

'If it's only short term, I suppose you can have it,' Alma agreed reluctantly.

'Of course it's short term.' Mike greeted the headwaiter as if he were a long-lost cousin.

Alma opened her handbag and removed the key to the flat from the inside zipped compartment. Mike took it from her and dropped it into his pocket.

'Good evening, George.' He took the menu the waiter handed him. 'What are the specials today?'

'Tiger prawns fried with leeks on a bed of noodles as a starter and prime Scottish steak with all the trimmings as an entrée, Mr Baldwin.'

'That sounds good, we'll both have it,' Mike said without consulting Alma. 'You've kept our usual table?'

'Of course, sir.' The waiter escorted them to it. 'I'll send over the wine waiter, Mr Baldwin.'

'Life is good, Alma.' Mike looked at the sun dipping down behind the buildings that bordered the water. 'But I've a gut feeling that it's about to get even better, for both of us.' He picked up her hand and kissed her fingertips.

Gail felt mentally and physically drained as she opened the café. A week ago she had asked Ivy to meet the children from school so she could go to the doctor's. He had been kind and sympathetic, arranged all the counselling she needed and made an appointment for her to have an abortion at a local clinic. Tomorrow was the big day. And she was dreading it.

She knew that she should be relieved, but although she had made the decision to terminate her pregnancy for Martin's sake even more than her own, she couldn't stop thinking about the child she was carrying as a person in its own right.

'What was that?' Mavis shrieked, breaking in on Gail's reverie as a terrible whine came from upstairs. The building shook, rattling the cutlery in the trays and the plates on their stacks.

'I have no idea.' Gail gripped the counter as the whine escalated and the building continued to vibrate. Dust wafted down from the ceiling, coating the tables, chairs and counter.

'Something's going on upstairs.' Mavis's eyes widened. 'Do you think squatters have moved in? The papers said some of them are violent. They could be doing drugs – or worse.'

'If it's squatters they're exceptionally noisy ones,' Gail said abruptly, not wanting to delve into what Mavis's idea of 'worse' might be.' She picked up the telephone and dialled the number Alma had given her when she had moved out of the upstairs flat.

'Mike Baldwin's,' Alma answered.

Gail wondered briefly what had possessed an independently wealthy woman like Alma to behave more like Mike Baldwin's housekeeper than his live-in lover. Had he sapped her confidence, or was she simply so besotted with him she was behaving like his slave?

'It's Gail. I'm telephoning from the café.' Gail held up the telephone receiver as the deafening noise filled the café again. 'Did you hear that?'

'What on earth is it?' Alma asked.

'I was hoping you could tell me. It's coming from upstairs, and every time it starts the building shakes.'

'Oh, that'll be the machines Mike put into the flat.'

'What machines?' Gail demanded.

'He's gone back into manufacturing. He's got girls making travel-bags upstairs.'

'In your flat?'

'It's only temporary. As soon as he gets back on his feet he'll rent a factory. He said it'll only be a week or two, maybe a month at the most. 'Bye, Gail.' Alma hung up as the excruciating noise began again, making conversation impossible.

Gail turned to see the first customers of the day walk into the café.

'What the hell is that bloody din?' Don Brennan complained.

'People working upstairs,' Gail answered ambiguously.

'Let me know when they've gone because I'm not taking my breaks in here until they've finished.'

'Killing elephants and cutting up the corpses,' the driver with him suggested, as he walked out behind Don.

When the building started shaking again, Gail reached for the *Yellow Pages*. She flicked through until she had found the number she wanted.

'Is that Environmental Health?' she asked the person who answered her call.

★

'You having me on?' Martin Platt asked Kevin Webster, as they sat hunched over pints of beer and packets of nuts in a corner of the Rovers.

'I wouldn't do that,' Kevin protested, 'not over something like this. Sally told me she met Gail in the chemist. Sally was that pleased about our baby and she could see Gail was upset about something, so she took her home with her. And that's when Gail told her that she's having your baby and she can't go through with the pregnancy because she doesn't think it's fair for you to be a father at your age.'

'I'm not some stupid kid,' Martin said angrily.

'Hey, you don't have to tell me that. There's only a couple of years between us, remember. You pleased about it, then?' Kevin asked.

'Of course I'm pleased about it. It's my baby.'

'As you've never talked about Gail, I thought this thing between you and her must be casual. A fling.'

'It's not a fling. It's been going on for months. I've a good mind to go round there now.' Martin finished his pint.

'At this time of night?' Kevin made a face. 'Bet's already called time and Sally told me that Gail's hospital appointment is for tomorrow.'

'In the abortion clinic?'

'Shh, keep your voice down. Gail's probably having an early night and won't thank you for waking her.'

'She told me she was busy tonight.' Martin frowned. 'Who's going to the clinic with her?'

'No one, as far as I know. Sally offered, but Gail told her she'd prefer to manage by herself.'

'What time's she's going in?'

'Ten o'clock in the morning. That's one of the reasons she didn't want Sally to go with her. Sally's been having terrible morning sickness.' A warm fuzzy feeling stole over Kevin every time he spoke about Sally and their coming baby. 'Anyway, you're a hospital porter. There can't be that many abortion clinics round here. If you wanted to find out which one she's booked into, I'm sure you could.'

'Thanks for telling me, mate.' Martin picked up their glasses from the table and dropped them on the bar as he and Kevin headed for the door. Gail might or might not have had an early night, but with her appointment fixed for early in the morning, he doubted that either of them would get much sleep.

The next morning Martin Platt followed Gail as she dropped Sarah off at her child-minder's before taking Nicky to school. He watched as she waved to Nicky from the gate after she'd left him with his friends in the playground. When she crossed the road and stood under the bus shelter, he walked up behind her and tapped her shoulder.

She turned and glanced away nervously. 'I can't stop to talk now, Martin. I'm in a hurry.'

'I know, and I know where you're going. Kevin told me last night.'

She paled, conscious of the other people standing in the queue around them. Martin guided her out of earshot.

'Sally had no right to tell Kevin anything about my private affairs—'

'I'm glad she did,' Martin interrupted. 'Please, Gail, I'm begging you, don't kill my baby.'

'Do you think I haven't thought this out? It's you I'm thinking of, Martin. You're ten years younger than me. I've two children besides this one, and these days three count as a big family. And kids are expensive. It's not just their food, it's clothes and shoes and toys. If you take me and them on, there'll never be any spare cash. Brian and I used to argue about money all the time. You can't possibly want to get tied down.'

'I can't think of anything I'd rather do with my life,' he said earnestly. 'You mean the world to me, Gail. The kids are just the icing on the cake.'

'Nicky and Sarah?'

'And our baby too.' He smiled as he looked at her waistline.

'You want this baby?'

'Our baby,' he corrected her. 'Yes, I've never wanted anything more. Please, Gail,' he wrapped his arm round her shoulders, 'seeing as how we've both skived off work for the day, can we go back to your house and talk about this?'

'Come on, Mike,' Peter Ingram hectored. 'Whatever else you've been, you've always been a realist. I've been asking around. I know the Environmental Health people shut down that sweatshop you set up in the flat above Alma's café. And you're not exactly flush after that last deal of yours went sour. Your creditors are pressing, you need to earn some money and quickly.'

'Not enough to work for you,' Mike broke in.

'I need a salesman,' Peter continued, as if he hadn't heard Mike's remark. 'You could sell sand to the Arabs if you put your mind to it. Come to work for me and we'll both make a lot of money.'

'I haven't worked for anyone except myself else since I was sixteen, and I'm not about to change my ways now,' Mike retorted.

'I'm an easygoing bloke.'

'The hell you are. You're anything but.'

'You refusing my offer wouldn't have anything to do with you poaching my customers, would it?' Peter asked.

Mike stared at the ceiling. He knew Peter had heard that he'd formed a new company called Phoenix Fabrics. He wondered if Peter had also heard that he hadn't found any alternative premises since Environmental Health had closed down his makeshift factory in Alma's old flat, or if he was simply fishing for information.

'You're not even going to deny it, are you?' Peter's colour heightened. 'You bastard, you *have* poached my customers!'

'They haven't been complaining to you about me, have they, Peter?' Mike enquired smoothly. He was worried about how he was going to fill the orders he'd taken, but as there were still two weeks to go to the first deadline, he was confident no one had yet found out that he wouldn't be in a position to deliver.

'Of all the unscrupulous—'

'A minute ago you wanted me to work for you. Don't tell me you made me an offer before you checked all the facts, Peter?' Mike stepped back as the other man stood up. For a split second Mike thought Peter intended to thump him and he retreated to the door. Hearing a thud, he turned to see that Peter had keeled over. He ran to him but even before he stooped to feel the pulse in Peter's neck, he could see that he was dead.

'There's no need to fuss over me,' Gail protested, as Martin lifted her feet on to the sofa and covered her with a rug.

'I disagree. If I'd done a little more fussing before, perhaps you wouldn't have had that fall at work today.'

'I slipped—'

'Which is a dangerous thing for a woman in your condition to do, especially at five months. I made a decision today. I'm giving up my job as a hospital porter to help you run the café. And,' he prepared to shout down any opposition she made, 'I'm moving in here so I can look after you and the kids properly. Before you say a word, there are loads of jobs that need doing that you aren't up to tackling. And now that the kids are used to me being around, it won't come as such a shock if they see me living here and sleeping in your bed.'

'If you move in with me permanently, everyone is going to know that we're living together.'

'Practically everyone in Coronation Street knows that already,' he reminded her.

'There's one who doesn't.' She didn't want to think about how her mother-in-law would react when the street's gossips told her that she was living with a man ten years younger and, what was more, they were having a baby together.

'Gail, I love you. My moving in here is the sensible solution to our problems. I refuse to put your health or the baby's at risk by letting you cope with the kids and your job any longer on your own. And that's final.'

'I never knew you could be so masterful, Martin.'

'Is that a "yes" to me moving in?'

'I suppose it is.'

'Right, you stay there. I'll make the kids beans on toast

for tea, and when they're safely tucked up in bed, I'll make us something more exotic.'

She smiled as he tucked the blanket round her legs. 'I like the sound of that.'

'Good.' He kissed her. 'Now, do as you're told. Lie there and rest – and that's a hospital porter telling you.'

'I can't believe you're doing this to me, Mike. You told me you'd changed. Everyone warned me that you never would, but I didn't believe them.' Alma watched Mike in mounting dismay as he lifted her cases out of the walk-in wardrobe in his Docklands flat.

'You didn't believe them because you didn't want to, Alma. I asked you to move in with me. You did. I never promised you anything other than a good time and we've had many of those.' Mike hated scenes, and he knew from Alma's white face and her dark eyes brimming with tears that she was about to make one.

'You have absolutely no morals.'

'I never said I did.'

'Don't you feel anything for anyone?' she questioned soberly.

'Of course. Seize the girl and the moment, that's me.' He grinned, refusing to take her seriously.

'How could you make love to Peter's widow, on the day of Peter's funeral, when you'd never even met her before?'

'You know what widows are, Alma, vulnerable, in need

of a man's shoulder to cry on. I gave Jackie Ingram what she needed most – comfort.'

'You bastard.'

'Feel free to call me names if it makes you happier.'

'To make love to Peter's wife on the day of his funeral is despicable enough, but then just to stroll in and take over Peter's business when he was hardly cold . . .'

'I didn't have to "take it over". Jackie was so grateful for my sound business advice, she handed it to me on a plate.'

'And then to bring her here! To the flat we share. To make love to her in the same bed we sleep in every night and invite her to move in with you when you're still living with me!'

'My flat, my bed, Alma. My possessions all paid for by me,' he reminded her strongly. 'I chose to share them with you. Now I choose to share them with Jackie.' Mike looked at his watch. 'Much as I'd like to stay here and chat, I have things to do, people to see and a factory to run. Leave the keys on the hall table when you go. Jackie will need them. Oh, and be sure that you're gone within the hour – it might be embarrassing if you two run into each other. For you, that is.' He slipped on his jacket and went to the door. 'Jackie knows all about you. The clinging girlfriend I've had a lot of trouble persuading to move out.'

Gail and Martin were helping Sally to carry the last of her Christmas shopping into her house on Christmas Eve when she doubled over and clutched her stomach. Insisting it was just a twinge, she went into the kitchen to make tea and pour orange squash for Nicky and Sarah. Gail and Martin exchanged glances, and Martin went to the telephone while Gail followed Sally into the kitchen and watched with an experienced eye as she lifted cups and saucers down from the cupboard.

'You really should go to the hospital, Sally' Gail advised.

'It's too soon. Everyone says first babies take for ever to come.' Sally's face creased in pain – again.

'I was watching you when we went round the super-market. Admit it, the pains have been coming for hours.'

'Minor cramps,' Sally said dismissively.

Martin slipped his hand over the mouthpiece on the telephone receiver and shouted to Gail in the kitchen. 'Mark says Kevin's out on a breakdown thirty miles away.'

'You've got to get to the hospital, Sally,' Gail told her in a firm voice.

As another pain gripped Sally, she nodded. 'I won't argue with you any more.'

'Tell Kevin to go straight to the hospital when he comes in.' Martin set down the receiver and dialled Don Brennan's number.

'Is your case packed?' Gail asked.

'It's upstairs in the bedroom.' Sally doubled over as another pain took hold. Gail raced up the stairs as fast as her own almost full-term pregnancy would let her.

'Can I do anything?' Martin asked, feeling helpless.

'I didn't think it was going to hurt this much,' Sally gasped.

Martin fought a bout of nausea. It was Sally now, but it would be Gail any time soon, and much as he wanted a baby he couldn't bear the thought of Gail going through the agonies of labour.

'I'll come to the hospital with you.' Gail ran back into the living room, and Martin took the case from her.

Sally shook her head. 'There's no need, Gail. You have to look after Nicky and Sarah . . .'

'I can do that,' Martin offered.

'I've probably got hours to go yet, and Kevin will be there long before the birth to hold my hand,' Sally insisted. 'You two lock up here and go home.' She glanced to where Nicky and Sarah were perched side by side in Sally's armchair, looking at a comic Gail had bought for them. 'You have to prepare for Father Christmas's arrival.'

Martin went to answer the door. He returned with Don Brennan and together they helped Sally into the back of the taxi.

'We shouldn't have let her go by herself,' Gail said to Martin as they watched Don drive round the corner. 'Her pains were coming really close together.'

'She'll be fine.' Martin hoped that he sounded more

convincing than he felt. It was the first time he had seen a woman in labour and it had traumatised him. He returned to Sally's house to make sure that the doors were locked.

He and Gail were rounding the corner of Coronation Street and Rosamund Street when they saw Don Brennan's cab pulled up high on the pavement so as not to block the traffic.

'Sally!' Gail shouted.

Don opened the back door of the cab and called to them for help. But he was too late. By the time Gail and Martin reached him they could hear a baby crying.

'I never thought we'd be in here together.' Brimming with maternal pride, Sally lifted her baby out of the cot and held her up for Gail to admire. 'Kevin and I decided during visiting last night that we're going to call her Rosie, because she was born in Rosamund Street.'

'If I'd known you'd give birth so soon, I'd never have let you go off alone in that taxi.' Gail managed a smile, although she was worn out from her own labour.

'Why not? Don Brennan proved himself a good midwife. We wouldn't have done any better if we'd been in here, would we, my precious?' she asked her baby solemnly.

'Gail?' A nurse wheeled a cot towards her. 'Are you in a fit state to take delivery of your son?'

'Oh, yes.' Gail smiled as the nurse lifted him from the cot and handed him to her.

'Have you and Martin decided on a name yet?' Sally looked at the door. The clock above it said two minutes to seven, but she had caught a glimpse of feet in the narrow gap between the floor and the door and she hoped that Kevin was waiting to see them. Or, even better, that the ward sister would open the door early.

'David – David Platt. I've asked Martin to register him in his name.' Gail pushed aside the shawl and examined her son's fingers. He was so small, so perfect and so like Martin that she wanted to cry, which was a ridiculous thing to do when she had never been happier in her life.

Kevin and Martin stood impatiently outside the maternity ward. Both were holding bunches of forced hothouse flowers and behind them in the corridor a choir was singing 'God Rest Ye Merry Gentlemen', to remind them that it was Christmas Day. As if either of them could forget it. Martin, Gail, Nicky and Sarah's Christmas dinner had been left abandoned and uneaten on the table and Martin had roped in Rita Fairclough to babysit while he rushed Gail to hospital. Kevin and Sally's turkey was still at the bottom of their fridge.

'Who would have thought Gail and Sally would go into labour within a day of each other?' Kevin said.

'I saw your baby when they let me come up with Gail

from the labour ward this afternoon. She's . . . pretty.' Martin wasn't quite sure what else to call Sally's baby. It had looked rather red and wrinkled in comparison to his David, whom he'd already decided was going to turn into a fine strong lad.

'You said Gail was dishing up Christmas dinner when the pains came.'

'We never got to eat it,' Martin told him.

'If you're hungry we could go out for a curry and a jar after visiting,' Kevin suggested.

'On Christmas Day?'

'I forgot.'

'I've got to get home because I've left the kids with Rita, but you're welcome to come back with me, if you like. I can't promise you a curry, but we've plenty of food and drink in the house.'

'Ta.' Kevin smiled. 'I'd like that.'

The doors to the ward opened, and Martin and Kevin saw Gail and Sally sitting up in neighbouring beds, both nursing their babies.

Chapter Forty-Five

'Ken Barlow has spent every New Year's Eve in the Rovers since I started working here as a barmaid,' Bet said to Alec Gilroy, as she looked around the crowded pub.

'He wasn't here last year,' Alec pointed out.

'Last year he was off gallivanting with that Wendy Crozier who broke up his marriage.'

'And now that he's footloose and fancy-free he could be seeing in the New Year with a dozen women. That's what most men would call celebrating,' Alec said archly.

'Oh, yes?' She crossed her arms and gave him a fierce look.

'Only joking, my darling wife.' He patted her behind playfully.

Surprised by how well her marriage to Alec was working out, considering the impetuous way they had rushed to the register office, Bet gave him a smile before glancing along the bar. 'Looks like we've hit a lull. I'll be back as soon as I can.'

'Hey, where are you off to?' Alec shouted, as she lifted the flap in the counter and walked out from behind the bar.

'I'm just going to pop round to Ken's flat and see if he wants to join us.'

'And if he's with a woman, or slams the door in your face?'

'I'll shout "Happy New Year" through the letter-box.'

'Put your coat on,' Alec shouted, but Bet slipped out in her thin silk blouse and satin skirt. 'If you catch your death of cold, don't blame me,' he muttered.

'What was that, Alec?' Jack Duckworth set four empty glasses on the counter.

'Nothing. What can I get you, Jack?'

Bet knocked on the door of the flat above the mini-market and, to her surprise, it opened. Ken had obviously left it on the latch, which meant he'd either just gone out for a moment or was in and hadn't bothered to lock the door.

'Ken?' When he didn't answer she walked up the stairs and tapped on the door of the living room. 'Ken?'

'Who is it?'

'It's me, Ken.' She pushed open the door to see him slumped forward over the coffee table. 'I called round to see if you wanted to come to the Rovers to welcome the New Year in. Practically the whole street's there.'

'I'd rather be by myself,' he mumbled, without looking at her.

She eyed the row of pill bottles set out in front of him; set beside them was a glass and a half-full bottle of whisky.

'How did you get in?' he asked, lifting his head to look at her.

She could see that he'd been drinking but he wasn't drunk – yet. She sat beside him. The pill bottles were all full and she breathed a sigh of relief.

'What's this?' She picked up one of the bottles.

'Pills.'

'That must be some headache you've got.'

'Heartache more like.'

'Is this all over Deirdre?' She saw no point in mincing her words.

Ken nodded wretchedly. 'I've lost her, Bet.'

'You lost her a year ago, Ken,' she said bluntly.

'I didn't realise it then. Now I know that I'll never get her back.'

'Good!'

'Good?' Ken repeated, as indignation won over self-pity.

'Now you've finally realised that you've lost her perhaps you'll stop hounding her. And don't say you haven't been. I've seen you standing outside her house late at night and

I've also heard that you have an odd habit of turning up wherever Phil Jennings happens to be.'

'Coincidence,' Ken muttered.

'Time to move on.' Bet picked up the bottles of pills.

'Where are taking them?'

'Where they belong.' She walked into the bathroom, lifted the toilet lid, opened the bottles and tipped their contents into the pan, then flushed it. 'Get your coat. You're coming to the Rovers with me. Who knows? You may even meet a woman worth a second look.'

'I only want Deirdre.'

'I don't recommend that as an opening gambit if you do meet someone. And, remember, relationships work both ways. She'll have to think you're worth a second look too. And the way you are at the moment, any woman in her right mind will walk right past you.'

'I heard you've opened a repair shop in one of those new units Maurice Jones has built on the site of Mike's old factory.' Alec Gilroy cleared away Phil Jennings's sandwich plate from his table in the Rovers.

'Business is booming,' Phil boasted. 'I've so many machines out in pubs, clubs and arcades that I needed somewhere to bring them for repair. The kind of use they're getting, bits wear out from time to time.'

'I suppose there's a fair profit in those machines.' Alec tried and failed to sound casual.

Phil wondered what he was after. 'There is,' he agreed.

'If you're looking for somewhere to invest your money, I've been thinking of opening a nightclub in the old Graffiti Club premises.'

'Oh, yes?'

'Could be a real money-spinner. The place is big enough to hold a crowd and partition an area off for machines.'

'People in clubs aren't interested in playing arcade games, Alec.'

'The nightclub idea alone is worth going for. What do you say? Me and you – partners?'

'Sorry, Alec.' Phil finished his beer. 'You're just too small fry to interest me.'

Alec glared at Phil's back as he left the pub. 'The nerve of the man,' he muttered, as he dumped Phil's plate and glass in the washing-up tray beneath the counter.

'What man?' Bet asked.

'That Phil Jennings. Swanning round with Deirdre, opening up amusement arcades all over the place. It's not right for our local councillor to have an affair with a man with his interests. Hey, Alf,' Alec shouted to Alf Roberts across the bar, 'the council elections are coming up. You standing against Deirdre?'

'I'm too busy with the shop to bother with all that now.' Alf picked up his glass and walked to the bar.

'In my opinion, we need you back in to run things properly.'

'Like you needed me the last time when you voted me out?'

'Where's your fighting spirit? You only lost by seven votes.' Alec pulled a couple of pints. 'Why don't you and me sit down quietly in that corner and talk about it?'

Raquel Wolstenhulme, a sales assistant at Bettabuy's, pouted sexily at Curly Watts, flicked her blonde hair back out of her blue eyes and gave him the glad eye as they built up a promotional display of cornflakes in the centre aisle of the supermarket. After he had been awarded his HND in business studies, Curly had been taken on as a management trainee and, apart from a minor argument with Brendan Scott, from Head Office, over the way he'd handled a customer complaint, he felt he was doing well.

'Do you really think I've a chance of taking the title, Mr Watts?' Raquel cooed seductively.

'I think it's already yours.' He gave Raquel a warm smile as a prelude to asking her out.

Raquel knew exactly what he was about to do, but although she liked him, she had greater ambitions than dating a trainee manager at Bettabuy's. She burned to become a model, and she saw the staff beauty competition for the title of Miss Bettabuy Northwest as a stepping-stone towards that end.

'You're very attractive,' Curly complimented her. In

fact, he thought she was the most stunning girl he'd ever met.

'Thank you for saying so, Mr Watts.'

'If you want someone to go with you to the competition, I'd be happy to drive you.'

'I'd like that very much indeed.' She put her hand on the same packet of cornflakes as Curly and gave him a huge smile. Then Curly saw the manager walking down the aisle towards them, and tried to concentrate on the pyramid they were building. But it was difficult. He felt happier than he had since Shirley Armitage had walked out on him.

'Come on, Deirdre,' Phil Jennings coaxed, as he drove her into Manchester for a night out. 'All's fair in love, war and politics.'

'I was looking forward to a good clean fight against Alf Roberts, and then Alec Gilroy tells me you've been spreading rumours about Alf and one of his supporters, Vivian Bartlett.'

'I did see them together.'

'Doing what?' she asked suspiciously.

He winked at her. 'Campaigning.'

'I don't need you putting your oar in, Phil,' she said crossly. 'I either win this seat fair and square or I don't win it at all.'

'Just trying to help.'

'Well, I don't need your help,' she said firmly.

'Not even after we go to bed tonight?'

'You're impossible.' Her anger dissipated and she laughed.

'Come on.' He parked the car. 'Let's go and see the film.' He kissed her before he opened his door. 'We'll continue this discussion on the way home.'

Ken Barlow had just made a pot of coffee and put it on the kitchen table next to the stack of marking he'd brought home from school when there was a thundering at the door. He opened it to see Alf Roberts, red-faced and angry.

'Like a cup of coffee?'

'No, I bloody well wouldn't. I'm here to tear that out of your window.' Alf strode across the room.

'Touch it and you'll be sorry,' Ken threatened as Alf moved towards Deirdre's election poster.

'I'm not having it displayed in the window of my flat.'

'As long as I pay you rent, it's my flat and I'm a free citizen. I can put up any poster I want.'

'You can't put up a bloody poster for a councillor who doesn't even run a clean campaign. Do you know what Phil Jennings has been saying about me?'

'That's Phil, not Deirdre.' Ken refused to get side-tracked into a discussion about Phil, whom he hated even more than Alf did. 'It's a free country, Alf. How would it look if it got out that you wouldn't even let your tenant canvass for the opposition?'

Alf dropped his hand and went to the door.

'If that was your idea of canvassing for votes, it won't be only me who'll be supporting the opposition,' Ken shouted after Alf as he walked down the stairs.

'Good luck,' Curly whispered, as Raquel disappeared through the door that led to the stage. He took his seat next to his housemate, Angie Freeman, and waited for the Miss Bettabuy Northwest beauty pageant to begin. His heart sank as the judges filed into the box to the side of the stage. In the middle was Brendan Scott from Head Office. If Brendan had seen him walk in with Raquel, she had no chance of winning.

'Problems?' Angie asked, seeing him frown.

'See that man sitting in the middle of the judges.' Curly deliberately looked to the opposite side of the theatre.

'What about him?'

'We fell out. If he's twigged that Raquel's with me, she stands no chance. I was trying to help her and all I've done is set her back. She was really hoping to win this title and get noticed. She wants to be a model.'

'If she wants to be a model, she can wear my designs in the end-of-year show at college,' Angie offered.

'She wants to be a professional,' Curly said despondently, as Brendan glared at him.

'Even professionals have to start somewhere. You'd be surprised at the people who come to a student fashion show hoping to spot talent. Anything can happen, for the models as well as the designers.'

'Quiet, it's starting.' Curly beamed as Raquel walked on stage in a bikini.

In the pub after the show, Angie sat between Curly and Raquel trying to work out who was the most disappointed, him or her.

'All I wanted to do was help,' Curly said miserably.

'You tried.' Raquel sipped her drink. 'And it's not all bad news. Angie's asked me to model her clothes for the student fashion show.'

'And you might be spotted by a top photographer or a scout for a fashion-house, whisked off in a limousine to London, put up in the Ritz and photographed for a really big glossy magazine,' Angie said cheerfully, attempting to lighten the gloom.

Curly tried to smile. He didn't mind Raquel having a successful modelling career but the last thing he wanted was for her to be taken away from Weatherfield and him. As yet he hadn't done any more than hold hands with her, but now, having seen her in a bikini, he wanted to do a whole lot more.

'Alf, I want a word.' Ken accosted Alf Roberts in the Rovers the night before the council elections.

'What about?' Alf adopted an innocent expression, although he knew what Ken wanted to see him about.

'The poster I put up in my window supporting Deirdre in the council elections – you went into my flat and tore it down.'

'It's *my* flat and I told you I didn't want it in the window.'

'I pay the rent, I live there, it's *my* flat. People fought and died so we could have free speech in this country.'

'And you weren't one of them.' Alf drew back his fist and punched Ken, who ducked and floored Alf with a rugby tackle.

'Stop it, the pair of you!' Bet yelled, as Alec stood back and made no attempt to stop the men rolling around on the floor of the bar.

A flash momentarily lit up the scene.

'Ta, very much. This is going to look great on the front page of the *Gazette*. I can see the caption now. 'Prospective Councillor in Brawl with Opposition Supporter.' The young man who had taken the photograph held his camera high in the air to protect it as he ran out of the door.

The estate agent handed Alma Sedgewick a brochure and an envelope. 'These are the details of the house, Mrs . . .'

Alma thought rapidly. The last name she wanted to give was her own. 'Baldwin,' she snapped decisively. Pushing her dark glasses further up her nose, she took the sheaf of papers the agent handed her.

'The key is in the envelope. Don't forget to return it before lunch because we have other viewings booked.'

'I will.' Alma left the office, climbed into her car and drove to Jackie Ingram's house. It was as grand a mansion as the one Mike had bought for Susan, but it was set in far larger gardens. Alma parked the car in the drive, checked that none of her hair had slipped out from beneath her headscarf, walked to the door and opened it.

The décor was red plush and gilt, the sort of interior design a *nouveau riche* businessman might go for. She glanced into the downstairs rooms. They were all expensively furnished, but devoid of ornaments and personal knick-knacks. The place had the impersonal air of a furniture showroom and she wondered if Jackie had packed her treasures away or taken them to Mike's flat in Docklands.

Heart pounding, she ran up the stairs and went into the bedrooms. All of them were just as bare. She opened the walk-in wardrobes. There was nothing personal in the entire place except . . .

She stared at the satin duvet cover on the bed. Then she opened her handbag, took out a metal nail file and attacked it, plunging in the point again and again, as she imagined Mike and Jackie lying naked beneath it. She didn't stop until the duvet was a mass of shredded satin and stuffing.

'I didn't expect to see you back at work so soon after having a baby,' Ivy Brennan snapped at Gail, who was standing behind the till in the café.

'It's my job, Ivy.' Gail struggled to keep her temper. She had never stopped Ivy from seeing Nicky and Sarah, but since Martin had moved in Ivy hadn't missed an opportunity to make snide remarks about her 'toy boy', the baby and the effect her behaviour was having on Nicky, who was at a particularly impressionable age. It would have been bad enough if Ivy had only made the remarks to her, but she knew that Ivy made them in Nicky's presence as well.

'It's half-term.' Ivy said abruptly.

'I know, Ivy.' Gail moved along the counter. 'Can I get you something? Tea, coffee?'

'Who is looking after my grandchildren?'

It didn't escape Gail's attention that Ivy hadn't asked after the new baby. 'Martin,' she replied.

'That's disgusting, allowing a young lad like that to look after your children.'

'Martin is very good with Nicky and Sarah, *and* little David,' Gail added pointedly in an effort to provoke Ivy into asking after the new baby.

'You're not fit to be a mother!'

The customers turned towards them as Ivy continued to rant. After a few minutes, Gail decided that she couldn't take any more. 'If you want something, Ivy, I'll be happy to serve you, but if you only came in to call me names, I'll have to ask you to leave because you're upsetting my customers.'

'I wouldn't want to eat here anyway,' Ivy said loudly, making sure that everyone heard her.

'You all right?' Mavis asked Gail, after Ivy had left.

'I've been better.' Gail glanced around the tables. 'If you're all right here for a moment, I'll take a break out the back.'

'I can cope,' Mavis assured her.

Gail went into the kitchen and stared blindly out of the back window into the builder's yard. She and Martin were happy, living together with the children. It hadn't been an easily won happiness: after the trauma of her marriage and frequent break-ups with Brian she had been constantly on the look-out for problems, but so far – superstitiously she touched wood – there hadn't been any. Until now.

Since the day she had come home from hospital with David, Martin had pleaded with her to marry him. She wanted to – oh, how she wanted to – but she couldn't help feeling that sooner or later he would come to resent being tied to her, Nicky, Sarah and David so young. Then he'd go looking for the youth she'd stolen from him by making him a father before he'd reached his twenties.

And there was Ivy. However hard she tried not to let her ex-mother-in-law's comments hurt, they did. She wondered how Ivy would react if she did marry Martin. Would it prove to Ivy once and for all that they were serious about their relationship and that Martin was capable of shouldering the responsibility for bringing up Nicky and Sarah? Or would it only goad Ivy into making even more public scenes like the one she had just made in the hope of disrupting their lives?

'There's more to life than being a councillor, Deirdre,' Phil Jennings consoled her as he and Deirdre walked into her house after the ballot count.

'I know.' She tried to put Alf's triumphant smile to the back of her mind. 'It's just that I really enjoyed the job and I haven't a clue what I'm going to do now.' Deirdre sat down and put her head in her hands.

'I know what you are going to do,' Phil said confidently, sitting in the chair opposite hers. 'You can work for me. I need somebody to front the business, chase sales and do the books.'

'I don't want you inventing a job for me to make me feel better.' She said disconsolately.

'I most certainly am not. It's a real position within my company, and after you've done it for a week, you'll believe me. In fact, I was thinking of advertising for someone. If you want to start with the books,' he nodded to the briefcase standing in the corner of the room, 'you can look at them when you've a spare minute. But for now I think you need some tender, loving care.' He left his chair and offered her his hand. 'And the best place to administer that is bed.'

'Mike.' Gail ran out of the café when she glimpsed him walking out of Phil Jennings's workshop. 'I was hoping to see you.'

'You haven't heard I'm spoken for?' he teased.

'I've heard that you're marrying Jackie Ingram. Congratulations,' she murmured, not knowing what else to say to him, although the word almost stuck in her throat after listening to Alma's account of the way he had treated her since Peter Ingram had died.

'Next weekend.' He grinned. 'I've just been having a word with my best man, Phil, about the arrangements. If you want to come you'll be more than welcome.'

'Thanks, but I'll be busy running the café.'

'If you change your mind, you know where it is.'

'No.'

'We're having the reception in Greenacres.' He named the newest, most expensive and fashionable venue in Manchester. 'Well, if you didn't want to talk to me about my wedding, it must be something else. And I warn you now, you can save your breath if you're going to try to persuade me and Jackie not to prosecute Alma for malicious damage after she ruined Jackie's duvet. She made the mistake of parking her car outside the estate agent's so they could take down her number and trace her after the damage had been discovered.'

'I didn't know . . .'

'Then forget I said anything. Jackie and I have decided to let the matter drop anyway.'

'Perhaps I shouldn't be talking to you at all considering the way things are between you and Alma, and with you getting married to Jackie . . .'

'You can't stop now you've started.'

'The yearly rent on the lease on the café and the flat above it has been doubled. There's no way I can afford to pay any more than I am already, and Alma says it wouldn't be sound business sense for her to pay it either, so she's closing down the café and moving away.'

'She told you that's what she's going to do?' Mike looked serious.

'Yesterday morning.'

'Do you know who owns the lease?'

'I wrote the name down when Alma mentioned it. I knew I'd never remember it otherwise.' Gail handed him a piece of paper.

'Don't worry, I'll take care of it.'

'What will you do?'

He tapped his nose. 'Wait and see.' He climbed into his car.

'Congratulations,' Gail shouted again as he drove away.

Chapter Forty-Six

Mike slipped his arm round Jackie's waist as they posed for photographs with Phil and Deirdre in the manicured gardens of Greenacres. Mike was feeling particularly smug: not only had he married Peter Ingram's money, he had used some of Jackie's to form a new company, Alcazar Holdings, and its first acquisition had been the lease of Alma's flat and the café. Alma had no idea that he was her landlord, and every time he thought about the papers he had signed the day before, he couldn't help smiling.

'Just one more of the bride and groom, by themselves this time,' the photographer shouted.

Phil and Deirdre moved behind the photographer.

'And one of the happy couple kissing.'

The photographer clicked his button as Mike dutifully kissed Jackie's lips.

'That's it, all finished.'

'And about time,' Mike said, as the man packed up his gear. 'I'm parched. Who's for drinks?'

'We all have been for hours,' Phil said sullenly.

Deirdre looked at him. Phil had been in a peculiar mood ever since he had suggested that she take over his books and she wondered if it was because he had expected her to start on them right away. She had tried to explain that she couldn't just hand over everything she had been working on to Alf after the election, that she needed time to brief him on the projects she had been nurturing, but he hadn't been sympathetic.

'This is a lovely place,' she said, as she took Phil's arm.

'Isn't it?' Jackie agreed, clinging to Mike as she tiptoed over the lawn, wary of her stiletto heels sinking into the grass. 'We should buy something like this, Mike.'

'Neither of us knows the first thing about running a hotel.'

'Not as a hotel, as a house for our retirement.'

'Our what?' Mike exploded.

'Retirement. I'm putting the factory up for sale next week. I know it's not worth much but I'm prepared to take whatever I can get for it.'

'Are you mad?' Mike stopped walking and stared at her.

'I have no intention of taking a back seat while you spend all your time running the business. I had years of that with Peter. I want to sell up, retire and spend time with you.'

'Doing what exactly?' The thought of being locked up in a claustrophobic marriage spending time with Jackie made his blood run cold.

'Having a good time.'

'No one can make a career out of being married.'

Deirdre and Phil went into the house when Jackie and Mike started arguing, but after he had taken a glass of champagne from the waiter, Phil went to the window and watched them. He was furious with Mike for refusing to give him a loan when he had asked for one a few days before.

'Trouble in Paradise?' he asked Jackie, as she walked in ahead of Mike, with a grim expression on her face.

'A minor disagreement,' she snapped.

'Mike's last marriage didn't last long – come to that, none of his relationships have either.'

'You knew his wife?' she asked, downing one glass of champagne and reaching for another.

'Yes.' Phil didn't want to get sidetracked into talking about Susan. 'What did you mean earlier when you said your factory wasn't worth much?'

'I considered selling it after Peter died, but the agent who came round to value it said even if he could sell it, which he doubted, he wouldn't get a good price.'

'Did you know the agent?' Phil asked.

'He was a friend of Mike's. He was the one who suggested I ask Mike to take it over.' Her face clouded. 'You don't think Mike asked him to give me a deliberately low valuation . . .'

Phil smiled. 'I'm not saying anything, Jackie. It's for

you to draw your own conclusions, but after losing almost everything he owned in that Spanish land deal that went sour, Mike needed a job.'

'The bastard!' Jackie's face hardened, and she crossed the room to where Mike was regaling his guests with a dirty joke.

Phil watched her push her new husband out into the corridor. Mike's previous marriage had lasted a full year but he had a feeling this one wasn't going to last a week.

Deirdre checked Phil's books with mounting horror. He owed money to every supplier and tradesman he dealt with and, on her calculations, the machines weren't bringing in enough profit to cover a fraction of the repayments he had to make if he was ever going to clear them. As if that wasn't enough, he had no assets. The arcades and the machines were all leased, the rent hadn't been paid on the buildings for months and the firms who owned the machines were threatening to repossess them. She wondered if Phil had asked her to look at his books because he hadn't been able to bring himself to tell her she was living with a man who was about to go bankrupt.

The front door opened. She glanced at the clock. It was half past two, too early for Tracy to come home from school.

Phil walked in. Blood was pouring from a cut above his eye and his face was covered with bruises.

'What on earth happened?' She rushed over to him, momentarily forgetting the horror of his books.

'What do you think happened?' he asked sarcastically. 'I bumped into a fist.'

'Someone you owed money to,' she suggested.

'Then you finally looked at the books.' He went into the kitchen, ran the tap, soaked a tea-towel and pressed it over his eye.

'You're about to go bankrupt.'

'Tell me something I don't know. Look, Deirdre, the guy who did this hasn't finished with me and he's not the only one who wants to rearrange my face. I've stashed away some cash—'

'Then pay off some of the money you owe.'

'Have you gone crazy? I'm using it to get far, far away from here. Somewhere warm where the wine and the living are cheap.'

'I won't go with you.'

'I'm not asking. I'm taking my wife.'

'Your wife!' Shocked, Deirdre fell back into a chair. 'You never said anything about being married.'

'You never asked.'

She thought back to when she had first met Phil. He had chased her and, newly separated from Ken, she had been flattered to think that another man could want her. No, she had never asked, but neither had he volunteered the information. Disgusted with herself for allowing him to use her, she sat staring into space as he ran upstairs. A few moments later, he returned with his suitcase. He picked up his briefcase.

'This is going into the river. 'Bye, Deirdre, it was nice knowing you.'

He walked down the passage and out of the house and, she hoped, out of her and Tracy's lives for ever.

She got up and went to the bathroom to wash her hands and face. Then she put on a layer of foundation, lipstick and mascara. When she returned to the hall, she saw that Phil had left the key she'd given him on the board. She picked it up and walked to the mini-market. Alf Roberts was standing behind the till, talking to Vera Duckworth.

She waited until Vera had left before she approached Alf. 'Congratulations. I'm sorry the election got so dirty between us.'

'So am I, Deirdre, but it wasn't your fault. It was Phil's. What can I do for you?'

'I've been thinking, now you're a councillor again you won't have much time to run this place.'

'No, I won't.' He leant on the till. 'Want your old job back?'

'Yes, please,' she murmured, grateful to him for not making her beg.

'I can't thank you enough for introducing me to your housemate, Curly. The students' fashion show was in this huge, plush hotel, and the clothes Angie had designed were the best, really stunning. And this photographer – he's professional and everything – he took loads and loads of photographs of me,' Raquel gushed. 'I know you and Angie told me it was going to be a good show, but I had no idea it was going to be *that* good. And this photographer, well, he knows people in London. And he said I could make it big there as a model if I had the right contacts. And he's prepared to introduce me to people. He's setting up appointments next week for me. And these people he knows, they're putting me up in a hotel and everything. And it's all down to you telling Angie that I wanted to be a model. I can't thank you enough.' Raquel wrapped her arms around Curly's neck, hugged him and kissed his cheek.

As Curly returned her embrace, he wished Raquel had never met Angie. Bettabuy's just wasn't going to be the same without her there to cheer him up.

Gail waited impatiently for Martin to come home from his weekly night out at the Rovers with Kevin. She had prepared a special supper of chicken salad and bought a bottle of wine to go with it. She had laid the table with her best cloth, glasses and china, and rehearsed the speech she wanted to make to him a dozen times in her head. When the door opened, she jumped up and stood in front of the table so he wouldn't see straight away what she'd done.

'Hello, love.' He kissed her cheek. 'I picked up some gossip in the Rovers. You know Mike Baldwin got married last weekend? Well, apparently he and Jackie quarrelled on their wedding day. She's already left him and ordered her lawyers to pay him to give her a quick divorce. Alec reckons Mike will get a hundred grand.' He glanced over her shoulder at the table. 'What's all this in aid of? Wine, chicken salad – it looks gorgeous. We celebrating something I don't know about or,' his face clouded, 'something I've forgotten?'

'No.' She knelt in front of him and looked up into his eyes. 'Will you marry me?'

'You're not having me on? After all the times I've asked you and you said no . . .'

'I've been thinking about it. I've been selfish, Martin. We *are* happy together. To be honest, I've never been happier in my life. But sometimes I think we're almost too happy and I've been afraid that if we married it would spoil our relationship. Brian and I were fine until we married.'

He helped her to her feet. 'I'm not Brian.'

'I know.' She returned his kiss. 'Want some supper?'

'Can I give you my answer first, the way I want to?'

'I already know it's yes.'

'I love you.'

'And I love you. Just one thing. Can we have a small wedding?'

'The smallest you can organise. Now that you've finally agreed to marry me, you can have whatever you want, love, provided I can give it to you.'

When they left the Rovers at closing time, Ken and Alma Sedgewick were still laughing about the way Jackie had ditched Mike less than a week after they'd got married.

'I know it's bitchy of me,' Alma said, 'but I feel Mike's finally got what he deserves.'

'I couldn't agree with you more.'

'You know something, Ken, it's good to sit and talk to a man as uncomplicated as you after living with someone like Mike. I enjoyed tonight more than I've enjoyed a night out in years.'

'It doesn't have to end now. Would you like to come up to my flat for a coffee?'

'Just coffee?' Alma raised her eyebrows.

'I'm not offering any more – at the moment.'

'Then I'd be delighted.'

He opened the door alongside the entrance to the mini-market, and she walked up the stairs ahead of him.

'You didn't have the guts to come round and tell me yourself!' Ivy railed at Gail. 'I had to find out from Vera Duckworth, who took great delight in telling me that a friend of hers had seen your name and that of the toy-boy you live with posted in the register office under forthcoming marriages. The thought of you marrying him and letting him live in the same house as my Brian's children—'

'Martin's a man, not a boy. I love him and he loves me. He's the father of my baby and he's good with all of my children,' Gail said softly, looking out of the window into the garden when Martin was playing with Nicky and Sarah. 'And I'd be happier if you kept your voice down, Ivy, it's not good for Nicky or Sarah to hear you shouting at me.'

'Not good? Now you're telling me how to behave in front of my grandchildren!' Ivy was almost purple with indignation.

'I am their mother.'

'What kind of a mother marries a boy half her age? Well, I'm not standing back and allowing him to move permanently into the same house as Nicky and Sarah.'

'You have no choice, Ivy. Nicky and Sarah live with me, I'm marrying Martin and . . .' Gail braced herself. '. . . he's making a formal application to adopt Nicky and Sarah so we can change their name to Platt.'

'Over my dead body!'

'Can't you think of Nicky for once?' Gail pleaded. 'What it's like for him at school. I'm going to be Mrs Platt. His brother's name is David Platt. He and Sarah want the same name as the rest of us.'

'Nicky's keeping his father's surname,' Ivy said flatly.

'And I know exactly how to make sure of it. I'm going to alter my will and leave Nicky my house, but only on condition he keeps the name Tilsley.'

'Do whatever you want, Ivy. I can't stop you.'

'You'd change his name to Platt, and deprive him of his inheritance?'

'Nicky can decide what he wants to do when he's old enough. But for now, all Martin and I want is to be left in peace so we can bring up our children and remain as happy as we are now. So, please, don't try making trouble between me and Martin the way you did between Brian and me.'

'Of all the nerve . . .'

'If you want to see the children, go and see them, Ivy. If you don't, I'll have to ask you to leave because I have to make the Sunday dinner.'

Ivy glared at her. 'I'll go, but don't think you've heard the last word on this subject. Because you haven't.'

'You wanted the wedding to be small and quiet, Gail, and it was, but it was still perfect.' Sally Webster blotted her eyes carefully with a tissue so as not to smudge her mascara. She always cried at weddings and Gail's had been no exception. She turned round and looked at Gail and Martin, who were sitting in the back of the mini-bus Kevin had borrowed from work for the day. Nicky and Sarah were sitting alongside Alma Sedgewick, who was asking them about school, and Rosie and David were making noises at each other from their adjoining car seats.

'Looks like it's not that small.' Kevin pulled up outside Gail's house. 'You've another couple of guests waiting.'

'Do you know them, Gail?' Martin asked, peering through the window.

Gail shook her head. 'I'll go and see what they want.' She left the van. 'Can I help you?' she asked the couple, as Martin helped Kevin unload the children from the van.

'Social Services.' Both the man and the woman showed Gail their identity cards. 'We're sorry to disturb you, Mrs Tilsley—'

'Platt,' Martin interrupted, joining Gail. 'We've just got married.'

'Congratulations.' The woman gave them a cold smile. 'We are here to investigate allegations that you are an unfit mother.'

'That's ridiculous!' Martin exclaimed furiously.

'Shouting or losing your temper isn't going to help the situation, sir.' The man moved protectively closer to his female colleague. 'We are legally obliged to look into all allegations of neglect or abuse of children.'

The woman glanced back at Kevin, Sally and Alma, who were standing with the babies, Nicky and Sarah. 'Are those your children, Mrs Platt?'

'Three of them are.' Gail felt sick. She knew exactly who had made the allegations against her and why.

'Could we talk to the older children – alone, please?'

The man and woman talked to Nicky and Sarah for an hour, then left. As soon as they had gone Martin reached for his jacket.

'You can't go anywhere,' Gail pleaded. 'It's our wedding day. Kevin, Sally and Alma are here—'

'I won't be long,' he interrupted.

'Please don't go.' Gail knew he was going to see Ivy. 'If you say something to her now, she'll only try to make things even more difficult for us.'

'It's about time someone started making things difficult for *her*. Keep the champagne on ice. Please stay and keep Gail company,' he said to Kevin and Alma. 'I won't be long.'

Martin strode the short distance to Coronation Street and knocked on the door of number five.

Don Brennan answered. 'Martin, this is a surprise.' Don's greeting was warm but guarded. He liked Gail, Martin and the children, but he was aware of how Ivy behaved towards them and couldn't imagine why Martin had called. 'It's nice to see you. Come in.'

'Is Ivy here?'

'Yes.' Don lowered his voice. 'But I warn you, you're not exactly her favourite person at the moment.'

She's not exactly mine either.' Martin walked through to the living room.

Ivy was sitting in a chair reading the paper. She looked up as he strode in. 'How dare you come into my house?'

'And how dare you telephone Social Services and tell them Gail is an unfit mother,' Martin interrupted fiercely.

'What? Ivy, is this true?' Don looked from Martin to his wife.

Ivy flushed. 'Gail *is* an unfit mother. Look at the things she's done to those children since Brian died. Allowing this – this boy to live in her house. Carrying on with him in front of Nicky and Sarah.'

'Gail and I are no longer "carrying on", Ivy. We were married an hour ago,' Martin informed her brusquely. 'And Nicky and Sarah couldn't be happier for their mother and me.'

'This time you really have gone too far, Ivy. Gail couldn't care better for those children if she tried.' Don turned to Martin. 'I'll sort this out and see that Ivy withdraws the allegations.'

'That's all Gail and I want.' Martin continued to stare at Ivy but she averted her eyes. 'That, and to be left alone to live our lives in peace.'

'You can walk round to Gail's and apologise to her now,' Don ordered Ivy as soon as Martin left.

'I'll do no such thing. She *is* an unfit mother,' Ivy

repeated, braver with her husband than she had been with Martin.

'You're not the warm, loving woman I married three years ago, Ivy. Not any more. You've become hard and bitter. I've been thinking of leaving you for the last few months, and this has helped me to make up my mind. I know you're still grieving for Brian, that's understandable, and I've made allowances. But what you've done to Gail, that boy and your own grandchildren is despicable. I'll pack my bags.'

Ivy ran to Don and clung to him. 'Please, don't leave me, Don. If you go I'll have nothing left. First I lost Brian, and now Martin's married Gail he'll take Nicky and Sarah . . .' Unable to continue, she buried her head in his chest.

He pushed her away from him and held her at arm's length. 'Martin and Gail are entitled to a life of their own, and Gail's never stopped you from seeing Nicky or Sarah, has she?'

'No,' Ivy answered, in a small voice.

'Then start behaving like a grandmother. Consider the children's feelings and put them before yourself and your own petty jealousy.'

'I'll go round to Gail's as soon as I pull myself together.'

'It might not hurt for her to see you the way you are. At least you'd prove to her that you're human,' he said acidly.

'I'm sorry, Don. You won't leave me, will you?'

Don shook his head.

'Perhaps it might be better if we moved away from here to somewhere where I wouldn't have to see Gail and the children every day. They remind me of Brian – and I miss him so much.'

'Where do you want to go?' Don asked.

'Does it matter? I haven't had a job since the factory closed. Perhaps I could find one in another area. And you can drive your taxi anywhere in the country.'

'You wouldn't mind selling this house?'

'No.' At that moment Ivy meant it. 'No, I wouldn't, Don.'

Mike Baldwin walked into the Rovers and blanched at the sight of Ken Barlow and Alma Sedgewick standing together at the bar. Ken's arm was round Alma and she was laughing at something he was saying. The last time he had called in at the mini-market he had overheard Ivy Brennan telling Vera Duckworth that Ken and Alma had become an item, but he had assumed that was just gossip. Now he was looking at them together, it was obvious that they were far more than just friends.

'Drink, Mike?' Alec Gilroy asked.

'Later. I've just remembered something I have to do.' Mike left the Rovers, walked down the street to number one and knocked on the door.

When Deirdre opened it, he asked. 'Feel like coming out for a drink?'

'So you can flaunt me in front of Ken and Alma? No, thanks, Mike.'

'Not at all, I just thought that since Phil pushed off, you must be feeling lonely—'

'Not for your company, Mike. Not now, and not ever again.' She closed the door in his face.

Chapter Forty-Seven

'I might have an early Christmas present for you,' Martin said to Gail, as he scrubbed baking potatoes in the sink for their tea. 'I was talking to Kevin earlier. You know that Maurice Jones has put number eight Coronation Street on the market? Well, yesterday he reduced it to thirty-eight thousand for a quick sale. I thought we might buy it.'

'That's an awful lot of money, Martin.'

'I had a word with the bank manager this morning. Our savings will more than cover the deposit, and with what we're making in the café, he'll give us a mortgage and the repayments won't be any more than the rent we're paying the council now. So, what do you say? Do you want to own your own house?'

'It's something I've always wanted.' She thought wistfully of the house Brian had sold to raise money for his garage. 'But . . .'

'I know what you're going to say. It's Coronation Street

and there's Ivy.' He dropped the last clean potato on the draining-board.

'Yes.'

'Her house has only been on the market for six weeks. It will be sold, I promise you. And you can't live your whole life in fear of Ivy, Gail.'

'You're right,' she said decisively. 'And I've never liked the thought of bringing up the kids in a council house. It's a wonderful early Christmas present, thank you.' She went to kiss him but the baby chose that moment to wake. She picked him up out of his carrycot and cuddled him.

'Did you hear, Nicky, Sarah?' she called to where the other two were sitting in front of the television, watching a video. 'Martin and I are going to buy a house. The very first house we'll own.'

'Good,' Nicky said. 'Will I have my own room?'

'You'll have to share with David when he's older,' Martin warned.

'At least he's a boy.'

'And I'll have *my* own room?' Sarah asked hopefully.

'Unless we have a baby sister for you.' Martin winked at Gail.

'One expense at a time.' She smiled.

Alma and Ken were sitting in the living room of her flat sharing a bottle of wine and a cuddle on her sofa. Ken could scarcely believe how close they had become in such a short time, and he regretted giving in to Tracy's impassioned plea that he join her and Deirdre for Christmas dinner: it had meant changing his plan to spend the day with Alma.

'You sure you don't mind?' he asked Alma. 'To say there's nothing left between me and Deirdre is the understatement of the century. Frankly, I think she'd be happier if I lived at the North Pole, but I don't like disappointing Tracy.'

'Of course I don't mind you spending Christmas Day with Tracy.' Alma forced a smile to conceal her disappointment.

'I promise I'll make it up to you on Boxing Day.'

'I'll hold you to that.' She entwined her fingers with his.

'What are you going to do?'

'It will be nice to have a day to myself.'

'I have a present for you.' He handed her a beautifully wrapped box.

'It looks lovely, Ken, thank you.'

'That's just the wrapping.' He checked the time. 'As it will be Christmas Day in four minutes you can open it.'

'I'm still keeping yours until Boxing Day.'

'Good. That will give me something to look forward to.'

She untied the silver ribbon and peeled back layers of gold paper to reveal a jeweller's box. She opened it to see a finely wrought gold bracelet nestling on a bed of dark blue velvet. 'It's lovely, Ken, thank you.' She kissed his cheek, and when he returned her embrace, tears pricked the back of her eyes at the thought of the long, lonely day that lay ahead of her. 'You'd better go.' She pushed him gently away from her. 'If you don't, you won't get up in time to enjoy your Christmas dinner, and Deirdre will be angrier with you than she already is. Wish Tracy a happy Christmas from me.'

'I will and thank you, Alma.'

The following morning, Ken walked up Coronation Street on his way to Deirdre's. The for-sale signs had been taken down and the front door and window of number eight had been freshly painted. Nicky and Sarah Platt's home-made poster was still pinned to the door, FATHER CHRISTMAS PLEASE STOP HERE, and the sound of the small Platts running around inside brought a smile to his face.

Alma had told him that Martin and Gail had been distraught when Ivy Brennan had changed her mind about leaving Weatherfield and taken number five off the market. Ken understood how they felt. He wondered if there was such a thing as a happy family where everyone got on well with everyone else. He checked his carrier-bags to make sure that he had brought everything he'd intended. A good bottle of wine for Deirdre and him to drink with their dinner and a box of chocolates that, hopefully, she wouldn't object to. And two bags of presents for Tracy that Alma had helped him choose.

Tracy opened the door before he knocked – she had

been looking out for him. He stepped inside without noticing the car that was driving up the street in the direction of Alma's flat.

Mike rang Alma's bell and waited. When she opened the door, in a flowing blue kaftan, he handed her an enormous parcel.

'Half a dozen bottles of the finest, ready-chilled champagne and a box of champagne truffles. Merry Christmas, Alma.'

Glad that he and Deirdre had managed to remain polite, even though the atmosphere between them had been strained, Ken kissed Tracy goodbye, thanked Deirdre for his Christmas dinner, left number one and walked towards the café. He recalled the wine and canapés he had taken over to Alma's the night before. Perhaps there was a film on television they could watch or perhaps they'd just sit in front of the fire sharing the wine and talking. He was looking forward to a peaceful domestic evening with a woman he didn't have to treat with kid gloves after the strain of Christmas dinner with Deirdre.

He had to ring the bell twice before he heard Alma's footsteps on the stairs. She opened the door and he was surprised to see her in her dressing-gown.

'I'm sorry – were you asleep?' he asked, concerned that

she was ill or, worse, depressed because he'd spent the best part of the day with Deirdre and Tracy.

'Not at all, Ken.' Mike stood at the top of the stairs, naked apart from a towel wrapped round his waist. 'We were in bed but we weren't asleep.'

Ken couldn't bring himself to look at Alma. He turned and walked away. Was there any woman who wouldn't run to Mike Baldwin the moment he snapped his fingers at them? He recalled the urgency with which Tracy had pleaded with him to join her and Deirdre for Christmas dinner and wondered how Baldwin had known that he wouldn't be with Alma. Baldwin wouldn't have stooped to use a child to get his own way with Alma, would he?

Bet Gilroy picked up the post from behind the door of the Rovers and carried it into the kitchen in her and Alec's private quarters. She flicked through the letters and dropped them on to the table next to Alec, who was eating toast and marmalade. 'You're getting a lot of letters lately from Sunliners Cruises,' she commented, picking up her tea.

Alec took the letter off the top of the pile and opened it. 'They've offered me a position as director of entertainment.'

'On board a cruise ship?'

'It's difficult to cruise on dry land,' he answered.

'It's too early in the morning to be funny, Alec,' she snapped.

'Of course on board a cruise ship,' he said curtly.

'Surely you're not going to take it. We have the Rovers—'

'The brewery will buy it back off us.'

She sat opposite him and tried to look him in the eye, but he continued to study the letter. It was then she realised he'd already made up his mind to take the job. 'We can't sell the Rovers,' she protested, angry that he hadn't even discussed the offer with her.

'Why not? You can't expect me to give up a job opportunity like this, Bet. Do you realise how the director of entertainment lives on a cruise ship? It will be the high life all the way, the best cabin, the best food, non-stop sunshine, calling in at all the most scenic ports in the world. It's being paid to take a long holiday. We'll live like royalty. You'll never have to pull another pint.'

'You expect me to go with you?'

'You're my wife, Bet. Of course I expect you to go with me.'

Bet sat back in her chair and studied her husband. She had married him expecting to run the Rovers with him until her retirement, which still seemed a long way off. She couldn't believe what she was thinking. She couldn't bear the thought of leaving the Rovers Return: the pub meant more to her than Alec and their marriage.

'I'm not going with you, Alec.'

'You can't run the Rovers on your own.'

'I did once before.'

'And you made a right mess of it,' he reminded her.

'That was five years ago. I'm older now, and wiser, and I've had a lot of experience. Face it, Alec, it's me who does the lion's share of the day-to-day work, including the bookkeeping. I'll ask the brewery to let me stay on as manager.'

'And if they say no?'

'They won't,' she replied, with more confidence than she felt.

'You do realise that if you don't go with me it will mean a separation.'

'In every way,' she agreed.

'I don't want to lose you.'

'Then you should have thought of that before you took the job.'

'How did you know . . . ?' Embarrassed, he fell silent.

'I know you, Alec. It's obvious from the way you've been talking that the letter you're holding is just crossing the Ts and dotting the Is on the contract you've negotiated. The last thing I want is a separation, but you're forcing it.'

'No, Bet. If anyone is ending our marriage, it's you.'

Curly Watts's boss, Reg Holdsworth, had been attracted to Rita Fairclough since the day he had moved into number twelve Coronation Street and seen her cleaning her front windows. And that was before he had discovered that since she had kicked out her live-in lover, Alan

Bradley, she was an eligible and comparatively wealthy widow. Although Rita had been friendly enough she had never accepted his invitations to dinner or to have a drink with him. He had been incensed when she started dating Ted Sullivan, a retired toffee salesman, whom he knew from the time when Ted had done business with the confectionery department of Bettabuy's.

Reg had made it his business to look into Ted's affairs and he'd warned Rita to be on her guard when he'd discovered that Ted had inherited a small fortune after his first wife had died in mysterious circumstances. However, all his attempts to discredit Ted had come to nothing. Oblivious to his warnings, Rita continued to see Ted – if anything more frequently than before. But, even so, Reg nurtured hopes that one day she would see through Ted and go out with him. Which was why he was shocked to see Ted and Rita, suitcases in hand, leaving her house early one morning when he was on his way to work.

'Off somewhere, Rita?' he asked.

'Ted and I are going to Florida for a holiday.' Rita looked up at the grey, overcast March sky. 'It will be nice to see the sun for a change.'

Unable to trust himself to speak civilly, Reg nodded and went on his way.

'The worst bit of any holiday is the travelling,' Ted said, as he and Rita drove to the airport in a taxi.

'But it will be worth it when we get off the plane. At least, I hope it will. I've only ever seen Florida on the television, and then it seemed to be all blue skies, blue sea, stretches of white sand and that long road built over the sea down to those islands . . . what are they called?'

'The Florida Keys,' Ted answered. 'And Florida isn't so different from the television images we see. In fact, I'm thinking of retiring there.'

'Really?' Rita asked, surprised.

'I've no family to keep me in this country, and no job any more. I can afford a house there. Houses are cheaper in some parts of Florida than they are here. It will be interesting to see what you make of the place. Perhaps your reaction will help me make a decision one way or the other.'

'You'll never guess who's back in Weatherfield,' Angie Freeman said to Curly, as she heated a tin of spaghetti hoops for her tea.

'Who?' Curly asked, disinterested. Reg Holdsworth had nitpicked and found fault with every single thing he'd done in Bettabuy's that day, and he was feeling particularly miserable.

'That friend of yours who used to work with you. The girl . . . the pretty one who modelled my designs for me in the end-of-year show. I know she was named after a film star, I just can't remember which one.'

'Raquel?' Curly suggested eagerly.

'That's the one.'

Curly smiled. The day might have been lousy, but the evening looked promising.

'You'll never guess who she's moved in with, though,' Angie added. 'Des Barnes in number six. His wife only ran off a couple of months back. I can't remember her name either.'

'Steph.' Curly was shattered that the love of his life was living with a married man – and a philandering one at that. He'd heard a lot of stories about Des Barnes since he'd moved into the street, all of them spicy.

'She's telling everyone she's his lodger. But everyone in the street says Des's spare room hasn't even got a bed in it.'

Curly grunted. Why hadn't he found the courage to declare his feelings to Raquel when they'd worked together? If he had, they might be together now. He felt as though Raquel had only returned to the area to taunt him with his inadequacies.

'Alma?' Mike Baldwin called from his car, as she left her flat to walk to the corner shop.

Furious at the way Mike had made his presence in her flat known to Ken, and suspecting that he had only knocked her door on Christmas Day to break up their growing intimacy, she quickened her pace and ignored him. But he left his car, caught up with her and forced her to stop.

'I've tried telephoning you, I've tried writing to you, but you haven't answered one letter or call, and I must have left over fifty messages on your answering-machine.'

'That should tell you something,' she retorted.

'What?'

'That I don't want to talk to you,' she said, staring at his hand in the hope that he would relax his grip.

'You've put the leasehold of the café and the flat up for sale.'

'So, now I know you can read.'

'Look, Alma, if this is about what happened on Christmas Day—'

'You set that up, and don't deny it. You wanted to make me look a fool and you wanted to hurt Ken Barlow by proving that you could have any woman he went out with. And you succeeded. You've broken us up. Tell me, Mike, does it make you feel happy now you've succeeded in making both Ken and me miserable?'

'I care for you, Alma.'

'Pull the other one, Mike. If you care for people you want the best for them. You asked me to move in with you, and you said you loved me. Then you threw me out so you could move Jackie Ingram into your flat and marry her. Just as I started to pick up the pieces of my life and build a relationship with Ken, you come along and wreck every-thing,' she said furiously.

'I know I've been a rat. Tell you what, I'll give you the

lease on the flat and the café to make amends. Then you'll own it freehold and you can double your asking price.'

'Even if you owned the lease, you could never make up for what you've done.'

'I do own the lease, Alma,' he said quietly. 'Why do you think the landlord changed his mind about doubling the rent a couple of months back? Gail told me what had happened and that you were thinking of selling the place, so I bought the lease and instructed my solicitor to leave the rent as it was.'

'You really do own it,' she said, in bewilderment. There was no other way he could know the details he had sketched out.

Taking advantage of her shock, he guided her gently to his car. 'Why don't we drive somewhere quiet and talk about this?'

'Like the Rovers so you can flaunt me in front of Ken?' she enquired.

'Not the Rovers. We'll go to another nice quiet little pub I know.'

Before Alma realised what was happening she was sitting in Mike's car and he was heading out of Weatherfield. 'Do you mean what you said about giving me the lease on the café and the flat?'

'After the way I've treated you, it's the least I can do.'

'No strings attached?'

'Absolutely none.'

'In that case I'll take it.'

'Good.' He pulled into a pub car park, drove into a parking bay, killed the engine and turned to her. 'I would like to ask you a question. No matter what your answer, I promise you that you'll get the lease. Will you marry me?'

Alma didn't have to think about it. 'No, Mike, I'll never marry you for one simple reason. I'll never be able to trust you again.'

Martin Platt came home from the afternoon shift at the hospital to discover that Gail had made them a special supper of Italian chicken and pasta.

'The children asleep?' he asked, as he sat at the table.

'Finally.' Gail placed the casserole dish on the table. 'They were disappointed that you weren't there to give them a goodnight kiss, but I told them they could save it for the morning when they wake up.'

'That'll be me up at five, then.' He smiled at her as she sat opposite him.

'Do you mind?' she asked anxiously.

'I love it.' He grinned as he helped himself to pasta. 'This looks great.'

'I thought we'd celebrate your first week back as a hospital porter. It seems to have gone all right, from what you've told me.'

'It seems like I've never been away,' he agreed, 'and it's

gone a lot better than you think. Do you remember me telling you how I saved that elderly woman who was stuck in a lift with me?'

'By giving her the kiss of life when she collapsed, yes.'

'They called me into the main office today and asked if I'd like to train as a nurse.'

'What did you say?'

'Yes. Even when I'm training, the money will be as good as I'm getting now, and when I qualify, I'll be earning a lot more. That has to be better for the kids – and us. What do you think?'

Touched by his eagerness and the way he was always thinking of her and the children, Gail put her hand over his. 'I think I have a very special husband, who'll make a great nurse.'

Rita Fairclough and Ted Sullivan walked slowly along the smooth stretch of sand that led down to the sea. The sun was a huge crimson ball that sank lower on the horizon with every passing minute. The sea sparkled, a deep cerulean blue, and pelicans flew in and out of the waves in search of fish.

'This is just like a sunset in a romantic film,' Rita said, as Ted slipped his arm round her waist.

'I love you, Rita.' He enveloped her in his arms and kissed her. 'These past two weeks here with you have been perfect.'

'I love you too,' she whispered softly.

'Then marry me.'

'Yes.'

'You don't want time to think about it?' he asked.

'Not one minute.' She wrapped her arms round him and hugged him.

'There is something you should know.' He took her hand in his and led her along the shoreline.

'You have another wife somewhere?'

'No, nothing like that.' He paused, then went on, 'I look all right at the moment, Rita, but I'm not. I have a brain tumour.'

Rita felt as though someone had hit her with a sledgehammer. 'Have you seen a doctor?'

'I've seen so many doctors, consultants and the insides of so many hospitals in the last few months I couldn't face seeing any more. When they all told me the same thing, that I have only months to live, I decided I wanted to do some living that wasn't inside a hospital ward. I meant to see some of the world, and enjoy what pleasures were left to me. I never thought I'd meet someone like you, or fall in love.' He caressed her face with his fingertips. 'I meant what I said about loving you. I only wish we could have more time together. But facing death has made me philosophical. I may only have a few months to live but I intend to make every day I have left count. And I'm going to pack as much living into them as I possibly can. If you still want to marry me, and I wouldn't blame you if you didn't after what I've just told you, I think we can make those months last for ever. Do you want to change your mind?'

'No.' Rita held him close.

'You sure about this? The last thing I want is for you to feel sorry for me.'

'I don't feel sorry for you, Ted, I love you,' Rita said firmly. 'And I agree. What's important is not the time we have left, but how we live it.'

Chapter Forty-Eight

'I can't believe you've agreed to marry Mike Baldwin after everything he's done to you, Alma.' Bet Gilroy set a tray of drinks in front of Alma, Gail, Sally, Emily, Deirdre, Mavis and Audrey who had gathered in the Rovers to celebrate Alma's hen night.

'When I received the official notice that Jackie was citing me as co-respondent in her divorce case, Mike paid her thousands to leave my name out of it,' Alma confided. 'He also gave me the lease on the café and the flat before I agreed to marry him. But, most of all, he's promised me faithfully that he's turned over a new leaf. From now on he's going to concentrate on building a new life for both of us.'

'Mike Baldwin has turned over more new leaves than an army of locusts,' Deirdre said cynically. 'He promised Susan exactly the same thing when she married him against Ken's wishes.'

'I wouldn't trust Mike further than I could throw him,

and he's too heavy for me to pick up,' Bet put in. 'But as this is your hen night, Alma, I think we've said enough about your groom.' She sent Deirdre a cautionary glance.

'Speak as you find,' Gail said. 'When I asked Mike for help when the lease of Alma's flat and café doubled, he sorted out the problem within a couple of days and he never asked for so much as a thank you.'

Emily could see that Alma was determined to go ahead with the wedding, no matter what, so she lifted her glass. 'To the bride and groom, and their future happiness,' she said.

'The bride and groom.' Bet and Deirdre tried to look and sound sincere, but both found it difficult, knowing what they did about Mike.

'Jackie,' Bet said in surprise, when she turned to walk back to the bar and bumped into Mike's ex-wife. 'Can I get you a drink?'

'No,' Jackie said. 'I just wanted a word with this fool before she makes a complete idiot of herself.' She jerked her head towards a secluded table in the corner. 'Can you spare me five minutes, Alma?'

Heart pounding, Alma left the table and joined her.

'I've changed my mind about that drink,' Jackie shouted to Bet. 'Two gin and tonics, treble, please. I'll pay.'

'I'll bring them over.'

'You really intend to go through with this marriage to Mike?' Jackie asked, after Bet had brought their drinks.

'Yes,' Alma replied, toying nervously with her glass.

'Then more fool you, that's all I can say. You do know that it was his idea I named you as co-respondent in the divorce.'

'He told me he had to pay you thousands to keep my name out of it,' Alma countered.

'The only thousands Mike Baldwin has were mine until I stupidly married him. I smelt a rat when he changed his mind about my citing you halfway through the proceedings. But, then, that's Mike for you. Devious, underhand and downright criminal, if he thinks he can get away with it.' Jackie opened her handbag, reached for her compact and reapplied her lipstick.

'He's given me the lease of my flat and the café,' Alma protested, feeling the need to say something in Mike's favour.

'Which he bought with my money.'

'He promised me he's turned over a new leaf.'

'That old chestnut.' Jackie returned her compact to her bag, closed it and drank half of her gin in a single swallow. 'If you want to believe that, I can't stop you. I think you're being an absolute fool in going ahead with the wedding after what I've told you, but it's your choice.' She finished her drink. 'Good luck, Alma. You're going to need it.'

Alma continued to sit at the isolated table after Jackie left the pub. The other women whispered among themselves for a few minutes and eventually Emily left the group and walked over to her.

'You coming back to join us, Alma?' she ventured.

Alma gave her a brittle smile. 'In a few moments.'

'We couldn't help overhearing what Jackie said.' Emily sat beside her.

'Jackie does have rather a loud voice,' Alma said.

'Are you still going to go through with the wedding?'

Alma sipped her gin and tonic. 'Now I know the truth, I can confront Mike with it and use it to make sure that he never lies to me again.' She left her chair and walked across to the others. 'What a lot of long faces for a hen night,' she said, in a resolutely cheerful voice. 'I hope you aren't going to be this miserable at the wedding tomorrow.'

Ken Barlow was cleaning the board in his classroom at the end of the day when there was a tap at the open door. An attractive blonde woman came in. 'Mr Barlow?'

'Yes?' Ken answered warily. Years of experience had taught him that not all parents were friendly, particularly if a child had spun a tale about being ill-treated by a member of staff.

'I came to thank you. My son Mark Redman is a friend of Nicky Platt's. Mark and Nicky told me you stopped the fifth-formers bullying them.'

'I did no more than any teacher would if they noticed anything untoward going on in the school. Not that there's much bullying in the school – occasionally a few of the older boys get a bit boisterous with the younger ones, as they did with Mark and Nicky, but I think it's safe to say that Nicky and Mark won't be bothered by that particular crowd again.'

'I just wanted to let you know how grateful I am that you stepped in.'

'It's my job,' he said, ending the discussion. 'Can I give you a lift home? I'm heading up Coronation Street way.'

'Yes, please. I'm Maggie Redman – but, then, you know my surname from Mark. I live just a few streets away.'

'Mark not with you?'

'No, he's having tea with Nicky tonight.'

As they left the school, Ken tried to remember everything that Mark had told him about his mother. He had never mentioned a father, and before he dropped Maggie off at her house, Ken decided that he'd ask her for a date.

A police car pulled up outside Rita Sullivan's house and she rushed to the window. She and Ted had married on the beach of their hotel at sunset before they had left Florida. Their holiday had been perfect, and they would have stayed longer but Ted's condition had begun to deteriorate. Hoping against hope that his doctors could do something for him, she had arranged flights home but since their return to Coronation Street it had become increasingly obvious that he was getting worse.

Even on a good day he was confused and unable to carry out the simplest task. Things like switching on the radio or television or putting bread in the toaster were beyond him. And although she allowed him to go out by himself, because he refused to be 'mollycoddled', she always waited anxiously, scarcely daring to breathe until he was safely back home.

She opened the door to the two policemen supporting Ted, who was comatose, between them.

'Mrs Sullivan?'

'Yes. Could you help my husband inside, please?'

'Does he often get drunk like this?' the younger constable enquired unpleasantly, as they shouldered Ted inside.

Rita's voice was icy. 'He's not drunk, Constable.'

'We found him lying on the pavement in the middle of town. If he hadn't been carrying a letter with this address on it, we wouldn't have known where to bring him.'

'He has a brain tumour,' Rita revealed.

Both constables glanced away from her, unable to meet her eye.

Before they had a chance to mumble their apologies, Rita said, 'Thank you for bringing him home. If you lay him on the sofa, I'll telephone the doctor. It was good of you to take the trouble.'

'This isn't the way I expected to see my son get married,' Vera Duckworth complained, loudly enough for her voice to carry to Lisa Horton, her son Terry's pregnant girlfriend. She'd decided that Lisa's parents disapproved of the marriage even more than she and Jack did, because they were conspicuous by their absence. The register office was empty, apart from the registrar, her, Jack, Lisa, Terry and the two prison warders who flanked him.

Terry had been refused bail and was being held on remand in Strangeways prison on a charge of grievous bodily harm. It was he who had insisted the wedding go ahead: he had told Jack and Vera that marrying in handcuffs was a trivial price to pay if it meant that his child could be registered as his.

The registrar began the service. Lisa, wearing a new dress and holding a bunch of flowers, and Terry stepped forward. Halfway through the ceremony, Terry lifted his cuffed hands and slipped the ring his father had bought for him on to Lisa's finger.

When he and Lisa were formally declared to be Mr and Mrs Duckworth, Terry held up his handcuffed wrists and looked pathetically at the warders. 'A photograph for the family album?'

The guards exchanged glances. The younger of the two stepped forward and unlocked the cuffs. A few seconds later Lisa was in tears, being comforted by a furious Vera and Jack. Terry had run out of the room and the building with the warders in hot pursuit.

'He never loved me,' Lisa sobbed, into Vera's best

jacket. 'He couldn't have. He would never have run off if he did.'

Vera looked at Jack over Lisa's shoulder, wishing she could contradict her.

'Ted, this is crazy,' Rita chided gently, as she drove him into town. 'Are you sure you want to go bowling?'

'I'm sure.' He gave her the strained, lopsided smile that she knew meant he had a headache.

'You don't look well enough to be out of the house, let alone go bowling.' She drove into the car park.

'I just want to . . .'

'Live a little,' she finished for him. 'I know.' She parked the car and switched off the lights.

'Thank you for understanding and loving me.' He tried to cover her hand with his but misjudged the distance, as he had done so often lately. 'I don't want to stay at home and wait for death to take me.'

'I know, darling.'

She helped him out of the car and they walked into the bowling alley arm in arm. While she was helping him change his shoes, he slumped forward. Rita knelt beside him and cradled him in her arms. When she tried to lift his head, she saw that he was unconscious and breathing oddly.

'Would you please get someone to call an ambulance?' she asked the man sitting beside them. 'My husband is dying.'

She continued to kneel on the floor with Ted's head in her lap while the staff kept the rest of the customers away from them. By the time the paramedics came, she didn't need them to tell her that Ted was dead.

'I have your weekly order all packed, Ken,' Deirdre said, when he walked into the shop after school one Friday.

'Thank you.' He wondered why they found it so difficult to talk to each other after living together for so many years as man and wife. Was it the result of the hurt he had inflicted on her by his betrayal? Or all the small hurts they had caused each other since?

He picked up the box and was surprised to see Deirdre turning the OPEN sign to CLOSED on the door. She taped a piece of paper alongside it.

'What does that say?'

'"Back in five minutes",' she informed him. 'Can I talk to you?'

'For about thirty seconds, then someone will be hammering on the door.'

'I won't answer.' She followed him up the stairs to his flat. 'You've been going out with Mark Redman's mother, Maggie, haven't you?' She watched him set the box of groceries on his kitchen table.

'No one can blow their nose around here without the world knowing about it. You have any objections to my going out with Maggie?' he enquired belligerently.

'No. It's just that there's something I think you should know. Mark Redman is Mike Baldwin's son.'

Ken felt as though someone had punched him in the stomach. He didn't want to believe what Deirdre had told him. He wondered if there was a woman in Manchester Mike Baldwin hadn't slept with.

'As far as I can make out, Mike and Maggie had a brief affair years ago. She wouldn't have anything to do with him afterwards, or take the money he offered her for Mark.'

'Then she has nothing to do with Baldwin now?'

'Hasn't for years. I just thought you should know the facts before you heard them from someone else.' Deirdre went to the door.

'Deirdre, thank you,' he murmured.

'I hope if the situation was reversed you would do as much for me.' She closed the door behind her and returned to the shop.

'That was a great meal, Maggie.' Ken pushed his chair back from the table as she set coffee in front of him.

'I wondered if you enjoyed it. You've hardly said a word all evening.'

'I was thinking about the future.' He looked across the table at her. 'I know that Mark is Mike Baldwin's son.'

'That's nothing to do with you,' she said quickly.

'I couldn't agree with you more. But you've lived

around here for years. You must have heard something about the run-ins I've had with Baldwin.'

'I know your ex-wife had an affair with him just after you were married. And that he married an ex-girlfriend of yours.'

'The fact that Mark is his son shouldn't affect us—'

'But it does?'

'It won't if we don't let it. We're both adults, we can move on.' He gave her a smile. 'And if we don't let it affect us, perhaps we can build some kind of a future together, you, me and Mark.'

'Mike has offered me money more than once for Mark. I won't take it and I won't allow him to control or disrupt Mark's life, the way he seems to disrupt and control every other person's life around him.'

'I admire your independence,' Ken said.

'Just my independence?' she teased. 'I have a fruit flan in the kitchen.'

'Sounds good. I'll get that,' he offered, as the doorbell rang. Maggie walked into the kitchen and Ken went down the passage into the hall. He opened the door. Mike Baldwin was standing on the step.

'Can I help you?' Ken enquired coldly.

'I called to see Mrs Redman about a personal matter.' Mike was as frosty as Ken, but failed to conceal his shock at seeing Ken in Maggie's house.

Maggie stood behind Ken. 'There are no personal matters between you and me, Mr Baldwin.'

'You heard Mrs Redman. Goodnight.' Ken closed the door in Mike's face.

'She just stood there and had the gall to say it to my face,' Vera Duckworth raged at Jack. 'Just stood in front of me and said, "I've left your Terry and I'm living with Des Barnes now." To think she married our Terry only six months ago and now her and little Tommy, our grandchild . . .'

'There's nowt that we can do about it,' Jack said bluntly. 'And in my book it's difficult for Lisa to leave our Terry when he's locked up in Strangeways for three years. Seems to me that our Terry was the one who did the leaving when he did what he did to get banged up. Not to mention when he ran away from her at the register office only to get caught halfway down the street.'

'So you don't care that our grandson Tommy is living across the street with our daughter-in-law and Des Barnes, who's had more women in and out of that house since his wife left him than you've had pints in Rovers? And you haven't heard the worst of it. Lisa told me that Des is selling the house and they're moving away together. Her, little Tommy and Des.'

'She has her own life to live, love,' Jack said practically. 'You can't blame her for doing just that. Or what she thinks is best for her and Tommy. Everyone round here knows about our Terry, it might be as well for her and the boy if they make a fresh start somewhere new, where people haven't heard the gossip.'

Vera sat down abruptly. 'Why does life have to be so complicated? All I want is for Lisa and Tommy to live with our Terry close to us, where we can keep an eye on them.'

'With our Terry put away that's not an option, and with the way our Terry's been behaving, good luck to the pair of them, that's what I say.'

Vera shook her head in despair. No matter what Jack said, she wasn't happy that her daughter-in-law and grandson were living with Des Barnes, and she was even more unhappy with Terry for getting himself into a situation where he was serving three years in prison. She wondered what had happened to the lively, mischievous boy she had brought up, because the last time she had seen Terry, there hadn't been any trace of him left.

Mike's solicitor left the chair behind his desk, held out his hand and shook Maggie Redman's.

'It's very good as you to come in, Mrs Redman. Mr Baldwin and I appreciate it.'

Maggie nodded at Mike, who was sitting in one of the two chairs set in front of the solicitor's desk.

'Right, we all know why we're here.' The solicitor gave a small, embarrassed cough.

'I want my son, Mark, to have the best education money can buy.' Mike looked at Maggie. 'Is that such a terrible thing for a father to want? I've visited an excellent boarding school—'

Maggie shook her head. 'I am not prepared to allow my son to go to any boarding school.'

'Think of the education he'll get, the friends he'll make,' Mike protested.

For once Maggie felt she had the upper hand. 'If you really want to pay for Mark's education, you can pay for him to attend the local private school, Oakhill. I've looked around it and it seems to provide a better education than the local comprehensive.'

'Right, we'll . . .' Mike saw Maggie glare at him and rephrased what he was about to say. 'Mark can go there, and I'll make him a monthly allowance.'

'You can make him an allowance, but anything above pocket-money level will have to be invested in a savings account,' Maggie told him.

'Agreed,' Mike said.

'Well, now that's sorted, all that seems to be left is to work out the exact sums of money involved,' the solicitor said efficiently. 'I'll telephone Oakhill this afternoon, find out their fees and ask when Mark can start.'

'I checked with the headmaster. He can start at the beginning of next term,' Maggie informed him.

'Very good, Miss – Mrs Redman, Mr Baldwin. I'll set everything in motion.' The solicitor rose to his feet and shook their hands.

Mike opened the door and followed Maggie outside.

'Thank you,' he muttered.

'For allowing you to pay my son's bills?' She turned a stony face to him.

'For allowing me to contribute, if only financially, to Mark's education. I know this hasn't been an easy decision for you to make. Not with Ken in your life.'

'Ken and I have finished,' Maggie informed him coldly. 'At first we thought we could cope with you being Mark's biological father, but it appears there is too much history between you and Ken for the two of you to share anything.'

'I'm sorry.'

'No, you're not,' she contradicted him.

'Would you like to go for a coffee or a drink?'

'This is purely a business arrangement, Mike. Don't ever fool yourself that it can be anything else.'

'And Mark?' he questioned. 'Someday he's going to have to be told that I am his father.'

'He already knows. Tracy Barlow told him. And at the moment he doesn't want to see you. If he ever does, I'll let you know. Goodbye, Mike.' Maggie walked away, holding her head high, leaving him more determined than ever to build a relationship with his son.

Ken Barlow came home from school just as Deirdre was finishing in the shop.

'Do you mind if I walk you home?' he asked.

'You heard?'

'Yes. To be honest, I hoped to see Tracy back at school today. She has four GCSEs, and pupils have come back with less to gain extra qualifications. She's bright, Deirdre, she could do more with her life than work as an assistant in Maggie's shop as a trainee florist.'

'Maggie said she'll keep an eye on her and make sure she does all the right examinations to get a recognised qualification. But that's not why you're walking me home, is it?' she probed, wondering if he'd heard of Tracy's latest escapade.

'One of the girls in her class told me that Tracy has moved in with her boyfriend, Craig Lee. She's only sixteen, Deirdre.'

'Do you think I haven't thought of that?' Deirdre interrupted fiercely, and Ken realised he'd touched a raw nerve.

'I'm sorry. I only wanted to say that if there's anything I can do to help, like talk to Tracy or provide a shoulder for you to lean on, I'm here.'

'I couldn't stop her, Ken.'

Ken recalled his own problems with Susan and Peter. 'I know just how you're feeling. Remember how I tried to stop Susan from marrying Baldwin? I knew she was heading for disaster, but all I could do was stand back and watch her make her own mistakes.'

'Then you don't blame me?'

'No more than I blame myself for all the mistakes I made with Susan . . . Sorry that came out wrong. I do blame myself for Susan because I wasn't there for her when she was growing up. But you were with Tracy, Deirdre, and so was I. Believe me you have absolutely nothing to reproach yourself with over Tracy's upbringing.'

'Deirdre, Ken.' Lisa Duckworth waved to them as she left Des's house. 'I'm off to buy a bottle of wine to celebrate,' she shouted. 'Des and I have found a house and they've accepted our offer.'

'Congratulations!' Ken called. He turned back to Deirdre, who screamed. He heard a screech of brakes and the thud of a car hitting something. He turned – to see Lisa lying in the road. 'Call an ambulance!' he yelled to Deirdre, and ran towards the girl.

Chapter Forty-Nine

Vera and Jack were sitting in the waiting room immediately outside the intensive-care ward, when two prison officers brought Terry into the hospital. This time he was firmly cuffed to one. 'How is she?' he asked.

Vera shook her head, too choked to speak.

'The doctor's been in, he said it's not looking good,' Jack muttered, feeling the need to say something to his son, although he had not forgiven him for using his wedding to try to escape from prison.

A nurse walked out of the cubicle. 'Mr Duckworth?' She looked at Terry. 'You can go in now.'

'I won't try to leg it,' Terry assured both the warders.

'You won't get far if you do, because we'll be right behind you, son.' The warder to whom Terry was handcuffed produced a key and unlocked the cuffs. Terry rubbed his wrist, squared his shoulders and walked past the nurse into the cubicle. One of the prison officers followed as far as the door.

Lisa was lying, pale and unconscious, on a bed, her dark

hair brushed loose to her shoulders. Des Barnes was sitting next to her, holding her hand. Terry took one look at him and curled his hand into a fist. Before the warder could stop him, he punched Des. The officer sprang forward, wrapped his arm across Terry's neck and gripped him in an armlock.

'Have some respect for your wife and the place, Duckworth,' he whispered harshly, in Terry's ear. 'One more trick like that and you'll be back inside, dying wife or not.'

The machine suspended above Lisa screeched alarmingly. The nurse rushed over and pushed a red panic button. A doctor and a second nurse ran in. Before she had time to usher Des and Terry out of the cubicle, the doctor had pronounced Lisa dead.

The warder pushed Terry into the waiting room and snapped the handcuffs back on to his wrist. Des walked out slowly behind them, tears streaming down his face. Vera and Jack didn't have to ask what had happened. Swallowing hard, Vera stepped forward.

'I want Tommy, Des.'

'Take him,' Des mumbled brokenly. 'I couldn't cope with him anyway.' As the warders led Terry away, Des walked down the corridor in the opposite direction. Pushing the fire doors open, he continued to walk on, solitary and alone.

Ken stood on the station platform and studied the people leaving the train, searching for Deirdre. She was one of the last to get off. She came towards the gates pulling a wheeled suitcase and carrying a couple of carrier-bags. When she saw him waiting for her, she smiled and quickened her pace.

'I wasn't expecting anyone to meet me. It's good to see you, Ken.' Risking a rebuff, she kissed his cheek.

Ken took her suitcase from her. 'When Tracy told me that you were coming back today, I thought you might like to see a familiar face after two months away. Besides, you must be exhausted after the journey. How's your mother?'

'On the mend.' Deirdre moved the carrier-bags into her other hand and stretched her cramped fingers. 'The doctor warned me it could be a slow recovery but he also said it's difficult to predict the after-effects of a stroke like the one she's had. But having said that, between the district nurses, home helps and the neighbours popping in, she's managing well enough. She was the one who told me she didn't need me any more. Not that I'm going to abandon her,' she added, lest Ken think she was being heartless. 'I'll go up again in a month or so to see how she's getting on.'

Deirdre had been horribly lonely at her mother's. The highlight of her days had been the visits from the medics and home help. The downside had been the endless stream of her mother's elderly friends and relatives who had wandered in and out of the house, demanding cups of tea and describing in nauseating detail their aches and pains. She stole a sideways glance at Ken. It was wonderful to see a comparatively young, healthy man who could walk without the aid of a stick.

Ken led the way to the short-stay car park, opened the boot of his car and stowed Deirdre's luggage in it. 'The car's open,' he said, when he saw she was waiting for him to open the passenger door. He held up his keys. 'Central locking, remember.'

'I wondered if you fancied stopping off and having a drink somewhere on the way home,' she suggested shyly. 'As a thank-you for picking me up.'

'I'd like that,' he climbed into the driving seat and she sat alongside him, 'but I have to get back. I've just moved out of the flat above the mini-market into number twelve and I've a million and one things to do just to get straight. I haven't even made up my bed.'

'You've bought number twelve from Reg? Tracy wrote and told me that he'd left the area to take a job with a freezer firm.'

'Not bought, rented,' Ken told her. 'And that brings me to the main reason why I wanted to pick you up. I remembered you warning me that Mark Redman was Mike Baldwin's son because you were afraid I'd hear it from someone else. Well, I'd like to reciprocate.'

'This isn't about Tracy, is it?' Deirdre was instantly transformed into the archetypal anxious mother.

'No, it's nothing to do with Tracy.' Ken turned the wheel and swung out of the car park into the stream of traffic. 'I might not approve of her living with Craig at her age, but as far as I can make out, they're happy enough. Do you know Denise Osbourne?'

'The hairdresser? Of course I do.' Deirdre wondered why Ken had mentioned her. 'She was at school with Tracy.'

'She's a couple of years older than Tracy.'

'What's that got to do with anything?' Deirdre asked bluntly.

Ken glanced across at her and decided there was no tactful way he could break the news. 'She's having my baby.'

Deirdre's jaw dropped. She stared at him in disbelief. Nursing her mother had given her time to take stock of her life, and the one thing she had done that she didn't regret was to have Tracy. And of all her disastrous relationships with men, the only one that made any sense had been her marriage to Ken. Older and wiser than when she had thrown him out for having the affair for which she now felt partly to blame – she hadn't worked any harder than he had to save their marriage – she had returned prepared to suggest that they might try living together again.

'Please say something, Deirdre.'

'What is there to say? You've made a girl young enough to be your daughter pregnant.'

'I'm not proud of my behaviour,' he said. 'Denise asked me out after she'd cut my hair. I was flattered, one thing led to another and, no she didn't seduce me. I knew what I was doing – or at least, I thought I did. What I wasn't bargaining for was that she'd get pregnant and make me a father again at fifty. But it happened, and I accept full responsibility for what I've done.'

'It never crossed your mind that she might have a child when you took her to bed?'

'I don't want to go into details, Deirdre. As I said, it happened, and I've accepted the consequences.'

'Do you love Denise?' Her heart was thundering so loudly she was certain he could hear it.

'Love doesn't come into it, for me or her. In fact, the one thing I am sure of is that Denise doesn't love me. But she's determined to go ahead and have the baby, and this is one child that I'm not going to walk out on. I'll be there for it, no matter what,' he said resolutely.

Deirdre had returned prepared to fight for Ken. Given the history between them, she was confident that she could have seen off a rival. But a child was different. Ken felt guilty that he had not being there for Susan and Peter when they had been growing up, and he'd been devastated when Tracy had refused to listen to his advice about staying on at school instead of moving in with her boyfriend. She knew that she could never persuade him to put her and their relationship before Denise's child.

Rita Sullivan breathed in the fresh, salty sea air and looked across at Sally Webster who was watching Rosie playing on the sand with a bucket and spade.

'It's good to get away from Coronation Street.' Rita recalled the last time she had sat on a beach, with Ted in Florida. As she pictured his face the memories flooded back, threatening to overwhelm her. 'It was kind of you and Kevin to invite me to come on holiday to Blackpool with you, Sally. I won't forget it.'

'It was kinder of you to come with us,' Sally said. 'We enjoy your company, especially Rosie.'

'I don't like to pry,' Rita picked up a handful of sand and allowed it to trickle through her fingers, 'but I can't help noticing things between you and Kevin are tense. Are you quarrelling about something? Me, for instance?' She had finally broached the question uppermost in her mind.

'Not you, Rita, I wouldn't have said we liked your company if we didn't, and I would never have asked you to come to Blackpool with us if I hadn't meant it.'

'At least you're honest.'

Sally bit her lip.

'Is it anything I can help with?' Rita asked. 'If it isn't, I'll shut up and never mention it again.'

'It's nothing anyone can help with,' Sally murmured. 'I'm pregnant and Kevin is furious.'

'I'd have thought he'd be pleased.'

'He said we can't afford another child and, much as I hate to admit it, he's right.'

'What are you going to do?'

'I don't know . . . have an abortion, I suppose.' Sally's voice wavered.

'You know that Ted left me quite well off?' Rita asked.

'No.' Sally was staring at Rosie again. 'I thought his sister inherited all his money.'

'She was furious when she read Ted's will – she even took me to court and told the judge Ted was insane and didn't know what he was doing the last few months of his life. Ted would have been so angry and upset if he'd known. Still, the judge allowed his will to stand and, as his wife, I inherited everything. If it would help I'd be happy to give you and Kevin five thousand pounds to help with the cost of bringing up this baby – and before you say you don't want it, remember it *is* only money.'

'I don't know what to say, Rita,' Sally said, as startled by Rita's admission that she was wealthy as she was by her offer of help.

'You and Kevin have given me something that no one else has. Unselfish friendship without thought of anything in return.' Rita waved as Kevin stepped on to the sand carrying four ice creams. 'I'd be happy to do something for you in return.'

'They didn't release you for good behaviour, I know,' Jack Duckworth challenged his son.

'Parole.' Terry lifted his son on to his lap. 'This one's grown into a lump of a lad.' He studied Tommy, who stared curiously back at the father he didn't know.

'He's ever so bright for a two-year-old, Terry,' Vera gushed proudly. 'He can do all his wooden jigsaws, and he loves stories. Books are his favourite, aren't they, Jack?' She continued, without waiting for Jack to grunt his customary reply, 'He plays for hours with his books, looking at the pictures and trying to say the words that go with them. And he's been talking in whole sentences for months. He's only quiet now because he's a bit shy with strangers. Not that you're a stranger – or you won't be once he gets to used to seeing his dad every day. He was walking before he was ten months old and now he runs about everywhere.' Vera returned to the kitchen and began ferrying food to the table for their tea.

Jack eyed his son warily. He knew that Terry had come straight home from prison because he didn't have anywhere else to go, but he still suspected him of having an ulterior motive.

Terry balanced Tommy on his foot and kicked his leg, bouncing the little boy up and down. 'He seems a bright nipper but, then, he's probably inherited my brains.'

'You'll be that proud of Tommy when you get to know him properly, Terry. Are you staying for good?' Vera set the butter dish and salt cellar on the table.

'Just until tomorrow. I'm taking Tommy up to Blackpool to the Hortons.'

'I could see they took Lisa's death hard at the funeral,' Vera said sympathetically. 'It must be awful to bury your own daughter. But Tommy will be a comfort to them. How long do you think you'll be there?'

'We won't be coming back, Mam. Well, I might, but Tommy won't.'

'You can't do that. You can't take Tommy away from me—'

'He's my son, Mam. I can do whatever I like with him,' Terry interrupted.

'But I've brought Tommy up ever since Lisa died,' Vera protested. 'Your father and I are the only mam and dad he knows. You can't take him away from us . . . He won't know where he is. It'll be like dumping him on strangers.'

'The Hortons aren't strangers, they're Tommy's grand-parents too,' Terry reminded his mother brutally.

'But they haven't seen him since Lisa died. They haven't changed his nappies or put him to bed every night.'

'If they haven't, it's because you took Tommy from Des

and didn't give them a chance to get a look-in. It's like you said yourself, Mam, they've lost Lisa and Tommy's all they've got left.'

'Please,' Vera begged. 'I'm not thinking of myself or your father, but Tommy. Think what it will be like for him—'

'He's not thinking of Tommy or you, Vera,' Jack interrupted. 'Only of himself.' He looked his son in the eye. 'How much did the Hortons pay you to hand Tommy over to them?'

Tommy started wriggling so Terry set him down and the child immediately ran to Vera.

'I'll ask you again,' Jack said. 'How much did they pay you to hand Tommy over to them?'

Terry shifted uneasily in his chair

'Then I'm right, they *are* paying you.'

Terry got up and went to the door. 'Pack Tommy's clothes tonight, Mam. We'll be leaving on the nine o'clock train tomorrow.'

Gail looked at Nicky in despair. She had been prepared for him to be difficult during his teenage years but she hadn't been prepared for the depth of his anger and aggression towards her and Martin.

'If my father was here now . . .' he shouted.

Gail flinched at the repetition of what had become Nicky's favourite phrase. 'Your father would say exactly the same as I'm saying to you,' she retorted, deciding to fight back instead of keeping quiet in the hope of maintaining peace in the house. 'He'd want to thump you for smoking and running wild, and for not giving a thought to your brother or sister or how Martin and I feel . . .'

'My father would have hated Martin. He's a wimp who works as a nurse and everyone knows that's women's work,' Nicky said contemptuously.

'Your father wasn't tough, Nicky.' Gail wondered where he'd got his ideas about Brian from.

'Gran told me he used to ride a motorbike.'

'A lot of people ride motorbikes but that doesn't make them tough.'

'I've had enough of you badmouthing my dad.'

'I don't,' Gail protested uneasily, hearing Ivy's voice in her son's. 'I loved him, I married him, I had you and Sarah—'

'I'm moving out.'

'To where?' Gail was suddenly grateful that Ivy had gone on a religious retreat.

'I'm moving in with Don. He said he'd be glad of my company.' Nicky omitted to mention that Don had told him he'd be welcome only if his mother and Martin agreed he could stay with him. 'And I'll be glad to get away from you, Martin and this house!'

'Did you hear that?' Gail asked Martin, as he walked downstairs after Nicky had packed his rucksack and left.

Martin nodded. 'I had a word with Don yesterday on my way home from work. We decided that the way Nicky's been behaving lately, it might be as well to give him some breathing space. And Don promised he'll be as tough on him about his smoking as we are. I've a feeling that Nicky is about to find out that Don won't allow him to run any wilder than we have.'

'I hope so.' Gail burst into tears.

'Don't worry, love, he'll be back.' Martin took her into his arms and held her close, hating himself for wishing that the boy would stay with Don permanently.

Curly remained at the bar of the Rovers after Raquel had served him his pint. When Des Barnes had thrown her out to move Lisa Duckworth into his house, Raquel had been glad to take the barmaid's job and live-in accommodation Bet Gilroy had offered her. It had worked out well for both women. Bet had found herself with a reliable barmaid more or less at her beck and call, and from the day she had moved into the Rovers Return, Raquel had felt at home. She and Bet had become close, and although she hadn't entirely given up her ambition to become a model, she was more content as a barmaid than she had ever been as an assistant at Bettabuy's.

'I hear you've got yourself a job as a manager now, Curly.' Raquel gave him his change.

Curly nodded. 'I'm manager of Soopa Soopa.'

'I always knew you'd go far. Is the shop any better than Bettabuy's?' she asked.

'It's different. I've been meaning to ask you a favour.' He blushed as she touched his hand.

'Anything, Curly, I haven't forgotten how kind you were to me the night I didn't get the Miss Bettabuy Northwest title.'

'It's Soopa Soopa's staff Christmas dinner-dance next week.'

'That's nice.'

'It could be.' He cleared his throat awkwardly. 'You see, I've told everyone at work that I'm engaged and they're expecting to see my fiancée.'

'But you're not engaged, are you?' she asked, in bewilderment.

'You know what girls who work in a supermarket are like,' he mumbled, embarrassed.

'We used to tease you.' She laughed.

'That's why I told them I had a fiancée.' He grabbed the excuse she'd handed him in an attempt to save his face. 'I don't suppose you'd come to the dinner with me and pretend to be my fiancée, would you? The dinner is two weeks this Saturday.'

'I don't see why not, Curly. I owe you a favour, and we've known each other long enough for me to pretend we're engaged.'

'Thank you.' Curly breathed a sigh of relief.

'I'll clear the night off with Bet. It's so far in advance, it won't be a problem.' She saw Bet frowning at her from the other end of the bar. 'I have to serve other customers now, Curly, but I'll look forward to a fortnight Saturday,' she whispered as she left him.

'I've never seen you like this, Deirdre.' Emily Bishop sipped the drink Deirdre had bought her as they sat in the Rovers watching Curly chat up Raquel.

'I've never felt like this before about any man,' Deirdre confessed. 'But I know what everyone's thinking. I see it on their faces whenever I start talking about him in Bettabuy's.'

'How do you like working there?' Emily asked, hoping to steer the conversation away from the love of Deirdre's life. Since she had returned from a holiday in Morocco – a break Deirdre had treated herself to after nursing her mother – all she could talk about was Samir Rachid, a waiter she had met in her hotel who had swept her off her feet.

Deirdre wrinkled her nose. 'Bettabuy's isn't like the mini-market. I was more or less my own boss there – but I couldn't expect my job to be kept open while I nursed my mother. You do understand, don't you, Emily? I mean, about me and Samir.'

'Yes,' Emily murmured, summoning all her patience.

'I don't need anyone to tell me that Samir's not much older than Tracy, and everyone has a fling on holiday that comes to nothing when they get home. But me and Samir aren't like that, Emily. This is the real thing, I'm absolutely sure of it. I love him and he loves me. We've written to each other every single day since I left Morocco. If I had the money, I'd send him an airline ticket and invite him over for Christmas.'

'If money is all that's stopping you,' Emily said recklessly, 'I'll lend you enough for a ticket.'

'Would you?' Deirdre's eyes sparkled. 'I'll pay you back as soon as I can. It's just that I'm a bit short at the moment, having taken all that time off to look after my mother.'

'I'll give you a cheque tomorrow. Same again?' Emily picked up their empty glasses.

'Please.' Deirdre hardly knew what she was saying. She was too excited by the prospect of seeing Samir again. 'You'll understand when you meet him, Emily. He's so gentle, kind – and good-looking, of course. You're going to fall in love with him just as I have.'

'I hope not.' Emily smiled. 'I've a feeling you'd never forgive me if I did.'

'I'll organise a really traditional English Christmas,' Deirdre said excitedly. 'I'll buy a real tree, decorate it, hang stockings embroidered with our names on the mantelpiece, put presents under the tree, a wreath on the door, buy a turkey . . . You must join us for Christmas dinner.'

Emily smiled, glad that she had made Deirdre so happy. 'I'd like that.'

'Good, that's settled.' Deirdre sat back in her chair, her thoughts lost in the moonlit garden of a Moroccan hotel. 'We're going to have the best Christmas ever, Emily, you just mark my words.'

'I can't believe you made Denise Osbourne pregnant!' Tracy screamed at Ken. 'A man your age and a girl like her – it's disgusting! Aren't you ashamed of yourself?'

'I'd be lying if I said I was happy about it.' Ken had been dreading telling Tracy about the baby, and with good cause. Tracy had taken the news even more badly than he had expected.

'You'll be a lousy father to this baby just as you've been a lousy father to me, Susan and Peter,' she yelled hysterically.

'I'm sorry you feel that way, Tracy.' He knew it was useless to try to reason with her when she was in this mood.

'I wish you that you and my mother would act your age. Do you know she's living with a twenty-one-year-old Moroccan waiter? You've only got to look at them together to see he's only using her so he can live in this country. And now you get a girl less than half your age pregnant . . .'

'I know this can't be easy for you, Tracy—'

'You don't know the first thing about me, or what I feel. This is my flat, mine and Craig's, so get out!'

Hating himself for having hurt his adopted daughter, Ken walked slowly back to his house. But his conversation with Tracy had only made him all the more determined to be a good father to the child Denise was carrying.

Chapter Fifty

'I appreciate that your country is warmer and sunnier than it is here. I was there, remember,' Deirdre said to Samir, as they cuddled on the sofa, which she'd pulled as close to the gas fire as she dared. 'And I know you find my country confusing.'

'Cold, noisy, confusing, frightening.' Samir recited words he'd learnt from his dictionary, which he'd never needed to know while working as a waiter in his native Morocco. 'But you are here and that makes this place lovelier than anywhere else in the world.'

'You say such beautiful things.'

Samir kissed her and Deirdre felt as though they were the only two people on the planet. She wished she could capture that emotion so she could show it to the immigration officials who had just interrogated Samir and her. They had given both of them a hard time, but had been particularly unpleasant to Samir.

'I love you, Deirdre,' he said, when he finally released her.

'And I love you.'

'Why didn't those people know that today? Why did they think that I love your cold country more than you?'

'Because they don't know or understand you or me, Samir. If you married me you could live here as my husband.'

'And they wouldn't bother us again?' he asked.

'No, they wouldn't,' she assured him. 'You could take the job you were offered in that Moroccan restaurant and we could live here together.'

'In the cold.'

'In the cold,' she repeated, smiling at him, 'but summer is coming.'

'It is hot then?' he asked hopefully.

'No, but sometimes it gets warm.'

'With you I am always warm, so we will get married. Soon, I hope.'

'Very soon.' Deirdre returned his kiss and tried to forget the arguments she'd had with Tracy since Samir had arrived. Once Samir and she were married, Tracy, and the neighbours, would come to accept him. They would have to, because from the very first moment she had met him, Samir had become her whole life.

Denise Osbourne gasped as her labour pains intensified. A nurse walked into her cubicle wheeling a cot and she knew the birth wouldn't be that long. 'Has he got here yet?' she snapped.

'We sent for Mr Barlow half an hour ago but it's a fair drive from Weatherfield to here. I doubt if he'll arrive for another half-hour and that's if he got the message.'

Denise relaxed as the contraction ended.

The curtains parted and Ken walked in. He smiled at her. 'I'm glad I'm in time. How are you?'

'How do you think I am? In bloody agony.' She moaned as another pain took hold.

The midwife gave Ken a sympathetic glance. 'It won't be long now, Mr Barlow.'

Ten minutes later Ken was holding his son. 'He's beautiful,' he gasped, too smitten by the baby to spare a look for Denise.

'Have you thought of a name for him yet?' the midwife asked.

'Daniel,' Denise said, in a voice that would brook no argument. 'But you can give him his second name if you like, Ken,' she conceded, in response to the besotted expression on his face.

'Daniel Albert, if that's all right with you?'

'It's what I expected after all the stories you told me about Albert Tatlock.'

'I didn't think you listened to them,' he said, in surprise.

'I heard some.'

'You can have another ten minutes and then we'll be

moving you to the maternity ward, Miss Osbourne,' the midwife said, on her way out of the cubicle. 'You can pick up a card giving you the visiting times on your way out, Mr Barlow.'

'Thank you.' Ken waited until the midwife left, then deposited Daniel gently in Denise's arms. 'I promise you, Daniel Albert Barlow . . .'

'Osbourne,' Denise corrected.

'Daniel Albert Osbourne, I'll always be around when you need me,' Ken vowed.

'I'll tell him about that when he's old enough,' Denise warned.

'I'd expect you to,' Ken replied.

'You're the last person I expected to see, Deirdre – Rachid now, isn't it?' Mike Baldwin said as Deirdre walked into his office. 'I thought you'd be enjoying all the delights a honeymoon can bring. Married life not going too well?'

'It's going fine, Mike.'

'That's not what I heard. A little bird told me Tracy left the register office in tears and Immigration was looking into your case. Something about your husband using you to get a residency permit.'

'That's why I'm here, Mike. Samir and I are in love, but Immigration refuse to believe it. They've interrogated us four times since we were married and now they're threatening to deport Samir.'

'You can't blame them. There *is* something of an age difference between you two. And if you've come here asking for help, I warn you, I haven't any pull with Immigration.'

'I know you haven't and I haven't come to ask you for help. Samir and I have decided to go back to Morocco.'

'To live?' Mike couldn't have been more surprised if she'd told him she was about to take up residence on the moon.

'Yes. And we need money to set ourselves up there so I have to sell the house quickly. You're the first person I thought of who'd have the cash available to put in an offer. As I'm not in a position to wait, you can have it for knockdown price for a quick sale.'

'Furnished?' he asked astutely.

'Furnished,' she reiterated. 'I can hardly take Albert Tatlock's antiques to Morocco with me.'

'Then I'll give you the full market price, Deirdre, and take the furniture off your hands. When are you thinking of leaving?'

'As soon as we have the money for our flights.'

'I'll get my solicitor on to it right away and tell him to have the contracts drawn up by tomorrow. As soon as I get your signature, I'll give you the cheque.'

'As much as I hate putting money into Mike Baldwin's pocket, I love this house.' Ken carried Denise's case into number one Coronation Street. He looked at Albert's furniture and felt at home for the first time since Deirdre had thrown him out of the house on New Year's Day, five years before. He set Denise's suitcase down beside the sofa. 'Can I get you a cup of tea?'

'Please.' Denise laid the carrycot on a chair, took her coat off and sat down. 'You won't expect too much of this relationship, will you?' she asked Ken, as he returned with a tea-tray. 'As I said, I'm willing to give it a go, for Daniel's sake, but we haven't much in common. And there is the age difference . . .'

'I know.' Like Denise, Ken felt their relationship would not stand the test of time but he was passionate about being involved in Daniel's upbringing. He had been shattered when his solicitor had told him that, as Denise hadn't named him as Daniel's father on his birth certificate, he had no paternal rights. Which was why he was prepared to work hard to keep things friendly between him and Denise.

'One sugar or two?' he asked, as he picked up her tea.

Martin walked into the living room to find Gail standing by the window, staring into space. She turned when she heard his step and looked at him expectantly.

'It's true,' he said. 'Ivy died of a stroke this morning.'

'She's really dead.'

'She's really dead, Gail.' He took her hand and led her

to the sofa. 'I spoke to Don, and what she said is true. She has left the house to Nicky on condition he reverts to the name Tilsley. But Don isn't happy about it. He warned me that he intends to contest the will and he won't let any of us over the threshold.'

'I can't believe it,' Gail whispered. 'She's really dead.'

'Nicky is going to have to be told about the house and Don contesting Ivy's will.'

'Must he?' she pleaded. 'He's been going through such a rough patch lately. He's only just moved back in with us after quarrelling with Don.'

'Nicky's been going through a rough patch!' Martin exclaimed crossly. 'What about the rest of us? He's been playing us off against Don and Ivy for months.' His temper cooled when he saw the stricken expression on Gail's face. 'He's your son, Gail, it's only natural that you feel protective towards him.'

'I know he's been difficult lately. To be honest, I haven't known which way to turn the last couple of months. I know I haven't been paying proper attention to you or Sarah and David. But lately I've felt as if everything is falling apart . . .'

She began to cry and Martin took her in his arms to comfort her. 'We'll sort out Nicky,' he promised her. But he couldn't help wondering if he was making an assurance he wouldn't be able to keep. Ivy might have gone, but she had primed Nicky so well that he sensed they might be exchanging one troublemaker in the family for another.

'What the hell happened, Ken?' Deirdre whispered, after she'd rushed into the intensive-care ward where Tracy was lying connected to a dialysis machine. It was four o'clock in the morning and Ken hadn't left the hospital for three days. He rose from the stool he'd been sitting on and reeled. He was so tired he was light-headed.

As Tracy was sleeping peacefully, he held his finger to his lips and pointed to the door. He led the way to the waiting room and Deirdre followed. Samir was sitting there with his head in his hands, suitcases piled at his feet. They had driven straight from the airport to the hospital. One month in Morocco and here Deirdre was back again.

'Tracy collapsed in a nightclub last Saturday night after taking ecstasy,' Ken told Deirdre, 'and they brought her straight here. It was touch and go for forty-eight hours. When she started to recover, they discovered that her kidneys were damaged.'

Deirdre sank on to the chair beside Samir and he reached out and held her hand. She clutched it, returning the pressure of his fingers, and Ken realised they were so close there was no need for words between them.

'If I'd been here . . .' Deirdre murmured.

'You wouldn't have been able to do a thing,' Ken countered firmly. 'The last couple of years Tracy's been so headstrong she hasn't listened to you, me or anyone else.'

'Does she know she has kidney damage?'

'The doctor told her when she came round this morning. She became hysterical and said she'd rather die than live on a dialysis machine. I had some tests in the hope that I could give her one of my kidneys, but my tissue isn't compatible with hers.'

Deirdre went to the door. 'I'll see about getting a test now. If mine is compatible, she can have one of mine.'

Samir leapt to his feet. 'No, Deirdre. If you give your daughter a kidney you will not be able to have our children. If she needs a kidney she can have one of mine.'

Ken had never before seen such a look of loving concern on anyone's face. So much for all the gossips in Coronation Street who had thought the Moroccan was only out for what he could get from Deirdre.

'There is no guarantee that your kidney will be any more compatible than mine, Samir,' Ken said. 'And neither does it follow that a mother and daughter have the same tissue type,' he warned Deirdre.

'I have to try.'

'And I will have the test as well,' Samir insisted.

'No,' Deirdre shook her head. 'There's no point, Samir.'

'I will still have it,' he repeated stubbornly.

Rita Sullivan left her house and walked up Coronation Street. She had been friendly with Bet Gilroy for years, but this was the first time Bet had invited her to have morning coffee in her private quarters at the Rovers and she wondered what Bet wanted from her.

Bet showed her straight into the living room. It had a deserted, unused air about it, which was hardly surprising given the number of hours Bet spent behind the bar. She watched Bet pour two cups of coffee and decided to cut to the chase.

'You have a problem you think I can help with, Bet?' she asked bluntly.

'Yes.' Bet didn't even try to pretend that she'd asked her over for a sociable chat. 'The brewery has put the Rovers up for sale. They want sixty-eight thousand pounds for it. I haven't anything like that kind of money.'

'I doubt many people have,' Rita said, wondering how much Bet knew about her finances. Between Len's insurance money, the rent from the builder's yard, the Kabin and the money Ted had left her, she could have afforded to buy the pub three times over and have a considerable amount of cash to spare. Only she didn't want to buy the Rovers Return. Especially if Bet Gilroy continued to run it. Much as she liked Bet and valued her friendship, she was cool-headed enough to grasp that, on past form and behaviour, Bet was not a good financial risk.

'I hoped the bank would lend me the money. But they wouldn't. I've asked around . . .'

Rita suspected that meant Bet had asked Mike Baldwin for the cash and he'd turned her down.

'. . . But no one is prepared to lend me what I'll need.' Bet sat and faced Rita. 'You're my last hope. Will you give me a private loan?'

Rita didn't even ask Bet how much she wanted. She shook her head, knowing that if she did lend Bet the money she'd never see it again.

'You could be a sleeping partner. You'd own half the Rovers – more if you want,' Bet offered recklessly. 'I'll carry on doing all the work and running the place on a day-to-day basis and pay you half the profits.'

'And keep up the repayments on the loan?'

'Of course,' Bet assured eagerly.

'Look at it from my point of view, Bet,' Rita said. 'The profit this place makes would never allow you to meet the repayments on the loan *and* give me a return on my investment.'

'You're my last hope.'

'I'm sorry.' Rita meant it. She was fond of Bet and hated disappointing her.

'I don't have a single friend in this street,' Bet said

cuttingly. 'After all the favours I've done for people over the years . . .'

'That's not true and you know it. I am very fond of you, Bet—'

'Then lend me the money! I know you have it.'

'If I loaned money to everyone who asked me, I'd have none left. I'm sorry I can't help you.' Rita stood up.

'You do realise this means that I'll have to leave the Rovers, and if I leave the pub I may as well leave the street,'

'Do whatever you think is right for yourself, Bet.' Rita opened the door. 'I wish you well, wherever you go,' she said calmly, refusing to cave in to emotional blackmail.

Bet sat in her chair, staring at the coffee pot and cups for half an hour after Rita had gone. She'd exhausted every possibility of getting a loan so there was no point in hanging around the Rovers. The deadline the brewery had set for the sale was only four days away. She got up and went upstairs, fetched her suitcase from the boxroom and began to pack.

'Denise not here?' Deirdre asked, as Ken showed her into the living room of number one. Her breath caught in her throat as she looked around. The room was exactly as it had been when she and Ken had lived in the house together.

'Denise took Daniel and moved in with her brother-in-law a couple of days ago. They've been having an on-off affair for years.'

'I'm sorry, Ken.'

'So am I, but about Daniel not Denise. I never expected our relationship to last. And then again, sitting in the hospital with Tracy made me realise that kids need you more when they're growing up – especially during their teenage years – than when they're babies. Denise will look after Daniel well enough for now, and hopefully he'll come to me in the future when he needs me. You and Samir comfortable lodging in the street?' he asked, deliberately changing the subject.

'Comfortable enough,' she replied. 'The hospital rang earlier with the result of the tests. You were right about me not having the same tissue type or blood group as Tracy, but Samir does.'

'*What?*'

'I find it difficult to believe as well, but he's already left for the hospital. He's determined to donate a kidney to her. I spoke to the doctor on the phone and he said what he told us before, that a person only needs one kidney to function. But I still feel that it's a lot to ask of Samir.'

'He loves you very much, Deirdre.' Ken experienced a sudden pang of regret for all that he and Deirdre had once had, and he'd thrown away.

'And I love him. But this is an awful sacrifice for him to make for my daughter.'

The telephone rang and Ken went into the hall to answer it. He spoke for about five minutes, glancing back at Deirdre at intervals. When he set down the receiver, he went to her and gripped her arms. 'We have to go to the hospital straight away.'

'Tracy—'

'Not Tracy. Samir. He's been found unconscious on the road outside the hospital. The police said it looks as though someone has beaten him up.' He reached for his car keys. 'I'll drive you there.'

Raquel had hated leaving her job and room in the Rovers, but the brewery had put in a temporary manager and he had told her in no uncertain terms that he didn't want her working or living there because he preferred to bring in his own team. She'd had nowhere to go so she'd moved in with Curly. It wasn't ideal, because ever since she had pretended to be his fiancée at the Soopa Soopa Christmas party, he had been telling everyone they were a couple. He'd even got her a job at the supermarket, and she felt as though he was pushing her into a hole she didn't quite fit.

She brushed away a tear as she sat on a pile of boxes in the Soopa Soopa warehouse and hoped that no one would track her down. Curly meant to be kind, but his insistence as manager that she be spared the menial jobs, like stacking shelves and polishing fruit, had made her unpopular with the other girls, who felt she was getting special treatment and resented her for it.

And then there was last night – every time she thought about what she had done she wanted to die of shame.

Curly was so good to her and she had repaid him by sleeping with Des Barnes. She didn't even know why. She'd lived with Des and he'd thrown her out of his house as soon as he'd fancied Lisa Duckworth, and he hadn't changed. She knew he was a rat who'd treat her just as badly as before if she went back to him. But she hadn't been able to stop herself. And that amounted to a betrayal of Curly and his feelings for her.

'Raquel, why are you hiding in here?' Curly walked into the warehouse and crouched at her feet. 'Has someone upset you?'

His kindness on top of the guilt she felt hurt more than she would have believed possible. 'No, Curly.'

'Then what's wrong?'

She tried to get a grip on her emotions. 'Curly, I know you want to marry me . . .'

'I've asked you often enough.'

'Marry me now, in a register office with strangers as witnesses. Promise me you won't tell a soul about the wedding?' she demanded frantically.

'If that's what you want, Raquel,' he replied, too grateful to her for accepting his proposal to wonder at her motive. 'But do you mind if I book us a honeymoon? Something really special?'

She looked up at him, hoping against hope that she was doing the right thing. 'We'll go anywhere you like, Curly, anywhere at all,' she said dully.

'I am sorry, Mrs Rachid, but your husband is brain dead.'

Ken wrapped his arm round Deirdre's shoulders as the doctor made his pronouncement. They looked at Samir's body, still linked to the life-support machine.

'But he's breathing.' Deirdre picked up Samir's hand, oblivious to Ken's touch on her shoulder.

'I've kept him on the life-support machine because I understand from my colleague that your husband's tissue type is compatible with your daughter's and he had offered to donate one of his kidneys to her. Now that he is clinically dead, his organs could help other people besides your daughter to live, Mrs Rachid. But,' knowing Deirdre was in shock, the doctor looked awkwardly from Deirdre to Ken, 'in order to use his organs, we need your consent.'

Deirdre stared blankly at the doctor, and Ken realised she hadn't taken in a word he'd said.

'Deirdre,' he murmured, 'if you sign that form they can use Samir's kidney to save Tracy. His other organs could save other people's lives. Samir is dead but you have to think about what he'd want you to do.'

'Samir never had a selfish bone in his body.'

'I know, Deirdre.' Ken took the form from the doctor and placed it on the cabinet beside her. He removed his pen from his top pocket and pushed it into her hand.

'You sign here, Mrs Rachid.' The doctor pointed to the line at the bottom of the form.

As soon as Deirdre had scribbled her name, the doctor nodded to the nurse and waiting porters. Ken gripped Deirdre's shoulders.

'Come on, I'll buy you a cup of coffee in the waiting room.'

Deirdre slipped from his grasp and rushed to the bed. At a signal from the doctor, the porters stopped. Deirdre held Samir's hand, touched his forehead and kissed him for the last time. Ken reached her just before she collapsed.

Ken looked at his watch, left his chair and paced from one end of the waiting room to the other. He pulled some change out of his pocket and put it into the coffee machine. He returned with two plastic cups to where Deirdre was sitting, staring stony-faced and dead-eyed into space. She hadn't said a word since she had kissed Samir goodbye.

'Mrs Rachid, Mr Barlow.' The surgeon joined them, still in his green cap and gown. 'The transplant went well and the tissue type is such a good match we're not antic-ipating any problems with rejection. I see no reason why your daughter shouldn't make a full recovery.'

Deirdre burst into hysterical cries. Overwhelmed by the depth of her grief Ken embraced her. She relaxed, still sobbing, against his shoulder.

'There is nothing you can do here now, Mr Barlow,' the doctor said. 'I suggest you take Mrs Rachid home. You can both call in tomorrow morning to see your daughter. She should have come round by then.'

Deirdre looked at the doctor and then at Ken. 'I don't know why Samir had to die. He was so good, so wonderful . . . I never, never want to see Tracy again as long as I live.'

'That is an understandable reaction, Mrs Rachid,' the doctor said, in his best bedside manner.

Ken led Deirdre away before she could say anything else. He knew her better than the doctor did: Deirdre always meant what she said. Hopefully, in time, he could persuade her to change her mind.

Chapter Fifty-One

Jack Duckworth came home late from the Rovers, sat at the table and waited for Vera to serve him with the Welsh rarebit she'd put into the oven for his supper.

'That temporary manager of the Rovers told me he's not putting in a bid for the pub.'

'I'm not surprised,' Vera said. 'He's not exactly a bundle of laughs, is he?'

'I was thinking about that money my brother Cliff left me.'

'You only had the letter from the solicitor this morning and you've spent that money ten times over,' Vera reminded him. 'It's only a couple of hours since you were round at Des Barnes's asking if he's still keen on selling number six because you fancied the garden.'

'It'd be nicer to own a pub than a house with a garden.'

'It would an' all,' Vera agreed, 'as long as you didn't drink the profits.'

'I'd still buy you that engagement ring.' Jack grabbed Vera as she passed his chair and gave her a hug. 'It's bothered me for years that I wasn't able to afford a proper one before we were wed.'

'Are you serious about buying Rovers?' She sat next to him at the table.

'I'll talk to the brewery tomorrow and see what's what. This looks good.' He ferried a forkful of cheese to his mouth. 'Who'd have thought it? You and me, publicans.'

'Only if the brewery agrees,' Vera warned him.

'They'll grab at the chance of laying their hands on a cash sale, love, you'll see, and now that our Cliff has left us all right, we have the cash to spare.'

'You're the last person I expected to see on our doorstep,' Martin Platt said to Don Brennan, when he opened his door to him. 'If you've come here to cause trouble, I'm telling you now, get back to your own house. Gail and the children have enough to do coming to terms with Ivy's death as it is, without you coming round making things worse.'

'I'm not here to cause any trouble, Martin.'

'No?' Martin enquired sceptically.

Unconvinced, he was about to close the door when Don said, 'I've been thinking. I wondered if it would help if I bought the house off Nicky.'

Martin stepped back. 'If you're serious, I suppose you'd better come inside so we can talk about it.'

Don trailed awkwardly behind Martin into the living room. After the way he had thrown Martin out after Ivy's death and told him that no Platt would be allowed over the doorstep of number five again, he knew he had no right to expect a warm welcome. Nicky, Sarah and David were sitting on the floor around the coffee table playing Monopoly and Gail was clearing away the tea-things.

'Don was asking if it would help matters if he bought Ivy's house from Nicky,' Martin explained.

'That's for Nicky to decide,' Gail said. 'It's his house, Ivy left it to him.'

'What do you say, Nicky?' Don hovered at the door as no one had asked him to sit down. 'Can I buy the house off you?'

'Can I have the money straight away?' Nicky asked.

'No, you cannot,' Gail said flatly. 'It will be invested until your twenty-first birthday.'

'That's not to say you couldn't have some of it for things like your education.' Martin tempered Gail's pronouncement when he saw Nicky's face fall.

Nicky shrugged. 'You can buy it, Don.'

'I'll pay the full market price.' Don might have been talking to Nicky but he was looking at Gail and Martin. 'I'll get an estate agent in tomorrow to value it.'

'Now that's settled I'll see you out, Don.' Martin opened the door and walked down the passage.

Don hesitated in the hall. 'Gail and the children haven't seen anything odd lately, have they, Martin? Here or in the street?'

'In what way?'

'I don't know, just something odd.'

'If you're asking if we've heard the story about Vera Duckworth seeing Ivy's ghost in the street, the answer is yes,' Martin told him. 'But given Ivy's behaviour during her life, don't you think this is the last house in the street that she would haunt?'

'I suppose so,' Don conceded.

Martin opened the door. 'Have you seen her, Don?'

Don shook his head.

'Then I doubt Vera saw anything other than a ghost conjured by her own imagination,' Martin said. 'Given Ivy's temperament, she'd be more likely to haunt her husband, if only to nag him, than Vera Duckworth.'

Ken Barlow sat on the edge of the bed in his spare room and watched Tracy stuff her clothes into a bag.

'It makes sense, Dad. I have friends in Blackpool who'll put me up until I get on my feet again. There are plenty of jobs going up there and now I have a clean bill of health from the hospital I'm bound to get something. So, what more could I want, apart from a mother who talks to me?'

'She'll come round, Tracy,' Ken said quietly. 'Just give her time. She's not come to terms with losing Samir yet.'

'And she won't while I'm around to remind her that I've his kidney. Face it, Dad, she's devastated at the thought of me being alive instead of Samir.'

'She's not, Tracy. She loves you—'

'Funny way she has of showing it. Look, I'm not just going to Blackpool to get away from her. There's better prospects for me there and I'll not be sorry to leave the street.'

Ken felt that Tracy was right. The last couple of years had been disastrous for her. She had broken up with Craig, taken drugs, and he had the feeling that if her kidneys hadn't failed, worse might have happened. 'Your mam and I both love you very much.' His words sounded trite and inadequate but he couldn't think of anything more profound to say.

'Time I went, and before you start, I promise to behave myself.'

'Promise?' he repeated seriously.

'Solemn promise, hope to die.' She spat on her finger and crossed herself.

'And you'll telephone me?'

'At least four times a week. Is that enough?'

'It'll have to be.' Ken knew he wasn't going to get a better offer out of her. 'I'll want your telephone number as soon as you've got one. Here, I'll take that.' He lifted the bag from the bed as soon as she had zipped it shut. 'I'll drive you to the station – and take this.' He put his hand into his pocket and pulled out two twenty pound notes.

'You've already given me money.'

'This is extra – for porters among other things. Don't you dare carry your bags yourself. You might have had a clean bill of health from the hospital, but you've been warned not to do any heavy lifting for at least a year.'

'When was the last time you saw a porter at a station?'

Ken couldn't remember. 'You'll just have to make eyes at the nearest man with a strong arm, then, won't you?'

'You telling me to pick up a bloke?' she teased.

'Definitely not. Come on, or you'll be late.'

As he followed her down the stairs and out of the house, he hoped he was doing the right thing in allowing her to go to Blackpool. But beneath the guilt he felt at not having been able to stop her experimenting with drugs was relief that she was moving away from Coronation Street.

'I never realised we had so much stuff, Vera.' Jack carried a box marked BATHROOM up the stairs at the Rovers. 'I haven't sat down for more than two minutes since the brewery accepted our offer for the pub.'

'The move wouldn't have been anywhere near so bad so if you hadn't told those Mallets that they could start renting number nine this week. If I'd had a couple of days to sort the packing properly, get all the boxes over here, then clean the house, everything would have gone much more smoothly.'

'They wanted a house in a hurry so I grabbed the chance of renting to them. You can't moan at me for that,' Jack protested.

'All I'm saying is, it would have made for a smoother move—'

'Jack, Vera?' Betty shouted up the stairs. 'There's a reporter here to see you.'

'I'll see to her.' Jack pushed the box he was carrying on to the landing and ran back down the stairs.

'What reporter?' Vera asked suspiciously.

'One I talked to,' Jack called back airily.

'What did you talk to a reporter about?' Vera pressed, refusing to be fobbed off by Jack's excuses.

'No publicity is bad publicity,' Jack answered evasively. 'And you know what people are when they hear a ghost story.'

'Jack Duckworth, if you've gone and told the newspapers that I saw Ivy Brennan's ghost . . .' Vera picked up the box that Jack had abandoned and threw it at him.

Jack dodged round Betty and raced into the bar – as the box of towels burst open at the foot of the stairs.

'Good to see you, Deirdre.' Alec Gilroy greeted her when she entered the corner shop, carrying her purse and a shopping bag.

'I didn't know you were back, Alec,' Deirdre said. But, then, she didn't know anything that had been happening in the outside world. She had spent the two months since Samir's death hiding in Ken's spare room.

'Sunliners travel agency has sent me to take over their Rosamund Street branch.' Alec gave her a small smile. He hadn't been back in Weatherfield for more than five minutes before he had been regaled with the full story of Deirdre's marriage, her return from Morocco, the tragic death of her husband and his lifesaving donation of a kidney to drug-taking Tracy. 'Have you come back to live here permanently?'

'I've just moved into one of Mike's new flats. He's converted and restored a Victorian house in Crimea Street. He offered it to me almost rent-free in return for caretaking duties.'

'Don't suppose you want a job as well?' he ventured.

'Doing what?'

'I need an assistant in the travel agency. Running an office will be child's play to someone with your experience, Deirdre, and there's cut-price travel on offer,' he added, as an incentive.

Remembering her last holiday and meeting Samir, Deirdre felt that she never wanted to leave the country again. She reflected on the oddities of life. She had tried to shut herself away after Samir had died, and slowly but surely Ken had coaxed her, first to leave her bed and then to leave her room. He had cooked meals for her, and if it had been with the intention of making her feel guilty that he was working full time and doing the housework and cooking, his ploy had worked. Because here she was, shopping for tea. Then, the first time she had left Ken's house, she had run into Mike, who had offered her the flat, and now she was being offered a job.

'Will you take the job?'

'Why not, Alec? I've nothing better to do. Thank you for thinking of me.'

'I'm the lucky one for getting you, Deirdre. When can you start?'

'Whenever you like. As I said, I've nothing better to do.'

'How about tomorrow? See you at nine o'clock?'

'See you then. Now, if you'll excuse me, I have shopping to do.' She picked up a basket and walked along, looking at what was on offer on the shelves of the mini-market.

Don Brennan's new girlfriend Josie Clarke snuggled up close to him in bed and ran her fingers through the hairs on his chest.

'I'm telling you it's a real money-spinner, Don. I saw the valuation on Mike's desk when I took the invoices in to him today. That garage is worth an absolute fortune and Mike only bought it because he has been making so much money from his designer sportswear manufacturing business he didn't know what to do with it. He has absolutely no interest in running the place. He's only been to see Kevin Webster and the boys who are managing it once since he bought it last month and he leaves everything to them. You're a taxi-driver, you know all about cars. You should own that garage, not Mike. If we go into partnership and buy it off him, we'll soon be making so much money we won't know what to do with it.'

'Why would Mike sell it to us if it's worth a fortune?' Don asked suspiciously.

'Because I happen to know that he needs cash to buy another factory that's just come on the market.'

'You need money to make money, Josie,' he reminded her strongly. 'And I haven't any spare to buy the garage.'

'I have enough saved to put down a deposit and you have this house. Any bank will let you use it as security against a sure thing like the garage,' she coaxed.

'You want us to become business partners.'

'I'll be your sleeping partner.' She giggled. 'In every sense of the word. I wouldn't want Mike to find out that I'd tipped you off, or that I owned half the garage or, worst of all, that we were sleeping together. He'd sack me on the spot.'

'I wondered when the wind would blow you back this way,' Jack Duckworth said to Terry, as he walked into the Rovers.

'I've a surprise for you and Mam.' Terry beckoned to

someone standing outside and a small boy tottered in clutching a suitcase almost as big as himself.

Vera gasped and clapped her hand over her mouth.

'Your grandson, Mam,' Terry said.

'Tommy, you've grown so big and you've changed so much in a year . . .' Vera rushed out from behind the bar but she hesitated as Tommy looked up at her with enormous frightened eyes. 'He doesn't remember me, Terry.'

'He soon will. You're his grandmother.'

'He can't stay in the bar,' Jack warned Vera. 'No children allowed in here, remember.'

'I know. I'll take him into the back and make him a meal. Are you hungry, Tommy?'

When he nodded, Vera offered him her hand. 'You'll have to tell me what you like to eat.' Tommy stared at her hand for a moment, then took it. They walked behind the bar and into the private quarters.

Terry looked around the Rovers. 'Very nice. You've done well for yourself, Dad.'

'If you've come back here thinking you can put your hand in the till you can clear off to wherever you came from now.'

'That's a nice way to greet your son after he's been away for the best part of a year,' Terry griped. 'I thought you'd like to see Tommy.'

'For a holiday?' Jack asked warily.

'For good.'

'The Hortons know you've got him?'

'They know all right,' Terry snapped.

'They stopped paying you?' Jack asked shrewdly.

'They knew the deal. Two thousand a year on the nose, or lose Tommy.'

'What kind of a father sells his own son?'

'One who wants the best for him.' Terry leant on the bar. 'If they can't afford to pay me off, they can't afford to buy Tommy the things he needs to be looked after properly.' He put his hand in his pocket and slammed a five-pound note on the bar. 'I'll have a pint.' He turned his back to Jack and studied the crowd of regulars. 'Nice little goldmine you've bought yourself here.' He eyed a group of girls sitting at a table and settled on one in particular.

'That's Tricia Armstrong,' Jack told him. 'She's got a bit of a reputation around here, not to mention a young lad who's running wild. Stay away from her.'

Terry noticed the almost empty glass on the table in front of her.

'Before you give me my change, I'll have a vodka and orange, a double – no, make that a treble.'

Shaking his head, Jack poured the drinks and put them with Terry's change on the bar. Terry scooped up the coins and pocketed them carelessly. He picked up his beer and the vodka and orange, then sauntered across the bar,

allowed him into her bed '. . . who wants to pull out because they're not getting any return on their money. If I'm going to keep the garage going I need to find a new business partner who is prepared to invest.'

'Don't look in this direction,' Kevin said shortly. 'If things don't improve around here Tony and I'll be off looking for new jobs.'

Don tossed his pen down on his desk. 'So, what you're saying is Baldwin swindled me when he sold me this garage.'

'Way I heard it, you went to him and asked to buy it. And you can't blame him for grabbing the chance when you offered.'

Don closed the books. If he'd had enough money to buy Josie out, he'd have given it to her just to get her off his back. But the niggling thought that Baldwin had deliberately swindled him preyed on his mind.

And Josie worked for Baldwin. He had bought the garage on her recommendation – had Josie and Baldwin joined together to scam him? Whichever way he looked at the situation, one thing was certain: he had to buy Josie out simply because he couldn't stand any more pressure from her to repay her investment.

The problem was, who to approach to invest in the garage. Clearly, Kevin and Tony weren't interested. But, then, they worked in the garage and had inside knowledge. Then it came to him. There was one person who had money to invest, money that wasn't doing anything. He left the garage and went to Gail and Martin's house. He knocked at the door and Nicky opened it.

'Hi, Nicky.'

'Hi.' Nicky wandered into the living room. Don followed him, glad that the boy appeared to be alone.

'You do anything with the money I paid you for the house?'

'Mam and Martin put it away for me.'

'In a building society?' Don guessed correctly.

'Whatever.'

'I've a better investment than that in mind. How would you like to own half a garage?'

Gail opened the kitchen door. 'I don't believe I heard you say that, Don,' she said, in disgust. 'How dare you? Kevin was only telling Martin the other day that he couldn't understand how anyone in their right mind would buy the garage from Mike Baldwin because it's not making any money. And now you've discovered you're losing money, you're looking to cut your losses by selling my son a bankrupt business. Get out!' She stepped threateningly towards Don. He was aware that there was something faintly ridiculous about a woman of Gail's size threatening him, but he didn't laugh. Instead, he backed away.

'Get out, stay out and don't come back!' she shouted from the doorstep, as he ran into his house.

★

'Good news?' Jack Duckworth asked Terry, as he opened a letter at the breakfast table.

'Reasonable.' Terry took a cheque from the envelope, folded it and stuffed it into his back pocket. 'Mam in the kitchen?'

Jack nodded, his mouth full of bacon and egg.

Terry ruffled Tommy's hair on his way out of the room. 'Mam,' he shouted, 'where are you? I've had a letter from the Hortons and they're meeting Tommy and me off the afternoon train. We'll have to leave in an hour.'

Jack heard Vera's voice thick with tears as she answered Terry, then they began to argue. He looked across at Tommy, who was solemnly eating toast and marmalade. The envelope Terry had opened was still on the table. He picked it up and removed the letter Terry hadn't bothered to read.

Enclosed one cheque for ten thousand pounds. I will put a stop on it until you sign a residency order for Tommy so you will never be able to take him away from us again. When he is returned to us, you will get your money, Geoff Horton.

Chapter Fifty-Two

Don Brennan lit his first cigarette of the morning and gazed in despair at the mail the postman had brought that morning. The bank had written to inform him that they'd foreclosed on the loan they'd given him to buy the garage, taking the business into receivership. He was also being prosecuted for driving under the influence of drink in his taxi after a lunchtime boozing session during which he'd tried to drown his financial sorrows. As he'd been well over the limit when the police caught up with him, he knew he would lose his licence and along with it his livelihood. Life just wasn't worth living.

Although it wasn't even nine o'clock in the morning, he went to the sideboard and lifted out a bottle of brandy.

'Gail Platt?'

'Yes.'

Gail looked at the tall, good-looking, fair-haired man on her doorstep and knew instinctively who he was.

'I'm your brother, Steve Reid.'

She smiled. 'Mam's told me all about you.'

'I wanted her to come with me and introduce us, but I think she finds this situation a bit strange.'

'Please, come in, we have so much to talk about.'

'We do,' he agreed. He looked around her living room. 'This is really nice,' he added.

'Thank you. Would you like a cup of tea or coffee?'

'Coffee, please. We Canadians are more like Americans in our tastes, we're not great tea-drinkers like you folks.'

'You here for a holiday?' she asked, from the kitchen.

'Business. I work for a sportswear firm, you may have heard of it, K-bec. I'm here to place an order with a new supplier – that's if they can come up with the goods. But the upside is that I get to meet you for the first time. It's great to have a little sister.'

Gail brought the coffee and set it on the table. 'I can't wait for Martin and the children to meet you.'

'Audrey told me a lot about you so perhaps I could start by filling you in about me. Audrey said you've never been to Canada.'

'I haven't, but I'd like to go.'

'We'll have to see what we can do about that.' Steve winked at her and Gail smiled back. Steve was so easy to get on with, she already felt as though she'd known him all her life.

★

Kevin waved to Martin Platt as he walked up the back lane behind Coronation Street. He had great news and he couldn't wait to share it with someone.

'Guess what, Martin?'

'Judging by that grin on your face, I'm guessing *Playgirl* has chosen you to be the centrefold mechanic of the month.'

'Very funny. The bank manager called round the garage this afternoon and asked Tony and me if we wanted to buy the place.'

'You said you wouldn't touch it with a bargepole in its present state,' Martin reminded him.

'And I wouldn't if the bank wanted us to pay anything like the amount Don did for the place. But all they want from us is enough to cover their loss.'

'You said all the equipment is outdated.'

'It is, but as we're picking up the building and the goodwill for a song, we can afford to re-equip the place. We could never have afforded Mike Baldwin's asking price, but buying it off the bank will leave us with enough money to invest in new tools and a few other things we need. And Tony and I have worked out that if we both take a small wage cut, we'll soon have one of the most up-to-date repair facilities around here.' Kevin fell silent for a moment. 'You hear an engine running?'

Martin sniffed. 'I can smell one.'

They looked back up the lane.

'It's Don's garage.' Martin charged up to the door. 'It's locked.'

Kevin picked up a brick that had fallen from one of the back walls. Martin took it and brought it down hard on the lock. Kevin lifted the door and they reeled back coughing. Kevin peered into the fume-filled garage. He made out a figure slumped in the front seat of the car, took a deep breath and dived in to turn off the engine. Martin was behind him and together they managed to drag Don into the lane. Miraculously he was still breathing. They laid him on his side and slumped on the ground with their backs to the wall, gulping in great lungfuls of fresh air.

'Good job we came along when we did,' Kevin said, when he could speak.

'I only hope Don thanks us when he's regained consciousness,' Martin commented, watching him retch.

'Martin, we've been waiting for you to come home,' Gail said, when Martin walked into the house.

Martin had meant to tell Gail and the children about Don, but when he saw their smiling faces and the special meal Gail had laid on he decided that the news about Don's attempted suicide could wait.

'Do you know who this is?' Gail asked him.

Martin looked at the blond stranger sitting at his table. 'Your brother.' He offered Steve his hand. 'I'm pleased to meet you.'

'Steve thinks we should all go on holiday to Canada. He said we can all stay in his house. What do you think?' Gail demanded eagerly.

Martin saw that Gail, Nicky, Sarah and David were all waiting for his verdict. He thought of Ivy and the problems she had caused them, Don's attempted suicide and the trip they would soon have to make to the hospital. 'I think a family holiday in Canada is exactly what we need, and a brilliant idea. How soon can we go, Steve?'

Curly straightened the vase of flowers he'd set in the centre of the dining table and checked the casserole he'd put into the oven. When he was certain that he couldn't make anything more perfect than it already was, he went into the kitchen, took the wine he'd bought out of the fridge and opened it. He was returning the bottle to the fridge to keep cool when the front door opened. He rushed into the hall.

'Hello, love.' He tried to kiss Raquel but she avoided him, dropped her suitcase and walked into the living room.

'The meal's all ready for you.'

'So I see.' She sat in one of the armchairs and looked up at him.

'Take your coat off. I'll pour us a glass of wine while you tell me about your week. Then I'll take your case upstairs.

You can unpack while I serve the meal, and then we'll sit down and enjoy it together. Afterwards we can—'

'I'm not stopping, Curly,' she broke in abruptly.

'You have to go back to the course?' His face fell.

If hadn't been for the assertiveness training that Raquel had undergone as part of her course, she might have taken the easy option and fallen in with the plans he'd made for them. She looked Curly in the eye. 'I applied for a job with an international firm last week. I heard this morning that I've got it.'

'That's great news, love.' He tried to look enthusiastic.

'It's a wonderful job and good money. I told them I'll take it. It's something I've been working towards my whole life, Curly.'

'I won't stand in your way. I want to support you however I can.'

'The job's not round here.'

He shrugged. 'The good thing about being a super-market manager is that I can get a job anywhere. There are supermarkets in every town in Britain.'

'It isn't in Britain. It's in Kuala Lumpur. And I'm going there alone.'

Silence reigned in the room, and for the first time since she had married Curly, Raquel didn't feel suffocated in his company.

'Alone . . .'

'I only came back to tell you the news. I need to go

upstairs and pack the rest of my things.' She looked at her watch. 'I've ordered a taxi to pick me up and take me to the station. It will be here any minute now.'

'But we haven't been married a year,' Curly remonstrated. 'I had plans for our anniversary—'

'It's not your fault, Curly, it's mine,' she interrupted, not wanting to sit through a detailed explanation of what she was missing by walking out on him. 'I shouldn't have married you. You can divorce me on any grounds you like.'

Ten minutes later a car horn sounded outside, and Raquel left the house.

'Isn't Mam looking well, Ken?' Deirdre prompted him when she walked into Ken's house with Blanche Hunt. 'You'd never think she'd been ill.'

Ken kissed his ex-mother-in-law's cheek. 'No, you wouldn't. You look very good, Blanche,' he complimented her. 'And the weather couldn't be better, considering it's November. This is going to be a proud day for all of us.'

'I told Deirdre this isn't the way I expected to see my only granddaughter married,' Blanche complained. 'In a register office, wearing a dress that cost fourteen pounds in a charity shop.'

'It was what Tracy wanted,' Ken explained. 'I offered to buy her a more expensive dress but she insisted she wanted that one.'

Blanche glowered. 'I suppose it's something that you two are both going to the wedding after the upset of the last year.'

'It was more than an upset, Blanche.' Ken couldn't believe that Blanche had dismissed Deirdre's tragedy as an 'upset'.

'Do you know the first thing about this Robert Preston Tracy's marrying? Because if you do, no one's thought to tell me anything about him,' Blanche grumbled.

'I told you, Mam, he's a carpet-fitter.' Deirdre glanced at herself in Ken's mirror and straightened her hat.

'Don't you know anything else about him?' Blanche demanded imperiously.

'Tracy loves him,' Ken suggested.

'And after everything she's done, you think she's capable of choosing a husband for herself and settling down?' she enquired sceptically.

'We'd better make a move.' Ken opened his front door. 'If we don't, we'll be late and we don't want to hold up the proceedings.' He caught Deirdre's eye. She flashed him a look of gratitude – and something else, or had he imagined it? He suddenly realised that they could still communicate without words. Perhaps there was something left between them after all.

Although Deirdre had insisted that she never wanted to see Tracy again, he had managed to talk her into attending the wedding where Tracy had failed so he must still have some influence over her. He opened the front passenger door for Deirdre but Blanche sat in the seat before he could stop her.

'I'm sick whenever I sit in the back,' she informed him tartly, when he tried to protest.

He squeezed Deirdre's hand sympathetically as he helped her into the back of his car. When she responded with a smile he wondered what the future might bring. Maybe – just maybe – Tracy's wedding would prove a new beginning, not only for her and Robert but also for him and Deirdre.

Two months after he had placed K-bec's sportswear manufacturing order with Mike Baldwin's Underworld, Steve Reid was back in Mike's office. He opened his brief-case and pulled out the full range of clothes K-bec had licensed Mike to produce.

'I didn't realise you'd come back. Here for a holiday with Gail and Martin?' Mike enquired. 'They told me they had a fantastic time in Canada – so fantastic that Nicky decided to stay out there to continue his education. Studying sport, or so Martin said.'

'I'm not here on holiday, Mike.' Steve ignored the pleasantries. 'K-bec sent me. Tell me, where have you seen these lines before?'

Mike fingered the shirts, shorts and sweaters. 'They look like K-bec's range.'

'They look like them,' Steve said shortly, 'only these are rip-offs bought at markets around here. K-bec believe they came out of the back door of your factory. And until an investigation proves otherwise your contract with K-bec is cancelled.'

'You can't prove anything!' Mike shouted.

'I can have a damned good try. And just in case you think you can clean up here and destroy any evidence you have lying around, I've already informed the police about this.' Steve took the shorts and T shirt Mike was holding and tossed them back into his briefcase.

Sally Webster, Mike's factory manager, walked into the office after Steve had left. 'I warned you it would only be a matter of time before K-bec found out you were selling their designs to market traders. What do you want me to do?'

'Stop listening at my office door,' Mike snapped, recalling Steve's warning about the police. If they had the factory under surveillance they'd certainly pick up on any unusual activity.

'Shouldn't I warn the girls?'

'That's the last thing you should do. Say one word, one single word, one whisper to any of the girls, and you'll be out on your ear.' Mike left his chair and picked up his jacket. 'I'm taking an early lunch.'

'You always want more, don't you, Mike?' Alma railed, after he had told her about Steve's visit. 'It's not enough for you to make a decent profit – you always have to go that extra illegal mile. Didn't you think an international firm like K-bec would notice a few market traders in the Midlands, selling cut-price copies of their goods?'

'They're not copies!' Mike exclaimed. 'The goods I sold to the traders were indistinguishable from what went out through the front door. And I don't need you to go on at me as well.'

'You never face the truth, Mike, that's your problem.'

Mike had gone to Alma hoping for sympathy. They had been married a year and although he sensed that she wasn't entirely happy, he had always been able to rely on her to support him – until now. Disappointed, he walked out to his car. He was convinced that the police were watching his every move and decided to go back to the factory. His office was quiet – or it would be if he shut the door and locked out Sally Webster.

He needed time to think and plan his next move. The warehouse was stacked high with K-bec merchandise, ten times more than he had been contracted to manufacture. And, although the business with the traders had been strictly cash, no questions asked, there were all the receipts and invoices from his fabric suppliers, of which they would hold copies. And the wages records of the hours the girls had put in and been paid for, which had been sent on to Inland Revenue.

He slipped his key into the ignition. He needed to do

some serious thinking and get his story straight. The sooner the better. There was no saying when the police might call. For all he knew they might already have enough evidence to pounce on him.

'You girls celebrating?' Don Brennan asked Sally Webster, who was buying a round of drinks at the bar of the Rovers.

'One of the girls' birthdays,' she explained.

'You don't look as though you're happy about it,' he slurred.

'Just tired. We've been working flat out on a big order.' She handed Jack the money for the drinks and wished Don would leave her alone. Her conversation with Mike was preying on her mind. It was all very well for the girls to be celebrating, but she had overheard Steve Reid cancel the K-bec contract and she knew they could all be out of a job soon.

'It's not right.' Don staggered as he banged his fist on the bar. 'You girls work like hell and Mike Baldwin pockets the profit.'

'You turned communist now the Russians have turned capitalist, Don?' Jack Duckworth laughed.

'It's not right,' Don repeated drunkenly. 'Baldwin messing with people's lives. Hiring and firing them like that.' He clicked his fingers in the air. 'Swindling people out of their hard-earned money. It's not right.'

Sally ferried the drinks she'd bought to the girls.

'Course it's not right, Don,' Jack crooned. 'Now, why don't you go home and sleep it off?'

Don struggled to focus on Jack, finished his drink and left the pub.

'Well done, love,' Vera said to Jack. 'Now you've got rid of Don you can take out the glasses and wash them.'

'That's Betty's job.'

'She's collecting the girls' glasses. You know what their conversation is like when they've had a few. I thought I'd spare your blushes.'

Don stood in the street, breathing in deeply in the hope that his head would stop spinning. He walked down to the other end of Coronation Street, leant against the door of the shuttered mini-market and looked across at Mike's factory. Then he fumbled in his pocket for his lighter, crossed the road, walked past the Kabin and up to the factory gate.

He tried to climb it three times before he succeeded. The waste-bins were ranged in front of the factory door. He opened one. It was filled with paper and scraps of material. Slowly, deliberately, he removed a piece of paper and wrapped it round a pile of scrap cloth. He lit it, pushed it through the factory's letter-box, then went back to the bin, made another paper and cloth sausage and lit that one too.

He didn't stop making fireballs until he saw flames licking up inside the windows of the factory.

'I hope you're insured for this place.' The police constable stood alongside Mike as he stared at the ashes of what had been his factory

'I am. I just hope they pay out.' If the insurance company ever heard of the conversation he'd had with Steve Reid, Mike doubted he'd collect a penny. The fire was too convenient, given what he'd had to hide. 'Have you any idea what caused it?'

'The firemen haven't said anything to us, except that it began by the door. You going to start up again?'

'It's too soon for me to make any plans, Constable. I'll have to talk to my insurance company first.'

'Mr Baldwin.' A man in a suit walked through the cordon towards him. 'Do you know if anyone bears a grudge against you?'

'I'm a businessman, Officer. I take it that you are an officer?' Mike asked.

The man pulled a warrant card from his pocket and showed it to Mike. 'Detective Sergeant Smith.'

'As I was saying, Detective Sergeant Smith, I'm a businessman and businessmen have enemies. Why do you ask?'

'A call came into the station last night, just before the fire was reported. The caller said he'd seen you setting fire to your factory and you'd boasted that you were about to do it for the insurance money.'

'That's ridiculous!' Mike protested.

'Just as a routine check, where were you yesterday evening around ten o'clock?'

'Out with my wife. We had dinner with friends and we were with them from eight until about one o'clock in the morning. Then my wife and I drove home.'

'Would you mind if we checked that, Mr Baldwin?'

'Be my guest.' Mike took a notebook from his pocket and scribbled down the name and address of his friends. He tore out the page and handed it to the officer, who was clearly impressed.

'Someone was seen acting suspiciously around here about ten o'clock. You've no idea who it might have been?'

Mike shook his head.

'If you had set fire to the factory, you would hardly have telephoned us to report it before the fire brigade arrived.'

'I like to think I'm cleverer than that,' Mike said dryly. 'If you should hear anything . . .'

'We'll keep in touch, Mr Baldwin. Good morning.'

'I didn't know where else to come,' Trisha Armstrong said to Vera Duckworth, as she stood embarrassed and heavily pregnant in the bar of the Rovers. 'I tried writing to Terry at the address he gave me, but if he got my letter, he never replied.'

'Surprise, surprise,' Jack muttered.

'Never mind him, love.' Vera consoled her. 'Sit down, and I'll make you a nice cup of tea.'

'The baby's due in eight weeks. And it is Terry's.'

'I don't doubt it.' Jack Duckworth recalled warning Terry off Tricia. He reflected that he should have known that his caution would be enough for Terry to head straight for her.

'No one wants to employ me when I'm this far gone, I can't afford to pay the rent on the flat and it's not just the baby. I've got Jamie, and his teachers keep on at me about how badly behaved he is at school.'

'You did the right thing in coming here, love. You and Jamie can stay here until the baby's born,' Vera assured her.

'We'll take care of you.' Despite his earlier assertion that she was a troublesome tart, with an even more troublesome lad, Jack felt sorry for the girl, or any girl for that matter who was taken in by his son.

'When you've finished your tea, Trisha, I'll go back to your flat with you and help you pack your things. Then we'll pick Jamie up from school and get you settled in here. It'll be nice to have a young lad around the place again. And a baby's arrival to look forward to.' Vera's eyes misted over as she thought of Tommy.

★

'Same again, please, Betty.' Mike set his whisky glass on the bar.

'Mike bloody Baldwin, drowning his sorrows!' Don Brennan mocked him from the corner of the bar where he had been drinking all afternoon.

'Hello, Don.' Mike softened his voice in the hope of appeasing Don, who was obviously and aggressively drunk.

'Not quite the entrepreneur now, are you, Mike?' Don lurched towards him. 'Aw, did his factory burn down?'

'We don't want any trouble, Don,' Jack warned him.

'I'm talking to my friend Mike here.' Don leant towards Mike and Mike moved back before he could touch him. 'His factory burnt down,' he informed Jack solemnly, as if it was the latest news.

'Did you burn it down, Don?' Mike asked conversationally.

'What if I did?' Don questioned belligerently. 'You can't prove a thing one way or the other.'

'The police know it's arson, but they also know that I didn't do it. The insurance company paid out in full this afternoon, and it's all thanks to you, Don. You've done me a bigger favour than you can ever know.' Mike smiled. All the evidence that K-bec would have used against him had gone up in smoke.

Infuriated, Don swept his arm across the counter and sent all the glasses flying. 'I'll get you, Mike Baldwin,' he threatened. 'If it takes my last breath, I'll get you, and then you'll be sorry.'

Chapter Fifty-Three

Alma Baldwin was the first customer of the day in Gail's café the following morning.

Gail waved to her from behind the counter as she walked in. 'Hi, Alma. Would you like coffee or tea?'

'Neither,' Alma replied brusquely. 'Mike told me that your brother cancelled K-bec's orders with his Underworld Company before the factory burnt down.'

'Steve doesn't own K-bec, he just works for them,' Gail explained.

'Well, I thought I'd let you know that I've sold the flat upstairs and this café to Roy Cropper for fifty thousand pounds. I hope you get on well with him, but then again he did say he might want to run the place himself.' Alma walked out, knowing that Gail was staring at her back.

'Just like a bent penny – you can't stop turning up, can you?' Jack Duckworth greeted his son sourly when Terry walked into the Rovers in the second week in

March. 'There's a girl upstairs who's just had your baby.'

'Sure it's mine?'

'Your mother says there's no doubt about it from the dates, or the way you were carrying on with her the last time you were here.'

'Then I'm a father again.' Terry grinned.

'As you haven't asked, I'll tell you. It's boy called Brad. And this girl hasn't any family that you can sell him to.'

'Mine's a pint.'

'Not until you've gone upstairs and seen the girl and the baby,' Jack said firmly.

Wary of annoying his parents the minute he walked through the door in case they kicked him out, Terry went into the private quarters and ran up the stairs. Vera was on the landing, closing one of the bedroom doors behind her.

'Hello, Mam.' He stooped to kiss her.

'Tricia wrote to you about the baby. When she didn't get a reply, we wondered if you'd moved and hadn't got the letter.'

'I came to see them,' he said, trying to recall what his father had told him. 'It's a boy and she's called him Brad.'

Vera smiled, hoping that Terry had come back to take care of his family. She opened the door and said, 'Tricia, look who's here.'

Tricia turned around in her chair. 'Terry!' She jumped to her feet and ran across the room to hug him.

'Let's have a look at him, then.' Terry frowned. The girl looked familiar and he didn't doubt that, as his father had said, he'd slept with her. But he had no memory of doing so.

Still smiling, Vera closed the door on them and returned downstairs. 'I think our Terry's turning over a new leaf,' she told Jack when she joined him behind the bar.

'And I just saw a purple flying pig dive-bomb the street,' Jack said sourly.

Don had spent every evening for the past week driving his taxi. Wary of his drink-driving ban, he carefully avoided police cars while cruising the area around Mike Baldwin's house with his for-hire sign switched off. He had been living on a knife-edge of uncertainty ever since he had got drunk in the Rovers and confessed that he'd set fire to the factory. Baldwin might have laughed at him and insisted that the destruction of the factory had been to his advantage, but he knew sooner or later Mike would tell the police about what he'd done. And before the law caught up with him, he wanted to hurt him in a way he couldn't laugh off.

Suddenly, he saw the chance he'd been waiting for. Alma Baldwin was walking down the drive of their house with a bundle of letters in her hand. He turned his taxi round and drove slowly behind her, then accelerated past. He slammed on the brakes and stopped ahead of her, dived out of the driver's seat, ran to her and clamped his hand over her mouth. He dragged her into the back of his cab, shut the door and pushed down the childproof locks before he returned to the driver's seat.

'I told your husband I'd get my own back on him, and I will,' he threatened Alma.

Alma banged on the window and screamed for help, but the streets were deserted. The cars travelling in the opposite direction were driving too fast for her to attract their occupants' attention.

Don put his foot down and charged ahead, joining a stream of traffic on a main thoroughfare. Terrified that he was going to rape her – or worse – Alma crouched on the back seat and gripped the door-handle so tightly that the plastic bit into the palm of her hand. 'Don, please, why you are you doing this to me? I've never hurt you.'

'Your husband has. I warned him I'd get him and he laughed at me. Well, let's see if he's still laughing after I've finished with you.'

'Whatever Mike's done to you, wouldn't it be more sensible to sit down and talk about it?' she pleaded, desperately trying to keep a grip on her emotions.

'The time for talking has long gone,' he growled.

'Please, Don—'

He drove even faster, staring intently at the road ahead, although from the number of cars that had to swerve, the flashing lights and blaring horns, Alma doubted that he was concentrating. She gritted her teeth and tried to remember everything she had heard about being kidnapped. She recalled a television programme and a police adviser saying, 'Talk to the kidnapper. Try to establish a relationship with him or her . . .'

She took a deep breath. 'Don, please, tell me what Mike has done to you. Perhaps I can help . . .'

'Shut up!' Don shouted hysterically. Alma had been talking non-stop for what seemed like days, although the clock told him they'd only been driving around for two hours.

'Don, you do realise that I'm not here with you of my own free will,' Alma persisted. 'You can't just pick people up off the streets and imprison them in your car. That's kidnapping. It's a crime. Look, I don't want to be here and I don't think you want me to be here, not any more. So why not be sensible? Take me home. You can drop me off outside my house and I promise I'll never tell a soul about this. Especially Mike . . .'

Kidnapping – crime – kidnapping – crime. The words whirled around in Don's mind and all he could think of was the police closing in. *Arson – drink-driving – kidnapping—*

'The police don't have to be involved,' Alma asserted,

as if she could read his thoughts. 'They will never hear about this, not from me, I swear it.'

Kidnapping – crime – kidnapping – arson – drink-driving – kidnapping. Don had a sudden very real image of the police closing in on him. He looked through the windscreen. The river Irwell was on their left. He pressed his right foot to the floor, turned the wheel sharply and hurtled his taxi down the bank at full speed.

Don slumped, sobbing, over the steering-wheel as water poured into the cab. Alma fought a tide of panic that had risen as rapidly as the water level inside the taxi. She had to think, coolly, coherently. The water covered her ankles and seconds later she could feel it, cold, clammy, swirling around her knees. She leant forward and opened the glass panel that separated her from Don. She sprang the childproof locks, then struggled with the back door until she had opened it.

She kicked off her shoes, closed her mind to the freezing temperature of the river and trod water. She glanced back at Don, still slumped sobbing in the driver's seat as water rose steadily on the inside of the windows. Unable to leave him to drown, she turned back, reached out to the driver's door and fought to open it. As soon as she succeeded, she dragged Don out, hooked her elbow beneath his chin and swam to the bank.

★

Alma closed her hands around the glass of whisky and ginger ale Mike had poured for her, snuggled under a blanket and leant towards the fire.

'We've charged Mr Brennan with arson and attempted murder, Mr Baldwin,' the constable advised Mike.

'Is he in jail?' Mike asked coldly. Two hours earlier the police had called to tell him that Alma was in hospital but that she'd been discharged. When he'd rushed round to pick her up, he'd been appalled to hear of her ordeal and, anxious to blame anyone for Don's behaviour except himself, he'd taken out his anger on the police, berating them for allowing a dangerous lunatic to roam the streets.

'Mr Brennan's in hospital at the moment, sir, but I think I can assure you that once he is tried he will be put away for quite a long time.'

'If they gave him life, it would be too short for what he's done,' Mike snapped.

'I will keep you and Mrs Baldwin informed of further developments, sir.' The officer nodded to Alma. 'Goodnight, Mrs Baldwin.'

'Goodnight, Constable. I'll show you out.' Still seething, Mike escorted the man to the door.

'Why don't you let me take some of the load around here?' Terry Duckworth asked Jack, as he watched his father total the account books.

'Like, for instance?'

'That cash. I could take it to the bank for you – save you a trip.'

Jack watched Terry eye the pile of banknotes. They'd had an unusually busy couple of days in the Rovers and there was over six hundred pounds waiting to be banked.

'All right,' Jack agreed. 'Just give me a couple of minutes to fill in the deposit form and you can go. Why don't you nip up and see Brad and Tricia while I get it ready?'

'I'll do that.'

While Terry climbed the stairs, Jack went into the living room. He set the pub takings down next to a cloth cash bag and picked up yesterday's newspaper.

Vera was closing the pub after the lunchtime trade when Terry came storming into the bar.

'Where's Dad?' he demanded angrily.

'You want me?' Jack emerged from the cellar.

'There weren't any notes in that bag, only a few coins and piles of cut newspaper,' Terry shouted.

'Then I expect you looked a proper fool when the cashier opened the bag.'

Terry bit his lips and looked away. He had been nowhere near a bank since he'd left the Rovers. And he'd been about to board a train when he had discovered what his father had done.

'I suggest you pack your bags and go wherever it is you live now,' Jack advised. 'You're not much use to Tricia and Brad or Tommy. And you're certainly no damned use to your mother and me.'

'So.' Natalie Horrocks sat on the edge of the desk in the garage and hitched up her skirt. She looked sideways at Kevin. 'I'm your business partner now that Tony's decided to move away.'

Kevin stared at the expanse of leg Natalie had uncovered and his heart beat faster. Sally had been in Scarborough for over a month nursing her mother and she had taken the girls with her. He missed them but, looking at Natalie, he realised there could be advantages to having an absent wife. 'It will be nice to have someone to talk to about the business.' His voice was suddenly hoarse.

'Perhaps we could start talking about it tonight?' Natalie suggested. She lifted her eyebrows. 'Over a bottle of wine?'

'My telephone number is down as an emergency number for the garage.'

'No problem. I'll bring the wine over to your house. What kind of take-away do you like? Chinese or Indian?'

'Indian.' Kevin's throat constricted even more.

'Eight o'clock suit you? That will give you time to clean up.' She fingered the sleeve of his oil-stained overalls.

'Fine,' he croaked, his voice reduced to a whisper.

'I am afraid there's no doubt about it,' the doctor told Gail and Alma, as they sat in the waiting area of the ward Don had been taken to. 'Mr Brennan has cancer. He has been asking to see both of you, but I urge you to be careful. Any upset could worsen his condition.'

'We'll be careful,' Gail assured him. 'Can we see him now?'

'I'll take you to him.'

Gail and Alma followed the doctor down the ward. Don was in a cubicle at the end. Lying flat on his back in bed, he looked pale and sickly.

'Thank you for coming,' he murmured. 'I need to say sorry to both of you. I've done such terrible things . . .'

'You don't have to say any more to me.' Alma pulled a chair up to his bed. 'I survived.'

'But I need you to say it, Alma,' Don begged. 'Please, forgive me.'

Alma glanced up at Gail, who was brushing a tear from her eye. 'I forgive you, Don. Now, let's just forget it, shall we, seeing as no harm was done?'

'And you?' Don clasped Gail's hand.

'I've nothing to forgive you for,' Gail said.

'Thank you, both of you,' Don said. 'For giving me peace.'

★

A week after Rita Sullivan had heard that Natalie Horrocks had taken over Tony's partnership in the garage, she saw Natalie leaving Kevin's house in the middle of the afternoon. She crossed the road and ran up to her.

'Natalie . . .'

'Haven't seen you for ages, Rita, but then I've been busy.'

'Ruining your business partner's personal life,' Rita accused her.

'I don't know what you mean.'

'Oh, yes, you do. Kevin has a good wife in Sally and two adorable daughters who need their father. It's not just his life you're trying to ruin, Natalie, it's theirs too.'

'I'm not ruining anyone's life.'

'Just having a bit of fun?' Rita asked ironically. 'I intend to have a word with Kevin about your "fun", and if that doesn't bring him to his senses, I'll write to Sally. She's too good a friend for me to stand back and watch her made a fool of by the likes of you – and Kevin, who should know better.'

Mike Baldwin wondered if his life would ever get back to what passed as normal when he opened his door to see a policeman – again. 'Can I help you?' he asked wearily.

'Can I come in, Mr Baldwin?'

'It's not convenient.' Mike's tone was polite but icy. 'We have invited friends over for dinner.'

'I'm hear to warn you and your wife that we were transferring Mr Brennan from the hospital to prison when he absconded.'

'That lunatic has escaped!'

'We know from what your wife and Mrs Platt told us that he made his peace with them, but from what the nurses say he still seems to bear a grudge against you. I take it you haven't seen him around here?'

'No, and if he does show up, I'll kill him after what he did to my wife.'

'We can't condone the general public taking the law into their own hands, Mr Baldwin.'

'You'd rather set lunatics free to kill *us*?' Mike enquired sarcastically.

'We'll ask the local patrols to keep an eye open. I know you're rebuilding your factory. Is it open yet?'

'Monday.' Mike had just signed a partnership with Angie Freeman to produce a range of lingerie and he remembered her saying that she intended to drop off some patterns at the factory. 'One of my business partners has gone to the factory tonight. She borrowed my wife's car.'

'Alone?'

Mike nodded. 'I'll make my excuses to my guests and I'll be with you.'

Mike and the officer saw the fire from Coronation Street. The constable hit his siren and switched on the flashing blue light as he drove towards it. A crowd had gathered alongside the viaduct, all of them staring at a ball of flames in front of the towering walls. When Mike left the car, he could make out the outline of a car in the flames. Firemen were training a hose on the blaze but, given its ferocity, it was little more than a token gesture.

'I'm sorry, Mike, Don took Alma's car.' Angie Freeman moved close to Mike. 'I saw him break into it through the window but by the time I got to the car park, he'd driven off. I phoned the police but he didn't get far.' She looked to the car.

'Don was in that?'

'People here said he drove head on into the viaduct. The car burst into flames at the moment of impact. There was nothing anyone could do.'

One of the firemen joined them. 'The flames were too intense to attempt a rescue, sir, and frankly there was no point in us even trying. If the driver wasn't killed in that crash, he would have been dead seconds later.'

'I've heard about your trouble with the taxman, Jack. Word is, you owe him seventeen thousand pounds and you can't pay.' Alec Gilroy shook his head as he stood at the bar of the Rovers with the Duckworths. 'The taxman is one person you don't want to annoy. He can do too many annoying things back.'

'I told you not to go blabbing our business to

everyone.' Vera flashed Jack an angry look to remind him that she blamed him for the mess they were in because he was in charge of the accounts.

'I might be able to help you,' Alec said.

'How?' Jack asked eagerly, hoping Alec that would offer to lend them the money they needed.

'I've been made redundant by Sunliners. They're cutting back on middle management and asked Deirdre to run the office. But sound economic sense for them leaves me at a loose end with some redundancy money. So, supposing I pay your tax bill . . .'

'And we can pay you back so much a week?' Vera suggested hopefully.

'No,' Alec said sharply. 'I'll pay your bill and give you a little extra in return for a fifty per cent share of the Rovers. What do you say, Jack? Shall we become partners?'

'This pub is all I've ever dreamed of,' Vera said mournfully. 'The last thing I want to do is sell half of it to anyone.'

'We don't have any choice, love.' Jack tried to put his arm round her but she shrugged it off.

'You can go to the bank and ask them to loan us the money we need,' she snapped.

'I tried, but they turned me down.'

'When?' she demanded suspiciously.

'This morning.'

'I won't be an interfering partner, Vera,' Alec promised.

'You and Jack can continue to run the Rovers exactly the way you have been doing.'

'You'll interfere with our profits,' Vera snapped, 'because you'll be making off with half of them.'

'But on the other hand you won't have any debts,' Alec said evenly. He offered Jack his hand.

Kevin walked into his house, saw the suitcases in the hall and shouted, 'Rosie! Sophie!' The girls came rushing to meet him, locking their arms around his neck. He swung them both off their feet while Sally hung back in the doorway.

'No kiss from my wife?' Kevin smiled.

'You have five minutes to pack before I throw you out.'

'Sally,' he said, 'don't tell me you've been listening to gossip.'

'Girls, into the living room and close the door behind you.'

Sally so seldom spoke sharply to them that the children did as she asked. She waited until they'd closed the door before confronting Kevin with her evidence.

'I went round to Natalie's house when I arrived. I saw you standing in front of her bedroom window – naked.'

'Sally, please . . .'

'Five minutes,' she repeated.

*

Ken Barlow faced Sue Jeffers across the table she'd set up in the staffroom at his school.

'This is a particularly tough time for me,' he explained. 'I've just been forced to agree to let my son Daniel live in Scotland with his mother, which means I'll hardly ever see him. And now you tell me that the school governors want to make me redundant.'

'It's nothing personal, Ken, just policy. Long-serving teachers get paid twice as much as new graduates so it makes sense for schools to make their older staff redundant and get two younger ones for the same cost.'

'I'm aware of the economics,' he informed her. He sat back and gazed over her head out of the window. 'It's strange. All my life I've been saying I'll do more of this or that when I retire. Now that I'm facing it, I haven't a clue what to do with myself.' He started as he felt Sue's stockinged foot slip up his trouser leg.

'Maybe, just maybe, we could stave off your retirement for a while. Tell me, Ken, what are you doing this evening?' she asked.

'I'm very glad you came into Sunliners looking for a cruise,' Deirdre said to her new boyfriend. She couldn't believe her luck: tall, dark, handsome and so caring, Jon Lindsay was an airline pilot who flew out of Manchester airport. Better still, he had his own detached house in a salubrious area. And he was an excellent cook. He had just made them a superb dinner of smoked salmon pâté, steak *au poivre* and Normandy pear flan.

Jon finished clearing the table, wiped his hands on a tea-towel and pulled Deirdre on to the sofa beside him. 'I have something to tell you and you're not going to like it.'

'What?' she asked apprehensively.

'I'm going to have to move out of this house this week.'

'I don't understand – you said it was yours.' Deirdre sat up and looked at him.

'It is, but my ex-wife and children are taking possession of it. Part of the divorce settlement. However, what do you say to us moving in together?'

'I'd say I like the idea,' she murmured, as he unbuttoned her blouse.

'I've seen a four-bedroom house in Didsbury I like. It's going cheap because the owners are emigrating and want a quick sale. The bank needs ten thousand pounds deposit. I have five but I can't come up with more immediately because I've been left a bit short after paying for the divorce.'

Deirdre thought of the money she'd banked when she'd sold number one Coronation Street to Mike. Money she and Samir would have used to buy a house in Morocco – if they'd had the chance . . . 'I can come up with the other five. I can give you a cheque now if you like.'

'Good, because if you do we can move in this weekend.' Jon filled both their wine glasses. 'Let's toast our future – together.'

Chapter Fifty-Four

'It's good of you to help me to move in, Ken,' Deirdre said, as he carried her suitcases into the house Jon had bought for them in Didsbury. It was the first time she'd seen it. Jon had dropped the address and keys off at her flat the evening before when he'd barely had time to kiss her before he left for work.

'I haven't anything better to do,' Ken said. Sue Jeffers had been forced to resign by the school governors when they discovered that she had blocked their move to make him redundant. So both of them had been thrown out of a job, and as a result their 'relationship' had never progressed beyond a one-night stand.

'This is nice, isn't it?' Deirdre looked around the hall and up the stairs, then opened the doors that led into the living and dining rooms.

'It is.' Ken straightened his back. 'Deirdre, you do know that Jon Lindsay isn't an airline pilot?' he said gently. When Deirdre had told him she had given Jon a cheque for five thousand pounds for a deposit on a house, he'd been worried that she'd fallen prey to a con-man. No one around Weatherfield had heard of a Jon Lindsay and, concerned for her, he'd driven out to the airport and made a few enquiries. There, he'd discovered that Jon Lindsay managed one of the airport shops.

'He told me he'd been grounded,' Deirdre answered evasively. When she'd booked a flight for a client shortly after meeting Jon, she'd mentioned his name to the girl on the airline desk and she'd told her that Jon wasn't a pilot.

When she'd confronted him with his lie, he'd told her that he'd only said he was a pilot because he was afraid of losing her. After he'd kissed her and begged forgiveness, she'd agreed she'd forget it – if he promised never to lie to her again. And he had, so convincingly that she was sure that from that moment on, there would be absolute trust between them.

Ken didn't push the point. 'I hope you'll be happy here, Deirdre. It's a fine place.' He meant it. The house was large and more comfortable than number one Coronation Street – the entire area was upmarket. He only wished he was the one moving in with her, but they seemed destined to miss every chance they'd ever been given to get back together.

'Thank you, Ken.'

'I'll push off.'

'It might be as well. Jon will be home soon.'

'He must be glad you came along when you did. It

would have been a pity to miss this place.' He stepped out into the well-laid-out front garden.

'What do you mean, miss it?'

'He must have been about ready to exchange contracts when he met you.'

'The people selling it wanted a quick deal. Jon finalised everything in three days.'

Ken looked quizzically at her, but wary of meeting Jon – and knowing he wouldn't like him on principle because he had Deirdre – he waved to her and walked out through the gate.

Deirdre turned and looked up at the house. Ken was right: it was a fine place and much better than any house she had lived in before. She went inside and walked around the rooms. Jon had told her that he'd bought some furniture from the people who were selling the house, a suite for the dining room, a three-piece suite for the living room, a bed for the master bedroom, which had fitted wardrobes. The kitchen was equipped with china and cutlery, but the patterns weren't to her taste.

She hugged herself in excitement at the thought of the shopping expeditions she and Jon would have. She contemplated the bedroom while she unpacked and hung away her clothes and imagined it in various colour schemes. She didn't like the heavy gold wallpaper on the walls: it reminded her of a club or a pub. Perhaps they should go for something floral. She recalled the décor in John's old house. He had told her his ex-wife had chosen it and she wondered what his taste was.

She went downstairs. She had shopped in the mini-market and bought chicken joints, vegetables and potatoes to make a casserole. She filled the sink with water and began to clean the potatoes.

When nine o'clock came and went and there was still no sign of Jon, she wondered if he had been delayed at his old house. Perhaps he had a lot of packing that she could help with. He'd warned her that she couldn't telephone because his ex-wife had arranged to have the number changed. She called a taxi, and gave the driver the address.

She had been right: Jon hadn't left his old house. But what she hadn't expected to see was him standing in the drive with his arm round his wife's waist, and his two children standing in front of him as they waved goodbye to an elderly couple who were driving away. While she continued to sit in the taxi and watch, he kissed his wife, then chased the children into the house.

She told the taxi-driver she had made a mistake and asked him to drive her back to the house. She switched off the oven, repacked her clothes and sat up for the rest of the night watching the telephone. It didn't ring. Jon might have bought this house for them, but when she had seen him he hadn't looked like a man about to leave his family.

When dawn broke, she opened her handbag and took out the banker's card Jon had given her for their joint account. She waited until seven o'clock, then rang for a taxi and asked the driver to take her to Sunliners. At eight she telephoned Mike Baldwin, who told her that as he hadn't let her flat yet, she was welcome to move back in.

As soon as the banks opened, she shut the shop and took the banker's card to withdraw her five thousand pounds from the joint account Jon had set up. She handed a withdrawal slip and the card to the girl at the till. The girl looked at it, passed it to a colleague and asked Deirdre to wait. A few minutes later a door opened at the end of the counter and the manager said,

'Mrs Rachid, could you come this way, please?'

She followed him into a small office.

'I'm afraid I'll have to ask you to stay here while I telephone the police.'

'I don't understand.'

'You have just used a banker's card belonging to a Captain Jenkins in a fraudulent attempt to withdraw five thousand pounds from his account. You have some explaining to do but, frankly, I'd prefer it if you do it to the police.'

'Ken, please.' Deirdre ran her fingers through her hair and bit her lips in an effort to keep hysteria at bay. 'I've just been sacked from Sunliners, the police have charged me with fraud and I wouldn't even have anywhere to live if Mike Baldwin hadn't given me the flat back. People cross the street if they see me walking towards them. Practically everyone seems to believe I'm guilty.'

'That's hardly surprising, Deirdre.' Ken paced to the window in her living room. 'I smelt a rat when you told me that Jon had bought the house in a couple of days. No one can buy a house that quickly.'

'You didn't say anything when you helped me move in.'

'I wasn't thinking straight.' Ken was angry with himself for being too full of self-pity over his redundancy to spare more than a passing thought for what Deirdre was getting herself into. 'Did you go to the solicitor's to sign any papers with Jon?'

'I told you, I just gave him the cheque and a couple of days later he gave me the address and the key and told me to move my things in.'

'And it didn't occur to you that the house belonged to Captain Jenkins and Jon just assumed his identity?'

'Of course not. I loved Jon, he loved me, I trusted him . . .' She fought back tears when she realised she'd spoken in the past tense.

'Jon told you he was a pilot and you'd found out he'd lied to you about that before I told you.'

'How do you know?'

'I can always tell when you're lying, Deirdre. And you were lying when you told me he'd been grounded, weren't you?'

She fought back tears as she nodded.

'You have to face it, Deirdre. Jon's a con man. A shop manager well placed to watch the real Captain Jenkins fly in and out of Manchester airport. And as the man was rarely home, all Jon had to do was break into his house, assume his identity and, bang, he got himself a double life. With you as his live-in lover. Are you sure you didn't know Jon was pretending to be this Captain Jenkins?' he pressed.

'I'm sure,' Deirdre said tearfully. 'Do you really think I'd go along with something like this—?'

The doorbell interrupted them. Ken went to answer it, leaving Deirdre to dry her tears. His lip curled disdain-fully when he saw Mike Baldwin.

'I've come to see Deirdre.'

'She's in the living room. I was on my way out.' Ken picked up his coat and left the flat.

Deirdre was standing at the window watching Ken walk to his car when Mike came in.

'Ken thinks I knew Jon was a con-man. I didn't!' she protested fiercely. *'I didn't!'*

Mike took her into his arms and stroked her hair. 'I believe you, Deirdre.'

946

'Do you? Really?' She looked up at him through her tears.

'Of course I believe you. Here.' He slipped his hand into the inside pocket of his jacket and handed her a passport and an airline ticket.

She opened the passport and found herself looking at a photograph of herself. A stranger's name and address was printed beneath it.

'I know a fellow who prints those things. I asked him to do it as a rush job. I found the photograph in a box of bits and pieces.'

'You keep mementoes of your past?' she whispered incredulously.

'Just as well in your case,' he said. 'The airline ticket is for a flight that leaves for Spain in four hours. I thought you'd want to get away until things cool down here.'

'You think they're going to send me to jail, don't you?'

'I don't think it, Deirdre, I know it. Fraud is a serious crime. Where's your suitcase?'

Ken was still sitting in his car outside Deirdre's flat when he saw Mike emerge carrying a suitcase. A few seconds later Deirdre followed. When she climbed into Mike's car, Ken started his engine and followed them to the airport. He watched Mike drop off Deirdre and drive away. He drove to the short-stay car park and found a bay.

Ken caught up with Deirdre at the check-in desk. He

tapped her shoulder as she was about to lift her suitcase on to the scales. 'Can we talk?'

'There's people waiting here,' a man behind Deirdre complained loudly.

'Please, take the lady's place. We won't be a moment.' Ken took the passport and ticket from the girl behind the desk, picked up Deirdre's suitcase and walked to the back of the queue.

'I . . .' Deirdre looked at him but couldn't say any more.

'Please, Deirdre,' he begged, 'don't do this. There's no point in running away. The police will hunt you down wherever you are. And things will be so much worse for you because you tried to run. Can't you see that?' He set down her case and opened her passport. 'Baldwin? I don't know why I'm asking. This is just the sort of stupid thing he would know how to do.'

'He said it would be best if I went away until things cooled down.'

'There's only one way to deal with this, Deirdre, and that's head on. If you don't stay and fight now, you'll spend the rest of your life looking over your shoulder.'

When a tear formed in the corner of her eye, Ken opened his arms and she ran to him. He held her close as she shuddered.

'You won't have to do this alone, Deirdre, I promise you. I'll be with you every single step of the way. I won't let you down.'

She pushed him away. He picked up her suitcase, wrapped his free arm round her shoulders and led her out to the car park.

Ken parked his car outside Deirdre's flat. 'I wish you'd move in with me, just until the worst is over.'

'I really am better off alone,' she said stubbornly.

'If you need me for anything at all . . .'

'I'll telephone.'

He felt in his pocket and produced the false passport and ticket Mike had given her.

'I'd rather you kept those,' she said.

'I'll destroy them,' he warned her.

'That's probably just as well.' She opened the car door. 'Do you mind if I don't ask you upstairs? I really would prefer to be alone.'

'OK.' But it wasn't OK. Ken was worried about her and afterwards, whenever he thought about it, allowing Deirdre to leave his car and walk up to her flat alone with her suitcase was one of the hardest things he'd had to do in his life.

Unused to being at home all day, Deirdre prowled restlessly around her flat unable to settle to anything. She almost jumped out of her skin when the doorbell rang at eleven o'clock. She walked down the stairs, slipped the chain on the door and opened it a crack. She stepped back in amazement when she saw Jon outside.

'Can I come in?' he asked, as if there was nothing wrong and they were still together.

She released the chain and opened the door.

'Thank you.' He walked up the stairs ahead of her. When he went into the living room, she picked up the telephone and dialled the number the police had given her.

'I've called the police and they're on their way,' she announced, when she entered her living room to find him sitting on her sofa, relaxed and unconcerned.

'Good. I was about to suggest you do just that.'

'You're a con-man. You took five thousand pounds of my money and told me you'd used it to put a deposit on a house for us. You gave me a banker's card belonging to another man. You stole his house, his identity, his bank account . . .'

'Deirdre,' he whispered her name softly in a voice she could imagine him using to his children, 'you are delusional.'

'I'm delusional!' she exclaimed. 'We'll see what the police say when they arrive.'

'We will, won't we? Would you mind passing me the newspaper so I can catch up on events while we wait?'

An interminable ten minutes later the doorbell rang. Deirdre ran downstairs and showed in two constables. When they walked into her living room, Jon rose to his feet and shook their hands.

'I am so glad you came, constables,' he said easily. 'Perhaps now we can finally clear up this misunderstanding.'

Jon did most of the talking. Deirdre tried to interrupt him, but the constables reminded her that she'd put her side of the story to them the day before when they'd been called to the bank. They both made copious notes when Jon told them how she had masterminded the whole plan. How she had visited him in the airport shop he managed, and watched the pilots come and go, and how she had suggested that it would be easy to impersonate one of them, and clean out their bank accounts and houses, because they were so seldom in the country for any length of time. When she continued to protest that Jon was lying, they downed their pencils.

'Mr Lindsay, Mrs Rachid, would you mind coming down to the station so we can get both your statements on record?'

Hoping that the truth would come out if they did, Deirdre fetched her coat.

Mike and Ken were waiting in the public area of the police station when Deirdre emerged from an interview room with the solicitor Mike had engaged for her. Ken was appalled by the change in her after just twenty-four hours. She looked pale and drawn, almost haggard, and her eyes were wild, like those of a cornered animal.

Mike looked expectantly at the solicitor, who said, 'The charges are obtaining money and property by deception. The case will come up in about six weeks to two months. And I warn you now, the legal costs will be high.'

Before Ken could open his mouth, Mike said, 'Send me the bill and don't spare any expense. Deirdre is innocent. All we have to do is prove it.'

Leanne Battersby leant on her elbow and looked down at Nicky Tilsley who was lying naked beside her in her narrow bed. Since they had started going out together they had taken to playing truant from college in the afternoons and spending their stolen time in her bedroom.

Nicky loved Leanne, but although he would never have admitted it, part of the attraction was her family. The Battersbys were the roughest people in the street and he knew that his mother and Martin would be horrified if they knew he was going out with her.

'You know that your mam and dad would never approve of me.' Leanne snuggled down and rested her head on his shoulder.

'Martin's not my dad,' Nicky corrected her.

'Your mam and Martin then.'

'He can't tell me what to do. No one can. I learnt to be independent when I spent last year in that Canadian school. I'm my own person. I love you and I want to marry you. No one, including my mam and Martin, is going to stop me.'

'You have to be eighteen to marry without their permission. You have another whole year to go and I've two. That's for ever,' she said dramatically.

'Maybe not. We could elope,' he suggested.

'Go to Gretna Green?' She smiled. 'If we did that it wouldn't only be your mam who would be furious.'

'If we were married, there would be nothing that my mam or anyone else could do about it.' Nicky picked up his watch from her bedside cabinet.

'What are you doing?'

'Checking to see if the banks are still open. They will be for another hour. I could go down and draw money out of my account. Then we'll go to the station. There's bound to be a train leaving for Scotland tonight. You game?'

'All I need is time to put my clothes on.'

'There's only one thing you can do,' Alec Gilroy told Jack and Vera Duckworth. 'I've checked the accounts and you're in so much debt that you'll have to sell your half of the Rovers. And since I own the other half, it makes more sense for me to buy it from you than for you to look for a stranger to sell it to.'

Vera sighed as she looked at Jack. They'd had several heart-to-hearts about the state of their finances, and Jack had already warned her that the only way they could clear their debts was to sell the pub.

'Can we still run the Rovers for you, Alec?' Vera asked.

'Of course. But, there'll be a bit to spare when I buy you out, so why don't you go on holiday? I know it's September but the weather's quite warm and Blackpool will be nice at this time of year.'

'I think we'll do just that,' Jack said. 'Alec, you're a real mate.'

Nicky and Leanne were returning from Gretna Green when they saw the Duckworths get on the train in Manchester. Nicky took care that the Duckworths didn't see them. He grabbed Leanne's hand, hitched his rucksack higher on his shoulders and pulled her towards the gate.

'Ready to face my mam and martin and your mam and dad?'

'Yes,' she answered defiantly.

They took the bus to Coronation Street and sat side by side smiling at each other the whole way. When they left the bus they went straight to number five.

Gail and Martin rushed to the door as soon as they heard Nicky's key in the lock.

'I know you phoned to tell us you were all right, but Martin and I have been worried sick . . .' Gail saw someone move behind Nicky and noticed Leanne for the first time.

'We're fine, Mam.' Nicky held up Leanne's left hand and pointed to her wedding ring. 'We're married.'

'You can't be. You're not old enough,' Martin told him.

'We went to Scotland and that's where we were married. And we're staying married.' Nicky stared at his mother and Martin, daring them to say otherwise.

'You married Leanne Battersby?' Gail gasped.

'I'm going to be a good wife to Nick, Mrs Platt,' Leanne promised 'You'll see, I'm going to be the best wife there has ever been.'

'You can't change the locks, Alec,' Betty Williams warned Alec, as he followed the locksmith from the front door of the Rovers Return to the cellar.

'I own the Rovers. I can do whatever I like with it, Betty.'

Betty nodded to Natalie, who had taken a barmaiding job in the Rovers after her brief marriage to Des Barnes had ended when he'd died of a heart attack. Natalie backed out through the door and ran to the public telephone outside the corner shop.

'You told Vera and Jack that they could continue to run the Rovers for you,' Betty reminded him, 'and now you're going back on your word.'

'I promised they could before I took a long, hard look at the accounts. Jack Duckworth could run Rothschild's

Bank into the ground, let alone the Rovers Return,' Alec told her. 'As long as those two remain in charge, the pub will never make any money. Now, if you'll excuse me, Betty, I need to make sure that every single lock in the place is changed.'

Deirdre's hands were shaking so much she had trouble holding her handbag as she walked into court with her solicitor, Mike and Ken.

'Don't worry, it's going to be all right,' Mike whispered in her ear.

Ken caught her hand and gave it a reassuring squeeze as her solicitor led her down to the dock.

Deirdre sat through what seemed to be a never-ending rigmarole. A jury was sworn in, the prosecuting counsel and her solicitor spoke for what seemed like days rather than hours. And as she looked at the people around her, the lawyers and the judge in their wigs and robes, the jury watching every move she made, the scene took on a surreal tinge.

Jon sat in the dock alongside her. He was barely three feet away and she couldn't even bring herself to look at him after the way he had tricked her.

At lunchtime someone brought her a sandwich that she couldn't eat. She wanted the trial to begin so Jon would be put into the witness box. She was convinced that once he was sworn in and his hand was on the Bible he would be forced to tell the truth, the whole truth and nothing but the truth.

But the prosecution's first witness was Ken Barlow.

Chapter Fifty-Five

Ken fought to keep his temper under control as he faced the prosecuting counsel. He was trying to explain why he couldn't answer his questions with a simple 'yes' or 'no', with the result that the counsel was repeating his question ad nauseam.

'Mr Barlow,' the prosecutor broke in brusquely, 'for the last time, did Deirdre Rachid tell you that Jon Lindsay was a pilot?'

'We had a conversation but—'

'Mr Barlow, did Deirdre Rachid or did she not tell you that Jon Lindsay was a pilot?'

'Yes, but—'

'Thank you, Mr Barlow.' The prosecutor turned to the jury to gauge their reaction to his triumph. 'And did you or did you not tell Mrs Rachid that Jon Lindsay was the manager of a shop at the airport?'

Ken felt as thought he was damning Deirdre but he couldn't lie when he was on oath. Not even to save Deirdre. 'Yes,' he muttered, tight-lipped.

'And what did Deirdre Rachid say when you told her that Jon Lindsay managed a shop at the airport?'

'She said that he'd told her he'd been grounded.'

'And you believed her?' the counsel pressed mercilessly.

'Not entirely.'

'Yes or no, Mr Barlow.'

'No.'

'Were you aware that Deirdre Rachid visited Jon Lindsay at his airport shop several times during the month before she gave him the cheque for the five thousand pounds that she alleged he asked her for to put a deposit on a house that they could live in together?'

Ken shook his head.

'Mr Barlow,' counsel prompted.

'No,' Ken replied reluctantly.

'Therefore she must have known that Jon Lindsay was not a pilot.'

'I wasn't aware that she had visited him at his shop,' Ken retorted.

'And did Mrs Rachid tell you that she gave Jon Lindsay a personal loan of five thousand pounds?'

'No. She told me that she had given him the money to pay half of the deposit on a house he was buying for them to live in.'

'Did you see this house, Mr Barlow?'

'Yes, I took Mrs Rachid—'

'Was it furnished?'

'I only saw the downstairs rooms.' He caught the prosecuting counsel's eye. 'The downstairs room were furnished.'

'And would you like to put a value on this house?'

'I have no idea what it's worth.'

'But it was a large, detached house in an expensive upmarket area, was it not?'

'Yes,' Ken answered, wondering where the question was leading.

'Wouldn't you say that five thousand pounds was somewhat low for a deposit on such a house?'

'Deirdre – Mrs Rachid told me that she had given Jon Lindsay the cheque to cover half of the deposit.'

'And it didn't occur to you that ten thousand pounds was low for a deposit?'

'I didn't think about it,' Ken replied honestly.

'And did Mrs Rachid tell you that she had viewed the house with Mr Lindsay?'

'She told me that he had picked out the house.'

'And you didn't think it odd that she was moving in less than a week after she gave Jon Lindsay the deposit?'

'I thought the house purchase had gone through somewhat quickly.'

'Did you comment on that fact to Mrs Rachid?'

'No.'

'Thank you, Mr Barlow.' The prosecutor looked at the

jury. 'The prosecution wishes to call the next witness, Your Honour.'

'I found myself a job,' Leanne announced to Gail, as she walked into the house after a day in the café. 'I'm going to work for Rita Sullivan in the Kabin as a shop assistant and general dogsbody and I'm going to earn enough for Nick to stay on in college.'

'If determination counts for anything, Leanne, you certainly have enough of it,' Gail said. Despite what she thought of the Battersbys she was warming to Leanne. Whatever else, the girl certainly wasn't afraid of hard work and she couldn't help but like her. But she still hadn't forgiven Nicky for marrying at seventeen.

'I called round to see Ashley Peacock at number four on the way back,' Leanne said brightly. 'She has a room to let and I took it for me and Nick.'

'You're welcome to stay here, Leanne.' Gail was stung by Leanne's announcement that they'd be moving out, although she and Martin had discussed the situation and agreed that the house wasn't big enough for six of them.

'I know that,' Leanne said easily, 'but now we're married, I think Nick and I should stand on our own feet.'

'I can understand that.' Gail remembered how she'd felt when she'd had to share a kitchen with Ivy Tilsley after she'd married Brian. 'But you're welcome to call in and see us any time you like.'

'I know that,' Leanne said chirpily. 'Do you want me to lay the table for tea?'

'Please,' Gail answered. 'I'd be grateful if you would.'

'Jon Lindsay.' The judge turned to the dock and peered over his spectacles at Jon, who was looking resolutely forward, ignoring Deirdre who was standing beside him. 'The jury has found you guilty as charged of obtaining money and property by deception. I believe that, given the weight of evidence against you, they have brought in the only verdict possible. However,' the judge paused and Deirdre felt as though his eyes were boring into her, 'you have fallen prey to the wiles of a lying, manipulative woman who used you to secure a house for herself. Therefore I sentence you to two hundred hours of community service, a non-custodial sentence which I believe reflects your wrongdoing but accepts that you were little more than a pawn in the deception.'

He turned to Deirdre. 'Deirdre Rachid, you stand convicted of obtaining money and property by deception. I hereby sentence you to eighteen months in prison.'

Mike and Ken stared at Deirdre in disbelief and mounting horror. Her solicitor looked back at Mike. The policewoman behind Deirdre bent towards her and whispered something too low for Mike or Ken to hear.

Deirdre turned and allowed the officer to escort her

from the dock. She turned back gave Ken and Mike one last imploring look, and shouted, 'I'm innocent.'

After she left the court Mike glared at Jon. 'I'd like to wipe the smirk off that bloody man's face once and for all,' he muttered darkly to Ken.

Alec Gilroy walked into the Rovers and went to the bar where Natalie Barnes was pulling a pint. 'They still upstairs?'

'Yes.' Natalie didn't have to ask who he was referring to. The Duckworths had cut short their holiday in Blackpool and returned to the Rovers when she had telephoned to tell them that Alec had changed the locks. They had walked in during evening opening hours, retreated to the rooms upstairs and barricaded themselves in.

Alec had done his best to dislodge them. He had turned off the heating and tried to starve them out, but the regulars had rallied round, sending up food and oil heaters.

'Do you want a drink?' Natalie asked.

'Half a pint.' Alec dug in his pocket to make a point. The Duckworths had never paid for their drinks while they had worked behind the bar and their habit of taking cash from the till whenever either of them ran short had contributed to, if not created, their debt problems.

'Last time you were here, you mentioned you wanted to move to Brighton to help your granddaughter, Vicky, set up her wine-bar.'

'What of it?' he asked.

'Nothing.' Natalie was conscious of Betty moving closer so she could eavesdrop. 'I was just thinking that she could probably do with an older head to give her some sound business advice.'

'She could.'

'Then sell the Rovers Return to me,' Natalie suggested.

'I wouldn't let it go cheap.'

'I wouldn't expect you to. I have a bit set aside, and I could sell my share of the garage. What do you say?'

Alec held out his hand. 'I say getting the Duckworths out of the Rovers Return will be your problem as soon as the papers are drawn up and signed. You can send the cheque to Brighton, care of the wine-bar. Shake on the deal.'

'As soon as we've agreed a price.' She smiled.

'How is Deirdre holding up?' Emily asked Ken as she showed him into her living room where Mike Baldwin was looking through a sheaf of legal documents the solicitor had sent him.

'As well as anyone can be when they're locked in a prison cell with a violent disturbed woman and only let out for a few hours a day to consort with other hardened criminals,' he replied grimly. 'She admitted today that they're giving her sedatives.'

'That's hardly surprising,' Emily said angrily. 'She's

innocent and she has no business being locked up in that place.'

'Proving her innocence is the problem.' Mike flicked through a file and set it to one side.

'I feel guilty now for persuading her to stay and face the charges.' Ken sat on a chair and took the cup of tea Emily handed him.

'And so you should,' Mike snarled.

'I believed in the justice system in this country.'

'And it failed her.'

'If I could have broken her out of that place today I would have—'

'We're here to set up a campaign to clear Deirdre's name, not argue among ourselves,' Emily interrupted, as both men's tempers flared.

Mike stared blankly at the papers. 'And we're going about it the wrong way.'

'What do you mean?' Emily asked.

'We know Deirdre's innocent, but a trial failed to prove it, and we have no new evidence to support her case. So, instead of trying to prove Deirdre innocent, perhaps we should try to prove Jon Lindsay's guilt.'

'How?' Ken rubbed his eyes. He was exhausted. He had hardly slept since Deirdre had been sent to prison two weeks before. Every time he closed his eyes he imagined her locked in a cell in the grim, grey building he had visited. Unable to bear the thought, he had taken to pacing around the house until dawn broke. And as he paced, he remembered. Every room at number one held memories, some happy, some bitter, but all relating to his and Deirdre's life together.

'For all we know, Jon Lindsay might have form.'

'Form?' Emily questioned Mike blankly.

'A prison record. Even if he doesn't, there might be something in his past. Other women he's duped or fleeced of their money.'

'It's certainly worth a try,' Emily agreed. 'Where do we start?'

'With some people I know who are good at asking questions and, more importantly, getting answers,' Mike said resolutely. He parried the disapproving look on Ken's face. 'You have a better idea? I'm listening.'

Ken shook his head.

'Then I'll start first thing tomorrow.' Mike picked up the papers he had strewn over Emily's dining table, shuffled them together and stuffed them into his briefcase. 'Goodnight, Emily.' He kissed her cheek, nodded to Ken and left.

Kevin Webster had never been so angry in his life and his anger was directed at his wife. He sat across the dining table from her and said, 'I can't believe you inherited fifty thousand pounds from your mother and you won't give me a penny to buy Natalie out of the garage.'

'The money is mine,' Sally said steadfastly. 'I can do what I like with it and, before you say another word, I think you're forgetting that it was *my* inheritance, not your earnings from the garage, that just paid for us to have a family holiday in Florida.'

'We had never had your money and my money before—'

'That's because we never had any money.' She rounded on him hotly.

'I've kept you and the girls, haven't I?'

'Barely!'

'I bought a house—'

'Only because Hilda Ogden sold it to us at a knock-down price.'

'You're a selfish bitch,' he hissed.

'For keeping my own money?' Sally sneered. 'I'm perfectly within my rights not to want to invest in your garage.'

'Well, seeing as we now have "your money" and "my money" I'll tell you what I'll do. I'll stop giving you house-keeping and you can use "your money" to pay the bills, buy the girls' clothes and shoes and stock up the fridge. See how you like that.' Kevin left the table and strode out through the door.

Sally didn't even look after him. She was too busy thinking about the affair she'd embarked on with Greg Kelly, who'd moved into the flat over the mini-market. He had such plans for them – and the girls – and she'd promised him that she would bankroll a clothing business he was starting up in competition with Mike Baldwin.

She only wished she'd found the courage to tell Kevin why she wouldn't give him the money to buy Natalie's share of the garage. It was simple: she no longer loved him. She shivered when she thought of Greg and the way he made her feel when they made love. When they talked, they really talked – about life, the love they shared, which was so important to them.

Her future would be so much more exciting with him than with Kevin, who only cared about the garage and drinking with his mates in the Rovers.

She slipped out of the living room and ran upstairs. Both Rosie and Sophie were fast asleep, curled in their bunk-beds, their cheeks flushed with sleep, their arms loosely wound round their teddy bears. They wouldn't wake. They never did after they were put to bed. She stole from their bedroom, closed the door and crept back down stairs. She picked up her coat, took off her slippers, slid her feet into her shoes and left the house. She closed the front door and headed down the street towards the mini-market.

Deirdre's solicitor walked into the court waiting room and approached Mike, Ken and Emily.

'The judge ordered Deirdre Rachid's immediate release on bail, pending further investigation. He was impressed by the evidence of the woman you found who told him how Jon had tricked her in exactly the same way he had Deirdre.'

'Deirdre won't have to return to prison?' Emily asked.

'She's on bail, but in my opinion the investigation will clear her name, so the answer is, no, she probably won't,' the solicitor assured her.

'That is such a relief.' Emily clasped Ken's hand. 'Isn't it?'

'It's wonderful news.' So wonderful that Ken was having a problem absorbing it.

'What happens now?' Mike asked.

'As the judge said, Deirdre has been released pending further investigation. Your witness has provided the police with several new leads. Two officers have already left with instructions to apprehend and arrest Jon Lindsay. I need to have a word with you, Mike.'

Mike didn't ask what it was about. It had cost him a small fortune to retain the solicitor to work on Deirdre's case, and he had yet to pay her for the work she had done on the appeal. Unable to meet the costs from his private account he had used Underworld's cash, but he was concerned about his partner Angie and his wife Alma finding out just how much money he had siphoned from the business to fund Deirdre's court costs.

But – he looked across as the door to the court opened and Deirdre emerged – it was worth every penny to get her out of prison, and if he had to pay as much again to keep her out, he would do it gladly.

'You take Deirdre home, Ken.' He felt for Underworld's cheque book in his inside pocket. 'I'll sort out a few details with the solicitor.'

'I can't thank you, Emily and Mike enough.' Deirdre leant back in the front passenger seat of Ken's car and watched the world speed past the window. She had only been incarcerated for three weeks, but the world seemed vast, huge and unbelievably colourful after the grey drabness of life behind bars.

Deirdre looked so thin, fragile and exhausted that Ken had longed to sweep her into his arms and hug her when they had left the court but he had settled for kissing her cheek. And even now, when he was driving her home, there was a gulf between them, a new strain that had nothing to do with their divorce or estrangement.

'Mike and Emily were like dogs worrying a bone,' Ken told her. 'They simply wouldn't let the verdict stand as it was. But if it hadn't been for the evidence of that other woman Jon duped, whom one of Mike's friends found, you'd probably still be inside.'

'It meant a great deal to me to know that the three of you believed I was innocent,' Deirdre said fervently.

'Your solicitor told us that the police have already gone to arrest Jon.'

'I hate the thought of anyone – even Jon – being locked up in a prison,' she said, too exhausted after her ordeal to take any pleasure in the news.

'Deirdre, come and stay with me so that I can look after you,' Ken pleaded. 'You shouldn't be by yourself, and as the house was ours for so long, you know you'll be comfortable there. I promise I won't put you under any pressure. You can do whatever you want whenever you want to.'

'Thank you for inviting me, but I want to go back to my flat.'

'Please . . .'

'I know you mean well, Ken, but all I want at the moment is my independence.'

More than anything else he wanted to ask her if there was still a chance for them to have a future together. But he was sensitive enough to realise that it was neither the time nor the place for that. First, she had to get used to being free again and making decisions for herself. But soon – very soon – he intended to ask her out to dinner. And then?

He didn't dare speculate as to what her answer might be.

'Angie Freeman came round earlier with a copy of Underworld's bank statement,' Alma said, as Mike poured brandy after their evening meal.

'If she had a query, she should have come to me,' Mike said, but he knew what was coming.

'You spent an absolute fortune paying Deirdre Rachid's

legal bills and you took the money from the Underworld account.'

'I had no choice.' There wasn't enough in my personal account to cover the costs,' he said.

'Angie was furious.'

'If she had come to me I would have explained that I intend to replace the money in the Underworld account as soon as I am in a position to do so.'

Alma looked him in the eye. 'Tell me, Mike, why did you spend a fortune paying solicitors to free Deirdre Rachid?'

'Because I knew she was innocent.'

'You had no other reason?'

'Like what?'

'It's cost you a business partner,' she said ignoring his question. 'Angie Freeman said there was no way she wanted to be involved in a partnership with someone who didn't treat her as an equal. She's gone to London and she told me to tell you she's not coming back.'

Mike shrugged. 'I've run the business alone before, I can do so again.'

'She wants you to return the money she invested.'

'There's enough left in the account to cover it.' He swirled the brandy in his glass and sipped it.

'Admit it, Mike, you're still in love with Deirdre.'

'I am not in love with Deirdre Rachid,' he said. 'And before you say another word, it was Ken Barlow who drove her home from the court today, not me.'

'You were lovers—'

'That's ancient history and I've never denied it. You knew all about Deirdre and me when we married.'

'And you're still in love with her.'

'Believe what you want to believe, Alma,' he shouted angrily, his temper roused. 'You will anyway, no matter what I say.'

'What am I supposed to believe? When Angie showed me Underworld's bank statement today I felt sick. No man pays out that kind of money to help a woman unless he's in love with her.'

Mike finished his brandy and picked up the bottle. 'I'm going into my study to get some peace.'

'Admit it, Mike, you're still in love with Deirdre.'

Mike turned back when he reached the door. 'When you're in this mood, Alma, I could easily get used to being in love with almost anyone else. Happy now?' he asked savagely, as tears started in her eyes.

Chapter Fifty-Six

The six pints Kevin had drunk quickly in the Rovers Return hadn't cooled his anger. If anything he was even more incensed when he walked into the house than when he'd left it. He hung his coat in the hall, went into the living room, switched on the light and looked around.

The room had an oddly deserted air. Nothing appeared to be out of place but he sensed that something was wrong.

'Sally?'

When she didn't answer, he left the living room and charged upstairs. The bedroom doors were open and he could see that the girls' bunk-beds were empty. Their wardrobe doors were open and there were no clothes hanging inside. He yanked out a drawer. That, too, was empty and there were no toys on the shelves he had put up alongside the bunks.

He went into the bedroom he shared with Sally. Her wardrobe was empty too, and there was a note on her pillow. He flicked it open and read.

Have taken girls and moved into the flat above the mini-market with Gregg Kelly. I'll use some of the money I inherited from my mother to pay for the divorce. Good luck with the garage, Sally.

'Eighteenth birthday parties are supposed to be memorable occasions,' Nick Tilsley said sombrely, as he watched the ambulance drive away from Coronation Street. 'I'll certainly never forget mine.'

Leanne slipped her arm round his waist as they watched Gail try to comfort Audrey.

'It's such a shock,' Audrey cried. 'One minute Alf was fine, laughing and joking with all of us, and the next he was lying back in the armchair . . . gone . . .'

'I know it's no comfort, Audrey,' Martin helped Gail to lead her mother back into the house, 'but it's the way I would choose to go. A quick heart attack, over and done with in an instant. No lingering illness, no long stays in hospital.'

'Only a selfish person would say that.' Audrey wept. 'Think of the way Gail and the children would feel . . .'

'Come on, Mam,' Gail coaxed, 'there's a splash of Christmas whisky left in the sideboard. I think we could all do with a drink.'

Nick watched Martin and his mother take his grandmother into the house, but he was reluctant to follow them.

Sensing his mood, Leanne said, 'Do you want to go for a walk or something?'

He nodded. 'I certainly don't want to go back in there for a while.'

'I have something to tell you that might make you feel better.' Leanne slipped her arm through his as they headed towards Viaduct Street.

'After seeing Alf die like that, I could do with some good news.'

'It's the best,' Leanne said proudly. 'You're going to be a father.'

Nicky pulled away from her. 'You're pregnant?'

'Yes.' Shocked by his reaction, Leanne fought back tears.

'But how? You're on the Pill . . .'

'Remember that bout of gastric flu I had a couple of months back? Well, the doctor said sometimes that's all it takes for the Pill to stop working.'

'The last thing I want is to be a father at my age,' Nicky hissed. 'We have no house, no security. I'm still a student, I don't want a kid cramping our style before we've even had time to find out what our style is.'

'I thought you'd be pleased.' Leanne allowed the tears to fall unchecked down her cheeks.

'No way! I don't want to be a father. If you're pregnant, you'll just have to have an abortion.'

'Nick . . .'

'I don't want to talk about this. If you really are pregnant promise me that you'll have an abortion and never say another word about it.'

Too much in love with Nicky to argue with him, she nodded.

'Go back to the house,' he ordered her roughly. 'I need to be alone.'

Still crying, she ran back up the street.

'I'm here, as you demanded. Now tell me, what's so important that you could only talk to me about it face to face?' Kevin asked Sally, as they sat in one of the pubs in central Manchester two months after she had taken the girls and left him.

'I want you to take the girls back to live with you, Kevin.'

Kevin had imagined Sally making several different demands of him, but that hadn't been one of them. 'Why? You were quick enough to take them with you when you walked out on me to live with Greg.'

'That was before I discovered what Greg was like.'

'I heard you set him up in business. Doing well, is he?' Kevin goaded her, knowing full well that Greg had gone bankrupt.

'No,' she replied quietly.

'I can't say I'm sorry to hear it.'

'Did you also hear that he lost most of my money and

beat me up when Mike Baldwin made mincemeat of his plans to sell to Mike's buyers?' She flicked her blonde hair back from her face.

He stared, shocked by the black, purple and yellow bruises on her cheek and round her eyes. 'Have you been to the police?'

'No. I just want to get the girls away from him to a safe place. I've talked to Rita Sullivan and I'm moving in with her, but I'm afraid that he might come after me and I don't want him to hurt the girls or for them to see him beating me up . . . again.'

'Rosie and Sophie saw him do that to you?'

She nodded.

'I'll kill the bastard!'

'No! Please, Kevin, promise me you'll take care of them.'

He was tempted to tell her that if she'd let him buy Natalie's share of the garage business she would have had something to show for the money her mother had left her. But when he looked at the beaten, cowed expression on her face he couldn't say anything that would make her feel worse than she already did.

'Don't worry, I'll look after the girls. You take care of yourself and if you need anything . . .'

'I'll be fine, thank you, Kevin.' She left her drink untouched on the table. 'I'll meet the girls from school and bring them straight to your house, if that's all right with you. I've already packed their things and left them with mine at Rita's.'

'I'll come home from the garage early to settle them in.' He closed his hand over hers. She returned the pressure then slipped it from his fingers.

Sally and Rita were drinking coffee in Rita's living room and watching the New Year celebrations in Edinburgh on television. Somehow, the jocularity of the Scottish revellers only made them feel even more miserable. It hadn't been a happy Christmas for either of them. Rita had spent most of it in tears, recalling her last Christmas and New Year with Ted, and Sally had spent most of the time imagining the kind of Christmas and New Year's Eve she would have had if she had still been living with Kevin and her daughters.

'Did you hear that?' Rita asked, as a noise resounded from the kitchen. 'It sounded like a window breaking.'

'Perhaps it's just kids letting off fireworks in the back again.' Sally didn't even believe her own explanation. Heart thundering, she pushed in front of Rita as they both left their chairs. 'Let me look.'

Before Sally reached the door, it opened and Greg ran towards her. An explosion in her head blurred her vision and sent her reeling into the wall. She fell to the floor. The room wavered out of focus as he continued to kick and hit her. She heard Rita screaming, and she was vaguely aware of someone rushing into the room and lashing out.

She groaned as strong arms lifted her from the floor and on to the sofa. She looked up to see Nick Tilsley.

'Leanne's calling the police.'

'Thank you,' Rita murmured thickly, and Sally realised that Greg had hurt her too. 'I tried, but I couldn't stop him laying into you, Sally,' she said apologetically.

'You shouldn't even have tried.' Sally looked up at Nicky. 'Thank you,' she murmured gratefully.

'You can certainly pick them,' he said wryly, 'but don't worry, I don't think he'll be back round here. Not tonight any road.'

'Well?' Mike asked impatiently, as Alma returned to the dining room after answering the telephone.

'The doctor said I'm fine. There was no trace of cancer, it was a cyst.' She picked up her toast and marmalade and looked at it as if she'd never seen toast before.

Mike heaved a sigh of relief. Two weeks earlier Alma had discovered a lump in her breast. They had both endured fourteen days of uncertainty when the surgeon had refused to speculate on whether or not the lump was cancerous until it had been removed and tested.

'It was benign, and that's an end to your problems?' he asked, needing reassurance that she really was healthy.

'Yes.' She watched him fold a letter he had been

reading and stuff it back into its envelope. 'What's that?'

'Nothing,' he answered carelessly. 'Just an invoice for Underworld.'

She looked at the envelope again. The address was handwritten. Strange for a business envelope. But, relieved by her news, she put it out of her mind.

'Any plans for today?' Mike asked.

'Audrey Roberts asked if I'd go shopping with her. She's been terribly depressed since Alf died.'

'Bend the credit cards as much as you like,' he said generously. He'd had an exceptionally good month's trading and he'd managed to buy Angie Freeman out of her partnership. He folded the envelope into his pocket and stopped to kiss her on his way out. 'I'm off to the factory, love, we'll celebrate your good news, tonight.'

Mike drove straight to his office at Underworld. He took the envelope from his pocket, opened the safe, removed the business cheque book and wrote out a cheque for ten thousand pounds. At half past ten, his office door opened and Deirdre, who'd accepted his offer of a job, showed in Julia Stone, a sales representative for one of the chain stores. He waited until Deirdre had left.

'There's no need for you to sit down, Julia. I have your cheque.' He tore it from the book and pushed it across his desk towards her. 'But I warn you, I've only been paying your blackmail demands because my wife was ill. This morning she was given a clean bill of health so that's the last you'll get from me. You can take the photographs your accomplice took of us in that seedy little hotel room and show them to the world, for all I care.'

Julia pushed the cheque back towards Mike. 'It's not me who's blackmailing you, Mike. The whole idea was Greg Kelly's. He was upset when you blocked his plans to sell the goods he produced to your customers. And he blames you for losing all the money he borrowed from Sally Webster.'

'And why exactly did you go along with this?' Mike asked sceptically.

'You weren't the only one he was blackmailing. I used to be a prostitute, but now I'm a respectable buyer. There are a lot of pornographic photographs of me around, and Greg has some. My bosses would sack me if they ever came to light.'

'Why are telling me this now, and not before?'

'Because I want out of this. Greg promised to give me back the negatives if I went along with his scheme to fleece you, but every time I ask for them he finds an excuse not to give them to me – only the photographs, to remind me just how bad they are. Now I believe he never intends to give the negatives to me.'

Mike took the cheque and tore it into tiny pieces.

Julia opened the door. 'If I were you, I'd go and see

your wife. If I don't return with the money, Greg may well push those photographs he took of us through your letter-box today.'

Mike drove home at lunchtime to find Alma staring at the photographs of him and Julia that had been taken when they had been making love. She had set them out on the sofa and he had to concede that they were explicit. There was no doubt about what was going on and it was point-less for him to do anything except own up to his infidelity.

He walked over to the drinks tray and poured himself a whisky. 'We were going through a bad patch. You thought I was having an affair with Deirdre. I wasn't, but after you refused to believe me, I met Julia. She offered, and I thought why not live up to the reputation you'd given me?'

Alma turned and slapped him soundly across the face.

'Alma!'

'I'm doing what I should have done years ago. Moving out of this house and away from you. I'm sick and tired of your wheeler-dealing, your lies, your lack of integrity, but most of all I'm sick and tired of you and your philan-dering ways. Goodbye, Mike, you'll be hearing from my solicitor.'

'I can't believe I heard what you just said about me,' Leanne reproached Nicky, as he returned to their table at the Rovers.

'Said what?' Nicky asked, confused.

'You told Betty and Natalie that I had a miscarriage.'

'You want me to tell everyone you had an abortion?' he whispered.

'I should never have listened to you,' Leanne said bitterly. 'Look at your mother, she wasn't happy when she found out about her pregnancy last month but she didn't run to the clinic and have an abortion. And Martin didn't make her.'

'You made the best decision for both of us,' Nick said. 'And now we can both go to Canada with Gran when she goes there for Steve's wedding. We can stay on afterwards, find jobs, a house of our own, and build a new life without worrying about anything other than ourselves. You've no idea what life is like out in Canada, Leanne. It's fantastic, and so different from here. You're going to love it.'

Leanne shook her head. 'I'm not going with you, Nick.'

'What do you mean, you're not coming?' he demanded furiously.

'When you made me abort our baby, you killed my love for you. Loving someone means wanting the best for them, and killing our baby wasn't the best for me or our child. You go to Canada, Nick, you go there by yourself.'

Nicky leant back in his chair. 'Don't think I won't do just that.'

'That's fine by me.'

As Leanne left the Rovers, Nicky picked up his glass. Miranda Peters was standing alone at the bar and he had fancied her for quite a while. Now that Leanne had walked out on him he was able to join her – with an almost clear conscience.

'I simply couldn't bear the thought of you living all alone in this flat another moment, Deirdre.' Blanche turned to the taxi-driver. 'Set the suitcase down over there, please.' She opened her purse. 'Six pounds, you said.'

'That's right.'

She handed him six pounds and fifty pence.

'It's nice to see you, Mam,' Deirdre said when Blanche had come back upstairs after seeing the driver out, 'but I'm fine, I really am. I'm working for Mike at the factory and I have my friends, so I'm hardly sitting here night after night pining for company.'

'But you have no man in your life,' Blanche Hunt pointed out logically. 'And that's your own fault. Ken was so supportive when you were in jail. The poor man was worried sick about you. I could hear it in his voice every time I telephoned.'

'We're friends.' Deirdre didn't bother to conceal her irritation with her mother's blatantly transparent attempts to matchmake her back with Ken.

'Shall we have a cup of tea?' Blanche asked. 'And do you have Ken's telephone number handy? I thought perhaps we could cook a special meal tonight and invite him over.'

'I can't believe you've taken a job collecting trolleys at Freshco's supermarket,' Tracy said as she sat on the arm of Ken's sofa and watched him lay the table.

'And I can't believe that you've left Robert. Come on, Tracy, a year ago you couldn't wait to marry him. Things can't be that bad between you,' Ken replied.

'I was mistaken about him, and before you say another word, you and Mam have made plenty of mistakes like that in your lives. I could even list them. There was Mike Baldwin and Denise Osbourne and—'

'That's enough,' Ken said sharply – she had hit a raw nerve. 'And if my experience is anything to go by, walking away from your marriage instead of working to save it is the worst mistake you'll ever make. In the long run you'll only end up hurting yourself.'

'So you want to give your marriage to Mam another chance?' she fished.

'I want to lay the table so we can eat and get to the Rovers in time for the surprise sixtieth birthday party your mother is throwing for me.' Ken brought in the salt and vinegar and set them in the centre of the table. 'Does she know that you've left Robert?'

Tracy made a face. 'I've gone to her place a couple of times to tell her but Gran is always sitting there, listening in.'

'I was hoping Blanche would have gone home by now.'

'I think she's dug in for life,' Tracy said. 'Want me to butter that bread?'

'Please, the fish and chips are almost ready.' Ken glanced round the room and checked his pockets. The envelope was nestling in his inside jacket pocket. He had tackled Mike Baldwin the last time he had seen him and asked if he could reimburse the costs of Deirdre's solicitor's bills. To his surprise Mike had agreed without an argument but, then, perhaps it was as obvious to Mike as it was to him that he and Deirdre were getting on better than they ever had before. He hadn't plucked up courage to ask her to move back in with him yet, but it was only a matter of time. Maybe even tonight.

'Supposing I tell your mother and Gran about your and Robert's problems for you?'

Tracy wrinkled her nose. 'Do you have to?'

'Frankly, yes.'

'I told you, I don't want to get back with Robert.'

'Let's just talk about it, shall we, Tracy?' Ken suggested.

'New Year's Eve, 1999, we won't be back in our house until the new millennium,' Deirdre said, as Ken closed and locked the door of number one Coronation Street behind them.

'It's not as if we're going far.' Ken laughed, and they stepped next door into the Rovers Return.

'New Year's Eve, and we'll be looking at the same faces we look at in here all year round.'

'Do you mind?' Ken had been so happy since Deirdre had moved back into his house and his life, and was anxious to please her.

'No.' She smiled. 'You?'

Ken remembered what Bet Gilroy had said to him ten years before on New Year's Eve when she had visited him in the flat above the mini-market and found him drunk and contemplating suicide. Her voice echoed back to him over the years.

'Get your coat. You're coming to the Rovers with me. Who knows? You may even meet a woman worth a second look.'

'I only want Deirdre.'

'I don't recommend that as an opening gambit if you do meet someone. And remember, relationships work both ways. She'll have to think that you're worth a second look too. And the way you are at the moment, any woman in her right mind will walk right past you.'

He wished he could see Bet again to tell her that she had been so right.

Deirdre's prediction was correct: the same faces they saw every day and evening were in the pub, all the neighbours, some of whom had become close friends and some who hadn't. They exchanged pleasantries and the whole time

Ken kept his arm firmly fixed round Deirdre's waist, especially when they walked near Mike Baldwin and the new woman in his life, Linda Sykes, who was hotly tipped by the gossips to become the next Mrs Baldwin as soon as Alma had divorced him.

While Ken bought a round of drinks, Deirdre fell into conversation with Alma, Audrey, Rita, Gail and Sally. He glanced at the clock. It was a quarter to twelve. He left his beer on the table in front of Deirdre, slipped outside and looked down the street.

It was a fine, dry, cold night. Lights shone in some of the windows, illuminating the deserted road and pavements. Nothing had changed since he had grown up in this street – and everything had.

The houses looked better for having had money spent on them, and since everyone had switched to gas or electric heating the air was cleaner. He glanced at his own door and thought he saw Albert Tatlock standing there, touching his flat cap to him. And, for no reason in particular, he remembered another evening back in 1960 when he'd jumped off the bus and walked home. It had been freezing cold and raining, but he'd been reluctant to go home despite the cold because his father thought he had become a snob, and mealtimes were an ordeal to be endured because of the way his father constantly berated him.

He listened hard and thought he could hear Elsie and Dennis Tanner's voices raised in anger behind the closed door of number eleven. Ena Sharples, Minnie Caldwell and Martha Longhurst had been walking up the street towards the Rovers Return for their milk-stout nightcaps in the snug.

He'd walked into his house. His father, collar abandoned, was sitting at the tea-table in braces and shirtsleeves, his mother dressed in a flowered overall, serving tea.

'We're not good enough for you now . . . I bet you don't tell those high and mighty pals that you hobnob down the university with, what your mother does to bring in money to keep you in the lap of luxury . . . You'd best watch out, Ida, he'll have you changing into an evening gown to eat your meal next.

'We're not good enough for you now . . .'

He thought of all the people who had left Coronation Street. Dennis Tanner going to Bath, Elsie Tanner realising her ambition to run a wine-bar in Portugal, his father winning the Premium Bonds and buying his detached house in a nice area, going up in the world and becoming a snob, doing the very thing of which he had accused his sons – forgetting their roots. Concepta, Harry and Christopher Hewitt moving to Ireland, only for Harry to return on the day of Elsie and Steve Tanner's wedding to die under Len's van.

So many people – so many lives that had touched his in one way or another. Suddenly the street seemed crowded with smiling people who were waving to him and wishing him well.

'Not good enough,' he whispered into the darkness.

His father had been afraid that he'd turned into a snob who would reject his upbringing, and here he was standing in the street on the brink of a new age when so many others had come and gone.

His brother David with his wife Irma, smiling at him from outside the corner shop at the other end of the street . . . David had at least achieved his dream of emigrating to Australia before he had died there at an absurdly young age. Stan and Hilda Ogden, with the massive bulk of Eddie Yeats beside them, Len Fairclough, Jerry Booth and Ray Langton at Len's yard. Ernest Bishop kissing Emily goodbye on the doorstep of number three on that last fateful morning . . .

'There you are.'

Ken turned to see Deirdre standing in the doorway of the Rovers behind him.

'It's five minutes to midnight, Ken, time to welcome in a new millennium.'

He opened his arms and she went to him. He kissed her.

'A new millennium, a new beginning for us.' As Ken pushed open the door of the Rovers Return, Natalie turned up the television and the first chimes of Big Ben echoed through the bar. He lifted his glass and touched it to Deirdre's, then lifted it to all the regulars. 'To the new millennium, our future and the future of Coronation Street.'

As the toast echoed around him, he glanced back through the open doorway. They were still there, his friends, his past, his ghosts – and they would always be there for him and the new residents. No matter what life threw at them, they were neighbours – and friends. But Coronation Street had always been like that and always would be. Because whatever else it was home – and more than good enough for him.